FUNCTIONAL DISORDERS OF MEMORY

Edited by

JOHN F. KIHLSTROM

HARVARD UNIVERSITY

FREDERICK J. EVANS

THE INSTITUTE OF PENNSYLVANIA HOSPITAL
AND UNIVERSITY OF PENNSYLVANIA

LEA LAWRENCE ERLBAUM ASSOCIATES, PUBLISHERS
1979   Hillsdale, New Jersey

DISTRIBUTED BY THE HALSTED PRESS DIVISION OF

JOHN WILEY & SONS

New York   Toronto   London   Sydney

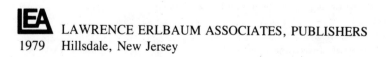

THE EXPERIMENTAL PSYCHOLOGY SERIES

Arthur W. Melton • *Consulting Editor*

Lawrence Erlbaum Associates, Inc., Publishers
62 Maria Drive
Hillsdale, New Jersey   07642

Distributed solely by Halsted Press Division
John Wiley & Sons, Inc., New York

Library of Congress Cataloging in Publication Data

Main entry under title:

Functional disorders of memory.

Includes bibliographical references and indexes.
1. Memory, Disorders of.   I. Kihlstrom, John F.
II. Evans, Frederick J.
BF376.F86   616.8'523   79-1049
ISBN 0-470-26698-8

Printed in the United States of America

Contents

Foreword

Memory allows people to use prior experiences to appreciate the familiar, to be alert to the novel, and to plan effectively for the future as a projection from the past. The integration of experience through memory is ordinarily quite successful despite occasional gaps and distortions. Sometimes, however, there are failures that leave the person for a shorter or longer time bereft of the anchorages that memory provides to sustain orderly behavior and experience. The most investigated of the failures are those incidental to organic brain damage produced by tumors, disease, or destructive accidents. Patients suffering from organically caused problems are readily studied, because their conditions are frequent and they are accessible in hospitals. Failures of another kind are called functional, because they appear to have psychological causes, and the brain damage, if any, is not detectable; not infrequently, the lost memories can be restored. These functional deficiencies or abnormalities have been less systematically studied, and it is to the credit of the editors that they have detected this omission in the current crop of books on memory. The authors, in their own ways, show how much is already known in these neglected areas and where further investigation might be pursued with profit.

It is worth recounting something of the background that has led to the current importance of these endeavors. The focus of interest in scientific psychology shifts from time to time not only from one major topic to another but from one aspect to another within an area of inquiry. During the first 75 years after Ebbinghaus's pioneer studies of memory in 1885, the study of learning and memory remained primarily focused on acquisition, typified by the curve of improvement with practice. The materials studied were chiefly rote verbal learning (Ebbinghaus had invented nonsense syllables for this purpose) or motor learning, as of mazes, mirror-drawing, or other skilled tasks. In this context, retention was studied as a by-product of the conditions of acquisition—part—

whole learning, massed versus distributed practice, length of list to be learned, and so on. The degree of permanence of the acquired knowledge or habits was investigated, along with the positive (or negative) transfer of what was learned to new learning. With the rising interest in animal learning, the study of overt movements predominated; gradually the conditioned-response theories refined the earlier associationist or functionalist interpretations, without greatly changing the style of experimentation.

What amounted to a paradigmatic shift occurred in the late 1950s as the study of human learning turned away from the traditional laboratory studies based on acquisition to focus primarily on memory according to encoding, storage, and retrieval, with interpretations based on information processing and cognitive psychology. With this shift the contrast between short- and long-term memory came to the fore, after the initial empirical work of the Petersons on short-term memory in 1959 and the theoretical proposals of Atkinson and Shiffrin in 1965. With this new impetus, the older and well-known distinction between immediate memory and enduring memory became subjected to precise experimental analysis. Because the strictures of the earlier behaviorism were relaxed, the phenomenology of what was happening began to be examined, and control processes became invoked, such as rehearsal to hold short-term memories in storage long enough to transfer them to more enduring storage. In 1972 Tulving revived another older distinction—that between the recollection of events dated in the personal past as against the recall of something such as the meaning of a word whose original learning might have been long forgotten. He assigned new labels, *episodic* memory for the dated ones and *semantic* memory for the non-dated ones, and these new terms again brought the differences between these processes into prominence.

The study of functional disorders of memory takes on new meaning against the background of the careful and precise studies of the last two decades, and in the chapters that follow the distinctions just referred to reappear repeatedly. In addition to throwing more light on topics already familiar, a number of new topics emerge from the dim background into the foreground—topics such as childhood amnesia, the effects of aging, the temporary amnesias in everyday life and in psychotherapy, and the dissociative aspects of posthypnotic experiences, fugues, and multiple personalities.

It is always important to be on the alert for a narrowing of focus, lest experimenters go off in specialized directions in which what they study communicates only to those who are within the community of specialists. A book of this kind, by widening the field of view, provides a testing ground for what has been going on in the center and in this way maintains the vitality and pertinence to the basic problems of the real world with which all psychological investigations begin.

Ernest R. Hilgard
Stanford University

Preface

The past two decades have witnessed an enormous burst of activity as investigators have attempted to gain a better understanding of memory. Although there are a number of excellent books available summarizing the knowledge that we have acquired so far, it is fair to say that almost every important construct in the literature remains the focus of a major theoretical controversy. Is the central metaphor for memory dynamics "organization" or "interference"? Is the act of remembering reproductive or reconstructive? Is the relationship between perception and memory best characterized by "depth of processing," "encoding specificity," or something else? Is there really a distinction between recall and recognition? Does memory possess a unitary structure, or is it composed of multiple storage systems such as short-term and long-term memory, or episodic and semantic memory? Despite all this activity, therefore, it is not altogether clear how much we know for certain about the processes involved in remembering and forgetting.

Part of the problem is that until very recently, most investigations of memory involved college students performing relatively trivial tasks under sterile laboratory conditions. Although this practice may have been ideal for some lines of research, in the final analysis it has placed severe limitations on our vision of memory: first, because few laboratory paradigms adequately represent memory as it is experienced and employed in everyday life; and second, because much more remembering is observed than forgetting. In this respect the current "Bartlett revival," with its interest in memory for extended prose and other meaningful material as well as in the occurrence of systematic distortions in memory, has been a tonic for the discipline—despite the conceptual ambiguities of schema theory.

It is our conviction that the study of amnesia—broadly construed—similarly illuminates aspects of remembering and forgetting that are obscured in conventional laboratory investigations of memory, and that amnesia can serve as an important proving ground for advances in memory theory. Others in the field seem to agree, as many investigators have become increasingly interested in the pathology of memory. However, this interest has been focused on those memory disorders that are associated with specific lesions or other definite disease processes in the central nervous system—Korsakoff's syndrome and similar amnesias, aphasia, dementia, and the like. Another domain, which encompasses the "functional" amnesias, has been virtually ignored. Yet these amnesias are frequently encountered in the clinic, the laboratory, and in everyday life; and they clearly represent subjectively compelling disruptions in the operation of memory. Research on at least some of these topics has progressed at a rapid pace, but the relevant literature remains scattered and difficult to access and has not been sufficiently integrated with the theories and constructs emerging from laboratory research on normal memory.

The aim of this volume, then, is to present a comprehensive account of the current state of knowledge concerning the functional disorders of memory. Each of the contributors to the volume has provided a summary of the results of research in a given topic area with emphasis on his or her own particular interests or program of investigation. The resulting papers cover such clinical phenomena as dissociative amnesia, momentary forgetting by patients in psychotherapy, and repression; amnesias associated with special states of consciousness such as convulsive seizure activity, sleep, hypnosis, and general anesthesia, as well as drug-induced, state-dependent learning; and disorders and anomalies observed in normal waking consciousness outside the laboratory and clinic, such as depersonalization and déjà vu, infantile and childhood amnesia, and the memory deficit observed in the aged. Almost all the work discussed involves human subjects, although in two cases—infantile/childhood amnesia and state-dependent learning—there are investigations of the phenomena in infrahuman species that cannot be ignored. We did not mean by our choice of title to revive the old "organic vs. functional" dispute in psychiatry and neurology, but only to specify a certain subset of phenomena within the pathology of memory where physiological considerations are less dominant; in fact, many of the authors have offered speculations concerning the psychobiological aspects of their topics.

We explicitly requested that our authors integrate the various phenomena and their theoretical accounts of them with the wider literature on normal memory. In each case, it turns out that the functional disorders of memory speak directly to one or more current theoretical debates. Consideration of both the anomalies of memory encountered in the psychopathology of everyday life and the memory difficulties observed in the aged call for reconsideration of the relationships between recall and recognition, and between the episodic and semantic components of memory. Research on infantile and childhood amnesia, traumatic amnesia, and the effects of anesthesia support the notion that encoding conditions, especially the extent to which the new memory is processed at the time of perception, are especially critical for later remembering. Other phenomena, such as dream recall and state dependency, illustrate the importance of similarity between the contexts in which learning and remembering take place. Studies of repression, including momentary forgetting during psychotherapy, remind us that memories possess motivational and affective qualities as well as spatio-temporal and linguistic features and that these relationships with personality can affect recall in important ways. The clinical cases of hysteria, fugue, and multiple personality indicate that memories can be rendered unconscious in other ways besides repression; and hypnosis, as well as other altered states of awareness, provides techniques for the study of divided consciousness.

The individual chapters, then, do not merely reflect the theoretical advances already made in other subdisciplines of memory and cognition. By providing perspectives on memory that are not available to the investigator who focuses on "normal" cognition as manifested in the usual sorts of laboratory experiments, they contribute directly to the development of a more adequate account of the processes involved in remembering and forgetting. The papers in this volume, and the volume itself, are meant to be construed as questions rather than answers. For that reason, we have decided not to provide the kind of integrative summary chapter that is usually expected from editors. The range of phenomena covered and the questions they pose for our understanding of memory are too diverse to permit any concise summary; and the state of contemporary cognitive psychology is such that it would be premature to offer much in the way of theoretical speculation.

A number of individuals and organizations assisted us in the editing of this volume. We are particularly grateful to Arthur W. Melton and Lawrence Erlbaum for their early interest and consistent support, and to our contributors for sharing our enthusiasm for the work. Special thanks go to our families and colleagues for putting up with us while we brought the book together; and to Ernest R. Hilgard for inspiring the enterprise and providing the foreword. Preparation of the volume was supported in part by Grants #MH 29951 and MH 19156 from the National Institutes of Mental Health, United States Public Health Service, and in part by a grant from the Institute for Experimental Psychiatry.

John F. Kihlstrom
Frederick J. Evans

DISORDERED AND ANOMALOUS MEMORY IN EVERYDAY LIFE

1 Everyday Anomalies of Recall and Recognition

Graham Reed
York University

This chapter is concerned with some everyday memory anomalies experienced routinely by normal people; they are puzzling to the individual but so commonplace as to evoke little discussion. Also to be considered are some classical psychogenic phenomena such as *déjà vu* and depersonalization. These have been meticulously documented in the psychiatric literature, but that does not mean that they are associated exclusively with mental illness. On the contrary, although they may occur only rarely in any given individual's lifetime, they seem to be experienced in some degree by the majority of normal people. They have been described by many writers, from Dostoyevsky to Oscar Wilde. Yet psychologists have tended to avoid both groups of phenomena. Memory disturbances associated with brain damage have always attracted the interest of experimental psychologists, but their psychogenic counterparts are rarely to be found indexed in textbooks of general, experimental, or cognitive psychology. Clinicians have discussed some of the classical phenomena but in terms of motivational or psychoanalytic theories. Occasionally, psychogenic memory anomalies have been described and discussed in cognitive terms (e.g., in an excellent little book by Talland, 1968). But with the exception of one attempt by the present writer (Reed, 1972), there has been no systematic analysis using a cognitive or information-processing approach.

Here, a collection of mnemonic anomalies are described and briefly discussed in cognitive terms. Later, attention is drawn to the significance of some of them in relation to issues in contemporary memory research. The approach taken throughout is of the "reconstructive" variety, deriving directly and unashamedly from the work of Sir Frederic Bartlett.

1

Many of the phenomena discussed later may be technically classified as examples of paramnesia. The crucial feature in any definition of paramnesia is that it involves some degree of *distortion* of recall as opposed to forgetting. (The latter includes a range of degrees of recall failure, the most extreme type of course being *amnesia*.) It was this element of distortion that Bartlett emphasized in his classical study, *Remembering* (1932). Bartlett pointed out that simple omissions or attenuation of recalled material can be explained in terms of any "trace" model of memory. But such models do not provide a ready answer to the problem of why so many recollections involve not attenuated versions of original material but elaborations or distortions of it. It is easy to see how a trace might "decay"; it is less obvious how it can "grow," especially when the growth is in different directions from the original representation. It was this observation, coupled with a consideration of the storage problems implied by associationist formulations, that led Bartlett to assert that memory must involve *dynamic organization.* Recall, he asserted, cannot simply be a question of the retrieval of inert traces. Distortion must surely reflect an active process of *reconstruction*. Bartlett reluctantly called the necessary cognitive structures *schemata*, a term borrowed from the neurologist Sir Henry Head. New information, Bartlett argued, was not stored intact but was incorporated into a number of extant schemata. Perhaps it should be stressed that a "schema" is not merely a grouping or a static concept. Bartlett conceived it as plastic and dynamic, undergoing continual change as new material is incorporated. The same term and conceptualization are of course central to the theories of Piaget, for whom schemata are continuously enriched through the function of "accommodation" to new input. (A highly sophisticated version of the "schema" approach is presented in detail by Piaget & Inhelder, 1973.) This presumption of structures undergoing constant modification differentiates the schema approach from such theories as that of Anderson and Bower (1974), whose "nodes"—although interconnected by vast numbers of associations—seem to be static concepts. On this sort of model, changes in the network are accomplished by increased associations, not by changes in the structures themselves.

Bartlett hypothesized that remembering was the process of activating the relevant schemata and drawing upon them to reconstruct the search target. On this argument, distortions are readily explicable. The reconstructive process might well overdraw on some contributory schemata or overemphasize the contribution of one or more at the expense of others. Now it must be admitted that the concept of schemata is sketchy, and difficult to examine experimentally. Furthermore, it raises as many questions as it answers. How, for instance, are the appropriate schemata identified? How are their respective contributions determined? How are their relevant features extracted? What determines the synthesis of these features, and what sort of "match" mechanism is employed to establish acceptable criteria and quality control? However, it must be pointed out that these questions and many others like them offer a challenge to *every* theory of memory. Meanwhile, Bartlett's model, however shaky, can be shown to encompass both everyday and experimental findings as well as any other and better than most. Its main features have been drawn upon, with or without attribution, by several contemporary theorists. Indeed, descendants of the very associationists assailed by Bartlett are now finding it necessary to borrow some of his postulations to bolster up their positions. And ironically, as Baddeley (1976) has pointed out, the development of computers has made Bartlett's theoretical ideas seem much more viable.

THE PHENOMENA

The "I Can't Quite Place Him" Phenomenon

Perhaps the most common of the paramnesias is the everyday experience of encountering a relatively well known person but being unable to identify him. In most cases the problem occurs when the other person is met outside of the context with which he is normally associated by the observer. To make things more complicated, the "I can't quite place him" experience often leads to a perplexed and preoccupying attempt to "place" the familiar person appropriately. This may involve running through a series of possible hypotheses that can lead to quite incorrect attribution with subsequent social embarrassment.

As an undergraduate, I was in the habit of taking morning coffee in a café near the psychological laboratories, where I habitually sat at a particular table with my classmates. Every day there appeared at an adjoining table a slightly older man. He was familiar to me, and I consistently greeted him as an acquaintance. But after some weeks, I realized one day that he was not a fellow student, and the embarrassing realization dawned that our acquaintance dated back a couple of years to a shared army service. The next day, I hastened to the adjoining table, addressed him by name, and apologized for having so far failed to engage in appropriate reminiscence. "The problem, Corporal Jenkins," I explained earnestly, "was that I didn't quite place you out of uniform." He regarded me closely for several seconds. "My name *is* Jenkins," he replied at last, "and as it happens, I *was* a corporal in the Army, though we never met there. Perhaps I ought to remind you that we both work most evenings as coleaders in the local youth club!"

The most interesting characteristic of the "I can't quite place him" phenomenon is that it seems to represent *recognition without complete recall.* In this, it has something in common with the more dramatic phenomenon of déjà vu, which is described later. However, in the present case there is an objectively sound basis for recognition, whereas in déjà vu there is not.

The "Know the Face, Not the Name" Phenomenon

A milder version of the "I can't quite place him" phenomenon is that where another person is recognized and appropriately identified, but his name cannot be recalled. Here the issue is much simpler, because it seems to involve merely partial forgetting; recall is present but is attenuated. The situation can therefore be handled by all models of memory in terms of the deployment of attention in the original situation. When we meet someone initially, we usually have ample opportunity to observe and register his physical characteristics. We can code these in a number of ways, thus facilitating subsequent search and increasing the chances of correct retrieval. Typically, we pay less attention to the name. We probably hear it only once as introductions are made; indeed, we may never catch it in the first place. Certainly, unless we have been studying Dale Carnegie, we do not practise the name. And there is no obvious linkage in most cases between the perceptible characteristics of a person and the abstractness of his name. Furthermore, both given name and surname are probably familiar to us, but this merely makes recall more difficult, because they are thus insufficiently discriminable. We are more likely to recall a name correctly and with appropriate attribution if the name is foreign to us, or otherwise unusual.

An interesting point of relevance to the present case is that in everyday parlance we say that we "recognize" a person's face, posture, voice, gait, etc. We never say that we "recognize" his given name if it is a familiar one. Thus we may say: "I know that man—I recognize his face." We never say: "That man is called Bill—I recognize his name." In relation to a person's name, we only employ the term *recognize* if the name is novel (e.g., 'Ah yes—Orumbajobi, I recognize that name") or if the combination of given and surname is for us unique (e.g., "Harriet Q. Watkins? Yes—I recognize that name"). This apparent truism may have some significance for theories of memory, especially since laboratory studies of recognition typically involve the presentation of material that is familiar to the subject—digits, letters, or words. This point is reexamined later. Meanwhile, it may be pointed out that in the case of familiar names, "recognition" of a person usually subsumes not his name per se, but the *association* between the person and the name.

The "Time-Gap" Experience

It is not at all uncommon for motorists to "wake up" during the course of a journey, to realize that they have no conscious recollection of covering the miles since, for example, the last town. Understandably, they usually interpret this in terms of time, reporting, for example, "a slice out of my life" or "a lost half hour." For this reason, Reed (1972) coined the term *time-gap experience* in his discussion of the phenomenon.

The gap in consciousness would be readily explicable had the individual been asleep. But part of the strangeness of the experience is due to the fact that his "waking up" was preceded by the continuous performance of a complex activity. He must have been awake to have got to the point where he "woke up."

Even more disturbing for the individual is the inexplicable blank in awareness of the passage of time. Our particular culture trains us to be clock-watchers, and much of our social organization is rooted in strict temporal structuring. The continual reference to clock time is an integral part of our workaday lives, as is our ability to gauge temporal duration. But more importantly, any break in personal time is alarming. The awareness of oneself as an individual is inextricably associated with a sense of the *continuity* of one's existence.

The key to this part of the puzzle is that what the time-gapper is reporting is not a question of time per se. Our awareness of time and its passage is determined by *events*, either external or internal. What the time-gapper describes as the loss of a slice of time (i.e., the failure to register a temporal segment) is really the failure to register or recall a series of external events that would "normally" have functioned as time markers. He fails to recall them, presumably because he did not pay conscious attention to them. The joker here is that the time-gapper registered *other* events—his passenger's conversation, the car radio, or, more commonly, the internal events of his own thoughts. His perturbation regarding the loss of a slice of time may be rapidly assuaged by pointing out that under other circumstances, these other events would be accepted as time markers. His problem is that he persists in counting as "appropriate" only those events that he classes as proper to his ostensible pursuit—driving a car along the road. The individual recalls a sequence of events of this type (let us call them X's) leading up to, for example, the limit sign outside the last town, X_{100}. He now wakes up to perceive event X_n—a major intersection, for example. He can recall no X events between X_{100} and X_n, but his knowledge of the distance covered implies that there must have been many of them. Thus—a gap in time—because the individual fails to take into account all the Y and Z events that would have been accepted happily as "appropriate" time markers in some other situation (e.g., sitting in the garden).

Having solved the time-gapper's problems, we can now turn to the underlying theoretical problem. Is it possible for a subject to fail to attend to a class of events while successfully engaging in a complex skill, the performance of which is largely dependent upon reactions to, and feedback from, that very class of events? The answer may be found in a brief consideration of the nature of skilled behavior. From the Bartlettian viewpoint, skilled performance is hierarchically organized. But most other theorists would also agree that elementary components become progressively habitual and automatized (i.e., not subject to conscious awareness). (Indeed, as the exponents of any complex skill know, de-automatization of particular elements can detract from the smooth performance of the whole sequence.) The experienced driver no longer needs to "pay attention" to each bodily movement or the positions of the controls as he, for example, steers, decelerates or changes gear. In the same way, the implications of routine external cues become predictable; the driver does not need to engage in continual conscious assessment of every individual event. He can afford to reserve attention for judgments of input at a strategic level. While the situation is undemanding and predictable, such strategic assessments are unnecessary, and the driver can "switch to automatic pilot." Attentional resources can be deployed elsewhere. But any "emergency" signal or other significant change in the situation will demand the assessment of probabilities, the setting up of hypotheses, the making and implementation of decisions. All this requires the focusing of conscious attention and thus a switch back to "manual control." But, it may be argued, such significant situational changes are a characteristic of driving. The answer to that is that the "time-gap experience" only occurs after a long stretch of undemanding driving. The incursion of the first relatively significant change is responsible for the time-gapper's "waking up."

The foregoing approach offers one explanation of why a prolonged series of events is not accessible to recall for the time-gapper. He did not consciously attend to the events, because they did not register above his "significance threshold." Presumably they were registered at some level beyond the sensory one (otherwise they could not have been deemed routine). But the suggestion is that they did not require further processing and were held only transiently in short-term memory. Of course, there is the possibility that although information about the events is not *accessible*, it might still be *available*, to use Tulving and Pearlstone's (1966) terminology. Unfortunately, we have no evidence that might clarify this point. It is quite possible that if prompted, offered retrieval cues, or merely urged to "try harder," the time-gapper might retrieve enough information to dispel his uneasiness.

Underwood (1976) has noted an alternative to the explanation offered here: that the time-gapper does, in fact, attend to the "missing" events but forgets each one completely. Again, as he points out, this is a question not yet answered by experiment. Its resolution has, of course, considerable relevance for the classical examination of the merits of single-channel as opposed to parallel processing of information.

The "Fleeting Thought" Experience

There can be few scholars who have not experienced the disconsolate feeling that they have grasped a new idea, achieved an insight, or glimpsed a problem but then been unable to identify it. The experience usually occurs during active attempts to follow up a particular line of thought or in the course of some cognitive activity. The "fleeting thought" may be felt to be important, but not directly relevant to the task in hand. Its consideration is therefore adjourned until the task is completed or until a "natural break" occurs in the preoccupying train of thought. By that time, however, it has disappeared, much to the frustration of its progenitor, who is left not only with a sense of certainty that he had the thought in question but also that it was one of some importance or novelty. The experience is usually described in such wistful terms as: "It was there at the back of my mind, but I wanted to finish what I was doing. If only . . ." or: "I had it by the tail, but I didn't grab it properly at the time, and it got away."

The intriguing problem here is that the individual finds it impossible to retrieve the "fleeting thought," because he does not know what it was about. In other words, he has no mnemonic handles to facilitate recall nor, usually, sufficient clues to limit the area of search. He is a treasure seeker who is not only unaware of the nature of the treasure but also has lost his maps.

In psychological terms, a "fleeting thought" usually occurs in the context of problem-solving activity, when the subject is running through alternative permutations of schemata in the search for an appropriate conceptualization or reconceptualization. Given that the "fleeting thought" experience is valid in the sense that it reflects a cognitive event, it seems likely that what has happened is that one of the permutations has been identified as of interest. It may indeed have provided an "answer" but not to the question under consideration (this incidentally, may be of interest in the analysis of creative processes of scientific insights). However, because of the ongoing task, the new schematic synthesis is not sufficiently processed to enable subsequent retrieval. In fact, it may not be enunciated semantically; its very domain may not be identified.

The ironic possibility emerges that the "fleeting thought" must indeed represent a novel conjunction of ideas, or it would be identified sufficiently to enable it to be reconstructed later. In that case, it is highly probable that it is of more interest than the "answer" being sought.

Remembering to Remember

At one time it was quite usual for people to tie knots in their handkerchiefs to remind themselves of some task to be accomplished during the day. A common sight was that of absent-minded individuals bemusedly contemplating the knots tied in their handkerchiefs by their more efficient wives. A busy day ahead was symbolized by the fact that a man could have so many knots in his handkerchief that he would be unable to blow his nose on the way to work. Presumably, the handkerchief was selected as the vehicle for mnemonic prods, because it was in constant use or was displayed prominently in the breast pocket. Changing fashions and the incursions of Kleenex tissues have led to a decline in the handkerchief as the customary bearer of "reminders." Instead, a range of idiosyncratic indicators may be identified. People tie pieces of string around their pinky fingers, wind rubber bands around their wrists, make ink marks on their thumbnails, or apply scraps of sticky tape to their cuffs.

Visible "reminders",of the sort described must be distinguished from written memoranda, lists made out for reference, notes entered in diaries or pocket-books, inscriptions on cards or kitchen slates, and so on. All these *aides-memoire* are explicit—they state what is to be remembered. The difference between them and "reminders" of the handkerchief-knot variety is subtle but profound. For, unlike the *aides-memoire*, the latter do not carry any information whatsoever about *what* is to be remembered. They serve merely as reminders that *something* is to be remembered. They exhort their possessor only to "remember to remember."

This distinction must surely pose a problem for memory theorists. At one level, it is true, the observation can be accounted for in many associationist models: The tying of the string (knot, etc.) lays down a trace in association with the thought of, for example, posting a letter later in the day. Subsequent sight of the string reactivates the associated trace. But can the matter be as straight-forward as this? There is something peculiar about this facile pairing of a physical activity with a meaningfully unrelated intent. On the other hand, contiguity theorists might well argue that temporal simultaneity is sufficient to establish appropriate association. But in that case, every other event present at the time of tying the knot could be predominant at later recall. How does the knot observer distinguish, for example, "post letter" from the chair he was sitting on when he tied the knot, his contemporaneous awareness that his wife was calling him for breakfast, that it was almost time to leave for work, that the radio announcer was summarizing the news, that he was also remembering to put on his jacket, and so on? The associationist might postulate the operation of semiselective attention. But he is now in danger of implying a "will to remember," which would presumably be a most unacceptable concept for him.

The core of the problem seems to be that contemporary memory research is focused on the relationship between an explicit event or piece of behavior (e.g., studying a list of words or attending to some visual or auditory stimulus) and its subsequent recall. In the present instance, the relationship is between a past physical event and a future one. However, the past physical event was at least temporally parallel with a thought about the future physical event, which may be termed a mental event. So now we have *three* events: an original event that is not itself recalled, a semantically unrelated mental event, and a subsequent physical event, semantically related to the latter but not to the former. And to make matters more complicated, the mental event apparently translates itself by a sort of Knight's Move into the second physical event. This translation lends itself to description in volitional terms. Posting a letter is a nice, safe piece of explicit behavior; but its antecedent appears to be "intent to post a letter," another concept that is currently very unfashionable.

It is possible, of course, that "remembering to remember" might be more appropriately considered, not in terms of memory per se, but as an example of what Flavell (1977) has termed "metamemory."

The "Feeling of Knowing"

There can be few people who do not frequently assert that they know something quite well, even though they cannot recall it. The "feeling of knowing" phenomenon (or FOK, to use its somewhat less than euphonious acronym) is characterized by an irritating mixture of surety and bafflement. The individual is convinced that he knows but frustrated by his inability to demonstrate his knowing. The inaccessible material may be almost any sort of information. But the feeling is most often reported in reference to some encapsulated semantic gobbet—a name, a word or synonym, a dimension, a date, a sequence, a definition, or an identifying feature. We are more likely to experience FOK in the face of our inability to recall the name of the general who fell during the American assault on the Queenston Heights than during our failure to summarize the whole pattern of events associated with the War of 1812.

The first question to be asked about FOK is whether it has any validity—that is to say, whether the subjective conviction does in fact reflect our state of knowing It is possible that FOK assertions are merely made to put a brave front on sheer ignorance. (There is another level of validity, of course. Is the subject "really" experiencing FOK, *regardless* of whether this reflects any underlying cognitive process of state? But this is not amenable to examination in objective terms.) The validity of the feeling might be indicated by seeing whether the subject could produce the information given further clues, probes, or associations. It could also be assessed by exploiting the fact that recognition tests are generally easier than recall tests. Having failed to recall, the subject might yet demonstrate the validity of his FOK by recognizing the information in dispute. The latter technique was in fact used by Hart (1965). Subjects were given a recall test of general information. They were asked to indicate whether or not they felt they knew the answers they were unable to recall. They were then given a multiple-choice test version of the same material. The results on two such experiments demonstrated that "FOK experiences are relatively accurate indicators of memory storage." Subjects proved able to predict generally which items they might be able to remember and which they would not.

A more intense variety of the general FOK experience is that where we feel not only that we know an unrecalled item but that we are so close to recalling it that it is "on the tip of our tongue." For some reason, TOT has excited much more interest than FOK. The report of an ingenious study by Brown and McNeill (1966) has subsequently been accorded the status of a classic. Subjects were presented with lexical definitions of uncommon words and were required to provide the words defined. When a TOT state was reported, the subjects were asked to describe as much as they could about the word—its initial letter, number of syllables, suffix, syllabic stress, and so on. Analysis of these reported features showed definite "generic recall." Both partial descriptions (letters) and formal characteristics (syllables, stress, etc.) tended to be correct, as did words claimed to be of similar sound or meaning. In other words, the subjects seemed to be able to produce criteria and identify possible multiple matches. Recall failure was due to an inability to define *all* the required criteria. But if the correct word was produced during the running-through of possibilities, the subject would recognize it as being correct immediately.

It should be noted that despite their intrinsic interest and methodical ingenuity, neither of the aforementioned studies has demonstrated more than that the FOK and TOT experiences can be shown to have objective validity. A complete conceptual analysis has yet to be made.

The apparent paradox of the phenomena is that they suggest that we can recognize that we have something available for recall without recalling it and before it is available for recognition. We mention levels of recognition later. Meanwhile, it may be suggested that FOK and TOT are reconcilable with the reconstructive approach to remembering. As argued earlier, information is not stored as discrete items, except for material that is deliberately rehearsed by rote and overlearned. Most information is coded and processed by assimilation into a variety of relevant schemata. Thus recall involves not the retrieval of the original items intact but the identification and activation of the appropriate schemata. Remembering consists of a reconstructive process that draws upon appropriate schemata and synthesizes their contributions. On this view, the FOK and TOT experiences accompany this cognitive organization and reflect the activation of some of the required schemata. The item of information is in process of being reconstructed. FOK is an apposite signal that a control model has been established, even though certain elements must yet be introduced to allow a final synthesis.

Cryptomnesia

Cryptomnesia is usually defined as the revival of an experience without the attributes of memory. In other words, a memory is not experienced as such but is thought to be a "first time" event. This is very common, particularly where integrative ideas and the solutions of problems are concerned. The individual comes up with an answer related to him in the past but one that has for him a novel flavor and that he therefore proudly identifies as original. In academic circles where ideas are continually interchanged, cryptomnesic claims are frequent and in extreme cases may lead to allegations of plagiarism. By definition, of course, the cryptomnesic cannot acknowledge his sources. To complicate matters, cryptomnesic "chains" can readily be observed. The graduate student may excitedly announce his brand-new "breakthrough," to the irritation of his supervisor, who had suggested it months before but who failed to realize that he had heard it from a colleague, who in turn. . . . Ironically enough, however, the originator of a subsequent cryptomnesic idea is often the individual himself. At a late state in preparing this chapter, I suddenly achieved a neat and unexpected insight that was excitedly incorporated in the text as a "new" idea. A subsequent review of my background notes revealed that I had recorded the "new" idea two months previously.

For most of us, it is probable that cryptomnesic experiences are everyday occurrences. We do not realize this, because in most cases we are never faced by the evidence that would disprove our assumptions of originality. But in any case, the vast majority of our "new" solutions and ideas are probably so mundane that we do not consider them worthy of celebration. We regard them as "original" but unexciting.

In the present context, the interest of cryptomnesia lies in the fact that it constitutes an everyday example of *recall without recognition*. This is a real-life situation that has not been explored in memory research and that presents basic problems for some current theories. These are discussed later. For the present, it may be observed that the fact that cryptomnesia is experienced most commonly in association with formal knowledge or, to use Tulving's (1972) terminology, in relation to "semantic" memories suggests one variable in recognition failure. That is that formal material is not richly personalized. The writer's approach would be that it has not been incorporated across many schemata and is therefore recalled with fewer identifying clues and less "richness" of processing. Its schematic shallowness does not favor an accompanying sense of familiarity, which is what determines recognition.

Checking

"Checking," in the sense it is used here, refers to those behaviors undertaken to confirm that some action or task has been completed. The subject experiences a nagging uncertainty that will not let him rest until a check has been completed. The action checked is usually one of a routine nature, carried out to serve domestic security, orderliness, or economy. The classical examples are locking doors; switching off lights, water faucets, and gas taps; adjusting thermostats; replacing implements and utensils; and putting out the garbage. Checking is referred to in most general textbooks of clinical psychiatry, usually in descriptions of obsessional states. In its extreme forms, it is commonly associated with compulsive disorders. But in milder forms, it is very common among normal people, although admittedly it is more generally reported by those with what are usually termed obsessional personality traits.

This sort of checking is usually assumed to reflect absent or attenuated memory. The checker, it is postulated, is unable to remember whether he has in fact, for example, locked the back door. He now confirms this by visual inspection. Unfortunately, this is only half the story; the elicitation of more detailed accounts rapidly reveals that the phenomenon is much more complicated.

Habitual checkers usually report that they *can* recall having previously locked the door. Sometimes they rationalize their checking on the grounds that it is necessary because it is always possible that somebody could have subsequently unlocked the door and then forgotten to relock it. But checking is often carried out only a few minutes after the initial action or in a situation where it would be impossible for another person to have reversed it. In either case, the checker may recall his initial action quite clearly.

Among habitual checkers, their checking is seldom limited to a single verification. The individual may lock the back door before settling down for the evening, check an hour later, check again before going to bed, and still find it necessary to get out of bed and go downstairs for a final check. (Ironically enough, this may become a vicious circle, because he now has to check that he switched off the downstairs lights before he returned to bed.) The point here is that checking does not seem to consist merely of some verification of a hazily remembered situation. But that there is a confimatory element present is suggested by the fact that the checker is eventually satisfied; except in pathological cases, he does not enter into an endless spiral of checking his checking.

The writer is not aware of any psychological study of everyday checking. Certainly, it would seem difficult to explain the phenomenon in terms of any currently fashionable theory of mnemonic processes. Two possible lines of approach are noted here.

Insightful checkers often observe that they have no doubt that they can recall, for example, locking the door. But this is a routine action. They do it every night and thus cannot be sure whether what they are recalling is the most recent episode or some earlier one. Their doubts have to do with the *temporal ordering* of the event, rather than the event itself. The regular, repetitious nature of the event tends to diminish the "recency effect" that gives a subjective freshness to our recollections of recent occurrences and that diminishes with the passage of time. Whatever accounts for this characteristic, it is well attested by everyday experience. Yet it has not been closely examined by contemporary memory theorists who have concerned themselves mostly with the parallel phenomena associated with immediate recall or sensory registration.

The second possibility is that checking may in some way be related to the nature of the *memory image*. Reed (1977) has reported some tentative findings regarding characteristics of remembering among a group of patients with obsessional personality disorders. One such finding was that by comparison with that of nonobsessional controls, the obsessional's memory imagery was restricted to the visual modality and was relatively "detached." Although the imagery was vivid and reported in detail, it was "seen" as though from outside the viewer. This indicates some weakness in *redintegration*, as though the personal flavor of the experience in question has not been completely synthesized with the objective event. If this interpretation is correct, it would suggest that for the checker, what is unsatisfactory is not *what* he recalls but *the quality of the recalling* itself.

Again, contemporary theorizing has so far shed little light on the nature of personal reminiscence despite Tulving's (1972) contribution, which is discussed later.

Déjà Vu

"The only time I have ever visited Quebec City was when I was at high school. We were walking down the hill in the old quarter when I suddenly felt convinced that I'd been there before. . . ."

This is a typical report of *déjà vu* (literally: "already seen")—the experience that one has witnessed some new situation previously. Perception of the current scene is accompanied by a compelling sense of familiarity. This usually lasts for only a few seconds, though in some pathological cases, the sensation may be prolonged or even continuous. It is often accompanied by a conviction that one knows what is to happen next; "I even knew that the street led down to the little square. . . ."

The phenomenon is often reported by psychiatric patients and is known to be associated with temporal lobe lesions and focal epilepsy. But it seems to be experienced on occasion by the majority of normal people, usually in youth or under conditions of fatigue or heightened sensitivity.

Déjà vu has excited interest and debate for many years, so there is no need here to give more than the briefest account of the various explanatory approaches proposed. In summary, the vast majority examines the phenomenon in terms of recall in one way or another. Understandably, the sensation of having previously experienced the event in question suggests to the individual concerned that he is somehow recalling a previous occurrence. The present event is taken to be a "second" occurrence; mystification and interest is thus focused on the posited "first" one. Since the paradox of déjà vu is that the individual knows that in fact he has not previously experienced the event in the normal way, many "explanations" assume that he must have experienced it in some abnormal way. One group of "explanations" thus posits psychical or magical processes, attributing unusual powers to the individual and interpreting the phenomenon in terms of precognition, revelation, telepathy, mediumship, or reincarnation. All of these are put forward as ways in which the individual could have gained his knowledge of that "first" occurrence. A more subtle hypothesis is that the "first" experience took place in a dream, a proposition that accords well with the dreamlike quality of déjà vu itself.

A variation of the recall approach is that taken by a number of psychological and psychiatric authorities who have classified the phenomenon as an example of *paramnesia*. For them, the question becomes not one of how the individual can remember something he has not experienced before but of why he should think that he has not experienced it before. A "first" occurrence is assumed and the postulated "forgetting" explained in terms of repression of a painful or ego-threatening experience.

A more prosaic psychological explanation, though of the same "recall-focused" variety, is that although the individual has, for example, never walked along the street in question, it shares so many features with other streets he has actually visited that he is reminded of them; i.e., he has partial recall. Technically, this would be an example of *restricted paramnesia*, like the "I can't place him" phenomenon. But in the latter case, the individual is well aware of those aspects of the situation that have been previously experienced (e.g., the other person's appearance, expression, and voice). The perplexity arises from the inability to reconstruct the *whole* of the previous experience (the context of previous encounters). In déjà vu, *all* the new experience seems familiar, and so do the ensuing events.

Finally, there is a theory based on neurological function, which again takes a "recall" approach. This argues that the cerebral hemispheres may temporarily lose synchronicity. Thus the anomalous feeling of familiarity may be due to the fact that one side of the brain is receiving input (the "first" occurrence) a microsecond before the other (which appropriately registers a "second" occurrence).

A more fruitful psychological approach to the consideration of déjà vu may be to de-emphasize the recall aspect, with its presumption of a "previous" or "first" event, and examine the experience in terms of its other name: "*fausse reconnaissance*" (false recognition). Instead of "Why is the observer unable to recall the previous situation?" the question reverts to "Why does the observer feel that he recognizes the present situation?" This, indeed, was the approach taken by Pierre Janet, the first psychologist to identify, describe, and analyze the experience. He argued that the problem was not to do with how the observer *remembers* a previous situation but with how he *perceives* the present one. We return to déjà vu when we discuss the nature of recognition.

Jamais Vu

The *jamais vu* experience is the converse of déjà vu. The individual reports that a situation or scene well known to him seems to lack familiarity. He is fully aware that he has experienced it before on many occasions and is disturbed because he does not feel that it is familiar. Patients have been known to complain that their bedrooms sometimes seem unfamiliar, although they know that nothing has been changed.

Jamais vu has not been discussed as much as déjà vu, probably because it is much rarer. The writer knows of no report of its occurrence among normal people. On the other hand, normal people occasionally refer to fleeting experiences of this type; the "unfamiliar" reaction seems to occur when some slight change in the normal arrangement of a room has taken place, for example. As soon as the change has been identified, the sensation disappears. In other words, the individual has responded to a change in the *organization* of a well-known visual display. The individual components have remained the same. Both the totality and its elements are so well known that they are normally "taken for granted." Conscious attention is focused upon them only when some reorganization constitutes a mismatch with the observer's established expectancies. The ironic outcome is that in such cases, the observer experiences some absence of familiarity only when he starts to pay attention to the situation.

The importance of jamais vu for the present discussion is that it is the classical example of recall without recognition. Whereas cryptomnesia represents a failure to recognize known ideas, jamais vu represents a failure to recognize regularly experienced *percepts*. And unlike the cryptomnesiac, the jamais vu victim is fully aware of appropriate recall.

A bizarre phenomenon that has some features in common with jamais vu is *l'illusion des sosies*, which has occasionally been reported in cases of paranoid illness. The patient recognizes appropriately all the individual attributes of another person but is unable to recognize the other person as such. Eventually he becomes convinced that the other person—usually a close friend, relative, or spouse—must be a double or impostor. The phenomenon is discussed by Reed (1972).

Depersonalization and Derealization

Under conditions of severe stress, it is not unusual for people to experience a strange feeling of personal unreality. "I felt as though I was a zombie. I knew I was behaving normally, but every movement seemed unnatural somehow. . . ." The individual is aware of what he is doing and perceives the environment as unchanged. But he has a dreamlike sense of himself as being different, unreal, and nonspontaneous, which may take the form of feeling detached from his physical self. This is termed *depersonalization*, as opposed to *derealization*, where the individual feels himself to be unchanged but his environment to be unreal.

Both phenomena figure prominently in psychiatric problems, particularly in anxiety and phobic states. But they are commonly encountered by normal people in the face of physical danger, anxiety, bereavement, social embarrassment, fatigue, or convalescent weakness. They have often been reported by military aircrew and combat troops as being experienced during action. "I felt like it was somebody else in that cockpit. . . ." "Oddly enough, I was quite calm—it was all like some sort of dream. . . ." Similar reports have been given by shipwreck survivors, explorers, and concentration camp victims. A less dramatic but well-known example is the state of mind of the tyro actor, public speaker, athlete, or entertainer during his first appearance before a large audience. His initial panic may give way to a feeling of unreality or a dreamy sense of "being away from it all." In extreme cases, the individual may feel not only that he is unreal but also that he has become detached from his body and is observing it from outside ("ego-splitting"). "I could hear this voice drooling on. Suddenly I realized it must be mine!" "There was a Madame Tussaud's figure propped up against the lectern. I was floating about six feet above its head, watching it."

These sorts of experience have been variously interpreted by psychoanalysts as flight from the fear of psychic castration, eroticization of thinking, or narcissistic self-scrutiny. Psychiatric theories have included the view that they constitute an abortive form of schizophrenia. Their relationship to anxiety is generally accepted; one argument is that they are merely expressions of fear. More positively, they can be regarded as defense mechanisms that allow the individual to function *despite* his fear. On the latter view, they are examples of *dissociation of affect*, a detachment from or walling-in of surges of emotion that would otherwise have a disintegrative effect.

Although this is not usually commented upon in the literature, depersonalization and derealization probably also occur in happier contexts, such as falling in love or winning a major lottery prize. And of course they may be induced by the ingestion of alcohol or hallucinogenic drugs. Indeed, the inculcation of a subjectively "unreal" state is often the reason for taking the drugs in the first place, as it is for participating in many mystic rituals and social or religious rites.

In non-drug-induced instances, the experience of depersonalization has certain characteristics that are important for both nosological precision and theoretical discussion:

1. The individual feels himself to be *changed* or altered in some way.
2. This change is associated with a sense of *unreality*.
3. He retains *insight*—he appreciates that the change and unreality are subjective.
4. He retains his sense of self, despite the changes.

In derealization, the same characteristics apply, except that the sense of change has reference to the environment, not to the individual. And here it must be stressed that despite subjective distortions, there appears to be no disorder of sensory function. What has changed is not the perceptible characteristics of the input but its significance.

Depersonalization and derealization, with related phenomena such as "dissociation of affect" and "ego-splitting," can be studied from a variety of viewpoints. Reed (1972) has discussed them in terms of cognitive organization, and the whole topic of dissociation is examined by Nemiah in Chapter 10. For present purposes, it will suffice to observe that these phenomena can be regarded as examples of attenuated or disordered *recognition* in its true sense. Input—on one hand personal, on the other contextual—is registered appropriately and with no failure of recall. But the qualities of familiarity and personal reference—the crucial characteristics of recognition—are absent or distorted.

GENERAL DISCUSSION

The majority of the phenomena outlined evoke affective response in the individual ranging from mild puzzlement or irritation to fears about his mental state. The degree of affect, it may be suggested, is a function of the amount of discrepancy between the experience and some cognitive assessment. At the "mild" end of the scale, the discrepancy is relatively small or of little significance. For instance, the first of our phenomena may be described by the individual as: "I feel sure that I know this person. Thus I should be able to remember his name, and yet I cannot." Here the discrepancy refers merely to an incomplete match. At the "severe" end, the discrepancy is at once more clear-cut and more profound. For instance, déjà vu may be described as: "I feel sure that I know this place. Yet I have never been here before." Here the discrepancy is total: the experience is completely contradicted by objective assessment.

At the same time, the effect seems to be enhanced by the intensity of personal attribution involved. And the reader will doubtless have noticed that one characteristic shared by all the phenomena is their *personal flavor*. This observation, of course, applies not only to anomalous instances like these under discussion but to all everyday remembering. Indeed, it could scarcely be otherwise. For *what* is selected and processed as well as *how* it is remembered are specific to the individual rememberer. The selection of input is determined by the individual's interests and needs and its organization by his level of cognitive development and his particular range and weighing of schemata. Whether it is accessible to retrieval and, if so, the form in which it is retrieved are also obviously individualized, each being a function not only of the retrieval cues available but of the nature of the earlier organization. Yet for almost a century, memory researchers, instead of studying these individual differences, have vainly attempted to eliminate them. Ebbinghaus (1885/1964), in his classical attempt to apply the precise methodology of the physical sciences to the study of the higher mental processes, deliberately set out to elicit "isolated responses" by using "simple" stimuli. He had rapidly realized that stimuli evoke different, highly individualized responses because each stimulus had different meaningful connotations for each observer. His solution to this "problem" was to present meaningless stimuli, this giving all subjects a zero start, as it were. Meaninglessness, he argued, could be assured by the use of nonsense material. Unfortunately, as we now know, subjects are quite capable of investing *any* stimuli with their own "meanings," especially if they are aware that they will be required to recall the material at a later date. Despite this, generations of memory and verbal learning researchers have continued in the Ebbinghaus tradition. Where nonsense material has been abandoned, it has been replaced by lists of words, often "controlled for association." But the central interest has remained the same—to eliminate or at least control individual differences. The approach used in the present chapter is, of course, that individual differences are at the heart of the matter. After a critical discussion of Ebbinghaus' assumptions, Bartlett (1932) condemned the use of "artificial" material and attempted to employ "the sort of material most closely resembling that commonly dealt with in real life." The appropriateness of the material he selected may be open to question. But his general theoretical principles have not only withstood the test of time; they seem to be slowly emerging triumphant. Contemporary researchers of the mainstream associationist persuasion are now beginning to consider Bartlett's ideas. This change is partly due to necessity; many experimental findings are difficult to explain without recourse to a "restructuring" approach. But much of the credit must go to Neisser's (1967) provocatively brilliant and influential work. The central issue of individual differences is still skated around. But it seems to be now generally accepted that at least the phenomenological distinction between "logical" or "formal" knowledge and "personal" knowledge has validity. The implications of the individual nature of the range and development of schemata may not be palatable as yet to the majority of mainstream researchers. At the same time, with honorable exceptions such as Eagle and Mulliken (1974), they have avoided consideration of the roles of interest and affect. But the central fact that input is personalized now seems undeniable. And this immediately implies not only that recall performance will reflect the idiosyncrasies of personal processing but that the subjective experience associated with recall will have a personal flavor.

"Episodic" and "Semantic" Memory

Changing attitudes among contemporary theorists in this regard were heralded by Tulving's (1972) presentation at the Pittsburgh conference of the distinction between "semantic" and "episodic" memories, which won immediate acceptance. Despite its recent introduction, it has already assumed classical status. "Semantic memory" we are told, is "a mental thesaurus, organized knowledge a person possesses about words and other verbal symbols, their meaning and referents, about relations among them, and about rules, formulas, and algorithms for the manipulation of these symbols, concepts and relations . . ." (Tulving, 1972, p. 386). "Episodic memory," on the other hand, "receives and stores information about temporally dated episodes or events, and temporal–spatial relations among these events. A perceptual event can be stored in the episodic system solely in terms of its perceptible properties or attributes, and it is always stored in terms of its autobiographical reference to the already existing contents of the episodic memory store" (Tulving, 1972, p. 385).

This all sounds suspiciously like new terminology for the old categories of "logical" memories as opposed to reminiscence. And it has much in common with Piaget and Inhelder's (1968, 1973) distinction between "memory in its strict sense" and "memory in the wider sense." There is no doubt that it is a useful and important distinction that merits reemphasis. But does it go far enough? Basically, Tulving's "episodic" memory holds information that is temporally coded—information about when things occurred and in what context. As we observe later, contemporary recognition studies are essentially about this "when-ness," rather than about "recognition" in its normal, phenomenological sense. It could be argued that memory researchers were forced to recognize the classical distinction if any theoretical sense was to be made of their work. This would account for the fact that Tulving's emphasis is somehow more restricted than the classical one. "Episodic" memory necessarily refers to personal variables associated with the acquisition of particular pieces of information. But as its very title suggests, it is more concerned with the *occasion* of the acquisition and the placing of that occasion in time. The classical equivalent— "personal" memory—also has reference to occasions. But its emphasis is upon the subjective flavor of the experience, the meaning of the information for the individual in question, its investment with personal significance. This would imply that the timing of the event must be considered in relation to the personal history of the individual. In information-processing terms, the significance of input is determined by the current state of the system, which will determine its coding and differential processing. Its subsequent retrieval is in turn determined by the processing employed.

According to Tulving's formulation, conventional memory tasks are categorized as "episodic." As we shall see, such tasks are indeed to do with temporal order—that is what the experiments are all about. But it would be hard to think of anything more neutral and less personalized than the perusal of, for example, lists of words. Indeed, affective components are deliberately excluded, ego-involvement is minimal, and individual differences are ignored. Thus, the temporal aspect of "episodic" memory can be recruited to enhance conventional studies of memory whereas the implications of the personal aspect are conveniently suppressed. It may reasonably be suggested that this is putting the cart before the horse.

But quite apart from the uses to which it has been put, Tulving's distinction is itself not beyond criticism. First of all, *all* information acquired by the individual must originally be "episodic"; its initial acquisition must have taken place at some time and must necessarily have involved the individual acquirer.

Second, there are difficulties inherent in the idea that we possess two complete memory systems that are independent, though they may be interactive in certain situations. The presumption raises a number of questions. Presumably, input must be allocated to one system or the other. How is that decision made? At what stage? By what criteria? If the systems are independent, is there any possibility of interchange as well as interaction? And if not, how does information ever enter the "semantic" store, given that initially it must have been "episodic"? Whatever the allocation criteria, system independence suggests a clear cutoff in allocation, with no overlap. Given that my knowledge of πr^2 is a characteristic piece of "semantic" knowledge, it must somehow figure in my "semantic" system. But supposing that I initially acquired that particular piece of information on a specific and memorable date (my birthday, for example) in a context of particular autobiographical significance (e.g., during a violent thunderstorm, while in the throes of my first love affair); what went into my "episodic" system?

It may be suggested that a more plausible and economical approach to Tulving's distinction would be to hypothesize in terms of schematic integration. Far from being independent, schemata are highly interactive and hierarchically organized. Autobiographical significance may readily be conceptualized as a degree of "saturation." If my knowledge of the length of the Amazon River was initially acquired in a routine classroom setting and a relatively neutral affective context, it will doubtless have a low "saturation" and may be termed "formal" or "semantic." My knowledge of πr^2 on the other hand, is a piece of formal information but is stamped with a high "saturation" level.

What is still open to question in this approach is how the subjective attribution of "I-ness" or "personalization" comes about. At what stage does it develop— input, encoding, processing, search, or final retrieval? Or, in Bartlettian terms— initial perception, schematization, or reconstruction? Is it a question of some sort of labeling or graduated bench mark; or is it to do with the operation of a special "personal" schema? Bartlett himself proposed that it was due to the range of schemata available. He argued that schemata were determined by "appetite and instinct" in early stages of organic development and, of much more importance at advanced human levels, "interests and ideals." These determinants are highly individualized, so that the very process of schematization involves the attribution of a "personal stamp." This explains differences between individuals. But as it stands, it does not explain intraindividual differences in the intensity of "personal flavor." To cover these, Bartlett would doubtless posit schematic "loadings" related to affective and interest factors in the individual's history. The word *history* reminds us of the temporal element in personalization. We have already noted, in reference to the "time-gap experience," how important to our self-conceptualization is the sense of personal continuity.

The problem is made even more complicated by the fact that a pronounced personal flavor may be attached to *false* memories. Incorrect recollections are often maintained with certainty and experienced as richly personalized. And déjà vu is the classical example of faulty recognition that is nevertheless experienced with conviction and overwhelming personal reference. This point has been emphasized by Piaget and Inhelder (1973): " . . . there is no intrinsic, qualitative difference between the contents of a false memory and those of a true one: a false recognition gives the same *déjà vu* impression (and the same impression of I-ness) as a correct recognition, and the same is true of reconstruction. There is nothing, moreover, that entitles us to distinguish 'reconstructed' from pure, or false from correct, recall [p. 398].'' They go on to demonstrate that it is not ''the subject's self-identity which confers their individual identities upon the memories and localizes them in the past [p. 398]'' but rather the reverse. In other words, information does not receive a graduated ''personal'' bench mark at the input stage. The personal flavor of memories is a function of the whole system operating during the process of reconstruction.

Recall and Recognition

The central feature of recognition, as it is defined by contemporary memory researchers, is that it is a case where remembering has perceptual support. Because the ''target'' material is presented, usually in association with alternative choices, the event remembered from a previous occasion is present at the time of remembering. Even on this simple criterion, several of the phenomena outlined involve ''faulty'' recognition. Déjà vu is the classical example of an anomaly in this respect, recognition being reported in response to a situation *not* previously encountered. If this may be termed a case of ''false positive'' responding, then jamais vu and cryptomnesia are ''false negatives,'' for here recognition is absent in a situation that has in fact been previously experienced. The ''Face, but not the name'' and the ''I can't quite place him'' phenomena are examples of a mixed type. Here, recognition is reported, but recall is patchy or abbreviated. On the other hand, in depersonalization and derealization, recognition is attenuated, though recall is complete. All these phenomena, then, involve some dissociation between recognition and recall, which is of significance for theorizing. Until relatively recently, most psychologists assumed that recall and recognition represented equivalent measures of remembering, the difference being one of degree, inasmuch as recognition was ''easier'' than recall. As Adams (1967) pointed out, it was the assumption that ''recognition and recall are indicants of the same underlying memory state [p. 263]'' which probably accounted for the fact that relatively few investigations or conceptual studies of recognition had been reported up to that time. Clearly, any naturally occurring examples of nonequivalence must offer difficulties for that assumption. The interesting question is whether contemporary models can accommodate them any better.

The standard earlier approach to the difference between recall and recognition has been termed the ''threshold hypothesis.'' This assumes that the probability of an item being remembered depends on the ''strength'' of the item. The item will be recognized if its strength is above the ''recognition threshold.'' More strength is required to bring it above the ''recall threshold.'' Thus the difference between recognition and recall, it is argued, is merely one of degree. The underlying processes are assumed to be the same. Kintsch (1970) has summarized the evidence for and against the "threshold hypothesis," pointing out that any variable that affects recall and recognition differentially impugns the validity of the hypothesis. But just as damaging would be any situation where the order of the thresholds is the opposite of that postulated. The hypothesis can allow for only three situations: (a) that where the strength of an item is so low that it is below both thresholds and is thus neither recognized nor recalled; (b) that where the strength is above both thresholds and the item may be both recognized and re-called; and (c) that where the strength is above the recognition threshold but below the recall threshold, so that the item may be recognized but not recalled. Of our phenomena, the "Face, not the name" and the "I can't quite place him" examples can both be covered by the third alternative. But jamais vu and cryptomnesia should not be possible on the "threshold hypothesis"; in these cases, recall is operating in the absence of recognition. A similar problem applies to depersonali-zation and derealization. And what of déjà vu? Here we have recognition with-out recall but in a situation where ostensibly there is nothing to recall.

The déjà vu paradox also eludes explanation by another hypothesis, which at first sight seems potentially more fruitful. This is the hypothesis proposed by Adams (1967), which suggests that recall and recognition reflect different sets of information stored in memory. Recall, it is hypothesized, draws upon verbal traces, whereas recognition utilizes pictorial traces. In our present instances, it will be noted that, with the exception of cryptomnesia, they are all to do with perceptual, as opposed to linguistic, material. There is ample evidence that information in different modalities is coded separately, and Paivio (1971) and others have proposed that semantic memory may operate at two levels, one linguistic and the other utilizing sensory imagery. However, as it stands, Adams' hypothesis offers no solution to our cases of recognition failure.

During the last seven years, considerable excitement has been engendered by the "Two-Stage Theory" (Anderson & Bower, 1972; Kintsch, 1970) and its various elaborations. In its most basic form, this approach argues that recall involves two independent processes—search (retrieval) and decision. Recogni-tion involves the decision element only; it is a subprocess of recall and therefore qualitatively different.

The two-stage approach is not only elegant and parsimonious; it has the advantage of avoiding the difficulties inherent in the previous two hypotheses. Its assumption of separable processes enables it to handle certain differential changes in recall and recognition while making unnecessary any recourse to more than one type of memory system. However, any attempt to apply the approach to encompass the phenomena under discussion runs into similar difficulties to those posed for the "threshold hypothesis."

We have just observed that the basic two-stage theory can accommodate differential changes in recall and recognition. This is so, but it should be noted that this applies in only one direction. The theory allows for situations where a variable affects recall while leaving recognition invariant. But the opposite situation cannot occur, according to the theory. For an item to be correctly recalled, it must pass through the two stages of retrieval and decision. As recognition involves the decision stage, it is logically impossible for recall to occur without recognition. A number of experimental studies (e.g., Tulving & Thomson, 1973; Watkins, 1974) have reported clear superiority of recall over recognition of word lists presented in different contexts. In the present instance, jamais vu, cryptomnesia, depersonalization, and derealization are all examples of recall without appropriate recognition and can therefore be no better handled by the standard two-stage theory than they could by the threshold hypothesis.

In more recent versions of the two-stage theory (Anderson & Bower, 1974; Kintsch, 1974), the problem has been resolved by postulating that retrieval occurs during recognition as well as during recall. But this, of course, diminishes the central point of the original theory and raises the question of whether a two-stage approach is useful.

The most recent development in comparison of recall and recognition is the interesting tendency of some authorities to revert to the older, standard view that the two are substantially the same (Lockhart, Craik, & Jacoby, 1976; Tulving, 1976). After a detailed criticism of the various versions of two-stage theory, Tulving (1976) has presented an approach based on what he terms *Episodic Ecphory*. The latter is defined (Tulving, 1976) as "the process by which information stored in a specific memory trace is utilized by the system to produce conscious memory of certain aspects of the original event [p. 40]." (Tulving uses the term merely to reserve the word *retrieval* to designate the first of the two hypothesized stages in the two-stage theory.) It is proposed that recall and recognition represent basically similar processes. Remembering (either by recall or recognition) springs from interactions between trace information, resultant encoding, and retrieval information. Recall and recognition differ only with respect to the nature of the available retrieval information. In recognition, this is present in a literal copy of the event to be remembered; in recall, only noncopy cues are available.

Tulving's proposal adds nothing to Bartlett's reconstruction approach. The only major difference is that he does not emphasize the nature of the processing and organization of input. He makes no reference to schematization, and his use of the term *trace* suggests that he conceives of information as being coded and stored intact. Thus he can argue (1976):

> An important consequence of the conceptualization of ecphory as a joint product of information from two sources is that the system never retrieves anything "incorrectly". Whatever is retrieved by the episodic system is determined by the information available in the store, by the specified temporal date of the original

event, and by any additional ecphoric information that is provided . . . the output from the ecphoric system is never "wrong", only the input into the system may be [p. 65].

If we take this literally, it suggests that when applied to our recognition phenomena, Tulving's view can account satisfactorily only for the paramnesias and the "time-gap" experience. The present writer's argument, derived directly from Bartlett, would be that "wrong" or anomalous remembering (whether in recall or recognition) is the product, not of the input into the system, but of how that input is organized *within* the system.

Reconstructed schematic material, in the present view, can seldom be a precise copy of the original input. Except in very undemanding or practised tasks, recall material will include condensation, reordering, interpretations, distortions, or elaborations. Bartlett demonstrated that such changes are accentuated during a series of recalls or reproductions. It may be suggested that in a series of recollections, we are not recalling the original event at all, but our last recollection of it. The longer the series, the more the remembered version will differ from the original, because each further recollection will involve, for example, elaborations of elaborations. If this line of argument is applied to the recognition situation, an interesting implication emerges. Recognition involves the acceptance of a "good fit" or match of currently perceived material with recalled, imaginal material. The better the subjective match, the more pronounced will be the accompanying sense of familiarity. Clearly, the more an original event has been recalled (or reminisced about), the more modifications will have been introduced and therefore the weaker the "fit" between our current reconstruction and any re-presentation of the actual original. At some point we may fail to recognize the original, because in many ways it will no longer match our reconstruction. This was demonstrated in a study by Belbin (1950), who left unsuspecting subjects in a waiting room for 2 minutes; on the wall facing them was a poster. The experimental subjects were then asked to recall as much as they could about the poster, prompted by standardized questions. The control subjects were engaged for the same length of time in the performance of an unrelated task. All subjects were then shown the original poster and asked if it was the one they had seen in the waiting room. Fourteen of the 16 control subjects recognized it, whereas only 4 of the 16 experimental subjects did so. Now conversely, it is equally possible that a good subjective match may be made (and therefore a feeling of familiarity may be evoked) with material that differs considerably from the original, given that the differences happen to be in line with the modifications developed during reconstruction.

Here may be the key to the apparently intransigent problem of déjà vu. Our reconstructive remembering of, for example, a street scene may provide a close match with the scene currently perceived. If we know for certain that we have never been on this particular street before, then the feeling of familiarity accompanying the match is highly perplexing. It may be that what constitutes the experience of déjà vu is this perplexity, resulting from the discrepancy between objective knowledge and subjective response in a situation of heightened affect.

Without doubt, many memory researchers will complain that it is neither fair nor relevant to discuss the foregoing phenomena in terms of their theories of recognition. These refer to "recognition" as a measure of *performance* or behavior, whereas our phenomena are to do with *experience*. But this would surely be a sorry admission.

The verb *recognize* has several dictionary definitions, of which the relevant one is "know again, identify as known before." The essential feature is the *feeling of familiarity*. Technical definitions concur, defining recognition as: "the feeling of familiarity when a previously encountered situation is present. . .". The memory researcher may on the one hand assert that he is interested, not in recognition as such, but in a method that *measures* recognition. In that case he can scarcely deny the association of his work with everyday, real-life instances of the very experience he claims to be measuring. On the other hand, he may claim that experiences or feelings have nothing to do with what he is studying. In that case he is not studying recognition and should retitle his method forthwith. Furthermore, he should cease to discuss his findings in terms of familiarity and desist from projecting them into discussions of recognition. They have applicability only to discussions of measurement or experimental technique.

This should not be taken to imply that conventional "recognition experiments" are pointless or trivial; on the contrary, they play a significant part in the study of remembering. But they have probably told us little about recognition as such. And it is quite possible that the difficulties encountered in conceptualizing recall and recognition are due to the assumption that laboratory recognition tests *do* measure recognition. It is quite reasonable to compare scores on different types of tests. But to extrapolate those findings in the analysis and comparison of underlying processes is valid only if the tests are differential measures of those processes. In the present instance, we are probably comparing chalk with cheese. At the risk of oversimplification, it may be proposed that recall is an operation or process evidenced by performance; recognition is a feeling or quality of experience. Recall can reasonably be expressed in terms of amount—for example, by the number of list items correctly recalled. Recognition, on the other hand, cannot be expressed in the same terms. Its measurement would surely involve ratings of familiarity, not numbers of items remembered. Comparisons of numbers of items can thus tell us nothing about recognition or its relation to recall. But they can give us important insights into remembering as a function of external retrieval cues, which is highly apposite to the consideration of hypotheses such as that of Tulving (1976).

The (so-called) recognition method also offers a way into the investigation of two other topics of fundamental importance in the study of memory. It would seem that the method measures not recognition but *context effects* and *temporal ordering*. The subject presented with a number of words and asked to judge whether they include any of the list he studied an hour before must surely ask himself two related questions: (a) "Were any of these among that list?" (b) "Were any of these among those I studied an hour ago?" Given that they are within his vocabularly, he recognizes *all* the words because they are all familiar to him. They may be words that he uses every week of his life. Thus he cannot discriminate between the "target" words and the alternatives in terms of recognition. He discriminates by trying to reconstruct the original list and assessing individual words in relation to that earlier context of other words that constituted the original list. At the same time, he essays a temporal judgment, a sort of recency effect assessment. "I see or hear all these quite frequently. But which ones did I see an hour ago?" The experience of relative recency or temporal distance and our attempts to "place" events in temporal order (perhaps over personal time, rather than calendar time) are interrelated features that are obviously central to the study of remembering. The literature on short-term memory is replete with relevant findings, but the details of medium- and long-term memory are less well documented, although there have been several laboratory studies in recent years. Murdock (1974) has integrated a number of findings that suggest that the encoding, storage, and retrieval of information may be conceptualized on a "conveyor-belt model". Incoming items of information are conceived as suitcases dropped upon an endless airport loading ramp. The further a particular item (suitcase) has moved along the belt, the less distinctive it becomes and the more time it takes to search for and retrieve it. Murdock is avowedly concerned only with laboratory studies of "reproductive" memory. It would be of major theoretical importance to know how far his model might apply to longer-term, "real-life" remembering.

We have not so far considered what cognitive states or processes are accompanied by the experience of recognition—the "feeling of familiarity." Reed (1972) has discussed this, pointing out that we do not, for example, say: "I recognize that. It is an object!" A pronounced experience of recognition occurs when we have run through a series of categorizations; for example, it is a chair, it is a rocking chair, it is old, the seat has been repaired, etc. Only then do we announce triumphantly: "I recognize that chair! It was old Uncle Harry's!" Reed suggested that the intensity of familiarity is related to the level of conceptualization attained. The higher the level in the hierarchic organization, the more schemata have been subsumed. Thus, perhaps the degree of familiarity experienced is proportional to the number of schemata contributing to the match. It may also be suggested that this is relevant to the question of "personal flavor" discussed above. Perhaps the richness of the personal quality of remembering is also a function of the level of schematic synthesis, leading to more satisfactory redintegration.

Interestingly enough, Craik and Lockhart (1972) suggested the same sort of explanation but in reference to recall of different types of information under different recall conditions. They suggested that the memory trace might fruitfully be considered as the by-product of perceptual processing. The trace's durability is a function of "depth of processing"—the degree of elaboration, or position in a hierarchy of analyses ranging upward from the level of physical characteristics to that of symbolic categories. It is a further sign of changing times in memory research that this suggestion was received with enthusiasm. But despite its initial appeal, the "depth of processing" idea becomes somewhat less plausible after due consideration. Although it is straightforward to describe the running-through of hypotheses in the "chair" example above, it is harder to envisage the same sequential process taking place at perception. At the same time, the Craik and Lockhart model suggests a continuum between, for example, the physical analysis of a word and its semantic analysis—which is a very difficult idea to accept. Furthermore, there is clear evidence for separate channels in memory for different modalities. How may the level of processing in one of these be compared with that in another? Perhaps significantly, Craik's own subsequent work (e.g., Craik & Tulving, 1975) has cast considerable doubt on the "depth of processing" model, leading to radical modifications along the lines of "spread" as opposed to "depth." Nevertheless, the Craik approach, with its emphasis on processing and the study of constituent operations and its acceptance of reconstruction as well as scanning as a mode of retrieval (Lockhart, Craik & Jacoby, 1976), suggests a most hopeful rapprochement between the Ebbinghaus and the Bartlett approaches.

As we noted in the introduction to this chapter, experimental psychologists have fought shy of any serious consideration of anomalous memory phenomena. This is perhaps understandable, because by their very nature they are scarcely susceptible to laboratory examination. The experiences cannot be "turned on" at will, their "natural" occurrence is difficult to predict, and their experimental simulation tends to be either tautologous or so attenuated as to be of dubious relevance. Nevertheless, they offer a potentially rich field of investigation. And the general unwillingness to accommodate them within cognitive psychology is surely regrettable, for their study can contribute significantly to our understanding of mnemonic processes. Admittedly, it is unlikely that such study on its own will lead to any major theoretical breakthrough. But at the very least, it can act as a touchstone or check on the validity of existing models. As Baddeley (1976) puts it: "One way of deciding which of the wealth of newly discovered phenomena is worth pursuing is to ask oneself whether it is likely to survive outside the sheltered world of the psychological laboratory [p. 374]." Any realistic theory of normal memory must be able to account for such well attested phenomena as those described here.

REFERENCES

Adams, J. A. *Human memory*. New York: McGraw-Hill, 1967.

Anderson, J. R., & Bower, G. H. Recognition and retrieval processes in free recall. *Psychological Review*, 1972, *79*, 97–123.

Anderson, J. R., & Bower, G. H. A propositional theory of recognition memory. *Memory & Cognition*, 1974, *2*, 406–412.

Baddeley, A. D. *The psychology of memory*. New York: Basic Books, 1976.

Bartlett, F. C. *Remembering: A study in experimental and social psychology*. Cambridge, England: Cambridge University Press, 1932.

Belbin, E. The influence of interpolated recall upon recognition. *Quarterly Journal of Experimental Psychology*, 1950, *2*, 163–169.

Brown, R., & McNeill, D. The "tip of the tongue" phenomenon. *Journal of Verbal Learning and Verbal Behavior*, 1966, *5*, 325–337.

Craik, F. I. M., & Lockhart, R. S. Levels of processing: A framework for memory research. *Journal of Verbal Learning and Verbal Behavior*, 1972, *11*, 671–684.

Craik, F. I. M., & Tulving, E. Depth of processing and the retention of words in episodic memory. *Journal of Experimental Psychology: General*, 1975, *104*, 268–294.

Eagle, M. N., & Mulliken, S. The role of affective ratings in intentional and incidental learning. *American Journal of Psychology*, 1974, *87*, 409–423.

Ebbinghaus, H. *Memory*. New York: Dover, 1964. (Originally published, 1885.)

Flavell, J. H. *Cognitive development*. Englewood Cliffs, N.J.: Prentice-Hall, 1977.

Hart, J. T. Memory and the feeling-of-knowing experience. *Journal of Educational Psychology*, 1965, *56*, 208–216.

Kintsch, W. Models for free recall and recognition. In D. A. Norman (Ed.), *Models of human memory*. New York: Academic Press, 1970.

Kintsch, W. *The representation of meaning in memory*. Hillsdale, N.J.: Lawrence Erlbaum Associates, 1974.

Lockhart, R. S., Craik, F. I. M., & Jacoby, L. Depth of processing, recognition and recall. In J. Brown (Ed.), *Recall and recognition*. London: Wiley, 1976.

Murdock, B. B., Jr. *Human memory: Theory and data*. Hillsdale, N.J.: Lawrence Erlbaum Associates, 1974.

Neisser, U. *Cognitive psychology*. Englewood Cliffs, N.J.: Prentice-Hall, 1967.

Paivio, A. *Imagery and verbal processes*. New York: Holt, Rinehart & Winston, 1971.

Piaget, J., & Inhelder, B. *Memory and Intelligence*. London: Routledge & Kegan Paul, 1973.

Reed, G. *The psychology of anomalous experience: A cognitive approach*. London: Hutchinson University Library, 1972.

Reed, G. Obsessional personality disorder and remembering. *British Journal of Psychiatry*, 1977, *130*, 177–183.

Talland, G. A. *Disorders of memory and learning*. Harmondsworth, Eng.: Penguin, 1968.

Tulving, E. Episodic and semantic memory. In E. Tulving & W. Donaldson (Eds.), *Organization of memory*. New York: Academic Press, 1972.

Tulving, E. Ecphoric processes in recall and recognition. In J. Brown (Ed.), *Recall and recognition*. London: Wiley, 1976.

Tulving, E., & Pearlstone, Z. Availability versus accessibility of information in memory for words. *Journal of Verbal Learning and Verbal Behavior*, 1966, *5*, 381–391.

Tulving, E., & Thomson, D. M. Encoding specificity and retrieval processes in episodic memory. *Psychological Review*, 1973, *80*, 352–373.

Underwood, G. *Attention and memory*. Oxford: Pergamon Press, 1976.

Watkins, M. J. When is recall spectacularly higher than recognition? *Journal of Experimental Psychology*, 1974, *102*, 161–163.

2 Childhood Amnesia and the Development of a Socially Accessible Memory System

Sheldon H. White
David B. Pillemer
Harvard University

What I have in mind is the peculiar amnesia which, in the case of most people, though by no means all, hides the earliest beginnings of their childhood up to their sixth or eighth year.

—Sigmund Freud, *Three Essays on the Theory of Sexuality*

Let us imagine for a moment that the mental stock of an adult is distributed in his memory like books in a well-arranged library, and it becomes at once clear that it must be as difficult to get the necessary ideas from the memory of a child, as it is to find books in a badly-organised library. This analogy is extremely tempting.

—Ivan Sechenov, *The Elements of Thought*

Several factors combine to make childhood amnesia of special interest for cognitive psychology. The phenomenon, as originally described by Freud, appears to be one of a recall deficit; adults usually cannot recollect their earliest experiences.

There is a large literature of research on memory, beginning with Ebbinghaus, extending through the voluminous verbal learning literature of the 1940s, most recently dealing with studies of short- and long-term memory and the analysis of metamemory. Besides the literature on memory, there is much work on cognition and cognitive development. Given that memory and cognitive development have been so abundantly explored in the research literature, it would seem natural to seek to find connections between the research findings and the psychoanalytic phenomenon. That is the general purpose of this paper.

29

But as soon as one seeks to do this, some problems present themselves. The varied research literature on memory has been confined within boundary conditions that have not allowed full exploration of the kinds and conditions of memory discussed under infantile amnesia.

The sine qua non of experimental research on memory has been some kind of index of veridicality. Generally, in memory experiments, it has seemed necessary to establish exactly what it is that has to be remembered, so that comparisons can be made between material available for memory and the substance of that which is recognized, recalled, described, or paraphrased. So there have been experiments on recall of nonsense syllables, words, nonsense figures, pictures, stories . . . in every case, on something that is there, perceptible to the experimenter as well as the subject, and available for exact comparisons between the experience and the memory.

In contrast, Freud's phenomenon of infantile amnesia manifests itself in a kind of remembering that is found in great frequency in everyday life but that has not been popular in laboratory research, because indices of veridicality are not easy to establish. People constantly tell one another stories about conversations they had, about life at the office, about what they did last summer, about a movie or a book, about their schooling or their childhood. They are remembering autobiographical experiences, but, in so doing, they are transforming temporally ordered sequences of perceptions and actions into temporally ordered sequences of words. Veridicality is an issue in such remembering (we are apt to say of some people that they "make up stories" or "you can't believe what they say"), but absolute diagnoses of veridicality are out of the question. The original events that form the basis of the recall do not exist in a form allowing for exact comparisons between the input and the memory. People are notoriously idiosyncratic in their portrayal of experience in words. Contemporary artists offer dramatic illustrations of this—Pirandello's *Right You Are If You Think You Are*, the movie *Rashomon*, Lawrence Durrell's *The Alexandria Quartet*. In each of these works, a group of characters recall the same set of events in such divergent ways that it is hard to believe they are talking about the same history. Obviously, ordinary interchange among humans depends on the assumption and the fact of some veridicality in narrative recall. But the fact remains that such veridicality is always approximate, vulnerable to errors of omission and deliberate commission, and not susceptible to the kinds of exact study and confirmation traditionally to be found in psychological studies of memory phenomena.

A second problem is that Freudian memory is not simply recollection, experience told over. Freudian memories—Freudian cognitions in general—have a mythical quality, conveying accurate information as part of the surface structure but carrying impressions of the emotional valences of the world in their deep structure. So Freudian memories are capable of at least two kinds of veridicality—accuracy in protrayal of what the Freudians would call secondary process thought and fidelity to the emotional resonances of primary process thought. The message from psychoanalysis is that content accuracy is always and everywhere at the mercy of emotional fidelity, so that distortions of the rational appear constantly in human thought. In contrast, the psychological research literature focuses exclusively on rational correspondence of memories with events and, what is more, attempts to separate sharply terms like *memory, cognition, emotion, motivation*, etc. There are, then, extremely serious problems in attempting an alignment between experimental "memory" and psycho-analytic "memory."

These difficulties have severely limited experimental analysis of infantile amnesia. There has been occasional discussion of the concept since Freud first introduced and popularized it. However, in our present investigation we uncovered only one major recent experimental publication (Campbell & Spear, 1972) dealing with the rapid forgetting of early experiences, and this study based its analyses primarily on animal data. The authors wryly note: ". . . the entire phenomenon of infantile amnesia appears to have been repressed by the scientific community rather than investigated systematically" (Campbell & Spear, 1972, p. 216).

The reader must certainly wonder why two chapters of the present volume resurrect the repressed. There are at least three major reasons why a reconsideration of childhood amnesia may offer important insights for current psychological theory and practice.

Despite its uncertain empirical status, Freud's proposition of infantile amnesia is a cornerstone of a large and diversified body of contemporary psychoanalytic practice. Hence, the alignment of the concept with current data should be of great interest and usefulness to mental health practitioners.

Although psychoanalytic theory does not lend itself easily to controlled experiments (Sears, 1943, 1944), the experience of recent years shows that the theory can serve as a nucleus for interesting aggregations of data collected in laboratory settings (Bowlby, 1969, 1973). A middle level of discourse is possible that integrates the insights of the clinic and the laboratory and that may suggest or sharpen ideas on both sides.

Simply because it cuts across the common topic distinctions in psychology—e.g., learning, memory, cognitive development, emotion—a phenomenon like infantile amnesia provides an occasion for drawing together material from different research specialties. An argument developed in a later section of this paper is that several current accounts of infantile amnesia that appear to be distinct and disparate are really not. The accounts may be taken as interlocking elements, each of which makes its essential contribution to an enlarged view of the phenomenon.

THE PHENOMENON AS ORIGINALLY DESCRIBED BY FREUD

Freud introduced the phenomenon of childhood amnesia early in his psycho-analytic theorizing, at the time of his *Three Essays on the Theory of Sexuality*

(1905b/1953): "What I have in mind is the peculiar amnesia which, in the case of most people, though by no means all, hides the earliest beginnings of their childhood up to their sixth or eighth year [p. 174]."

He describes this amnesia further, in his series of lectures delivered at the University of Vienna in 1915–1916 and published as *Introductory Lectures on Psychoanalysis*. In those lectures, he repeatedly alludes to a blockade of early memories as in the following quotes (1916–1917/1963):

> In analyzing each separate hysterical symptom one is usually led to a whole chain of impressions of events, which, when they recur, are expressly described by the patient as having been till then forgotten. On the one hand, this chain reaches back to the earliest years of life, so that the hysterical amnesia can be recognized as an immediate continuation of infantile amnesia which, for us normal people, conceals the beginnings of our mental life [p. 283].

> The majority of experiences and mental impulses before the start of the latency period now fall victim to infantile amnesia—the forgetting which veils our earliest youth from us and makes us strangers to it. The task is set us in every psychoanalysis of bringing this forgotten period back into memory. It is impossible to avoid a suspicion that the beginnings of sexual life which are included in that period have provided the motive for its being forgotten—that this forgetting, in fact, is an outcome of repression [p. 326].

Some essential ambiguities begin at this point. Freud is claiming the existence of a universal or near-universal phenomenon of human memory. Humans lose contact with their earliest memories. The memories are there but they have been "veiled"; there is an "amnesia" for them. We are to assume that humans have memories going back behind the amnesia, perhaps a great many of them, but that they have been walled off. It seems a little incredible that humans have many, many memories of the earliest years of life, blockaded by repression but potentially all there and expressible. If the starting point of human memories at 6 or 8 is not a natural one, is there perhaps some other starting point behind the amnesia?

Freud offers a claim of a near-universal human phenomenon, something applying to "most" people. It is apparent that the claim is not based upon widespread and systematic surveys. It comes from psychoanalytic encounters with patients, a kind of experience that is not available to most people reading Freud. What is there about the clinical experience that leads toward or tends to sustain such a broad claim?

According to Freud, the successful treatment of neurotic and hysterical disorders requires that these memory gaps be filled in by the patient: "In the further course of the treatment the patient supplies the facts which, though he had known them all along, had been kept back by him or had not occurred in his mind. The paramnesias prove untenable, and the gaps in his memory are filled in" (Freud, 1905a/1953, p. 18).

As most people understand psychoanalytic therapy, childhood amnesia is a central target of the treatment. Neurosis arises from emotionally painful memories of early childhood that have been repressed, that reside in the unconscious, and that act as the nuclei of symptom formation. The goal of psychoanalytic therapy is to penetrate the blockade of the amnesia and to release the memory and the pent-up emotion associated with it. With the catharsis of the emotion, the nuclear neurotic factor is dissipated. In order to be successful, psychoanalysis must bring about the recovery of childhood memories.

This kind of claim about the existence and meaning of childhood amnesia is widely understood as a central assertion of psychoanalytic theory. It exists as a stereotype in many modern writings about psychoanalysis. One finds subsequent psychological commentators on Freud at times expressing skepticism about the existence of a latent store of childhood memories, at times trying to rationalize the claim, and at times trying to reinterpret it. They argue that some kind of modification of memory takes place in early childhood but that the phenomena of memory development are not quite as Freud described them. The last tactic, reinterpretation of the claim, is of course a little awkward for research psychologists who do not have access to Freud's "data base," the experience of psychoanalysis, and who therefore must be a little uncertain about what kinds of modifications of the phenomenon might be possible while still retaining consistency with clinical experience.

Despite the persistence until the present day of a popular image of childhood amnesia as involving repressed memories to be recovered by therapy, an examination of some of Freud's later writings does not make it clear that he held to this exact view. As early as 1899, he was aware of a paper published by the Henris, (Henri & Henri, 1897), documenting a study in which 123 adults had responded to a questionnaire about their early memories of childhood. Early memories going back to between 2 and 4 years of age were reported by 88 people in the study. Freud says that it is quite reasonable that such memories might exist: "Actually, however, a normally highly developed child of three or four already exhibits an enormous amount of organized mental functioning . . . and there is no obvious reason why amnesia should overtake these psychical acts, which carry no less weight than those of a later age" (Freud, 1899/1974, p. 304).

Many of the childhood memories found by the Henris seem to point to momentous happenings—births, fires, illnesses, etc. But a minority of the memories seem to be for trivial and insignificant events, and Freud argues that these are "screen memories." What is being remembered is a displaced event associated with, and replacing, an emotionally laden memory that is not recovered by the individual.

Turning to the memories that seem on the surface straightforward, Freud notes that they show some peculiarities. For example, in a majority of the reasonable-looking memories, the subjects see themselves as children in the midst of the recollected event. One does not see oneself going through an event, and many of the Henris' subjects were explicitly disturbed by this implausibility in their recollections. From this peculiarity, and from others, Freud ultimately concludes that the entire corpus of data collected by the Henris must represent reconstructions. Traces of early childhood experiences are brought forward in time until, at a later age, the actual memories (that is, extended narrative symbolizations) are constructed.

In 1917, Freud offered an analysis of what he took to be a screen memory of early childhood offered in an autobiography written by Goethe when he was 60. Goethe recalled that when he was 4, stimulated by some mischievous neighbors, he playfully threw all his parents' crockery out in the street and smashed it. One of Freud's patients had had exactly the same memory, and Freud constructs an argument that Goethe's memory and the patient's memory stemmed from the same source; the event had actually happened in both cases, but it represented a desire to throw a brand-new sibling out into the street. The adult does not recall the desire to get rid of the sibling. He recalls the crockery smashing, but the memory is deceptive because what is really "memorable" to the person are his hostile feelings toward the sibling.

In these analytic papers on screen memories, it is not clear that Freud is expressing the presently held stereotype of a blockading of early memories. He seems to be arguing that fragmentary memory traces are the raw material for fully formed narrative memories that the child is only capable of constructing at older ages. This kind of view seems implicit in a later statement of childhood amnesia: "You are all familiar, of course, from your own experience, with the remarkable amnesia of childhood. I mean the fact that the earliest years of life, up to the age of five, six, or eight, have not left behind them traces in our memory like later experiences" (Freud, 1916–1917/1963, pp. 199–200).

Memories in narrative form do not exist before 5, 6, or 8 years. It is not that they are not available. They are not there. What are available are nuclear memories of powerful and emotionally significant events. In some people, repression has displaced the hot core of the memory, so that what appears to the adult is a bland surrogate. Therapy acts not so much to recover a childhood memory but to reconstrue an existing memory and to find that aspect or associate of the memory that has been screened.

Summarizing the foregoing discussion, we appear to find in Freud's several presentations of the phenomenon of childhood amnesia two descriptions of the phenomenon that are almost but not quite the same. The two pictures appear in papers that are interspersed with one another in time. One might epitomize the two pictures as the *blockade* model and the *selective reconstruction* model.

In the blockade model, children form memories of their experiences during the preschool years, but those fully formed memories are not available to adults because a wall of repression arising at 6 or 8 years of age acts to blockade them. This blockade model is the generally held understanding of the phenomenon, the sterotyped view, in some part because it agrees so well with the "hydraulic metaphor,'' which is generally useful to individuals attempting to understand the psychodynamics of psychoanalytic theory.

In the selective reconstruction model children do not create fully formed narrative memories of their experiences during the preschool years, because they are unable to. They retain traces, fragments, images. All elaborated memories of early childhood are reconstructions occurring after 6 to 8 years of age when the early traces are worked up into stories. Distortions of psychopathology occur when some early traces are not worked up or are worked up in a misleading way and are thus ''forgotten.''[1]

As we have endeavored to show, these two differing accounts are present in Freud's writings. Why did he offer two accounts? The blockade model was probably his first. This kind of model fits well with the therapeutic notions of catharsis and abreaction with which Freud began his psychiatric practice. It is consistent with the hydraulicism of classic Freudian theory. Conceivably, Freud developed the selective reconstruction model as an alternative, but he was not able to work out the extended reconstruction he would have had to perform on other terms of his theory in order to fully realize the implications of this alternative view. It is possible that he periodically entertained the two hypotheses and that, in fact, the degree of ambiguity created by the differences between these two versions was not of great consequence for psychoanalytic therapy. He could live with the uncertainty. Or it is possible that he periodically came upon cases whose nature favored first one construction and then the other. For example, the trend of later research that we discuss has more and more favored the selective reconstruction model. Yet one can identify among modern psychiatric writings a classic account of adult psychopathology, Grinker and Spiegel's *War Neuroses* (1945), that clearly fits the blockade model.

The ambiguity has been consequential for subsequent researchers interested in psychoanalytic phenomena. Most researchers have directed their attention first toward the phenomenon of childhood amnesia construed in terms of the blockade model; finding that more and more implausible, they have developed a view of the phenomenon that looks like an elaboration of the selective reconstruction model.

STUDIES OF ADULT RECOLLECTIONS OF CHILDHOOD

Studies like that of Henri and Henri (1897) have been undertaken by a number of modern writers, exploring adult recall of childhood experiences.

---

[1]Frank Sulloway has directed us to private correspondence of Freud to Fliess on December 6, 1896, in which Freud outlines a hierarchical system of human memories. His treatment would today be called an information-processing analysis of human memory. In the terms of his system, Freud identifies repression as a ''failure of translation'' from a lower-order to a higher-order level of processing. Note that this private analysis in correspondence was written shortly before the 1899 publication on screen memories in which Freud seems to be appealing to the cognitive selective reconstruction model.

Age of the First Reported Memory

A central question has been to determine the subject's age at the time of his earliest remembered experience. Early studies conducted by Dudycha and Dudycha (1933a, 1933b) on college students and a review of the previous literature by these authors (Dudycha & Dudycha, 1941) consistently present the average age of the earliest reported memory at about 3½ years.

A later study (Weiland & Steisel, 1958) dealt with the age of earliest memory for a mixed psychiatric population composed of schizophrenic, character disorder, psychoneurotic, and prepsychotic patients. The subjects' ages at the time of testing ranged from 5 to 18 years. The majority of the reported memories of all diagnostic groups fell within the years 2 through 6. The accuracy of subjects' memories and age estimates in these studies is open to question. However, these results indicate that normal and abnormal subjects usually report at least one memory during the period supposedly shrouded by amnesia.

Changes in the Number of Early Memories

Waldfogel (1948) investigated the number of early memories that subjects reported for different age periods in their childhoods. He asked college students to record all memories for events occurring prior to their eighth birthday. Students were allowed 85 minutes for responding. As was the case in the earlier studies, the average age of the earliest recollection was about 3½ years. In addition, Waldfogel determined: (1) that the average college student reported about 50 memories before his 8th birthday, and (2) that the number of early memories increases with the subject's reported age at the time of the experiences. The rate of increase was shown to accelerate with each succeeding year up to age 5 and then decrease (see Fig. 2.1). Waldfogel presents data from other studies of children's memory and vocabulary development that also demonstrate ogival age curves like that generated by the adult recall of childhood data. Waldfogel (1948) concludes:

> When the memories were plotted according to the age of their origin, it was found that there was an increment from year to year which took the form of an ogive and seemed to parallel the growth of language and memory during childhood. This suggested, first, that memory for childhood events might be related to the level of mental development of the time of their occurrence; and, second, that factors besides repression determine the extent and content of childhood recollections. Indeed the relatively large number of memories from the early years (elicited under far from ideal conditions) and their gradual increase with age stand in apparent contradiction to the Freudian doctrines of infantile amnesia [p. 32].

Waldfogel is here, as do many of the modern theorists, reacting to the blockade model of the Freudian phenomenon. It is unfortunate that neither he nor the other students of adult recollections appear to have considered the plausibility of memories before 6 as did Freud (1899/1974).

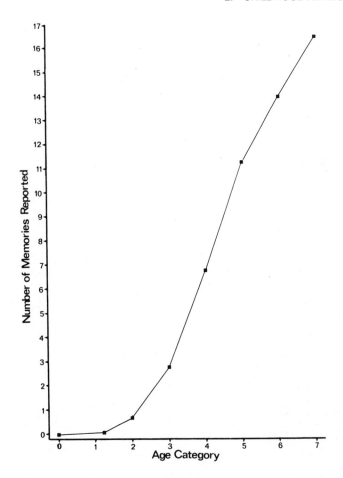

FIG. 2.1.   Average number of memories reported by college students as a function of estimated age at the time of the remembered experiences (after Waldfogel, 1948).

Sex Differences

Several of the studies of early memories demonstrate slight sex differences, with a younger average age of earliest recall for women than for men. Dudycha and Dudycha (1941) report sex differences in earlier studies ranging from 2 months up to more than 1 year. Waldfogel (1948) estimated that the average age of first recall was 3.23 years for females and 3.64 years for males. Schachtel (1947) describes a study by Ruth Benedict that suggested that "European men usually show a more extensive and persuasive amnesia for their early childhood than women [p. 24]."

If, as Waldfogel (1948) suggests, the retrieval of early memories is related to the rate of mental development in childhood, then one could conceivably expect females to exhibit slightly superior recall of early events. In their definitive survey of the literature on sex differences, Maccoby and Jacklin (1974) note that: "Tests from age 2 to 7 do come closer to measuring abilities that will be involved in later intelligence, and when there is a difference in this age group, it favors girls [p. 65]." The studies investigating the age of the earliest memory support this prediction of a slight sex difference, as already noted. However, Waldfogel found the average total number of early memories before age 8 to be almost identical across sexes.

Emotional Content of Early Memories

Most sources (Dudycha & Dudycha, 1933a, 1933b, 1941; Waldfogel, 1948) agree that positive or negative emotions usually accompany early remembrances. Purcell (1952) attempted to relate the assessed psychological security of college students to their memories of childhood. he concluded that "the emotional impressions ascribed to childhood memories are as significantly related to security feelings as the emotional impressions ascribed to adult memories [p. 437]." These results were taken to be in contradiction to Freud's description of the affectless character of available early memories: "The great variety and intensity of emotion accompanying these early experiences challenges the contention that childhood memories are for the most part banal screen-memories" (Waldfogel, 1948, p. 32).

Taken as a body, it is not clear that the studies of adult recollections of childhood have offered a significant test of the Freudian hypothesis of childhood amnesia. They reveal a pattern of gradually rising frequency of memories that seems quite similar to that pattern offered in the Henris' data; unfortunately, the authors do not apply tests for the plausibility of the earliest memories similar to those outlined by Freud. They acknowledge that the apparent memories may rest upon omissions, distortions, substitutions, fabrications, or reconstructions (Dudycha & Dudycha, 1941; Waldfogel, 1948). In one case (Dudycha & Dudycha, 1933b), the subjects were asked not to report experiences that had only been recounted to them, and they were asked to check with parents and with other individuals who were adults when the subjects were children as to the actual dates of occurrence of early experiences. But it is questionable whether these kinds of safeguards insure the accuracy of the adult recollections.

EXPLANATIONS FOR CHILDHOOD AMNESIA

Various lines of explanation for infantile amnesia have been offered in the psychoanalytic and research literatures. Causal mechanisms are proposed in these several arguments, but it would probably be an exaggeration to view the several sources as, say, contending theories. No very complete theory has been offered by anyone. It might be most accurate to view these accounts as metaphoric reflections or interpretations of the phenomenon in several frames of analytic discourse about psychological events. This section reviews these several accounts to prepare for later sections that try to present a more unified argument that may capture the sense of these several lines.

Repression

The dual aspect of Freud's description of infantile amnesia has been presented. However, his explanation for the phenomenon's existence relies exclusively on repression, a blockading of early memories. According to Freud (1905b/1953), the physical and mental experiences of early childhood are not forgotten. Rather they are rendered inaccessible to consciousness by repression:

> There can, therefore, be no question of any real abolition of the impressions of childhood, but rather an amnesia similar to that which neurotics exhibit for later events, and of which the essence consists in a simple withholding of these impressions from consciousness, viz., in their repression [p. 175].

The repression of one's earliest memories is seen as an unavoidable milepost in the lives of all normal children. An infant's existence is permeated by perverse and erotic fantasies. During the first 6 years of life, the child passes through psychosexual stages that focus successively on oral, anal, and phallic eroticism. During the phallic stage, the child's inherently bisexual constitution fuels his or her desire to alternatively replace the mother or the father as the primary love object of the remaining parent (Freud, 1925/1961).

Since the child's sexual desires with respect to his parents cannot be fulfilled, his instinctual impulses increasingly come into conflict with the restrictions of reality. This conflict culminates in the Oedipal complex (e.g., Freud, 1924/1961). At this point, children of both sexes abandon their fantasies of parental replacement, boys because of the threat of castration and girls due to the perceived futility of their childhood wishes. The resolution of the complex is accompanied by an identification with the parent of the appropriate sex, the formation of the superego, and the advent of the latency period. The remembrances of this period of life succumb to repression and are rendered unconscious. According to Neisser (1962):

> Freud saw childhood amnesia as the necessary outcome of the forces of repression. It serves to conceal the beginnings of our sexual lives. Once past Oedipal crisis, we cannot bear to think of the perverse and incestual passions which were once so strong. Any memory from infancy, no matter how innocuous the event itself might

have been, would risk bringing the old and dangerous emotions to the surface again [p. 61].

Freud (1924/1961) viewed the motivations for the resolution of the Oedipal complex and the repression of infantile wishes as twofold. First, the child experiences actual frustrations and perceived threats that demand the development of a more successful mode of functioning. In speaking of the cause of the decay of the Oedipus complex, Freud states that "analyses seem to show that it is the experience of painful disappointments" (Freud, 1924/1961, p. 173).

Second, Freud recognized the possibility that the psychosexual events of childhood might come as reflections of maturational sequences in development, a view that has been espoused by some later analysts (cf. Yazmajian, 1967). It is apparent that Freud believes that the repression of infantile sexuality constitutes a step in a near-universal, organically determined developmental progression (1924/1961):

Another view is that the Oedipus complex must collapse because the time has come for its disintegration, just as the milk-teeth fall out when the permanent ones begin to grow. Although the majority of human beings go through the Oedipus complex as an individual experience, it is nevertheless a phenomenon which is determined and laid down by heredity and which is bound to pass away according to programme when the next pre-ordained phase of development sets in. This being so, it is of no great importance what the occasions are which allow this to happen, or, indeed, whether any such occasions can be discovered at all [pp. 173–174].

Freud does not believe that environmental and organic explanations of repression and infantile amnesia are incompatible (1924/1961): "The justice of both these views cannot be disputed. Moreover, they are compatible. There is room for the ontogenetic view side by side with the more far-reaching phylogenetic one [p. 174]." Freud's position might be considered epigenetic (Fishbein, 1976). The plan of normal psychosexual development may be inherent. However, the fashion in which real experiences interact with the genetic plan actually determines the ultimate developmental outcomes.

The heart of the Freudian explanation for childhood amnesia is, then, a conflict between memory and repression. Repression is pictured as a blockading force. One does not find in Freud's writings an alternative treatment of repression that might describe it as a slightly different mechanism operating in accordance with the selective reconstruction model discussed earlier. One perceptive reviewer (Neisser, 1962) argues that there may be something to the phenomenon of childhood amnesia but that the explanation of its origin in terms of a repressive blockade seems entirely inadequate:

Nevertheless, despite these confirmations, Freud's theory of infantile amnesia has seemed less than adequate. It has almost no point of contact with any interpretation of ordinary adult remembering and forgetting; it relies on an unimpressive analogy with physical forces in opposition to one another; and it would seem to predict that a patient should readily recall his childhood years when his analysis was completed—a prediction which is never confirmed [p. 62].

As an alternative, following earlier writings of Schachtel, Neisser outlines a hypothesis of socially induced changes in memory organization that may be understood as an important element in a revised view of the repressive forces hindering recall of early childhood memories.

Socially Induced Changes in Memory Organization

Schachtel (1947) and Neisser (1962, 1967) begin with the view that memory is not a process of retrieving static unaltered traces but rather is the outcome of a reconstructive process. The child develops thought structures, called "schemata." These schemata are aroused by experiential inputs, are used as formats or frames of interpretation, and give the inputs meaning. In this process, the mental inputs are altered to fit the schemata ("assimilation"). The analysis is partly Piagetian. Assimilation and accommodation are taken in a familiar sense, but the "schemata" of Schachtel (1947) and Neisser (1962) are not sensorimotor plans but something like frames of reference. Schachtel refers to the schemata as "categories of memory," and Neisser uses the phrase "dimensions of cognitive growth." Progressive accommodations of schemata bring about modifications of the categories of thought as the child grows older.

Remembering involves reconstructing past events using the presently existing schemata: "Memory as a function of the living personality can be understood only as a capacity for the organization and reconstruction of past experiences and impressions in the service of present needs, fears, and interests" (Schachtel, 1947, p. 3).

Forgetting is an inability to reconstruct past events from the information provided by the present recall situation. According to Neisser (1967):

> For the attempted recall to succeed, the schemata I develop now, in the attempt to recall, must not be too different from those whose traces were established long ago. They can differ, but not so much that the present ones cannot incorporate the information stored earlier. Otherwise, the stored fragments of structure will be unusable, and recall will fail [p. 289].

The argument that retrieval of past events from memory requires that the existing memory structures or categories be similar to those used at storage provides the basis for explaining the inaccessibility of early experiences. Since schemata change with age, the recall of distant events should be difficult. In particular, the dramatic differences between adults' and children's categories prohibit easy recall of childhood experiences. According to Schachtel, (1947):

> The categories (or schemata) of adult memory are not suitable receptacles for early childhood experiences and therefore not fit to preserve these experiences and enable their recall. The functional capacity of the conscious, adult memory is usually limited to those types of experience which the adult consciously makes and is capable of making [p. 4].

Neisser (1967) offers this phenomenon as a direct explanation for childhood amnesia:

> The rather similar state of infantile amnesia—inability to recall one's own early childhood—is not reversible to any substantial degree. The reason, as Schachtel (1947) saw clearly, is that adults cannot think as children do; they no longer carry out attentive constructions in the way they once did. As a result, they cannot make use of any fragments of infantile constructions that they may still retain [p. 290].

These authors view the socialization of the child as the primary factor fostering the drastic changes in the child's schemata. Furthermore, these socially induced changes result in a developmental "discontinuity" at about age 6 in Western society. It is at this age that the child usually enters school. The child becomes reality oriented and responsible, and his schemata must reflect these changes.

A central factor influencing the construction of increasingly sophisticated schemata is the development of language. Schachtel (1947) argues that there is a great discrepancy between the infants' "precivilized, unschematized experience and the categories of civilized, conventional language [p. 10]." Not only does language influence memory by allowing storage of linguistic representations. Language also helps form schemata that in turn are instrumental in reconstructive memory (Neisser, 1962):

> The acceptable adult must want what his fellows want, or something fairly close to it; he must see what they see, and believe in the importance of what is important to them. It is especially necessary that he speak as they speak, and as he yields to the pressure for linguistic conformity he becomes committed to that particular language's somewhat arbitrary analysis of reality [p. 62].

In sum, these authors attribute the inaccessibility of early memories to emergent thought categories as the child grows older. These categories, formed in large part by linguistic discourse, act to bring the child into an adult society premised in some part on shared thought and judgment. A by-product of this progressive entry is a progressive inability to reconstruct full-blooded memories from the traces of early experiences. In Neisser's words (1962):

> This means that the universal amnesia for childhood is not primarily the result of anxiety or guilt, and is not based on an active process of suppression. It is, instead, a necessary consequence of the discontinuities in cognitive functioning which accompany growth into adulthood. From pre-verbal to verbal, from naive to sophisticated, from carefree to responsible, from weak to powerful—the cognitive accommodations which must accompany these transitions seem to make the past inaccessible [p. 63].

The distinction between Freud's position and Neisser's own does not seem as dramatic as this statement suggests. The major impetus for childhood amnesia in both cases appears to be the necessity of replacing infantile modes of functioning with more socially acceptable, "adultlike" forms of thought and behavior. The difference lies in the mechanisms underlying this development. Unlike Freud, who postulates genetic as well as environmental determinants of the psycho-sexual timetable, Neisser and Schachtel rely entirely on social causes. The reported suddenness of onset of childhood amnesia comes from a sudden social change. Neisser (1962) states that "In America, real childishness has to end by about the seventh year of life [p. 68]." Children go to school.

Both Schachtel and Neisser suggest that since the incongruities between the child's world and the socially oriented world of the adult are responsible for infantile amnesia, the phenomenon should be strongest in those populations that experience the severest cultural discontinuities. Neisser (1962) offers an interesting and potentially testable hypothesis:

> Wherever important differences between the customary assimilations of adults and of children are the rule, we can expect relatively less recall of childhood experience. Wherever the culture makes the transition relatively continuous, and particularly where the cognitive accommodations of adulthood are consistently based on those of the child, childhood memories should be more available. . . . Not only the thoroughness of the amnesia, but also the period that it covers should vary with the developmental pattern in the society [p. 68].

In this view, by implication, the "repression" of Freudian theory would have to be understood in terms of a match−mismatch between cognitive structures, schematizations, and events. Events for which schematizations exist can be understood, discussed, and remembered, and other events for which there are not schematizations are, effectively, "repressed." The unconscious is the unconstruable. Childhood amnesia at age 6 or 8 arises through a kind of accidental circumstance of social design. Children in Vienna and in the United States, entering school at age 6, are induced to change their memory categories, and this creates the amnesia. The repression of childhood memories is epiphenomenal, a by-product of social arrangements peculiar to Western societies and their institutions of schooling.

This hypothesis of socially mediated memory change is loose but plausible. There is evidence that not only Western societies but also nonliterate societies direct the child toward adult roles and responsibilities at ages 5 to 7 (Rogoff, Sellars, Pirotta, Fox, & White, 1975). However, the cognitive changes required of children in schooling societies may well be much more drastic.

One could explain the gradual emergence of memories found in Waldfogel's data as the result of an induced process of category shifting in childhood. Schachtel and Neisser do not have to appeal to maturational factors for their explanation. But we all know that children grow, and we can ask whether intrinsic changes in the child "place" the social process at a particular point in a maturational sequence that may, by its intrinsic nature, create or foster the loss of memory. Other authors consider this possibility.

Developmental Changes in the Sensory Environment

Another kind of argument pictures childhood amnesia as derived not so much from changes in schemas for interpreting sensory inputs as from changes in the sensory inputs themselves. There may be changes in sensory registration, the balance or salience factors among receptor systems, or perceptual processing, so that the older child comes not to "see" the cues that are associated with juvenile memories and capable of evoking them.

In their recent review of the evidence for age changes in memory functions, Campbell and Spear (1972) offer "growth-induced changes in body and physiological makeup [p. 223]" as a possible causal factor. Campbell and Spear suggest that physical changes may transform perception, so that, in effect, older children no longer see the cues that might trigger early memories. Campbell and Spear (1972) state the argument as follows:

> . . . to a young rat, a maze may look like a great cavern from which escape requires a massive effort, but on retest after a retention interval, the same apparatus may appear much different because the visual angles from which the apparatus is viewed have changed or because the size of the apparatus, relative to the animal's body size, is now much smaller. Similarly the child's view of the world changes from one which is populated by giants and distinguished by spots of gum underneath tabletops, to the adult view of the world as we know it. This hypothesis is so intuitively appealing that some psychologists have considered this the major mechanism underlying forgetting in infancy [p. 223].

This hypothesis proposes a relatively radical perceptual transformation occurring in preschool years, the passage from a world so "strange" that it is foreign to the child-become-adult. But children talk to adults from age 1 on; there must be some commonality of perceived experience to permit this. Of course, they share a limited universe of communication. Many things that adults perceive or talk about are not discussed with children, and, in turn, many interpretations of the world offered by children are taken by adults as cute, charming, or poetic. It is not clear that other modes of perception—hearing, smell, etc.—are radically transformed by physical growth alone. But there have been arguments that maturation may bring about significant shifts in sensory registration or perceptual processing—e.g., with corticalization, a shift from "near receptor" to "far receptor" dominance (Schachtel, 1959); with myelinization of association areas, an onset or increase of "cross-modal transfer" (Birch & Lefford, 1963). Not only external, but internal, sensory registration may change with maturation. Beach and Jaynes (1954) have offered the hypothesis that effects of early experiences on behavior may be irreversible because adults never again experience emotions as strongly as do the young.

Another kind of argument would hold that the cues of childhood become unavailable in the later years, not because of maturational changes, but because of ecological changes. "Reinstatement" refers to the improved retention of learned material that comes from exposure to the original learning conditions during the time between learning and recall (Campbell & Spear, 1972). Experiencing the conditions of an event "primes" its later recollection. This principle has been shown to be a factor in animal retention. Campbell and Spear argue that something like the principle could explain the forgetting of childhood events. Children move outward toward more and more differentiated behavior settings as they get older; this has been documented in systematic studies of the ecologies of childhood (Barker & Wright, 1955). Conceivably, there is a progressive loss of reinstatement opportunities as children less and less confine themselves to the scenes and people of early childhood.

There is, again, a researchable hypothesis in the argument. Children raised in an ecology of less broadly differentiated behavior settings should show less forgetting of early experiences. However, it is not certain how well this principle would explain a rapid change in the accessibility of memories around age 5. One learning setting that is common to all ages up to the college years is the ecology of the home.

The hypotheses discussed so far in this section have proposed a developmental change in sensory inputs, whereas earlier we dealt with Schachtel and Neisser's hypothesis of socially induced changes in schemata applied to sensory inputs. Some current evidence bears upon both lines of argument.

There is some evidence for a developmental shift in encoding categories (Bach & Underwood, 1970; Melkman & Deutsch, 1977; Underwood, 1969). Underwood (1969) has articulated an "attribute" theory of memory. Memories are composed of a number of attributes, which are established at encoding. These attributes serve as cues for discriminating between different memories and hence are critical to understanding recall and forgetting. Underwood states that there are developmental changes in the attributes that become established as characteristics of memories. "Primordial" attributes, such as acoustic and spatial attributes, are replaced by verbal attributes: "As a child ages, and particularly as he concomitantly is exposed to successive learning experiences in the school systems, the primary attributes developed in learning may change, with the associative verbal attributes becoming more and more common" (Underwood, 1969, p. 571).

Bach and Underwood (1970) detected a developmental change in the dominance of attributes on a word-recognition task. The acoustic attribute was dominant for second-grade subjects, whereas the verbal-associative attribute was dominant for sixth graders. Melkman and Deutsch (1977) investigated nursery school, second-, and fifth-grade children's recall of colored objects belonging to four conceptual categories. These investigators found that the use of conceptual categories as an organizing principle for recall increased with age, whereas the use of color decreased with age.

These studies indicate that there are developmental changes in memory attributes. In accordance with Schachtel's and Neisser's positions, Underwood (1969; Bach & Underwood, 1970) explains the shift to verbal-associative attributes by the child's entry into school. However, this shift is not complete or irreversible. Rather, the evidence suggests a change in the dominant or preferred attributes or mode of organization. The shift appears to be gradual and is not complete by 7 years of age; for example, Melkman and Deutsch (1977) observed an increased use of conceptual categories as an organizing principle of recall from second to fifth grade. The results of this study also suggest that "both color and conceptual categories are encoded by children of all ages [p. 94]" but that there is an age change in their effectiveness in memory tasks. Underwood (1969) states that certain situations may prompt older subjects to utilize the more primitive attributes:

> It sometimes seems that when a learning task made up of difficult letter sequences (e.g., consonant syllables) is imposed on adult S's, these S's are forced to revert to the more primordial attributes to master the task because these materials do not elicit the attributes commonly produced by more meaningful material [p. 571].

Neurological and Physical Development: Growth Waves and Brain Changes

There are a number of growth processes and central nervous system changes occurring during early childhood that could conceivably influence childhood memories in ways other than by changing sensory registration. A common way of talking about forgetting in nervous-system terms is to say that "over time the memory trace, as represented in the central nervous system, diminishes in strength" (Campbell & Spear, 1972, p. 230). This is not so much an explanation of the phenomenon as a translation. The phenomenon manifested in behavioral terms is now construed in a neural discourse. In order to account for infantile amnesia, one would now seek specific nervous-system factors that might explain unusually rapid memory decay in very young children. Is there anything in growth that might diminish the diminution in strength of memory traces over time?

Campbell and Spear (1972) outline several known central-nervous-system changes that occur during childhood. These include measurable changes in myelinization, cell differentiation, electrophysiological activity, concentrations and distribution of neurotransmitters, DNA and RNA production, protein synthesis, and metabolic rate. Variations in these factors have been shown to correlate with variations in memory. Conceivably, some progressive change occurring with growth could produce an ever-increasing capacity of the nervous system to "hold" memory traces firm over time. This is a rather vague supposition, far beyond the state of the art of our present ability to measure and analyze the growing child's nervous system. Nevertheless, the supposition is so entirely plausible as a line of possible explanation that it has to be kept in mind. We may in time find out that the nervous system holds memory traces better as children get older, and we may find out where and why.

Some other arguments or information about children's growth could also conceivably point to a maturational basis for the phenomenon of infantile amnesia.

Growth Waves in Physical and Mental Development

Some of Freud's followers came to believe in the possibility that the psychosexual stages of childhood might be based upon biological cycles of physical and psychic development. The argument is reviewed in some detail by Yazmajian (1967). Prenatal morphogenesis, it is held, shows a pattern of two consecutive cephalocaudal *growth waves* that are, in at least some aspects, recapitulationistic. The mouth opening, phylogenetically older, differentiates before the anal opening, which in turn differentiates before the genital opening. After the child is born, there is a third cycle of embryogenesis, but now the psychic structures of the child exhibit the same recapitulationistic pattern of development formerly shown by the physical structures. Oral, anal, and genital psychic stages of development appear, reflecting genetic canalizations of growth. This postnatal embryogenesis runs off until ages 6 or 7, where there is a programmed but suppressed adolescence.

In 1926, an influential thesis by Bolk, a Dutch anatomist, appeared that stimulated interest among psychoanalysts and anthropologists. Bolk advocated a principle of human evolution known as fetalization, neoteny, or pedomorphosis. The basic idea is that human evolution from an apelike progenitor took place through some factor or factors that acted to sustain immaturity. A number of factual comparisons between humans and apes are in line with this principle.

(For accounts of the Bolk thesis, see Yazmajian, 1967; Dobzhansky, 1962; and Gould, 1977.)

A number of factual comparisons between man and ape are not in line with the principle, and so the hypothesis that human development is that of an ape slowed down has been argued to this day. Nevertheless, some early psychoanalysts saw in Bolk's argument a possible basis for the rather dramatic events of psychosexual development at ages 6 and 7: the upwelling of sexual desire for the parent, the Oedipus conflict, the suppression of this sexuality and the onset of latency, and, presumably, the associated phenomenon of infantile amnesia. The argument, in brief, was that these events marked the completion of early psychic embryogenesis and the upwelling of an old adolescence that had been suppressed in evolution to permit humankind's long childhood and the later eruption of human adolescence (Yazmajian, 1967).[2]

This kind of argument would hold that there is a discontinuity in human growth at ages 6 or 7. Conceivably, the masking of earlier memories could result from such a discontinuity. Are there any other data supportive of the hypothesis of a discontinuity in physical growth at this time? There are some. Over the years, anthropometric studies of children's physical growth have produced various odd indications of discontinuity suggesting that there may be what is called in that literature a "mid-growth spurt." In the second edition of his book on adolescence, Tanner (1955) reviewed the evidence for such a phenomenon, but in at least one subsequent review (Tanner, 1970) he does not mention the possibility. Recently, Epstein (1974a, 1974b, 1978) has argued for "phrenoblysis" in human mental and neural growth, special periods of accelerated growth at ages 6 to 8, 10 to 12, 14 to 17, and possibly 2 to 4.

These several hypothecations of human growth waves or spurts are all tenuous, and one can create an illusion of solidity simply by the mere act of collecting them beside one another. However, other odd changes in reported sensory phenomena, motor organization, brain-wave patterning, and susceptibility to pathology exist in the several literatures on children's development. All this literature makes it abundantly clear that there are maturational events of consequence for psychological phenomena at this time. But it is far from clear

---

[2]One reason why psychoanalysts found the Bolk thesis appealing is that Freud had come very close to anticipating the argument. Chapter 10 of Frank Sulloway's thesis deals with Freud's use of evolutionary biology to resolve some basic psychoanalytic problems. It is argued that beginning in 1912–1913 with *Totem and Taboo*, Freud attributed neurosis to a unique "diphasic onset" of human sexuality. According to Sulloway (1978): "Unlike other animals, man's sexual life, and hence man's choice of a sexual object, Freud asserted, emerges in two major waves. An early epoch of sexual efflorescence, reaching its peak at the age of five, is interrupted by a period of latency and is then followed by a new wave of sexual development at the time of puberty. So literally did Freud subscribe to the biogenetic implications of this claim that, in 1939, and again in his posthumously published *Outline of Psycho-Analysis* [after Bolk], he suggested that man must be descended from an animal originally reaching sexual maturity at the age of five [p. 645]."

that these maturational events are interorganized together to create what would in effect amount to a stagelike change in human maturation.

Some Significant Brain Changes

A variety of maturational phenomena in the brain have been reported, but two might be noted here because of their possible specific significance for the phenomenon of infantile amnesia.

Recently, Altman, Brunner, and Bayer (1973) and Douglas, Peterson, and Douglas (1973) have argued that hippocampal maturation in rats is associated with the shedding of juvenile patterns of behavior and the emergence of characteristically adult behavioral characteristics. Rose (1976) noted that many of the cognitive changes found in children between 5 and 7 years of age look as though they might be potentiated by processes attributed to the hippocampus. He undertook an unusually careful and searching analysis of human neural and behavioral development. Significant hippocampal maturation occurs in human children at about 4½ years of age. Dentate granule cells mature in the hippocampus, activating a system that, at the very least, includes hippocampal – prefrontal circuitry. Rose reviews several research literatures: (1) information on the neuroanatomy of the hippocampus; (2) information on human brain development; (3) neuropsychological studies of hippocampal control of behavior; and (4) studies of the behavior of younger and older children confronted with conditioning and learning and discrimination tasks like those used with animals in hippocampal studies. Within the limits of the state of the art in these several literatures—and there are limits—a consistent and rather striking pattern emerges. Structurally, at least, there are signs of hippocampal and prefrontal maturation at this time in humans. Functionally, one finds a strong concordance between the behavioral literatures for animals and children. Children below 4½ years of age show a pattern of responses to experimental procedures like that of hippocampectomized animals; children after that age look like animals with an intact hippocampus.

Rose reviews the several behavioral-control functions that an enormous research literature has attributed to the hippocampus, including: (1) inhibition of unsuccessful or irrelevant behavior, prepotent responses, etc.; (2) regulation or control of voluntary movement; (3) memory consolidation; (4) memory retrieval; (5) control of orienting responses or their habituation; (6) modulation of arousal processes; (7) regulation of motivation or emotion; (8) cognitive mapping; (9) behavioral flexibility; and (10) control of attention. This is a lot of responsibility to attribute to one small brain configuration, but it must reasonably be borne in mind that we are not here dealing with phrenological localization of function. The hippocampus must be understood as an entity participating in control systems that span an immense amount of the architecture of the brain. For our present purposes, it is noteworthy that functions (3) and (4) are directly relevant to the discussion; hippocampal maturation could be associated with improvement in children's ability to store and/or retrieve memories. Subsequent discussion offers an argument that (8), an augmented ability to cognitively map, may well also be a factor in what appears to be a loss of early memories.

In Magda Arnold's two-volume review, *Emotion and Personality*, she argues that neural maturation involving the hippocampus is also a basis for the young child's growing ability to reduce impulsivity and to organize flexible and extended attention (1960, Vol. 2):

> Gradually, the child learns to consider several aspects of a situation one after the other, and so is able to prolong his attention by reducing the appeal of other things. . . .
>
> This alertness to one thing and unconcern for others seems to be made possible by the relay from the hippocampus to the caudate nucleus and the diffuse thalamic system. . . .
>
> Our hypothesis would explain why the EEG records of young children show delta and theta waves but no alpha rhythms. Even when these begin to appear (around three or four years of age), the EEG still shows mingled theta and alpha waves for some years, at least until about ten years of age. The delta waves in early childhood and the later theta waves seem to indicate impulsive reactions, with no attempt to appraise the situation accurately, and hence little imagination and memory activity [pp. 161–162].

If one assumes, under the selective reconstruction model, that all memories of early childhood are really constructions developed after 6 or 8 years of age, then a second relevant maturational factor might conceivably be the myelinization of parietal cortex. Milner (1967) reviews studies that show that myelinization of parietal cortex in humans is completed at about age 7. Myelinization studies of children's neural development have been undertaken because they are an available index of maturation, although it is not at all clear what the presence or absence of myelin sheathing tells us about actual neural functioning.

Children before 5 regularly show difficulties in the conceptual sorting of Vygotsky blocks and in Bender–Gestalt performance, which in adults would be taken as signs of "constructional apraxia" or "amorphosynthesis" and linked with parietal–occipital dysfunction (White, 1970). Some kinds of reading disability have traditionally been associated with parietal factors (Critchley, 1964). There is evidence that children before 6 regularly have trouble recalling stories as complete stories. They remember interesting fragments and incidents, but not until the school years will they use the fragments to attempt a reconstruction of a plot with a beginning, middle, and end (Maranda & Maranda, 1970). This appears to be one reason why a television show like *Sesame Street* directed toward preschoolers is built out of disconnected fragments. Common observation of preschoolers shows that television commercials seem to be a peculiarly exciting art form to them. The commercials are brief, vivid, often offer striking imagery, and they do not require extended assembly of information over time to enable comprehension.

Some kind of constructional factor associated with parietal maturation might be proposed as a basis for the selective reconstruction model of childhood amnesia. This would explain some of the data of cognitive development, but some important exceptions would have to be dealt with. There are circumstances, so far not well specified, under which very young preschoolers show extended and robust bouts of constructive play and extended "attention span."

INFORMATION-PROCESSING CHANGES AND CHILDHOOD AMNESIA

An account of childhood amnesia can be constructed that depends on changes in information processing with age. Such an account would emphasize internal organization, rather than socially induced reorganization of memory. An information-processing explanation would emphasize the fact that some central mental functions increase with age. Children respond to social pressures to think and act differently, because their capacity to think and act differently increases with age. The social pressures may be, in fact, predicated upon generalized cultural expectations that such changes are normatively to be expected.

In recent years, Juan Pascual–Leone (1970, 1972; Pillemer, 1976) has put forward an information-processing theory of cognitive development. He is an interesting bridge figure for our discussion. A trained psychiatrist, he obtained a second doctorate at Geneva where he studied Jean Piaget's genetic epistemology. In a series of recent writings, he and his students have elaborated an information-processing model of cognitive development, intended in part to articulate more precisely the Piagetian model of cognitive development but intended also to provide a more adequate theoretical basis for discussions of the interaction of cognition, affect, learning, and perception. Perhaps Pascual–Leone's theory can provide a discourse rich enough to address the complex nexus of causations surrounding infantile amnesia.

Pascual–Leone's Model of Human Cognitive Performance

Pascual–Leone's neo-Piagetian theory is one of several recently appearing "process" theories of cognitive development (e.g., Klahr & Wallace, 1970; Newell & Simon, 1972; Pascual–Leone, 1970). A goal of these theories is to explicitly represent the successive mental steps characterizing the subject's problem-solving processes. A particular focus of Pascual–Leone's work in this regard has been to provide explanations for the child's acquisition of the abilities described by Jean Piaget (e.g., Pascual–Leone, 1969; Pascual–Leone & Smith, 1969). Thus, the theory may be seen as a supplement to, and not a replacement for, Piaget's theory of cognitive development (Pascual–Leone, 1972).

According to the neo-Piagetian theory, human problem-solving takes place in discrete steps, and each step may be pictured as an assembly of discrete informational units. When a subject performs a task, he moves through a series of mental steps. These steps may be automatically generated by a stored program, as with habitual or overlearned activity, but what Pascual–Leone is most concerned with are nonautomated steps. How are steps in thinking generated when one tries, purposefully and consciously, to solve a problem? What is the internal structure of a single step?

Each step is composed of procedural units and informational units, both called *schemes*. The procedural, or *executive*, scheme directs the processing activity of the step. The information that is processed is represented as one or more additional schemes. Suppose one could determine what executive schemes and what substantive schemes are available to and activated by a subject. Suppose, also, that one has performed an adequate *task analysis* (a decomposition of a problem into the necessary strategic steps). Then, ideally, one should be able to predict whether a subject will or will not solve the problem.

According to the theory, the subject's problem-solving processes consist of sequences of mental operations, each of which involves the activation of one or more separate schemes. In explaining subject performance, it is necessary to determine which schemes are activated by a particular situation. The neo-Piagetian theory postulates several operators, termed *metaconstructs*, that may activate mental schemes. The metaconstructs represent the influence of directed attention, learning, affect, and perceptual salience in determining which schemes will be brought to bear on performance. Since it will be helpful to refer to these factors in constructing an explanation for childhood amnesia, each metaconstruct is now briefly described.

The *mental (M) operator* may be thought of as being analogous to a voluntary selective attention mechanism, directing schemes into a limited, active, immediate memory (e.g., Atkinson & Shiffrin, 1968; Norman, 1969; Waugh & Norman, 1965). The M operator activates or "boosts" schemes into consciousness, and the set of coexisting M-boosted schemes at any moment are envisaged as placed in a central computing space, M-space. The size of an individual's M-space determines the number of discrete chunks of information that he can activate simultaneously (or "think about"), using his voluntary directed attention.

According to Pascual–Leone (e.g., 1970), the size of an individual's M-space increases regularly with age. The amount of space (or energy) needed to activate the executive schemes that direct mental activities develops during the first 2 years of life. This directing component of voluntary mental activities often corresponds to the task instructions in psychological experiments. Children before 2 are creatures of habit or conditioning; they do not cognitively plan. The capacity to activate information in addition to executive schemes develops from the years 3 until adolescence. The number of separate schemes that an individual can activate (in addition to executive schemes) is one at ages 3 to 4 and increases by one additional unit for every 2 years of physical growth, until age 15. The hypothesized M-space estimates for normal subjects appear in Table 2.1. The original estimates were derived through analyzing a large number of Piagetian tasks for which age expectations were available (Pascual—Leone, 1969). Subsequently, a fair amount of converging empirical support for these estimates has been generated by Pascual—Leone and his associates (Case, 1972; De Avila, 1974; Parkinson, 1975; Pascual—Leone; 1970, Scardamalia, 1973).

An example may clarify the implications of the growth of M-space for understanding a subject's mental performance. A well-known psychological test is the backward digit-span. A subject is read a list of numbers, and the task involves remembering the numbers long enough to repeat them in reverse order. The transformational requirement interferes with the subject's attempts to "chunk" several numbers together into a larger numerical unit (Case, 1972); thus, the sequence of separate numbers must remain active in the subject's working memory for at least a brief time period. In Pascual—Leone's terminology, each number is said to occupy one unit of M-space. Using the M-space age estimates given in Table 2.1, it is then possible to predict the "number of numbers" that the average person at a given age will be able to correctly repeat backwards. For instance, an 8-year-old will likely have space enough to activate an executive scheme that directs the remembering and performing activities plus an additional three numbers. Assuming that the subject does not use elaborate rehearsal strategies, his predicted backward digit-span would be three.

The hypothesized increase in M-space is a central aspect of the neo-Piagetian theory. "Cognitive development," or a central aspect of it, is now construed in

TABLE 2.1
M-Space Age Estimates for Normal Subjects[a]

Estimated M-Space	Chronological Age (Years)
e	2
e + 1	3–4
e + 2	5–6
e + 3	7–8
e + 4	9–10
e + 5	11–12
e + 6	13–14
e + 7	15–adults

[a]*Note.* The element e corresponds to the space occupied by the executive schemes that direct M-operator activities. (After Pascual-Leone, 1969.)

the model as an increase in information-processing capacity. (For an independent, though very general, assertion of the same argument, see McLaughlin, 1963.) According to Pascual—Leone (1970, 1972), the maximum size of a subject's M-space determines his ability to think and sets upper limits on his cognitive performance in initial encounters with experimental tasks (before chunking of relevant schemes can occur). The growth of M-space is an important part of the explanation for infantile amnesia that follows.

Learning metaconstructs described by Pascual—Leone (1976) include two general types of learning, C (content) and L (logical); there are then two subtypes of L learning, LC and LM. Content (C) learning corresponds roughly to what Piaget calls "accommodation." C learning provides new cues by which a scheme can be activated. This scheme-enriching process occurs as a result of everyday experience and does not require conscious mental activity. When you look at a typewriter for the first time, you see a general shape and color. Continued experience with a typewriter enriches the perception by adding details. As a scheme becomes associated with more cues through continued use, its probability of activation is increased. The scheme itself becomes richer in information. C learning increases the intrinsic probability that a scheme will come into attention, its salience, by providing more features that may be noticed.

Structural (L) learning occurs whenever several schemes are repeatedly coactivated in determining the subject's performance. L (logical) learning combines the separate schemes into a larger functional unit, or "superscheme." Simply stated, schemes that are regularly activated together will in time come to be represented by (or "chunked" into) a single superscheme that is informationally equivalent to the set of separate schemes. The new superscheme may be activated by the cues of the original separate schemes.

There are two types of L learning, LC and LM. LC learning occurs "as a result of long practice in the simultaneous activation of co-functional schemes— practice which takes place tacitly (without the participation of M) in the context (i.e., the content) of daily experience. In fact, LC learning is the limit point or last step of C learning" (Pascual—Leone, 1976, p. 30). LC learning accounts for many of the integrated performance routines that comprise our daily activities. LC structures are not formed through conscious effort (application of M) but rather through experience. They are tied to the experiences that led to their formation, and thus these structures cannot be easily mobilized in an organized fashion through conscious thought independently of context. LC learning, in ordinary terms, would be something like purely associative learning.

LM learning also generates superschemes that represent the relationships among sets of subschemes. Unlike LC learning, however, LM structures arise as a result of the application of conscious mental effort: "LM learning takes place whenever a set of co-functional schemes are simultaneously and repeatedly boosted by the mental effort (mental attentional energy M) of the subject. . . . LM learning occurs wherever the schemes in question are simultaneously and repeatedly placed inside the subject's working memory M'' (Pascual–Leone, 1976, p. 30). LM learning involves the conscious and purposeful mental coordination of schemes and results in the linking together of two or more pieces of information. LM learning is very rapid and efficient. LM structures can be accessed in M-space through conscious thought.

We are here talking about two forms of what is usually called associative learning. Both forms associate skills or information together into coordinated systems, but the rules for both formation of the association and subsequent access to it are different. LC structures are formed when there is repeated exercise of a coordinated activity, or overlearning. LM structures are formed when there is repeated purposeful, voluntary coordination of schemes—when there is mental effort in Kahneman's (1973) terms. These LM scheme-systems may be retrieved from memory when any member of the system is purposefully activated. The distinction is somewhat like traditional notions of association under emotion versus association under contiguity, except that here there is the notion that the retrieval of the association depends on the conditions under which it was originally formed.

Pure cases of LC learning would be found in early infancy, when babies organize sensorimotor routines through pure exercise of function. Pure cases of LM learning would be found in adulthood, when, say, a subject mentally rehearses his way through a set of activities. Adult learning usually involves mixed LC and LM learning. If you learn tennis, you must begin with some conscious organization of a grip, a forehand stance, a serve, etc. You organize these in M, but a principal purpose of the M organization is to "pose" the system for LC learning. This consciously posed system, posed and exercised over and over, allows the gradual establishment of LC learning. This kind of sequence is one with which people are generally familiar as an automation sequence in human skill acquisition. But Pascual–Leone adds, as a new wrinkle, the argument that a parallel "posing" LM system is learned and perfected. Not only do you "groove in" your serves through practice; you learn hypothecation systems through which you purposefully organize your serve.

The *field-effects (F) operator* has received a great deal of attention from Pascual–Leone and his co-workers (e.g., Case & Globerson, 1974; Pascual–Leone, 1969, 1974). It is of limited importance for the purposes of this chapter, although it is of central importance in accounting for styles of perception and thought such as field dependence–independence (Witkin, Dyk, Faterson, Goodenough, & Karp, 1962). F accounts for a subject's sensitivity to salient perceptual cues. Thus schemes for salient cues present in the subject's sensory field will usually be activated by F and do not require activation by the M operator.

The *affective (A) operator* represents a range of motivations "from specific instinctual drives, such as hunger, thirst, sex, etc., to specific affects such as various types of object-bound fears, hopes, angers, likes, dislikes, loves, hates, etc." (Pascual—Leone, 1972, p. 23). Certain "cognitive states of affairs" activate the motivations that may increase or lower the probability of activation of corresponding cognitive schemes. The strength of the boost provided by the affective operator is proportional to the arousal of the individual at the moment. Pascual—Leone is here proposing a theoretical entity much like classical conditioning in the Pavlovian sense or cathexis in psychoanalytic terms. Objects in the world become invested with emotional meaning; they may become more or less accessible to thought because of the emotion.

Some major terms of Pascual—Leone's theory have now been discussed. It is important to keep in mind what the theory is and is not. It is not a totally quantitative, predictive theory—as some modern mathematical learning theories are for very limited domains of data. Nor is it simply a verbal argument disguised in formalisms. Some constraining and falsifiable theorems can be generated from the theory for limited sets of questions. But what it offers, first and foremost, is a synthetic discourse. Contained within the terminology system is an acknowledgment of central cognitive mechanisms now postulated within the literatures of genetic epistemology, information processing, cognitive style, and personality theory. It is an effort to hypothecate a mechanism system incorporating a set of locally hypothecated mechanisms. Following one modern terminology, it sketches out a "superframe" that is the locus of a set of "frames" (Minsky, 1975).

This kind of system is of particular interest to us here, because we deal with the phenomenon of infantile amnesia and because we are concerned with the possible intersection of research and clinical literatures in accounting for that phenomenon.

A Neo-Piagetian Model of Long-Term Memory: M-Boosted Learning and Retrieval

We can easily generalize Pascual—Leone's model to allow it to deal with long-term memory. Memory traces can be seen as "schemes." In fact, many of the schemes of Pascual—Leone's task analyses consist of learned information that is activated from long-term memory. In the experimental situations used by Pascual—Leone, the schemes are activated for the purpose of performing a psychological task. In attempting to remember childhood experiences, the task involves (a) activating the relevant schemes, and (b) actively processing the schemes in order to produce a meaningful symbolic reconstruction.

All of the theoretical metaconstructs play a role in the activation of information stored in long-term memory. For discussing infantile amnesia, it is useful to distinguish between purposeful acts of retrieval from long-term memory, which require use of the voluntary attentional operator M (or M-space), and involuntary remembering, which derives from the content learning (C) and affective (A) operators.

On the face of it, Freud's phenomenon of infantile amnesia implies, in contemporary terms, a retrieval problem. There has been storage. The information is there. But direct efforts do not locate it; hence the amnesia. Much recent evidence testifies to the child's growing use of more and more complex retrieval strategies as he moves toward adulthood (Flavell, 1977). Thus, infantile amnesia cannot rest on missing retrieval strategies in any simple sense. Adults, who have the largest M-space and the most elaborate retrieval strategies, are precisely the ones who show the missing memories. Maybe the incapacity depends on: (a) the types of storage operations that the child can perform, and (b) the fact that adults come to depend so heavily on purposeful, rational systems of access to memory.

As the child's information-processing capacity increases, one may predict a corresponding development toward more effective processing of to-be-remembered information. Suppose the following:

1. The child's information-processing capacity increases regularly with age.
2. Recall from long-term memory is facilitated by active information-processing at storage.
3. The experiences of very young children are stored before they can engage in effective information processing.
4. Older children engage in more and more elaborate processing of information.
5. An increase in information-processing capacity occurring at about age 5 might well be critical for voluntary address to long-term memory.

The first assumption supposes an orderly growth of information-processing capacity of a kind that has been regularly reported by Pascual–Leone and his associates in their M-space studies (Case, 1972; Parkinson, 1975; Pascual–Leone, 1970). The second assumption receives support from contemporary research on memory. The other assumptions are fairly direct extensions of the first two.

Current memory research provides considerable support for a relationship between active processing of information and subsequent retrievability (Craik & Lockhart, 1972; Craik & Watkins, 1973; Koulack & Goodenough, 1976; McCormack, 1976; Tulving & Thomson, 1973). The "levels of processing" theory of memory recently developed by Craik and his co-workers holds that retrievability varies directly with type of activity at processing. Craik and Lockhart (1972) describe a "flexible central processor [which] can be deployed to one of several levels in one of several encoding dimensions . . . this central processor can only deal with a limited number of items at a given time [p. 679]." Craik and Lockhart stress the importance of the particular encoding operations that are performed at storage in determining how well the target information will be remembered: ". . . long-term recall should be facilitated by manipulations which induce deeper or more elaborative processing [p. 680]."

Koulack and Goodenough (1976) investigated subjects' dream recall. They concluded that a person must awaken immediately after dreaming and think about the dream in order to remember it.

> Although information resides in a short-term store, we suggest that cognitive processing in the form of reorganization, chunking, recoding, and the like, facilitates the effective transfer of the information to (consolidation in) a long-term memory store. Without adequate processing of this sort, the information may still be located in the long-term store, but retrieval of the information is impaired [p. 976].

Tulving and Thomson (1973) in a different discourse emphasize the association of mental activity and remembering. According to their "encoding specificity" theory, only those items of information that are actively related to a target item during encoding will constitute part of the memory trace. These may serve as retrieval cues for the target item.

> . . . we assume that what is stored about the occurrence of a word in an experimental list is information about the specific encoding of that word in that context in that situation. This information may or may not include the relation that the target word has with some other word in the semantic system. If it does, that other word may be an effective retrieval cue. If it does not, the other word cannot provide access to the stored information because its relation to the target word is not stored [p. 359].

The subject must be able to concentrate on information in addition to the target item in order for effective retrieval cues to be formed. In the foregoing example, perceiving a *relationship* between the target word and other words is necessary if the nontarget words are to serve as retrieval cues. What this implies, of course, is that the broader the field of concentration—the more items involved—the greater would be the possibilities of access to memory of the target item.

The growth in M-space from one unit to two units may be particularly important in this regard. Prior to this development, the child can purposefully process but one unit of information (in addition to executive schemes) at a time. After the growth to two units of processing capacity, the child can simultaneously activate more than one informational chunk. The appearance of combinatorial processing abilities allows the subject to purposefully activate information in addition to the to-be-remembered item at storage, which may serve as retrieval cues in later recall situations. It allows the child, in Piagetian terms, to "decenter," to consider two aspects of a presenting situation together—for example, the relation of figure to ground. Since Pascual–Leone (1970) has provided data indicating that the average age of transition from one to two units of information-processing capacity is at about 5 years, an improvement in purposeful recall is to be predicted.

It will be remembered that Pascual–Leone distinguishes between LC and LM learning. LC and LM structures are reactivated by different types of situations. LC structures were not formed by conscious mental effort but rather through experience. They were not formed in M, and so they cannot be retrieved in an organized fashion in M. Thus, the activation of LC structures generally depends on internal or external retrieval cues that are similar to those present in the environment in which the structure was formed.

In contrast, LM structures are formed entirely as a result of directed mental effort. Hence, the M activation of one or more of the separate schemes may activate the whole LM structure. Thus, LM structures may be purposefully activated by the subject independent of context (assuming that an appropriate cue is activated during the memory search).

The bearing of this distinction on a theory of infantile amnesia may now be elaborated. Since LM structures are a result of the simultaneous activation of at least two schemes in M-space, such structures cannot be formed before age 5. The child's mental representations of complex events before this age must be of the LC type and are largely dependent on contextual or affective cues for their organized reassembly. In contrast, LM structures are accessible through M-operator (directed memory search) activities. It follows that certain memory structures that are formed after age 5 should be more accessible to purposeful recall. This could partially account for the difficulty adults have in recalling their earliest experiences.

The net effect of positing LC and LM learning mechanisms is to propose a dual memory system. The duality is similar to some standard psychological learning dualities—classical versus instrumental conditioning, respondent versus operant learning, associative versus cognitive function. But Pascual–Leone's duality is founded on a consideration of human learning, and it has some important and useful differences in properties from those derived from animal data.

LC memories are addressable by situational and affective factors. They are not known or felt as memories (unless, at a later time, the subject looks at his LC-organized behavior and considers it, which is tantamount to placing symbolic representations of the LC learning in M). LM memories, in contrast, are addressable through intentional behavior. This distinction does not mean that young children never attempt to intentionally retrieve learned information. By age 2, children have developed executive schemes or "plans," and they begin to use M. But the purposiveness that directs their behavior is limited; they show limited "attention span" except as situational cues continually reconstitute the temporal line of their behavior. The amount of schematic material that can be placed in M *is not yet sufficient for an intentional and easily addressable memory*.

What Pascual—Leone's theoretical apparatus asserts, in ordinary terms, seems to be this. Young children form ideas and behaviors, which become attached to situations. "Situations" can be external cues—sounds, sights, smells—or they can be internal—fear, excitement, joy. If a situation is repeated, it tends to bring back the memory. The memories so stored are fragmentary and brief—an idea, an image, a movement. We call them memories, but the child does not think of them as memories.

Older children become able to think about their ideas and behavior and, in thinking about them, manage them adaptively. To think simultaneously about an idea and the situation that first evoked it is to begin to know that the idea is a memory. This kind of "thinking simultaneously" causes idea combinations to go into a higher-order kind of memory designed for idea combinations. One can address this higher-order memory as humans ordinarily address one another's memory. One can ask, "Do you remember what we did last Sunday?" The signals contained in the question locate "Sunday" idea combinations that can then, using the planning powers of the higher-order "simultaneous thinker," be so worked and shaped that what the child puts out is an adequate and conventional narrative account of his ideas about last Sunday.

All memories put out through the higher-order system would be subordinated to "last Sunday"—relevant, as we would ordinarily say. Imagine the same question asked of a younger child. One might or might not get an appropriate first idea (children are only vaguely aware of things like "Sundays"), but the train of serial ideas and behaviors would seem "irrelevant" and "meaningless." Each idea produced by the very young child would serve as a situation evoking a next. "Sunday" might evoke "church"; "church" might evoke "new hat." One would obtain associative flow, with local couplings meaningful, but the overall string of ideas would not be well subordinated to an overriding intentionality.

As with any argument based upon developmental data, it must be understood that identifying the transition point as "age 5" in this discourse should be taken as a statistical abstraction. We use age 5 to refer to a distribution of incidence having a mode at age 5 with individual children distributed in a range of months and years around that mode. Furthermore, it seems to be the case here, as with many other developmental phenomena, that it is unlikely that change in the child comes in suddenly, absolutely, and completely. Observable growth changes in children (e.g., the move from creeping to walking) do not burst into existence overnight. It seems unreasonable to expect that hypothecated central events would come into existence suddenly and completely either. So one might well imagine that the central transition pictured by Pascual—Leone, the move from one to two units of M processing at "age 5," could very well serve as a substrate for the gradually rising ogival curve of frequency of childhood memories pictured by Waldfogel in Fig. 2.1.

In presenting Pascual—Leone's theory, we have described LC remembering as the only alternative to purposeful remembering. LC structures are formed through repetition of a situation, so that overlearning may occur. For example, if seeing Grandma and going for long walks occur together often enough, the two events may become associated or linked in the mind of the child. Occasionally, however, children and adults alike form memories that were apparently neither overlearned nor M processed. One emotional experience suffices. Brown and Kulik (1977) analyzed adults' recollections of President Kennedy's assassination and use the phrase *flashbulb memories* to refer to the strong memory traces that are recorded at moments of intense emotion. These memories contain a great deal of minute details that are seemingly not relevant to understanding the emotional content of the remembered experiences. If during a walk Grandma is suddenly hit by a car, the flashbulb may fire, recording such details as the color of the car and the trees in the distance as well as the central event. It is as if surpassing a certain emotional threshold triggers the shutter, and a mental picture is taken.

The flashbulb memories appear to be an extreme case of a "Now Print!" mechanism proposed by Livingston (1967a, 1967b) as a general basis for all reinforcement phenomena in learning. Moments of excitement, novelty, or satisfaction in ordinary experience might set off little flashes that, over time and repeated experience, would gradually create learning. Such a "Now Print!" mechanism might very well serve as an adequate neuropsychological basis for Pascual–Leone's LC learning. Siegel and White (1975) have argued that the "Now Print!" mechanism might establish the primary landmarks upon which children and adults, using constructive processes, form route maps and survey maps of spatial terrains. In memory, LC learning created through a "Now Print!" mechanism might establish "landmarks"—remembered traces, ideas, images—upon which children and adults, using constructive processes in M-space, form narrative memories and more complex ideas about their experience.

COMPOSITE CAUSATION AS ENVISAGED IN SOCIAL, BIOLOGICAL, AND PSYCHOLOGICAL FRAMES

narrative memories

We have reviewed several hypotheses about developmental discontinuities around age 5 that may account for infantile amnesia. In addition, we have repeatedly asserted that the several hypotheses need not be competing or mutually exclusive. It is quite likely that the rise in memories for events occurring after age 5 reflects social, psychological, and biological factors in interaction with one another. The picture of composite causation might look something like what follows.

Socialization processes normally foster a reorganization of memory. In the quote from Sechenov used as an epigraph to this chapter, it is argued that "it must be as difficult to get the necessary ideas from the memory of a child, as it is to find books in a badly-organized library." The quote deserves some careful consideration. It is doubtful if the memories of a young child are, in an absolute sense, badly organized. Young children use their memories well. They recognize things and people, know a lot about what to say and do, show fear or surprise or delight appropriately. All this says that their memories are in some sense well organized for practical dealings with things near at hand. What the memory is badly organized for is cooperation in symbolic discourse. Children use memories, but apparently some reorganizations are necessary if others are to get to them. There must be a performance system that produces symbols that can be read by others who will then understand what the child knows and remembers. Preschool children regularly organize such performance systems: dramatic play, the ability to work with paints and other media, and most notably language. Parents delight in helping their young children to speak, because, of course, it enables them to communicate with the child in a rather powerful way. The parent can "get" the child's ideas, and the child can get the parent's ideas. Both become able to address the memories of the other.

Language is a rather complex and demanding performance system. If one is to play the game of language well, if one is to make well-formed and complete grammatical sentences, then one must be able to express memory traces in a performance system that includes notations about who, what, where, when, and why. Such notations are often missing or inconsistent in the speech of preschoolers. We have the not infrequent situation where the tot comes in to the parent, very excited, and offers a great stream of language. The perplexed parent is concerned but confused, because he cannot make out from the child's discourse who has done what to whom.

The proper and consistent notation of sentences takes some time and development. Two-year-olds often speak in cryptic telegraphic utterances: "cup hot," "ice cream fall down." Parents simplify their speech when they talk to toddlers, but nevertheless they tend to expand and organize their telegraphic utterances. According to Brown and Bellugi (1964):

> The expansion encodes aspects of reality that are not coded by the child's telegraphic utterance. Functors have meaning but it is meaning that accrues to them in context rather than in isolation. The meanings that are added by functors seem to be nothing less than the basic terms in which we construe reality: the time of an action, whether it is ongoing or completed, whether it is presently relevant or not; . . . It seems to us that a mother in expanding speech may be teaching more than grammar; she may be teaching something like a world-view [pp. 141–142].

So the organization of adequate spoken language implicitly demands that the child become able to format his ideas in an organized symbolic framework denoting dimensions of time, space, and causation. Spoken language generally deals with things that are relatively proximal. It is supported by performance devices that are possible in face-to-face communication: vocal emphasis, gesture, and the apparatus of nonverbal communication. The onset of schooling brings about a demand that the child develop performance systems for reading and writing. The requirements for explicit notation are even more stringent in writing than in speaking. The communication pattern may have to locate and deal with distal circumstances of time, place, and person. Because of the absence of the auxiliary devices of face-to-face communication, these notations must be explicit and in the discourse (White, 1977).

In short, the development of spoken and written communication by children implicitly demands that they express their thoughts in a well-organized way and, if they are to respond to communications from others, that they be able to find memories in response to questions annotated according to the "world view" of the common culture. Some organization of access to memory must be created to permit this.

Changes in perceptual processing or encoding strategies must occur in childhood. Evidence at hand suggests that there may well be developmental changes in the sensory systems of children, and such changes, coupled with changes in the ecologies of childhood and their associated sensory surrounds, may well mean that older children have trouble reinstating the cues that would draw forth the memories of their early years. But developmental changes in perceptual processing do not entirely arise through accident of maturation or circumstance. One can argue that they must be there to support the development of the communication systems already envisaged.

It seems reasonable to believe that children and adults communicate by locating events on common maps of time, space, causation, etc. The data on children at about 7 years of age are full of the coming of dimensionalization. Piaget argues that children at about 7 years of age become generally able to ordinate things, and in book after book, Piaget and his associates have shown that children become able to deal with orderings of things or events in terms of time, space, causation, number, physical quantity, or causative contingency (Flavell, 1963). Not too long after orderings of the physical world appear, children begin to show evidence of categorization and ordination of the social world. These dimensionalizations are not inventions or discoveries of the child. The child is organizing the world in terms of conventional social dimensionalizations, in terms of what Berger and Luckmann (1967) have called "the social construction of reality." The child is explicitly recognizing that world view that Brown and Bellugi have argued is implicit in the organization of a fully grammatical speech.

If an event is to be located on a map, it cannot be perceived or encoded in any old way. Siegel and White (1975) have recently reviewed the organization of cognitive mapping in children. If a string of events across time are to be related together in a common mapping, then it is a logical requirement that each single event be annotated in such a way that it can later be related to the other events in a temporal string. Imagine an aerial photographer flying over a terrain, shooting still pictures. If he wants to aggregate the stills into a composite picture, then he has to make notations for each picture that will allow him to place it appropriately with regard to another and another.

If children develop socially given dimensionalizations, then they must become able to perceive or encode events in such a way that they can place them on such dimensions. They must become able to tell time, know the days of the week, what an inch or a foot or a mile feels like, something about streets and addresses and cities and towns. Then, in the course of their ongoing activities, they must register information that will allow them to make estimations of the locus of those activities according to such categorizations and dimensionalizations. Conceivably, it is this growing organization of perceptual processing that leads children more and more to treat conceptual attributes of an experience as most salient (Underwood, 1969). What we usually think of as ''cognitive development'' implies an emphasis on verbal categorization of the world (Luria, 1976).

Maturation prepares the way for higher-order developments in perception and memory. Recent data more and more clearly suggest that focal maturational events are necessary but not sufficient for the cognitive changes and that implicit in society's timetable for child development are some normative expectations about maturation and readiness.

Of most interest for our consideration of childhood amnesia are the possibilities that parietal maturation may facilitate the child's ability to construct sustained purposeful performance systems and the possibility that the maturation of a hippocampal – prefrontal system may relate to manifest changes in children's long-term memory and their ability to congitively map. Psychologists have generally been somewhat reluctant to consider maturational factors as causative for observed changes in child development, because, generally, the hypothesis that maturation is causal tends to put matters out of the hands of the psychologist; given the state of the art of our present knowledge of neural and neurological maturation, it often consigns explanation to the realm of the mysterious and unknown. The case for consideration of maturational causation seems a little better and clearer here. Known kinds of maturational change in children occur at sites where, according to existing neuropsychological analysis, there are known control functions dealing with observed developments in children's performance. Further exploration of these kinds of neural maturation may well shed some further light on the details of the development of perception, memory, and the organization of performance systems in childhood.

As children grow up, they develop a dual memory system, a private system and a socially addressable system. ''Repression'' occurs when private memories are not brought into the socially addressable system. Our discussion thus far has touched upon the social, psychological, and maturational factors bearing upon a gradually rising ability to construct symbolic narrative memories in childhood. Freud's selective reconstruction model implies that not all childhood memory traces are brought from the private into the social memory system, and Pascual – Leone's model allows us to imagine the implications of such a selective process.

In Pascual – Leone's model, the activation of memory traces can take place through the affective or contextual boosting of schemes. However, purposeful constructive processes that interorganize schemes would take place only when and if the schemes are M−boosted in a working memory of sufficient size. Generally, developmental enlargements of M-space occurring at age 5 seems sufficient for the construction of narrative symbolic memories. If people are to embed memory traces in rational categorizations and propositional statements, those traces must be processed in M-space.

We have so far discussed the development of a higher-order memory system in children only in terms of social pressures and social requirements for communication. But it may be important to recognize that this higher-order system may have some significant implications for the individual as well. Children use the performative symbol systems not only to communicate with others; they may well use them to express, and communicate with, themselves. If a child is to propositionalize about his own behavior, characterize it, explain it, think about it, that child may well have to actively process the material in M-space. Ideas not so construed by the child may have no clear locus. They may not be understood to be memories, or if they are, the causal pattern governing them may not be at all clear. This kind of failure to fully construe the self's ideas and patterns of behavior may be at the heart of Freudian repression.

A recent psychoanalytic paper by McGuire (1970) considers the possiblity of a dual memory system as the locus of repression, resistance, and recall of the past. The dual memory system is identified with the Freudian distinction between primary and secondary process and with Schachtel's contrast between a pre-socialized and socialized memory. The primary memory system is envisaged as unsocialized and "trans-schematic"; it does not follow the assembly rules of socialized forms of discourse, or what we have earlier referred to as performance systems. The secondary memory system is socialized in the sense that it delivers thoughts organized according to schematic forms of communication.

What is a "trans-schematic" memory? At its extreme, it might be an idea or a feeling intruding into consciousness that is not recognized as a memory. In order to grasp the fact that an image coming into mind is a memory, one has to associate a minimal propositionalization. This image did not just happen; it is associated with something that happened to me in the past. Easson (1973) has reviewed the psychoanalytic evidence for the Isakower Phenomenon, free-floating imagery experienced by some individuals that seems traceable to fragmentary feelings associated with nursing at the breast. There may be visual, tactile, and gustatory sensations, and there may be a feeling that the "sense of self becomes more fluid and indistinct [p. 61]." Typically, the memories come when the subject is falling asleep or just awakening. Their meaning or origin may not be known to the patient, although in the experience of analysis they are construed and given an origin.

This kind of workup and interpretation of an isolated memory fragment would, in the terms of the present discussion, consist in the construal of the scheme in M-space, leading the subject to understand where the idea was coming from, why the idea was there. The idea would cease to be "unconscious" in the sense that it could now be given a definite place in the subject's theory of the self.

The process of thinking about the self-as-feeler seems not too remote from what Piaget has construed as "reflective abstraction," the process of thinking about the "self-as-knower."

The acceptance of parallel memory systems has important consequences for a theory of repression. The model indicates that the "censor" that appears at age 5 and shrouds our earliest memories is not repression as represented in the stereotyped blockade model, but rather the increasing power of and reliance upon rational information-processing activities with age.[3] Only that information that is actively processed at storage becomes accessible via purposeful retrieval efforts. As a result, very early remembrances are not directly addressable through M operations and will usually be inhibited while M is active. When M is inactive, early memories may be activated by affective or contextual cues, although these images may not be recognized as memories. Through the use of free association, psychoanalysis may encourage the generation of affect-boosted memories, which are subsequently made "rational" through M processing.

The step that Freud did not take, in his alternation between the blockade model vs. the selective reconstruction model, was the reconsideration of repression and, subsequently, the work of therapy that removes repression. Some modern writers have argued for the psychoanalytic utility of a selective reconstruction model through, first, a reconsideration of repression (McGuire, 1970) and, second, a reconsideration of the work of the therapy (Rubinfine, 1967). Rubinfine discusses psychoanalysis as a process of reconstruction that works, first, through the creation of altered ego states that will allow the free production of drive organized schemas (affect-boosted schemes):

> The waking, fully conscious ego with its highly developed sense of self-awareness, clear-cut distinction between self and nonself and secondary process-dominated operations will have great difficulty cognizing memorial data of fantasies, events, conflicts, affects and defensive operations which occurred and were registered in former (archaic) ego states [p. 201].

---

[3]The possibility that 'repression' might be reconstrued as 'reconstruction' was stated by Piaget (1962) in his *Play, Dreams and Imitation*:

"In accordance with their hypothesis, the Freudians make the beginnings of memory coincide with those of mental life. Why is it that we have no memories of our first years, and more particularly of our first months, which are so rich in affective experiences? The Freudians reply that there has been repression. But the theory of reconstruction-memory provides us with a much simpler explanation. There are no memories of early childhood for the excellent reason that at that stage there was no evocative mechanism capable of organising them. Recognition memory in no way implies a capacity for evocation, which presupposes mental images, interiorised language, and the beginnings of conceptual intelligence. The memory of the two or three year old child is still a medley of made-up stories and exact but chaotic reconstructions, organised memory developing only with the progress of intelligence as a whole. (p. 187)"

The archaic schemas so brought forward are then subject to rational consideration by the patient. They are subject to ego function and incorporation in an understanding of objective reality.

> In this way drive organized schemas which repeat are converted into "recollections," i.e., representations rather than repetitions. When these schemas acquire "me-ness" in present-day consciousness, they are modified and integrated into present-day structure and autobiography. In other words, they are integrated into newly formed structure which I have referred to above as conceptually organized schemas [p. 202].

OTHER RELATED PHENOMENA: FREE ASSOCIATION, DREAM RECALL, AND MENTAL DISORDERS

In conclusion, it seems worth noting that the information-processing account of childhood amnesia implicit in modern psychoanalytic writings and formulated earlier using Pascual—Leone's theory may serve as a basis for interpretation of other issues arising in psychotherapy and psychopathology. Three such issues are briefly noted: free association, dream recall, and psychotic confusion.

The parallel memory model may provide a tentative explanation for the effectiveness of the psychoanalytic technique of free association for triggering early memories. The success of this technique may rely on the request made of the client not to think about "anything in particular," but to let his thoughts flow freely. The client's compliance may result in the suspension of M-operator activities. Since the subsequent activation of mental schemes may be determined primarily by the affective mood created by the situation, certain salient but "unprocessed" memories, including those corresponding to events that occurred before age 5, may be activated. This is especially likely if the current affective mood is similar to the predominant mood that accompanied a salient childhood incident. However, later experiences are likely to be more salient and will usually be more readily activated in adult contexts, even when the M operator is inactive.

The study by Koulack and Goodenough (1976) discussed earlier illustrates certain parallels between the inaccessibility of dreams and early memories. Psychoanalytic theory states that the content of dreams, like early memories, is unacceptable to the adult ego and is consequently censored or repressed. However, Koulack and Goodenough have demonstrated that dreams are likely to be recalled when the subject awakens at the time of dreaming and actively processes the dream content. Thus, the general difficulty of dream recall, like the recall of early experiences, appears to result from the subject's failure (or inability) to consciously process the information at storage. According to the explanation developed here, voluntary efforts to recall "unprocessed" dreams should meet with little success, whereas free-association techniques should demonstrate a limited amount of unprocessed dream recall, especially for affectively salient dreams.

Efforts to integrate information-processing concepts with psychoanalytic and other psychiatric theories may prove fruitful. In particular, psychiatric theories may gain considerable explanatory power through adopting the notion of a voluntary information processor that normally inhibits early and even adult recollections that rely primarily on affect for their activation. For example, it is possible that certain commonly observed pathological symptoms present in schizophrenia and other mental disorders (e.g., affect-laden thoughts) may result from information-processing malfunctions. In particular, a sudden disruption of normal M-operator activities is likely to result in intense confusion and distress. In the absence of purposeful information-processing operations, certain affectively charged thoughts or even early memories may occur with abnormally high frequency. These thoughts are likely to be perceived as foreign to the individual and to be labeled as fantasies or hallucinations.

There are obvious parallels between this position and theories that attribute schizophrenia to attentional disorders. For example, McGhie and Chapman (1961) note the apparent breakdown of directed attention in early schizophrenia:

> These patients appear to have lost the ability and freedom to direct their attention focally as required in normal concentration. Their attention is instead directed radially in a manner which is determined, not by the individual's volition but by the diffuse pattern of stimuli existing in the total environmental situation. In effect, what seems to be happening is that the individual finds himself less free to direct his attention at will. Instead, his control of attention is now being increasingly determined for him by concrete changes in the environment. To this extent, the patient feels "open," vulnerable and in danger of having his personal identity swamped by the incoming tide of impressions which he cannot control [p. 105].

These authors draw parallels between attentional disorders and other conditions in which directed attention is simply inactive:

> . . . the concept of control, direction and inhibition is central to the process of logical reasoning. In conditions of relaxed control, such as in the hypnagogic state and in sleep, our thinking loses this sense of direction and is no longer orientated towards reality. Logical sequences of ideas are replaced by merely associative sequences and the thought level passes from the abstract to the concrete. It is this very lack of control, direction and inhibition which characterizes the disturbances of thinking reported by our patients [p. 109].

This statement is in accord with the present model in which infancy, sleep, and certain pathological states are all characterized by the absence, inactivity, or malfunctioning of a voluntary information processor. As a result, the mental activities that occur are dominated by other factors, particularly affect.[4] It is hoped that information-processing theories such as Pascual–Leone's, which explicitly articulate an interaction between cognition and affect, may aid in uncovering the causes of mental disorders that are presently little understood.

ACKNOWLEDGMENTS

We would like to thank Bennett Simon for several helpful discussions of the phenomena of childhood amnesia as they appear in psychiatric practice. Frank Sulloway read a late draft of the manuscript and was able to lead us toward useful documentation in Freud's writings. Some of his contribution appears in two footnotes. Sulloway's remarkable historical analysis of Freud's work, *Freud as Psychobiologist: A Study in Scientific Revolution and Revolutionary Ideology*, is being submitted as a thesis to the Department of the History of Science at Harvard University. A published version is forthcoming.

REFERENCES

Altman, J., Brunner, R. L., & Bayer, S. A. The hippocampus and behavioral maturation. *Behavioral Biology*, 1973, *8*, 557–596.

Arnold, M. B. *Emotion and personality* (2 vols.). New York: Columbia University Press, 1960.

Atkinson, R. C., & Shiffrin, R. M. Human memory: A proposed system and its control processes. In R. W. Spence & J. T. Spence (Eds.), *The psychology of learning and motivation: Advances in research and theory* (Vol. 2). New York: Academic Press, 1968.

Bach, M. J., & Underwood, B. J. Developmental changes in memory attributes. *Journal of Educational Psychology*, 1970, *61*, 292–296.

Barker, R. B., & Wright, H. F. *Midwest and its children*. New York: Harper & Row, 1955.

Beach, F. A., & Jaynes, J. Effects of early experience upon the behavior of animals. *Psychological Bulletin*, 1954, *51*, 239–263.

Berger, P. L., & Luckmann, T. *The social construction of reality: A treatise in the sociology of knowledge*. New York: Anchor Books, 1967.

Birch, H. G., & Lefford, A. Intersensory development in children. *Monographs of the Society for Research in Child Development*, 1963, *28*, No. 5.

Bowlby, J. *Attachment and loss: Vol. I. Attachment*. New York: Basic Books, 1969.

Bowlby, J. *Attachment and loss: Vol. II. Separation: Anxiety and anger*. New York: Basic Books, 1973.

Brown, R., & Bellugi, U. Three processes in the acquisition of syntax. *Harvard Educational Review*, 1964, *34*, 133–151.

Brown, R., & Kulik, J. Flashbulb memories. *Cognition*, 1977, *5*, 73–99.

---

[4]This model may also be usefully applied to the phenomenon of apparent regression in old age. There is some evidence that the elderly demonstrate lower levels of cognitive functioning than middle-aged adults (Papalia & Bielby, 1974). If these changes are due to a weakening of the information processor, one may expect other factors to become increasingly dominant in senescence. This shift may be accompanied by a heightened availability of memories that rely primarily on affect or contextual cues for their activation.

Campbell, B. A., & Spear, N. E. Ontogeny of memory. *Psychological Review*, 1972, *79*, 215–236.

Case, R. Validation of a neo-Piagetian mental capacity construct. *Journal of Experimental Child Psychology*, 1972, *14*, 287–302.

Case, R., & Globerson, T. Field independence and central computing space. *Child Development*, 1974, *45*, 772–778.

Craik, F. I. M., & Lockhart, R. S. Levels of processing: A framework for memory research. *Journal of Verbal Learning and Verbal Behavior*, 1972, *11*, 671–684.

Craik, F. I. M., & Watkins, M. J. The role of rehearsal in short-term memory. *Journal of Verbal Learning and Verbal Behavior*, 1973, *12*, 599–607.

Critchley, M. *Developmental dyslexia*. Springfield, Ill.: Charles C Thomas, 1964.

De Avila, E. *Children's transformation of visual information according to nonverbal syntactical rules*. Unpublished doctoral dissertation, York University, 1974.

Dobzhansky, T. *Mankind evolving: The evolution of the human species*. New Haven, Conn.: Yale University Press, 1962.

Douglas, R. J., Peterson, J. J., & Douglas, D. The ontogeny of a hippocampus-dependent response in two rodent species. *Behavoral Biology*, 1973, *8*, 27–37.

Dudycha, G. J., & Dudycha, M. M. Adolescents' memories of preschool experiences. *Journal of Genetic Psychology*, 1933, *42*, 468–480. (a)

Dudycha, G. J., & Dudycha, M. M. Some factors and characteristics of childhood memories. *Child Development*, 1933, *4*, 265–278. (b)

Dudycha, G. J., & Dudycha, M. M. Childhood memories: A review of the literature. *Psychological Bulletin*, 1941, *36*, 34–50.

Easson, W. M. The earliest ego development, primitive memory traces, and the Isakower phenomenon. *Psychoanalytic Quarterly*, 1973, *42*, 60–72.

Epstein, H. T. Phrenoblysis: Special brain and mind growth periods. I. Human brain and skull development. *Developmental Psychobiology*, 1974, *7*, 207–216. (a)

Epstein, H. T. Phrenoblysis: Special brain and mind growth periods. II. Human mental development. *Developmental Psychobiology*, 1974, *7*, 217–224. (b)

Epstein, H. T. Growth spurts during brain development: Implications for educational policy & practice. In J. S. Chall & A. F. Mirsky (Eds.) *Education and the brain*. Chicago: University of Chicago, 1978.

Fishbein, H. *Evolution, development, and children's learning*. Pacific Palisades, Calif.: Goodyear, 1976.

Flavell, J. H. *The developmental psychology of Jean Piaget*. Princeton, N.J.: Van Nostrand, 1963.

Flavell, J. H. *Cognitive development*. Englewood Cliffs, N.J.: Prentice–Hall, 1977.

Freud, S. Screen memories. In J. Strachey (Ed.), *The standard edition of the complete psychological works of Sigmund Freud* (Vol. 3). London: Hogarth, 1974. (Originally published, 1899.)

Freud, S. Fragment of an analysis of a case of hysteria. In J. Strachey (Ed.), *The standard edition of the complete psychological works of Sigmund Freud* (Vol. 7). London: Hogarth Press, 1953. (Originally published, 1905.) (a)

Freud, S. Three essays on the theory of sexuality. In J. Strachey (Ed.), *The standard edition of the complete psychological works of Sigmund Freud* (Vol. 7). London: Hogarth Press, 1953. (Originally published, 1905.) (b)

Freud, S. Introductory lectures on psychoanalysis. In J. Strachey (Ed.), *The standard edition of the complete psychological works of Sigmund Freud* (Vols. 15–16.). London: Hogarth Press, 1963. (Originally published, 1916–1917.)

Freud, S. A childhood recollection from *Dichtung und wahrheit*. In J. Strachey (Ed.), *The standard edition of the complete psychological works of Sigmund Freud* (Vol. 17). London: Hogarth Press, 1955. (Originally published, 1917.)

Freud, S. The dissolution of the Oedipus complex. In J. Strachey (Ed.), *The standard edition of the complete psychological works of Sigmund Freud* (Vol. 19). London: Hogarth Press, 1961. (Originally published, 1924.)

Freud, S. Some psychical consequences of the anatomical distinction between the sexes. In J. Strachey (Ed.), *The standard edition of the complete psychological works of Sigmund Freud* (Vol. 19). London: Hogarth Press, 1961. (Originally published, 1925.)

Gould, S. J. *Ontogeny and phylogeny*. Cambridge, Mass.: Belknap Press, 1977.

Grinker, R. R., & Spiegel, J. P. *War neuroses*. New York: Blakiston, 1945.

Henri, V., & Henri, C. Enquête sur les premiers souvenirs de l'enfance. *L'Année Psychologique*, 1897, *3*, 184−198.

Kahneman, D. *Attention and effort*. Englewood Cliffs, N.J.: Prentice-Hall, 1973.

Klahr, D., & Wallace, J. G. An information processing analysis of some Piagetian tasks. *Cognitive Psychology*, 1970, *1*, 358−387.

Koulack, D., & Goodenough, D. R. Dream recall and dream recall failure: An arousal−retrieval model. *Psychological Bulletin*, 1976, *83*, 975−984.

Livingston, R. B. Brain circuitry relating to complex behavior. In G. C. Quarton, T. Melnechuk, & F. O. Schmitt (Eds.), *The neurosciences: A study program*. New York: Rockefeller University Press, 1967. (a)

Livingston, R. B. Reinforcement. In G. C. Quarton, T. Melnechuk, & F. O. Schmitt (Eds.), *The neurosciences: A study program*. New York: Rockefeller University Press, 1967. (b)

Luria, A. R. *Cognitive development: Its cultural and social foundations*. Cambridge, Mass.: Harvard University Press, 1976.

Maccoby, E. E., & Jacklin, C. N. *The psychology of sex differences*. Stanford, Calif.: Stanford University Press, 1974.

Maranda, P., & Maranda, E. L. *Structural models in folklore and transformational essays*. The Hague: Mouton, 1970.

McCormack, P. D. Language as an attribute of memory. *Canadian Journal of Psychology/Revue Canadienne de Psychologie*, 1976, *30*, 238−248.

McGhie, A., & Chapman, J. Disorders of attention and perception in early schizophrenia. *British Journal of Medical Psychology*, 1961, *34*, 103−116.

McGuire, M. T. Repression, resistance, and recall of the past: Some reconsiderations. *Psychoanalytic Quarterly*, 1970, *39*, 427−448.

McLaughlin, G. H. Psycho-logic: A possible alternative to Piaget's formulation. *British Journal of Educational Psychology*, 1963, *33*, 61−67.

Melkman, R., & Deutsch, C. Memory functioning as related to developmental changes in bases of organization. *Journal of Experimental Child Psychology*, 1977, *23*, 84−97.

Milner, E. *Human neural and behavioral development: A relational inquiry, with implications for personality*. Springfield, Ill.: Charles C Thomas, 1967.

Minsky, M. A framework for representing knowledge. In P. Winston (Ed.), *The psychology of computer vision*. New York: McGraw-Hill, 1975.

Neisser, U. Cultural and cognitive discontinuity. In T. E. Gladwin & W. Sturtevant (Eds.), *Anthropology and human behavior*. Washington, D.C.: Anthropological Society of Washington, 1962.

Neisser, U. *Cognitive psychology*. Englewood Cliffs, N.J.: Prentice-Hall, 1967.

Newell, A., & Simon, H. A. *Human problem solving*. Englewood Cliffs, N.J.: Prentice-Hall, 1972.

Norman, D. A. *Memory and attention*. New York: Wiley, 1969.

Papalia, D. E., & Bielby, D. D. V. Cognitive functioning in middle and old age adults. *Human Development*, 1974, *17*, 424−443.

Parkinson, G. M. *The limits of learning: A quantitative developmental investigation of intelligence*. Unpublished doctoral dissertation, York University, 1975.

Pascual−Leone, J. *Cognitive development and cognitive style: A general psychological integration*. Unpublished doctoral dissertation, University of Geneva, 1969. Revised version to be published by D.C. Heath, Heath-Lexington Books, Lexington, Mass.

Pascual−Leone, J. A mathematical model for the transition rule in Piaget's developmental stages. *Acta Psychologica*, 1970, *63*, 301−345.

Pascual−Leone, J. *A theory of constructive operators, a neo-Piagetian model of conservation, and the problem of horizontal decalages*. Paper prepared for the Canadian Psychological Association meetings, 1972.

Pascual−Leone, J. *A neo-Piagetian process-structure model of Witkin's psychological differentiation*. Paper presented at the 2nd International Conference of the International Association for Cross-Cultural Psychology, Kingston, Ontario, 1974.

Pascual−Leone, J. Metasubjective problems of constructive cognition: Forms of knowing and their psychological mechanism. *Canadian Psychological Review*, 1976, *17*, 110−125.

Pascual−Leone, J., & Smith, J. The encoding and decoding of symbols by children: A new experimental paradigm and a neo-Piagetian model. *Journal of Experimental Child Psychology*, 1969, *8*, 328−355.

Piaget, J. *Play, dreams and imitation in childhood*. New York: Norton, 1962.

Pillemer, D. B. *The prediction of human performance: An analysis of Juan Pascual−Leone's neo-Piagetian theory*. Unpublished special qualifying paper, Harvard Graduate School of Education, 1976.

Purcell, K. Memory and psychological security. *Journal of Abnormal and Social Psychology*, 1952, *47*, 433−440.

Rogoff, B., Sellars, M., Pirotta, S., Fox, N., & White, S. Age of assignment of roles and responsibilities to children: A cross-cultural survey. *Human Development*, 1975, *18*, 353−369.

Rose, D. H. *Dentate gyrus granule cells and cognitive development: Explorations in the substrates of behavioral change*. Unpublished doctoral dissertation, Harvard Graduate School of Education, 1976.

Rubinfine, D. L. Notes on a theory of reconstruction. *British Journal of Medical Psychology*, 1967, *40*, 195−206.

Scardamalia, M. *Some performance aspects of two formal operational tasks*. Unpublished doctoral dissertation, University of Toronto, 1973.

Schachtel, E. On memory and childhood amnesia. *Psychiatry*, 1947, *10*, 1−26.

Schachtel, E. *Metamorphosis*. New York: Basic Books, 1959.

Sears, R. R. *Survey of objective studies of psychoanalytic concepts*. New York: Social Science Research Council Bulletin, No. 51, 1943.

Sears, R. R. Experimental analysis of psychoanalytic phenomena. In J. McV. Hunt (Ed.), *Personality and the behavior disorders* (Vol. I.). New York: Ronald Press, 1944.

Sechenov, I. M. Elements of thought. In *Selected works*. Moscow/Leningrad, 1935.

Siegel, A. W., & White, S. H. The development of spatial representations of large-scale environments. In H. W. Reese (Ed.), *Advances in child development and behavior* (Vol. 10). New York: Academic Press, 1975.

Sulloway, F. *Freud as psychobiologist: A study in scientific revolution and revolutionary ideology*. Unpublished doctoral dissertation, Harvard University, 1978.

Tanner, J. M. *Growth at adolescence*. Springfield, Ill.: Charles C Thomas, 1955.

Tanner, J. M. Physical growth. In P. H. Mussen (Ed.), *Carmichael's manual of child psychology* (3rd ed.). New York: Wiley, 1970.

Tulving, E., & Thomson, D. M. Encoding specificity and retrieval processes in episodic memory. *Psychological Review*, 1973, *80*, 352−373.

Underwood, B. J. Attributes of memory. *Psychological Review*, 1969, *76*, 559−573.

Waldfogel, S. The frequency and affective character of childhood memories. *Psychological Monographs*, 1948, *62* (Whole No. 291).

Waugh, N., & Norman, D. A. Primary memory. *Psychological Review*, 1965, *72*, 89−104.

Weiland, I. H., & Steisel, I. M. An analysis of manifest content of the earliest memories of children. *Journal of Genetic Psychology*, 1958, *92*, 41−52.

White, S. H. Some general outlines of the matrix of developmental changes between five and seven years. *Bulletin of the Orton Society*, 1970, *20*, 41−57.

White, S. H. Social proof structures: The dialectic of method and theory in the work of psychology. In N. Datan & H. Reese (Eds.), *Life-span developmental psychology: Dialectical perspectives on experimental research.* New York: Academic Press, 1977.

Witkin, H. A., Dyk, B. B., Faterson, H. F., Goodenough, D. R., & Karp, S. A. *Psychological differentiation.* New York: Wiley, 1962.

Yazmajian, R. V. Biological aspects of infantile sexuality and the latency period. *Psychoanalytic Quarterly*, 1967, *36*, 213−229.

3 Experimental Analysis of Infantile Amnesia

Norman E. Spear
State University of New York at Binghamton

Infantile amnesia is a phenomenon easily appreciated because of our common difficulty in remembering events from early childhood. In practical terms, reference is to forgetting after a very long interval between infancy and adulthood. It may appear somewhat trivial to add that this interval encompasses the period of physiological and behavioral development from an immature to a mature organism, but the point probably cannot be overemphasized. The critical feature for infantile amnesia is that forgetting during this period is greater than that during a similar retention interval that does not begin until after the organism is mature. For instance, whereas a 20-year-old person would be quite unable to remember specific events accompanying her birth in a hospital, a 40-year-old can remember without difficulty a good deal about her stay in the hospital during an illness 20 years earlier; the greater forgetting for the infantile experience over the common 20-year duration defines "infantile amnesia."

Elsewhere in this volume (Chapter 2), White and Pillemer have discussed the importance of infantile amnesia for human behavior, the multitude of possible explanations for it, and some of the difficulties in analysis of this phenomenon with human subjects (also see Campbell & Coulter, 1976; Campbell & Spear, 1972; Spear, 1978). My purpose is to concentrate on the *experimental* analysis of infantile amnesia—essentially impossible with human subjects—through the application of psychobiological techniques using animals as subjects. Although interesting observations are on record concerning infantile amnesia in such animals as the dog and wolf (Fox, 1971) and even the frog (Miller & Berk, 1977), the subject of choice for most analytical studies in this area has been the rat (and somewhat less frequently, the mouse).

The frequent use of the rat will surprise no psychologist, in view of its ubiquitous role in the history of behavioral research. But beyond this precedent, several important factors promote the choice of the rat as the principal subject for these experiments. First, of course, such rodents are cheaper to acquire and maintain over long retention intervals than are larger animals—a not insignificant consideration in these days of limited research funds. Of greater significance analytically, means for testing the behavior of the rat are readily available and better understood than for other animals; and a great deal is known about ontogenetic changes in physiological features of the rat, including critical changes in those morphological and chemical features of the central nervous system that seem importantly linked to the processing of memories (Campbell & Coulter, 1976; Campbell & Spear, 1972; Spear, 1978). The rat reaches sexual maturity within 50 to 60 days after birth and has a correspondingly short period of immaturity in other respects; retention intervals that span the period between the rat's infancy and adulthood therefore need be only a month or two rather than the 10 to 15 years required for the human. And, as with all caged animals, a good deal of control can be exerted over the animal's experiences before and after learning of the critical episode to be tested for retention later.

I probably need not elaborate the value, demonstrated repeatedly throughout history, of applying animal models toward the understanding of biomedical problems of importance to human welfare. It is in this spirit that we may consider the use of rodents to study infantile amnesia, because the latter surely qualifies as such a biomedical problem. Moreover, the rat is of course altricial like the human, and the ontogenetic changes found in the rat's similarly structured central nervous system parallel in striking fashion those in the human. Whether the mechanisms of learning and retention in the rat coincide perfectly with those in the human is uncertain, but there seems a general agreement that at least at some level, the same or very similar mechanisms are involved.

For several reasons, the majority of studies establishing infantile amnesia in the rat have focused upon immature animals in the age range of 15 to 25 days. First, animals 25 to 30 days of age or older have not seemed to show exaggerated forgetting relative to adults, perhaps because most characteristics of their brains deemed potentially relevant for learning and retention are quite near adult levels. Second, rats much younger than 15 days of age have obvious sensory limitations (their eyes and ears have not yet opened) and also are markedly inferior to adults in terms of the conventional tests of instrumental learning and Pavlovian conditioning. This is not to say that such very young rats cannot learn and learn quite well, but only that in relation to adult behavior, quantitative differences in learning speed and probably also in the quality of behavior emitted make comparison difficult. At 15 days of age, however, the now attractive, furry animal with large (opened) eyes and ears is capable of adultlike mobility and can learn quite rapidly and attain adult levels of performance within a reasonably comparable period of training. Yet after an interval of a few weeks, these rats exhibit a good deal more forgetting than the adults; to my knowledge, no one has ever demonstrated significant retention by such infants after an interval of 4 weeks, except possibly in terms of relearning and even then only in special cases. This may be illustrated through recent research conducted in our laboratory by Richard Bryan. For strategic reasons that need not be described here, Bryan attempted to arrange conditions conducive to good retention by 15-day-old rats after a 28-day retention interval. The task involved Pavlovian discriminative conditioning that exposed the 15-day-old rat to a distinctive odor in conjunction with a mildly painful electric footshock and to a different odor in the absence of the footshock. These rats learn this task rapidly, showing significant conditioning after a single presentation of each contingency. But after about 10 complete experiments, including presentation of numerous pairings of the odor with the footshock, Bryan remained quite unable to find conditions that would reliably yield significant retention after a 28-day interval.

Briefly stated, the technical problem for proper assessment of infantile amnesia in the rat is in arranging conditions of learning so that for immature and mature animals, motivational factors (e.g., sensitivity to reinforcement) are equal and so is the amount learned prior to introduction of the retention interval. These conditions were approximated in a study in our laboratory with Michael Stoloff (Stoloff & Spear, 1976); we may use the results of this study as an illustration. The task was a simple spatial discrimination where a solution permitted rapid escape from a mildly painful footshock. Specifically, the apparatus was a T-maze in which the rats (15 or 36 days of age) learned to turn in a particular direction to enter a compartment free of the otherwise omnipresent footshock (.5mA for some animals, 1.0 mA for the others). The use of this type of escape learning conveniently solves or at least minimizes the motivation problem, because as Campbell and his associates have shown (e.g., Campbell, 1967) and Stoloff and Spear verified for the apparatus of the present experiment, aversion thresholds to footshock in the present range do not differ importantly for animals of the present ages. Figure 3.1 shows that although discrimination performance did not differ for 15- and 36-day-old animals at the end of training, the subsequent decrease in percentage of correct responses between a 1-day test and a 21-day test was greater for the younger animals. This greater forgetting by the more immature animals (i.e., infantile amnesia) was independent of the intensity of the footshock from which the animals escaped.

The data depicted in Fig. 3.1 do not provide an ideal illustration of infantile amnesia, because it is unclear that degree of learning was equal for animals of the two ages prior to the retention interval; some of the 36-day-old animals had attained perfect discrimination performance for several trials prior to the end of acquisition, and so these older rats may be said to have received overtraining and hence overlearning in comparison to the 15-day-old animals, relatively few of whom performed perfectly for a long period during acquisition. This technical problem is more clearly resolved with another task, a one-way active avoidance task, and somewhat older animals, in the age range of 21 to 25 days. In a study conducted several years ago in our laboratory, we determined that for a variety of

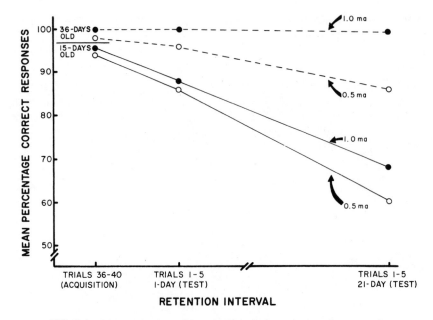

FIG. 3.1.   Mean percentage correct responses is shown for retention test performance of each of eight groups of rats. On each of two days these rats had received 20
acquisition trials on a discriminated (spatial) escape problem in a T-maze; in a three-
way factorial design, the rats were either 15 or 36 days old at the start of acquisition
training, escaped from a footshock intensity of either .5 or 1 mA and were tested
either 1 day or 21 days after the conclusion of acquisition training.

motivational conditions, the rate of learning one-way active avoidance is about
equal for animals 21 to 25 days of age and adults and that their terminal
acquisition performance (speed of avoiding) also does not differ. Furthermore,
avoidance performance for these two ages remains equivalent for at least 24
hours. Subsequent forgetting manifested at a test given 28 days later, however, is
significantly greater for the younger animals with any of several intensities of
footshock (Feigley & Spear, 1970).

Between the ages of 15 and 30 days, therefore, the rat's capacity for retention
over intervals of several weeks or more changes from virtual nonexistence on
Days 15 to 16 to adultlike levels at Day 30. During this same period, the rat
shows increase in basic muscular coordination, sensory capacities, and reaction
times; drastic increases in concentration and turnover rate of a variety of neurotransmitters in the brain; general increase in the rate of protein synthesis in the
central nervous system; and an increase of over tenfold in the number of synapses
found in the cerebral cortex. In some respects, even more dramatic changes
occur within earlier ages. Between 5 and 15 days of age, when the capacity for
learning certain tasks and manifesting this learning several hours later grows in
accord with a vast array of basic sensory capacities, we see also a drastically
increasing responsiveness to stress in terms of pituitary and adrenal hormones

believed to affect memory processing and a wide spectrum of changes in the central nervous system.

Lest we be swept away with enthusiasm over the richness of the relationships one might see between the ontogenesis of memory processing and neurophysiological features in the rat, it should be clear that a correlational analysis between physical growth and the processing of memories is nearer the beginning than the end of the road toward understanding infantile amnesia. A more important requirement for understanding is experimental analysis of the phenomenon. Methodological pitfalls pervade this experimental analysis, however, and a reminder of some of the basic ones is useful.

An especially difficult methodological issue is the ''comparative'' problem that arises in manipulations of any subject variable—whether species differences, sex differences, or whatever individual differences one wishes to ''manipulate.'' The basic problem of experimental design in the area is simple and classical: Subject variables cannot in fact be manipulated independently, and if we are to attribute retention differences to differences in age of the animal during learning, we must be certain that no other variable likely to influence test performance differs in value at differing ages. We must be certain, for example, that the immature and mature rat do not differ in their motivation, sensory detection or perception of events of the test, or in degree of learning established prior to the introduction of the retention interval. The obvious problem is that stating this basic principle of experimental design is a good bit easier than abiding by it.

For the case of infantile amnesia, discussions of these design problems and their solutions have appeared elsewhere (e.g., Campbell, 1967; Campbell & Spear, 1972); we should not, however, pretend that all the design problems have been solved. Furthermore, as analysis progresses, it is inevitable that certain features now viewed as explanatory will be brought under experimental control and will then be regarded more as methodological problems than as analytical solutions. For example, it has been suggested frequently that the encoding of environmental events is different for immature and mature animals, so that in effect, the content of a memory representing a common episode may actually be different for animals of different ages. If we someday are able to control precisely what is stored (as opposed to what is presented), we may then view age-related differences in encoding as a methodological shortcoming instead of an interesting explanation for age-related forgetting.

THE STATE OF THE EXPERIMENTAL
ANALYSIS OF INFANTILE AMNESIA

I find it useful to adopt a broad definition of infantile amnesia—which includes any deficit in retention associated with the state of immaturity. In practice, immaturity must of course have a referent, and I attend to this requirement. But the point is that I begin this analysis by treating infantile amnesia as the greater forgetting found in immature than mature organisms, regardless of whether the retention interval involves a relatively large chunk of the organism's life span or whether the source of forgetting is a retention interval at all. From this stance, for example, the finding of greater retroactive interference in immature than mature organisms, or greater susceptibility to amnesic treatments by the former than the latter, would equally qualify as instances of "infantile amnesia." At present, not much is gained by taking this broad view of infantile amnesia, because so little has been accomplished analytically, even with only the retention interval as a source of forgetting (and for the most part, the retention interval is the only source of forgetting that has been pursued at all systematically with respect to ontogeny). I simply believe that without this broad view, important relationships may be lost. I turn now to a brief review of the state of the experimental analysis of infantile amnesia.

In a pragmatic sense, the first step in analyzing infantile amnesia is to determine variables that alter the relationship between age and forgetting. We must seek specifiable circumstances under which the greater forgetting by immature than mature animals is minimized or eliminated and other circumstances where the usual retention deficit of immature animals is made still greater in relation to that of mature animals. And in doing so, we must achieve maximal experimental control over variables not of analytical interest. For example, it is useful to repeat that greater forgetting by immature than mature animals is of little interest if it can be attributed merely to the lesser learning by immature than mature animals. Degree of learning must therefore be equated, at least in operational terms. It should not be surprising that this frequently has been achieved. Immature animals, like human infants, are often remarkably adept at acquiring new information and holding it for short periods; it is in later retention tests where their poor performance contrasts with that of adults.

Of the studies of infantile amnesia that have applied the experimental method, many have served only to substantiate the basic phenomenon. This in itself is no easy research effort; it requires orthogonal variation in age and retention interval and the development of procedures whereby prior to the retention interval, immature and mature animals learn with about equal proficiency or at least to an equal degree.

A few studies have gone significantly beyond demonstration of the basic phenomenon, however, toward understanding at a level more advanced than description. For analytical purposes, these studies have varied in their success and may be considered in terms of two sets, those of largely methodological importance and those associated with a particular theory of infantile amnesia. The methodological studies of infantile amnesia have focused largely upon motivational factors. There has as yet been no systematic series of studies directed toward a particular theory of infantile amnesia. The tendency instead has been toward an isolated experiment or two to test one of a diverse set of possible theories. An example of these studies may be considered in terms of the conventional classification of independent variables (Underwood, 1957): environmental variables (e.g., treatments that are independent of the particular learning task), subject variables, and task variables.

Motivational Factors

Representative of experiments in this set are studies examining the influence of the intensity of the aversive stimulus (typically, footshock) on relative forgetting by animals of differing ages. If it can be determined for a particular aversive-conditioning task that forgetting is independent of the intensity of the aversive stimulus, for both young and old animals, then one can be less concerned that potential age-related differences in the aversion might confound the effects of age and retention interval and so preclude clear inferences about memory processing. To the benefit of such studies, other results also would lead to better understanding of the ontogeny of retention and forgetting.

The greater forgetting of a discriminated escape response by more immature animals has been found to be independent of footshock intensity for mice in the age range of 9 to 13 days (Nagy, 1975) and for rats 15 to 36 days of age (Stoloff & Spear, 1976). Similarly, the greater forgetting by weanling than adult rats appears not to depend on footshock intensity when retention of either active or passive avoidance is tested (Feigley & Spear, 1970). The issue cannot be said to be completely closed even for these tasks, because only a few intensities were tested in these experiments. The indications are, however, that forgetting is unaffected by shock intensity, regardless of the animal's age.

A similar strategy may be followed with respect to degree of original learning. For instance, Potash and Ferguson (1976, 1977) report that with sufficiently stringent criteria of original learning, weanling and adult rats did not differ in retention after a long interval. This was the case for both one-way active avoidance and passive avoidance tasks. In each of these particular experiments, however, ceiling effects of measurement appear to preclude firm theoretical decisions.

Environmental Variables

Campbell and Spear (1972) suggested that because of the higher levels of activity and exploratory tendencies among immature rats, they may be more likely than adults to encounter sources of retroactive interference during the retention interval or sources of proactive interference in close temporal proximity to original learning. Parsons and Spear (1972) tested this notion in terms of retroactive interference effects from experience in an enriched environment. Although exposure to the enriched environment during the retention interval did serve as a source of retroactive interference (for retention of active avoidance—

not for passive avoidance), the effect was about equal among weanlings and adults. The prediction of greater interference in the younger animals due to their greater probability of encountering the "enriched" sources of interference was, therefore, not confirmed. A subsequent study by Hurst and Spear (in preparation) employed a quite different method and additional control procedures, this time testing retention of a brightness discrimination (Kreshevsky maze) learned with food as reinforcer and testing whether exposure to an enriched environment might serve as a source of proactive as well as retroactive interference. Although prior environmental enrichment did facilitate acquisition, neither prior nor subsequent exposure to the enriched environment affected forgetting.

Holding number of encounters with an interfering task constant, Spear, Gordon, and Chiszar (1972) tested the relative susceptibility of weanling and adult rats to proactive interference in retention of active avoidance. The source of proactive interference was prior acquisition of passive avoidance. Although the younger animals showed more negative transfer from the passive avoidance to the learning of active avoidance, the deficit in retention caused by this prior learning was no greater for the younger animals than for the adults.[1]

Subject Variables

Campbell, Misanin, White, and Lytle (1974) compared infantile amnesia in the (precocial) guinea pig with that of the (altricial) rat. In most indices of central nervous system development, the guinea pig is practically mature at birth, but the rat does not attain comparable levels until 30 to 60 days postpartum. It was reasoned that if, relative to comparable adults, forgetting by young rats were greater than that of young guinea pigs, the source of the rats' greater infantile amnesia must be the relative immaturity of their central nervous system, because the experiential opportunities of the young guinea pigs and young rats may be presumed to be about equal. Campbell et al. (1974) conducted a thorough study involving two distinct types of learning tasks and comparisons of the retention of adult and young animals after each of several retention intervals. In contrast to the typically large and systematic effect found for the rat, no infantile amnesia could be detected in the guinea pig.

---

[1]A special case of environmental variable—the "structure" of the retention interval—has been included in a number of studies of infantile amnesia in our laboratory and in those of Professor Byron Campbell of Princeton University and Professor David Riccio of Kent State University. For our studies, the specific procedure has involved presentation during the retention interval of components of the training situation. This procedure has been found to alleviate forgetting. Spear and Parsons (1976) used this procedure to test a few theoretical issues such as the role of perceptual accommodation, or its failure, as a determinant of infantile amnesia. The tests indicated that failure in perceptual accommodation was relatively unimportant for the exaggerated forgetting observed in immature animals, but failure to maintain the memory in storage also seemed an unlikely explanation for even the youngest animals tested (rats, 16 days of age during original learning). We consider these and related experiments later.

The study of Campbell et al. is one of several possible approaches to determining the relative contribution of physiological immaturity and growth to infantile amnesia, compared to that of experiential factors. It is generally understood, however, that no single experiment will be crucial to deciding between these alternatives, and if the question is to be at all useful, its value will be in guiding the efforts of several kinds of investigations toward a deeper understanding of infantile amnesia, or of forgetting in general. Accordingly, a useful class of experiments in testing these alternatives concerns the relative forgetting attributable to metamorphosis, which in many respects involves more extensive physiological change than other comparable periods of growth. So far, the best study of this kind is that of Miller and Berk (1977, 1979). They tested the forgetting of African frogs trained at differing ages, including the especially important age for which metamorphosis occurred during the retention interval. Although infantile amnesia was indeed present with these animals, the effect was not enhanced when metamorphosis intervened between learning and the retention test. This argues for the importance of experiential factors in determining infantile amnesia, although as Miller and Berk astutely note, metamorphosis in this animal does not include especially exaggerated development of the central nervous system in relation to other periods of growth, and so conclusions must be tempered.

Task Variables

The "content of memory" issue (Spear, 1978) is central here; in other words, are certain attributes of a memory especially susceptible to forgetting? Operationally speaking, the more specific question here is whether certain kinds of learning tasks, or certain components of a given learning task, are forgotten especially rapidly by more immature animals. We now cite examples of this consideration.

Feigley and Spear (1970) compared weanling and adult rats in their forgetting of active avoidance responses. Although there were no age-related differences when retention was assessed with a go−no go test that did not present the aversive stimulus and so involved no specific reinforcement−response contingencies, the younger animals did exhibit greater forgetting than adults when tested in terms of a relearning measure. It was as if the weanling rats remembered the generally aversive character of the situation (because relative to nontrained controls, the former measure indicated emotional responding by animals of both ages) but had more forgetting of what to do about it than did the adults. A similar finding has been reported by Sussman and Ferguson (1976). They too observed little or no infantile amnesia in terms of a general activity measure, an index reflecting the general emotional responses conditioned to the circumstances of training, although substantial infantile amnesia was found in terms of instrumental responding.

Degree of infantile amnesia has seemed to vary for different kinds of tasks. It seems likely that this variation ultimately will be found to be lawful in terms of the specific storage requirements for memory acquisition, the nature of the retrieval cues available during testing, or the content of the memory that has been acquired. Coulter, Collier, and Campbell (1976) assessed retention in terms of a conditioned emotional response (CER) measure following an off-baseline procedure of Pavlovian conditioning, with tone as conditioned stimulus (CS) and footshock as unconditioned stimulus (UCS). Under these circumstances, rats conditioned when 17 to 22 days of age did not show infantile amnesia, although the effect was observed in still younger rats.

The off-baseline conditioning procedure excludes from the testing situation most extroceptive cues of original acquisition other than the CS. Therefore, Coulter et al. argued, growth-induced perceptual–motor changes could be largely discounted as a source of forgetting in the immature animals. On this basis, one might conclude that those studies showing infantile amnesia in rats 17 to 22 days of age have done so because for the particular learning tasks involved, growth-induced perceptual–motor changes were especially detrimental to later retention, whereas for the younger rats tested by Coulter et al. (11 to 16 days of age), some other factor was responsible for the infantile amnesia. Although of great interest and certainly plausible, other conclusions are equally plausible. Several relatively unique characteristics of the CER procedure used by Coulter et al. seem at least as likely to account for their results. For example, the conditioning procedure used by Coulter et al. required that training be distributed over 3 days. This contrasts with the more typical procedure in studies of infantile amnesia—massed training completed within a single day. Kessler (1976) and Kessler and Spear (in preparation) have found that with either of two quite different learning tasks (one identical to that of Coulter et al.; Kessler, 1976), forgetting is markedly reduced following distributed, compared to massed, practice. Furthermore, this benefit to retention following distributed practice is greater for immature rats than for adults, a remarkable finding to which we return later.

This study by Coulter et al. is very important, however, because it serves to emphasize growing indications that forgetting by immature animals, and perhaps infantile amnesia per se, may depend on the particular content of the acquired memory. Amsel (1979) has found that in contrast to the infantile amnesia readily shown for instrumental escape or avoidance learning, a disposition for general persistence acquired by rats about 18 days of age is subject to only slight forgetting after a long interval (a similar disposition acquired by still younger rats is forgotten rather rapidly, however). Rudy and Cheatle (1979) report that if rats 2 days of age are exposed to a particular odor at the time they are made ill with lithium chloride, significant aversion to that odor is manifested 6 days later. This is striking when one considers that previously, retention after as much as a single day had not seemed possible for the rat prior to 9 days of age, an estimate derived in terms of an instrumental escape response with footshock as the aversive stimulus (Misanin, Nagy, Keiser, & Bowen, 1971).

The purpose of this section has been to present merely the flavor of previous analytical investigations of infantile amnesia, hence the absence of detail. Several of these studies have important implications, however, and are discussed at greater length later.

THREE BASIC ASSUMPTIONS AND AN OPINION

The orientation and structure of our experimental analysis of infantile amnesia arises, like that of any other analysis, from a more or less explicit set of assumptions and dispositions. Of these, the following seem notable.

First, I assume that rate of ontogeny is genetically determined. This implies that the age of emergence of certain behaviors such as capacity for retention of a particular episode over a particular interval will differ not only between species but also between strains of the same species. Because of this and because learning and retention are so heavily dependent on the ontogeny of sensory capacities and response capabilities that may interact with the particular task used for testing, we choose not to orient our questions in terms of the critical age for emergence of certain aspects of memory processing. Such questions might ultimately be useful, but we simply feel that present knowledge leaves us unprepared to pursue them at this time. Instead, our analysis focuses upon differences in the characteristics of retention and forgetting for animals of differing levels of maturity ("maturity" obviously must have a referent, and we acknowledge this in the strategies for our research).

The second assumption is that performance factors associated with differential response capabilities or special dispositions may mask actual learning in immature animals. It is somewhat interesting that although sophisticated control conditions have evolved in the analysis of learning to help distinguish performance changes due to associative learning from those due to nonspecific systemic effects, there has been little or no progress in how to detect learning that might fail to be manifested behaviorally in spite of an appropriately acquired disposition. These circumstances lead to special problems in ontogenetic research.

Third, techniques for controlling (in this case, equating across ages) motivational determinants of behavior, degree of learning, and assorted simple performance factors are improving (e.g., Miller & Berk, 1979) but are unlikely to be perfect. More realistically, these techniques are unlikely to be adequate to permit precise parametric estimates of the magnitude of the difference in retention and forgetting for animals differing in maturation level. We believe the best approach, therefore, is to strive for generality of behavioral phenomena across methods of study—for differing apparatuses, tasks, motivation determinants, and degrees of learning. To supplement this approach, we find it useful to vary motivational determinants and degree of learning orthogonal to variables of specific analytical interest whenever the former factors are likely to confound ontogenetic conclusions. When it can be determined that motivational determinants and degree of learning do not significantly influence forgetting of animals at any age, then these factors are unlikely to confound conclusions about the ontogeny of retention and forgetting.

In addition to these three assumptions, this seems a good point to express an opinion about future research strategies. This opinion concerns the state of the technology available for assessing the ontogeny of learning and forgetting. I view the technical advances in this area thus far to be largely due to the motivational analysis concerning aversive stimuli (contributed by Byron Campbell and his colleagues), refinements of methods for assessing instrumental learning in neonates (by the laboratories of Michael Nagy, James Misanin, Elliott Blass, Abram Amsel, and Joseph Altman), and the more recent application of Pavlovian conditioning and acquired taste or odor aversions (e.g., Rudy & Cheatle, 1979; for further documentation, see Spear & Campbell, 1979). It is my opinion that the next advance in this area is likely through application of a research strategy initiated by Levitsky (e.g., 1975) and his colleagues in the study of malnutrition. The basic idea, advanced also by Melzack (1965) and many others (including, of course, Tolman, 1932), is that organisms (in this case, immature organisms) are likely to undergo a good deal of learning in situations where manifestation of that learning is not directed (by an experimenter) as essential for the animal's immediate welfare. Levitsky's interest in this kind of learning arose from difficulty in finding learning of the conventional "directed" variety to be sensitive to the effects of early malnutrition. He found, however, that important effects of early malnutrition did emerge in terms of tasks of the "latent learning" variety (e.g., see Blodgett, 1929; for a recent review of the latent learning literature, see Mackintosh, 1974) or for learning manifested to stimuli redundant to basic conditioning.

We already know that learning of this "nondirected" type is readily manifested in neonates in a variety of circumstances. For example, such effects are shown in terms of impairment to later learning caused by prior exposure to an extroceptive CS used later to control avoidance learning (Spear & Smith, 1978), prior exposure to the noncontingent footshock used later to control discrimination behavior (Rego, 1977), and prior exposure to odors to which the animal later is to acquire a conditioned aversion (Rudy & Cheatle, 1979). But how will this aid in the ontogenetic analysis of memory processing? Is it not likely that ontogenetic differences in latent learning or in the relative control acquired by redundant stimuli reflect only attentional differences and not differences in learning per se? This is indeed likely; but our interest is in retention and forgetting, and, at least within our conceptual framework of the requirements for manifestation of a memory (memory retrieval), the number of redundant-though-relevant stimuli encoded as memory attributes and present also at the retention test may be critical for memory retrieval. Moreover, the possibility that immature animals encode too few of such attributes is one hypothesis for infantile amnesia.

AN ORIENTATION FOR ANALYSIS
OF INFANTILE AMNESIA

The analysis proposed here may be understood by considering various levels of theory proposed to explain retention and forgetting. First, at a very general level not far removed from description, it has been asserted that forgetting is so obviously adaptive as to be explained in the manner of any basic organismic feature that survives evolution. Within the bounds of our present operational definition of retention and forgetting, it is hardly necessary to comment on the survival value of being able to recall (or otherwise act upon) needed information without simultaneously remembering all that has been learned; and the similar value of forgetting inaccurate, outmoded, or unpleasant information is equally obvious.

Another level of analysis has concerned the internal organismic mechanisms that accompany and perhaps cause forgetting. In the 6th century B.C. Parmenides implied that forgetting occurs as a consequence of disturbance in the appropriate relationship of light, dark, heat, and cold in the body. A century later, Diogenes suggested that forgetting was due to a disturbance in the proper distribution of air in the body. He based his decision on the observation that persons frequently breathe a sigh of relief upon remembering a previously forgotten event, thus becoming perhaps the first of a long line of scholars who have floundered in the difficult task of separating correlated physiological events from those that are more or less causal in memory processing. Plato's thinking on this matter led him, wisely, to be satisfied with his famous metaphor of forgetting as effacement of the etching (memory) on a waxed tablet (mind). In the 2nd century A.D., Galen returned to the question of which physiological mechanisms might be responsible for forgetting. His analysis implied that forgetting is a consequence of malfunction in the animal spirits presumed to reside in the lateral ventricles. Over 1500 years later, Descartes still held the animal spirits to be at fault in the occurrence of forgetting. His thinking, though, evolved a more detailed mechanism of forgetting: an impediment in the animal spirits' movement through pores in the brain when carrying messages between the pineal gland and the locus of the critical memory trace.

Today, the analysis of forgetting may be viewed as diverging along two types of explanations—one continuing the emphasis on physiological processes underlying the phenomenon (e.g. decay, disruption of consolidation), the other focusing upon the behavioral locus of the origin of forgetting together with environmental events that might disrupt processes responsible for remembering (e.g., encoding deficiencies, retrieval failure due to an inadequate number of kind of cues associated with original learning, mechanisms of interference that result from the acquisition of conflicting memories).

In reviewing and organizing the literature on retention and forgetting to guide research in our laboratory, we have adopted a somewhat different level of theoretical analysis. We have found it useful to treat "source of forgetting" as an intervening variable and to apply a somewhat functionalistic analysis (Spear, 1978). Although it is unnecessary to repeat here the details of the approach, a few brief remarks will be useful.

The interest in forgetting and retention implies that analysis begins from the point of established acquisition of a memory. For the purpose of experimental analysis, a further implication is that characteristics of the acquired memory (e.g., "degree of learning") be controlled precisely and a specific source for forgetting be introduced. Our approach emphasizes that more than one source of forgetting may be specified empirically. Defined operationally in terms of behavioral change, "forgetting" may be induced by the occurrence of any of several specific events apart from the largely unspecified occurrences that accompany a retention interval. A "source of forgetting" is any event that produces a decrement in learned performance (for consideration of associated events such as extinction treatments, see Spear, 1971, 1978), with the restriction that the decrement not be attributable to performance effects of a sensory or perceptual−motor nature. So long as forgetting from a specified source can be replicated with a variety of converging operations, the concept "source of forgetting" is no more tautological than conventional concepts such as "reinforcement." Thus events such as physiological trauma, certain cases of stimulus change, interpolated intervals of relative inactivity, and the acquisition or emerging accessibility of conflicting memories qualify as sources of forgetting. It is in this manner, as in the classical treatment of other concepts in psychobiology, that "source of forgetting" is treated as an intervening variable.

Is Infantile Amnesia Caused by a Relatively Unique Source of Forgetting?

The present approach implies this central question: Is the age-related change in capacity for retention (infantile amnesia) due to sources of forgetting that are relatively unique in immature animals or to the immature animal's greater susceptibility to those sources conventionally responsible for forgetting in mature animals? Stated another way, is greater susceptibility among immature animals to adult sources of forgetting sufficient to account for all the variance in retention attributable to age?

It is obvious from the discussion so far that for experimental purposes, the source of forgetting applied operationally in studying infantile amnesia is a retention interval involving unspecified events and behaviors. In terms of this manipulation, there would appear to be three subservient sources of forgetting that might be unique in immature, compared to mature, animals. The first of these is inadequate encoding of the to-be-remembered episode at the time of original storage. This deficiency might take the form of either inadequate quality of the memorial representation (in our terms, storing the wrong attributes) or inadequate quantity (in our terms, storing too few attributes). A second source of forgetting unique to immature animals might be growth during the retention interval. A third might be deficiency in the retrieval process or in its implementation.

These sources might conceivably act on forgetting by adults and so may not be completely "unique" to younger animals. But growth clearly is of a different kind in immature and mature animals, and problems of encoding (storage) and retrieval also may be qualitatively different in immature and mature animals. The alternative is that sources of forgetting acting to promote forgetting by adults during a retention interval (e.g., interference from conflicting memories) are the same as those responsible for infantile forgetting but are extraordinarily effective in promoting forgetting by the immature animals.

For the moment we may set aside the third potential source, age-related differences in the retrieval process or its implementation. Most experimental studies of infantile amnesia have ignored this factor, because when tested after a sufficiently long retention interval, all animals are adults. This may be a mistake for even this type of experiment, and special retrieval deficiencies in immature animals certainly might promote extra forgetting in these animals after relatively short intervals. We nevertheless withhold consideration of this factor.

Theories of infantile amnesia may be categorized roughly in terms of those holding that growth during the retention interval constitutes a unique source of forgetting and those believing that immaturity at encoding or storage constitutes the unique source. The following are examples of theories emphasizing growth as the relatively unique source of forgetting in immature animals:

1. The psychoanalytic repression of infantile memories links infantile amnesia directly with certain stages of ontogenetic development.
2. Exaggerated changes in the perceived context of a learned episode are viewed as causal in infantile amnesia, and these changes are due to the organism's growth between learning and remembering.
3. The "synaptic overlay hypothesis" views memories of certain episodes as permanently stored during infancy but rendered inaccessible later, due to morphological development in the central nervous system.
4. Ontogenetic changes in the chemical milieu of the central nervous system, especially in terms of neurotransmitter amounts and rate of turnover, induce forgetting by disrupting the electrochemical code required for manifestation of restored memory.

The following are examples of theories that emphasize immaturity at the time of memory storage as the major source of infantile amnesia:

1. Retention depends on redundancy in the memorial representation, and the limited storage capacity of the immature animal precludes or limits such redundancy.
2. The encoding of immature animals is deficient in terms of a failure to store a sufficient quantity of contextual attributes that may support later retrieval of the memory.
3. The neurochemical capacities of the immature animal are inadequate for permanent memory storage due to the demand on protein synthesis for basic physiological growth; i.e., because of general growth, little protein synthesis can be spared for storing memories.

In a practical sense, it is quite clear that growth during a retention interval and immaturity during storage normally are quite confounded. But it is not unreasonable to expect that with the proper research strategy, these alternatives may be untangled.

An Initial Strategy

How can we begin to test these alternatives? It would seem that a clear requirement initially is to determine variables that alter forgetting across a variety of sources of forgetting. If infantile amnesia reflects a unique source of forgetting, we would expect some degree of dissociation between those variables that alter forgetting in immature animals and those that alter it in adults. At the same time, we must realize, again, that dissociation is unlikely to be complete, because undoubtedly there are sources of forgetting common to immature and mature animals, and even those sources relatively unique to immature animals may be effective to some degree also in adults.

To decide between factors of growth and factors of encoding as explanations of infantile amnesia, the foregoing reasoning leads us to experiments that determine conditions under which infantile amnesia may be prevented or alleviated. It is notable that theories of infantile amnesia differ in whether prevention or alleviation is to be expected at all, without physiological intervention. Psychoanalytic theory expects alleviation of infantile amnesia; to a large extent, the success of therapeutic treatment is thought to depend on it. Theories emphasizing inadequate verbal representation by immature humans during learning (or perhaps improper representation, generally, in immature animals) imply that if one could only "break the code," infantile amnesia could be alleviated. If infantile amnesia is due to the exaggerated contextual change between infancy and adulthood, drastic reproduction of the context perceived during infancy should lead to its alleviation (see Tompkins, 1970). For another set of theories, in contrast, prevention or alleviation of infantile amnesia makes no sense without intervention in the neurophysiological development of the central nervous system. If the infant's neurochemical machinery (e.g., neurotransmitter activity, number of dendritic connections, etc.) is inadequate to maintain storage of a memory, or if morphological development enhances complexity in circuitry and precludes retrieval and behavioral manifestation of the memory, prevention or alleviation of infantile amnesia would seem unlikely without direct manipulation of CNS growth and structure.

In summary, a core strategy of experimental analysis would appear to rest on two questions: Is infantile amnesia due to a unique source of forgetting? And if so, is the unique source associated with growth during the retention interval or immaturity during storage? These questions lead us to the empirical study of variables that may prevent or alleviate infantile amnesia. The real analysis of infantile amnesia will begin when we identify treatments for prevention or alleviation of forgetting that differ in their effectiveness for immature and mature animals.

PREVENTION AND ALLEVIATION OF INFANTILE AMNESIA: SOME EMPIRICAL TESTS

Treatments that decrease forgetting may be classified operationally: Treatments having this effect when administered during acquisition of a memory may be said to "prevent" forgetting; treatments with this effect when presented following the source of forgetting may be said to "alleviate" forgetting. Conceptually, however, a clear distinction between "prevention" and "alleviation" of forgetting is difficult, because the content of the memory—the particular attributes that constitute the memory in storage—seems to determine which events will be effective in alleviating the forgetting later on (cf. "encoding specificity," Spear, 1976; Tulving & Thomson, 1973; Tulving & Watkins, 1975). Ultimately, then, both alleviation and prevention of forgetting are likely to be quite dependent on precisely what attributes of an episode are represented memorially. Still, the operationally based classification is useful as an initial approximation, and we apply it here with full appreciation for the underlying complications.

Prevention of Forgetting in Immature and Mature Rats

With degree of learning equated by arranging conditions to ensure equivalent retention performance immediately after learning, variation in certain circumstances of the learning episode may yield corresponding differences in infantile amnesia. Once such circumstances are identified, the mechanisms underlying the effect can be analyzed toward an answer to what processes of memory acquisition are responsible for variation in infantile amnesia, or why infantile amnesia occurs at all. For example, in spite of an equivalent degree of learning in terms of behavior shortly after training, there may be wide variation for immature compared to mature animals in the number or kinds of memory attributes stored, and the probability of later retrieval may depend importantly on precisely what attributes, or how many, were stored. Of particular importance to the problem of infantile amnesia, there is reason to suspect that during memory acquisition, immature rats may acquire different memory attributes than adults and perhaps fewer (or more) as well (Spear & Campbell, 1979).

Toward such an analysis, recent studies indicate at least one set of acquisition conditions that prevent forgetting of immature rats more than that of mature rats, and hence may be said to prevent infantile amnesia. In her PhD dissertation, Kessler (1976) gave preweanling rats Pavlovian conditioning under either distributed or massed conditions, then tested their retention with a CER (conditioned emotional response) paradigm after either a 1- or 28-day retention interval. Some rats received all nine of their conditioning trials at age 20 days ("massed" training), whereas others had three of their trials presented at age 18, three at age 19, and three at age 20 days ("distributed" training). Animals tested after a one-day interval showed equally good retention whether trained under massed or distributed conditions, but for those animals tested 28 days later, retention was quite significantly superior for animals given the distributed practice.

That distributed training benefits retention is a frequently reported effect, often profound in its magnitude. This phenomenon has been observed in studies using human as well as animal subjects and for a variety of learning tasks, though with only a few exceptions (e.g., Estes, 1955), this phenomenon has not received the theoretical attention it deserves (for a review, see Spear, 1978). Our immediate concern, however, is the ontogeny of this distributed-practice effect.

Kessler (1976) considered the possibility that this effect might be especially marked in immature animals. As a test, she replicated the foregoing experiment with adults. Although no effect of distributed practice was detected, an unequivocal conclusion about the effect of age was precluded by ceiling effects on the measurement of retention: apparently because adults in all conditions had maximal CS-induced suppression when tested, no significant forgetting was measured for these animals after *either* massed or distributed practice (as has been found previously with the CER measure; see Gleitman, 1971; Spear, 1971).

To resolve this question, Kessler and Spear (in preparation) applied a different technique to compare immature and mature animals in this distributed-training effect on retention. The technique involved Pavlovian differential conditioning with distinctive odors as CS+ and CS− and footshock as the UCS. From previous work in our laboratory by Richard Bryan, we knew that this task yields very effective learning in rats from 15 days of age to adulthood. The procedure is simply to pair the UCS with the CS+ but not CS− and to assess conditioning by the extent to which animals prefer the CS− over the CS+ when given a choice in an apparatus different from the conditioning apparatus. To ensure an absence of a ceiling effect on measurement of adult retention in this study, number of conditioning trials was varied (from 3 to 15), orthogonal to age, distribution of training trials, and retention interval.

The results of this study were unequivocal (see Fig. 3.2). The important conclusion may be stated quite simply: Forgetting by 17-to 19-day-old infants after 28 days (compared to that after 1 day) was about three times as great for those given massed training as for those given distributed training, for all levels of training. In contrast, retention by adults did not differ after distributed compared to massed training. This provides us the clearest example to date of a treatment that alleviates forgetting differentially for immature and mature animals and, through its analysis, a possible lead toward a fundamental source of infantile amnesia.

In analyzing the distributed-training effect further, Kessler and Spear determined additional results of interest for our proposed analysis of infantile amnesia. As one study in this series, the initial experiment was replicated in terms of the four primary independent variables (number of conditioning trials, distribution of trials, age of the animal during original conditioning, and retention interval), but either of two different kinds of retention tests was applied in order to assess the relative stimulus control acquired by CS+ and CS−. Specifically, some animals were tested in terms of their choice between CS+ (the odor previously associated with the footshock) and a neutral odor, whereas others were given a choice between CS− (the odor associated with the absence of shock) and the neutral odor. This experiment revealed the striking finding that the immature animals appeared to learn little or nothing about the CS−; after either a 1- or a 28-day retention interval; for either 3, 9, or 15 conditioning trials; and whether distributed or massed, the rats trained when about 20 days old showed about equal preference for the CS− and the neutral odor. In contrast, adult animals preferred CS− over the neutral odor. When the distributed-practice effect in retention was assessed in terms of the comparison between CS+ and the neutral odor (all animals preferred the neutral odor to CS+, of course), the adult animals did show some benefit to retention from distributed practice, but the benefit shown by the immature animals was far greater. In effect, then, the age-determined distributed-practice effect could be attributed primarily to the animals' response to CS+.

Although these effects alone do not directly provide an explanation for infantile amnesia, they do suggest that an important determinant of the effect is the circumstances under which the memory is stored and perhaps what is stored to represent the episode. One avenue for explanation is suggested in the following preliminary, three-part hypothesis:

1. The immature animal's capacity for processing information is more limited than that of the adult. The number of events in an episode the immature

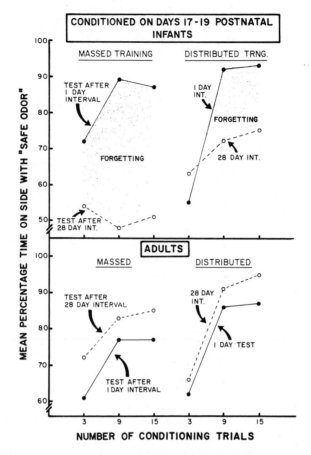

FIG. 3.2.   This figure shows mean retention scores for each of 24 independent groups of rats that had been given discriminated Pavlovian conditioning with one particular odor as CS+ and another as CS−, with footshock as the UCS. The point to be made from this figure is that regardless of number of conditioning trials, forgetting (assessed as the difference between performance of a group tested 1 day after conditioning and that of a group tested 28 days after conditioning) was greater for infants given massed conditioning trials than for those given distributed conditioning trials; but a corresponding difference was not found with the adult subjects. It may be noted that in fact adults showed no measurable forgetting whatever, with a trend toward reminiscence following either distribution of practice.

animal attends to, perceives, and hence learns will therefore be fewer than that of the adult within any single session of training.

2. If the training episode is repeated in a distributed manner so that upon its reintroduction the animal views it anew, the animal may attend to, perceive, and learn a different aspect of the episode than previously. In this way the immature animal given distributed training may represent, within its memory of an

episode, more events of the episode than if an extended massed session were given.

3. As described by Estes' stimulus fluctuation model (Estes, 1955, 1959), we may expect that during the interval between (distributed) conditioning sessions, the event(s) processed will return to the pool and other events will then have an equal probability of being processed upon the next exposure.

Consider an example of a simple conditioning situation in which there are, say, three events to be processed and used later to promote memory retrieval. One may call these events A, B, and C, and it is understood that they may be either internal to the organism or extroceptive cues. Let us say that the immature animal has a processing capacity of one event, whereas the mature animal has a processing capacity of three events. By "processing capacity of one event" is meant that upon a single exposure to a multi-event episode, regardless of duration but barring interruption or significant habituation to the attended event, the organism will incorporate only one event into its memory for that episode. With massed training, the immature animal will be expected to process only A; with training distributed over three sessions and replacement and resampling from the ABC pool between sessions, the number of different events processed will increase, possibly to as many as three. For the adult animal in such a simple situation, A, B, and C would all be processed with either massed or distributed training; and as attributes of the memory, they could be expected to promote retrieval with equal probability after either circumstance of training.

This simple model generates a number of predictions beyond the important age-related distributed-practice effect in retention. For example, the benefit to retention should depend less on the simple passage of time between practice sessions and more on the nature of the events interpolated between practice sessions. If the events are sufficiently disruptive of processing that, in effect, the event processed in the previous session returns to the pool from which a complete resampling must occur, then there should be some benefit to retention. Accordingly, experiments by Kessler (1976) implied that it was not the intertrial interval per se but rather whether or not the rat was returned to its home cage between conditioning trials, and Coulter (1979) has confirmed this.

Perhaps a more important prediction for our purposes concerns the role of redundant stimuli. I have suggested that redundant stimuli that are present during conditioning and incorporated as attributes of a memory, may be important for promoting retrieval of that memory; and evidence has been provided to support this notion (e.g., Spear, 1973, 1976). The foregoing analysis implies that immature animals may not incorporate as many redundant stimuli within their memorial representation of an episode as do adults. If true, the consequential deficiency in the effectiveness of memory retrieval (due ultimately to an insufficient number of cues at the retention test that correspond to memory attributes) may in part explain infantile amnesia.

Alleviation of Forgetting in Immature and Mature Rats

Forgetting from a variety of sources—e.g., amnesic treatments involving electrical or chemical insult to the brain, retroactive or proactive interference from conflicting memories, or retention intervals of intermediate or relatively long duration—may be alleviated if the subject is exposed to some critical portion of the original learning episode just prior to or concurrent with the retention test (Spear, 1973, 1976). The question here is whether such "reactivation treatments" might alter the extent of infantile amnesia. If so, the existence and nature of the effect would lead us to focus more closely on certain explanations of infantile amnesia while discarding, at least tentatively, some others. We discussed this earlier, noting that the simple fact of any alleviation of infantile amnesia would be quite contrary to some explanations of the phenomena. For example, to say that the immature rat has a retention deficit relative to adults because it is not yet equipped neurophysiologically to hold the memory in storage for more than a short period would be an untenable position if it were shown that the retention deficit caused by immaturity could be alleviated following a long retention interval.

For a number of years, we have been conducting tests in our laboratory to compare animals of different ages in their susceptibility to treatments intended to alleviate forgetting. Much of our initial work of this kind was reported by Spear and Parsons (1976). With retention intervals of several weeks' duration, a general result was that alleviation of forgetting by a reactivation treatment was no greater for immature than mature animals. In fact, the opposite relationship prevailed, with more alleviation among the more mature subjects. This suggested that the greater forgetting by immature animals may be due to deficiencies in initial storage of the memory. But in opposition to this notion, further studies showed reactivation treatments to be quite effective after shorter retention intervals of several days. This indicated that deficiency in initial storage by immature animals was an unlikely explanation and that it might be better to focus theoretical attention on forgetting-inducing processes present throughout the retention interval. One such process, the factor of "perceptual accommodation" in maturing animals, was discounted because of the equivalent alleviation of forgetting produced for immature animals by the techniques of "reinstatement" (multiple reexposures to training stimuli distributed throughout the retention interval) and "reactivation" (single exposure, just prior to the retention test). We emphasized, however, that certain factors limited our conclusions from this series of studies. First, the experiments in this series focused upon a single type of conditioning task. There were several good reasons for this strategy, including especially that the parameters governing behavior with this particular task had been studied extensively in our laboratory and others. Still, we maintain that as yet no one knows enough about animal behavior to permit reliance upon a single laboratory apparatus for establishing general principles of memory processing. A second limitation was that this particular task did not permit the level of control we prefer over degree of learning. Subsequently, therefore, we have conducted analogous experiments with the one-way active avoidance task that permits better control over degree of learning. The initial results have confirmed the basic ontogenetic relationship; reactivation treatments effective in alleviating the adult's forgetting with this task were less effective in alleviating that of weanling (22–24-day-old) rats.

A third limitation of these studies was that they did not test animals younger than 16 days of age, whereas two extensive studies conducted more recently have indicated that for two other types of learning episodes that also may be characterized as Pavlovian conditioning, infantile amnesia is not really evident for animals conditioned after the age of about 14 days. Coulter et al. (1976) report this relationship in terms of a CER index of retention and Campbell and Alberts (in press) in terms of retention of a conditioned taste aversion. Furthermore, studies of neonatal rats and mice in the age range of 7 to 12 days indicate extremely rapid forgetting of instrumental learning over periods of a few hours (for reviews, see Nagy, 1979; Spear, 1978). Finally, it is the behavior of these rats in the neonatal range, less than 15 days of age, that prompted the speculation by Campbell and Spear (1972) that infantile amnesia may in fact be due to storage deficiencies in very young animals but attributable to other factors in older but still immature animals.

To initiate assessment of whether retention deficits in neonatal rats could be alleviated by reactivation treatments, Gregory Smith and I employed a nondirectional active avoidance task. The avoidance response was "nondirectional" in that the animal could climb out of a shallow well in any direction to escape footshock or to avoid it if accomplished within 5 seconds of the onset of the CS. The CS was vibrotactile (because neonatal rats do not yet have their eyes or ears open), and the UCS and was a weak (.1mA) footshock. For the older animals (9 or 12 days old), we found that their drastic forgetting over a 24-hour interval could indeed be alleviated if the retention test was preceded by the reactivation treatment (noncontingent footshock). Ontogenetically, however, the relationship was like that of our previous studies: Forgetting was alleviated somewhat more for rats trained when 12 days of age than for those trained when 9 days old, and it was not alleviated at all in animals trained when 7 days of age. A summary figure of the influence of reactivation treatment for these animals is shown in Fig. 3.3 (also see Spear & Smith, 1978).

Is the forgetting seen in the 7-day-old animal therefore due to a simple storage deficit rather than to some factor associated with memory retrieval? We now believe the evidence represented in Fig. 3.3 is indecisive in this respect, because this avoidance task was quite difficult for the 7-day-old, and they could hardly be said to have learned it well, if at all. Also, more recent tests in our laboratory by Richard Bryan indicate that at least for Pavlovian conditioning, forgetting in the 7-day-old rat may be alleviated by a reactivation treatment administered 24 hours

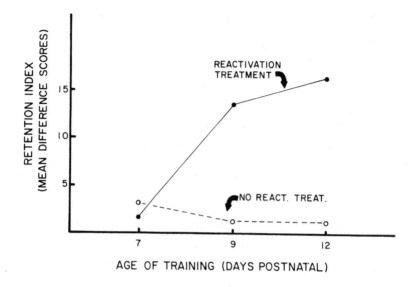

FIG. 3.3.   This figure shows the relative influence of a reactivation treatment on retention of nondirectional active avoidance by neonatal rats tested 24 hours after training. The index is determined by the difference in number of trials to "relearn" the avoidance task for rats trained on the task 24 hours earlier compared to those not previously trained (but given equivalent numbers and distributions of footshocks). The point to be made is that the influence of the reactivation treatment was no greater for animals 9 days of age than for those 12 days of age during training (the alternative trend was not significant). Conclusions about the influence of reactivation on rats 7 days of age during training are indeterminant, because these animals were so deficient in the original acquisition of the avoidance task (adapted from Spear & Smith, 1978).

after learning. For conditioning, these 7-day-old rats were given footshock in the presence of one distinctive odor (lemon or peppermint) but no footshock in the presence of the alternative odor. Twenty-four hours later, the animal's relative preference for the odors was assessed in terms of its spatial proximity to the sources of the alternative odor. Either of two kinds of reactivation treatments preceded this retention test. For one set of 20 animals, the reactivation treatment consisted of pairing one of the odors and the footshock, matched exactly as during conditioning but for a relatively brief period; for another set of 20 animals, the odor previously presented in the absence of footshock was now briefly paired *with* footshock. The forgetting ordinarily seen over 24 hours was alleviated in the former group in comparison with the latter. Because of its brevity, the reactivation treatment itself was not sufficient to result in this degree of preference without prior acquisition of the memory. Although the effects obtained in two such experiments were small, the suggestion is that for neonatal rats as young as 7 days of age, the age-related deficit in retention is at least partly due to deficiencies in retrieving the stored memory. The contribution of a deficiency in memory storage, if any, remains unclear.

Evaluative Comments

What I have presented here is a sample of the particular experimental analysis I have chosen toward understanding infantile amnesia. Most assuredly, this is not the only way to analyze this phenomenon, nor is it likely to be judged the best when, several years or centuries hence, scientists assess in retrospect how they came to understand infantile amnesia so completely.

It is therefore fortunate that an increasing number of laboratories are engaging in the experimental analysis of infantile amnesia and that the technology and methods underlying this analysis have improved sharply during the past few years. These points were illustrated clearly in a recent symposium at the State University of New York at Binghamton. Especially evident were the advances in this area even when considering, for the most part, only the rat and mouse as the psychobiological models for infantile amnesia (Spear & Campbell, 1979). Recent progress reported at that symposium included: (a) development of experimental preparations for assessing acquisition and retention with very fundamental behaviors in rats as young as 1 or 2 days of age (Campbell & Stehouwer, 1979; Rudy & Cheatle, 1979); (b) implementation of appetitive conditioning procedures for studying memory processing in the neonatal rat in association with the ontogeny of basic regulatory mechanisms involved in feeding (Blass, Kenny, Stoloff, Bruno, Teicher, & Hall, 1979) and with that of a relatively complex behavioral disposition—persistence (Amsel, 1979); (c) improvement of procedures for more effectively controlling degree of learning and motivational factors, to permit more precise estimates of the ontogeny of stimulus generalization as well as infantile amnesia (Miller & Berk, 1979); (d) perfection of procedures to study learning and retention in neonates within the context of psychopharmacology (Campbell & Stehouwer, 1979; Nagy, 1979); and (e) elaboration of questions and experimentally derived answers relevant to the prevention and alleviation of infantile amnesia (Coulter, 1979; Riccio & Haroutunian, 1979). It is to our good fortune, therefore, that the experimental analysis of infantile amnesia may be expected to advance so rapidly as to require that the present chapter be revised very soon.

ACKNOWLEDGMENTS

Research reported in this chapter was supported by funds from the National Science Foundation (Grants BNS74−24194 and BNS78−02360). The invaluable technical assistance and advice of Norman G. Richter and secretarial assistance of Teri Tanenhaus is gratefully acknowledged.

REFERENCES

Amsel, A. The ontogeny of appetitive learning and persistence in the rat. In N. E. Spear & B. A. Campbell (Eds.), *Ontogeny of learning and memory*. Hillsdale, N.J.: Lawrence Erlbaum Associates, 1979.

Blass, E. M., Kenny, J. T., Stoloff, M., Bruno, J. P., Teicher, M. H., & Hall, W. G. Motivation, learning, and memory in the ontogeny of suckling in albino rats. In N. E. Spear & B. A. Campbell (Eds.), *Ontogeny of learning and memory*. Hillsdale, N.J.: Lawrence Erlbaum Associates, 1979.

Blodgett, H. C. The effect of the introduction of reward upon the maze performance of rats. *University of California Publications in Psychology*, 1929, *4*, 113–134.

Campbell, B. A. Developmental studies of learning and motivation in infraprimate mammals. In H. W. Stevenson, E. H. Hess, & H. L. Rheingold (Eds.), *Early behavior: Comparative and development approaches*. New York: Wiley, 1967.

Campbell, B. A., & Alberts, J. R. Ontogeny of long-term memory for learned taste aversions. *Behavioral Biology*, in press.

Campbell, B. A., & Coulter, X. Ontogeny of learning and memory. In M. R. Rosenzweig (Ed.), *Neuromechanisms of learning and memory*. Cambridge, Mass.: MIT Press, 1976.

Campbell, B. A., Misanin, J. R., White, B. C., & Lytle, L. D. Species differences in ontogeny of memory: Indirect support for neural maturation as a determinant of forgetting. *Journal of Comparative and Physiological Psychology*, 1974, *87*, 193–202.

Campbell, B. A., & Spear, N. E. Ontogeny of memory. *Psychological Review*, 1972, *79*, 215–236.

Campbell, B. A., & Stehouwer, D. Habituation and sensitization of the fore- and hind-flexor reflex in the developing rat. In N. E. Spear & B. A. Campbell (Eds.), *The ontogeny of learning and memory*. Hillsdale, N.J.: Lawrence Erlbaum Associates, 1979.

Coulter, X. The determinants of infantile amnesia. In N. E. Spear & B. A. Campbell (Eds.), *The ontogeny of learning and memory*. Hillsdale, N.J.: Lawrence Erlbaum Associates, 1979.

Coulter, X., Collier, A. C., & Campbell, B. A. Long-term retention of early Pavlovian fear conditioning in infant rats. *Journal of Experimental Psychology: Animal Behavior Processes*, 1976, *2*, 48–56.

Estes, W. K. Statistical theory of spontaneous recovery and regression. *Psychological Review*, 1955, *62*, 145–154.

Estes, W. K. The statistical approach of learning theory. In S. Koch (Ed.), *Psychology: A study of science* (Vol. 2). New York: McGraw-Hill, 1959.

Feigley, D. A., & Spear, N. E. Effect of age and punishment condition on long-term retention by the rat of active- and passive-avoidance learning. *Journal of Comparative and Physiological Psychology*, 1970, *73*, 515–526.

Fox, M. *Integrative development of brain and behavior in the dog*. Chicago: University of Chicago Press, 1971.

Gleitman, H. Forgetting of long-term memories in animals. In W. K. Honig & P. H. R. James (Eds.), *Animal memory*. New York: Academic Press, 1971.

Hurst, D. D. & Spear, N. E. *Interfering and facilitating effects of environmental enrichment on learning and retention with appetitive conditioning in a complex maze*. Manuscript in preparation.

Kessler, P. G. *Retention of early Pavlovian fear conditioning in infant rats: Effects of temporal variables in conditioning*. Unpublished doctoral dissertation, State University of New York at Stony Brook, 1976.

Kessler, P. G., & Spear, N. E. *Distributed practice decreases infantile amnesia*. Manuscript in preparation, 1978.

Levitsky, B. A. *Malnutrition and the hunger to learn*. Paper delivered at the Cornell Conference on Malnutrition and Behavior, Cornell University, Ithaca, New York, 1975.

Mackintosh, N. J. *The psychology of animal learning*. New York: Academic Press, 1974.

Melzack, R. Effects of early experience on behavior: Experimental and conceptual considerations. In P. H. Hock & J. Zubin (Eds.), *Disorders of perception*. New York: Grune & Stratton, 1965.

Miller R. R., & Berk, A. M. Retention over metamorphosis in the African claw-toed frog. *Journal of Experimental Psychology: Animal Behavior Processes*, 1977, *3*, 343–356.

Miller, R. R., & Berk, A. M. Sources of infantile amnesia. In N. E. Spear & B. A. Campbell (Eds.), *The ontogeny of learning and memory*. Hillsdale, N.J.: Lawrence Erlbaum Associates, 1979.

Misanin, J. R., Nagy, Z. M., Keiser, E. F., & Bowen, W. Emergence of long-term memory in the neonatal rat. *Journal of Comparative and Physiological Psychology*, 1971, *77*, 188–199.

Nagy, Z. M. Escape learning in infant mice as a function of drive level and drive shift during acquisition. *Developmental Psychobiology*, 1975, *9*, 389–399.

Nagy, Z. M. Development of learning and memory processes in infant mice. In N. E. Spear & B. A. Campbell (Eds.), *The ontogeny of learning and memory*. Hillsdale, N.J.: Lawrence Erlbaum Associates, 1979.

Parsons, P. J., & Spear, N. E. Long-term retention of avoidance learning by immature and adult rats as a function of environmental enrichment. *Journal of Comparative and Physiological Psychology*, 1972, *80*, 297–303.

Potash, M., & Ferguson, H. B. *Acquisition and retention of a passive-avoidance response as a function of age and criterion*. Paper presented at meetings of the International Society for Developmental Psychobiology, Toronto, 1976.

Potash, M., & Ferguson, H. B. The effect of criterion level on the acquisition and retention of a one-way avoidance response in young and old rats. *Developmental psychobiology*, 1977, *10*, 347–354.

Rego, M. *The effects of thyroxine on learning and retention in the neonatal rat*. Unpublished master's thesis, State University of New York at Binghamton, 1977.

Riccio, D. C., & Haroutunian, V. Some approaches to the alleviation of ontogenetic memory deficits. In N. E. Spear & B. A. Campbell (Eds.), *Ontogeny of learning and memory*. Hillsdale, N.J.: Lawrence Erlbaum Associates, 1979.

Rudy, J. W., & Cheatle, M. D. Ontogeny of associative learning: Acquisition of odor aversions by neonatal rats. In N. E. Spear & B. A. Campbell (Eds.), *Ontogeny of learning and memory*. Hillsdale, N.J.: Lawrence Erlbaum Associates, 1979.

Spear, N. E. Forgetting as retrieval failure. In W. K. Honig & P. H. R. James (Eds.), *Animal memory*. New York: Academic Press, 1971.

Spear, N. E. Retrieval of memory in animals. *Psychological Review*, 1973, *80*, 163–194.

Spear, N. E. Retrieval of memories: A psychobiological approach. In W. K. Estes (Ed.), *Handbook of learning and cognitive processes (Vol. IV): Attention and memory*. Hillsdale, N.J.: Lawrence Erlbaum Associates, 1976.

Spear, N. E. *The processing of memories: Forgetting and retention*. Hillsdale, N.J.: Lawrence Erlbaum Associates, 1978.

Spear, N. E., & Campbell, B. A. *Ontogeny of learning and memory*. Hillsdale, N.J.: Lawrence Erlbaum Associates, 1979.

Spear, N. E., Gordon, W. C., & Chiszar, D. A. Interaction between memories in the rat: The effect of degree of prior conflicting learning on forgetting after short intervals. *Journal of Comparative and Physiological Psychology*, 1972, *78*, 471–477.

Spear, N. E., & Parsons, P. Alleviation of forgetting by reactivation treatment: A preliminary analysis of the ontogeny of memory processing. In D. Medin, W. Roberts, & R. Davis (Eds.), *Processes in animal memory*. Hillsdale, N.J.: Lawrence Erlbaum Associates, 1976.

Spear, N. E., & Smith, G. Alleviation of forgetting in neonatal rats. *Developmental Psychobiology*, 1978, *11*, 513–529.

Stoloff, M. & Spear, N. E. *Effect of shock intensity on discriminated escape behavior in infant and adolescent albino rats*. Paper presented at meetings of the Eastern Psychological Association, New York, 1976.

Sussman, P., & Ferguson, H. B. *Differential retention of classical and instrumental responding as a function of age and criterion*. Paper presented at meetings of the International Society of Developmental Psychobiology, Toronto, 1976.

Tolman, E. C. *Purposive behavior in animals and men*. New York: Appleton-Century-Crofts, 1932.

Tompkins, S. S. A theory of memory. In J. S. Antrobus (Ed.), *Cognition and affect*. Boston: Little, Brown, 1970.

Tulving, E., & Thomson, D. M. Encoding specificity and retrieval processes in episodic memory. *Psychological Review*, 1973, *80*, 352–373.

Tulving, E., & Watkins, M. J. Structure of memory traces. *Psychological Review*, 1975, *82*, 261–275.

Underwood, B. J. *Psychological research*. New York: Appleton-Century-Crofts, 1957.

4

Remembering and Aging

David Schonfield
University of Calgary

M. J. Stones
Memorial University of Newfoundland

BIOLOGICAL AND HISTORICAL BACKDROP

The early years of a human life span are reserved for an apprenticeship on how to cope with the environment into which an individual is born. Before being drafted into adult service, we learn to differentiate between important and less important changes in our surroundings, as well as to vary our responses accordingly. One obvious advantage of reliance on learning and thinking, rather than on innate stimulus – response connections, for adjusting to or mastering our environment is that acquired skills are not immutable. Members of the human species are not limited by previous accomplishments in their ability to survive when moving to a new environment or when the old environment itself changes. Early learning can be overlaid by new learning. Casual observation as well as experimental investigations disprove the proverbial statement that an old dog cannot learn new tricks but nevertheless provide some support for the hypothesis of greater difficulty in such acquisitions. Adults anticipate problems in learning to understand a foreign tongue, and from the perspective of an English-speaking adult, Chinese children seem highly intelligent for having mastered such a difficult language. Indeed, it would not be surprising if evolution, which endowed early human years with a readiness to absorb, had its counterpart in the later years in reduced ability to meet a demand for radically different types of proficiencies.

An early "explanation" of losses in mental capacity employed the concept of degeneration during the adult years, following previous years of maturation. A valuable aspect of the degeneration concept was that it could be couched in both psychological and physiological terminology. Thus, Thorndike, Bregman,

Tilton, and Woodyard (1928) proposed a lessening with age in the "sheer modifiability" of the nervous system on the basis of psychological data derived from learning experiments. Although Thorndike's framework of stimulus–response bonds is now outmoded, his transfer of training formulation remains important. Separating processes that are hindered and those that are helped by existing knowledge continues to be a useful approach for the psychologist of aging. Further, by specifying modifiability as one differentiating variable, Thorndike was implying that reproduction of old bonds should cause much less difficulty for the aged and the aging than establishing new bonds. As opposed to the catchall idea of degeneration, reduced modifiability leads to particular predictions and distinctions. New learning constitutes a problem, even though old memories may neither die nor fade away. Plasticity of the nervous system during early years continues its functional value into old age, so long as information provided by the environment can be processed according to acquired categories, so long as the acquired responses remain appropriate, and so long as the mapping between stimuli and responses remains compatible with earlier experiences.

The involvement of previously acquired current knowledge in examining differences in behavior strikes a contemporary, cognitive note. It almost dictates consideration of internal processes, instead of confining psychology to external manifestations. The possibility that difficulty in processing new information is due to the presence of old information restores memory to its deserved prominence in psychological studies. It probably is not, therefore, completely accidental to find a confluence of early investigations on aging and those on information processing during the 1940s and 1950s at Cambridge under Sir Frederic Bartlett (Welford, 1950). Genesis of the themes of storage and retrieval, timing of operations and stages, divided attention and limited capacity of the organism can be partly attributed to those early studies in gerontology.

REMOTE MEMORIES

Remote memories are those that have lasted a long time, and such aged memories seem an appropriate starting point for an examination of remembering among the aged or aging. If forgetting increases with age, a naive extrapolator might predict that the remoter the memory, the greater the deficit. However, many elderly people claim that their recall of events long past has not deteriorated, although they complain of their forgetfulness of recent happenings. With minimal encouragement, and often in the face of discouragement, older individuals indulge in autobiographical details of inordinate length. For a variety of reasons, this hearsay (or say-hear) evidence must be treated with circumspection. Nevertheless, it should not be arbitrarily dismissed, even though normal experimental controls are lacking.

If an individual of 80 volunteers to describe his 5th birthday party, he might begin by saying, "There were five candles on the cake." That kind of logical reconstruction clearly does not necessarily indicate the strength of remote recollections. Recounting incidents that occurred at the party, although more acceptable as testimony, is open to the objection that the same stories have probably been told, or at least recalled, at various times between the ages of 5 and 80. The likelihood of intervening reviews brings into question the validity of such evidence of remote remembering. Another fundamental objection is that the sampling of the population of memories is determined by the recollector. Ask the elderly man to recall incidents that occurred two days before his 5th birthday, and possibly he would excuse himself by saying that he was then only 4 years old. A more controlled sampling of remote memories to permit comparisons between age groups was recognized as a challenge by a few recent investigators.

The first systematic attack on the problem seems to have been reported by Schonfield (1969). He asked individuals aged from 20 to 85 for personal particulars, including the age they left school, the number and gender of their teachers in each grade, followed by a request to recall the names of each of these teachers. The dependent variable used in the study was the proportion of names recalled, and this is summarized in Table 4.1 by age group. Excluded from these proportions are cases where a specific teacher had been encountered since leaving school, as well as data from subjects who were themselves teachers and therefore likely to have seen some of the relevant names during their professional careers. It can be seen that the proportions of names recalled tends to drop with age, although changes are minimal between 40 and 70. No attempt was made to check the correctness of recall against historical records, but the respondents' manner of behavior during the interview makes it improbable that any conscious deception occurred. Subjects demonstrated that they were actively searching their memories, rejecting some of the retrieved names, and often recollecting specific attributes of, say, a grade 6 mathematics teacher while showing frustration at forgetting her name. The obvious drawbacks of the study make its

TABLE 4.1
Proportion of Possible Names Recalled[a]

Age Groups	Means
20 – 29	0.67
30 – 39	0.56
40 – 49	0.52
50 – 59	0.50
60 – 69	0.50
70 +	0.45

[a]Adapted from Schonfield (1969).

outcome merely suggestive, however. There seems to be some loss with age in the ability to recall well-known names, and certainly improved recall in old age is contraindicated. However, the evidence for forgetting is less impressive than that for recall. When a man of 60 can remember the names of 29 out of 37 teachers who taught him more than 40 years ago, one can only marvel at the efficiency of the human mind.

A much more elaborate and sophisticated investigation of remote memories was conducted by Bahrick, Bahrick, and Wittlinger (1975), using material from school yearbooks. Recognition, matching, and recall tests were administered to high school graduates between the ages of 17 and 74 whose graduating class included at least 90 students and who were in possession of a yearbook. Subjects were required to recognize which one of five names (first and surname) and which one of five portraits belonged to a classmate. In the matching task, a display consisted of either a portrait with the names of five classmates or a name with five portraits. For recall, only a portrait was presented, and the subject had to produce from memory the name of the individual portrayed. There were 10 items in each of the tests. An abridged version of results obtained by Bahrick et al. on three of their tests is shown in Table 4.2. The 18-year-old group, who had been out of high school for 3 months, and the 25-year-olds provide baselines for assessing age changes. It is obvious that considerable loss in recognition and matching scores occurs only after the age of 60—perhaps only after 70—and minimal change before then. However, recall, which requires active retrieval from long-term memory storage (Schonfield, 1965), shows a definite deficit by the 30s, a slight loss during middle age, and another large drop in old age.

Bahrick et al. obtained information from their subjects about size of class, years spent with classmates, class reunions, etc., that might have influenced original acquisition and rehearsal. The heroic task of formulating multiple regression equations based on these influences and estimating adjusted scores by age groups produced only minor changes, showing essentially the same trends as unadjusted scores. Other findings demonstrated that all groups were very confident about the correctness of their memories when they produced the right answers, although there was a slight lessening of confidence in the oldest group. Females, on the average, obtained higher scores than males, with a crossover to male superiority in the oldest group.

Warrington and Sanders (1971) used public events and well-known faces as material to investigate remote memories. Tests based on sampling of news reviews for various periods between 1930 and 1968 were administered to adults aged over 40. Questions posed to any respondent were confined to happenings that occurred and faces that were prominent while the subject was grown up, so that people aged 40 in 1969, for example, were only tested on post-1949 material. The performance of subjects in their forties and fifties was almost identical, both on recall and multiple choice, whatever period was being tested. However, memory deficits were found on all tests for those in their sixties, although forgetting of faces was minimal. The greatest drop in scores was usually between subjects in their sixties and seventies. Mean scores on the multiple-choice tests were higher than recall scores, and the difference between multiple choice and recall increased in older age groups. This supports the idea of a special retrieval difficulty with age but also demonstrates that forgetting after the age of 60 cannot be wholly attributed to retrieval problems. High correlations were obtained between memory scores for information acquired recently and in the distant past. There was, thus, no suggestion that age-associated memory loss was reduced when dealing with more remote memories. Squire (1974), in a multiple-choice study of public events, reported almost identical scores in his 50- and 60-year groups but replicated the evidence for memory loss in the seventies, with an even more pronounced deficit in the eighties.

In summary, the various investigations all demonstrate some forgetting of remote memories in old age and contraindicate the popular notion that the elderly have no loss when recollecting events of early life. Deficits may occur by the third decade of life, but there is noticeable stability from then until the sixties. Thereafter, deficits become more pronounced with each decade. Whether dealing with information acquired in school years or with public events learned during adulthood, the evidence seems conclusive that memory does deteriorate for most people by the age of 70. However, given the unknown strength of the original learning in remote-memory studies, it is impossible to compare the amount of age-associated forgetting of remote memories with the forgetting of recently acquired material. Therefore, there may well be a kernel of truth in the introspective reports of so many elderly people that childhood memories are more readily retrieved than memories for recent events.

TABLE 4.2
Retention of Names of Classmates by Age Group
(in percentages)[a]

Mean Age[b]	Name Recognition	Matching Name to Portrait	Name Recall for Portrait
18	91	89	67
25	85	85	51
32	87	83	37
44	81	78	37
52	82	83	33
66	69	56	18

[a]Adapted from Table 4 in Bahrick et al. (1975).

[b]The original paper divides groups according to months since graduation. The ages given in the present table assumed that graduation occurs on the average at the age of 18. The youngest group has been 3 months out of school.

EPISODIC, SEMANTIC, AND GENERIC MEMORIES

The remote memories discussed in the previous section are not easily pigeon-holed as either episodic or semantic, according to the taxonomic distinction and criteria proposed by Tulving (1972). Recollection of frequently encountered names and faces cannot be classified as episodic, since these are not temporally dated and spatially defined events. Even remembering public events does not necessarily meet the requirement of personal autobiographical reference, emphasized by Tulving as an attribute of every episodic memory. On the other hand, material used in remote-memory studies does not fit into the semantic classification, either, insofar as that involves the meaning of language or "a mental Thesaurus" (Tulving, 1972, p. 386). Lockhart, Craik, and Jacoby (1976) have pointed out that each semantic memory is formed from a series of episodic memories. The same kind of accretion occurs in many nonsemantic memories, such as knowledge of names or faces, and there is, therefore, a need for a less constricting term than *semantic* to include these nonepisodic memories that share other qualities of semantic memory. The suggested label is *generic*, notwith-standing the already overabundant proposed memory classifications, with semantic memories being considered as a major subclass of generic memory. Much of the material for investigations of remote memories falls under the heading of generic.

Each time a face is seen and attended to, or a name heard, a specific trace or an episodic memory results. However, when a face is seen, a name is heard, or even when an event is referred to repeatedly, generic, overlearned, and longer-lasting memories are also being established. Every episodic memory trace has reciprocal links with a number of generic memories. Bartlett's (1932) proposal that schema provide the basis for reconstructing specific memories has implications for the distinction between the generic and episodic classification. Schemata will usually be categorized as, and at the very least derived from, generic memories. The attempted reconstruction of an episodic memory from a schema involves a concurrent search for the specific trace or traces. If the specific trace is not contacted, the schema is embellished through imaginative processes, which eventuate in a sensible pseudomemory. If the memory search is successful and contact is made with the relevant specific trace, the episodic memory eventuates into a more veridical reproduction of the original episode. It is likely that an episodic trace is more susceptible to disintegration, since by definition it represents just one learning episode. For the individual's survival, repeated encounters are more significant than an accidental happenstance, unless the latter is associated with strong emotional arousal. Permanent storage of every episode could be an encumbrance to the human organism as it moves forward in time, as it ages. The cumulative record would increase with every incident encountered during each day of human existence, whereas the more important generic memories would change very little in a stable environment.

No environment, not even the most primitive, remains completely stable, and competence during the adult years is, therefore, demonstrated by ability to absorb additional generic memories. Knowledge of the meaning of words, as assessed in vocabulary tests, can be considered the quintessence of the semantic subclass of generic memories and does, in fact, show increases during middle age (Bromley, 1974). The difference between such vocabulary tests and material used in remote-memory studies should be emphasized. Generic recollection in remote-memory investigations is confined to knowledge acquired during a specific time period without, or at the most minimal, opportunity for subsequent reviews or reminders. On the other hand, words learned early in life are normally constantly reencountered. Confrontation with a new word should result in an episodic memory, even though its meaning may only be vaguely understood through association with known words. New words are likely to be of low linguistic frequency, but every recurrence adds strength to a fresh unit of semantic memory without detracting from the strength of other units. It is interesting to note, however, that a loss in vocabulary scores is consistently reported after the age of 65 or 70 (Botwinick, 1967; Bromley, 1974) and that these are the identical earliest ages for demonstrated loss of remote memories when tested by recognition and multiple-choice questions.

Laboratory studies of age differences in remembering have until very recently been almost exclusively concerned with material that becomes stored in episodic memory. Possible age differences in the influence of generic memories are often also considered. Generic memories and, more specifically, semantic memories provide the backdrop for dealing with all incoming stimuli. Episodic and generic memory systems are dependent on each other, and their interrelationships constitute focal points for future investigations.

RETRIEVAL FROM SECONDARY MEMORY

Investigators of age differences in remembering are bedeviled by the dilemma of separating the acquisition phase of learning from postacquisition phases. Experiments that suggest that memory deteriorates with age can often be explained by attributing lower scores of older groups to a learning, rather than a remembering, deficit. It then seems superfluous to hypothesize additional age-related impairment following acquisition. An extreme form of this doctrine reverts to the fact that amount remembered can itself be used as a measure of original learning. Therefore, by definition, poor recollection demonstrates poor acquisition. The opposite position is also tenable. It could be argued that because acquisition involves a memory component, memory loss is primary and learning loss is secondary. One implication of the confusing state of affairs is that limiting a discussion to a particular phase of learning or remembering is almost impossible. A central focus on retrieval cannot exclude some consideration of input and storage variables.

Recognition and Recall

The hypothesis of an age-associated difficulty in retrieving memories from storage was originally proposed (Schonfield, 1965; Schonfield & Robertson, 1966) as an interpretation of previous evidence that older adults were especially prone to errors of omission and demonstrated disproportionate loss in performing externally paced tasks, as well as tasks requiring shifts of attention. A common component implicated in each of the three kinds of relevant tests was the reclamation of stored memories. The postulated retrieval problem led to the prediction that the difference between recall and recognition scores would be greater in older than younger groups. Recognition, it was argued, does not demand active search or retrieval and should, therefore, show less deterioration with age than recall. That rather simplistic formulation is in accord with what has since become the sophisticated and elaborate generation-discrimination theory (Anderson & Bower, 1972; Brown, 1976b). The hypothesis was tested by presenting two lists of 24 words to subjects aged between 20 and 75—one list requiring recall and the other demanding the choice of target words among four distractors. The results, as seen in Table 4.3, showed no deterioration with age in recognition scores but a consistent drop in recall. Because of the absence of recognition loss, Schonfield and Robertson (1966) commented: "It is worth emphasizing that the original prediction was not that recognition would show no loss; it was that recognition scores would not deteriorate to the same extent as recall scores. A repetition of the present experiment, which showed some drop in older subjects' recognition scores, would not necessarily constitute evidence against the present hypothesis [p. 233]." Notwithstanding this statement, some critics have adopted the position that any lowering of recognition scores among older, compared to younger, groups constitutes a refutation of the retrieval hypothesis. A necessary prerequisite of disproving the recall–recognition discrepancy is the administration of both recall and recognition tests. However, support for the discrepancy is perhaps provided by the absence of age differences

TABLE 4.3
Mean Recognition, Recall, and Recognition Minus
Recall Scores by Age [a]

Age Range	Recognition	Recall	Recognition Minus Recall
20 – 29	20.01	13.78	6.42
30 – 39	19.48	12.30	7.17
40 – 49	19.53	10.01	9.47
50 – 59	19.90	9.57	10.24
60 +	20.09	7.50	12.59

[a]Adapted from Schonfield & Robertson (1966).

in recognition scores (Craik, 1971), since age-associated recall loss is so well established that it can be assumed without testing.

The clear-cut outcome of the Schonfield and Robertson study made it highly improbable that the results were a chance finding. In fact, almost all succeeding investigations have confirmed that the difference between old and young and recognition scores is less than on recall scores (e.g., Botwinick & Storandt, 1974; Harwood & Naylor, 1969; Johnson, 1972; Kausler, Kleim, & Overcast, 1975; Smith, 1975). That statement should be restricted to recognition tests where the subject is required to identify targets among distractors, following presentation of the list of targets. Often the recognition scores of older groups are slightly lower than those of the young—sometimes the difference being statistically insignificant, sometimes significant. The degree of recognition loss among older groups in the various experiments provides some pointers to deficits that occur even when item retrieval is not required. Most important of all is the suggestion that recognition scores tend to drop more frequently after the age of 65 (for example, Erber, 1974; Harwood & Naylor, 1969). A similar dividing line at the age of 65 has already been mentioned in connection with recognition of remote memories. The Schonfield and Robertson results provided a picture of retrieval by decades from the twenties onward but placed all people over 60—most of whom were in their sixties—in one group. However, changes that they documented there do not necessarily portray whatever further changes may occur in the aged (i.e., those over 65) or the senior aged (i.e., those over 75).

Some distinctive memory traces of targets are clearly necessary for identifying those items among distractors. When recognition fails, it can be assumed that the attribute permitting such discrimination is lacking. Therefore, losses with age in recognition scores direct attention to the possible age-associated variables causing difficulty in making the needed discriminations, or causing de-differentiation of the distinctive traces. Increasing the number of targets in a list, which also necessitates a proportional increase of distractors during testing, is one such variable. Although Kapnick (1971) did not find statistically significant age differences among adults between the ages of 20 and 62 in recognition scores even with a 40-word list, Erber (1974) reported poor performance by subjects over 65 on both a 24-word and a 60-word list. The major age loss occurred when the 60-word list was presented second. This difficulty in establishing or maintaining distinctive memory traces "second-time round" was also shown by Gordon and Clark (1974), who gave two acquisition trials and two recognition tests on the same list. Age differences (mean ages 25 and 72) on a d' measure were found on the second test but not on the first test. It seems likely that the distractors of the first recognition test reduce the distinctiveness of succeeding items. Older people are perhaps more prone to confuse targets with similar items presented in the experimental situation.

The only study that seems to show no increase with age in the difference between recall and recognition scores occurs in a highly complicated experiment performed by Adamowicz (1976). An example of the type of material he used is given in Fig. 4.1 and serves to illustrate the requirement for distinctive memory traces. Brown (1976a) has rightly pointed out that a test of recognition does not necessarily correspond to a process of recognition and that recognition may be mediated by processes of recall. In other words, presenting the target among distractors may be of no help, and a subject still has to rely completely on recall. This is almost certainly the case in the Adamowicz study. If someone cannot recall which of the target small squares were blacked in, it is improbable that he will recognize the correct design. Support for that assumption is provided by the identical scores apparently obtained on the recall and recognition tests by members of the younger group.[1] They were not aided by the presence of the target, and the older group could not be expected to overcome the hypothesized retrieval deficit unless distinctive traces were available.

Most commentators by now accept the generalization that older groups usually show reduced deficits on recognition tests requiring the identification of a previously presented target. Contention, however, has arisen on the interpreta-

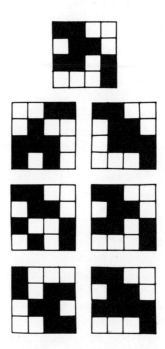

FIG. 4.1.   An example of matrix used in the recognition study of Adamowicz (1976). The pattern at the top is the original target (from Adamowicz, 1976).

---

[1]When no specified age is given for a group labeled as "young," it should be assumed throughout the chapter that the mean age was between 18 and 23.

tion of this finding. The retrieval hypothesis certainly does not receive unanimous support, and alternative explanations have been proposed.

Alternative Explanations

The relatively high performance of older groups on recognition tests has been explained by McNulty and Caird (1966, 1967) as due to the effectiveness of partial input images and by Drachman and Leavitt (1972) in terms of partial learning. Partial input images imply that memory traces established by middle-aged or older persons often represent less than the complete items. Partial learning means that the trace itself may be as complete as among the young but has less signal strength. According to both explanations, the attenuated trace is assumed to suffice for recognition, although not for recall. Increasing difficulty with age in recalling is thus blamed on poor acquisition and resultant poor storage, without recourse to a retrieval deficit.

The partial input hypothesis can be tested by the provision of distractors in a recognition test that share common features with the target item. That, according to McNulty and Caird (1966), should result in a disproportionate lowering of scores in older groups compared to the young. Had the prediction been confirmed, the outcome might still be due to greater susceptibility with age to retroactive interference from the similarity between target and distractors at the time of retrieval (Schonfield, 1967). Be that as it may, investigators have found no decrease in scores among the aged even when the alternative choices provided in a recognition test differed from the target by only one letter (Hartley & Marshall, 1967; Schonfield, Trueman, & Kline, 1972; Smith, 1975). Partial input learning, according to McNulty and Caird (1967), should not be considered as confined to structural letter components but to include what they termed association-type aspects. A study by Smith (1975) provides support for the idea that semantic relations among targets and distractors cause slightly greater problems for older age groups. False recognitions among synonyms of target words increased significantly from 0.92 out of a possible score of 15 at ages 20 to 29, through 1.3 at ages 50 to 69, to 1.7 at ages 70 to 90. Although these differences could only account for a small part of reported age effects on recall or recognition scores, they underlined the importance of separating structural from semantic factors in experiments on age and memory.

Opponents of the retrieval hypothesis have tended to take an either—or viewpoint: If older people "suffer from" partial input images or partial learning, or indeed any acquisition deficit, older people must be considered to have no special retrieval difficulty. That approach follows the classical science method of hypotheses confrontation. Proponents of the retrieval hypothesis, however, have no need to deny age-associated learning deficits, although these too could be partly due to retrieval problems during the acquisition phase (Schonfield & Robertson, 1966).

The loci of loss under dispute can be clarified by using Brown's (1976a) analysis of internal representations contributing to word-list learning, recall, and recognition. Brown separates the unit word code from complex attribute codes of the word and both of these from contextual tagging codes. The unit word code uniquely specifies the target and is accessed in an all-or-none manner. Attribute codes represent various associations of the target word including structural components, imagery, and other mnemonic devices employed during acquisition. Contextual tags refer not only to the list itself; they also encompass other subjective or external features of the environment that occur during the acquisition of a particular list. A possibly important contextual tag, not mentioned by Brown, might result from the very intention to learn. The suggestion that intention to remember enhances the probability of recollection is opposed to the prevalent orthodoxy among psychologists (Craik & Lockhart, 1972; Hyde & Jenkins, 1973), although some reservations about that position are now being voiced (Postman & Kruesi, 1977). In any case, it seems at least feasible that an internal tag could result from an active organism repeating to itself, ''I want to remember this item.'' Whatever the attributes of the contextual codes may be, a conscious attempt to reinstate some of these occurs during recall. If they lead directly to the tagged unit word code or indirectly by way of attribute codes, success is achieved. The retrieval hypothesis states that the routes from tagging codes either to unit target codes or to attribute codes, or from attribute codes to unit target codes, are more liable to obstruction with advancing age. In recognition, the problem of obstructed pathways is obviated. The suggestion of partially learned images implies that an abbreviated unit target code or fewer and less complete attribute codes are established during learning but that there is nothing amiss with the pathways. Success is achieved in recognition, because these attenuated codes with their contextual tags afford adequate discrimination from distractors. Partial learning implies a higher threshold with age in the unit target code and perhaps also in attribute codes but again nothing amiss with the pathways. Both alternative explanations assume the absence of a recognition advantage to older groups in the situations where there is presumptive evidence for equal acquisition among young and old.

The special relevance of the Bahrick et al. (1975) remote-memory study to the issue of equated acquisition is obvious. There is no reason for suggesting that one generation is likely to be better or worse in learning the names of its school fellows. Nevertheless, Table 4.2 demonstrated the maintenance of recognition scores compared to the precipitous drop with age in recalling names. It is difficult to envisage how those results could be interpreted to accord with anything but the retrieval hypothesis. A disparity between the remote generic memories and remembering word lists is worthy of note. The names of classmates are encountered often, so that their internal representations share many groups of overlapping contextual tags. Such contextual tags seem functionally equivalent to attribute codes. Therefore, the difference between attribute and context codes perhaps only occurs in episodic memory but disappears in semantic and generic memories.

An experiment that attempted to exclude a storage deficiency while demonstrating age-associated retrieval difficulty was performed by teLinde, Schonfield, and Adam (1976). They capitalized on the well-established finding that vocabulary test scores increase in middle age and decrease minimally in old age. This of itself has been interpreted as showing the absence of semantic memory loss (Eysenck, 1975). However, success in a vocabulary test does not depend on retrieving a uniquely specified response for each item, and that may be the reason why an age decline is absent. An obstruction in the pathway to a unit word code in a vocabulary test may be compensated by one of many synonymous attribute codes, all eventuating in the award of identical scores. By reversing the usual procedure, so that the definition was provided and the requirement was to produce a specific word, teLinde et al. (1976) anticipated that evidence for the retrieval deficit in semantic memory would be manifested. Alternate items of the Wechsler Adult Intelligence Scale Vocabulary subtest were used for word production and the remaining items for a traditional definition test. Definitional phrases by themselves were found to constitute too difficult a task, and the first letter of the target word was given as an additional cue or clue for word production. The cues for Items 1 and 30, for example, were: an article of furniture to sleep or rest in, B__; a building or architectural structure, especially one of imposing size, E__. Results confirmed the prediction of a greater difference between definition and word-production scores in an older group (mean age 62.3) than in a younger group. Age disparities were in fact rather small, although significant statistically. The older group was superior in its knowledge of words as demonstrated by higher definition scores but not in the word production that required retrieving specific target items from semantic memory.

Brief mention should be made of Botwinick's (1973) suggestion that age differences in recall and recognition can be explained in terms of overall difficulty. He seems to claim that older age groups show disproportionate loss when tasks become more difficult for the young. Recognition is easy for the young and therefore should show little loss with age, whereas the opposite is true of recall. In fact, there are numerous studies where performance of the young deteriorates without a disproportionate deficit in the old. Botwinick himself, in a discussion of his own experiment on card sorting (Botwinick, Robbin, & Brinley, 1960), distinguished between difficulty that caused no special problem with age and complexity that did. And sometimes the aged demonstrate a deficit, whereas the young do not (Schonfield & Wenger, 1975). Increased difficulty is not an adequate summary of studies that have shown age deterioration and therefore cannot be used as an explanation of a specific finding.

Different Meanings of Recognition

Identification of a target is the common theme underlying the usage of the word *recognition*. However, the degree or amount of identification varies greatly among different so-called recognition tests, thereby necessitating diverse underlying mental processes. The kind of identification required in the various situations determines whether age-associated difficulties increase or decrease. Borrowing once again Brown's (1976a) terminology, the performance of older adults is determined by the amount and type of contextual tags that a situation demands. If only one relatively short list of items has been encountered, the contextual tags corresponding to "that is an old item" seem to be readily accessed on the presentation of target items in the recognition test. But if the requirement is for more specific information, which necessitates discriminations among overlapping contextual codes, age deficits are likely to be manifested. The answers to questions such as: "Was the item in list 3 or list 10?" "Was the item associated with stimulus X or some other stimulus?" "Who is this person?" demand access to more stored information than is required for recognizing an item as having recently been encountered in a clearly differentiated and unusual experimental situation. The presence of the target item in such a test bypasses the hypothesized difficulty in reaching or retrieving the unit word code, but the context tag *old* does not suffice for success.

An experiment by Kausler, Kleim, and Overcast (1975) illustrates two different identification requirements, both of which are sometimes labeled as recognition tasks. Young and middle-aged (median age 47) subjects were given verbal discrimination instructions and one study trial of 25 word pairs, one member of each pair being denoted as right. Without warning, a recognition test for both right and wrong old words among new distractors was administered, and afterwards subjects were asked to identify the right words. Significant age differences were not found for recognizing old items, but the middle-aged group was significantly worse at identifying the right items. Target words in the recognition test afforded access to unit word codes and their accompanying context tag *old*, but the middle aged were less efficient in reaching the contextual tag corresponding to *right*. The difference between the two tasks parallels the classical distinction between response learning and associative learning.

It is worth noting that in everyday speech, the claim of recognition does not seem justified by merely identifying a person as previously encountered. It would be odd for someone to say, "I recognize you, but I don't know who you are." Recognition requires more than the knowledge of having seen a person before; recollection of some attributes as well as specific context is needed before one can say, "Now I recognize you; you are Miss Smith who. . . ." On the other hand, the classical psychology recognition test often merely demands identification as "old."

Identifying a word as a member of a category, which is also labeled as recognition, demands yet a different kind of knowledge. Success on this semantic task requires access to attribute codes, rather than to context tags. Time or latency is the usual measure employed, and Eysenck (1975) reported that a group of middle-aged London teachers (age range 55−65) were slower than young adults on this type of recognition task. Latencies for the young and middle aged were between 0.5 second and 0.75 second, and resemble the well-established age differences in complex reaction time. Eysenck (1975) contrasts the middle-aged deficit in recognition with the superiority of the same group in producing an exemplar from a designated category starting with a specified letter. Mean latencies were 2.29 seconds for the middle aged and 2.86 seconds for the young when a suitable exemplar of the category−letter combination was low in dominance, i.e., retrieved infrequently according to established norms. Eysenck interprets his results as suggesting that older people retrieve information from semantic memory faster than the young but are slower in making decisions. It must be admitted that the good showing of the middle aged on the retrieval task is somewhat surprising, but an adequate analysis of internal processes occurring during such a long silent interval between stimulus and response is well-nigh impossible. The advantage of the middle aged in this particular experiment is perhaps best explained as due to their professional experience as teachers. Retrieval from semantic memory may well improve with practice during the middle adult years. Indeed, there would be little hazard in betting that a person of 60, who had been completing crossword puzzles each day for 20 years would be faster at accomplishing that task than a novice of 25.

Category Instance Fluency

A fluency test in the sense of category instance generation (CIG) requires the production of as many exemplars as possible from a given category, usually defined by a common concept or an initial consonant. Scores are based either on the number of category instances generated in a fixed time or on the time taken to generate a specified number of instances. This task and the one used by Eysenck (1975) have similar components. Fluency obviously requires repeated retrievals from semantic memory, and therefore age differences in scores could serve as a useful corroboration or refutation of the retrieval hypothesis.

Category retrieval has been described as "almost a pure test of retrieval from old store" (Drachman & Leavitt, 1972, p. 308), but of course other aspects of stored information and speed of performance are also involved. Correlations of above .40 have been reported between CIG and Wechsler Memory Scale scores (Strother, Schaie, & Horst, 1957), which suggest quite close links between the ability to recall from episodic and semantic memory systems. Similar correlations have been found between CIG and vocabulary (Isaacs & Akhtar, 1972). Clearly, knowledge of word meaning is likely to be associated with ability to retrieve appropriate words. Correlations between CIG and IQ, covering the age range from the twenties to the seventies, were found by Schaie (1958) to exceed .60, but since this was based on group and timed intelligence subtests, the speed factor may have been particularly important.

The results of all relevant experiments show poorer performance on CIG tasks by elderly groups of over 60, compared to the young (Schaie, 1958; Schaie & Strother, 1968; Strother et al., 1957; Stones, 1976a, 1976b, 1977), although the age difference was not significant in an experiment reported by Drachman and Leavitt (1972). Whether responses had to be written or spoken, whether the categories were determined by initial consonants or common concepts, the findings seem quite consistent. Beyond the age of 60, Strother et al. (1957) found no additional decrements for groups of superior elderly. On the other hand, Isaacs and Akhtar (1972) show a distinct loss by the senior aged (over 75) compared to those between 65 and 74. Those authors go so far as to propose that their Set Test, made up of four CIG scores, should be used as a general measure of mental functioning in the elderly. The evidence on age of loss onset in CIG is conflicting, with Schaie and Strother (1968) reporting a decline as early as the twenties in the only longitudinal study, Stones (1976a, 1976b, 1977) finding a difference between initial letter CIG and common concept CIG, and Eysenck (1975) reporting an improvement in middle age. The vocabulary levels of the various middle-aged groups might have been influential in causing the discrepancies, since vocabulary is correlated with CIG performance and increases on the average, but not universally, during middle age.

Stones (1976a, 1976b, 1977) devised a test of category recall that was shown in pilot work to be independent of vocabulary level. Phase I of the task follows the CIG paradigm with instances being generated from five or six categories. Phase II (CIGR) involved re-presentation of the category titles in the same order as previously presented, with unlimited time allowed for regeneration of the Phase I instances. The index of retrieval was the proportion of initial instances regenerated during Phase II.

Some representative results of studies using CIGR are contained in Table 4.4. In Experiment 1, categories were defined by initial consonant, and generation of 10 instances per category was required during Phase I. The old group displayed much longer initial generation times, and all age groups differed significantly from each other in the proportion of instances subsequently regenerated, i.e., CIGR performance. This result was replicated by further experiments in the series but only where categories were defined by initial consonants. When category cuing was by common concept, as in Experiment 2, levels of recall were much higher, and no age effect was obtained in CIGR performance.

There are, of course, problems in comparing proportions of a fixed number of category instances in Experiment 1 with proportions of varying and age-related numbers of instances in Experiment 2, but other studies show that this is not a

TABLE 4.4
Age, CIG, and CIGR Performance in Two Experiments[a]

Groups	Experiment 1			Experiment 2		
	Mean Age	CIG[b]	CIGR	Mean Age	CIG[c]	CIGR
Young	18	50 sec.	.51	18	13.12	.79
Middle aged	44	63 sec.	.42	50	9.34	.78
Old	71	109 sec.	.34	77	8.52	.79

[a]Adapted from Stones (1976a, 1977).

[b]Mean time to generate 10 instances per category.

[c]Mean number of instances generated with a 45 second time limit imposed per category.

fundamental variable. The difference between age effects on CIGR with initial consonants versus common concepts parallels findings on distractors in recognition tests discussed earlier and the findings on cuing mentioned in later sections of this chapter. These results suggest that storage of attribute codes according to meaning becomes comparatively more important with age, whereas storage of structural attribute codes is less prevalent. At what age the changes begin to affect retrieval and to what extent the size of category population is a relevant influence await future experimentation.

Cuing at Recall

Supplying a cue during recall can be considered as serving a function similar to recognition in overcoming retrieval deficits. Insofar as the association between cue and target item is strong and overlearned, the cue should bypass any obstruction in the mental pathways leading to the unit target code. For example, if the target word is *apple*, there may well be little difference between providing the word *apple* itself in a recognition test or supplying the cue "fruit." However, obstructions might still occur between a cue such as "fruit" and a target such as "lichee," the block perhaps being partly caused by some form of perseveration of words more highly associated with fruit. The thoughts of oranges and lemons may prevent the retrieval of "lichee." It would also not be surprising if a retrieval deficit prevented successful recall when numerous target items are served by one cue.

Experiments have invariably shown the expected special advantage given older groups when conceptual category cues are provided in comparison to cueless recall. Lawrence (1967) gave one learning trial to young and old (mean age 75) groups of an unblocked 36-word list consisting of six examples of each of six categories, without advance knowledge of the list's makeup. Higher scores were obtained by the young group in free recall, but age differences were not statistically significant when a cue card with the six category names on it was available during recall. Similar advantages for a middle-aged group (mean age 58) were reported by Johnson (1972). Hultsch (1975) informed his young, middle-aged, and old subjects (age ranges: 18–34; 50–64; 65–83) before presenting a list in blocked order that the 40 words consisted of members of 10 familiar noun categories. The count of number of categories recalled, based on at least one exemplar per category, showed age differences in uncued recall but not in cued recall. However, even in cued recall, total scores as well as number of words per category were highest for the youngest group, with a nonsignificant difference between the two older groups. Hultsch interpreted his findings as demonstrating that trace-dependent and cue-dependent forgetting increased with age. In other words, there were both retrieval and storage problems.

The sole result that purported to contradict the retrieval hypothesis comes from Drachman and Leavitt (1972), where the cues provided at recall for a 35-word list were initial letters of the words. The older group (mean age 68) derived no special benefit from this type of cuing. In fact, the cues were of no functional value to either young or old on the first of three learning trials—cued and uncued groups earned equal scores. Sharing the 26 letters of the alphabet among 35 initial letters seems in any case a questionable procedure. Smith's (1977) findings suggest that the presence of initial letters at the recall stage may lower scores, as can be seen by comparing the performance of the structural groups in the top graphs of Fig. 4.2. As opposed to the inadequacy of structural cues, semantic cues at output benefited the older groups more than the young (age ranges: 20–39; 40–59; 60–80), although total recall scores remained much lower with increasing age. In Smith's study, each of the 20 words in the list represented a different taxonomic category and had a different initial letter. Thus, for the target words *Astronomy, Mumps,* and *Wagon,* one group in each age range had no cues at recall; another group was shown A___, M___, W___; and another group, A Science___, A Disease___, A Toy___. The reason why letter or structural cues are disadvantageous is probably that these interfere with more efficient spontaneous strategies for reaching the unit target code. The special advantage of semantic cues demonstrates the increased age-associated importance of semantic attribute codes. Spontaneously used strategies for recall seem less successful in utilizing these and thereby overcoming retrieval deficits.

The studies discussed in this section have been confined to situations where cues are provided at the time of recall but where no special instructions are given, nor mnemonic aids suggested, during the acquisition phase. It can be assumed that cues that lead to successful retrieval mirror existing systems of storage. Whether the storage systems wholly depend on strategies adopted during acquisition, as is stated by the encoding specificity principle (Tulving & Thomson, 1973), or are only partly so determined, the division between input cues, treated in the next section, and output cues is somewhat arbitrary.

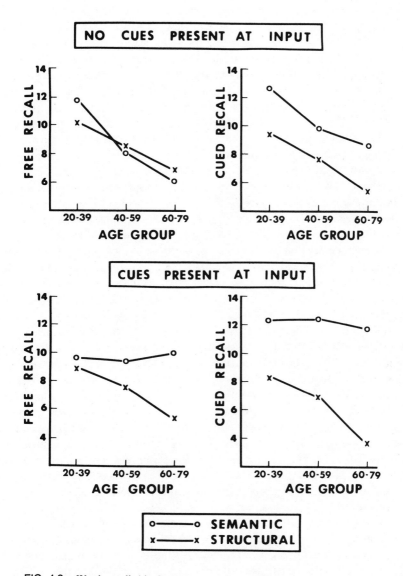

FIG. 4.2. Words recalled in Cued and Uncued conditions in the experiment by Smith (1977).

ORGANIZATION AND MEDIATORS DURING ACQUISITION

The classical separation of acquisition, retention, and the remembering or retrieval stages of learning has almost disappeared in the era of cognitive psychology. Adequate understanding of retrieval processes requires consideration of coding operations and vice versa—the nature of coding operations is illuminated by comparing successful and unsuccessful retrieval. The discussion in this section, therefore, overlaps with the earlier treatment of the retrieval hypothesis. There are, however, some heuristic advantages in a provisional separation of input and output variables. At the very least, it avoids a premature conclusion that all age deficits should be classified as retrieval deficiencies. Inferior strategies during acquisition can cause incomplete storage or inadequate learning as well as retrieval difficulty, but the retrieval difficulty in older groups might also occur even with the most efficient strategy. Tulving's (Tulving & Pearlstone, 1966) distinctions between trace-dependent and cue-dependent forgetting or between availability and accessibility are obviously pertinent but seem to ignore the fact that forgetting implies that there was something in storage to be forgotten. Extra confusion is caused, because the term *storage deficiency* can mean either that the item was not placed in storage or that once in storage, it became unavailable and lost. In any case, there probably are special difficulties for older people at the acquisition stage, which result in poor performance on a remembering test and which should not be labeled as a retention or storage or retrieval deficit.

The studies of Lawrence (1967) and Smith (1977), described earlier, provide useful bridges between the issues of input and output. In one of Lawrence's experiments, the cue card with names of the relevant six categories was shown before list presentation, and subjects were told that all test words belonged to those categories. The number of words recalled was not significantly higher than in the no-list condition, and there was certainly no special advantage to the older group (mean age 75). On the other hand, Smith's results, as can be seen in the bottom panels of Fig. 4.2, showed rather surprisingly that age differences disappear when semantic cues are provided during input. When the cues were presented again during recall, still more improvement was found, but that was equal for the three age groups. The contradiction between the Lawrence and Smith results is more apparent than real. Whereas each item in Smith's 20-word list belonged to a different taxonomic category, and these categories were associated with their respective targets at the time of acquisition, Lawrence had 36 items with 6 members per category, and the category names were proffered before the list was presented. Smith's procedure represents the epitome of depth-of-processing procedures (Craik & Lockhart, 1972), which should result in durable and distinctive traces—the cuest targets imaginable. The real surprise, therefore, is that only an average of 12 words out of 20 were recalled by even the young group. Smith's results on structural cues at input parallel those for output;

their effect is to reduce scores in all age groups, as can be seen from comparing the two graphs on the left of Fig. 4.2. The very worst performance is shown in each age group when structural cues are provided both at input and output (right bottom panel of Fig. 4.2). It can be concluded that unsuitable "cues" given either during acquisition or during recall prevent optimal functioning of spontaneously produced strategies in all age groups.

Experimental manipulations in the Smith and Lawrence experiments can be classified under the general heading of *mediation*. Any coding operation occurring during acquisition that aims to enhance remembering through inserting additional links leading to a target word is termed *mediational*. In paired-associate learning, the additional link attempts to strengthen bonds between cue and response, whereas in free and serial recall, the links may be between different items in a list. A metamorphosis from free recall to a paired-associate paradigm occurs when the same cue is provided for each item at acquisition and recall stages, as in Smith's study. Following Paivio (1971), it is useful to distinguish between imagery mediation and verbal mediation. The concern of aging studies is to examine the influence of mediation on age-associated differences in recall.

Age differences in the incidence of spontaneous mediator utilization have been investigated through careful coding of introspective data. Hulicka and Grossman (1967) and Rowe and Schnore (1971) asked their subjects for reports on methods used to learn individual paired associates after they had recalled lists and without prior hints about the value of mediational devices. Young samples in both studies (mean ages 16.1 and 18.4) used mediators much more frequently than the elderly (mean ages 74.1 and 72.8). However, the middle-aged group (mean age 50.4), included in the Rowe and Schnore investigation, reported slightly more verbal and imagery mediators than the teenagers.

In addition to the subjects in Hulicka and Grossman's experiment, who had no special instructions, one group was told to form an image that included both items of each paired associate, another group was provided with a linking phrase, and another group was instructed to form an image suggested by the phrase. All of these manipulations resulted in higher recall scores and greater frequency of mediator utilization among the elderly, but the effects were not quite so consistent in the young. Self-image instructions produced the greatest improvement in recall in both age groups. Nevertheless, the elderly group that profited most from the mediational instruction still had poorer recall scores than the young group that received no mediational suggestions. In a further study, Hulicka, Sterns, and Grossman (1967) examined the effect of providing unlimited time to create mediators and to produce responses compared to that of paced schedules when all participants were advised to form their own images or phrases linking each paired associate. The results showed no diminution of age differences in the unpaced condition, both young and old groups benefiting equally.

The reports of subjects in the two Hulicka studies about the techniques employed in learning showed that the elderly were particularly deficient in their use of visual mediators. They also complained much more frequently than the young that associated pairs were too odd to make connections. Later research has therefore examined variables such as concrete versus abstract words and providing subjects with pictures representing the words, which might facilitate establishment of images. Such variables complicate the assessment of age differences, since the young also benefit when appropriate mediators are readily aroused, and recall may then become almost perfect. Older groups may seem to benefit disproportionately from the manipulations, since they have room for improvement, whereas the young nudge, but cannot raise, the ceiling. Hulicka overcame this problem by having twice as many paired associates in the lists for young groups as in those for the old, and then analyzed her results in percentages.

The ceiling difficulty occurs in the Rowe and Schnore (1971) study mentioned earlier, where half the word pairs in the list represented concrete objects and half were abstract. Age differences in learning were much smaller on the concrete items, which are known to facilitate recall, but both young and middle-aged groups had almost perfect scores on the very first trial. The same problem arises in Canestrari's (1968) experiment, where one group each of young and older (mean age 62.4) subjects was presented with a sketch illustrating both words of a pair. Thus, the paired associate "red-heart" was depicted as a red heart. Other groups were either encouraged to form an image for each pair or provided with verbal mediators. A differentially greater improvement in learning scores occurred among the older groups where the experimenter provided either of the mediators, with the pictures having the greatest benefit. Again, the young had "nowhere to go," since they made hardly any errors even without the mediators.

Ceiling limitations for a young group constitute no objection to findings when both a middle-aged and elderly group are included in an experiment and the manipulated variable affects the former but not the latter. This occurs in two experiments reported by Mason and Smith (1977). In the first experiment, subjects learned peg word mnemonic devices as aids in the recall of lists made up of 10 concrete or 10 abstract words. A significant interaction between age and list type demonstrated that the middle aged (age range 40–59) had disproportionate benefits on the concrete list compared to both the old (age range 60–80) and the young (age range 20–40). In the second experiment, with different subjects belonging to the same age ranges, one-half of the members in each group were instructed to use visual imagery in learning abstract and concrete lists. The results showed that the middle aged improved greatly with the imagery instructions and that all age groups improved equally on the concrete word list compared to the abstract words. The likelihood of ceiling effects in the young group in both experiments does not invalidate the conclusions that the middle aged benefit more than the elderly from concrete words when all age groups use the peg word device, and that similar middle-aged benefits accrue from imagery instructions whether the words are concrete or abstract.

Different problems arise in attempting to interpret the results of a paired-associate learning experiment by Treat and Reese (1976), with two age groups (mean ages 29.7 and 69.5), different imagery instructions, and varied anticipation times, inspection times, and interval times (2:2:6; 6:2:2; and 2:6:2 seconds). The authors summarize their results for the first test trial as showing: "With self-generated imagery and the longer anticipation time, the old performed as well as the young [p. 119]." This conclusion, however, is based on analysis of co-variance "corrected" for education, occupation, and vocabulary. That procedure makes the whole exercise rather suspect, especially as scores of the young on vocabulary were very high compared to the elderly, possibly because a timed test was used. It is also not clear how the manipulated time variable operated during the first and only presentation of paired associates read aloud by the experimenter. When the experimenter provided the suggested images, presentation must have taken longer than in the conditions without instructions and self-generated image instructions. Further, a repeated utterance of test items must have occurred when the experimenter suggested the images. It would seem wise to suspend judgment about the conclusions claimed by Treat and Reese until the balancing between groups is clarified or until the experiment is repeated with perhaps a less sophisticated methodology.

The major conclusion suggested from the various mediation studies is that the elderly are deficient in spontaneous utilization of such aids to memory, especially in the case of imagery mediators. Recall is greatly improved when elderly subjects are instructed to create their own mediators and allowed adequate time to do so, as well as when lists are made up of concrete items. Nevertheless, the recall of the elderly remains depressed compared to the young, and the benefits derived from interventions are probably no greater than among the young. The middle aged are likely to reap the greatest advantage through help in using memory aids. The drawback of the ceiling confound to the theoretical interpretation of the results does not detract from the important practical value of applying the derived principles in an effort to reduce memory problems that often plague older people.

FORGETTING STORED INFORMATION

The belief that passage of time alone could cause forgetting has been considered as anathema by psychologists of almost every persuasion since the heyday of Gestalt theory. Some heterodoxy was allowed for decay of short-term or primary memories, but once stored in secondary memory, causes of forgetting more specific than trace fading have been demanded. Interference has been, of course, the popular explanation of reduced recall, and it is sometimes argued that if forgetting increases with age, interference susceptibilities must also have increased. The concept of interference, as employed in that covert syllogism, is extremely fuzzy compared to the operational definitions elaborated by inter-ference theory. Certainly, the consecutive learning of AB, AC lists—different responses to the same cue—is the sine qua non, as Kausler (1970) puts it, for retroactive and proactive interference according to the theory. But before inserting the extra list and seeking a theoretical explanation for increased forgetting with age, it might be helpful to establish first that increased forgetting is a justifiable generalization.

Are there age differences in recall following the learning of one list? In order to answer the question fairly, it is necessary to cover the objection to the layman's notion that memory deteriorates with age and to ensure that original learning has been equated among age groups. Hulicka and Weiss (1965) tackled the problem by giving groups of younger (mean age 38) and older (mean age 68) subjects a fixed number of trials on a paired-associate task, whereas other groups of the same age learned to a criterion of one errorless trial. There was one further group of elderly subjects in an overlearning condition, where additional trials amounting to 40% of those needed to reach criterion were administered. As ex-pected, the "fixed trials" younger group showed far superior recall than the old group after 5 minutes and 20 minutes. Based on the number of trials required to reach criterion by the other groups, the old group had not "learned" the list, but the young had. Surprisingly, recall scores of the old group allowed to reach criterion were slightly higher than the parallel younger group when tested 20 minutes and 1 week after learning. This study deserves careful analysis, because it is frequently quoted as demonstrating the absence of age-associated memory deficits and retrieval problems. The group labeled here as "younger," and called "young" by Hulicka and Weiss, had a mean age of 38 years; better recall might well have been expected in a really young group. All subjects were male, hospitalized veterans, and refusals to participate were much more frequent among older patients. The question of uncontrolled reviews between acquisition and delayed-recall testing is always a problem but is likely to be accentuated among a group of male veterans living together in a ward. Finally, among the old subjects, the over-learning group had much lower scores after 1 week's retention than the criterion group, which suggests that one or both old groups behaved anomalously. Whether or not lower recall would be expected for the elderly 15 minutes after criterion learning is a moot point, but after a day or week, most studies show that the young remember more than the old. Hulicka and Weiss' results demonstrate that not all members of middle-aged groups have better recall than all the elderly, but confirmation of the findings from other studies is necessary before a generalization can be made.

Significantly lower scores for delayed recall by the elderly (mean ages 62 to 72) compared to young groups, following learning to a criterion of one error-less trial have been reported by: Wimer (1960), after 24 hours; Hulicka and Rust

(1964), after 24 hours and 1 week, but not after 15 minutes; Davis and Obrist (1966), after 48 hours. On the other hand, the superiority of the middle aged over the elderly (mean ages 45.1 and 68.8) did not reach significance in a study by Desroches, Kaiman, and Ballard (1966) at 1 hour and 1 day, and the groups obtained equal scores 1 week after learning. Smith (1974) compared the middle aged to a young group (age ranges 20−30 and 45−55) after 24 hours, and few errors were made by either group. A trend was found for better retention by the young following part learning and better retention by the old following whole learning. All in all, the evidence strongly suggests that people of 70 show more forgetting within 24 hours than young adults, even without experimentally controlled intervening learning. Some middle-aged groups resemble the young, whereas others resemble the elderly in their achievement on memory tasks.

Retroactive Interference

Only a handful of investigators have been prepared to face the pitfalls, logistics, and statistics involved in comparing different age groups on first-list recall following the learning of AB, AC lists, together with the appropriate controls. (Someone, some time, should study how time limits for doctoral dissertations influence the development of psychological theories.) There is the problem of persuading elderly folk to come to the laboratory, sustaining their motivation, and avoiding their frustrations as they attempt to master paired associates in one list after another, often having to relearn the first list once again. Because the learning of any list may take more than 20 trials, dropout rates are understandably high, especially when the material consists of nonsense syllables. In any case, it is difficult to assess the effect of retroactive interference when an older group takes twice as long as the young to learn an intervening list. To make matters worse, spread of scores increases with age, and groups that are initially equated, or at least not significantly different on something like vocabulary, behave dissimilarly on the learning tasks. Some learn to learn quickly, some slowly. And when the old groups are not causing methodological problems, the young ones are.

An additional complication arises because of the predilection of psychologists to attribute age differences to learning rather than to memory deficits. When an elderly group demonstrates a recall loss in the retroactive interference paradigm, the disappearance of age differences may be helped through analysis of covariance, "correcting" for differences in original and intervening learning scores. There may be some logical justification for such procedures in dealing with relearning scores—although even then there are statistical objections—but if remembering following criterion learning is under investigation, the method is difficult to defend or even to comprehend. The present summary of findings is confined to remembering and excludes relearning measures.

Two studies report no age differences following interpolated learning. In an experiment conducted by Wimer and Wigdor (1958), both young and elderly (mean age 72.6) groups who had learned AB and AC lists to a criterion of two consecutive errorless trials responded correctly to less than one out of the four originally paired associates. The low score must have been due to the very short anticipation interval of 1 second allowed for responding. Given this floor, the absence of age differences can probably be discounted. In Hulicka's (1967) study, two young and two old experimental groups (mean ages 15.5 and 70) learned AB, AC with additional appropriate control groups who learned AB. Half the subjects learned AB to a criterion of an errorless trial, and the remainder were given a prescribed six trials on AB. The results, according to Hulicka, showed that interpolated learning had equivalent effects on the two age groups when original learning was taken to criterion. Interference was said to be greater for the elderly in the "six trials" situation. The analyses certainly demonstrated just that, although the raw scores of the various experimental groups shown in Table 4.5 throw doubt on the interpretation. Exactly the same recall scores were obtained by both the elderly experimental groups, and therefore the manipulation did not affect them. The difference between learning to criterion and the "six trial" group is confined to the young. The reason why recall is better following six trials of first-list learning is presumably due to an over-learning effect. As can be seen in Table 4.5, only 3.1 trials were required to reach criterion by the young, so that the young "six trials" group overlearned the first list, which therefore became less susceptible to the AC interference. Nevertheless, correct recalls were considerably higher in the young than in the old criterion group. These detailed comments are not intended as criticisms of the experimenters—anyone who has performed gerontological experiments will have faced similar issues and published similar results—but those who have not yet undertaken aging research need to be alerted about the pitfalls.

The remaining studies all demonstrate some age losses in remembering after intervening learning. In each of the experiments, a variable other than age and straightforward retroactive interference was manipulated. Gladis and Braun (1958) compared young, middle-aged, and old groups (age ranges 20−29,

TABLE 4.5
Trials to Criterion and Retention of List 1
(Following List 2 Learning)[a]

| | Number of Trials on List 1 | | Correct Recalls (Maximum 7) | |
	Criterion	"6 trials"	Criterion	"6 trials"
Young	3.1	6	4.5	5.9
Old	6.4	6	3.4	3.4

[a]Adapted from Hulicka (1967).

40−49, 60−72) in an AB, AC' design, with four degrees of similarity between responses in the first and second lists. The number of items recalled and correctly associated decreased with increasing age, but the authors discounted the age effect because it evaporated on analysis of covariance. There was no age by degree of similarity interaction, all groups showing greater interference as similarity of responses decreased. Schonfield and Trueman (1970) also found age effects but no interaction with an AB, AC; AB, DC; AB, EF design, using subjects between 20 and 80. Decade differences were usually very slight, and sometimes the mean score for a younger decade was exceeded by that of an older decade. The extra variables in this study involved consecutive recall and multiple-choice testing during acquisition and for assessment of interference. Paradigms and testing methods were both significant statistically, but the absence of interactions with age suggested that weakening of associations as well as unavailable responses were both implicated in age-associated forgetting. Traxler (1973) as well as Dale (1975) combined an investigation into both retroactive and proactive interference in their studies, testing recall by the modified-modified-free-recall (MMFR) method, i.e., all stimuli presented on one sheet and responses from both tests required. Traxler had three paradigms and also examined short and long anticipation intervals. Dale had two paradigms and examined losses after 15 minutes and 24 hours. The story remains the same— age differences in favor of the young are almost invariably significant, but interactions are not.

The general conclusion must be that retroactive interference, as defined by interference theory, does not increase disproportionately with age. The learning of an extra list before a recall test merely allows the age differences to appear more quickly.

Proactive Interference and Negative Transfer

The only studies using AB, AC and AB, DE paradigms for assessing proactive interference seem to be those of Traxler (1973) and Dale (1975), mentioned earlier. Traxler included an additional AB, DB paradigm and also manipulated the time allowed for responding. Recall of the second list 2 minutes after learning to criterion was very high, but even so, the young group (mean age 27.4) performed better than the old (mean age 68.8). Neither the factors of paradigm nor anticipation time was significant statistically. Dale gave the modified-modified-free-recall test to half the members of each group after 15 minutes and to the remainder after 24 hours. The results are presented in Table 4.6. The young groups obtained significantly better scores than the old (mean age 71) at both intervals. The interval itself was also found to be significant, but once again not the paradigm employed nor any interactions. There is a trend in Dale's results that hints that the difference in scores between experimental and control groups decreases over time for the aged and increases for the young. Other analyses

TABLE 4.6
Proactive Inhibition: MMFR Scores on List 2
(Maximum 8)[a]

	AB, AC		AB, DE	
	After 15 minutes	After 24 hours	After 15 minutes	After 24 hours
Young	7.63	6.0	7.75	6.88
Elderly	5.88	5.75	6.63	5.88

[a]Adapted from Dale (1975).

performed by Dale suggested that the age difference was primarily due to a weakening of associations rather than to difficulty in retrieving responses. These suggestions may constitute important signposts for better understanding of the processes of forgetting with age, but they await future confirmation.

The indication from the proactive and retroactive experiments is that the internal representations of newly learned bonds in aging individuals weaken in strength at a decelerating rate for about 24 hours and perhaps eventually reach a plateau. This occurs without any specific response competition at the time of recall and does not seem easily explicable in terms of concepts newly introduced to interference theory (e.g., response-set interference). Learning a prior or succeeding list of paired associates seems to accelerate, but not to increase, age-associated memory losses.

The lack of help from interference theory in explaining memory loss with age should not be confused with the notion that proactive interference in its more nebulous sense increases with age. Although information newly acquired by older people may not cause additional memory loss of subsequently learned material, nevertheless, the mass of stored knowledge, which presumably increases day by day, may still be the nub of the forgetting problem. Compared to new knowledge, much of existing knowledge is likely to be overlearned, consisting in large part of generic memories, and therefore should fare better in any remembering sweepstakes. It is intuitively appealing to suggest that forgetting increases because there is more to forget. Unfortunately, it would be difficult either to test this proposition or to separate it operationally from a fading hypothesis. Is there any difference between saying that general proactive inhibition increases with age and suggesting that newly stored associations and memories are more prone to fade in elderly organisms?

The evidence for increased interference with age in learning, as opposed to remembering, seems reasonably conclusive. Stored memories of strong relationships cause special problems in learning relevant new relationships. This is probably best described as an increase in negative transfer and stems originally from Thorndike (1928). However, it could also be argued that problems for the aged occur when positive transfer from stored memories is of no avail. A number of studies have shown that: Age differences in learning measures are minimal when paired words have high associative strength according to established norms; age differences increase as the associative strength decreases or when pairings are strange and meaningless; age differences are large when established associations have to be divorced and partners swapped (see, for example, Boyarsky & Eisdorfer, 1972; Gladis & Braun, 1958; Korchin & Basowitz, 1957; Lair, Moon, & Kausler, 1969; Zaretsky & Halberstam, 1968). It is important to emphasize that the increase of negative transfer seems to occur throughout the adult years and is not confined to differences between the young and elderly. Similar increases in negative transfer with age occur in motor learning of incompatible responses (Ruch, 1934; Simon, 1967). Insofar as learning, by definition, involves the acquisition of new information and new associations, a case could be made for subsuming all age-associated learning deficits under the general heading of negative transfer.

PRIMARY MEMORY AND SPANNING THE SPAN

An extensive review of the literature relevant to primary memory has recently been provided by Craik (1976), and it is unnecessary to dwell on the points that he covered so cogently. Briefly, numerous experiments demonstrate that there is no age loss or, at the most, minimal loss in digit/word spans and primary memory. Age decrements appear if some reorganization of a span is demanded, such as output in reversed order from that of input. Older groups also have lower performance when a task demands divided attention or parallel processing. This occurs when there are two input sources and when simultaneous perception and review or simultaneous review and performance are required. Dichotic listening, for example, shows a loss with age, even though merely one digit has to be recalled from each ear. Speed of memory search when using Sternberg techniques slows to some extent by middle age and even more among the elderly. The intercept of the latency function in such tasks, representing the time required for decision and response, also increases with age.

Substantive theoretical and practical issues are raised as to what happens when the material to be remembered exceeds the capacity of primary memory. Clearly, the contents of primary memory are subject to sequential turnover—first in, first out; last in, last out. Primacy effects are demonstrated by older groups, although some data suggest that it is not as clearly demarcated as among the young. The transfer from primary to secondary memory seems to pinpoint an important locus of aging loss. Some authorities explain this as due to fading in short-term memory. Others claim that this specific problem is another example of negative transfer and/or interference. Craik (1976) prefers an explanation in accordance with his depth-of-processing principle; because of shallow processing retrieval cues become less well established than among the young. The various interpretations all lead to the next question: Why more fading? Why more negative transfer? Why shallower processing? Whatever the eventual answers may be, at present one can merely reiterate the principle that functioning requires increased attention with age (Schonfield, 1974).

INTELLIGENCE AND COMPETENCE

Reliable age trends in adult intelligence with important implications for memory have been obtained from standardized tests, although these tests were not originally designed with memory in mind. Typically, results conform to a classical aging pattern that has been replicated both with cross-sectional and longitudinal designs (Botwinick, 1976). This pattern involves a general maintenance of abilities until advanced age on tasks that are predominantly verbal but show an age decline of earlier onset on tasks that involve spatial components, often called performance tests. Although the performance tests tend to be timed and verbal tests untimed, the decline does not appear fully attributable to speed reduction (Doppelt & Wallace, 1955; Storandt, 1977).

Age trends in the organization of intellectual abilities yield a less consistent picture than raw scores. Factor analyses of intelligence test results usually reveal factors of general intelligence and memory. Authors disagree as to whether the memory factor becomes more (Cohen, 1956) or less (Berger, Bernstein, Klein, Cohen, & Lucas, 1964; Radcliffe, 1966) prominent with advancing age. Wechsler (1958), relying on the findings of Cohen (1956), suggests that compared to the young, older persons depend more on the retrieval of stored information as a problem-solving strategy and less on the general intelligence factor.

The distinction between utilization of previously acquired information (memory) and coping with novel information (general intelligence) was placed on firmer theoretical and empirical footings by Horn and Cattell (1966, 1967). They proposed that intellectual abilities are broadly organized around two main dimensions of fluid and crystallized intelligence. Fluid intelligence resembles Spearman's (1927) general factor, as well as Hebb's (1949) ability A, and is thought to depend on the integrity of the central nervous system. Attainment levels are influenced positively by neural maturation and negatively by the cumulative effects of insults to the central nervous system. Measures of crystallized intelligence reflect culturally directed learning. An important component comprises generalized solution instruments (Horn, 1970), or learning sets (Harlow, 1949), that permit the solution of novel problems by the transfer of skills acquired through solving earlier problems. The empirical validity of the fluid versus crystallized distinction was supported by factor analysis on a wide range of tasks. The crystallized factor showed greater saturation than the fluid factor on tests requiring retrieval of stored information. Horn and Cattell (1966, 1967) report a much steeper age decline for fluid than for crystallized abilities, which in a way supports Wechsler's (1958) assertion that memory assumes increased importance with age for the maintenance of intellectual capabilities. The assumption that the elderly come to rely more on memory than on general intelligence has to be reconciled with the evidence for age impairment in memory retrieval: Retrieval loss might lead to the expectation of a marked decline in crystallized intelligence. However, tests saturated with that factor usually involve the kinds of generic memories and overlearned skills that are least affected by a retrieval deficit.

Horn and Cattell (1966, 1967) explain the decline of fluid intelligence in terms of diminished competence. That hypothesis of reduced capacity due to neural decrement is opposed to the notion espoused by Denny (1974) and Hornblum and Overton (1976) of a performance deficiency. The performance deficiency is supported by evidence of improvement following brief intervention. The elderly tend to resemble children in the styles used for object sorting, but Denny found that 83% of his elderly group readily adopted a strategy more sophisticated than that to which they had previously been exposed. Denny concluded that higher-level sorting skills were so easily established that an interpretation of diminished functions was untenable. Similarly, Hornblum and Overton (1976) demonstrated the beneficial effects of feedback training with elderly subjects deficient in area- and volume-conservation skills. The improvements generalized to tasks both similar and dissimilar to that utilized for training and appeared to persist for at least 6 weeks. These studies demonstrate that the elderly may fail to use stored skills that could benefit task performance. Although the possibility of diminished competence cannot be discounted, the relevant information must have been retained to an appreciable extent for brief training to have been so effective. It appears probable that stylistic or situational factors, perhaps interacting with impaired retrieval, are responsible for the failure of elderly people to capitalize fully on old storage.

Retrieval impairment may contribute directly to the age decline apparent in other tasks included in intelligence scales, especially those that involve retention of unfamiliar material. An example is provided by the Digit Symbol subtest of the WAIS, which requires the substitution of symbols for digits on the basis of a code. Several studies show that the steep age decline on this task is not fully explicable in terms of response speed or spatial factors (Botwinick & Storandt, 1973; Kaufmann, 1968; Storandt, 1976). Schonfield and Robertson (1968) endeavored to demonstrate that retrieval of unfamiliar material from short-term memory was a possible reason for the age decline. In their experiment, elderly subjects performed a sorting task and coding task, each involving digits and unfamiliar symbols. Performance was deficient where the response items were symbols, but unfamiliarity of stimulus items had little influence. The results seem to show that the need to retrieve unfamiliar material in order to make a response, be it in sorting or in coding, causes special difficulties to the aged.

The involvement of memory in intellectual functioning is somewhat paradoxical. The elderly come to rely increasingly on retrieval from storage for tasks of a highly practiced nature. With unfamiliar tasks, retrieval impairment may contribute directly to age decline. Between these two extremes are tasks where stored material might contribute, perhaps indirectly, to task performance but fails to be utilized by the elderly.

THE PAST AS MORE THAN PROLOGUE

A search for loci of age-associated memory losses would be doomed to failure if all types of remembering deteriorated in parallel and at uniform rates. The aim of research has been to delineate processes that show age deterioration from those that do not. Data rarely reveal the decade in life when deficiencies become pronounced, since experiments are usually confined to one older and one younger group of subjects. Such analyses are in any case complicated by the ability of the human organism to compensate for a loss in one function through greater reliance on intact capacities. The salient area for maintained competence is that of primary memory. Providing that sensory losses can be bypassed, older people seem as effective as the young in immediate recall of registered information. The biological utility of this capacity is inestimable, since it permits the aging organism to remain alerted to change in its immediate surroundings and also provides the basic building block for fresh learning. If the new information is encountered sufficiently often, the elderly will be capable of long-term retention of the additional knowledge. However, engrams of temporary oddities become more liable to disintegration with age. It is in the secondary memory store where search for changes has to be concentrated.

It can be taken as axiomatic that an individual's existing mental structures, the product or memory of the past, provide the backdrop for dealing with and inducing fresh experiences. These interrelated structures consist of schematized recollections of unique incidents and what we earlier called generic memories, including Tulving's semantic thesaurus. Capacity of the repository for storing new information may in a sense remain unlimited as the aging adult moves forward in time. Nevertheless, many potential cues that could aid reclamation of new specific memories have already been earmarked, and frequently used, for earlier memories. Overloading of cues can perhaps be considered as a cause of the age-associated retrieval problem and of the obstructions in the pathways to the unit target code. Very specific items—a number, a name—experienced in new situations have already had so many attached consorts that they may not create distinctive traces in secondary memory, even among young adults, unless given extra attention. Shapiro (1951) reports that graduate students obtained lower scores than children on a reading comprehension test that required answers to very specific questions. Another piece of the jigsaw puzzle may fall into place from the evidence of a greater tendency among the aged for oscillation (Hull, 1943) of successful retrieval over time. Robertson (1972) and Robinson (1975) both provide data suggesting reduced consistency over trials in recall from secondary memory. Retrieving of specific items or reaching unit target codes, however, is certainly not the only memory problem of the aged. The evidence is strong that newly stored associations are more liable to weaken or to become de-differentiated with increasing age. Whether the disintegration should be considered as due to the influence of a general form of proactive inhibition or just fading is a matter of taste.

Of the many topics not covered in this chapter, "remembering to remember" is likely to develop into a research area and therefore deserves a brief mention. In everyday life, a person often says to himself, "I must remember to do X," and often does remember in accordance with the delayed command. The notion of dynamic memories is a major facet of Freud's theory but has not been investigated by experimental psychologists. Reports by older adults and an observation by Schonfield (quoted in Welford, 1958, p. 211) suggest that fulfillment of delayed command becomes less efficient with age. When told to press a button on completion of a task, elderly subjects constantly forget to do so, notwithstanding reminders; as people grow older, the required memory does not so readily "pop up" into consciousness. This type of intentional recall is very different from, but possibly as important as, memorizing word lists in a laboratory.

The psychological literature is unanimous on one generalization to reduce memory problems: Better learning produces better recall and recognition. The improved acquisition can come from a variety of techniques—overlearning, imagery, deeper processing, progressive part-learning, discovery method (Belbin, 1969), or slower pacing (Arenberg, 1967). Borrowing Masters' (1975) beautiful phrase, we conclude that "the cogs of memory lose a few teeth" in old age, but extra learning can compensate for the loss.

ACKNOWLEDGMENTS

The work of the authors has been supported by National Research Council Grants APA-89 and A-9945. The first author is indebted to his university for the award of a Killam Resident Fellowship while writing this chapter.

REFERENCES

Adamowicz, J. K. Visual short-term memory and aging. *Journal of Gerontology*, 1976, *31*, 39–46.

Anderson, J. R., & Bower, G. H. Recognition and retrieval processes in free recall. *Psychological Review*, 1972, *79*, 97–123.

Arenberg, D. Age differences in retroaction. *Journal of Gerontology, 1967, 22,* 88−91.

Bahrick, H. P., Bahrick, P. O., & Wittlinger, R. P. Fifty years of memory for names and faces: A cross-sectional approach. *Journal of Experimental Psychology: General, 1975, 104,* 54−75.

Bartlett, F. C. *Remembering.* Cambridge: Cambridge University Press, 1932.

Belbin, R. M. *The discovery method: An international experiment in retraining.* Paris: Organisation for Economic Co-operation and Development, 1969.

Berger, L., Bernstein, A., Klein, E., Cohen, J., & Lucas, A. Effects of aging and pathology on the functional structure of intelligence. *Journal of Consulting Psychology, 1964, 28,* 199−207.

Botwinick, J. *Cognitive processes in maturity and old age.* New York: Springer Publishing, 1967.

Botwinick, J. *Aging and behavior.* New York: Springer Publishing, 1973.

Botwinick, J. Intellectual abilities. In J. E. Birren & K. W. Schaie (Eds.), *Handbook of the psychology of aging.* New York: Van Nostrand Reinhold, 1976.

Botwinick, J., Robbin, J. S., & Brinley, J. F. Age differences in card sorting performance in relation to task difficulty, task set and practice. *Journal of Experimental Psychology, 1960, 59,* 10−18.

Botwinick, J., & Storandt, M. Speed functions, vocabulary ability and age. *Perceptual and Motor Skills, 1973, 36,* 1123−1128.

Botwinick, J., & Storandt, M. *Memory related functions and age.* Springfield Ill.: Charles C. Thomas, 1974.

Boyarsky, R. E., & Eisdorfer, C. Forgetting in older persons. *Journal of Gerontology, 1972, 27,* 254−258.

Bromley, D. B. *The psychology of human ageing* (2nd ed.) Harmondsworth, Middlesex, England: Penguin Books, 1974.

Brown, J. An analysis of recognition and recall and of problems in their comparison. In J. Brown (Ed.), *Recall and recognition.* London: Wiley, 1976(a).

Brown, J. (Ed.). *Recall and recognition.* London: Wiley, 1976(b).

Canestrari, R. E. Age changes in acquisition. In G. A. Talland (Ed.), *Human aging and behavior.* New York: Academic Press, 1968.

Cohen, J. A comparative factor analysis of WAIS performance for four age groups between 18 and 80. *American Psychologist, 1956, 11,* 449.

Craik, F. I. M. Age differences in recognition memory. *Quarterly Journal of Experimental Psychology, 1971, 23,* 316−323.

Craik, F. I. M. Age differences in human memory. In J. E. Birren & K. W. Schaie (Eds.), *Handbook of the Psychology of Aging.* New York: Van Nostrand Reinhold, 1976.

Craik, F. I. M., & Lockhart, R. S. Levels of processing: A framework for memory research. *Journal of Verbal Learning and Verbal Behavior, 1972, 11,* 671−684.

Dale, P. *Differences between young and elderly adults in proactive and retroactive interference.* Unpublished thesis, University of Calgary, 1975.

Davis, S. H., & Obrist, W. D. Age differences in learning and retention of verbal material. *Cornell Journal of Social Relations, 1966, 1,* 95−103.

Denny, N. W. Classification abilities in the elderly. *Journal of Gerontology, 1974, 29,* 309−314.

Desroches, H. F., Kaiman, B. D., & Ballard, H. T. Relationships between age and recall of meaningful material. *Psychological Reports, 1966, 18,* 920−922.

Doppelt, J., & Wallace, W. Standardization of the WAIS for older persons. *Journal of Abnormal and Social Psychology, 1955, 51,* 312—330.

Drachman, D. A., & Leavitt, J. Memory impairment in the aged: Storage versus retrieval deficit. *Journal of Experimental Psychology, 1972, 93,* 302—308.

Erber, J. T. Age differences in recognition memory. *Journal of Gerontology, 1974, 29,* 177—181.

Eysenck, M. W. Retrieval from semantic memory as a function of age. *Journal of Gerontology, 1975, 30,* 174−180.

Gladis, M., & Braun, H. W. Age differences in transfer and retroaction as the function of inter-task response similarity. *Journal of Experimental Psychology, 1958, 55,* 25−30.

Gordon, S. K., & Clark, W. C. Adult age differences in word and nonsense syllable recognition memory and response criterion. *Journal of Gerontology*, 1974, *29*, 659—665.

Harlow, H. F. The formation of learning sets. *Psychological Review*, 1949, *56*, 51−65.

Hartley, J., & Marshall, I. S. Ageing, recognition and partial learning. *Psychonomic Science*, 1967, *9*, 215−216.

Harwood, E. & Naylor, G. F. K. Recall and recognition in elderly and young subjects. *Australian Journal of Psychology*, 1969, *21*, 251−257.

Hebb, D. O. *Organization of behavior*. New York: Wiley, 1949.

Horn, J. L. Organization of data on lifespan development of human abilities. In L. R. Goulet & P. B. Baltes (Eds.), *Lifespan developmental psychology*. New York: Academic Press, 1970.

Horn, J. L., & Cattell, R. B. Age differences in primary mental ability factors. *Journal of Gerontology*, 1966, *21*, 210−220.

Horn, J. L., & Cattell, R. B. Age differences in fluid and crystallized intelligence, *Acta Psychologica*, 1967, *26*, 107−129.

Hornblum, J. N., & Overton, W. F. Area and volume conservation among the elderly: Assessment and training. *Developmental Psychology*, 1976, *12*, 68−74.

Hulicka, I. M. Age differences in retention as a function of interference. *Journal of Gerontology*, 1967, 22, 180−184.

Hulicka, I. M., & Grossman, J. L. Age-group comparisons for the use of mediators in paired-associate learning. *Journal of Gerontology*, 1967, *22*, 46−51.

Hulicka, I. M., & Rust, L. D. Age-related retention deficit as a function of learning. *Journal of the American Geriatric Society*, 1964, *12*, 1061−1065.

Hulicka, I. M., Sterns, H., & Grossman, J. Age-group comparisons of paired-associate learning as a function of paced and self paced association and response times. *Journal of Gerontology*, 1967, *22*, 274−280.

Hulicka, I. M., & Weiss, R. L. Age differences in retention as a function of learning. *Journal of Consulting Psychology*, 1965, *29*, 125−129.

Hull, C. L. *Principles of behavior*. New York: Appleton-Century-Crofts, 1943.

Hultsch, D. F. Adult age differences in retrieval: Trace-dependent and cue-dependent forgetting. *Developmental Psychology*, 1975, *11*, 197−201.

Hyde, T. S., & Jenkins, J. J. Recall for words as a function of semantic, graphic and syntactic orienting tasks. *Journal of Verbal Learning and Verbal Behavior*, 1973, *12*, 471−480.

Isaacs, B., & Akhtar, A. J. The Set Test: A rapid test of mental function in old people, *Age and Ageing*, 1972, *1*, 222−226.

Johnson, L. K. Memory loss with age: A storage or retrieval problem. *The Gerontologist*, 1972, *12* (3,4), 53.

Kapnick, P. L. *Age and recognition memory*. Unpublished Ph.D. dissertation, Washington University, St. Louis, Missouri, 1971.

Kaufmann, A. Age and performance in oral and written versions of the substitution test. In S. S. Chown & K. F. Riegel (Eds.), *Psychological Functioning in normal aging and senile aged*. Basel, Switzerland: S. Karger, 1968.

Kausler, D. H. Retention—forgetting as a nomological network for developmental research. In L. R. Goulet & P. B. Baltes (Eds.), *Lifespan developmental psychology: Research and theory*. New York: Academic Press, 1970.

Kausler, D. H., Kleim, D. M., & Overcast, T. D. Item recognition following a multiple item study trial for young and middle-aged adults. *Experimental Aging Research*, 1975, *1*, 243−250

Korchin, S. J., & Basowitz, H. Age differences in verbal learning. *Journal of Abnormal and Social Psychology*, 1957, *54*, 64−69.

Lair, C. V., Moon, W. H., & Kausler, D. H. Associative interference in the paired-associate learning of middle aged and old subjects. *Developmental Psychology*, 1969, *1*, 548−552.

Lawrence, M. W. Memory loss with age: A test of two strategies for its retardation. *Psychonomic Science*, 1967, *9*, 209−210.

Lockhart, R. S., Craik, F. I. M., & Jacoby, L. Depth of processing, recognition and recall. In J. Brown (Ed.), *Recall and recognition*. London: Wiley, 1976.

Mason, S. E., & Smith, A. D. Imagery in the aged. *Experimental Aging Research*, 1977, *3*, 17−32.

Masters, J. *The field marshal's memoirs*. New York: Doubleday, 1975.

McNulty, J. A., & Caird, W. K. Memory loss with age: Retrieval or storage: *Psychological Reports*, 1966, *19*, 229−230.

McNulty, J. A., & Caird, W. K. Memory loss with age: An unsolved problem. *Psychological Reports*, 1967, *20*, 283−288.

Paivio, A. *Imagery and verbal processes*. New York: Holt, Rinehart & Winston, 1971.

Postman, L., & Kruesi, E. The influence of orienting tasks on the encoding and recall of words. *Journal of Verbal Learning and Verbal Behavior*, 1977, *16*, 353−369.

Radcliffe, J. A. WAIS factorial structure and factor sources for ages 18−54. *Australian Journal of Psychology*, 1966, *18*, 228−238.

Robertson, E. A. *Age differences in primary and secondary memory processes*. Unpublished thesis, University of Southern California, Los Angeles, 1972.

Robinson, J. K. *Changes with age in structuring of information for utilization in memory*. Paper delivered at Tenth International Congress of Gerontology, Jerusalem, 1975.

Rowe, E. J., & Schnore, M. M. Item concreteness and reported strategies in paired associate learning as a function of age. *Journal of Gerontology*, 1971, *24*, 470−475.

Ruch, F. L. The differentiative effects of age upon human learning. *Journal of General Psychology*, 1934, *11*, 261−268.

Schaie, K. W. Rigidity—flexibility and intelligence: A cross-sectional study of the adult. *Psychological Monographs*, 1958, *72*, (462, Whole No. 9).

Schaie, K. W., & Strother, C. R. A cross-sequential study of age changes in cognitive behaviour. *Psychological Bulletin*, 1968, *70*, 671−680.

Schonfield, D. Memory changes with age. *Nature*, 1965, *208*, 918.

Schonfield, D. Memory loss with age: Acquisition and retrieval. *Psychological Reports*, 1967, *20*, 223−226.

Schonfield, D. *In search of old memories*. Paper delivered at Eighth International Congress of Gerontology, Washington, D.C., 1969.

Schonfield, D. Translations in gerontology: From lab to life. *American Psychologist*, 1974, *29*, 796−800.

Schonfield, D., & Robertson, B. Memory storage and aging. *Canadian Journal of Psychology*, 1966, *20*, 2, 228−236.

Schonfield, D., & Robertson, E. A. The coding and sorting of digits and symbols by an elderly sample. *Journal of Gerontology*, 1968, *23*, 318−323.

Schonfield, D., & Trueman, V. Recall and recognition tests of paired associate learning. *The Gerontologist*, 1970, *10*, 3(2), 36.

Schonfield, D., Trueman, V., & Kline, D. Recognition tests of dichotic listening and the age variable. *Journal of Gerontology*, 1972, *27*, 487−493.

Schonfield, D., & Wenger, L. Age limitation of perceptual span. *Nature*, 1975, *253*, 377−378.

Shapiro, M. B. An experimental approach to diagnostic psychological testing. *Journal of Mental Science*, 1951, *97*, 748−764.

Simon, J. R. Reaction time as a function of SR correspondence, age and sex. *Ergonomics*, 1967, *10*, 659−664.

Smith, A. D. Partial learning and recognition memory in the aged. *International Journal of Aging and Human Development*, 1975, *6*, 359−365.

Smith, A. D. Adult age differences in cued recall. *Developmental Psychology*, 1977, *13*, 326−331.

Smith, S. L. *Age differences in part and whole learning*. Unpublished thesis, University of Calgary, 1974.

Spearman, C. *The abilities of man*. New York: Macmillan, 1927.

Squire, L. R. Remote memory as affected by aging. *Neuropsychologia*, 1974, *12*, 429−435.

Stones, M. J. *Aging and memory for a self-generated episode*. Paper delivered at Canadian Association on Gerontology, Vancouver, 1976(a).

Stones, M. J. *An intra-familial study of aging and memory*. Paper delivered at Canadian Psychological Association annual conference, Toronto, 1976(b).

Stones, M. J. *Memory for self-generated verbal material*. Unpublished manuscript, 1977.

Storandt, M. Speed and coding effects in relation to age and ability level. *Developmental Psychology*, 1976, *12*, 177−178.

Storandt, M. Age, ability level, and method of administering and scoring the WAIS. *Journal of Gerontology*, 1977, *32*, 175−178.

Strother, C. R., Schaie, K. W., & Horst, P. The relationship between advanced age and mental abilities. *Journal of Abnormal and Social Psychology*, 1957, *55*, 166−170.

teLinde, J., Schonfield, D., & Adam, J. *Retrieval, age and semantic memory*. Paper delivered at Canadian Association on Gerontology, Vancouver, 1976.

Thorndike, E. L., Bregman, E. O., Tilton, J. W., & Woodyard, E. *Adult learning*. New York: Macmillan, 1928.

Traxler, A. J. Retroactive and proactive inhibition in young and elderly adults using an unpaced modified free-recall test. *Psychological Reports*, 1973, *32*, 215−222.

Treat, N., & Reese, H. W. Age, pacing and imagery in paired-associate learning. *Developmental Psychology*, 1976, *12*, 119−124.

Tulving, E. Episodic and semantic memory. In E. Tulving & W. Donaldson (Eds.), *Organization of memory*. New York: Academic Press, 1972.

Tulving, E., & Pearlstone, A. Availability versus accessibility of information in memory for words. *Journal of Verbal Learning and Verbal Behavior*, 1966, *5*, 381−391.

Tulving, E., & Thomson, D. M. Encoding specificity and retrieval processes in episodic memory. *Psychological Review*, 1973, *80*, 352−373.

Warrington, E. K., & Sanders, H. I. The fate of old memories. *Quarterly Journal of Experimental Psychology*, 1971, *23*, 432−442.

Wechsler, D. *The measurement and appraisal of adult intelligence*. Baltimore, Md.: Williams & Wilkins, 1958.

Welford, A. T. Age and skill. *The Nineteenth Century and After*, 1950, *148*, 98−105.

Welford, A. T. *Ageing and human skill*. Oxford: Oxford University Press, 1958.

Wimer, R. E. A supplementary report on age differences in retention over a 24-hour period. *Journal of Gerontology*, 1960, *15*, 417−418.

Wimer, R. E., & Wigdor, B. T. Age differences in retention of learning. *Journal of Gerontology*, 1958, *13*, 291−295.

Zaretsky, H. H., & Halberstam, J. L. Age differences in paired-associate learning. *Journal of Gerontology*, 1968, *23*, 165−168.

DISRUPTED MEMORY IN SPECIAL STATES OF CONSCIOUSNESS

5 Amnesia Following Electroconvulsive Shock

Ralph R. Miller
Nancy A. Marlin
Brooklyn College of the City University of New York

This chapter focuses upon what has been learned about memorial processes through the use of electroconvulsive shock. Observations of memory impairments from the clinical literature are briefly reviewed, followed by an examination of the more extensive and well-controlled research of the animal laboratory. It is not our intent to comprehensively review the vast literature concerning electrically induced amnesia, but rather to discuss phenomena and studies that have important theoretical implications.

The area has been encumbered by controversy, and almost every report of new phenomena has been followed by one or more failures to "replicate." Sometimes these failures have proven to be the more reliable finding; the reader will be so informed in those instances that we see fit to cite such effects. When a phenomenon has been reliably observed in a large majority of the independent laboratories examining the effect, we have usually omitted reference to the noncorroborative studies as well as the oft-appearing subsequent papers illuminating the sources of discrepancy. For purposes of convenience, most of the figures depict data from our own laboratory, but for each effect discussed, the original report is cited along with select follow-up studies that have been of special theoretical value or have introduced critical control groups.

MEMORY DISTURBANCES FOLLOWING ECT

Electroconvulsive therapy (ECT) for select behavioral disorders was first introduced in 1938 as a substitute for the chemically induced shock therapy that was prevalent at the time. ECT was soon heralded as an effective treatment for many classes of mental illness and, relative to therapies such as insulin or metrazol shock, had the advantage of a brief and readily controllable period of primary action. However, it was soon discovered that the therapeutic benefits of ECT were limited to patients with affective disorders and acute psychoses, and even in those cases ECT was frequently accompanied by adverse effects such as memory impairment (Zubin & Barrera, 1941). Much of this memorial deficit receded with the passage of time after treatment, but some fraction of the malfunction lasted long enough to be objectionable.

An extensive series of studies initiated by Cronholm and his associates (e.g., Cronholm & Molander, 1957, 1961, 1964) and continued by Ottosson (e.g., 1960, 1966) and other researchers have probed the memorial consequences of ECT and their interaction with the therapeutic effects of ECT. Cronholm's studies were among the first to differentiate between ECT-induced alterations of learning and alterations of retention—a distinction that is still overlooked by some researchers today. Even among those attuned to the distinction, there is no universally accepted procedure for unambiguously identifying ECT-induced memory deficits because of the acquisition differences observed in ECT patients before and after treatment (Harper & Wiens, 1975). This problem is further aggravated by the ethical restraints on using appropriate control groups. With the foregoing qualification in mind, it appears that except for a brief period of post-treatment confusion, ECT improves learning performance in patients with affective disorders. Prior to treatment, these patients generally suffer from impaired learning, the impairment probably stemming from poor attentional processes. The long-term improvement in acquisition capabilities following ECT is generally regarded as a consequence of the improved mental health of the patient (e.g., better motivation and concentration) rather than the result of ECT action upon specific learning mechanisms (Cronholm & Ottosson, 1961).

Anterograde amnesia, decreasing in severity as the temporal interval between treatment and subsequent learning increases, is a common memorial consequence of ECT. To be properly evaluated, it must be differentiated from the learning deficit ordinarily caused by confusion in the first few hours after ECT (Ottosson, 1968). Furthermore, the extent of anterograde amnesia has been found to depend on such variables as ECT current intensity and electrode placement. Under ordinary therapeutic conditions, anterograde amnesia is appreciable for the first 24 hours after treatment and is still detectable a week later, but appears not to extend as long as a month (Cronholm & Molander, 1957, 1961, 1964). Ordinarily, no spontaneous recovery of material lost to anterograde amnesia is observed. Although anterograde amnesia is of considerable interest, retrograde amnesia has been regarded to be of greater theoretical consequence; hence this review primarily focuses on the latter.

When ECT is interpolated between acquisition and testing, retrograde amnesia for the newly acquired information is commonly observed (e.g., Cronholm & Lagergren, 1959). Testing within a couple of hours following ECT reveals pronounced amnesia reaching back at least several hours prior to treatment. However, when the test is delayed much longer after treatment, spontaneous recovery of almost all information acquired more than an hour prior to treatment is seen. Pronounced retrograde amnesia appears to remain only for events immediately preceding treatment, and even here amnesia is far from complete. For instance, Cronholm and Lagergren (1959) report that more than 50% of the information acquired 5 seconds prior to ECT onset could be recalled 2 hours after treatment. The high percentage of information that spontaneously returns following retrograde amnesia indicates that much if not all such amnesia is caused by a retrieval failure. Surprisingly, even though this fact was well known for many years, the storage-failure explanation of retrograde amnesia dominated the 1960s. This bias apparently stemmed from the models of memory that were fashionable at the time, emphasizing the small residue of amnesia for events immediately prior to ECT for which spontaneous recovery was not usually observed.

Testing at some uniform time after ECT—such as 2 hours, so as to minimize posttreatment confusion and the effects of muscle relaxants administered prior to ECT—the retrograde gradient for ECT-induced amnesia is typically seen to be steepest over the 10 to 30 seconds immediately prior to ECT administration and levels off to a virtual absence of amnesia for events occurring more than an hour prior to treatment (e.g., Cronholm & Lagergren, 1959). In contrast to this widely held view, Squire (1975) found evidence of amnesia for events that occurred more than 30 years before treatment. As such old memories are apt to be stored as stably as any information will ever be, Squire's data further support a retrieval-failure explanation of most ECT-induced retrograde amnesia. Consistent with this view, spontaneous recovery of these ancient memories was clearly evident on a test 2 weeks after treatment and appeared to be complete 9 months later (Squire & Chace, 1975).

The early attempts to explain ECT-induced amnesia were generally founded upon the consolidation-interference theory of Müller and Pilzecker (1900). These researchers postulated that retroactive interference could be produced by a later arriving stimulus disrupting the memory trace of the target information prior to the stabilization of the trace. For instance, Duncan (1949), building upon the then prevailing two-stage model of memory (e.g., Hebb, 1949), proposed that ECT obliterated all information in short-term storage so that any information not already encoded in long-term storage was permanently lost.

Therapists using ECT to treat behavioral disorders were relatively unconcerned with the understanding of memory processes per se. The divergence of interest between clinicians and students of memory was augmented by the observation that ECT-induced amnesia was not correlated with the consequent improvement in mental health, commonly measured as recovery from endogenous depression (Ottosson, 1966). This conclusion is based on data indicating that the therapeutic value of ECT depends largely on the neural convulsion, whereas the memorial deficit depends primarily on applied current intensity (Cronholm & Ottosson, 1960, 1961; Fink, 1974; Ottosson, 1960, 1962). The foregoing observation effectively eliminates the possibility that amnesia is instrumental in producing the desired clinical consequences.

Taking advantage of the apparent independence of mechanisms responsible for amnesia and therapeutic effects, clinicians have adopted a procedure of unilateral administration of ECT to the nondominant hemisphere, thereby minimizing the memorial deficit while still providing therapeutic benefits (d'Elia, 1970; Frost, 1957). However, d'Elia (1976) has recently pointed out that in contrast to treatment of the dominant hemisphere being damaging to verbal memory, treatment of the nondominant hemisphere appears to be selectively detrimental to memory of spatial information.

EARLY EXPERIMENTS RESEARCH: PARAMETERS OF ECS-INDUCED AMNESIA WITHIN THE CONSOLIDATION-FAILURE MODEL

In order to experimentally test the consolidation-failure explanation of retrograde amnesia, Duncan (1949) turned from the administration of ECT in clinical situations to electroconvulsive shock (ECS) in the animal laboratory. In that oft-cited study, rats received one active-avoidance training trial per day for 18 days. Following each daily training trial, subjects were given ECS at a fixed time ranging from 20 seconds to 14 hours later. Retention of the active-avoidance training was inferred from the rats' behavior on the last training trial and their average performance over all trials. Duncan noted that the longer the delay of ECS after each training trial, the better the performance on the last test trial was; a delay of 60 minutes or more between training and ECS appeared equivalent to no ECS (See Fig. 5.1A). He concluded that consolidation began soon after acquisition and took between 15 and 60 minutes to complete. However, careful inspection of his data indicates that with ECS delays as short as 20 to 40 seconds considerable acquisition occurred by Trials 7 to 12, and performance deteriorated after this point (see Fig. 5.1B). This aspect of the data, overlooked by Duncan in his initial analysis, is incompatible with the consolidation-failure position that he believed his results supported. Despite the interpretive error, Duncan's studies with experimental animals marked the starting point of a long series of experiments using ECS and other retention-impairing and facilitating agents to probe the relationship between time and memory formation.

In 1960, Coons and Miller demonstrated that repeated ECS can act as an aversive stimulus. The punishing effect of ECS was apparently why Duncan's (1949) animals that received ECS soon after actively avoiding ceased to do so over repeated trials. To avoid the aversive effects of ECS, subsequent studies used a single ECS, which Coons and Miller showed had little or no aversive

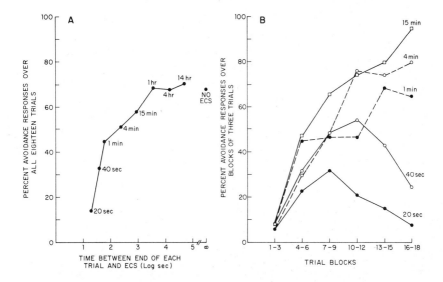

FIG. 5.1.   Redrawn from Duncan (1949). Panel A represents average performance over all 18 trials as a function of the training−ECS interval. The gradient appears to asymptote between 15 and 60 minutes. Panel B illustrates average performance over blocks of three trials of those treatment groups alleged to have had consolidation impaired by ECS. It can be seen that the 20- and 40-second groups, comprising the animals that performed worst over the 18 trials, did display considerable acquisition around Trials 7 to 9 but then deteriorated in performance apparently due to the aversive effects of multiple ECS.

consequences. Moreover, most researchers turned to using passive-avoidance rather than active-avoidance tasks, so that any aversive effects of even a single ECS would not be mistaken for amnesia. Passive avoidance also facilitated one-trial learning. This minimizes the length of the acquisition period, thereby reducing the ambiguity in time between learning and ECS relative to multiple training tasks.

In the decade following the Coons and Miller (1960) report, a number of empirical studies, ordinarily with rodents as subjects, have parametrically examined the relationship of experimental retrograde amnesia to several task, treatment, and subject variables. For example, the retrograde amnesia gradient was found to interact with the degree of learning. Specifically, increased footshock intensity during training was found to reduce the amnesia for given intervals between learning and ECS (Ray & Bivens, 1968). An increase in footshock duration yielded smaller though similar effects (Chorover & Schiller, 1965). Moreover, increased delay of reinforcement increased the resultant amnesia to a proportionately greater degree than it reduced apparent learning (Robustelli, Geller, Aron, & Jarvik, 1969). In respect to ECS treatment parameters, increases in ECS current intensity were found to enhance the resultant amnesia (Dorfman & Jarvik, 1968b; Miller, 1968), and prolonged ECS was observed to have a similar although less potent effect (Alpern & McGaugh, 1968). In keeping with the pharmacological rule of thumb equating dosage to body weight, Miller and Spear (1969) found that the ECS intensity necessary to produce a given degree of amnesia is directly related to the body weight of the animal. Consistently, skull screw electrodes and transcorneal electrodes were found to produce more amnesia than equivalent ECS current delivered through the more commonly used transpinnate electrodes, probably because the former two means of application deliver a larger percentage of the applied current to the brain than does the latter preparation (Dorfman & Jarvik, 1968a). Variations in the internal, neurohumoral states of the animals themselves have been implicated in a study by Stephens and McGaugh (1968), demonstrating that, all other factors being equal, the degree of amnesia is a function of the time of treatment in the subject's diurnal cycle.

Despite the variability introduced by all the foregoing factors, the great majority of the one-trial-ECS studies examining the retrograde gradient for amnesia have found that the gradient approaches an asymptote of essentially no amnesia somewhere between 10 and 30 seconds after learning is terminated (e.g., Chorover & Schiller, 1965, 1966; Quartermain, Paolino, & Miller, 1965), although there are occasional studies reporting gradients that take as much as an hour to reach asymptote (Kopp, Bohdanecky, & Jarvik, 1966).

If the foregoing (and subsequent) remarks were solely limited to passive-avoidance tasks that could be learned in one trial, there would be grounds for questioning the value of research with experimental retrograde amnesia. However, to the extent that the various effects described in this review have been tested, they appear to generalize to other tasks. For example, Lewis, Miller, Misanin, and Richter (1967) demonstrated retrograde amnesia for one-trial active-avoidance training following ECS, suggesting that *memory* rather than propensity for locomotion was being altered. Concordantly, Tenen (1965) showed that a retrograde gradient for an appetitively motivated task could be obtained. And Schiller and Chorover (1967) obtained the basic phenomenon in a simultaneous-choice situation.

The assertion that there are at least two distinct physiological states in which acquired information can be represented receives support from a number of sources other than the ECS literature. Compelling evidence is found in the juxta-position of two facts: that initial representation of acquired information must be in the form of ongoing afferent neural transmission begun immediately after receptor stimulation, and that hibernators (Gerard, 1963) and nonhibernators (Riccio, Hodges, & Randall, 1968) can retain information during periods in which hypothermia has radically attenuated neural activity. We hereafter refer to the former storage mechanism as *active storage* and the latter as *passive storage* to avoid confusion with the seemingly parallel but probably not equivalent cognitive concepts of short-term storage and long-term storage (e.g., Atkinson &

Shiffrin, 1968). The most commonly postulated relationship between active and passive storage, by these or other names, is that growth of trace strength in the latter is directly related to the momentary trace strength in the former until some limiting value of strength in passive storage is approached (see Fig. 5.2). Active storage strength for a particular event appears to be a function of the degree of current acquisition and, more recently, has been recognized to also depend on retrieval from passive storage in the presence of appropriate cues. *Consolidation time* is ordinarily defined as the interval necessary for passive storage to approach its presumed asymptotic limit.

A few qualifications of the foregoing model are in order. First, there is little reason other than parsimony to assume that there are only two storage mechanisms; the arguments supporting this position insist only that there be *at least* two

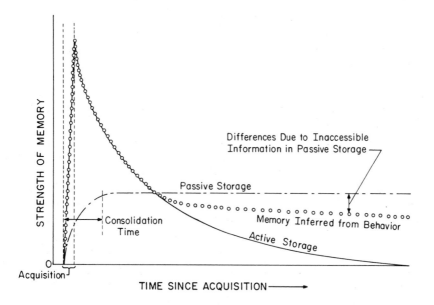

FIG. 5.2. This diagram illustrates a commonly hypothesized relationship between active storage and passive storage. Traditionally, initial encoding in passive storage has been thought to occur in the first 10 to 30 seconds after acquisition, although subsequent processing and further modification of passive storage probably occurs after this time. Recent data described later in the text suggest that input may in fact take as little as 0.5 seconds. "Thinking about the information," called *covert rehearsal* by cognitive psychologists, postpones the decay of active storage and often augments passive storage. If passive storage is subject to spontaneous decay at all, the rate is relatively slow. Rehearsal clearly improves observable retention. This probably results in part from enhanced access to information already in passive storage and in part from additional information, largely redundant, entering passive storage. The observed retention function also depends on the nature of the retention test.

mechanisms. Second, some researchers have objected to the semantics of referring to ongoing neural transmission as storage mechanism; they feel that
"storage" connotes something inactive. However, the present use of "active
storage" is analogous to speaking of information being stored in a temporal
pattern of voltage fluctuations in a telephone line, or energy being stored in a
rotating flywheel. Third, there is no reason to believe that active and passive
storage are mutually exclusive; information is not a conserved quantity. It is
assumed that specific information can be transferred from one storage system to
the other without loss from the first as is the case for the hypothetical memory
system illustrated in Fig. 5.2.

Other than quibbling about the choice of names used for the different stages of
storage, few researchers then or now would dispute the validity of the basic
model represented in Fig. 5.2. The real argument centers on such details as the
magnitude of time required for consolidation and whether or not the experimental
retrograde amnesia paradigm is a valid measure of this interval.

From Duncan's (1949) pioneering studies until the mid-1960s, the large
majority of the experiments published were interpreted as lending support to the
(unmodified) consolidation-failure hypothesis, which is perhaps best summarized
by McGaugh (1966). The only real development of this theory over that period
was the recognition that the alleged consolidation time is to some degree
dependent on the forementioned task, subject, and treatment variables. The
assumptions implicit in the consolidation-failure hypothesis are illustrated in
Fig. 5.3.

As can be seen in Fig. 5.3, when ECS is delayed even momentarily after
information input, an enduring residue of nondisrupted information can be
expected and is in fact seen. If repeated training trials are administered, each
followed by ECS, these residues can be expected to summate. A number of
investigators have reported data consistent with this prediction (e.g., Kesner,
McDonough, & Doty, 1970). However, this observation is also compatible with
several alternate hypotheses concerning ECS-induced amnesia that are described
later. Additionally, Hinderliter, Smith, and Misanin (1973) have reported that
ECS delivered alone 24 hours prior to training followed by another ECS will
reduce the amnesia produced by the second ECS. This latter observation is not
predicted by the traditional consolidation-failure hypothesis nor, for that matter,
by most of the more contemporary explanations of experimental amnesia.

Upon closer inspection, the seemingly straightforward prediction of the consolidation-failure hypothesis concerning memorial residues after ECS that has
been delayed following acquisition depends on assumptions that may be valid but
that probably would have been rejected by most advocates of the consolidation-
failure position. For *any* bit of information to survive ECS, it would have to have
been consolidated prior to ECS, assuming that ECS obliterates all information
encoded in active storage, which appears to be a plausible assumption on electrophysiological grounds. As even a short delay in ECS after learning tends to

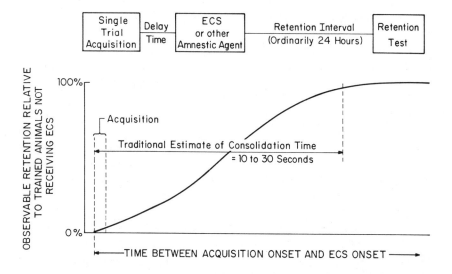

FIG. 5.3.   Retrograde amnesia is maximal in animals receiving ECS immediately following training and is progressively attenuated in animals with an increasing interval between ECS and training as illustrated in this hypothetical experiment. Minimally, ECS obliterates all information in active storage. Traditional theory assumed that information already in passive storage was unaffected and that residual memory evident after delayed ECS was caused by some information having been consolidated sufficiently prior to ECS to render it invulnerable. More likely, in the face of present evidence, is that initial consolidation is so rapid that ECS does not appreciably disrupt it. Instead, ECS is seen to impair access to select information in passive storage.

reduce amnesia, retaining the consolidation-failure view requires the conclusion that consolidation for at least some information must be a very rapid process measured in fractions of a second and is perhaps limited in the amount of information that can be consolidated at one time, suggesting a bit-wise serial mechanism. Alternatively, the process may be limited in the number of redundant traces of the entire learning event that can be consolidated at once, consistent with a chunk-wise serial mechanism. The latter possibility is consistent with the observation that a small percentage of the subjects in most groups of amnesic animals display good retention even with immediate ECS following a very brief learning trial. This empirical point is frequently obscured by statistical presentations that emphasize measures of central tendency. In either case, the improvement in retention with even slight delays of ECS indicates that a more rapid consolidation is possible than was ordinarily acknowledged by the consolidation-failure viewpoint. Further evidence supporting very rapid consolidation is discussed later in this chapter.

The preceding remarks have been concerned with varying the interval between learning and ECS while holding all other parameters constant. When experience during the delay interval is manipulated, the situation becomes more complicated. Davis and Agranoff (1966) found that "detention" in the training apparatus after acquisition could potentiate the amnestic effect of puromycin in goldfish. Robustelli and Jarvik (1968) and Robustelli, Geller, and Jarvik (1968) showed a similar increment in amnesia could be obtained in rodents, using ECS as the amnestic agent. Moreover, they established that the enhancement of amnesia was an interaction rather than merely an additive consequence of ECS-induced amnesia and the attenuation of performance seen to be caused by detention alone. They also determined that a delay between training and the initiation of detention diminishes the effect, and that detention in any novel enclosure could be substituted for detention in the training apparatus with only a partial diminution of the effect.

Paralleling the detention effect, Miller, Misanin, and Lewis (1969) found that a novel stimulus, specifically a flashing light, presented between training and ECS potentiates ECS-induced amnesia. One explanation of both of these effects is that consolidation is delayed until completion of the learning event, which is defined by a break in the impinging novel stimulation. However, other data presented in the next section force us to the conclusion that detention and other forms of stimulation after acquisition are better conceived of as prolonging the postacquisition vulnerability of retrieval processes, a position that we discuss in detail later.

We have recently finished a series of studies that yielded results that superficially contrast with the detention effect. Using one-trial training, the interval between the beginning of the final environmental link in acquisition (reinforcement initiation) and ECS onset was covaried with the interval between the termination of acquisition (reinforcement offset) and ECS onset. With both appetitive or aversive reinforcement, we found that ECS vulnerability begins to decline with the reinforcement offset rather than onset, provided that reinforcement duration is not so prolonged (about 10 seconds) as to "lose its novelty." For example, in the aversive case, 1 second of footshock followed 4 seconds after offset by ECS yielded less amnesia than if footshock was presented during the entire 5-second interval between reinforcement onset and ECS. The greater degree of learning expected from 5 seconds of footshock relative to 1 second creates a bias against the observed effect; hence, we must conclude that the 4 seconds of reinforcement-free processing time was of greater value in protecting the memory than was the mere strengthening of the memory trace by 4 additional seconds of footshock. As the 4 seconds between footshock offset and ECS onset were passed in the training apparatus, we might have expected a small enhancement of amnesia due to detention rather than the appreciable attenuation of amnesia that was actually observed. However, detention effects are ordinarily found when detained animals are compared to animals spending the detention interval in their home cages, whereas the attenuation-of-amnesia effect that we obtained depends on a comparison with animals receiving continuous reinforcement in place of post-reinforcement detention. Moreover, most detention studies have used intervals of 10 to 30 minutes, whereas our recent experiments dealt with intervals two orders of magnitude less. If our studies and the detention effect studies are viewed on a continuum with respect to stimulation during the learning—ECS interval (in order of increasing stimulation: home cage, training apparatus without footshock, apparatus with footshock present), the apparent discrepancy is resolved; information processing that immunizes memories to ECS occurs at a rate inversely related to the rate of novel information impinging upon the organism.

Despite its pervasiveness, the consolidation-failure explanation of ECS-induced amnesia was not without its critics in the early 1960s. The previously mentioned report of Coons and Miller (1960) was only one of a number of papers suggesting that ECS was an aversive reinforcer of instrumental behavior rather than an amnestic agent. Though clearly correct for most multi-ECS paradigms, this explanation was found to be lacking in respect to passive-avoidance tasks and single-ECS studies (Madsen & McGaugh, 1961; McGaugh & Madsen, 1964).

A second early alternative to the consolidation-failure position was the suggestion that ECS acted as a US in a classical conditioning paradigm. In one version of this hypothesis, the CR was hypothesized to be a partial neurological convulsion that interfered with the response indicative of retention of the experimenter-defined learning task (Lewis & Adams, 1963). A second version proposed that the CR was a general inhibitory state reflecting a UR postulated to be the post-ECS comatose state (Lewis & Maher, 1965). Both of these variations suggest interference with test performance rather than memory per se. These hypotheses can handily explain a failure to actively avoid but do not clarify why the suggested competing responses should interfere with, rather than enhance, a passive-avoidance response. Furthermore, a number of studies have reported data directly contradictory to the conditioning hypothesis itself (e.g., King, 1967).

Another explanation of ECS-induced amnesia was offered by Pinel and Cooper (1966a, 1966b). They proposed that the Kamin effect, a temporary deficit in performance sometimes seen 1 to 4 hours after aversive training, reflected a postconsolidation incubation process in passive storage after the information was lost from active storage. ECS, they suggested, truncated this process that was essential for the manifestation of long-term retention. Their hypothesis was given rather short shrift, as it assumed that the retrograde gradient for ECS-induced amnesia requires several hours after acquisition to reach asymptote (comparable to the observed gradient for the Kamin effect), whereas most studies of the retrograde amnesia gradient observed asymptotes that were reached within seconds or minutes.

Given the glaring inadequacies of these early alternatives to the consolidation-failure view, it is not surprising that the consolidation-failure position was almost universally accepted in the late 1960s. However, a series of observations over the following decade have caused researchers to completely reconsider the issue.

CONTEMPORARY RESEARCH: PHENOMENA INCONSISTENT WITH THE CONSOLIDATION-FAILURE MODEL

Several memorial phenomena have been discovered in recent years that are inconsistent with the seemingly tidy explanation of ECS-induced amnesia offered by the consolidation-failure hypothesis. We describe these phenomena in some detail, because they not only refute the "traditional" explanation of experimental amnesia but they also illuminate some important aspects of memory functioning.

Early Testing

In most studies of induced amnesia, animals are tested for retention 24 hours after receiving training and ECS. The reason for this choice is often arbitrary or dictated by convenience for the researcher. In principle, the choice of a training–test interval should make no difference in the amount of amnesia observed; the consolidation-failure hypothesis predicts that failure of information to enter passive storage will yield amnesia at any and all times after training. Geller and Jarvik (1968) were the first to test this prediction. They found that in mice, amnesia does *not* appear immediately following ECS but takes several hours to develop. Miller and Springer (1971) essentially replicated this observation in rats (amnesia developed over the 30 minutes following ECS) and also determined that the apparent retention seen shortly after ECS was truly memorial in nature and not caused by factors such as changes in general activity levels. The results of this latter study are illustrated in Fig. 5.4.

A digression at this point is in order. In addition to ECS, there are numerous other sources of experimental retrograde amnesia. These agents were commonly regarded as falling into one of two categories: those such as ECS, hypoxia, and hypothermia, which were thought to disrupt newly acquired information in active storage prior to the formation of a passive trace; and those such as cycloheximide and actinomycin-D, which were thought to allow normal active storage processes but temporarily inhibit the formation of a passive trace (Agranoff, 1971). The latter category, composed of antimetabolites, was assumed to interfere with retention by inhibiting protein and/or RNA synthesis believed necessary for the formation of passive traces. When these antimetabolites are injected into animals immediately subsequent to learning, initially no effect upon retention is observed, but amnesia is seen to develop over a period of several hours. This decrement in retention was thought to reflect the normal loss of information from active storage without any relevant information in passive storage upon which to draw.

Although antimetabolite and ECS-like amnestic agents were assumed to have highly dissimilar modes of action, the primary empirical distinction between the two resultant behavioral syndromes was that antimetabolite-induced amnesia develops over several hours after training, whereas ECS-induced amnesia was

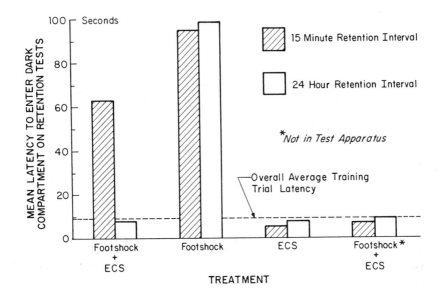

FIG. 5.4.   Experimental amnesia develops over an hour or two subsequent to ECS (or an injection of an antimetabolite) that immediately follows training. In this experiment with rats (Miller & Springer, 1971), no differences between behavior at the two retention intervals occurred after footshock alone or ECS alone. However, fear seen 15 minutes after footshock plus ECS vanished before the 24-hour retention test. The right-hand group also received footshock plus ECS, but outside the test apparatus. These animals indicate that the long latencies of the rats receiving training footshock plus ECS are a memorial effect. A consolidation-failure explanation of ECS-induced amnesia would predict that amnesia should appear immediately after ECS.

originally thought to appear full-blown immediately following ECS. Obviously the observation of retention over an extended period of time after ECS belies this distinction. Moreover, we find that the properties of the two kinds of amnesia are similar in respect to other newly discovered amnesia phenomena to be described. This similarity has prompted a number of researchers to reconsider the initial contention that these two families of amnestic agents act through different neural mechanisms. Although there is no doubt that both types of amnestic agents have the physiological consequences originally attributed to them, it now appears that each type of agent has a number of additional biochemical and physiological effects and that some common but yet unidentified consequences may well be responsible for all experimental amnesia.

Insulation Against Amnesia

A number of treatments administered prior to ECS have been identified as insulating an animal against the amnestic consequences of ECS. Some of these are pharmacological, whereas others involve environmental manipulations. In the former category, for example, Essman (1968) reported that pre-ECS injections of the serotonin antagonist DBMC attenuates subsequent experimental amnesia. In the category of environmental manipulations, Lewis, Miller, and Misanin (1968) found that if rats were permitted to explore the training apparatus for three sessions of 5 minutes each prior to one-trial passive-avoidance acquisition, ECS failed to produce the amnesia seen to develop in animals that were given only 5 seconds of preexposure to the apparatus in each pretraining session. Without ECS, this difference in preexposure duration had no obvious effect on performance during the retention test despite care having been taken to avoid ceiling effects. These results are illustrated in Fig. 5.5. As animals apparently learn about the topology of the apparatus during pretraining exposure, this phenomenon has come to be called the "familiarization" effect.

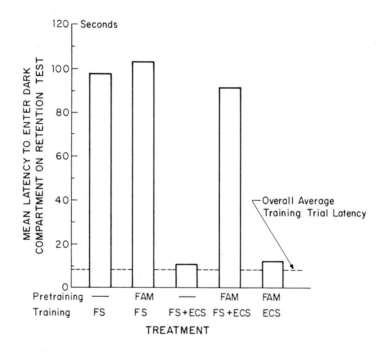

FIG. 5.5.   Pretraining familiarization (FAM) with the training apparatus in the absence of footshock (FS) prevents the subsequent development of amnesia despite ECS immediately following the training FS (Lewis, Miller, & Misanin, 1968). This effect has been obtained even when the interval between footshock onset and ECS onset is only 0.5 seconds. ECS is thought to obliterate all information in active storage independent of its action upon passive storage. Thus, the familiarization effect suggests that rats are able to place information in passive storage less than 0.5 seconds after acquisition.

Our thinking in 1968 was still strongly influenced by the consolidation-failure view of experimental amnesia. We hypothesized that familiarization reduced the amount of information that an animal had to consolidate on the training trial; and, assuming some sort of sequential consolidation process, consolidation during training could be completed more rapidly by animals having had pretraining familiarization. It was further assumed that the time from footshock onset to ECS onset determined the maximal amount of time an animal had to consolidate the crucial information about the task. In the initial familiarization studies, a 5-second footshock was followed immediately by ECS, so that the animal had 5 seconds to consolidate the information about footshock. Possibly the familiarized animal could consolidate the relevant information within that time, whereas the nonfamiliarized animal could not. To test the likelihood of this, Lewis, Miller, and Misanin (1969) performed another study similar to their previous one but reduced the interval between footshock onset and ECS onset to 500 milliseconds. They found that even with only a half second to consolidate information about footshock, familiarized animals failed to display amnesia. As in the previous study, appropriate control groups assured that the effect was actually due to specific memory of training.

The studies already described and those yet to be described in this chapter cast doubt upon the view that experimental amnesia ordinarily results from interference with consolidation. However, there appear to be no grounds for rejecting the premise of traditional theory that ECS erases active storage, thereby obliterating all information that is not already represented in passive storage. Accepting this assumption, we must conclude that the familiarization studies demonstrate that rats *can* consolidate information into some sort of chemical/structural format in less than 500 milliseconds. If animals have the facility to consolidate information within 500 milliseconds of receipt in this particular situation, the possibility must be entertained that similar rates of consolidation may apply in other situations. An important implication of this rapid consolidation process is that extremely rapid biochemical processes subserving passive storage must exist and should be sought by researchers. There is probably a multitude of biochemical reactions involved in passive storage, some of which may occur far more slowly than this, but there must be at least one biochemical process that can occur within one-half second and is capable of fully encoding the relevant information. It is possible that pharmacological agents that protect newly acquired information when administered prior to training and ECS (e.g., Essman, 1968) act through a mechanism similar to that which produces the familiarization effect; however, there is presently no evidence to support this view. It is noteworthy that most interpretations of the pharmacological studies have attributed their effects to neurological arousal produced in the animal, which is not a plausible explanation of the familiarization effect. Further research with both types of isolating agents is clearly required.

Amnesia Following Reactivation

The assertion that ECS-induced amnesia results from the prevention of consolidation requires that amnesia occur only for newly acquired information. Many studies have found that information acquired more than 10 to 30 seconds prior to ECS is not subject to experimental amnesia. However, Misanin, Miller, and Lewis (1968) asked whether it was the age of a memory per se or actually the time since the information had last entered active storage that determined its vulnerability to ECS. They trained animals and then, on the next day, used a stimulus from the training situation to reinstate memory of training in active storage. The question asked was whether the information would again become vulnerable to ECS when reactivated at this later time.

Their rats were maintained on a water-deprivation schedule to assure that they were thirsty at the time of experimentation each day. Over a number of days, each rat was placed in an enclosure with a filled water tube and was permitted to drink a fixed amount. After all animals had learned to rapidly approach the water and lick, each was returned to the enclosure with the water tube removed. On this trial, a tone was presented and followed immediately by a footshock. Previous research had shown that a single pairing of this tone and footshock was adequate to make the tone a fear-inducing stimulus as indicated by its ability to suppress a rat's drinking. It was also known that ECS administered immediately following the footshock caused amnesia for the tone−footshock association; i.e., rats would continue to drink when the tone came on during testing as if they never had had the tone−footshock conditioning trial. In the present study, 24 hours after the tone−footshock pairing, the tone was presented and was followed immediately by ECS in an apparatus dissimilar to the training enclosure. On the next day, each rat was tested with the tone while it was drinking in the conditioning enclosure. It was found that ECS produced amnesia for the tone−footshock association provided the ECS immediately followed the tone. The data from this study are illustrated in Fig. 5.6, and confirming data are to be found in a number of other independent reports (e.g., Robbins & Meyer, 1970; Schneider & Sherman, 1968). Apparently ECS is capable of producing amnesia for information acquired 24 hours earlier, information that may reasonably be assumed to be well represented in passive storage by this time. In the face of this finding, we must seek a mechanism by which amnestic agents can influence the use of information already established in passive storage in addition to whatever ECS does to information that is uniquely in active storage.

Preliminary data from our own laboratory indicate that the degree of amnesia produced by the reactivation method depends on the interval between the onset of the reinstating cue and the onset of the ECS. This parallel with the traditional retrograde gradient for experimental amnesia is consistent with a number of other effects that traditionally were obtainable only with treatments administered soon after training but that are now found to be producible at other times after acqui-

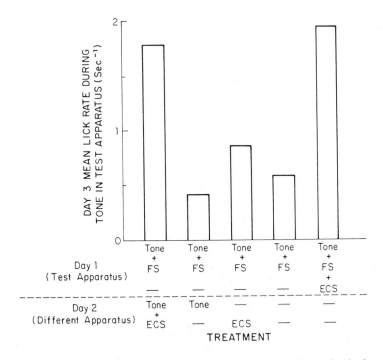

FIG. 5.6.   ECS produces amnesia for 24-hour-old memories of tone–footshock (FS) association when the tone used in original training is presented immediately before the ECS is delivered (Misanin, Miller, & Lewis, 1968). The resultant amnesia is quite similar to the amnesia seen when ECS immediately follows original training. The various control groups indicate that the reinstatement effect is the product of memorial factors. These results suggest that ECS is capable of acting upon information that is already consolidated in passive storage.

sition provided the treatment is preceded by a reinstating cue. For example, Gordon (1977) has reported that a low dose of strychnine, which appears to enhance retention of newly acquired information, can also enhance retention of information acquired days earlier provided that reinstating cues are presented immediately prior to injection. Apparently the representational state of a memory trace is more important than its age in determining its malleability.

Permanence of Amnesia

The view that experimental amnesia results from the obliteration of information in active storage before the information can be encoded in passive storage predicts that the observed memory loss will be permanent. Yet ECT-induced amnesia and clinical amnesia produced by head injuries are well known to dissipate in large part, if not completely, with time after the injury, with the older memories returning first (Ervin & Anders, 1970). This, plus the previously discussed problems with the traditional explanation of experimental amnesia, caused a number of researchers to look for recovery from amnesia in a laboratory situation. The earliest experiments followed the lead from the clinical literature and merely lengthened the retention interval from the conventional 24 hours to multiple days and even weeks, but no evidence of spontaneous recovery of memory was commonly observed. An exception was a report by Zinkin and Miller (1967), but Herz and Peeke (1968) determined that the Zinkin and Miller results depended on the use of repeated test trials for the same subjects and hence do not constitute a *spontaneous* restoration of memory. Having failed to obtain spontaneous recovery, several researchers, again following examples from the clinical literature, attempted to "remind" the amnesic animals of the training experience under circumstances that prohibited further relevant learning. Beginning with a study by Koppenaal, Jagoda, and Cruce (1967), these efforts met with considerable success. As electrophysiological recordings indicate that ECS obliterates information uniquely stored in active memory, recovery from amnesia in a situation that excludes new acquisition must be interpreted as supporting consolidation in passive storage during the interval between acquisition and ECS, i.e., extremely rapid consolidation.

Given the theoretical importance of the recovery effect, it is appropriate here to review a few "reminder" experiments performed in our own laboratory a few years ago (Miller & Springer, 1972a). Using a shuttlebox, rats were given a single passive-avoidance training trial in which footshock was followed immediately by ECS. Twenty-four hours later, some of the amnesic animals were placed in an apparatus dissimilar to the shuttlebox and, independent of their behavior, were given a footshock similar to that received during training. On the next day, all animals were tested for retention. Those subjects that received only ECS after training exhibited amnesia, but those that also received the "reminder" shock displayed appreciable retention. Appropriate control groups were included to assure that the recovery from amnesia was due to restoration of memory specific to training. The results of this experiment may be seen in Fig. 5.7. They provide direct evidence that experimental amnesia is caused at least partially, if not entirely, by a failure to retrieve information still present in the amnesic animal and still potentially accessible. Other studies in this series determined that neither the time between ECS and the reminder treatment nor the time between the reminder treatment and the test trial was critical to the effect.

The importance of this finding prompted Miller, Ott, Berk, and Springer (1974) to test its generalizability to learning situations involving approach to reward rather than passive avoidance of punishment. The specific task consisted of letting a water-deprived rat find a saccharine-flavored water supply in a novel enclosure. On first exposure, the typical subject took several minutes to locate the water tube and then drank voraciously. In this particular study, the experimenter removed the water tube after an electronic circuit indicated that the animal had

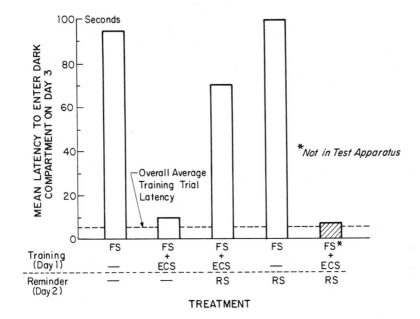

FIG. 5.7. A reminder footshock (RS) is seen to restore memory when given to an amnesic rat outside of the test apparatus 24 hours after a training footshock (FS) and ECS (Miller & Springer, 1972a). This restoration of memory without the possibility of any relearning indicates that the amnesia was caused by a failure to access information present within the animal while it was amnesic, i.e., a retrieval failure. All training was in the shuttlebox that was used for testing except for the right-hand group, which was included to determine if the reminder effect was the result of recovery of specific memory for training. These results are in stark contradiction to the traditional view that experimental amnesia is permanent.

emitted 10 licks, which typically took less than 1.5 seconds after the tube was located. If the animal was returned to the apparatus on the next day, it located the tube and started to lick within a few seconds unless it had received ECS immediately after the 10 licks on the previous day. Thus, we had a one-trial training task motivated by a reward and ECS-induced amnesia for that learning. As a reminder treatment, some of the amnesic rats were exposed to saccharine-flavored water on the next day in an apparatus quite different from the enclosure used in training. This produced recovery of memory as demonstrated on a subsequent test trial. The results, analogous to the reminder studies that used aversive reinforcement, argue for the generality of the reminder effect.

In the report of Miller et al. (1974), the appropriateness of labeling the "reminder" effect as such was discussed. At that time, it was not yet clear which qualities of the reminder situation were instrumental in reversing amnesia. Consequently, a number of stimuli were examined to determine their potential to reverse amnesia. Previous research (unpublished) had convinced us, not surprisingly, that saccharine-flavored water but not footshock, outside the training situation, could reverse amnesia for the location of saccharine-flavored water and that footshock but not saccharine-flavored water, outside the training situation, could reverse amnesia for the location of footshock. In general, the higher the similarity of the reminder stimulus to the stimuli present during training, the more pronounced was the reminder effect. Finally, it was determined that reminder stimuli did not have to be reinforcers such as footshock or water. A reminder effect was obtained merely by exposing an amnesic rat to the training environment in the absence of the reinforcer. This assured that no relevant new learning about reinforcement contingencies took place. The effectiveness of this reminder treatment is consistent with data reported by Sara (1973) and also helps to identify the mechanism underlying the allegedly spontaneous recovery from amnesia reported by Zinkin and Miller (1967), who inadvertently gave their animals apparatus cue reminders in the form of multiple test trials. The amount of exposure to apparatus cues necessary to obtain a reminder effect (which is larger than the exposure necessary when the reinforcer is the recovery agent) is critical, as too little exposure fails to yield recovery and too much exposure produces extinction of initial learning once the animal recovers from amnesia.

Although the studies just described indicate that it is appropriate to refer to recovery from amnesia achieved through stimulus presentation as a "reminder" effect, it should be noted that pharmacological agents have also proven effective in reversing experimental amnesia. For example, Rigter and Van Riezen (1975) report that injections of select pharmacological agents ($ACTH_{4-10}$) can produce recovery of memory of punishment. These findings could be considered akin to the reminder effect, since the reminder stimuli produce neuroendocrinological effects as a consequence of their action upon sensory receptors. In this light, the pharmacological agents that produce a recovery of memory can be considered as having similar effects upon the nervous system, except that use of a hypodermic syringe bypasses the sensory receptors. Ultimately any complete biological model of memory will have to incorporate the important role of hormones in regulating information processing in the nervous system. Consistently, a number of investigators have demonstrated the modulating effects of exogenous hormones upon memory processes outside the framework of experimental amnesia (e.g., Gold & Van Buskirk, 1976).

RECENT EXPLANATIONS OF EXPERIMENTAL AMNESIA

Retrieval-Failure Hypotheses and the Catalog Model

The consolidation-failure explanation of experimental amnesia has proven to be highly resilient in the face of what is now strong evidence of its inadequacy. There are many reasons for this, the most important of which is probably the historically rooted theoretical bias of many investigators. The chain of events between presentation of training stimuli and the performance of an animal on a test trial has many links in it, and a break in any one would result in a disruption of test performance. A tradition started by Müller and Pilzecker (1900) and continuing through Hebb (1949) and Duncan (1949) has led researchers to focus their attention rather myopically on the consolidation process. The sole observation lending support to this emphasis upon consolidation was the fact that the retrograde gradient for amnesia is anchored to the learning event, whereas the time between administration of the amnestic agent and testing was commonly believed to be inconsequential. As consolidation is surely a process that must occur soon after acquisition, it is not unreasonable to suspect that a consolidation failure is involved in the behavioral deficit. However, there are other memorial processes in addition to consolidation that likely occur soon after learning.

If consolidation is conceived as a laying down of a structural/chemical representation of acquired information, it is plausible that there is an additional process occurring soon after acquisition that enables retrieval of this information at the time of testing. As this process is not necessary for storage but is for later accessing of the acquired information, it seems reasonable to refer to the process as an aspect of the overall retrieval process, one that occurs soon after acquisition rather than at the time of testing. Some researchers would rather reserve the word *retrieval* exclusively for processes that occur at the time of the retention test and instead would prefer to speak of a disruption of *encoding subsequent to initial consolidation*. There is no basis for argument here; the difference is merely a matter of how one chooses to define *retrieval*. In either case, ECS-induced amnesia is clearly construed as a failure to retrieve stored information due to a deficit in postconsolidation encoding at an earlier stage of information processing.

We find it helpful to refer to an analogy of a library in which purchasing and shelving a book is comparable to information acquisition and consolidation by an organism and in which making an entry in the card catalog is comparable to that aspect of the retrieval process that occurs soon after acquisition (Miller & Springer, 1973). Borrowing from this analogy, we hereafter refer to this aspect of retrieval as *cataloging*. Cataloging is conceived to be quite independent of initial consolidation but essential for later access to the acquired information without resorting to a laborious and time-consuming search of long-term—i.e., passive—storage.

It is cataloging and not initial consolidation that we believe to be primarily disrupted by ECS (and other amnestic agents) in most if not all experiments reported to date. One reason that cataloging is more vulnerable than consolidation is that initial consolidation into *mass storage* appears to be so rapid as to occur prior to (or perhaps despite) ECS, whereas stabilization of the catalog trace appears to be delayed in time. The basis for this delay is probably functional; perhaps the delay lasts until the stream of novel information input is broken sufficiently to inform the animal that the learning event is complete. This is in agreement with the general finding that temporal proximity is the most important single factor in determining which stimuli will be associated.

The retrieval-failure explanation of experimental amnesia, currently favored by a number of investigators including ourselves, parallels a rising interest in retrieval processes in animal learning (e.g., Spear, 1973) and in human cognition (e.g., Tulving, 1974). Consistent with the consolidation position, we have little doubt that the electrical storm that ECS induces in the nervous system obliterates all acquired information not represented in some sort of structural/chemical format. However, the familiarization experiments (Lewis, Miller, & Misanin, 1969) suggest that initial consolidation is a very rapid process that can reach a self-sustaining point in less than 500 milliseconds. Reminder treatment apparently facilitates access to the relevant information that was consolidated in passive storage between acquisition and ECS. In addition to triggering action potentials in a multitude of neurons, ECS is known to have many physiological "side effects" (e.g., Nielson, 1968; Oke, Mendelson, & Justensen, 1974). It is likely that one or more of these supposed side effects is in fact responsible for disruption of what we have chosen to call the cataloging process. It seems reasonable to conceive of the cataloging system as essentially a small segment of passive storage in which a number of stimulus dimensions have been defined as salient, probably through some sort of genetic control. Since the catalog trace, an extremely abbreviated memory of the learning event, is assumed to contain the storage locations for only the most salient stimuli composing the complete trace, it is likely that it stabilizes after the global trace for the complete learning event has been laid down in passive storage. This is necessary because functional location addresses cannot be stored until they have been assigned, and the *most* salient cues of the learning event cannot be ascertained until the learning event is complete. Since the catalog trace is a memory in its own right, many questions concerning the dynamics of the catalog system may be raised. At this time we are not prepared to offer many answers to these questions; however, the similarities of our catalog system and mass storage to the recognition and semantic components respectively of Simon's (1976) LTM are highly suggestive.

The most important phenomenon supporting the retrieval-failure hypothesis is recovery from amnesia induced by either reminder manipulations or pharmacological agents. These studies indicate that at least some if not all experimental amnesia is attributable to a retrieval failure. The theorizing we have indulged in concerning a cataloging process as an important component of retrieval is obviously a more specific statement than is necessary based solely on the recovery of memory studies. Many researchers subscribe to the retrieval-failure position without necessarily accepting our notions concerning cataloging.

In addition to the reminder effect, each of the other phenomena previously described is consistent with the retrieval-failure hypothesis and can be integrated into our somewhat more specific catalog model. For example, the familiarization effect argues not only for rapid consolidation but for the occurrence of much of the ultimately necessary cataloging concerning apparatus stimuli during the pretraining sessions. The reactivation effect suggests that even long after establishment, the catalog trace is still subject to disruption whenever it is called into use. The phenomenon least readily incorporated into our theory of a special catalog trace in passive storage is the delayed development of amnesia following treatment. Here we can only paraphrase the observation and say that the amnestic agent starts a degradation of the consolidated, but still unstable, catalog trace that occurs over time rather then preventing its initial consolidation. The detention phenomenon may be viewed as a consequence of the continuing presence of the environmental cues or other novel stimuli maintaining the instability of the catalog trace of the particular learning event on hand.

Salvaging the Consolidation-Failure Hypothesis

The retrieval-failure position, whether in the general sense or the more specific catalog version of which we have spoken, has met with considerable resistance from the proponents of a consolidation-failure hypothesis. Cherkin (1970) has argued that anything that occurs soon after acquisition is, by definition, a consolidation process. This definition of consolidation is less useful than the conventional definition; however, given Cherkin's definition, we do not see any conceptual difference in view between what he calls consolidation failure and what we call retrieval failure.

A second attempt to defend the consolidation-failure position has been offered by Cherkin (1972) and Gold, Haycock, Macri, and McGaugh (1973). These researchers have proposed that the typical amnesic animal has managed to consolidate some informaton concerning the learning event, but not enough to behaviorally manifest itself during a retention test. They suggest that treatments resulting in apparent recovery of memory are, in fact, magnifying the small degree of residual memory that was consolidated prior to ECS. To support this supposition, Gold et al. (1973) presented data indicating that a weakly trained animal will show an improvement in test performance following a reminder treatment that excludes the possibility of learning in a naive animal. There are two problems with this position. First, DeVietti and Haynes (1975) have demonstrated that there are distinct differences between weakly trained animals and amnesic animals. Second, Gold et al. (1973) assume that there is a substantial information deficit in the typical "weakly" trained animal. It is equally probable that the animal alleged to be weakly trained is exhibiting a performance deficit rather than an informational deficit. If this is true, there could be merit to the claim that there is a similarity between "weakly trained" animals and amnesic animals without the similarity lending support to the consolidation-failure hypothesis.

A third attempt to salvage the consolidation-failure position has been offered by Schneider, Tyler, and Jinich (1974). Based on the observations of Mendoza and Adams (1969) and Hine and Paolino (1970) that autonomic indices of retention such as heart rate and defecation often fail to indicate amnesia at the same time that amnesia is observed when skeletal indices are monitored, they constructed the following hypothesis. ECS, they suggest, disrupts consolidation of instrumental learning but not of classical conditioning. If an amnesic animal is returned to the training situation for a retention test, the apparatus cues act as CSs and, assuming an aversive US, evoke fear as a CR. In the course of this retention test, the animal instrumentally learns to avoid locations in which shock was previously given with motivation being provided by the conditioned fear. Foot-shock outside of the training apparatus on a subsequent reminder trial serves to amplify the newly acquired instrumental association, and, when the animal is returned to the training apparatus for a second retention test, overt avoidance is now observed. The major problem with this hypothesis is that it is incapable of dealing with reminder studies in which a between-subjects design was used. In these experiments the amnesic animals were reminded without a test trial intervening following ECS, and evidence that the amnesic animals were in fact amnesic is provided by control groups (Miller & Springer, 1972a, 1972b). In studies such as these, there is no opportunity for instrumental learning prior to the reminder shock. The hypothesis also has difficulty dealing with appetitive studies in which a reminder effect was observed (Miller, Ott, Berk, & Springer, 1974). Not only is there a question as to what the classically conditioned response would be in a case such as this, but the information dealt with was of a discriminative rather than of a go−no go nature.

Despite the initial problems with the hypothesis of Schneider, Tyler, and Jinich (1974), a number of studies were performed to further probe the proposition. Springer (1975) found that whereas autonomic indices of memory (changes in heart rate and defecation) are less vulnerable to ECS than somatic indices (changes in lick rate), with sufficiently high ECS current intensities, a retrograde gradient for amnesia can be observed in heart rate and defecation as well as locomotor behavior. Using a high enough ECS intensity to produce amnesia as indexed by autonomic measures as well as skeletal measures (180 mA), Miller and Kraus (1977) found that the reminder effect could still be obtained, even using a between-subjects design in which animals only received one test trial. These observations suggest that there are only quantitative rather than qualitative differences between autonomic and somatic indices of memory. Moreover, the quantitative differences between autonomic and somatic metrics appear no greater than between pairs of autonomic indices (Miller & Kraus, 1977) or between pairs of somatic indices (Carew, 1970).

We conclude that none of the attempts to date to incorporate the reminder phenomenon into the framework of the consolidation-failure hypothesis have been notably successful.

State-Dependency Models

Two distinctly different explanations of ECS-induced amnesia based upon state-dependent learning have been proposed. Both of these hypotheses are specific models within the retrieval-failure framework. The first of these, proposed by Nielson (1968) and DeVietti and Larson (1971, Exp. 1), suggests that newly acquired information is consolidated extremely rapidly, e.g., before ECS is delivered. Then, the stress of training (ordinarily involving footshock) and ECS are assumed to induce brain amine and excitability levels (Nielson & Fleming, 1968) and AChE levels (Adams, Hoblit, & Sutker, 1969) in the subject that are distinctly different from the ''normal'' states that existed at the beginning of training. These altered physiological states are assumed to require some number of seconds to develop and are thought to persist up to 72 hours after ECS, which is far longer than the traditional 24-hour retention interval. Consequently, the animal is in an *altered* state during testing that interferes with retrieval. Despite some consistent data, there are two major pieces of evidence contradicting this position. First, the model would suggest increments in amnesia with decreasing ECS−test intervals, rather than the generally observed decrement in amnesia with the decreasing ECS−test intervals that normally accompany increasing training−ECS intervals. Second, the model predicts spontaneous recovery of memory with longer retention intervals as the animal returns to its ''normal'' physiological state. However, the vast majority of the relevant literature does not support this expectation (e.g., Herz & Peeke, 1968; Zornetzer & McGaugh, 1969).

A second state-dependent model of ECS-induced amnesia has been proposed by Thompson and Neely (1970). They hypothesize that it is the physiological state, not at the moment of information acquisition, but at the time of consolidation that must be reproduced to permit retrieval of information from long-term storage. This model implicitly assumes that information uniquely in short-term storage must have survived ECS and that consolidation occurs *after* ECS while the animal is in the physiological state induced by ECS. The model further requires that the animal recover from the ECS-induced state within 24 hours in order to accommodate the amnesia ordinarily observed on the traditional 24-hour retention test. This recovery period of less than 24 hours sharply contrasts with the 72-hour recovery period assumed by the previously described state-dependent model (Nielson, 1968). As unlikely as the Thompson and Neely state-dependent model of ECS-induced amnesia may appear, it does predict a retrograde gradient for amnesia with slowly fading retention following ECS. Unfortunately, attempts to verify this hypothesis by reinducing the post-ECS state prior to testing have proven unsuccessful (McGaugh & Landfield, 1970). Moreover, Miller, Malinowski, Puk, and Springer (1972) have presented evidence suggesting that Thompson and Neely's (1970) data were more likely produced by a reminder effect rather than being due to ECS-induced retrograde amnesia being state-dependent.

Although both attempts to explain ECS-induced retrograde amnesia through state dependency have proven unsuccessful, there appear to be grounds for believing that the anterograde gradient for ECS-induced amnesia (Kopp, Bohdanecky, & Jarvik, 1967) is due to state-dependent learning. DeVietti and Larson (1971, Exp. 2) and Overton, Ercole, and Dutta (1976) have presented data suggesting that ECS induces a temporary, altered brain state that interacts with "normal" brain states such that manifest retention depends on a common state during acquisition and testing. Relatively little research has been done on anterograde amnesia, because it is presently of less theoretical interest, and one of its tests requires that animals be trained soon after ECS, which is a problem in light of the known effects of ECS upon acquisition as distinct from retention (Ottosson, 1968).

Postacquisition Interference

Peters, Calhoun, and Adams (1973) and Hinderliter, Smith, and Misanin (1976) have proposed that ECS creates a temporary postacquistion state during which information acquired immediately prior to ECS is particularly vulnerable to stimulus interference. Since others have suggested that contiguously acquired memories are prone to interfere with one another (e.g., Spear, 1973), the present hypothesis can be seen as suggesting a prolongation of a normal memory process. Essentially the animals' functional definition of *contiguous* is thought to be expanded. Though one might wonder about the physiological mechanism underlying such an alteration in information processing, it is noteworthy that this hypothesis is capable of explaining the gradual decay of retention following ECS. The foregoing studies supporting this hypothesis both reported that maintaining an animal under conditions of stimulus deprivation following ECS attenuates the resultant retrograde amnesia. Unfortunately, other studies have not yielded results consistent with this hypothesis. Adams, Calhoun, Davis, and Peters (1974) found that under select conditions, stimulus deprivation following training and ECS resulted in greater amnesia relative to that in animals that spent the post-ECS period in their home cages. Moreover, Calhoun, Prewett, Peters, and Adams (1975) have reported that darkness was the most important component of their post-ECS stimulus-deprivation environment in attenuating amnesia. This latter observation is surprising in respect to the post-ECS interference hypothesis, given that the rat is a nocturnal animal and vision is not believed to be one of its more salient stimulus modalities. Despite the foregoing problems, we have been attracted to this hypothesis, because it is consistent with a number of phenomena from outside the ECS literature. Over the last 4 years, we have completed more than 30 unpublished studies attempting to reduce ECS-induced amnesia through posttreatment stimulus deprivation. In the process we have parametrically varied a large number of task and treatment variables but have not obtained any reliable reduction in amnesia. Although we are forced to tentatively reject the postacquisition stimulus-interference hypothesis that postulates that stimulus deprivation should attenuate memory, it does appear that various environmental manipulations after treatment can, for reasons not yet clear, increase or decrease experimental amnesia. The similarity of these effects to the recovery from amnesia induced by reminder or pharmacological agents should be noted.

A Single-Trace, Two-Process Model

Gold and McGaugh (1975) have recently outlined a memory system that deviates widely from previous concepts. They speak of specific information being represented as a single trace that is stabilized over time by a second process not specific for particular information. They suggest that the numerous manipulations that enhance or attenuate memory are due to changes in the rate of the nonspecific, stabilization process. Gold and McGaugh (1975) have discussed the considerable merits of this position at length. For example, they point out that if ECS disrupts the nonspecific process, the memory trace should decay slowly over time to a level below the performance threshold. This is consistent with the previously described slow decay of manifest retention over time after ECS.

Like any new hypothesis, the model of Gold and McGaugh (1975) raises numerous questions. For instance, the model as stated suggests that the nonspecific process should stabilize all newly acquired information uniformly. However, in their paper on reactivation, Misanin, Miller, and Lewis (1968) reported that although a tone—ECS pairing interfered with retention of a previous tone—footshock pairing, the tone—ECS treatment did not interfere with the animal's retention of the apparatus—footshock associations that were acquired at the same instant as the tone—footshock association. The nonspecific aspect of the stabilization process in the Gold and McGaugh hypothesis fails to explain how one memory can be diminished while a second memory of identical age and comparable affect fails to be attenuated.

The question may also be asked as to how different is the Gold and McGaugh model from more traditional theory. For example, if the specific process prior to stabilization were defined as short-term storage and the specific process after stabilization were defined as long-term storage, differences between the present and traditional views become hard to discern, leaving only the lack of differences in the physiological processes underlying the two stages to distinguish the present model. The real issue, then, is whether the supposed single trace has the same physiological format before and after stabilization. Gold and McGaugh's claim that newly acquired memories are enhanced by the nonspecific process, whereas older memories are not, suggests that there is some basic biological distinction between new and old memories. If this is the case, it may be misleading to speak of a single trace.

We are personally inclined to equate Gold and McGaugh's specific memory process with what we have previously called passive storage and to attribute the consequences of treatments that they believe affect their hypothesized nonspecific process as being due to action upon our information-specific catalog process. Moreover, we feel that the evidence that the initial electrochemical representation of acquired information is qualitatively different from the long-term representation is too compelling to overlook.

Possible Physiological Mechanisms Underlying Retrograde Amnesia

A number of investigators have pointed out specific physiological and biochemical alterations produced by amnestic agents that they feel may be the bases for experimental amnesia. However, for none of the proposed mechanisms is there sufficient evidence to permit us to distinguish whether the observed physiological/biochemical modification is a cause or merely a correlate of the memorial deficit.

The number of physiological alterations reputed to be induced by ECS are great, and we only itemize those that plausibly may influence retention. Plum, Posner, and Troy (1968) noted that ECS causes local cerebral hypoxia. Aird (1958) has reported that ECT increases cerebral vascular permeability for a period of several days. Furthermore, it comes as no surprise that changes in several neurotransmitter substances are found (Weil–Malherbe, 1955). Ottosson (1974) chronicles numerous studies showing the effect of electroshock convulsions upon the pituitary adrenocortical system and neuronal permeability to various ions. Oke, Mendelson, and Justensen (1974) have reported that ECS produces a temporary drop in cerebral temperature. Wetsel, Riccio, and Hinderliter (1976) have used this last observation as a basis for suggesting that decreased brain temperature may be a common consequence of most if not all amnestic agents. Kety (1974) has reviewed a number of effects of electroconvulsive shock upon brain catecholamines. Dunn, Giuditta, Wilson, and Glassman (1974) summarize the numerous effects of ECS upon neural RNA and protein synthesis, the latter of which has been independently implicated in memorial processes. Essman (1968) has shown that by pharmacologically defending brain serotonin levels, ECS-induced amnesia can be attenuated. And of course the potential of ECS to disrupt electrical activity in the brain has not been overlooked, this being the original basis for experimental interest in ECS. Several specific hypotheses concerning ECS-induced electrophysiological alterations and memory have been offered. For example, Zornetzer (1974) proposed that amnesia is intricately related to the appearance of secondary after-discharges observed after convulsive treatment. Chorover and DeLuca (1969) have presented evidence that both the behavioral and neuroelectrical response of the brain to ECS depend on the electrical state of the brain immediately before treatment. And Landfield and McGaugh (1972) have demonstrated that ECS decreases theta activity, which has often been discussed as being critical to memorial processes. It is presently not clear which if any of the above modifications resulting from ECS is responsible for experimental amnesia. Moreover, it must be kept in mind that a physiological/biochemical explanation is a complement to, not a substitute for, an explanation at the cognitive level of analysis.

Localization

Although technically not ECS, electrical stimulation of specific brain regions with the intent to alter retention has become a popular research probe to locate exactly where in the brain ECS has its primary memorial effect. A long list of such studies with significant effects upon retention could be assembled; we only attempt to convey the flavor of these studies here. The interested reader is advised to consult Kesner and Willburn (1974) for a thorough review. Researchers intent upon locating anatomical sites critical for different stages of information processing have been strikingly successful in pinpointing "hot spots," and in fact may have undercut their initial intention by the breadth of their success. For example: In a particularly well designed study, Kesner and Connor (1972) found that immediate postacquisition stimulation of the hippocampus interfered with long term storage, whereas stimulation of the midbrain reticular formation interfered only with short-term memory; however, stimulation of the amygdala interfered both with short-term storage and long-term storage. Haycock, Deadwyler, Sideroff, and McGaugh (1973) reported that they could disrupt retention by stimulation of the caudate-putamen complex or the dorsal hippocampus. Gold, Bueno, and McGaugh (1973) were able to induce amnesia in rats through electrical stimulation of the cerebral cortex.

So many "critical" locations have been identified that the overall picture is currently a complicated mesh of many interactive locations. In mammals, current data suggest that, minimally, the limbic system is necessary for normal processing and that the cerebral cortex is a site of passive storage though not necessarily a unique one. To further complicate the model, motivation, sensory modality, and other task variables apparently interact strongly with anatomical localization of memory processes. Though it is not surprising that stimulation of a specific anatomical location can produce a variety of retention deficits at different stimulation levels and sometimes even apparent enhancement at others (e.g., Landfield, Tusa, & McGaugh, 1973), it is food for thought to learn that identical electrical stimulation of the brain can facilitate retention of one task and, with the same delay between acquisition and stimulation, can impair retention of another task (Zornetzer & Chronister, 1973). Adding to the already complicated picture, Gold, Hankins, Edwards, Chester, and McGaugh (1975) reported that post-training stimulation of the amygdala facilitated retention of a passive-avoidance task when a low intensity footshock was used in training, whereas the same stimulation impaired retention when a more intense footshock was used in training. Furthermore, when electrical stimulation of a specified site affects memory functioning, it is still not clear whether the effect is due to primary action at that location or to modification of neural processes elsewhere. Obviously a lot of work needs to be done before some semblance of order can be extracted from the localization studies. However, in the long run, we may expect to learn a great deal from this approach. Unfortunately, some of the investigators in this area have failed to pay proper heed to the lessons learned from the use of global ECS; i.e., these studies frequently overlook such important factors such as the rate of development of amnesia, the permanence of amnesia, the possibility of using local brain stimulation to interfere with established memories, and the effects of pretraining environmental and pharmacological manipulations upon amnesia induced in this way.

CONCLUSIONS

Looking back upon 30 years of research with ECS to probe the nature of memory, we see that a great deal about information processing has been learned, but at the same time a lot of effort was expended unnecessarily. A primary fault to be found with the literature has been the tendency of investigators to permit their theoretical biases to too strongly influence their interpretation of data. Logical analysis alone makes clear that a memory failure may be due to either a storage or a retrieval deficit. Although the retrograde amnesia paradigm does not permit confirmation of a storage failure, it is possible to document a retrieval failure by subsequent recovery from amnesia. For this reason, retrograde experimental amnesia appears to be a more useful probe for studying retrieval processes than storage processes.

As a matter of general approach, we recommend that future studies devote themselves more to studying memory and less to studying amnesia. In particular, when an animal shows a retrieval deficit, one cannot be certain of the source of that deficit, because each amnestic agent has a number of known consequences and heaven knows how many unknown effects. However, if one of the known consequences of a particular amnestic agent is the disruption of a particular physiological process, and if the agent at a particular time after acquisition does *not* induce amnesia, then we can conclude that the disrupted physiological process is not crucial to information processing at the time the agent was administered.

Despite the foregoing reservations, research with ECS has taught us a great deal concerning mnemonic processes. Assuming that ECS does minimally obliterate all information uniquely represented in ongoing neural transmission, we must conclude that initial consolidation is possible in less than 500 milliseconds. It now appears that most experimental amnesia is due to a retrieval deficit rather than a storage deficit, thereby placing the ECS literature more in the mainstream of current animal behavioral and cognitive trends. We have found that reactivated memories are manipulable in a fashion comparable to newly acquired memories. This observation has stimulated a number of parallel studies using treatments other than ECS that have collectively established the generality of the high degree of equivalency between new and reactivated memories. And finally, it appears that there are certain memorial processes that are initiated only by the termination of novel information flow to the organism or completion of reactivation induced by appropriate stimuli. Whether ECS-induced amnesia will continue to be a fruitful method for investigating mnemonic functioning in the future remains to be seen, but over the last few decades, it has clearly increased our knowledge of memory processes.

ACKNOWLEDGMENTS

The preparation of this chapter was supported in part by NSF Research Grant BMS75-03383 and the Faculty Research Award Program of The City University of New York. R. R. M. is supported by NIMH Research Scientist Development Award MH-00061. Thanks are due to Alvin Berk and John Sullivan for their critical reading of a preliminary version of the manuscript and to Joan Wessely for her assistance in typing the manuscript.

REFERENCES

Adams, H. E., Calhoun, K. S., Davis, J. W., & Peters, R. D. Effects of isolation on retrograde amnesia produced by ECS in multiple trial learning. *Physiology and Behavior*, 1974, *12*, 499–501.

Adams, H. E., Hobbit, P. R., & Sutker, P. B. Electroconvulsive shock, brain acetylcholinesterase activity and memory. *Physiology and Behavior*, 1969, *4*, 113–116.

Agranoff, B. W. Effects of antibiotics on long-term memory formation in the goldfish. In W. K. Honig & P. H. R. James (Ed.), *Animal memory*. New York: Academic Press, 1971.

Aird, R. B. Clinical correlates of electroshock therapy. *Archives of Neurology and Psychology*, 1958, *79*, 633–639.

Alpern, H. P., & McGaugh, J. L. Retrograde amnesia as a function of duration of electroshock stimulation. *Journal of Comparative and Physiological Psychology*, 1968, *65*, 265–269.

Atkinson, R. C., & Shiffrin, R. M. Human memory: A proposed system and its control processes. In K. W. Spence & J. T. Spence (Eds.), *The psychology of learning and motivation* (Vol. 2). New York: Academic Press, 1968.

Calhoun, K. S., Prewett, M. J., Peters, R. D., & Adams, H. E. Factors in the modification by isolation of eletroconvulsive shock-produced retrograde amnesia in the rat. *Journal of Comparative and Physiological Psychology*, 1975, *88*, 373–377.

Carew, T. J. Do passive avoidance tasks permit assessment of retrograde amnesia in rats? *Journal of Comparative and Physiological Psychology*, 1970, *72*, 267–271.

Cherkin, A. Retrograde amnesia: Impaired memory consolidation or impaired retrieval? *Communications in Behavioral Biology*, 1970, *A5*, 183–190.

Cherkin, A. Retrograde amnesia in the chick: Resistance to the reminder effect. *Physiology and Behavior*, 1972, *8*, 949–955.

Chorover, S. L., & DeLuca, A. M. Transient change in electrocorticographic reaction to ECS in the rat following footshock. *Journal of Comparative and Physiological Psychology*, 1969, *69*, 141–149.

Chorover, S. L., & Schiller, P. H. Short-term retrograde amnesia in rats. *Journal of Comparative and Physiological Psychology*, 1965, *59*, 73–78.

Chorover, S. L., & Schiller, P. H. Reexamination of prolonged retrograde amnesia in one-trial learning. *Journal of Comparative and Physiological Psychology*, 1966, *61*, 34–41.

Coons, E. E., & Miller, N. E. Conflict versus consolidation of memory traces to explain "retrograde amnesia" produced by ECS. *Journal of Comparative and Physiological Psychology*, 1960, *53*, 524–531.

Cronholm, B., & Lagergren, A. Memory disturbances after electroconvulsive therapy. 3. An experimental study of retrograde amnesia after electroconvulsive shock. *Acta Psychiatrica et Neurologica Scandinavica*, 1959, *3*, 283–310.

Cronholm, B., & Molander, L. Memory disturbances after electroconvulsive therapy. 1. Conditions 6 hours after electroconvulsive treatment. *Acta Psychiatrica et Neurologica Scandinavica*, 1957, *32*, 280–306.

Cronholm, B., & Molander, L. Memory disturbances after electroconvulsive therapy. 4. Influence of an interpolated electroconvulsive shock on retention of memory material. *Acta Psychiatrica et Neurologica Scandinavica*, 1961, *36*, 80–89.

Cronholm, B., & Molander, L. Memory disturbances after electroconvulsive therapy. 5. Conditions one month after a series of treatment. *Acta Psychiatrica Scandinavica*, 1964, *40*, 212–216.

Cronholm, B., & Ottosson, J.–O. Experimental studies of the therapeutic action of electroconvulsive therapy in endogenous depression. *Acta Psychiatrica et Neurologica Scandinavica*, 1960, *35* (Suppl. 145), 69–101.

Cronholm, B., & Ottosson, J.–O. Memory functions in endogenous depression. *Archives of General Psychiatry*, 1961, *5*, 193–199.

Davis, R. E., & Agranoff, B. W. Stages of memory formation in goldfish: Evidence for an environmental trigger. *Proceedings of the National Academy of Science*, 1966, *55*, 555–559.

d'Elia, G. Unilateral electroconvulsive therapy. *Acta Psychiatrica Scandinavica*, 1970, (Suppl. 215, Whole).

d'Elia, G. Memory changes after unilateral electroconvulsive therapy with different electrode positions. *Cortex*, 1976, *12*, 280–289.

DeVietti, T. L., & Haynes, D. A. Reminder: Similar and differential effects in amnesic and weakly trained rats. *Physiological Psychology*, 1975, *3*, 265–269.

DeVietti, T. L., & Larson, R. C. ECS effects: Evidence supporting state-dependent learning in rats. *Journal of Comparative and Physiological Psychology*, 1971, *74*, 407–415.

Dorfman, L. J., & Jarvik, M. E. Comparative amnesic effects of transcorneal and transpinnate ECS in mice. *Physiology and Behavior*, 1968, *3*, 815–818. (a)

Dorfman, L. J., & Jarvik, M. E. A parametric study of electroshock-induced amnesia in mice. *Neuropsychologia*, 1968, *6*, 373–380. (b)

Duncan, C. P. Retroactive effect of electroshock on learning. *Journal of Comparative and Physiological Psychology*, 1949, *42*, 32–44.

Dunn, A., Giuditta, A., Wilson, J. E., & Glassman, E. The effect of electroshock on brain RNA and protein synthesis and its possible relationship to behavioral effects. In M. Fink, S. Kety, J. McGaugh, & T. A. Williams, (Eds.), *Psychobiology of convulsive therapy*. Washington, D.C.: Winston, 1974.

Ervin, F. R., & Anders, T. R. Normal and pathological memory: Data and a conceptual scheme. In F. O. Schmitt (Ed.), *The neurosciences: Second study program*. New York: Rockefeller University Press, 1970.

Essman, W. B. Changes in ECS-induced retrograde amnesia with DBMC: Behavioral and biochemical correlates of brain serotonin and antagonism. *Physiology and Behavior*, 1968, *3*, 527–531.

Fink, M. Induced seizures and human behavior. In M. Fink, S. Kety, J. McGaugh, & T. A.

Williams (Eds.), *Psychobiology of convulsive therapy*. Washington, D.C.: Winston, 1974.

Frost, J. Unilateral electroshock. *Lancet*, 1957, *19*, 157−158.

Geller, A., & Jarvik, M. E. The time relations of ECS induced amnesia. *Psychonomic Science*, 1968, *12*, 169−170.

Gerard, R. W. The material basis of memory. *Journal of Verbal Learning and Verbal Behavior*, 1963, *2*, 22−33.

Gold, P. E., Bueno, O. F., & McGaugh, J. L. Training and task-related differences in retrograde amnesia thresholds determined by direct electrical stimulation of the cortex in rats. *Physiology and Behavior*, 1973, *11*, 57−63.

Gold, P. E., Hankins, L., Edwards, R. M., Chester, J., & McGaugh, J. L. Memory interference and facilitation with posttrial amygdala stimulation: Effect on memory varies with footshock level. *Brain Research*, 1975, *86*, 509−513.

Gold, P. E., Haycock, J. W., Macri, J., & McGaugh, J. L. Retrograde amnesia and the "reminder effect": An alternative interpretation. *Science*, 1973, *180*, 1199−1201.

Gold, P. E., & McGaugh, J. L. A single-trace, two-process view of memory storage processes. In D. Deutsch & J. A. Deutsch (Eds.), *Short-term memory*. New York: Academic Press, 1975.

Gold, P. E., & Van Buskirk, R. Effects of posttrial hormone injections on memory processes. *Hormones and Behavior*, 1976, *7*, 509−517.

Gordon, W. C. Susceptibility of a reactivated memory to the effects of strychnine: A time-dependent process. *Physiology and Behavior*, 1977, *18*, 95−99.

Harper, R. G., & Wiens, A. N. Electroconvulsive therapy and memory. *Journal of Nervous and Mental Disease*, 1975, *161*, 245−254.

Haycock, J. W., Deadwyler, S. A., Sideroff, S. I., & McGaugh, J. L. Retrograde amnesia and cholinergic systems in the caudate−putamen complex and dorsal hippocampus of the rat. *Experimental Neurology*, 1973, *41*, 201−213.

Hebb, D. O. *The organization of behavior*. New York: Wiley, 1949.

Herz, M. J., & Peeke, H. V. S. ECS-produced retrograde amnesia: Permanence vs. recovery over repeated testing. *Physiology and Behavior*, 1968, *3*, 517−521.

Hinderliter, C. F., Smith, S. L., & Misanin, J. R. Effect of pretraining experience on retention of a passive avoidance task following ECS. *Physiology and Behavior*, 1973, *10*, 671−675.

Hinderliter, C. F., Smith, S. L., & Misanin, J. R. A reduction of ECS-produced amnesia through post-ECS sensory isolation. *Bulletin of the Psychonomic Society*, 1976, *7*, 542−544.

Hine, B., & Paolino, R. M. Retrograde amnesia: Production of skeletal but not cardiac response gradients by electroconvulsive shock. *Science*, 1970, *169*, 1224−1226.

Kesner, R. P., & Connor, H. S. Independence of short- and long-term memory: A neural system analysis. *Science*, 1972, *176*, 432−434.

Kesner, R. P., McDonough, J. H., & Doty, R. W. Diminished amnestic effect of a second electro-convulsive seizure. *Experimental Neurology*, 1970, *27*, 527−533.

Kesner, R. P., & Willburn, M. W. A review of electrical stimulation of the brain in the context of learning and retention. *Behavioral Biology*, 1974, *10*, 259−293.

Kety, S. S. Biochemical and neurochemical effects of electroconvulsive shock. In M. Fink, S. Kety, J. McGaugh, & T. A. Williams, (Eds.), *Psychobiology of convulsive therapy*. Washington, D.C.: Winston, 1974.

King, R. A. Consolidation of the neural trace in memory. ECS-produced retrograde amnesia is not an artifact of conditioning. *Psychonomic Science*, 1967, *9*, 409−410.

Kopp, R., Bohdanecky, Z., & Jarvik, M. E. A long temporal gradient of retrograde amnesia for a well discriminated stimulus. *Science*, 1966, *153*, 1547−1549.

Kopp, R., Bohdanecky, Z., & Jarvik, M. E. Proactive effect of a single ECS on stepthrough performance of naive and punished rats. *Journal of Comparative and Physiological Psychology*, 1967, *64*, 22−25.

Koppenaal, R. J., Jagoda, E., & Cruce, J. A. F. Recovery from ECS-produced amnesia following a reminder. *Psychonomic Science*, 1967, *9*, 293−294.

Landfield, P. W., & McGaugh, J. L. Effects of electroconvulsive shock and brain stimulation on EEG cortical theta rhythms in rats. *Behavioral Biology*, 1972, *7*, 271–278.

Landfield, P. W., Tusa, R., & McGaugh, J. L. Effects of posttrial hippocampal stimulation on memory state and EEG activity. *Behavioral Biology*, 1973, *8*, 485–505.

Lewis, D. J., & Adams, H. E. Retrograde amnesia from conditioned competing responses. *Science*, 1963, *141*, 516–517.

Lewis, D. J., & Maher, B. A. Neural consolidation and electroconvulsive shock. *Psychological Review*, 1965, *72*, 225–239.

Lewis, D. J., Miller, R. R., & Misanin, J. R. Control of retrograde amnesia. *Journal of Comparative and Physiological Psychology*, 1968, *66*, 48–52.

Lewis, D. J., Miller, R. R., & Misanin, J. R. Selective amnesia in rats produced by electroconvulsive shock. *Journal of Comparative and Physiological Psychology*, 1969, *69*, 136–140.

Lewis, D. J., Miller, R. R., Misanin, J. R., & Richter, N. G. ECS-induced retrograde amnesia for one trial active avoidance. *Psychonomic Science*, 1967, *8*, 485–486.

Madsen, M. C., & McGaugh, J. L. The effect of ECS on one-trial avoidance learning. *Journal of Comparative and Physiological Psychology*, 1961, *54*, 522–523.

McGaugh, J. L. Time-dependent processes in memory storage. *Science*, 1966, *153*, 1351–1358.

McGaugh, J. L., & Landfield, P. W. Delayed development of amnesia following ECS. *Physiology and Behavior*, 1970, *5*, 1109–1113.

McGaugh, J. L., & Madsen, M. C. Amnesic and punishing effects of electroconvulsive shock. *Science*, 1964, *144*, 182–183.

Mendoza, M. E., & Adams, H. E. Does electroconvulsive shock produce retrograde amnesia? *Physiology and Behavior*, 1969, *4*, 307–309.

Miller, A. J. Variations in retrograde amnesia with parameters of electroconvulsive shock and time of testing. *Journal of Comparative and Physiological Psychology*, 1968, *66*, 40–47.

Miller, R. R., & Kraus, J. N. Somatic and autonomic indexes of recovery from ECS-induced amnesia in rats. *Journal of Comparative and Physiological Psychology*, 1977, *91*, 434–442.

Miller, R. R., Malinowski, B., Puk, G., & Springer, A. D. State-dependent models of ECS-induced amnesia in rats. *Journal of Comparative and Physiological Psychology*, 1972, *81*, 533–540.

Miller, R. R., Misanin, J. R., & Lewis, D. J. Amnesia as a function of events during the learning–ECS interval. *Journal of Comparative and Physiological Psychology*, 1969, *67*, 145–148.

Miller, R. R., Ott, C. A., Berk, A. M., & Springer, A. D. Appetitive memory restoration after electroconvulsive shock in the rat. *Journal of Comparative and Physiological Psychology*, 1974, *87*, 717–723.

Miller, R. R., & Spear, N. E. Memory and the extensor phase of convulsions induced by electroconvulsive shock. *Psychonomic Science*, 1969, *15*, 164–166.

Miller, R. R., & Springer, A. D. Temporal course of amnesia in rats after electroconvulsive shock. *Physiology and Behavior*, 1971, *6*, 229–233.

Miller, R. R., & Springer, A. D. Induced recovery of memory in rats following electroconvulsive shock. *Physiology and Behavior*, 1972, *8*, 645–651. (a)

Miller, R. R., & Springer, A. D. Recovery from amnesia following transcorneal electroconvulsive shock. *Psychonomic Science*, 1972, *28*, 7–9. (b)

Miller, R. R., & Springer, A. D. Amnesia, consolidation and retrieval. *Psychological Review*, 1973, *80*, 69–79.

Misanin, J. R., Miller, R. R., & Lewis, D. J. Retrograde amnesia produced by electroconvulsive shock after reactivation of a consolidated memory trace. *Science*, 1968, *160*, 554–555.

Müller, G. E., & Pilzecker, A. Experimentelle beiträge zur lehre von gedächtnis. *Zeitschrift für psychologie und physiologie der sinnesorgane*, 1900, *1* (Suppl. 1), 1–288.

Nielson, H. C. Evidence that electroconvulsive shock alters memory retrieval rather than memory consolidation. *Experimental Neurology*, 1968, *20*, 3–20.

Nielson, H. C., & Fleming, R. M. Effects of electroconvulsive shock and prior stress on brain amine levels. *Experimental Neurology*, 1968, *20*, 21–30.

Oke, A. F., Mendelson, J., & Justensen, D. R. Cortical hypothermia is a sequela of electroconvulsive shock. *Nature*, 1974, *248*, 437−439.

Ottosson. J.−O. Experimental studies of memory impairment after electroconvulsive therapy. *Acta Psychiatrica et Neurologica Scandinavica*, 1960, *35* (Suppl. 145), 103−131.

Ottosson, J.−O. Seizure characteristics and therapeutic efficiency in electroconvulsive therapy: An analysis of the antidepressive efficiency of grand mal and lidocaine-modified seizures. *Journal of Nervous and Mental Disease*, 1962, *135*, 239−251.

Ottosson, J.−O. Memory disturbance after ECT—a major or minor side effect? *Excerpta Medica Congresa Series. Psychosomatic Medicine*, 1966, *134*, 161−168.

Ottosson, J.−O. Psychological or physiological theories of ECT. *International Journal of Psychiatry*, 1968, *5*, 170−174.

Ottosson, J.−O. Systematic biochemical effects of ECT. In M. Fink, S. Kety, J. McGaugh, & T. A. Williams (Eds.), *Psychobiology of convulsive therapy*. Washington, D.C.: Winston, 1974.

Overton, D. A., Ercole, M. A., & Dutta, P. Discriminability of the posticatal state produced by electroconvulsive shock in rats. *Physiological Psychology*, 1976, *4*, 207−212.

Peters, R. D., Calhoun, K. S., & Adams, H. E. Modification by environmental conditions of retrograde amnesia produced by ECS. *Physiology and Behavior*, 1973, *11*, 889−892.

Pinel, J. P. J., & Cooper, R. M. Incubation and its implications for the interpretation of the ECS gradient effect. *Psychonomic Science*, 1966, *6*, 123−124. (a)

Pinel, J. P. J., & Cooper, R. M. The relationship between incubation and ECS gradient effects. *Psychonomic Science*, 1966, *6*, 125−126. (b)

Plum, F., Posner, J. B., & Troy, B. Cerebral metabolic and circulatory responses to induced convulsions in animals. *Archives of Neurology*, 1968, *18*, 1−13.

Quartermain, D., Paolino, R. M., & Miller, N. E. A brief temporal gradient of retrograde amnesia independent of situational change. *Science*, 1965, *149*, 1116−1118.

Ray, O. S., & Bivens, L. W. Reinforcement magnitude as a determinant of performance decrement after electroconvulsive shock. *Science*, 1968, *160*, 330−332.

Riccio, D. C., Hodges, L. A., & Randall, P. K. Retrograde amnesia produced by hyperthermia in rats. *Journal of Comparative and Physiological Psychology*, 1968, *66*, 618−622.

Rigter, H., & Van Riezen, H. Anti-amnesic effect of $ACTH_{4-10}$: Its independence of the nature of the amnesic agent and the behavioral test. *Physiology and Behavior*, 1975, *14*, 563−566.

Robbins, M. J., & Meyer, D. R. Motivational control of retrograde amnesia. *Journal of Experimental Psychology*, 1970, *84*, 220−225.

Robustelli, F., Geller, A., Aron, C., & Jarvik, M. E. The relationship between the amnesic effects of electroconvulsive shock and strength of conditioning in a passive avoidance task. *Communications in Behavioral Biology*, 1969, *3*, 233−239.

Robustelli, F., Geller, A., & Jarvik, M. E. Potentiation of the amnesic effect of electroconvulsive shock by detention. *Psychonomic Science*, 1968, *12*, 85−86.

Robustelli, F., & Jarvik, M. E. Retrograde amnesia from detention. *Physiology and Behavior*, 1968, *3*, 543−547.

Sara, S. J. Recovery from hypoxia and ECS-induced amnesia after a single exposure to training environment. *Physiology and Behavior*, 1973, *10*, 85−89.

Schiller, P. H., & Chorover, S. L. Short-term amnestic effects of electroconvulsive shock in a one-trial maze learning paradigm. *Neuropsychologia*, 1967, *5*, 155−163.

Schneider, A. M., & Sherman, W. Amnesia: A function of the temporal relation of footshock to electroconvulsive shock. *Science*, 1968, *159*, 219−221.

Schneider, A. M., Tyler, J., & Jinich, D. Recovery from retrograde amnesia: A learning process. *Science*, 1974, *184*, 87−88.

Simon, H. A. The information storage system called "human memory." In M. R. Rosenzweig & E. L. Bennett (Eds.), *Neural mechanisms of learning and memory*. Cambridge, Mass.: M.I.T. Press, 1976.

Spear, N. E. Retrieval of memory in animals. *Psychological Review*, 1973, *80*, 163−194.

Springer, A. D. Vulnerability of skeletal and autonomic manifestations of memory in the rat to electroconvulsive shock. *Journal of Comparative and Physiological Psychology*, 1975, *88*, 890–903.

Squire, L. R. A stable impairment in remote memory following electroconvulsive therapy. *Neuropsychologia*, 1975, *13*, 51–58.

Squire, L. R., & Chace, P. M. Memory functions six to nine months after electroconvulsive therapy. *Archives of General Psychiatry*, 1975, *32*, 1557–1564.

Stephens, G., & McGaugh, J. L. Retrograde amnesia—effects of periodicity and degree of training. *Communications in Behavioral Biology*, 1968, *1*, 267–275.

Tenen, S. S. Retrograde amnesia from electroconvulsive shock in a one-trial appetitive learning task. *Science*, 1965, *148*, 1248–1250.

Thompson, C. I., & Neely, J. E. Dissociated learning in rats produced by electroconvulsive shock. *Physiology and Behavior*, 1970, *5*, 783–786.

Tulving, E. Cue-dependent forgetting. *American Scientist*, 1974, *62*, 74–82.

Weil–Malherbe, H. The effect of convulsive therapy on plasma, adrenaline and noradrenaline. *Journal of Mental Health*, 1955, *101*, 156–162.

Wetsel, W. C., Riccio, D. C., & Hinderliter, C. F. Effects of artificial rewarming upon hypothermic-induced retrograde amnesia. *Physiological Psychology*, 1976, *4*, 201–206.

Zinkin, S., & Miller, A. J. Recovery of memory after amnesia induced by electroconvulsive shock. *Science*, 1967, *155*, 102–104.

Zornetzer, S. F. Retrograde amnesia and brain seizures in rodents: Electrophysiological and neuroanatomical analyses. In M. Fink, S. Kety, J. McGaugh, & T. A. Williams (Eds.), *Psychobiology of convulsive therapy*. Washington, D.C.: Winston, 1974.

Zornetzer, S. F., & Chronister, R. B. Neuroanatomical localization of memory disruption: Relationship between brain structure and learning task. *Physiology and Behavior*, 1973, *10*, 747–750.

Zornetzer, S. F., & McGaugh, J. L. Effects of electroconvulsive shock upon inhibitory avoidance: The persistence and stability of amnesia. *Communications in Behavioral Biology*, 1969, *A3*, 173–180.

Zubin, J., & Barrera, S. E. Effect of electric convulsive therapy on memory. *Proceedings of the Society for Experimental Biology and Medicine*, 1941, *48*, 596–597.

6

Memory Retrieval Processes During Posthypnotic Amnesia

John F. Kihlstrom
Harvard University

Frederick J. Evans
*The Institute of Pennsylvania Hospital
and University of Pennsylvania*

A person who has been deeply hypnotized is able to experience a wide variety of alterations in cognitive functioning in accordance with suggestions given by the hypnotist. The phenomena include subjectively compelling positive and negative hallucinations in all modalities, age regression and other changes in personality, and, perhaps, enhanced memory for past experiences (for comprehensive reviews of research on hypnosis, see Bowers, 1976; Evans, 1968; Hilgard, 1965a, 1965b, 1975, 1977; Orne, 1966a). After hypnosis has been terminated, moreover, the subject often awakens to find himself unable to remember the events and experiences that transpired while he was hypnotized. This difficulty in remembering, known as posthypnotic amnesia, is one of the hallmarks of the experience of hypnosis (for review see Cooper, 1972; Hilgard, 1966; Orne, 1966b).

Posthypnotic amnesia is particularly interesting, because it appears to be similar to other amnesias observed in the clinic, the laboratory, and the psychopathology of everyday life. The experience is rather like forgetting where one has laid down the car keys or blocking on an acquaintance's name at a cocktail party; it is also similar to the difficulty that people generally have in remembering their dreams and other events from the past night's sleep. In some respects, posthypnotic amnesia also parallels the "state-dependent" learning that can be induced in the laboratory by ingestion of alcohol, barbiturates, and other psychoactive substances. And historically posthypnotic amnesia has been viewed as

179

similar to the memory disturbances observed in clinical cases of hysteria, fugue, and multiple personality. In all of these instances, there is a compelling disturbance of memory that particularly affects personal experiences and other material with a strong autobiographical component. However, there is no recognizable disturbance of central nervous system functioning. Furthermore, the essential intactness of the critical memories is evidenced by their eventual recovery, as well as by subtle hints of their presence and activity during the amnesic period itself.[1]

These phenotypic similarities seem strong enough to suggest genotypic similarities among these amnesias as well. Because posthypnotic amnesia can be easily and reliably induced and lifted in a substantial number of normal human subjects without any trauma or other hazard, it may serve as a convenient laboratory model for the study of other amnesic processes. By conducting research on posthypnotic amnesia, then, we hope to learn more about the processes underlying the other functional amnesias; this knowledge in turn may be expected to shed light on the processes underlying normal remembering and forgetting.

POSTHYPNOTIC AMNESIA IN STANDARDIZED HYPNOTIC PROCEDURES

We begin by describing posthypnotic amnesia as it occurs in a typical laboratory setting. Research in hypnosis has been aided enormously by the development, beginning in the late 1950s, of a set of standardized hypnotic procedures designed for laboratory use: the Stanford Hypnotic Susceptibility Scales, Forms A, B, and C (SHSS:A,B,C), and the Revised Stanford Profile Scales of Hypnotic Susceptibility, Forms I and II (SPSHS: I, II), developed by Weitzenhoffer and Hilgard (1959, 1962, 1967); and the Harvard Group Scale of Hypnotic Susceptibility, Form A (HGSHS:A), a self-scored adaptation of SHSS:A developed for group administration by Shor and E. Orne (1962). The exact content of each of these scales varies, but the general format remains the same. Table 6.1 lists the items contained in two representative scales, HGSHS:A and SHSS:C, along with the relative frequency with which each scale item was passed by the unselected subjects included in the standardization samples (Shor & Orne, 1963; Weitzenhoffer & Hilgard, 1962). For expository purposes, our discussion focuses on HGSHS:A.

The HGSHS:A begins with a test of waking ''primary'' suggestibility (Evans,

---

[1]This is not to say that there are no differences between posthypnotic amnesia and the other functional amnesias. Whereas many of the other amnesias occur more or less spontaneously, posthypnotic amnesia must be suggested to the subject (Hilgard & Cooper, 1965). Moreover, relief of posthypnotic amnesia does not require the reinduction of the hypnotic state.

TABLE 6.1
Items in Specimen Standardized Hypnotic Procedures

Description	Scoring Criterion	% Passing
A. Harvard Group Scale of Hypnotic Susceptibility, Form A (HGSHS:A)[a]		
1. Head nodding	Head falls forward 2" before told to stop	86
2. Eye closure	Eyelids close before told to deliberately close them	74
3. Hand lowering	Extended arm falls 6" before told to drop it	89
4. Arm immobilization	Hand lifts less than 1" from resting position before told to stop trying	48
5. Finger lock	Hands clasped, fingers incompletely separated before told to stop trying	67
6. Arm rigidity	Extended arm bends less than 2" before told to stop trying	57
7. Hands moving together	Extended arms move to less than 6" apart before told to stop	86
8. Communication inhibition	Does not shake head "no" before told to stop trying	50
9. Fly hallucination	Outward acknowledgment of suggested effect	39
10. Eye catalepsy	Eyes remain closed when asked to try to open them	56
11. Posthypnotic suggestion	At least partial observable movement to touch ankle	36
12. Posthypnotic amnesia	Lists ⩽ 3 of Items #3–11 before amnesia canceled	48
B. Stanford Hypnotic Susceptibility Scale, Form C (SHSS:C)[b]		
0. Eye closure (not counted)	Eyelids close before told to deliberately close them	– –
1. Hand lowering	Extended arm falls 6" before told to drop it	92
2. Moving hands apart	Extended arms move more than 6" apart before told to stop	88
3. Mosquito hallucination	Outward acknowledgment of suggested effect	48
4. Taste hallucination	Experience both sweet and sour, either one strong or one with overt movements	46
5. Arm rigidity	Extended arm bends less than 2" before told to stop trying	45
6. Dream	Dreamlike imagery and action, not under volitional control	44
7. Age regression	Clear change in handwriting between chronological age and one of two suggested ages	43

(Continued)

TABLE 6.1
(Continued)

Description	Scoring Criterion	% Passing
8. Arm immobilization	Hand lifted less than 1″ from resting position before told to stop trying	36
9. Anosmia	Odor of ammonia denied and overt signs absent	19
10. Hallucinated voice	Answers questions realistically at least once	9
11. Negative visual hallucination	Reports seeing only two of three boxes	9
12. Posthypnotic amnesia	Lists ≤ 3 of Items #1–11 before amnesia canceled	27

[a]Item pass percent from volunteer sample, N = 132 (Shor & Orne, 1963).
[b]Item pass percent from volunteer sample, N = 203 (Weitzenhoffer & Hilgard, 1962).

1967): The subject is asked to close his eyes and imagine his head falling forward (Item #1). Then the experimenter proceeds with the formal induction of hypnosis, which contains instructions for eye fixation, relaxation, focused attention, and finally eye closure (Item #2). After the subject has closed his eyes, the experimenter administers a series of suggestions (Items #3–11), each of which calls for an alteration in subjective experience that is not in accordance with objective reality. For example, in Item #7 the subject is asked to extend his arms and feel his hands being drawn together as if by magnets; in Item #9 he is asked to feel a fly buzzing around his head, darting annoyingly at his face. The entire procedure lasts about 45 minutes.

Each suggested alteration in inner, subjective experience is associated with some behavioral index by which an external observer can gauge the subject's response to the suggestion. Returning to the examples, in Item #7 the subject's extended hands must move so that they are no more than 6 inches apart by the end of 10 seconds; in Item #9 the subject must wave his hand, grimace, or make some other overt acknowledgment of the presence of the fly. As Table 6.1 indicates, the items of HGSHS:A and SHSS:C vary in difficulty level. On SHSS:A, B, and C and SPSHS: I and II, the behavioral ratings are made by the experimenter; on HGSHS:A, because of the group setting in which the scale is administered, the subjects make retrospective self-ratings after hypnosis (and posthypnotic amnesia) is terminated. These self-ratings are highly reliable (Bentler & Hilgard, 1963; O'Connell, 1964; Shor & Orne, 1963). The number of items "passed" yields a score ranging from 0 to 12 by which subjects may be classified as low (typically scoring 0 to 4), medium (5–7), or high (8–12) in hypnotic susceptibility (in ordinary discourse, highly hypnotizable subjects are often referred to as "deeply hypnotized"). These scales have been constructed with considerable care and have quite adequate psychometric properties (Hilgard, 1965b).

Toward the end of the standardized scale, the experimenter administers a suggestion for posthypnotic amnesia. He says to the subject (Shor & Orne, 1962):

> Remain deeply relaxed and pay close attention to what I tell you next. In a moment I shall begin counting backwards from twenty to one. You will gradually wake up, but for most of the count you will still remain in the state that you are now in. By the time I reach "five" you will open your eyes, but you will not be fully aroused. When I get to "one" you will be fully alert, in your normal state of wakefulness. You probably will have the impression that you have slept because you will have difficulty in remembering all the things I told you and all the things you did or felt. In fact, you will find it to be so much of an effort to recall any of these things that you will have no wish to do so. It will be much easier simply to forget until I tell you that you can remember. You will remember nothing of what has happened until I say to you, "Now you can remember everything!" You will not remember *anything* until then . . . [p. 11].

After termination of hypnosis and testing of the prearranged posthypnotic suggestion (Item #11), the subject is asked to recount his experience of hypnosis. On HGSHS:A, the memory report is collected in written form in a specially provided response booklet, according to the following instructions (Shor & Orne, 1962):

> Now . . . please write down briefly in your own words a list of the things that happened since you began looking at the target. You should not go into much detail here on the particular ways in which you responded, but please try to mention all of the different things that you were asked to do . . . [p. 11].

After 3 minutes have passed, the amnesia suggestion is canceled by means of the prearranged reversibility cue, and the subjects are given 2 minutes more to report any additional memories that may occur to them:

> All right, now listen carefully to my words, *Now you can remember everything.* Please . . . write down a list of anything else that you remember now that you did not remember previously . . . (Shor & Orne, 1962, p. 11).

Similar wording occurs in SHSS:A, B, and C. In these individual procedures, memory reports are collected orally, and the testing continues until the subject reaches an impasse, at which point the reversibility cue is given.

Posthypnotic amnesia is assessed in terms of the number of items that the subject remembers after hypnosis, before the administration of the reversibility cue. Figure 6.1 shows the frequency distribution of recall during posthypnotic amnesia for the group of 691 subjects studied by Kihlstrom and Evans (1976, 1977). The subjects were all administered HGSHS:A in the standard manner; in addition, 391 of these subjects subsequently returned to the laboratory for an individual administration of SHSS:C. Although both HGSHS:A and SHSS:C contain 12 items, not all of these count in scoring the amnesia test; on HGSHS:A, Items #1 and #2, which occur before or during the induction of hypnosis, and #12, which is the amnesia suggestion itself, are not included. On SHSS:C, no suggestions are administered until the induction procedure is completed, so only #12, the amnesia suggestion, is not counted. Figure 6.1 shows the distribution of recall during both HGSHS:A (Panel A) and SHSS:C (Panel B).

On HGSHS:A, the distribution of recall during posthypnotic amnesia is

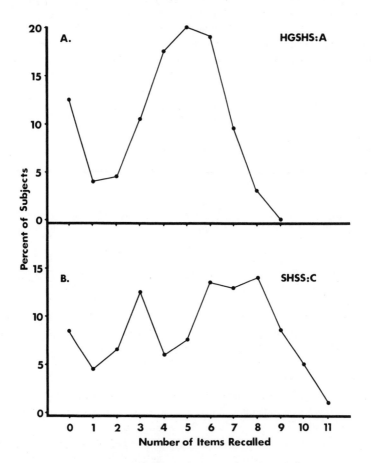

FIG. 6.1. Frequency distributions of recall on the initial amnesia test of HGSHS:A (top panel) and SHSS:C (bottom panel). Maximum number of items available for recall: HGSHS:A, 9; SHSS:C, 11. On both procedures, subjects recalling three or fewer items on this test are considered to meet the standardized criterion for posthypnotic amnesia.

bimodal, and most subjects recall a fair number of the suggestions that they received. Those subjects who recall no more than three critical items on the initial amnesia test are considered to pass amnesia according to the standard scoring criterion (reversibility is not counted in the standard procedure). This criterion is met by a minority of subjects: in the present sample, 31%. These amnesic subjects are typically the ones who have been most deeply hypnotized; in this sample, there was a significant point-biserial correlation of .35 between initial amnesia and corrected hypnotizability scale score. Similar results are apparent for SHSS:C; a total of 32% of the sample passed the amnesia suggestion according to the standard criterion, and the item-to-total correlation (point-biserial) for amnesia was .52.[2]

Inspection of the serial-position curves for either HGSHS:A or SHSS:C reveals three modes: Those items most frequently recalled are those at the very beginning and the very end (Items #3 and #11 on HGSHS:A, Items #1 and #11 on SHSS:C) and one approximately in the middle of the procedure (Item #7, hands moving together on HGSHS:A and age regression on SHSS:C). The curves themselves are reminiscent of others obtained for serially organized material retrieved from long-term memory (Roediger & Crowder, 1976). The serial-position curves for hypnotizable and insusceptible subjects are parallel, although of course the overall levels of recall are clearly diminished for the former group.

PHENOMENOLOGY OF POSTHYPNOTIC AMNESIA

Frequency distributions, item pass percents, and item-to-total correlations are helpful in understanding a phenomenon, but they can also be misleading in that they may obscure a great deal of interindividual variation in its manifestation. Posthypnotic amnesia is no exception. Some subjects, for example, awaken from hypnosis and seem blithely unaware that anything at all transpired while they were hypnotized. For them, hypnosis was induced and terminated, and that was all that seemed to happen. Much more typically, however, the amnesic subject recognizes a gap in his memory that corresponds to a discontinuity in his subjective experience, much like the experience following sleep. Such subjects are often chagrined and sometimes mildly distressed at their inability to remember what they were doing a few moments before. Hilgard (1965b) cites an

---

[2]At least two factors combine to diminish the item-to-total correlation for amnesia on HGSHS:A. First, the amnesia item is confounded by the "pseudoamnesic" performance of some subjects who for apparently motivational reasons fail to report items that they actually remember (Kihlstrom & Evans, 1976; Kihlstrom, Evans, Orne, & Orne, in preparation). Moreover, subjects' performance on HGSHS:A as a whole is somewhat contaminated by social contagion and other effects inherent in the group setting in which the procedure is administered (Evans & Mitchell, 1977).

excellent example of a subjective report of the experience of posthypnotic amnesia:

> "It was just like being on a merry-go-round and reaching for a ring. It's gone before you get a chance to grab it, and on the next time around, you almost get it, but not quite. It's always just out of reach [p. 181]."

In the face of this subjective failure of memory, some subjects will simply make up experiences: They will report "events" that bear no resemblance to what actually occurred. Other subjects, if they have had some previous experience with hypnosis, may report some of these past experiences as if they had just taken place. Still others will report only incidental events (e.g., a door slamming in the outside corridor) or particularly salient perceptual-cognitive changes associated with the induction or termination of hypnosis. These behaviors all appear to reflect a confabulatory tendency on the part of the amnesic subject. He has been asked to recall things that he does not remember but that he knows he should recall, and it is as if he is attempting to fill an awkward "silence" in his memory with something meaningful.

Even when the subject recalls a fair amount of his hypnotic experience, it is still possible to observe subtle effects of posthypnotic amnesia. In a study by Evans, Kihlstrom, and E. C. Orne (1973), typescripts of handwritten HGSHS:A memory reports taken from 167 subjects were prepared and submitted to blind raters for examination. The following two transcripts are representative of what subjects actually do on the amnesia test (numbers in brackets refer to the items of HGSHS:A, as listed in Table 6.1). The first report was written by a subject who scored in the range of high hypnotizability, 8 out of 12 points, on HGSHS:A:

> Became very tired. Eyes shut soon afterward [2]. Feel like I was floating. I made my arm stiff [6] and tried to hold out my left arm [4]. I felt a fly on my head [9]. I remember counting 1 to 20. Also holding out both of my arms [7].

The second report was written by a subject who achieved only a low score (3 out of 12) on HGSHS:A:

> We were told we were getting tired and drowsy. Our eyelids were heavy [2]. Then we were told to raise our left arm palm downward [3], then to interlock our hands [5], then to hold them straight in front of us palms toward each other, twelve inches apart [7]. Then we were told to touch our left ankle when we heard a tapping sound [11].

Note that in simple quantitative terms, the two subjects recalled precisely the same amount of critical material—four items, thus objectively failing the amnesia item. Nonetheless, it is also apparent that there are qualitative differences between the two reports. Aside from the interesting use of the first-person singular and active voice by the hypnotizable subject and the first-person plural and passive voice by the insusceptible subject (a difference frequently encountered), several of these qualities seem directly related to the effects of the amnesia suggestion on memory. In the first place, the insusceptible subject is proceeding systematically through the items in memory, recalling the suggestions in the same order in which they actually occurred. By contrast, the report of the hypnotizable subject seems rather more haphazard, with a kind of "afterthought" quality. We have more to say about this aspect of posthypnotic amnesia later. Second, the report of the insusceptible subject is clearly detailed, whereas that of the hypnotizable subject is more vague and fragmentary. For the sample as a whole, for example, Evans et al. (1973) found that hypnotizable subjects employed only an average of 5.1 words to describe each remembered suggestion, whereas insusceptible subjects used a significantly higher average of 7.7 words.

The vagueness in memory apparent during posthypnotic amnesia has been further studied by Kihlstrom and Evans (1978) in a different sample of subjects. In scoring amnesia protocols, we had noticed that occasionally a subject would remember some portion of one or more of the relevant suggestions without remembering the remainder. Sometimes the particular referent experience was fairly clear in that it was the only scale item related to the memory report (e.g., "Something about a fly"); but at other times this was not the case. In the latter instance, for example, a subject might report merely, "I did something with my hand," referring to any one of several separate and distinct suggestions concerned with movements of the hands and/or arms. Following the usage established by Brown and McNeil (1966), we have come to think of this phenomenon as a kind of *generic recall*: The subject seemed to have the general idea of the to-be-remembered material—that is, that it involved hands or arms or feelings of heaviness—but did not seem to have successfully completed the act of recall in the sense of being clear about details. In an analysis of two samples totaling 725 subjects, generic recall was found to occur significantly more often in the memory reports of the hypnotizable subjects than in those of insusceptible subjects (23% vs. 6%, respectively). Within the group of hypnotizable subjects, generic recall was most often found in those who were most completely amnesic. Moreover, there was a marked shift from generic to particular (or detailed) recall following cancellation of the amnesia suggestion. The relative poverty of the memory reports of hypnotizable subjects, including their vague, fragmentary, and generic qualities, appears to mark the partial influence of suggestions for posthypnotic amnesia, in spite of the occurrence of some recall.

REVERSIBILITY OF POSTHYPNOTIC AMNESIA

The hypnotized subject's memory does not remain incomplete, however. When the experimenter administers a prearranged cue, the critical memories appear to flood back into awareness, and the hitherto amnesic subject is now able to remember the events and experiences of hypnosis clearly and without difficulty. Figure 6.2, which presents data from the subjects studied by Kihlstrom and Evans (1976, 1977), illustrates the recovery of memory that takes place after the amnesia suggestion has been canceled. Here the 691 subjects have been classified as high, medium, or low in hypnotic susceptibility according to their scores on HGSHS:A. The shaded area of each bar shows the average number of items recalled on the test of initial amnesia (this is a recasting of the data of Fig. 6.1); clearly, on this test the hypnotizable subjects recall significantly fewer critical memories than do the insusceptible subjects. The white area shows the average number of new items recalled on the subsequent reversibility test, after the amnesia suggestion has been canceled; on this test the hypnotizable subjects recover significantly more new memories than do the insusceptible subjects, so that by the time the memory tests have been concluded, the hypnotizable and

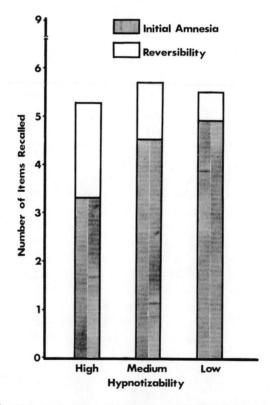

FIG. 6.2.   Mean recall on the initial amnesia test (shaded area) and mean number of new items subsequently recovered on the reversibility test (unshaded area) of HGSHS:A. Subjects have been classified as low, medium, or high in hypnotizability.

insusceptible subjects have recalled, on the average, about the same total amount of critical material.

The foregoing demonstration of the reversibility of posthypnotic amnesia is not unambiguous, however. Obviously, the correlation between initial amnesia and hypnotizability introduces the possibility of artifact in the correlation between subsequent recovery of memory and hypnotizability (Nace, Orne, & Hammer, 1974). Put simply, the hypnotizable subjects may recover more new items on the later test, simply because they have a larger pool of items left for recall after the first test is over and not because of any effects of the reversibility cue as such. Kihlstrom and Evans (1976) were able to obviate the ceiling effect problem by taking advantage of the less-than-perfect correlation between hypnotic susceptibility and initial amnesia obtained with HGSHS:A. In general, hypnotizable subjects recall less material during initial amnesia than do the insusceptible subjects; but some insusceptible subjects actually recall very little of their experience, and some hypnotizable subjects recall a fair number of the relevant memories. Given a large number of subjects, groups of hypnotizable and insusceptible subjects can be matched for level of recall during initial amnesia testing. If reversibility is independently correlated with hypnotic susceptibility, hypnotizable subjects should be observed to recover more new memories than their insusceptible counterparts after amnesia is lifted. We found this to be the case: At virtually all levels of initial amnesia recall, hypnotizable subjects recovered significantly more new items during reversibility than did the matched groups of insusceptible subjects. In fact, the insusceptible subjects typically recalled no more than a single additional item, no matter what their initial recall; we assume this to reflect normal reminiscence effects. Evidently, however, for the hypnotizable subjects the administration of the reversibility cue results in a substantial improvement in recall.

A closer inspection of the results, however, made it clear that although the recovery of memory after amnesia is lifted is quite substantial, it is still some-what less than complete. When a measure of total recall was derived by summing the number of memories reported on the initial amnesia test with the number of additional memories recovered on the subsequent reversibility test, it was found that the total recall for the 691 subjects averaged only about 5.5 of the 9 items, leaving about 40% of the critical material unrecalled at the conclusion of memory testing; in fact, only 3% of the sample recalled all 9 items even after post-hypnotic amnesia had been lifted. One would expect a few items to be omitted from recall inadvertently by subjects (Cooper, 1972), but a further analysis of the total recall data (Kihlstrom & Evans, 1977) showed that the postamnesia deficit in recall sometimes appeared to go beyond the bounds of ordinary forgetfulness. Most important for the purposes of the present discussion was the finding that among the hypnotizable subjects, those who passed the test of initial amnesia showed significantly less total recall than those who failed the amnesia test ($M = 4.27$ and 6.55, respectively). The initially amnesic subjects showed significant reversibility, but even so, their total recall was less extensive than that of their counterparts who were not amnesic. The difference in total recall after amnesia seems to reflect the residual effects of the amnesia suggestion, which persist despite the reversibility cue. The nature of this residual amnesia is not clear at this point, but it is likely that posthypnotic amnesia simply takes time to dissipate fully, in a manner analogous to the retrograde amnesia observed following head trauma.

Despite the finding of a small residual amnesia, the fact remains that post-hypnotic amnesia is reversible. Reversibility is the primary property of post-hypnotic amnesia, as it allows the temporary effects of the amnesia suggestion to be distinguished from the more permanent effects of ordinary forgetting (Hull, 1933; Orne, 1966). Amnesia cannot be assessed solely on the basis of the subject's initial level of recall. In the sample we studied (Kihlstrom & Evans, 1976), for example, a small number of insusceptible subjects met the standard-ized criterion for initial posthypnotic amnesia, but they largely failed to show reversibility; we called them *pseudoamnesic*. Moreover, a fairly large number of hypnotizable subjects failed to pass the amnesia item on the basis of their initial recall but nonetheless showed a substantial further improvement in memory after the suggestion was canceled; this we considered to reflect a *partial amnesia*. Considering reversibility allows the investigator to distinguish more precisely between amnesia and pseudoamnesia, and between partial amnesia and non-amnesia. Elsewhere (Kihlstrom & Evans, 1973) we have shown that joint consideration of initial amnesia and reversibility increases the strength of the relationship between performance on the HGSHS:A suggestion and overall hypnotic susceptibility and also improves the capacity of the amnesia item on HGSHS:A to predict performance on the later, more demanding SHSS:C (especially with respect to response to suggestions for amnesia).[3] On a theoretical level, reversibility is of fundamental importance, because it shows clearly that the hypnotized subject has attended to the critical material during hypnosis and that the corresponding memories have been actually encoded. Thus, the process of posthypnotic amnesia appears to temporarily affect the retrieval of the critical memories but not their acquisition or storage.

PARADOXICAL FEATURES OF POSTHYPNOTIC AMNESIA

Posthypnotic amnesia is routinely assessed by means of a simple test of free recall, as in the standardized scales described earlier. Under these circumstances,

---

[3]The concept of reversibility has been put to good use in resolving the puzzling discrepancy between the generally low hypnotizability of chronic schizophrenics and their relatively high level of response to suggestions for posthypnotic amnesia: The apparent amnesia is actually pseudoamnesia, an artifact of distraction (Lavoie, Sabourin, & Langlois, 1973; Lieberman, Brisson, & Lavoie, 1978).

where the task is to actively remember the critical material, deeply hypnotized subjects typically show a gross impairment of memory. Under other forms of testing, however, quite different results may be obtained. Thus, comparative analyses of recall and other measures of memory such as recognition, savings in relearning, retroactive inhibition effects, and psychophysiological response to critical items have shown that the various aspects of memory functioning are not all equally affected by suggestions for posthypnotic amnesia. Consideration of the details of the selectivity of amnesia will allow us to draw somewhat clearer conclusions concerning its nature (for a more complete listing of the relevant studies, see Kihlstrom, 1977).

The fact that an experience is not remembered does not mean that it cannot exert an influence on subsequent behavior and experience. This is true for post-hypnotic amnesia as it is for the unconscious ideas dealt with in clinical situations, and the impression can be confirmed through studies that assess the effect of memories covered by amnesia on other aspects of learning or skilled performance. For example, studies from Hull's laboratory by Strickler and by Coors (Hull, 1933) showed that subjects who could not recall material learned during hypnosis (paired associates or a path through a stylus maze, respectively) nevertheless showed considerable savings in relearning the same material post-hypnotically. A further experiment by Graham and Patton (1968) employed an ABA retroactive-inhibition paradigm. The subjects learned a list of adjectives in the normal waking state and another list during hypnosis. Amnesia was suggested for the learning of the interpolated list, and memory for the original list was then retested. A control group that did not receive the interpolated list showed 87.3% savings in relearning the original list. The amnesic group, however, showed a savings of only 54.8%, a figure that was not significantly different from that of 45.5% showed by a group that learned both lists in the waking state with no amnesia suggestions. Even though the subjects reported that they did not remember the items of List B, or even the fact that they had learned such a list, the amnesia did not reduce the retroactive inhibition produced by the interpolated learning.

In another experiment, Williamsen, Johnson, and Eriksen (1965) taught subjects a list of familiar words during hypnosis, followed by suggestions of amnesia for the learning. After awakening, the hypnotizable subjects showed very little memory for the words on an initial test of recall. Sometime later in the session, however, the subjects were shown a series of partial words and were asked to guess what they were. Half of the degraded items were the words that had been covered by the amnesia suggestion, whereas the other half were common words that had not just been learned. Despite their initial failure of recall, the amnesic subjects achieved significantly more solutions to the critical words than to the control words. In fact, their performance was no different than that of control subjects who simply learned the critical words in the normal waking state, with unimpaired memory on recall testing. Although the critical items were not remembered by the amnesic subjects, the material nevertheless remained "primed" somehow in memory, so that they could capitalize on their previous learning experience to achieve the required solutions.

The problem in amnesia, then, appears to reside in gaining direct access to memories that are available and active in memory storage. But even this is not strictly true, because it is sometimes possible to recall at least certain components of the critical material. In order to make this point most clearly, it is necessary to refer to the distinction between episodic and semantic components of long-term memory that has been articulated by Tulving (1972). The difference is similar to the distinction that Bergson (1896/1911) drew between remembrances and memoria. Episodic memories (remembrances) carry an essential component of autobiographical reference and are encoded in a specific, unique, spatiotemporal context; semantic memories (memoria) consist of knowledge—of the facts of the world, meanings of words, rules of mathematical and logical operations, and highly overlearned skills—that is stored independent of a particular experiential context. Of course, many memories have both an episodic and semantic component; when a person learns a new fact, he or she may remember both the experience of learning and how the new material fits into the storehouse of knowledge already possessed. When posthypnotic amnesia is suggested for such material, it is frequently found that the episodic component of memory, but not the semantic component, is affected.

Consider two further experiments from Hull's laboratory (reviewed in Hull, 1933). Patten gave hypnotized subjects practice in complex mental addition; Life gave subjects practice in learning nonsense syllables. On posthypnotic inquiry, the subjects in both studies denied memory for the trance events but showed substantial positive transfer when required to perform tasks similar, but not identical, to those that previously had been practiced. Evidently, the experience gained during the practice session was retained. Williamsen et al. (1965) provide a further example of this selectivity. After the initial recall test of posthypnotic memory, the subjects were asked to free associate to words that were close associates of the critical words. Those subjects who showed posthypnotic amnesia for the critical words nevertheless gave these same words as free associates to the appropriate stimulus items as often, and as quickly, as did waking control subjects. Amnesia affected the subjects' episodic memory for the recent learning experience but did not disrupt the network of associations in which those words were embedded in semantic memory.

Perhaps the most striking example of the dissociation between episodic and semantic memory in posthypnotic amnesia is provided by the phenomenon of posthypnotic source amnesia, named by Thorn (1960) and studied systematically by Evans and Thorn (1966) and Evans (1971). In a typical source-amnesia experiment, the experimenter teaches the hypnotized subject a set of obscure facts by administering a "test of general information" to the subject and informing him of the correct answers to those items that he misses. One question is: "An amethyst is a blue or purple gemstone; what color does it turn when it is exposed to heat?'' The subject typically does not know the answer, and the experimenter says, in passing, ''It turns yellow'' and goes on to the next question. Near the end of the hypnosis session, the experimenter administers the usual suggestion for posthypnotic amnesia. Upon awakening, most deeply hypnotized subjects fail to remember the previous general knowledge test, in which case the test is readministered. On this second administration of the test, however, a significant proportion of otherwise completely amnesic subjects will be able to answer the critical questions correctly. If the experimenter goes on to ask the subject how he knows a particular answer, the subject will frequently draw a blank or rationalize his knowledge; for example, ''Oh, I don't know, my girl friend is interested in gemstones, and she must have told me.'' In two studies reported by Evans (1971), source amnesia was shown by about one-third of deeply hypnotized, amnesic subjects but never by a group of insusceptible subjects who had been instructed to simulate hypnosis in accordance with the procedure described by Orne (1962, 1970, 1972). Source-amnesic subjects show effortless recall of facts learned during hypnosis but do not remember the circumstances under which the information was acquired. In short, retrieval from episodic memory is impaired, but retrieval from semantic memory is unencumbered.

With respect to the episodic component of memories covered by posthypnotic amnesia, it is often possible to produce the critical memories if the subject is not required to rely on active recall. One of the clearest indications of this comes from experiments that have compared recall and recognition measures of post-hypnotic amnesia. Williamsen et al. (1965) gave amnesic subjects a list containing the six critical words and six new, unfamiliar words with instructions to pick out those items that had been learned during hypnosis. The amnesic subjects recognized substantially more critical words than they had earlier recalled, although recognition-test performance still did not match that of the waking control subjects. In a more recent experiment, Kihlstrom and Shor (1978) compared a recognition test of memory for the suggestions contained on HGSHS:A and SHSS:C, confirming the earlier finding.

These diverse findings point to what might be called the ''paradox'' of post-hypnotic amnesia. This paradox resides in the apparent contradiction between the subject's assertion that he cannot remember something and the objective evidence of the dynamic presence of the ''lost'' memories in storage. Most of the major attempts to develop a comprehensive understanding of amnesia have taken this paradox as a starting point (for a review of these approaches, see Kihlstrom, 1977). For example, these facts have led some to dismiss posthypnotic amnesia as merely a phenomenon of motivated neglect, the subject playing the role of amnesic, but currently available evidence is largely inconsistent with this position (Ashford & Hammer, 1978; Kihlstrom, 1977, 1978; Kihlstrom, Evans, Orne, & Orne, in preparation). In the remainder of this chapter, we articulate an approach to posthypnotic amnesia that is rooted in contemporary cognitive psychology and present the results of some recent research intended to assess the adequacy of that point of view.

POSTHYPNOTIC AMNESIA AS DISRUPTED RETRIEVAL

In surveying the literature on posthypnotic amnesia that was available to him, Hull (1933) concluded that "the posthypnotic amnesia ordinarily met with, which appears superficially to be a complete wiping out of memory, is by no means complete [p. 138]." Of course, Hull based his conclusions on the trace-strength theory of memory that prevailed at that time. To the extent that post-hypnotic amnesia was analogous to forgetting, the memory traces seemed to be weakened somewhat but not entirely ablated. In terms of contemporary theoretical approaches to cognition, however, one might wish to interpret this same evidence quite differently, in terms of the selectivity of the disruption of memory functions in amnesia. We know from the fact that posthypnotic amnesia is reversible that amnesia affects retrieval functions rather than acquisition or storage processes. In a similar manner, the phenomenon of source amnesia underscores the selective disruption of episodic, but not semantic, memory. Moreover, a number of experiments show that the memories temporarily blocked by amnesia still interact (if only indirectly) with other ongoing cognitive activities, as in the relearning and retroactive-inhibition studies. The problem in amnesia, then, appears to have to do with gaining direct access to the critical episodic memories.

Here the comparison of recall and recognition during amnesia takes on added importance, because many current theories of memory retrieval contend that retrieval involves two distinct processes: a search through memory storage that generates candidate items suitable to the recall task, followed by a decision as to which candidate item so generated is most appropriate (e.g., Anderson & Bower, 1972, 1974). Recall memory is generally held to involve both the search and the decision processes, whereas recognition memory is said to involve decision only, because the presentation of the target item obviates the need to activate a search (for a dissenting view, see Tulving & Thomson, 1973, and Watkins & Tulving, 1975). The studies of Williamsen et al. (1965) and Kihlstrom and Shor (1978) show that recognition memory is substantially less impaired during amnesia than recall memory, suggesting that posthypnotic amnesia may involve that component of the retrieval process by which memory storage is searched for the candidate item, rather than the process by which candidates are tested against relevant decision criteria.

The search process itself is guided by various sorts of organizational cues and strategies by which the retrieval mechanism can work through the array(s) of associated memories. Without a sufficiently rich associational network, and without an adequate plan for searching through memory and sufficient cues to guide retrieval, the person will not be able to gain access to material that is available in memory (Tulving & Pearlstone, 1966). In this instance, there will occur a complete failure of memory or, in a less severe case, incomplete or vague and fragmentary recall. In the final analysis, then, organizational cues make recall as easy, efficient, and productive as it is for most of us most of the time. It follows, then, that when recall is difficult, inefficient, and unproductive, the impairment in memory is likely to reflect the disorganization of the search process in retrieval. This is especially the case if the memory deficit proves to be reversible and recognition memory remains intact. Posthypnotic amnesia seems to fit this description nicely. Accordingly, we have proposed that posthypnotic amnesia reflects a disruption of memory retrieval stemming from a disorganization of the process of memory search (Evans & Kihlstrom, 1973).

This proposal represented a shift in emphasis in the study of posthypnotic amnesia. It is immensely beneficial, of course, to be able to ground research in a comprehensive and sophisticated body of theory and to take advantage of research techniques that have already been developed in other contexts. With the benefits, however, have come some problems. Specifically, it is difficult to study the retrieval process in subjects who have forgotten everything. Whereas earlier work routinely studied the extent of forgetting in subjects who showed a complete recall deficit (or nearly so), we were required to focus our attention on subjects who were able to remember at least some of the critical material. Fortunately, our studies of the recovery of memory after posthypnotic amnesia (Kihlstrom & Evans, 1976) and the qualities of memory reports taken during amnesia (Evans et al., 1973; Kihlstrom & Evans, 1978) have clearly documented the partial effects of suggestions for posthypnotic amnesia. Specifically, among those subjects who show some posthypnotic memory despite the suggestion for complete amnesia, hypnotizable subjects still appear to find remembering more difficult, inefficient, and unproductive than do their insusceptible counterparts. In the following reported studies, the general research strategy is as follows: Exclude from consideration those subjects who recall virtually nothing during the test for posthypnotic amnesia, and compare the remaining hypnotizable and insusceptible subjects in terms of the organization of recall and other aspects of retrieval. So far we have examined some general aspects of the organization of recall, as well as considered in some detail one particular principle of memory organization: temporal sequence.

SUBJECTIVE ORGANIZATION OF RECALL DURING AMNESIA: COMMONALITIES AMONG SUBJECTS

The organization of recall draws upon many features of memory, including visual, orthographic, acoustic, semantic, and syntactic cues for verbal material; and sensory modality, frequency, salience, familiarity, emotional valence, and

spatiotemporal context for events and experiences with autobiographical reference (Bower, 1970, 1972; Tulving, 1972; Underwood, 1969). By focusing on
one set of organizational cues to the exclusion of the others, an experimenter
might lose sight of an important aspect of subjects' attempts at retrieval. Moreover, Tulving (1962) has noted that even in the absence of an explicit organizational principle by which a list of items might be organized for recall, subjects
will tend to employ idiosyncratic organizational schemes in their attempts to
remember the critical material. We wished initially to examine group differences
in the organization of recall without imposing on the data any specific pre-
conception of what shape that organization might take. Accordingly, we first
performed an analysis of what Tulving (1962) has termed the subjective
organization of recall.

This analysis employed two separate samples of subjects who had received a
series of standardized hypnotic procedures as part of other research. Sample A
consisted of 112 subjects, and Sample B contained 107 subjects; both received
HGSHS:A followed by an individual administration of SHSS:C. The subjects
were classified as low (0−4), medium (5−7), or high (8−12) in hypnotic
susceptibility according to their scores on SHSS:C.[4] After excluding those
subjects who showed complete posthypnotic amnesia (recall = 0 on the initial
amnesia test), there remained 23 to 40 subjects in each hypnotizability subgroup
in each sample. The analysis of subjective organization in recall for Sample A
was originally reported by Evans and Kihlstrom (1973); Sample B constitutes a
replication.

For each subject, a list was available showing each scale item that had been
recalled during posthypnotic amnesia testing as well as the exact order in which
the items had been recalled. Because recall data was gathered on the basis of only
a single trial, subjective organization was indexed by the *SO* statistic proposed by
Tulving (1962). In essence, *SO* is based on the frequency with which any item is
recalled following any other item, as tabulated in a contingency matrix similar to
that used in the calculation of χ^2 or the measurement of second-order behavioral
stereotypy (Miller & Frick, 1949). *SO* is essentially the ratio of the actual
organization observed in recall to the maximum organization possible. Typically, *SO* is calculated for a single subject and observed to increase as a function
of repeated study-test trials. However, Tulving (1962) has also indicated that
SO may be meaningfully calculated from test results taken from a single trial and
pooled across several subjects. In this case, *SO* represents an index of group
stereotypy in recall. A value close to 0 results when all the cells in the

---

[4]The parameters of hypnotic susceptibility were approximately the same in the two samples
(HGSHS:A scale score: Sample A, $M = 6.49$, $SD = 2.78$ and in Sample B, $M = 5.93$, $SD = 2.98$;
SHSS:C scale score: Sample A, $M = 6.25$, $SD = 3.11$ and in Sample B, $M = 6.12$, $SD = 3.29$. Sub-
jects in Sample A also received SHSS:B intervening between HGSHS:A and SHSS:C ($M = 6.68$,
$SD = 3.13$).

contingency matrix have approximately the same frequency—that is, all permutations of item pairs have the same probability of occurring in recall, and therefore the recall of each subject is idiosyncratic. A score close to 1, on the other hand, indicates that some permutations are very much more likely to be recalled than others—that is, that all the subjects in the group are recalling item pairs in approximately the same order.

Figure 6.3 shows the *SO* indices derived from HGSHS:A and SHSS:C for subjects of high, medium, and low hypnotic susceptibility. For both procedures

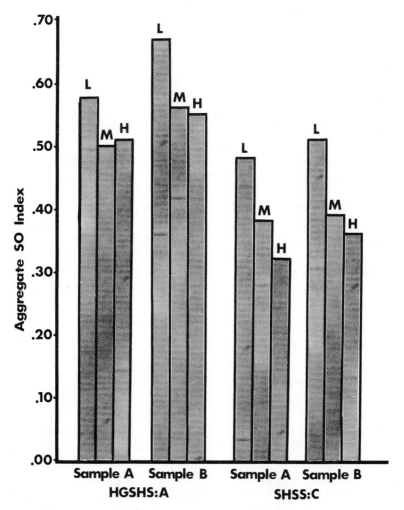

FIG. 6.3.   *SO* index of group stereotypy in the organization of recall on the initial amnesia test of HGSHS:A and SHSS:C. Subjects have been classified as low, medium, or high in hypnotizability.

and in both samples, there is less subjective organization in the recall of hypnotizable subjects than in that of insusceptible subjects. This difference is especially apparent on SHSS:C. Tests of statistical significance are not available for this kind of data, but the consistency of the pattern observed permits us to have some confidence in the results. During the time that amnesia suggestions are in effect, insusceptible subjects tend to recall those items that they can remember in a relatively consistent, organized, and stereotyped fashion, compared to the more idiosyncratic recall of the hypnotizable subjects. This is consistent with the hypothesis concerning disrupted retrieval processes; accordingly, we have continued to explore aspects of the organization of recall during posthypnotic amnesia.

TEMPORAL ORGANIZATION OF RECALL DURING POSTHYPNOTIC AMNESIA

A number of considerations suggest that of all the cues and strategies that could be used in organizing recall, for the kind of memory task under consideration here, spatial and especially temporal relations among the to-be-remembered items are probably the most salient and important (Neisser, 1967). As Tulving (1972) has pointed out, retrieval of any episodic memory requires the specification of the spatiotemporal context in which the to-be-remembered material was encoded. Moreover, as is the case with any series of personal experiences, the principal organizational rubric has to do with temporal sequence: Ask someone to recollect everything that he did yesterday, and there is a high likelihood that those events will be recalled in the temporal sequence in which they occurred. Accordingly, we decided to focus our attention on the temporal organization of recall during posthypnotic amnesia.

Differential Recall of the First Experience

The test of posthypnotic amnesia begins with the instruction that the subject should report everything that he remembers having occurred since the induction of hypnosis began, thus implying a specific temporal anchor point for the search process and probably implying temporal-sequence organization as well. In this respect it was interesting to note that the serial-position curves discussed earlier suggest a tendency for hypnotizable subjects to fail to recall particularly those suggestions that occurred early in the hypnotic procedure. More germane to the point, though, is the matter of *when* the subject recalls the early items if in fact he does. Table 6.2 presents this comparison for Samples A and B combined. On both HGSHS:A and SHSS:C, the first item was recalled first by the insusceptible subjects almost to the exclusion of the other items. Proportionately fewer of the more hypnotizable subjects, however, recalled the first item first; this was

TABLE 6.2
Differential Recall of the First Item in
Standardized Hypnotic Procedures by
Subjects of Low, Medium, and
High Hypnotic Susceptibility

	Hynotizability		
Group	*High*	*Medium*	*Low*
HGSHS:A			
Total N	60	51	68
Subjects recalling Item #3	48	42	61
Initial item recalled			
Item #3	39	36	58
Any other item	9	6	3
SHSS:C			
Total N	58	56	74
Subjects recalling Item #1	19	40	68
Initial item recalled			
Item #1	11	26	62
Any other item	8	14	6

Note. On HGSHS: A, Items #1 and #2 are not counted in scoring amnesia, as they occur either before or during the induction of hypnosis. For the purpose of this analysis, Item #3 is counted as the "first item" on that procedure.

especially the case for the most deeply hypnotized subjects (HGSHS:A: $\chi^2(2) = 5.27$, $p < .10$; SHSS:C: $\chi^2(2) = 15.28$, $p < .001$).

The findings with respect to the differential recall of the first item encouraged us to continue to look for group differences in the temporal organization of recall during posthypnotic amnesia, considering now the entire output of the subject. In order to determine whether subjects' recall was organized according to the chronological sequence of the suggested hypnotic experiences, order-of-retrieval scores were calculated for each subject who recalled at least three items on a particular recall trial. Specifically, Spearman rank-order correlation coefficients (*rho*) were calculated between the order in which each subject recalled those suggestions that he could remember and the order in which those scale items were actually administered during the hypnotic procedure. The resulting correlations were treated as scores representing the extent to which the order of recall followed the temporal sequence of events. Rho, of course, varies from $+1.00$ (items recalled in perfect temporal sequence), through 0.00 (no correspondence between order of administration and order of recall), to -1.00 (items recalled in reverse order). As a rule of thumb, recall was considered *ordered* when rho was found to be positive and statistically significant ($p < .05$, one-tailed); otherwise, rho was considered *random* (in practice, recall in perfect or almost-perfect reverse order is hardly ever observed). With this index in hand, we were ready to ask the question: How orderly is the recall of hypnotizable and insusceptible subjects under various conditions? In the remainder of this chapter, we describe a series of studies that bear on this question.

Temporal Sequencing of Recall During Amnesia

First, we wished to address the issue of temporal organization in recall during the time that the amnesia suggestion was in effect. For this analysis, we examined amnesia recall data from three separate samples of subjects, each of which had received one or more of the hypnotic susceptibility scales, including the suggestion and test for posthypnotic amnesia, under standardized conditions. Two of these samples, A ($N = 112$) and B ($N = 107$) have already been described in the section on the subjective organization of recall. The subjects in Sample C ($N = 488$) received one of four slightly modified versions of HGSHS:A as part of a formal experiment (Kihlstrom et al., in preparation). Again, the temporal sequencing of recall for Sample A was first reported by Evans and Kihlstrom (1973); Samples B and C, then, constitute replication studies. The subjects in Samples A, B, and C were classified as low, medium, and high in hypnotic susceptibility according to the best available measure: SHSS:C in the case of Samples A and B, HGSHS:A in the case of Sample C. Because HGSHS:A ratings of medium hypnotizability are somewhat unreliable, Sample C subjects scoring in the middle range (5 to 8 in this sample) were dropped from consideration.[5]

The principal results of the analysis are presented in Table 6.3, which lists the mean rho score for recall during amnesia for each hypnotizability subgroup on each standardized procedure. It is apparent that the insusceptible subjects consistently show a higher average rho score than do the hypnotizable subjects. The differences are significant in all cases ($p < .05$) except SHSS:B for Sample A, where the trend is in the appropriate direction. Note also that from sample to sample, the magnitudes of the mean rho scores, and the differences

---

[5]The parameters of HGSHS:A response for Sample C were $M = 7.09$, $SD = 2.58$. Because of the slightly higher mean scale score obtained in this sample, the criterion for high hypnotizability was adjusted to require a minimum of 9 items passed, instead of the usual 8 items.

TABLE 6.3
Temporal Organization of Recall (Rho) During Posthypnotic Amnesia

Procedure	Subjects with Recall ≤ 3	Low	Medium	High	t	p<
			Hypnotizability		Low vs. High	
		A. Sample A (N = 112)				
HGSHS:A	25	.80	.70	.67	1.94	.050
SHSS:B	32	.58	.17	.39	1.47	.100
SHSS:C	22	.55	.31	.08	3.34	.001
		B. Sample B (N = 107)				
HGSHS:A	27	.81	.71	.61	2.26	.050
SHSS:C	25	.68	.50	.16	3.59	.001
		C. Sample C (N = 488)				
HGSHS:A	97	.85	– – –	.68	2.90	.005

Note. Sample Ns are given in Table 6.4.

between them, remain fairly constant for a given procedure. When the scores for each subject were entered into contingency tables according to hypnotizability (low, medium, or high) and rho score (ordered or random), as shown in Table 6.4, the resulting chi-square tests were significant ($p < .05$) in each case except HGSHS:A for Sample B, where again the general trend was shown. Supplementary nonparametric analyses confirmed the essential trends.[6] Across the board, the subjects of relatively high hypnotizability showed a clear tendency to remember hypnotic events out of correct temporal order.

Of course, the distribution and set of possible values for rho varies with the number of items recalled. Thus, for $n = 3$, rho can take only the values $+1.00$, $+.50$, $-.50$, and -1.00; whereas for $n = 6$, rho can have the values of $+1.00$, $+.94$, $+.89$, $+.83$, $+.77$, . . . , and -1.00. Clearly, a minor error in sequencing "costs" the subject more at low levels of recall than at high levels. As has been noted previously, hypnotizable subjects generally recall significantly fewer items during amnesia than do insusceptible subjects. Thus it is possible that the

---

[6]For example, combining Samples A and B, the median rho scores for subjects of low, medium, and high hypnotizability were, respectively: on HGSHS:A, .92, .90, and .68; on SHSS:C, .70, .58, and .40. Kruskal–Wallis one-way analysis of variance by ranks showed that these differences were significant (HGSHS:A: $H = 26.57$, $p < .001$; SHSS:C: $H = 10.43$, $p < .005$), as did the Mann–Whitney U test comparing just the highs and lows (HGSHS:A: $U = 2109$, $z = 2.37$, $p < .001$; SHSS:C: $U = 2386$, $z = 4.22$, $p < .001$). Similar nonparametric analyses for a portion of Sample C are reported by Kihlstrom (1975).

TABLE 6.4
Frequency of Ordered and Random Recall (Rho)
During Posthypnotic Amnesia

Procedure	Hypnotizability	Temporal Sequence Ordered	Temporal Sequence Random	χ^2	$p<$
A. Sample A (N = 112)					
HGSHS:A	Low	22	15		
	Medium	12	11		
	High	8	19	5.75	.050
SHSS:B	Low	19	18		
	Medium	3	17		
	High	4	19	11.18	.005
SHSS:C	Low	22	18		
	Medium	6	21		
	High	3	20	13.04	.001
B. Sample B (N = 107)					
HGSHS:A	Low	16	12		
	Medium	10	15		
	High	10	17	2.61	.150
SHSS:C	Low	17	17		
	Medium	12	15		
	High	3	18	7.46	.050
C. Sample C (N = 488)					
HGSHS:A	Low	41	18		
	High	27	51	14.98	.001

generally lower rho scores of hypnotizable subjects are an artifact of the lower average recall shown by these same subjects. If this were the case, it would be expected that at low levels of recall, rho would be low for both hypnotizable and insusceptible subjects; and at high levels of recall, rho would be correspondingly high in both groups. Figure 6.4 shows the mean rho scores on HGSHS:A for hypnotizable and insusceptible subjects (i.e., excluding medium hypnotizables from consideration) for Samples A, B, and C combined. As in the earlier discussion of reversibility, the hypnotizable and insusceptible subjects have been matched for the number of items recalled during initial amnesia testing. Although the subsample sizes are necessarily small at some points (ranging from 7 to 40, median = 27.2), there is a clear overall trend for hypnotizable subjects to have lower mean rho scores than their insusceptible counterparts, regardless of the level of amnesia recall. This difference is statistically significant at most points on the distribution (recall = 3: $t(45) = 4.16$, $p < .001$; recall = 4: $t(57) = 2.81$, $p < .005$; recall = 5: $t(59) = 1.96$, $p < .05$; recall = 6: $t(50) = 1.90$, $p < .05$; recall = 7–9; $t(36) = .66$). Nonparametric tests confirmed this trend (Kihlstrom, 1975).

At each point on the distribution of posthypnotic recall, then, the rho scores of hypnotizable subjects were considerably lower than those of insusceptible subjects. These findings indicate that the generally lower rho scores shown by hypnotizable subjects are not merely artifacts of the fewer number of items recalled. Furthermore, they offer additional evidence supporting the concepts of partial amnesia and pseudoamnesia (Kihlstrom & Evans, 1976). Temporal disorganization is found among hypnotizable subjects even for those who recall five or six items during amnesia, indicating that the effects of the amnesia suggestion extend well beyond the cutoff established by the standardized criterion.

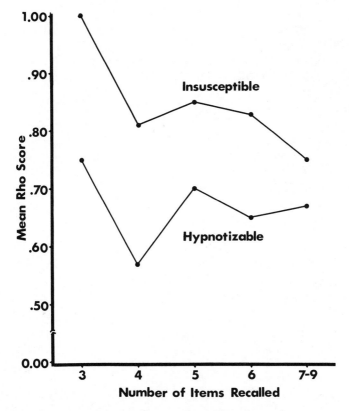

FIG. 6.4.   Mean rho index of temporal organization of recall on the initial amnesia test for hypnotizable and insusceptible subjects matched for the number of items recalled (HGSHS:A only; Samples A, B, and C combined).

And at relatively low levels of recall (three or four items), the insusceptible subjects do not show the same degree of temporal disorganization manifested by the hypnotizable subjects, suggesting that the mechanisms underlying poor memory performance are different in the two groups.

Temporal Disorganization as an Index of Partial Amnesia

If the disruption in temporal sequencing of recall that we have observed is actually a manifestation of partial posthypnotic amnesia, then it should show the expected relationships with other aspects of hypnotic response. These other variables include hypnotic susceptibility (i.e., standardized scale score) and both initial amnesia and subsequent reversibility (i.e., the number of items recalled on the two amnesia tests). In addition to being related to other aspects of concurrent hypnotic performance, temporal disorganization during amnesia should predict these same variables with respect to performance on a future hypnotic procedure. Accordingly, a series of analyses was performed using the combined Samples A and B where information was available concerning subjects' behavior on both HGSHS:A and SHSS:C (total $N = 219$). A portion of this analysis has been reported previously for Sample A alone (Evans & Kihlstrom, 1973).

Table 6.5 shows the mean rho for these subjects classified according to whether they met the criterion for reversibility after the cue was given to cancel the amnesia suggestion (collapsing across the three categories of hypnotic susceptibility). This analysis necessarily excludes those subjects who showed virtually complete initial amnesia, for whom rho scores could not be calculated ($N = 52$ on HGSHS:A; $N = 47$ on SHSS:C). On HGSHS:A the 46 subjects who showed reversibility after amnesia also tended to have lower rho scores during amnesia than did the 121 subjects who did not recover any substantial amount of new material after amnesia. This trend was highly significant on SHSS:C, where there were 66 reversers and 106 nonreversers.

TABLE 6.5
Mean Rho Score During Amnesia for
Subjects Passing and Failing Criterion for
Subsequent Reversibility

Samples A and B Combined ($N = 219$)

| Procedure | Reversibility | | t |
	Pass	Fail	
HGSHS:A	0.66	0.75	1.49*
SHSS:C	0.23	0.54	3.60**

* $p < .10$
**$p < .001$ (1-tailed)

Table 6.6 presents corresponding analyses relating the temporal sequence of recall during amnesia to general hypnotic susceptibility and to aspects of response to the specific suggestion for amnesia. As might be expected, those subjects with virtually complete amnesia on either HGSHS:A or SHSS:C showed the highest levels of hypnotic response. However, among the remaining subjects, there were substantial differences between those with ordered or random temporal sequencing in recall. For example, Part A of Table 6.6 shows that although those subjects with virtually complete amnesia on HGSHS:A achieved the highest overall scores on that scale (dropping the amnesia item itself in the calculation of HGSHS:A score), of the remaining subjects, those with random recall ($N = 89$) during amnesia scored significantly higher than those with ordered rho ($N = 78$). In the same manner, subjects with random rho recalled significantly fewer items on the initial amnesia test, and recovered significantly more new items on the subsequent reversibility test, than did their counterparts with ordered rho. The same trends are apparent in Part B, where the 109 subjects who showed random rho on SHSS:C proved to score higher on that procedure (again, SHSS:C score was corrected by dropping the amnesia item), recalled less on its amnesia test, and recovered more on the reversibility test than the 63 subjects with ordered rho. Finally, Part C of Table 6.6 shows that temporal sequencing has some predictive power, in that subjects with random rho on HGSHS:A scored higher on the later SHSS:C and also showed more initial amnesia and subsequent reversibility than those with ordered rho on HGSHS:A. In all instances the categories of complete amnesia, recall with random sequencing, and recall with ordered sequencing form a continuum of amnesic response. Like reversibility (Kihlstrom & Evans, 1976) and fragmentary recall (Evans et al., 1973; Kihlstrom & Evans, 1978), relatively random temporal sequencing appears to be a manifestation of partial posthypnotic amnesia.

A final aspect of the continuity among the three broad categories of amnesia was observed when the subjects were jointly classified according to the nature of their recall (i.e., complete amnesia, random recall, and ordered recall) on both HGSHS:A and SHSS:C. The resulting contingency table showed a significant relationship among the categories ($\chi^2(4) = 37.51$, $C = .38$, $p < .001$). Table 6.7, which presents the results for the hypnotizable subjects only (SHSS:C score ≥ 8), shows the actual nature of the relationship more clearly. Subjects who manifested complete amnesia on HGSHS:A tended to show it again on SHSS:C; if not, they overwhelmingly showed random rather than ordered recall. By the same token, subjects who showed random recall on HGSHS:A tend to be more completely amnesic on SHSS:C; if not, they show random recall again rather than ordered recall. This regular pattern ($\chi^2(4) = 15.18$, $C = .38$, $p < .005$) is consistent with the continuity hypothesis: Some subjects "fall back" from their group scale performance when they receive the more demanding SHSS:C; similarly, some subjects become more deeply hypnotized and respond more fully to amnesia suggestions once they have become familiar with the procedure.

TABLE 6.6
Relationship Between Temporal Sequencing of Recall During Amnesia and Other
Aspects of Hypnotic Response (N = 219)

Criterion	Complete Amnesia	Random Recall	Ordered Recall	F^a	t^b
A. HGSHS:A Amnesia Predicting Concurrent HGSHS:A Performance					
HGSHS:A Score[c]	7.08	5.83	5.15	8.65**	1.70*
HGSHS:A Amnesia recall[d]	0.83	4.55	5.30	211.32***	3.62***
HGSHS:A Reversibility recall[c]	2.52	1.17	0.73	29.15***	2.56*
B. SHSS:C Amnesia Predicting Concurrent SHSS:C Performance					
SHSS:C Score[c]	8.85	5.63	3.98	56.50***	4.07***
SHSS:C Amnesia recall[d]	0.85	5.81	7.54	179.91***	5.29***
SHSS:C Reversibility recall[e]	5.49	2.00	0.89	77.29***	4.11***
C. HGSHS:A Amnesia Predicting Future SHSS:C Performance					
SHSS:C Score[c]	7.27	5.98	4.76	12.77***	2.79**
SHSS:C Amnesia recall[d]	3.10	5.30	6.60	25.08***	3.07**
SHSS:C Reversibility recall[e]	3.62	2.30	1.78	8.55**	1.50

[a]Overall.
[b]Comparing random vs. ordered.
[c]Based on 11 items, excluding amnesia.
[d]Number of items recalled on initial amnesia test.
[e]Number of items recalled on subsequent reversibility test.
*$p < 0.05$ **$p < 0.005$ ***$p < 0.001$ (all 1-tailed)

TABLE 6.7
Consistency of Amnesia Performance:
Joint Classification of Subjects
Based on Category of Amnesia on HGSHS:A and SHSS:C
(Hypnotizable Subjects Only)

HGSHS:A Amnesia	SHSS:C Amnesia		
	Complete Amnesia	Random Recall	Ordered Recall
Complete	24	9	1
Random recall	11	23	2
Ordered recall	9	6	3

FURTHER STUDIES OF TEMPORAL SEQUENCING
IN POSTHYPNOTIC RECALL

So far we have focused on documenting the basic finding of relatively random temporal sequencing in recall during posthypnotic amnesia. We have twice replicated the effect first reported by Evans and Kihlstrom (1973), as has Crawford (1974). The same findings are obtained even when the classification of hypnotic susceptibility is based on HGSHS:A, rather than the more satisfactory SHSS:C. Further analyses of this data ruled out the possibility that the temporal sequencing effect was some kind of artifact of the low number of items recalled by hypnotizable subjects during amnesia, as well as some other statistical artifacts. Moreover, our data confirm that random temporal sequencing is located on a continuum of response to suggestions for posthypnotic amnesia and in fact is a manifestation of partial amnesia. In addition to these studies, we have carried out a number of smaller experiments to explore other aspects of temporal organization in posthypnotic recall. For reasons of economy and to reduce the subtle effect of experimenter-subject interactions, these studies have employed the group-administered HGSHS:A as the sole hypnotic procedure. Even so, the results have helped settle some questions, and raise others that are important, about the temporal organization of recall and posthypnotic amnesia.

Temporal Sequencing in the Absence of Amnesia

The analyses reported so far indicate that a relative lack of temporal-sequence organization is observed in the recall of hypnotizable subjects during the time that the suggestion for posthypnotic amnesia is in effect. However, it is possible that this apparent temporal disorganization may not be functionally related to the specific suggestion for posthypnotic amnesia. For example, the effect may be due to hypnosis alone. Hypnosis is generally considered to be a special state of consciousness, and the subject's failure to organize what he remembers according to temporal sequence (or any other principle) may reflect the manner in which those memories were encoded during hypnosis, or the cognitive sequelae of the transition from hypnosis to the usual waking state (Schwartz, 1978). Alternatively, it may be that the temporal disorganization seen during amnesia testing merely reflects a somewhat disorganized "memory style" present in hypnotizable subjects even in the waking state. Some of the research on the personality correlates of hypnotizability, for example, may be interpreted as suggesting that hypnotizable subjects are more disorganized in their personal lives than insusceptible subjects; they frequently become lost in thought or fantasy (Hilgard, 1970; Shor, Orne, & O'Connell, 1966; Tellegen & Atkinson, 1974), for example, and tend to arrive late for experimental appointments (Evans, Orne, & Markowsky, 1977).[7]

A further study, therefore, addressed both the "state-specific" and "memory style" hypotheses directly by analyzing various aspects of posthypnotic recall in subjects who were hypnotized but who did not receive any suggestions for amnesia. A modified version of HGSHS:A was administered to 72 introductory psychology students in the course of a lecture-demonstration on hypnosis. At the close of the usual hypnotic procedure, the standard suggestion for amnesia was deleted, but the subjects still were asked to recall everything that had happened while they were hypnotized, as in the standard test of posthypnotic amnesia. The subjects were classified as low, medium, or high in hypnotizability according to the usual criterion, and mediums ($N = 21$) were excluded from further consideration.

The overall HGSHS:A scores for this sample (based on 11 items after dropping amnesia) were similar to those obtained in other studies: $M = 6.47$, $SD = 2.56$. However, perhaps because of the circumstances of testing, the levels of recall shown were relatively low: Despite the absence of the amnesia suggestion, a few subjects recalled less than three critical items on the amnesia test. Because these subjects came in equal proportions from the pools of insusceptible (6/22) and hypnotizable (10/29) subjects ($\chi^2(1) = .36$), pseudoamnesia, rather than spontaneous amnesia, is a possibility here. Nevertheless, the important analyses concern the remaining 16 insusceptible and 19 hypnotizable subjects. They were not found to differ in terms of either the number of items recalled ($M = 5.81$ and 5.63, respectively; $t(33) = .36$) or rho score ($M = .89$ and .88, respectively; $t(33) = .23$). These figures contrast sharply with the differences in both the number of items recalled and the order of recall seen in the earlier analyses, when posthypnotic amnesia had been suggested to the subjects. Evidently the disruption in temporal sequencing observed in the earlier experiments is a specific effect of the amnesia suggestion and not a function of the subjects' waking memory style or the experience of hypnosis alone.

Effect of Instructions on Temporal Sequencing During Amnesia

Implicit in the studies that have been described so far is the assumption that the temporal disorganization of recall observed during amnesia reflects the inaccessi-

---

[7]In this context, it is important to note that among hypnotizable subjects, those who can experience posthypnotic amnesia do not appear to be more "forgetful" in ordinary waking life. In fact, studies comparing these subjects on tasks involving short-term auditory and visual memory, prose memory, free recall, incidental memory, and recollection of salient public events suggest that if anything, amnesic subjects may have *better* memories than nonamnesics (Evans & Kihlstrom, 1975; Kihlstrom & Evans, 1975; Kihlstrom & Twersky, 1978).

bility of temporal cues; in other words, that there is some impediment to adequate organization that cannot be easily transcended by the amnesic subject. On the other hand, the temporal disorganization observed during amnesia may arise from the subject's failure to employ temporal cues that in fact are readily accessible to him. If that were the case, the association between temporal disorganization and posthypnotic amnesia might be simply adventitious. The essential issue is the subject's possible neglect of temporal sequence; during amnesia, can the hypnotizable subject adopt the correct temporal sequence if instructed to do so?

Data from the experiment by Kihlstrom et al. (in preparation), discussed earlier, is relevant to this issue. In the experiment the conventional version of HGSHS:A was modified, so that a second recall test of posthypnotic amnesia was interpolated between the initial standardized test and the subsequent cancellation of the amnesia suggestion and testing for recovery of memory. This interpolated amnesia test was preceded by one of four kinds of treatments. The Retest group ($N = 115$) simply received a further recall test with no further instructions; a second, Cue, group ($N = 139$) was asked to recall the suggestions in the order in which they actually occurred during the hypnotic procedure. The other groups received instructions to exert extra effort in recalling the material or to be completely candid in reporting those events that they actually remembered. The most important comparisons for present purposes pertain to the Retest and Cue groups. Table 6.8 shows the mean recall and rho scores on Test 1 and Test 2 during amnesia for those hypnotizable and insusceptible subjects who recalled at least three items on Test 1, the initial standardized test of posthypnotic amnesia.

In accordance with the results obtained in the larger combined sample discussed earlier (Sample C), the hypnotizable subjects in both conditions showed substantially lower rho scores on Test 1 than did the insusceptible subjects (Retest: $t(39) = 2.69, p < .01$; Cue: $t(37) = 1.71, p < .05$). On Test 2

TABLE 6.8
Classification of Temporal Sequencing of Recall During Two Tests
of Posthypnotic Amnesia

Condition	Group	Total N	Subjects with Recall ⩾ 3	Rho During Amnesia Test 1	Test 2
Retest	Low	24	18	0.94	0.93
	High	38	23	0.62	0.71
	t			2.69**	2.71**
Cue	Low	19	16	0.87	0.96
	High	46	23	0.74	0.85
	t			1.71*	3.24**

*$p < 0.05$ **$p < 0.005$

in the Retest condition, there was essentially no change in temporal sequencing for the insusceptible subjects ($t(17)$ = .31), and the increment observed in the hypnotizable subjects proved not to be significant ($t(22)$ = 0.01). In the Cue condition, however, both groups of subjects responded to the instruction by showing a general increase in rho on Test 2 (insusceptible: $t(15)$ = 2.42, p < .025; hypnotizable: $t(22)$ = 1.79, p < .05). Despite the significant shift upward in the temporal organization of recall, however, the hypnotizable subjects continued to show a significantly lower average rho score than the insusceptible subjects ($t(37)$ = 3.24, p < .005). In relative terms, the changes in temporal organization for the hypnotizable subjects were of the same order of magnitude. Nonparametric analysis of these data (McNemar's test of the significance of changes applied to the shifts between ordered and random rho) showed essentially the same outcome. Explicit instructions to recall the items in correct sequence did not completely rectify the temporal disorganization observed in the hypnotizable subjects' recall on the initial amnesia test. Thus, the disorganization was not a function of their simple neglect of that strategy on the earlier recall trial.

We have documented the corresponding changes in the amount of material recalled across the two tests during amnesia elsewhere (Kihlstrom et al., in preparation) and will not detail those results here. On Test 1, there was, of course, a significant deficit in memory among the hypnotizable subjects in both Retest and Cue conditions, compared to insusceptible subjects. As we have shown, the hypnotizable subjects also showed a significant decrement in the temporal organization of recall. On Test 2, there was an increase in the amount of material recalled and in the temporal organization of recall, but a relative deficit on both measures persisted among the hypnotizable subjects in both groups. For both the extent of recall and the temporal organization of recall, the improvements shown by the hypnotizable subjects on Test 2 (while the amnesia suggestion remained in effect) were not different, relatively speaking, in the Retest and Cue conditions.

It appears, then, that during amnesia, hypnotizable subjects are relatively less able to recall their experiences in correct temporal sequence than are insusceptible subjects—even when they are requested to do so. A specific instruction to recall the items in order produced no more improvement in temporal sequencing among the hypnotizable subjects than was found for their counterparts who were uninstructed. Apparently, reminders are not sufficient to produce the correct temporal order in recall. The lower rho scores of hypnotizable subjects during amnesia seem to reflect their inability to gain access to and capitalize upon temporal cues, rather than their simple neglect of them.

Temporal Sequencing After Amnesia

What happens to the temporal organization of recall after posthypnotic amnesia is lifted? If the failure observed during amnesia is due (at least in part) to the amnesic subject's inability to employ temporal cues in the organization of recall, it would seem reasonable to expect that when memory is restored after the amnesia suggestion has been canceled, the subject would organize his recall according to temporal sequence.

Some evidence from studies previously described reinforces this expectation. During the initial standardized test of posthypnotic amnesia, those subjects with random rho scores recalled significantly less critical material than did those with ordered rho; this was especially true in the hypnotizable group. Moreover, if memory testing continues during the amnesic period, an improvement in recall also appears to be accompanied by an increase in temporal sequencing. During amnesia, then, there appears to be some regular correspondence between the extent of temporal organization and the amount of material recalled.

When one examines temporal organization after amnesia has been lifted, however, our preliminary studies suggest that a somewhat different picture may emerge. The subjects in the Retest condition of the experiment by Kihlstrom et al. (in preparation) provide the most complete data in this regard. Following the completion of Test 2, the reversibility cue was administered, and yet a third recall test was conducted on which the subjects were asked again to report everything that they now remembered of the events of the hypnosis session. On this Test 3, as on the two tests administered previously to this group, nothing was said about the manner of recall. A total of 15 hypnotizable subjects showed virtually complete amnesia on Test 1; on Test 3, after amnesia was lifted, they showed a significant increment in the number of items recalled as well as a high rho score. This, of course, is as we would expect. Somewhat more troubling findings were obtained in the groups of hypnotizable and insusceptible subjects who failed to meet the criterion for complete initial amnesia. The hypnotizable subjects showed the expected significant improvement in recall after the reversibility cue was given but surprisingly showed no substantial increase in the temporal organization of recall. The insusceptible subjects, for their part, showed (as expected) no significant change in recall after the reversibility cue was administered but surprised us with a significant drop in rho. These data contrast with the data taken during amnesia and from those subjects who show a virtually complete amnesia on initial testing, by showing that after amnesia has been canceled, the amount of material recalled and the temporal organization of recall do not always correspond.

These results also contrast with those obtained in another study in which the subjects were specifically instructed, after amnesia, to recall the items in correct temporal sequence. In this experiment, 90 subjects received a slightly modified version of HGSHS:A part of a lecture-demonstration given to an introductory psychology class. As before, the usual free-recall test of initial amnesia was given; this was followed by the reversibility cue and an instruction to recall everything that the subject remembered of the hypnosis session in the exact temporal order in which it had occurred. The HGSHS:A scores for this sample were comparable to those obtained in the other studies discussed: $M = 6.56$,

SD = 2.43. The subjects were classified as low, medium, and high in hypnotic susceptibility according to the usual criteria, and the medium subjects were excluded from further consideration. For the hypnotizable subjects who were completely amnesic on the initial amnesia test, there was substantial recovery of memory shown on the later postamnesia test; in addition, the level of temporal organization was relatively high. For the remaining subjects, who had at least some recall on the initial amnesia test, the level of temporal organization was significantly lower in the hypnotizable subjects than in the insusceptible subjects (M = .53 vs. .84, respectively; $t(41)$ = 2.68, p < .01), yielding another independent replication of the findings of Evans and Kihlstrom (1973). After the amnesia suggestion was lifted (resulting in a significant increment in the amount of material recalled by the hypnotizable but not by the insusceptible subjects), both groups listed the items in correct temporal order (M = .88 and .90, respectively). The ability of the hypnotizable subjects to place the items in correct temporal order when specifically instructed to do so after amnesia stands in apparent contrast to their relative inability to do so when similarly instructed *during* amnesia, and to their relative failure to do so spontaneously after amnesia.

We have not yet performed a definitive study of this matter, but it appears that we must be prepared to understand the failure of hypnotizable, partially amnesic subjects to recall the events and experiences of hypnosis in correct temporal sequence once amnesia has been lifted. Clearly they are capable of doing so in response to an appropriate instruction. Moreover, postamnesia temporal sequencing is relatively high for those subjects who were completely amnesic on initial testing. We suspect that temporal organization may be an important organizational strategy only the first time that a person tries to remember a series of events such as those with which we have worked. Once this material has been retrieved from long-term memory and placed in working memory, and assuming that it is not subsequently lost from working memory, different organizational strategies—or none at all—may be employed on subsequent recall trials. Such spontaneous shifting of strategies in subjective organization is quite commonly observed in conventional free-recall experiments. Moreover, although temporal cues may be most likely to be followed during amnesia, the administration of the reversibility cue may open up other possible organizational principles. Memory traces are stored with many attributes in addition to temporal tags, and retrieval may be organized in accordance with any of them (Bower, 1967, 1970; Underwood, 1969).

A SUMMARY, SOME CONCLUSIONS, AND SOME QUESTIONS

These experiments indicate that posthypnotic amnesia involves the loss of some cues and strategies by which memory retrieval is normally structured. This is particularly the case for one of the most salient principles by which memory for a series of personal experiences is organized: the temporal relationships uniting the individual events that make up the experience as a whole. While the amnesia suggestion is in effect, subjects who have been deeply hypnotized tend not to begin at the beginning and do not follow the temporal sequence of the events as they are recounting their experiences. Their recall seems in general to be more random and haphazard with a "catch-as-catch-can" quality that is not present in the memory reports of insusceptible subjects. These latter subjects, who have not been deeply hypnotized, tend to proceed in an orderly fashion during recall, following the chronological sequence of events. This deficit in temporal organization appears to be functionally tied to posthypnotic amnesia; it is not observed if hypnotized subjects do not receive the amnesia suggestion; and although there are some things that we do not yet understand clearly enough, it appears at least that these cues are accessible to subjects after amnesia has been lifted. In general terms, moreover, temporal disorganization in retrieval shows the expected relationships with other aspects of posthypnotic amnesia such as the number of items recalled during amnesia and the recovery of additional memories after amnesia has been lifted.

These findings, in turn, are consistent with our initial hypothesis about the disruption of retrieval processes in posthypnotic amnesia—that the subject's inability to capitalize on appropriate organizational cues and strategies renders the act of remembering difficult, inefficient, and unproductive. Although for methodological reasons these studies have been carried out largely with subjects who are experiencing only partial posthypnotic amnesia, we feel confident in extending our conclusions to cover the phenomenon in general terms. Source amnesia, for example, represents an extreme instance of the loss of temporal context cues. Perhaps complete posthypnotic amnesia involves the loss of an anchor point at which to begin the process of search and retrieval, or the extreme poverty of the tags associated with memories or of the associational network uniting them.

Armed with a new theory of memory provided by laboratory investigations of normal memory processes, we feel we have made significant progress in understanding the nature of memory-retrieval processes in posthypnotic amnesia. Nevertheless, there is clearly a great deal of empirical work remaining. Several questions are raised by individual exceptions to the group trends found in our studies. Some subjects recall events in the correct temporal order, for example, but the vagueness of their initial recall and their subsequent recovery of additional memories suggest that they are nonetheless partially amnesic; in such cases, it seems likely that some other retrieval cues and strategies have been disrupted. Recently, Spanos and Bodorik (1977; Bodorik & Spanos, 1977) have shown that subjects who are partially amnesic for a word list learned during hypnosis show a disruption of the normal organization of list items by taxonomic category. They have also performed a comparable analysis of the fate of subjective organization for unrelated words, but conclusions from the study are limited by difficulties in successfully indexing superordinate units of subjective organization and other methodological matters (Spanos, Bodorik, & Shabinsky, 1977). The shift from standardized scale items to word lists as the critical material in amnesia studies entails some sacrifice in ecological validity but gives the investigator the advantage of working with material that can be easily integrated with theories of memory search and retrieval emerging from the cognitive psychology laboratory.

In addition, subjects who show clearly random temporal sequencing still, obviously, remember some events; thus we are led to inquire into organizational cues and strategies that are not disrupted. It is possible to organize material according to its emotional valence (Clemes, 1964), for example, and several studies have shown that hypnotizable and insusceptible subjects do not differ in their tendency to favor the recall of suggestions that they have successfully experienced over items that they have failed (Hilgard & Hommel, 1961; O'Connell, 1966; Pettinati & Evans, 1978). We also need to know more about the vicissitudes of organization, temporal and otherwise, after posthypnotic amnesia has been lifted.

There are other, more general questions as well. What is the mechanism by which access to memories is blocked? The amnesia suggestion may function in a manner analogous to the cue in the instructed-forgetting paradigm studied by Bjork and others (Bjork, 1972; Epstein, 1972). The concept of dissociation, as revived by Hammer (1961) and by Hilgard (1973, 1976, 1977), is clearly important in amnesia, but more work is required before this notion can be formalized. How does the reversibility signal function to restore effective retrieval? The signal may be simply another retrieval cue, more effective than temporal sequence (and other cues) because of the manner in which the critical memories have been encoded or dissociated. Nevertheless, its dramatic effects, which often approach the "involuntary remembering" portrayed by Proust in *The Remembrance of Things Past* (Salaman, 1970), make us want to examine it more closely. Finally, we want to understand more about the properties of hypnosis that make this temporary, subjectively compelling disruption of memory possible.

The disrupted-retrieval hypothesis has unresolved problems, but we think that it has fared better than other hypotheses that have been offered (Kihlstrom, 1977, 1978). We note that our account of posthypnotic amnesia is consistent with accounts that have been provided for other amnesias (including many syndromes discussed elsewhere in this volume), as well as the vagaries of memory encountered in everyday existence. We expect to learn more about posthypnotic amnesia as we continue to learn about other normal and abnormal memory processes, and we hope that the study of posthypnotic amnesia will contribute in its own way to the further development of a comprehensive theory of remembering and forgetting.

ACKNOWLEDGMENTS

Preparation of this paper and the conduct of the research reported herein were supported in part by Grants #MH 19156 and #MH 29951 from the National Institute of Mental Health, United States Public Health Service, and in part by a grant from the Institute for Experimental Psychiatry. We thank our colleagues, Heather A. Brenneman, Thomas Carothers, A. Gordon Hammer, Pamela A. Markowsky, Emily Carota Orne, Helen M. Pettinati, Martin T. Orne, William M. Waid, and Stuart K. Wilson, for their comments during the research and writing; and Paul Rozin and Thomas E. Webb for permitting us access to their classes for some of the experiments reported here.

REFERENCES

Anderson, J. R., & Bower, G. H. Recognition and retrieval processes in free recall. *Psychological Review*, 1972, *79*, 97–123.

Anderson, J. R., & Bower, G. H. A propositional theory of recognition memory. *Memory & Cognition*, 1974, *1*, 406–412.

Ashford, B., & Hammer, A. G. The role of expectancies in the occurrence of post-hypnotic amnesia. *International Journal of Clinical and Experimental Hypnosis*, 1978, *26*, 281–291.

Bentler, P. M., & Hilgard, E. R. A comparison of group and individual induction of hypnosis with self-scoring and observer-scoring. *International Journal of Clinical and Experimental Hypnosis*, 1963, *11*, 49–54.

Bergson, H. *Matter and memory*. London: Allen, 1911. (Originally published, 1896.)

Bjork, R. A. Theoretical implications of directed forgetting. In A. W. Melton & E. Martin (Eds.), *Coding processes in human memory*. Washington, D.C.: Winston, 1972.

Bodorik, H. L., & Spanos, N. P. *Suggested amnesia and disorganization of semantic components of memory in hypnotic and task-motivated subjects*. Unpublished manuscript, Carleton University, Ottawa, Ontario, Canada. 1977.

Bower, G. H. A multicomponent theory of the memory trace. In K. W. Spence & J. T. Spence (Eds.), *The psychology of learning and motivation* (Vol. 1). New York: Academic Press, 1967.

Bower, G. H. Organizational factors in memory. *Cognitive Psychology*, 1970, *1*, 18–46.

Bower, G. H. A selective review of organizational factors in memory. In E. Tulving & W. Donaldson (Eds.), *Organization of memory*. New York: Academic Press, 1972.

Bowers, K. S. *Hypnosis for the seriously curious*. Monterey, Calif.: Brooks/Cole, 1976.

Brown, R., & McNeil, D. The "tip of the tongue" phenomenon. *Journal of Verbal Learning and Verbal Behavior*, 1966, *5*, 325–337.

Clemes, S. Repression and hypnotic amnesia. *Journal of Abnormal and Social Psychology*, 1964, *69*, 62–69.

Cooper L. M. Hypnotic amnesia. In E. Fromm & R. E. Shor (Eds.), *Hypnosis: Research developments and perspectives*. Chicago: Aldine-Atherton, 1972.

Crawford, H. J. The effects of marijuana on primary suggestibility (Doctoral dissertation, University of California at Davis, 1974). *Dissertation Abstracts International*, 1974, *35* (University Microfilms No. 74-29298).

Epstein, W. Mechanisms of directed forgetting. In G. H. Bower (Ed.), *The psychology of learning and motivation: Advances in research and theory* (Vol. 6). New York: Academic Press, 1972.

Evans, F. J. Suggestibility in the normal waking state. *Psychological Bulletin*, 1967, *67*, 114–129.

Evans, F. J. Recent trends in experimental hypnosis. *Behavioral Science*, 1968, *13*, 477–487.

Evans, F. J. *Contextual forgetting: A study of source amnesia.* Paper presented at the 42nd annual meeting of the Eastern Psychological Association, New York, April 1971.

Evans, F. J., & Kihlstrom, J. F. Posthypnotic amnesia as disrupted retrieval. *Journal of Abnormal Psychology*, 1973, *82*, 317–323.

Evans, F. J., & Kihlstrom, J. F. *Contextual and temporal disorganization during posthypnotic amnesia.* Paper presented at the 83rd annual meeting of the American Psychological Association Chicago, September 1975.

Evans, F. J., Kihlstrom, J. F., & Orne, E. C. Quantifying subjective reports during posthypnotic amnesia. *Proceedings of the 81st Annual Convention of the American Psychological Association*, 1973, *8*, 1077–1078.

Evans, F. J., & Mitchell, W. A. *Interaction between neighbors during group hypnosis: The independence of social influence and hypnotizability.* Paper presented at the 29th annual meeting of the Society for Clinical and Experimental Hypnosis, Los Angeles, October 1977.

Evans, F. J., Orne, E. C., & Markowsky, P. A. *Punctuality and hypnotizability.* Paper presented at the 48th annual meeting of the Eastern Psychological Association, Boston, April 1977.

Evans, F. J., & Thorn, W. A. F. Two types of posthypnotic amnesia: Recall amnesia and source amnesia. *International Journal of Clinical and Experimental Hypnosis*, 1966, *14*, 162–179.

Graham, K. R., & Patton, A. Retroactive inhibition, hypnosis, and hypnotic amnesia. *International Journal of Clinical and Experimental Hypnosis*, 1968, *16*, 68–74.

Hammer, A. G. Reflections on the study of hypnosis. *Australian Journal of Psychology*, 1961, *13*, 3–22.

Hilgard, E. R. Hypnosis. *Annual Review of Psychology*, 1965, *16*, 157–180. (a)

Hilgard, E. R. *Hypnotic susceptibility.* New York: Harcourt, Brace, & World, 1965. (b)

Hilgard, E. R. Posthypnotic amnesia: Experiments and theory. *International Journal of Clinical and Experimental Hypnosis*, 1966, *14*, 104–111.

Hilgard, E. R. A neodissociation interpretation of pain reduction in hypnosis. *Psychological Review*, 1973, *80*, 396–411.

Hilgard, E. R. Hypnosis. *Annual Review of Psychology*, 1975, *26*, 19–44.

Hilgard, E. R. Neodissociation theory of multiple cognitive control systems. In G. E. Schwartz & D. Shapiro (Eds.), *Consciousness and self-regulation* (Vol. 1). New York: Plenum Press, 1976.

Hilgard, E. R. *Divided consciousness: Multiple controls in human thought and action.* New York: Wiley-Interscience, 1977.

Hilgard, E. R., & Cooper, L. M. Spontaneous and suggested posthypnotic amnesia. *International Journal of Clinical and Experimental Hypnosis*, 1965, *13*, 261–273.

Hilgard, E. R., & Hommel, L. S. Selective amnesia for events within hypnosis in relation to repression. *Journal of Personality*, 1961, *29*, 205–216.

Hilgard, J. R. *Personality and hypnosis: A study of imaginative involvements.* Chicago: University of Chicago Press, 1970.

Hull, C. L. *Hypnosis and suggestibility: An experimental approach.* New York: Appleton-Century-Crofts, 1933.

Kihlstrom, J. F. The effects of organization and motivation on recall during posthypnotic amnesia (Doctoral dissertation, University of Pennsylvania, 1975). *Dissertation Abstracts International*, 1975, *36*, 2473B–2474B. (University Microfilms No. 75-24082)

Kihlstrom, J. F. Models of posthypnotic amnesia. In W. E. Edmonston (Ed.), *Conceptual and investigative approaches to hypnosis and hypnotic phenomena. Annals of the New York Academy of Sciences*, 1977, *296*, 284–301.

Kihlstrom, J. F. Context and cognition in posthypnotic amnesia. *International Journal of Clinical and Experimental Hypnosis*, 1978, *26*, 246–267.

Kihlstrom, J. F., & Evans, F. J. *Forgetting to count reversibility: What constitutes posthypnotic amnesia.* Paper presented to the 25th annual meeting of the Society for Clinical and Experimental Hypnosis, Newport Beach, California, December 1973.

Kihlstrom, J. F., & Evans, F. J. *Hypnotizability, amnesia, and waking memory for experience.* Paper presented to the 27th annual meeting of the Society for Clinical and Experimental Hypnosis, Chicago, October 1975.

Kihlstrom, J. F., & Evans, F. J. Recovery of memory after posthypnotic amnesia. *Journal of Abnormal Psychology,* 1976, *85,* 564–569.

Kihlstrom, J. F., & Evans, F. J. Residual effect of suggestions for posthypnotic amnesia: A re-examination. *Journal of Abnormal Psychology,* 1977, *86,* 327–333.

Kihlstrom, J. F., & Evans, F. J. Generic recall during posthypnotic amnesia. *Bulletin of the Psychonomic Society,* 1978, *12,* 57–60.

Kihlstrom, J. F., Evans, F. J., Orne, E. C., & Orne, M. T. *Attempting to breach posthypnotic amnesia.* Manuscript in preparation.

Kihlstrom, J. F., & Shor, R. E. Recall and recognition during posthypnotic amnesia. *International Journal of Clinical and Experimental Hypnosis,* 1978, *26,* 330–335.

Kihlstrom, J. F., & Twersky, M. Relationship of posthypnotic amnesia to aspects of waking memory. *International Journal of Clinical and Experimental Hypnosis,* 1978, *26,* 292–306.

Lavoie, G., Sabourin, M., & Langlois, J. Hypnotic susceptibility, amnesia, and IQ in chronic schizophrenia. *International Journal of Clinical and Experimental Hypnosis,* 1973, *21,* 157–167.

Lieberman, J., Brisson, A., & Lavoie, G. Suggested amnesia and order of recall as a function of hypnotic susceptibility and learning conditions in chronic schizophrenic patients. *International Journal of Clinical and Experimental Hypnosis,* 1978, *26,* 268—280.

Miller, G. A., & Frick, F. C. Statistical behavioristics and sequences of responses. *Psychological Review,* 1949, *56,* 311–324.

Nace, E. P., Orne, M. T., & Hammer, A. G. Posthypnotic amnesia as an active psychic process: The reversibility of amnesia. *Archives of General Psychiatry,* 1974, *31,* 257–260.

Neisser, U. *Cognitive psychology.* Englewood Cliffs, N.J.: Prentice-Hall, 1967.

O'Connell, D. N. An experimental comparison of hypnotic depth measured by self-ratings and by an objective scale. *International Journal of Clinical and Experimental Hypnosis,* 1964, *12,* 34–46.

O'Connell, D. N. Selective recall of hypnotic susceptibility items: Evidence for repression or enhancement? *International Journal of Clinical and Experimental Hypnosis,* 1966, *14,* 150–161.

Orne, M. T. On the social psychology of the psychological experiment: With particular reference to demand characteristics and their implications. *American Psychologist,* 1962, *17,* 776–783.

Orne, M. T. Hypnosis, motivation, and compliance. *American Journal of Psychiatry,* 1966, *122,* 721–726. (a)

Orne, M. T. On the mechanisms of posthypnotic amnesia. *International Journal of Clinical and Experimental Hypnosis,* 1966, *14,* 121–134. (b)

Orne, M. T. Hypnosis, motivation, and the ecological validity of the psychological experiment. In W. J. Arnold & M. M. Page (Eds.), *Nebraska symposium on motivation.* Lincoln, Nebraska: University of Nebraska Press, 1970.

Orne, M. T. On the simulating subject as a quasi-control group in hypnosis research: What, why, and how. In E. From & R. E. Shor (Eds.), *Hypnosis: Research developments and perspectives.* Chicago: Aldine-Atherton, 1972.

Pettinati, H. M., and Evans, F. J. Posthypnotic amnesia: Evaluation of selective recall of successful experiences. *International Journal of Clinical and Experimental Hypnosis,* 1978, *26,* 317–329.

Roediger, H. L., & Crowder, R. G. A serial-position effect in the recall of United States presidents. *Bulletin of the Psychonomic Society,* 1976, *8,* 277–278.

Salaman, E. *A collection of moments: A study of involuntary memories.* New York: St Martin's Press, 1974.

Schwartz, W. S. Time and context during hypnotic involvement. *International Journal of Clinical and Experimental Hypnosis,* 1978, *26,* 307–316.

Shor, R. E., & Orne, E. C. *Harvard Group Scale of Hypnotic Susceptibility, Form A.* Palo Alto, Calif.: Consulting Psychologists Press, 1962.

Shor, R. E., & Orne, E. C. Norms on the Harvard Group Scale of Hypnotic Susceptibility, Form A. *International Journal of Clinical and Experimental Hypnosis*, 1963, *11*, 39–47.

Shor, R. E., Orne, M. T., & O'Connell, D. N. Psychological correlates of plateau hypnotizability in a special volunteer sample. *Journal of Personality and Social Psychology*, 1966, *3*, 80–95.

Spanos, N. P., & Bodorik, H. L. Suggested amnesia and disorganized recall in hypnotic and task-motivated subjects. *Journal of Abnormal Psychology*, 1977, *86*, 295–305.

Spanos, N. P., Bodorik, H. L., & Shabinsky, M. A. *Amnesia, subjective organization, and learning for high and low imagery nouns in hypnotic and task-motivated subjects.* Unpublished manuscript, Carleton University, Ottawa, Ontario, Canada, 1977.

Tellegen, A., & Atkinson, G. Openness to absorbing and self-altering experiences ("absorption") a trait related to hypnotic susceptibility. *Journal of Abnormal Psychology*, 1974, *83*, 268–277.

Thorn, W. A. F. *A study of the correlates of dissociation as measured by hypnotic amnesia.* Unpublished bachelor's (honors) thesis, University of Sidney, 1960.

Tulving, E. Subjective organization in free recall of "unrelated" words. *Psychological Review*, 1962, *69*, 344–354.

Tulving, E. Episodic and semantic memory. In E. Tulving & W. Donaldson (Eds.), *Organization of memory*. New York: Academic Press, 1972.

Tulving, E., & Pearlstone, Z. Availability and accessibility of information in memory for words. *Journal of Verbal Learning and Verbal Behavior*, 1966, *5*, 381–391.

Tulving, E., & Thomson, D. M. Encoding specificity and retrieval processes in episodic memory. *Psychological Review*, 1973, *80*, 352–373.

Underwood, B. J. Attributes of memory. *Psychological Review*, 1969, *76*, 559–573.

Watkins, M. J., & Tulving, E. Episodic memory: When recognition fails. *Journal of Experimental Psychology: General*, 1975, *104*, 5–29.

Weitzenhoffer, A. M., & Hilgard, E. R. *Stanford Hypnotic Susceptibility Scale, Forms A and B.* Palo Alto, Calif.: Consulting Psychologists Press, 1959.

Weitzenhoffer, A. M., & Hilgard, E. R. *Stanford Hypnotic Susceptibility Scale, Form C.* Palo Alto, Calif.: Consulting Psychologists Press, 1962.

Weitzenhoffer, A. M., & Hilgard, E. R. *Revised Stanford Profile Scales of Hypnotic Susceptibility, Forms I and II.* Palo Alto, Calif.: Consulting Psychologists Press, 1967.

Williamsen, J. A., Johnson, H. J., & Eriksen, C. W. Some characteristics of posthypnotic amnesia. *Journal of Abnormal Psychology*, 1965, *70*, 123–131.

7 Disruption of Memory Functions Associated with General Anesthetics

Nilly Adam
Technion, School of Medicine

As part of the efforts to analyze memory functions into more basic processes, various cases of memory pathology have been examined in great detail. Behind this line of investigation usually lies the hope that under abnormal conditions, the dissection of a given cognitive function into its underlying components may be easier and that different aspects of a function that appear correlated in the normal individual may be found to be dissociated in pathological cases. A good example is the extensive investigation of unilateral and bilateral hippocampal destruction in man by Milner and her associates (for review, see Milner, 1970), which showed, among other findings, dissociation between verbal and nonverbal memory functions. Another relevant example is the analysis of memory recovery following closed-head traumas (Russell, 1971). The fact that retrieval of familiar memories covering a period of up to several years prior to the trauma may be impossible for a while, and then recovers, presents puzzling questions to consolidation theories.

Other cognitive functions besides memory processes are also impaired as a result of the effects on brain function of structural damage or drug administration. Consequently, the behavioral methodology in memory pathology research should permit memory effects to be differentiated from other psychological effects, among which disturbed attention and perception are of primary importance.

In the present paper we present an investigation of the use of general anesthetics to induce temporary and reversible disturbances in memory functions. The usefulness of these studies depends on the careful choice of behavioral methods, which should derive from a theoretical framework of memory functions and enable distinction among various aspects of memory processes.

This line of investigation has, of course, its practical side as well, e.g., delineating the time course and type of memory disturbance following clinical use of general anesthetics. Postoperative patients occasionally complain of a subjective feeling of deterioration in mental functioning for up to several weeks following surgery. These effects may not necessarily be due to the anesthetic drugs but to the body's reaction to the surgical procedure itself. In any case, we have very little data on cognitive functioning following surgical doses of anesthetics, and most of the available data concern personality rather than cognitive functions (Cronin, Redfern, & Utting, 1973; James, 1969). Head traumas, which have a diffuse effect on brain tissue, result in temporary deficits in learning that may last between a few hours to a few months. General anesthetics may produce similar effects, reinforcing our interest in the question of postanesthesia cognitive deficits.

Another important question is the possibility of cognitive deficits resulting from chronic exposure to trace concentrations of anesthetics. Operating room personnel who work in inadequately ventilated rooms are constantly exposed to this hazard. This possibility has recently aroused worldwide concern due to a relatively high incidence of various diseases in anesthesiologists. Moreover, recent studies on chronic effects of general anesthetics in rats (Quimby, Aschkenase, Bowman, Katz, & Chang, 1974; Quimby, Katz, & Bowman, 1975) have shown permanent morphological changes in nerve cells and permanent learning deficits in developing rats. Comparable data on humans are not yet available.

The investigation of the neurophysiological mechanisms of memory may benefit from the knowledge acquired on the association between the neurophysiological effects and the memory effects of general anesthetics. When we first started using anesthetics in our laboratory, we hoped to find differential effects of various general anesthetics that would be correlated with their differential neurophysiological effects. Unfortunately, although a clear distinction may be made between various general anesthetics on the neurophysiological level (Clark & Rosner, 1973; Rosner & Clark, 1973), most inhalation anesthetics studied to date produce very similar effects on memory functions. Thus, obviously, some neural action common to all anesthetics underlies the anesthetic effect on memory functions.

Over the years there have appeared a number of reports on patients who could recall sentences spoken while they were deeply anesthetized and operated upon. Trustman, Dubrovsky, and Titley (1977) have recently reviewed these reports, including the failures to observe this effect, and concluded that in all such reported cases there are important methodological deficiencies. In many of the cases, for example, there could have been a temporary decrease in the depth of anesthesia. Such a situation may well occur in the modern operating room, where the use of muscle relaxants permits surgery to be performed with lower drug concentrations than would be possible without such relaxants.

A clear distinction should be made between anesthesia and anesthetic influence. Anesthesia involves lack of consciousness. Effects of anesthesia on memory imply either effects on material learned prior to drug administration or disturbances in postanesthesia memory. In contrast, anesthetic influence may be studied using varying low concentrations of anesthetic and examining the subject's performance on memory tests during drug inhalation itself. Since the anesthetic effects are dose dependent, slight changes in drug concentration may result in behavior changes that will obscure the expected effects. For this reason, most of the studies reported here were performed with controlled gas concentrations. In the present chapter we review the effects of low controlled concentrations of various general anesthetics in clinical use on such memory processes as short-term span, search in short-term memory, retrieval of verbal and nonverbal information from long-term memory, and probability learning.

EFFECTS OF GENERAL ANESTHETICS ON
SHORT-TERM MEMORY

There is no general concensus yet as to the precise function of short-term memory (STM) storage. Many view this storage as a necessary step before registration in long-term memory (LTM), whereas some maintain that short-term memory has nothing to do with long-term memory registration but serves to aid speech perception (Warrington & Weiskrantz, 1973).

Avoiding these issues, the digit span is generally accepted as a measure of STM capacity. Steinberg (1954) showed negligible effects on the digit span during inhalation of 30% nitrous oxide (N_2O). Such concentrations of N_2O are about half the minimal concentration producing loss of consciousness. Much smaller concentrations of N_2O, such as exist in the operating room (typically 500 ppm), did produce a significant decrement in the combined index of both forward and backward digit span, as reported by Bruce, Bach, and Arbit (1974). They further reported similar effects with other general anesthetics—halothane and enflurane and their combination with N_2O (Bruce & Bach, 1975, 1976). Unfortunately, these reports do not specify the results separately for forward and backward span. From our experience, the main effect would be found for backward span, with negligible effects on the forward span. Deterioration in backward recall of digit series could reflect other anesthetic effects rather than direct effects on memory functions. We observed only very slight decrement in the digit span (not reaching statistical significance) with general anesthetics including diethyl ether, methoxyflurane, and enflurane in higher concentrations than those used by Bruce (Adam, 1973).

Digit span, word span, etc., may not be the best ways to test anesthetic effects on short-term capacities. More information can be obtained through the use of more complicated tasks such as search paradigms. We recently compared the effects of enflurane on search in short-term memory for three types of stimulus material using the Sternberg (1969) paradigm (Adam & Collins, 1977). Basically, the subject sees a series of stimuli (memory set) followed by a test stimulus to which he has to give a choice motor response—"yes" if the test stimulus was contained in the memory set and "no" if not. The size of the series determines the amount of search. Span in this task may be determined by the number of errors; but this paradigm also permits the assessment of search time in short-term memory. The data thus collected (plotted as reaction time as a function of memory set size) usually yield linear functions, the slopes of which give search time per item. The intercept is thought to be a measure of stimulus perception time plus decision time plus response production, an analysis that has received recent experimental support (Chiang & Atkinson, 1976).

We tested three types of stimulus material: digits, words, and common familiar pictures. All were presented visually, 20 times for each memory set size, with stimulus duration of 300 msec, interstimulus duration of 150 msec, and intertrial interval of 4 sec. Control and anesthetic conditions were run on separate days 1 week apart to prevent excessive fatigue. Figure 7.1 presents the linear functions best describing the average data. Digits and words gave similar linear search functions in control. Low concentrations of enflurane produced a significant elevation in the intercept of the function but no change in the slope for both digits and words. In other words, the anesthetic affected mainly the component reflecting stimulus reception time, stimulus evaluation time, and the execution of the motor response.

The same general conclusion pertains to the pictorial material. In contrast to verbal material, the search control functions for the pictures were not linear. Rather the slope approximated zero; or in other words, the functions indicated parallel rather than serial search. This confirms previous reports with nonverbal pictorial material (Bentin, & Adam, 1977; Cohen, 1973). The anesthetic increased the intercept markedly but had no effect on the slope, as may be seen in Fig. 7.1.

These data imply that the short-term memory functions tapped by the search task are not affected by the anesthetic. Rather, the drugged individual needs more time to perceive the stimulus, to evaluate its meaning in context of the task being performed, to choose the appropriate motor response, and to execute it.

On the other hand, measures of memory span in the same search task did show some deterioration of performance under the anesthetic influence. If the set size for which there was a sharp increase in error percentage may be taken as an indicator of short-term span, then the anesthetic decreased the span from an average of 8 in control to 7 in anesthetic condition for digits, from 8 to 6 for words, and from 7 to 6 for pictures, respectively.

Should this be taken to indicate drug effect on memory span but not on search speed in short-term memory? We tend to interpret the results differently. The observed effects on span do not necessarily indicate direct anesthetic effect on

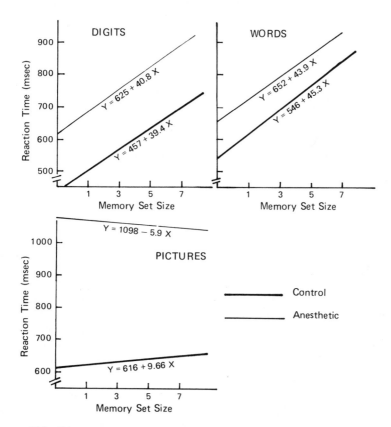

FIG. 7.1. Effects of general anesthetics on search functions in short-term memory for three types of stimulus material.

basic short-term processes such as the decay rate of the short-term trace, but they may be the result of short lapses in attention for long series and increased stimulus evaluation time. There are no investigations yet assessing directly the decay rate of items in short-term memory. Only such data will enable us to draw more definite conclusions. Available data on performance of brain-damaged patients on various short-term tasks indicate that only right-hemisphere parietal cortical lesions yield a faster decay rate of the short-term trace and then only with visual material (Butters, Samuels, Goodglass, & Brody, 1970). Methodological difficulties cast doubt on even this finding, indicating that a wide variety of cortical lesions do not affect the decay rate of short-term traces. The same will probably be found for general anesthetics.

Notice that stimulus presentation time in the search task was 300 msec, long enough to permit verbalization of pictorial material. Despite this, the search functions for the pictorial stimuli were different from those obtained for verbal material. We tried to use shorter presentation time (100 msec). This was possible in control testing but not during anesthetic inhalation, where brief stimulus presentation times yielded random performance, rendering it impossible to evaluate drug effects. The subject's inability to perform with fast presentation rates agrees well with our contention that general anesthetics mainly increase the time required for stimulus processing and execution of response in STM tasks. This observation also fits the reports of Bruce and Bach (1975, 1976) and Bruce, Bach, and Arbit (1974) that trace concentrations of halothane, N2O, and enflurane had a pronounced effect on performance of an audiovisual task. This task required detection of change in either visual or auditory stimulus presented at fast rates.

Behavioral methods do not adequately separate the cognitive elements of the search function. In contrast, average evoked potentials (or, as preferred by some, event-related potentials) have been shown to differentiate well among stages in information processing (Kutas, McCarthy, & Donchin, 1977). We therefore obtained event-related potentials (ERPs) during performance of the digit-search task described earlier (Adam & Collins, in press). More specifically, we were interested in the electrical changes preceding and following the presentation of the test stimulus that initiates the search process. The trigger stimulus for the averaging process was a warning stimulus preceding the test digit by 800 msec. The fixed time between the warning and test stimuli allowed the development of the contingent negative variation (CNV), the slowly developing negativity that anticipates imperative stimulus and is commonly thought of as reflecting preparatory processes. The subject saw series of 1, 3, 5, 7, 9, and 11 digits, and for each memory set size he saw about 90 different series produced randomly by a computer that controlled the whole experimental procedure. Stimulus parameters were identical to those used in the studies already described.

Figure 7.2 presents a typical set of waveforms obtained for a single subject for control testing, and Fig. 7.3 shows the effects of low concentrations of enflurane on the ERP waveform in six subjects. The main effects to be noticed are an increase of 33 msec on the average in latency of the early components (covering the first 250 msec), flattening of late components (latency over 260 msec), marked increase in latency and variance of the reaction time, and marked decrease in amplitude of prestimulus CNV.

There is ample evidence indicating that the early components reflect primary sensory processing (Simson, Vaughan, & Ritter, 1976) and that the later components reflect stimulus evaluation (Kutas et al., 1977). The flattening of late components does not necessarily imply the disappearance of electrical responses of late latency, since the averaging process would tend to flatten any component with a marked variable latency. Such an effect of the averaging procedure in our case is likely in view of the observed high variance of the reaction time under anesthetic influence and the known relation between reaction time and the late components' latency (Kutas et al., 1977). The only way to assess the late positive component that best reflects stimulus evaluation would be to analyze the

CONTROL ERPs FOR SET SIZES 1–11

C_Z–LINKED EARS

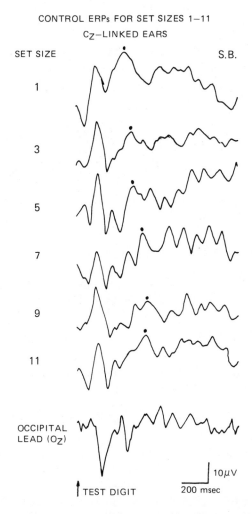

FIG. 7.2. Typical set of event-related potentials for a search task in short-term memory. The ERP following the test digit reflects the search process. The dot represents the peak of the late positive component termed P300. Latency of P300 increases linearly with memory set size up to 7 items and parallels the reaction-time function. Positivity is up.

records from single trials, thus avoiding averaging. This analysis is in progress at present. Preliminary results show that the late positivity may be measured in single trials although there is some decrease in amplitude during anesthetic inhalation, and that there is a high correlation between reaction time and late positivity latency. This strengthens the argument that increased stimulus evaluation time is the main contributor to the overt performance deficit in short-term

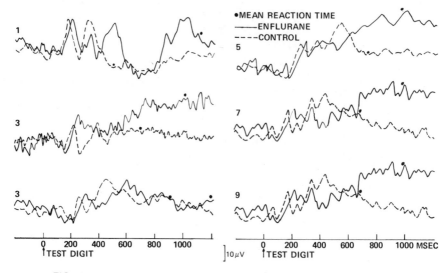

FIG. 7.3. Effects of enflurane on the ERP waveform evoked by a search task in short-term memory (see legend to Fig. 7.2.). Latency of early components is increased by the anesthetic. Numbers to the left of each trace indicate memory set size. Data represent six different subjects. Positivity is up.

memory tasks. We suggest that the data available today do not support specific anesthetic effects on basic short-term memory processes.

We further tested the effects of general anesthetics on STM with yet another nonverbal task—reproduction of sequences of spatially distributed lights. The display consisted of 10 lighted switches, 9 arranged in a circle and 1 in the center. The subject saw in each trial a sequence of lights, each turned on for 300 msec, followed immediately by the next light in the series. The subject had to repeat the sequence in exactly the same order as presented by pressing down the same switches. A 5-sec delay was introduced between presentation and response to assure fading out of afterimages. The testing procedure involved gradual increase in sequence length with two different series for each length. Any given sequence was repeated until the subject answered correctly twice consecutively but no more than eight times. This deviation from classical procedure for span measurement permitted assessment of learning.

In contrast to the slight effect on span observed with verbal and pictorial material, low concentrations of enflurane between .1% and .28% end-tidal had a marked effect on the span measured by this task. With most subjects, the span decreased by as much as three to four items during gas inhalation. The possibility that the anesthetic did not affect verbal STM but only nonverbal STM cannot be accepted; STM for pictorial material was not severely affected by the gas. Rather, independent evidence (Carmon, 1977) suggests that this specific task depends heavily on left-hemispheric functioning and may differ in this respect from other short-term span tasks we used. In later sections this interpretation is further developed.

EFFECTS OF GENERAL ANESTHETICS ON LONG-TERM MEMORY

Anesthetic gases affect the electrical activity of the whole brain. Although some sites are more affected than others, the reversible "lesion" produced by the anesthetic is shown to be diffuse by the EEG (Clark & Rosner, 1973; Rosner & Clark, 1973). Most diffuse brain lesions produce some LTM impairment, e.g., infectious diseases, closed-head traumas, and senility. Thus, anesthetic effects on long-term processes may be expected. Such effects could result from any number of reasons, such as impaired consolidation, impaired retrieval, greater susceptibility to interference, or defective encoding. Unfortunately, many of the existing reports fail to discriminate between the possible basic processes affected. As is often the case in science, the unknown is greater than the known, but we try to present a coherent picture of the current state of knowledge.

Effects on Old Material

The possible effects of low concentrations of general anesthetics on retrieval of familiar material were first investigated by Marshall (1937), who tested recall of known events during inhalation of subanesthetic concentrations of nitrous oxide. He reported no effects. Osborn, Bunker, Cooper, Frank, and Hilgard (1967) arrived at similar conclusions, although they used barbiturates, which differ from inhalation anesthetics in neurophysiological effects.

Recall of major events from the subject's life history may not be the ideal test of anesthetic effects on material already in LTM; more sensitive tests may be needed to reveal the effects. We preferred to teach the subject a verbal list prior to drug administration and observe his retention during gas inhalation (Adam, 1973). No impairment was observed. This was true for all inhalation anesthetics we tested, which included, enflurane, halothane, methoxyflurane, nitrous oxide, diethyl ether, and isoflurane.

In subsequent studies (Adam, 1976), we kept on looking for other indices of retrieval from LTM that might show some deficit. One such task was search in LTM. More specifically, the subject had to generate as fast as possible words beginning with a letter specified by the examiner, e.g., all words beginning with *b*. Such search is obviously guided by verbal cues. To test the possibility of material-specific effects, a task requiring visually guided search was also given, requiring the subject to name all countries in a specified continent, not according to alphabetical order, but rather by visually scanning the map from memory.

The results were clear-cut. The rate of word generation was drastically reduced by the anesthetic. When the cumulative number of words is plotted as a function of time in log—log coordinates, the functions obtained are linear, as may be seen in Fig. 7.4. The anesthetic reduced the slope from an average of .63 to .42. No such effect was found for visually guided search. Obviously, retrieval from LTM cannot be viewed as a unitary process. The nature of the cues required for the search (verbal, visual, acoustic nonverbal) determines the severity of the anesthetic effect.

Although these results could reflect various deficits, other data suggest that cue generation may be the affected process. In another task the subject heard a dictionary definition and had to provide the associated word as fast as possible. The experimenter helped, if needed, by providing cues (first letter of the

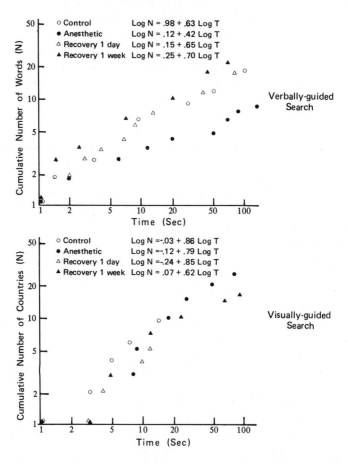

FIG. 7.4. Verbally guided and visually guided search functions in long-term memory. Data are plotted in log—log coordinates. Best fitting functions are given at the top of each graph.

searched-after word, second letter, etc.). The anesthetic increased significantly the number of cues the subject needed, more so for rare words than for high-frequency words in the language, as may be expected.

Evidently, retrieval of verbal information requires the use of verbal cues, which are generated by the person engaged in retrieval and which obviously require some active process on his part. The anesthetic affects this process. This deficit does not manifest itself in easy retrieval tasks; only very sensitive tests will reveal it. This deficit probably underlies the subjective feelings of some postoperative patients complaining of transient deterioration in verbal capabilities. Interestingly, the complaints come most often from individuals actively engaged in activities such as preparation of speeches and other sophisticated verbal communication. This pattern is consistent with our observations.

Effects on Acquisition and Retention of New Material

Acquisition of new material is not a good paradigm to study memory deficits induced by anesthetic, for the very obvious reason that knowing that acquisition is slower gives no information about the underlying affected processes. Nevertheless, acquisition has been the favorite paradigm in most reports. Inhalation anesthetics have been shown to slow down acquisition of lists of nonsense syllables (Parkhouse, Henrie, Duncan, & Rome, 1960; Steinberg & Summerfield, 1957) and acquisition of pictorial material (Parkhouse et al., 1960). These observations do not provide any insight into the mechanisms involved. For all we know, attentional factors may account for the observed deficits.

Retention of well-learned material is more informative. In our studies, therefore, we allowed as much time as needed for learning and assured the achievement of perfect learning as measured by immediate retention tests. To avoid interference effects, we chose to present just one verbal, visual, or acoustic list during anesthetic inhalation and to test recognition as a function of time from presentation. Recognition was tested again about 1 hour following termination of drug inhalation to assess recovery effects. We devote our discussion to three aspects of the results.

First, the effects were dose dependent. Since there were large individual differences with respect to effective doses, we prefer not to associate a particular concentration with particular specific deficits but will rather use the terms *lower* or *higher*, where *higher* refers to a concentration close to losing consciousness for any given subject and *lower* refers to about half of the higher dose.

Lower concentrations produced transient retrieval deficits for verbal material and no effects on either nonverbal visual or nonverbal auditory material (e.g., pictures and tunes; Adam, 1973). We refer to the retrieval deficit as transient, due to the recovery effect observed 1 hour after termination of inhalation. It is important to notice that by recovery, we do not mean simply that after recovery from drug effects new material could be learned and retrieved as efficiently as before drug administration; rather we mean that after recovery, the list learned during drug inhalation was recognized better than during drug inhalation. Similar recovery effects were observed 1 week after the learning of a verbal list presented following 6 hours of deep anesthesia (see Fig. 7.5). The use of recognition scores rather than recall render the transient retrieval deficit even more striking. We later return to the exact nature of the deficit.

Higher concentrations totally prevented retention of verbal material beyond immediate testing. This effect is also seen in Fig. 7.5. We do not have data on the fate of nonverbal visual material at higher concentrations. Recognition of nonverbal auditory material (tunes) was only slightly affected and only transiently. As a rule, subjects showing this pattern of results also had complete amnesia for all events occurring while at that anesthetic level. Thus, the presence of posttreatment amnesia provided an additional indicator of anesthetic depth.

As is often the case, the results are obvious but not the interpretation. The most attractive possibility is in terms of a consolidation deficit similar to that sometimes claimed in animal studies of retrograde amnesia induced by electroconvulsive shock. However, in view of the abundance of reports in the last few years demonstrating that most ECS effects are transient (e.g., Lewis, 1969), the consolidation explanation has no real support. The other alternative interpretation is, obviously, permanent inaccessibility of traces. We favor this explanation and return to this issue after presentation of the rest of the data.

The second aspect of the results we wish to discuss is the specific nature of the retrieval deficit at lower concentrations. Decreased retention during anesthetic influence may be the result of defective trace consolidation, of fast decay of

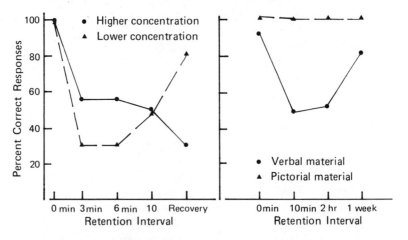

FIG. 7.5.   The graph to the left demonstrates the difference in retention pattern between lower and higher anesthetic concentrations for verbal material only. The graph to the right demonstrates material-dependent effects for lower concentrations only.

consolidated long-term traces, or of inaccessible traces. Fortunately, the presence of the recovery effect, i.e., the improved recognition of the anesthetic list after recovery from the drug effects, rules out consolidation deficit and fast decay as explanations, with the possibility of temporary inaccessible traces remaining as the plausible interpretation.

Temporarily inaccessible traces are a well-known phenomenon in memory pathology, e.g., transient retrograde amnesia following brain traumas. These examples, however, refer to old material; the transient retrieval associated with anesthetics involves new material, that is, anterograde amnesia. Are these observations related? Retrograde amnesia in memory pathology is usually accompanied by anterograde amnesia, involving impaired retention of new material, which may improve as in head traumas or be permanent as in bilateral hippocampal lesions. Although no one has yet shown recovery effects in these syndromes that are similar to those observed with the lower concentrations of general anesthetics, this may turn out to be the case at least for less severe cases. This possibility has not been tested carefully. Interestingly, Warrington and Weiskrantz (1970) have suggested that the permanent retention deficit for new material observed after hippocampal lesions should be interpreted in terms of retrieval deficit rather than storage deficit, i.e., permanently inaccessible traces. We have suggested that the memorial effects of higher concentrations of anesthetics may best be understood as permanent inaccessibility to traces. Such an interpretation would make more sense in terms of dose-dependent effects; as drug concentration increases, retrieval deficits become more severe, until no more retrieval is possible. Otherwise, one would have to conclude that low concentrations impair retrieval whereas higher doses impair storage in LTM.

Why is the trace less accessible during anesthetic inhalation? Is it due to ineffective encoding? In one of our studies we used a forced-choice recognition paradigm where the subject's error could be either an acoustically similar verbal item, a semantically similar verbal item, or an unrelated item (Adam, 1973). Subjects under anesthetic influence chose acoustically similar items much more frequently than is found in undrugged man. This indicates a decreased level of semantic coding and reminds us that a higher frequency of acoustic confusions has been observed in younger children (Felzen & Anisfeld, 1970). Thus, anesthetics impair retrieval because the encoding processes are not consistent with efficient retrieval. Possibly, anesthetics first impair functions maturing later in development. Whether this generalizes to other functions as well remains to be seen.

The third aspect of the results that merits discussion is the modality-specfic effect. Retention of common pictures and tunes is not impaired at the same anesthetic level at which retrieval deficits are observed for word lists. Is it possible that the observed effect is simply a function of task difficulty? It is an almost impossible task to deal with this argument, since even if we had some independent criterion of difficulty for normals, what may be easier for the normal may be more difficult to the drugged subject. The finding that retention of faces is also unaffected by anesthetic inhalation (James, 1969) adds some support to the modality-specific interpretation. In any case, the verbal task we used was so easy for normals (six-word lists) that we tend to attribute the results to material-specific effects rather than to task difficulty. Furthermore, the observation by Milner and her associates (Milner, 1970) that unilateral hippocampal lesion in man produces material-specific memory deficits that dissociate between verbal and nonverbal memory gives further support to our interpretation.

The verbal versus nonverbal dichotomy used to be adequate in describing hemispheric specialization. Such a dichotomy would encompass some material-specific anesthetic effects and fit well with the suggestion that anesthetics first impair later developing functions phylogenetically and ontogenetically, i.e., verbal functions associated with the left hemisphere. Recently, however, a shift has occurred toward a different dichotomy of sequential (analytical) versus parallel (holistic) modes of processing as best describing left- versus right-hemispheric differences. Are our data consistent with this latter dichotomy as well? It is not yet clear what memory processes are related to the sequential mode of processing and whether there is hemispheric specialization at all with regard to memory processes such as trace consolidation and trace decay. Therefore, the suggestion that general anesthetics first attack left-hemisphere functions would have to rely on independent cognitive tasks. Two pieces of data suggest that this may be the case:

1. The reproduction of light sequences discussed in the section on STM has been found to be very sensitive to left-hemisphere deficits in right-handed individuals (Carmon, 1977). General anesthetics severely affect performance in this task.

2. Identification and retention of faces is known as a good test of right-hemisphere functions in brain-damaged patients. General anesthetics do not affect face recognition (James, 1969).

Obviously, if this distinction is valid, our data would imply that all STM functions including what Sternberg (1969) termed sequential exhaustive search, of both verbal and nonverbal material, would show right-hemisphere preference or at least equal performance of both hemispheres. So would LTM functions such as storage and search of nonverbal material. The only functions that may show left-hemisphere preference would be search in LTM for semantic material and semantic encoding processes that are essential for retrieval of verbal material.

Why would search in STM for verbal material have a different hemispheric representation than search in LTM for verbal material? This is not a contradiction but is to be expected. There is ample evidence demonstrating the acoustic rather than semantic nature of verbal STM in normals. Acoustic codes are obviously possible for the right hemisphere. Accordingly, the subject under anesthetic influence uses acoustic encoding of verbal material in LTM, and young children show the same tendency. The emerging pattern is coherent and consistent. We expect that further cognitive tests will confirm the interpretation presented.

Effects on Probability Learning

We have already mentioned that most learning paradigms are not informative with regard to analysis of anesthetic effects. Probability learning, however, provides a useful paradigm to test perseveration effects of anesthetics following change of event probability subsequent to attainment of a stable learning level. To avoid verbal material, we chose the following task: A light was turned on either to the right or to the left of a warning signal with a preset probability (.8 for left in our case) unknown to the subject. At each single trial the subject had to predict in advance on which side he thought the light would appear. After 100 trials (enough to allow achievement of a stable response level), the probability of the left light dropped from .8 to .4 without the subject's knowledge, and 100 additional trials followed. Our reasons for expecting perseveration effects emanated from observations of perseveration with patients and animals suffering from hippocampal damage; the pattern of verbal memory deficits we observed with the higher doses of anesthetics is reminiscent of the cognitive pattern obtained with hippocampal lesions. We therefore intended to test whether other characteristics for hippocampal deficit, such as perseveration, would also be

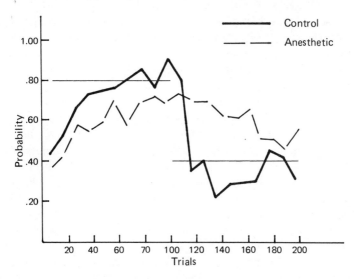

FIG. 7.6.   Effects of general anesthetics on probability learning. The thin horizontal lines represent the objective probability.

found for our volunteers breathing low anesthetic concentrations. We have data for enflurane only, but in view of the data already presented, we expect similar results with other drugs as well.

The perseverative nature of the subjects' responses is clearly seen in Fig. 7.6. Whereas it took the control subject an average of 29 trials to achieve the new response level appropriate to the changed probability, some drugged subjects required twice that amount, and others did not achieve at all the new response level (Bentin, Collins, & Adam, in press). Whether or not these observations imply that the hippocampal structures are extremely sensitive to the anesthetic action will have to await more electrophysiological data.

SIMILARITIES BETWEEN ANESTHETIC EFFECTS AND OTHER MEMORY PATHOLOGIES

Throughout this chapter we have mentioned the resemblance between the anesthetic effects on memory and other instances of memory pathology. Here this theme is further developed.

General anesthetics and marijuana share several effects in common. In our earlier work on time perception under anesthetic influence (Adam et al, 1971; 1974), we concluded that time perception is most sensitive to anesthetic effects; changes in this function had been observed before any other cognitive deficit could be detected. Interestingly, Marx (1974) has noted the same for marijuana intoxication. We have concluded that anesthetics do not significantly affect STM processes. Similarly, Darley, Tinklenberg, Roth, Hollister, and Atkinson (1973) have reported no effects of marijuana on STM. We further reported that anesthetics did not alter the slope of the search function in verbal STM but only increased the intercept. Darley, Tinklenberg, Hollister, and Atkinson (1973) have shown the same for marijuana. Anesthetics impair retention in LTM and so does marijuana (Darley, Tinklenberg, Roth, & Atkinson, 1974). Anesthetics do not produce state-dependent effects with recognition tests. Darley et al. (1974) have noted the same with marijuana, although they did observe state-dependent effects with recall measures (we do not have comparable recall tests). It might be interesting to search for encoding patterns under marijuana influence and specifically for recovery of retention of the type seen with anesthetics.

These similarities between general anesthetics and marijuana raise further questions. Entin and Goldzung (1973) have reported long-term residual effects of chronic use of marijuana on rate of acquisition. In view of recent observations of Katz and his group (Chang & Katz, 1976) on permanent learning deficits in rats after chronic exposure to a general anesthetic in young age, such possible effects should be studied in operating room personnel chronically exposed to trace anesthetic concentrations.

General anesthetics also share some common features with alcohol. Alcohol, similarly to anesthetics, does not affect STM functions, as far as has been studied (for review, see Ryback, 1971). Also, alcohol in high doses produces total amnesia for the whole period, such as was observed with the higher anesthetic concentrations as reported in previous sections of this chapter. Alcohol does not impair retrieval of well-known information but affects retention in LTM of newly learned material, similar to our observations with inhalation anesthetics.

General anesthetics also share some common effects with the Korsakoff syndrome. We have concluded that deficits in semantic encoding of verbal information account satisfactorily for the retention deficits observed under anesthetic influence. That is, efficient retrieval depends on efficient encoding for retrieval, which was found deficient. Similar conclusions have been reported for patients with Korsakoff syndrome (Cermak, Butters, & Goodglass, 1971; Cermak, Butters, & Moreines, 1974; Ritter & Buschke, 1974). Most interestingly, Fuld (1976) has observed in Korsakoff patients the spontaneous recovery of items after former retrieval failure with a testing procedure allowing 12 repeated recall trials. This parallels our observations of recovery with general anesthetics. According to Fuld (1976), deficits in semantic encoding do not account for the whole effect, and she suggested also deficits in contextual encoding, which is probably true also for subjects under anesthetic influence. Perseveration is another feature that shows similarities between general anesthetics and Korsakoff patients. The latter perseverate upon inappropriate hypotheses in a concept-detection task (Oscar−Berman, 1973) and also show perseveration in a probability-learning task (Oscar−Berman, Sahakian, & Wikmark, 1976) very similar to the task we used with general anesthetics.

Finally, the common effects of anesthetics and hippocampal lesions have been mentioned in some detail in former sections. Is there a common denominator behind all these manifestations of memory disturbances? If so, the hippocampus and its connections to the reticular system and cortex are the candidates indicated by the data available to date. Incidentally, the etiology of global amnesia following head traumas is also thought to involve the hippocampus due to insufficiency of basilar artery circulation causing ischemia of the hippocampus and reticular structures (Ryback, 1971). The effects of general anesthetics on the reticular system are well documented (Clark & Rosner, 1973; Rosner & Clark, 1973). More data are needed on anesthetic action in the hippocampus.

FINAL COMMENTS

We started by hoping to be able to correlate the differential neurophysiological effects of different general anesthetics with their differential effects on memory processes. Is seems that all general anesthetics we have studied produce similar memory effects despite differing neurophysiological action. This information indicates a common site of action as a factor in producing the observed effects. The involvement of the reticular system is obvious; the behavioral data also point to the hippocampus and its cortical connections. This supports observations of other instances of memory pathology. Besides the practical implications of our research, our findings contribute in several ways to theory of memory.

First, research with general anesthetics has provided further independent support for verbal-dependent versus verbal-independent memory functions, including encoding and retrieval. Second, it has provided support in favor of encoding/retrieval deficit interpretation rather than consolidation deficit interpretation of some disturbances in LTM retention. Third, this research has corroborated the developmental analysis of memory-encoding processes in terms of acoustic coding in young age with a shift toward predominantly semantic coding in older age. Moreover, the data indicate that the acoustic mode is still extant in the normal adult but is usually supplanted by the semantic mode. Fourth, it seems that at certain doses, the anesthetics primarily affect what is commonly termed left-hemisphere functions, enabling the study of hemispheric representation of memory functions. Finally, it is important to note that the data do not support the expectation that general anesthetics affect to a significant degree basic neurophysiological processes involved in memory formation such as memory trace decay or consolidation of traces. Rather, the observed effects may be explained by a deficit in the active verbal processes called into action during encoding and retrieval of verbal information. These active processes are obviously extremely sensitive to inhalation anesthetics and evidently to a host of other agents affecting the nervous system, as is indicated by the striking similarities in the effects on memory of alcohol, marijuana, anesthetics, and lesions to neural structures such as is seen in Korsakoff syndrome and hippocampal damage.

General anesthetics probably affect other cognitive functions with left-hemispheric representation. The use of controlled subanesthetic concentrations of anesthetics may yet prove to be an excellent tool in assessing hemispheric specialization, having the advantage of absence of chronic brain pathology.

ACKNOWLEDGMENT

Preparation of this paper was supported by the Israeli Ministry of Health.

REFERENCES

Adam, N. Effects of general anesthetics on memory functions in man. *Journal of Comparative and Physiological Psychology*, 1973, *83*, 294–305.

Adam, N. Effects of general anesthetics on search in memory in man. *T.-I.-T. Journal of Life Sciences*, 1976, *6*, 29–34.

Adam, N., Castro, A. D., & Clark, D. L. Production, estimation, and reproduction of time intervals during inhalation of a general anesthetic in man. *Journal of Experimental Psychology*, 1974, *102*, 609—614.

Adam, N., & Collins, G. I Search in short-term memory during inhalation of a general anesthetic in man. *T.-I.-T. Jounral of Life Sciences*, 1977, *7*, 53—58.

Adam, N., & Collins, G. I. Effects of enflurane on electrophysiological correlates of search in short-term memory. *Anesthesiology*, in press, 1978.

Adam, N., Rosner, B. S., Hosick, E. C., & Clark, D. L. Effect of anesthetic drugs on time production and alpha rhythm. *Perception & Psychophysics*, 1971, *10*, 133—136.

Bentin, S., & Adam, N. *Search in short-term memory for verbal and pictorial material*. Unpublished report, 1977.

Bentin, S., Collins, G. I., & Adam, N. Probability learning during inhalation of subanesthetic concentrations of enflurane. *British Journal of Anesthesia*, in press.

Bruce, D. L., & Bach, M. J. Psychological studies of human performance as affected by traces of enflurane and nitrous oxide. *Anesthesiology*, 1975, *42*, 194—196.

Bruce, D. L., & Bach, M. J. Effects of trace anesthetic gases on behavioural performance of volunteers. *British Journal of Anesthesia*, 1976, *48*, 871—876.

Bruce, D. L., Bach, M. J., & Arbit, J. Trace anesthetic effects on perceptual, cognitive and motor skills. *Anesthesiology*, 1974, *40*, 453—458.

Butters, N., Samuels, I., Goodglass, H., & Brody, B. Short-term visual and auditory memory disorders after parietal and frontal lobe damage. *Cortex*, 1970, *6*, 440—459.

Carmon, A. Personal communication, 1977.

Cermak, L., Butters, N., & Goodglass, H. Extent of memory loss in Korsakoff patients. *Neuropsychologia*, 1971, *9*, 307—315.

Cermak, L., Butters, N., & Moreines, J. Some analyses of the verbal encoding deficit of alcoholic Korsakoff patients. *Brain and Language*, 1974, *1*, 141—150.

Chang, L. W., & Katz, J. Pathologic effects of chronic halothane inhalation. *Anesthesiology*, 1976, *45*, 640—653.

Chiang, A., & Atkinson, R. C. Individual differences and interrelationships among a select set of cognitive skills. *Memory & Cognition*, 1976, *4*, 661—672.

Clark, D. L., & Rosner, B. S. Neurophysiologic effects of general anesthetics: I. The electroencephalogram and sensory evoked responses in man. *Anesthesiology*, 1973, *38*, 564—582.

Cohen, G. Hemispheric differences in serial versus parallel processing. *Journal of Experimental Psychology*, 1973, *97*, 349—356.

Cronin, M., Redfern, P. A., & Utting, J. E. Psychometry and postoperative complaints in surgical patients. *British Journal of Anesthesia*, 1973, *45*, 879—886.

Darley, C. F., Tinklenberg, J. R., Hollister, T. E., & Atkinson, R. C. Marijuana and retrieval from short-term memory. *Psychopharmacologia*, 1973, *29*, 231—238.

Darley, C. F., Tinklenberg, J. R., Roth, W. T., & Atkinson, R. C. The nature of storage deficits and state-dependent retrieval under marijuana. *Psychopharmacologia*, 1974, *37*, 139—149.

Darley, C. F., Tinklenberg, J. R., Roth, W. T., Hollister, T. E., & Atkinson, R. C. Influence of marijuana on storage and retrieval processes in memory. *Memory & Cognition*, 1973, *1*, 196—200.

Entin, E. E., & Goldzung, P. J. Residual effects of marijuana usage on learning and memory. *Psychological Record*, 1973, *23*, 169—178.

Felzen, E., & Anisfeld, M. Semantic and phonetic relations in the false recognition of words in third- and sixth-grade children. *Developmental Psychology*, 1970, *3*, 163—168.

Fuld, P. A. Storage, retention and retrieval in Korsakoff's syndrome. *Neuropsychologia*, 1976, *14*, 225—236.

James, F. M. The effects of cyclopropane anesthesia without surgical operation on mental functions of normal man. *Anesthesiology*, 1969, *30*, 264—272.

Kutas, M., McCarthy, G., & Donchin, E. Augmenting mental chronometry: The P300 as a measure of stimulus evaluation time. *Science*, 1977, *197*, 792–795.

Lewis, D. J. Sources of experimental amnesia. *Psychological Review*, 1969, *76*, 461–472.

Marshall, C. R. The influence of moderate and severe intoxication on remembering. *British Journal of Psychology*, 1937, *28*, 18–27.

Marx, M. R. Residual effects of recurrent use of marijuana on immediate and short-term memory processes (with special reference to LSD). *Dissertation Abstracts International*, 1974, *34*, (7-B) 3468–3469.

Milner, B. Memory and the medial temporal regions of the brain. In K. H. Pribram & D. E. Broadbent (Eds.), *Biology of Memory*. New York: Academic Press, 1970.

Osborn, A. G., Bunker, J. P., Cooper, L. M., Frank, G. S., & Hilgard, E. R. Effects of thiopental sedation on learning and memory. *Science*, 1967, *157*, 574.

Oscar–Berman, M. Hypothesis testing and focusing behavior during concept formation by amnesic patients. *Neuropsychologia*, 1973, *11*, 191–198.

Oscar–Berman, M., Sahakian, B. J., & Wikmark, G. Spatial probability learning by alcoholic Korsakoff patients. *Journal of Experimental Psychology*, 1976, *2*, 215–222.

Parkhouse, J., Henrie, J. R., Duncan, G. M., & Rome, H. P. Nitrous oxide analgesia in relation to mental performance. *Journal of Pharmacology and Experimental Therapeutics*, 1960, *128*, 44.

Quimby, K. L., Aschkenase, L. J., Bowman, R. E., Katz, J., & Chang, L. W. Enduring learning deficits and cerebral synaptic malformation from exposure to 10 parts of halothane per million. *Science*, 1974, *185*, 625–627.

Quimby, K. L., Katz, J., & Bowman, R. E. Behavioral consequences in rats from chronic exposure to 10 ppm halothane during early development. *Anesthesia and Analgesia*, 1975, *54*, 628–633.

Ritter, W., & Buschke, H. Free, forced, and restricted recall in verbal learning. *Journal of Experimental Psychology*, 1974, *103*, 1204–1207.

Rosner, B. S., & Clark, D. L. Neurophysiologic effects of general anesthetics: II. Sequential regional actions in the brain. *Anesthesiology*, 1973, *39*, 59–81.

Russell, W. R. The Traumatic Amnesias. *Oxford University Press*, New York, 1971.

Ryback, R. S. The continuum and specificity of the effects of alcohol on memory: A review. *Quarterly Journal of Studies in Alcoholism*, 1971, *32*, 995–1016.

Simson, R., Vaughan, H. G., Jr., & Ritter, W. The scalp topography of potentials associated with missing visual or auditory stimuli. *Electroencephalography and Clinical Neurophysiology*, 1976, *40*, 33–42.

Steinberg, H. Selective effects of an anesthetic drug on cognitive behaviour. *Quarterly Journal of Experimental Psychology*, 1954, *6*, 170–180.

Steinberg, H. & Summerfield, A. Influence of a depressant drug on acquisition in rote learning. *Quarterly Journal of Experimental Psychology*, 1957, *9*, 138–145.

Sternberg, S. Memory-scanning: Mental processes revealed by reaction-time experiments. *American Scientist*, 1969, *57*, 421–457.

Trustman, R., Dubrovsky, S., & Titley, R. Auditory perception during general anesthesia—myth or fact? *International Journal of Clinical and Experimental Hypnosis*, 1977, *25*, 88–105.

Warrington, E. K., & Weiskrantz, L. Amnestic syndrome: Consolidation or retrieval? *Nature*, 1970, *228*, 628–630.

Warrington, E. K., & Weiskrantz, L. An analysis of short-term and long-term memory deficits in man. In J. A. Deutsch (Ed.), *The physiological basis of memory*. London: Academic Press, 1973.

8

Remembering and Forgetting Dreaming

David B. Cohen
University of Texas at Austin

The study of memory for dreaming poses a unique validity problem: How do we know that the report is a valid reflection of the original experience? Prior to the advent of modern sleep research, it was maintained that much, if not all, "dream recall" was a fabulation constructed out of the waking process. However, discovery of objective indicators of the REM dreaming process (Aserinsky & Kleitman, 1953) helped to revive scientific interest in dreaming and to reestablish the credibility of the dream report. Once the validity of the dream report could be established to the satisfaction of most investigators (Rechtschaffen, 1967), factors that determine dream recall could be studied.

After briefly describing approaches to the validation of dream reports, I discuss the importance of the dream-recall process to theories of dreaming and review correlational and experimental data on two aspects of the recall problem: individual differences in dream-recall frequency (DRF) and situational changes in the probability of recall. Three general factors hypothesized to affect dream recall are evaluated: (a) *repression* (a psychodynamically motivated rejection from consciousness of ego-threatening fantasy); (b) *salience* (encoding factors such as intensity and inherent interest of the dream experience); and (c) *interference* (decoding factors largely affecting retrieval and including those implicating the construct of state dependency).

VALIDATION OF THE DREAM REPORT

Empirical Evaluation

The single most important determinant of current interest in the scientific investigation of dreaming was the discovery in the early 1950s of a correlation between clearly recalled dreaming experiences and an electrophysiological pattern of sleep characteristics that soon came to define REM sleep (e.g., low voltage, mixed-frequency EEG largely in the theta range, rapid and conjugate eye movements, and a paradoxical diminution of submental or chin EMG).[1] Some of the more extreme conclusions derived from this early work (Aserinsky & Kleitman, 1953, 1955; Dement & Kleitman, 1957), such as the supposition that mental activity is confined to REM sleep, have undergone appropriate modification (Foulkes, 1966), but the association between REM and dreaming remains compelling.

An era of psychophysiological research has provided an empirical basis for evaluating the validity of dream reports. Despite the still largely unexplored problem of individual differences, it became evident that certain characteristics of the dream report could be correlated with, and thus validated by, observable electrophysiological and behavioral events. For example, the subjective estimate of the length of a dream tends to be correlated with the duration of a REM period between gross body movements (Dement & Wolpert, 1958). The content of sleep talking during REM sleep, when observed, generally correlates with the content of recalled REM dreaming (Arkin, Toth, Baker, & Hastey, 1970). Sudden penile detumescence is correlated with anxiety content in the recalled dream (Karacan, Goodenough, Shapiro, & Starker, 1966).

More refined analysis of the kinds of psychophysiological correlates upon which dream-report validity could be more firmly grounded has met with mixed success, as shown in Rechtschaffen's (1973) masterly review. The most popular of these was the attempt to demonstrate that there is an association between direction of eye movement just prior to awakening and the pattern of events reported to have occurred in the dream.[2] Such an analysis requires proficient recallers as well as careful attention to details of reporting (Gardiner, Grossman, Roffwarg, & Weiner, 1975).

Psychophysiological paradigms suggested by Stoyva and Kamiya (1968) and Barber (1971) for evaluating the validity of reports about imagery, along with impressions derived from work with laboratory subjects, suggest that well-articulated reports are acceptable as valid indications of prior dreaming experience. Of course, to some extent, a certain degree of selective forgetting and/or spurious construction will be produced by situational as well as dispositional

---

[1]In adults, REM sleep occurs periodically throughout the night. The first epoch begins about 90 minutes after sleep onset. The REM component of the REM−NREM 90-minute cycle constitutes a greater portion of sleep time later in the night. Normally, about 22% of a night's sleep is expressed as REM sleep.

[2]Unfortunately, with the exception of highly specialized patterns such as optokinetic nystagmus, it is generally not possible to determine the content of simple visual fields from eye movement patterns during normal wakefulness, and thus it would indeed be fortuitous to isolate such correlations during sleep (F. J. Evans, personal communication, 1977).

factors. Nevertheless, it is generally assumed that the dream report provides a reasonable datum from which factors that influence amount, frequency, and quality of recall may be inferred.

Practical and Theoretical Implications

Once it is assumed that dream reports are not merely fabrications of the waking process, the question remains concerning what the report implies about the dreaming experience. A popular assumption is that dreaming involves "primary process" mental activity—something archaic, infantile, chaotic, bizarre. Murphy (1947) describes this view, so characteristic of modern industrial society. Sleep and dreaming "is a sad psychological waste that has no economic value except as a hostage to tomorrow's toil; its psychological product is industrial waste, occasionally salvaged by the psychoanalytic chemist, but for most people most of the time, so gross that it is not commercially worth the cost of claiming it. Nobody wants a 'dreamer'. Let's get down to business [p. 416]." He then counters by saying that "this attitude has resulted in one of the greatest instances of myopia to be found in contemporary psychology [p. 416]."

In fact, neither the rejectionist view nor its romantic alternative can adequately be evaluated in the absence of a careful assessment of the process through which we come to know about the dream experience. Thus, research on situational and dispositional factors that facilitate or inhibit dream recall has implications for our understanding of dreaming. For example, the impression that dreaming is a fragmented, sequentially illogical process may to some extent be an artifact of recall rather than a reflection of the actual experience. Sometimes a subject will spontaneously clarify later in the night a report given earlier. The revision suggests that the experience was in fact more rational and sequentially logical than the earlier report had suggested.

There are many other factors related to dream recall that will bias our conclusions about the nature of the dreaming experience. Reports obtained in the laboratory appear to contain less "primary process" thought than those obtained (even from the same subjects) after spontaneous and uncontrolled awakenings at home (Snyder, 1970). The average college student reports dreams that seem less bizarre than those reported by certain groups of psychiatric populations; yet it is data from the latter that have been most frequently used to develop theories about dream content and dream function. In addition, it is possible that only the most unusual or disturbing of dreams are likely to be recalled or remembered later, thereby contributing to a biased view about the dysphoric nature of the average dream (Goodenough, Witkin, Lewis, Koulack, & Cohen, 1974). Finally, clinical, lay, as well as scientific investigators may be biased with respect to which dreams are paid attention. Tversky and Kahneman (1974) have provided numerous examples of "heuristics" that bias judgments under conditions of uncertainty.[3]

There are at least two other issues regarding the nature of dreams that are raised by dream-recall data. First, it has been suggested that those very characteristics of mature and healthy ego function that we take for granted during wakefulness (e.g., evaluation, discrimination, judgment, impulse control, self-consciousness) are absent during the typical REM dream. In fact, Hartmann (1973) has offered a theory of catecholaminergic deficit to explain such psychological deficiencies in REM dreams. This empirically based view conflicts with the hypothesis that dreaming is an adaptive process that permits reorganization and metaprogramming of remote and recent information (Breger, 1967; Dewan, 1969; Shapiro, 1967), psychodynamic defensive problem resolution (Cohen & Cox, 1975), and creative insight (Krippner & Hughes, 1970). Surely, the catecholaminergic-deficit hypothesis, together with the view that dreaming is a crude and primitive process of little import, would make such adaptive hypotheses less tenable. In fact, an analysis of determinants of dream recall raises the possibility that it is just those kinds of characteristics said to be absent from typical dream experiences that are most difficult to recall. Careful attention to the reporting process, including recall and communication (Gardiner et al., 1975), may force us to revise our conclusions about the dream and its relationship to "external" (e.g., physiological, behavioral) correlates. For example, Molinari and Foulkes (1969) reported that awakenings from "quiescent" REM periods yielded dream reports that had a more cognitive than the "primary visual" quality found with awakenings during REM-active episodes. However, a later report (Foulkes & Pope, 1973) suggested that the difference was related to the kind of qualities to which the subject was spontaneously paying attention. Under more structured questioning, evidence of secondary process was obtained even during active REM. Again, it is likely that even under laboratory conditions that are ideal for recall, factors extraneous to the dream itself operate to bias the communication (and possibly the recall) of dream material. We cannot conclude that dreaming reflects poor "ego functioning" if the dream-reporting process is suspect.

Changes in dream content during the night can provide a basis for evaluating

---

[3]I suspect that our impressions about the nature of dreaming are biased by the high frequency of recall of the dreamy experiences that are associated with transitional states (e.g., Stage 1 without REM, the drowsy wakefulness typically associated with sleep onset) rather than the REM dream (Cohen, 1977c). If we accept a broad definition of the dream that includes such hypnagogic and hypnopompic experiences, and if these are statistically more frequent events in memory, then we will tend to think of dreaming as a "primary process" mental activity. But if we restrict our definition of a dream to REM experiences, then we will be less apt to characterize dreaming as a primitive and regressive phenomenon. Although the hallucinatory experiences of REM and other states have a superficial similarity, the evidence that REM sleep is functionally unique would encourage retaining a distinction between the two kinds of experience.

the problem of biases that affect dream recall. In one unpublished study, a group of male undergraduates rated both *quality of recall* and *ego functioning*, based on their estimates both on REM material obtained throughout the night and waking experience just prior to arriving at the laboratory. Quality of recall was rated on a 7-step scale indicating a composite of amount and clarity of visualization. Ego functioning was rated on seven 3-step scales (judgment, impulse control, social adjustment, etc.), and the ratings were averaged. Quality of recall increased over the night and was associated with an increase in estimated ego functioning (in fact, to levels comparable to presleep levels). Interpretation of these results is difficult. Either ego functioning in dreams is reasonably good but hard to recall earlier in the night, or both ego functioning and recall are different indications of a general intellectual competence that increases during the night. The data for the good dream recallers support the latter interpretation. The point is, however, that both situational and dispositional factors (e.g., early REM awakenings and generally poor recall) may artifactually influence precisely those characteristics of dream reports that would be important to the hypothesis that (at least some) dreams may be adaptive. Dement (1975) captures the problem of distinguishing between experience vs. recall of experience by suggesting that "our task in describing the dream world is roughly as difficult as if we were strolling casually without a care down the Champs Elysees, and we were suddenly plucked into the dream world to the accompaniment of a raucous buzzer where in the dim light of a dream bedroom a shadowy figure would begin a relentless interrogation about what we'd just been doing. One would surely forget a few things [p. 271]."

The second issue raised by the dream-recall literature is the sequencing of cognitive events. Dream reports often give the impression of sequential disorganization and patchwork quality. Faulty recall of (especially transitional) aspects of the dream experience (e.g., sequencing in the report reflecting recallability rather than actual sequence of material) may contribute to a biased impression of the logic of the dream experience. Consider the possibility that dream experiences are, in fact, to some extent discontinuous. The question then becomes one of the *relative* disorganization of this sequencing, i.e., relative to sequencing of cognitive activity that takes place during wakefulness. If we compare the "logic" of overt behavioral sequencing to the sequencing of cognitions, or at least recalled cognitions, we begin to appreciate the discontinuity of cognitive sequencing in *wakefulness*. Smooth performance, rational conversation, efficient problem solving all belie a certain kaleidoscopic temporal arrangement of conscious thought. We tend to underestimate the discontinuity of waking mentation while we overemphasize that of dreaming. Perhaps this is partially a function of the tendency for dreams to give equal emphasis to both the focal and the peripheral, a quality that promotes the view that dreaming is a schizophrenic process. Such a democratization of cognitive content would indeed be inefficient during wakefulness, though it may be a source of creative insight during dreaming. More relevant is the implication about recall of cognitive processes in general that emerges from a consideration of dream recall. We are not particularly skilled at recalling and describing the flow of wakeful mentation. Therefore we need to pay more attention to the process of dream recall, since this includes an additional demand, that of recalling information that is both incidentally learned and that is in some ways more difficult to recall.

INDIVIDUAL DIFFERENCES IN DREAM RECALL

Most of the early work on dream recall was in the form of correlational studies of individual differences in questionnaire or home dream-diary estimates of dream-recall frequency (DRF) and personality. Based on an implicit assumption that dreams often reflect potentially ego-threatening impulses and preoccupations, a typical expectation was that DRF would reflect the degree to which the individual relied on repression or denial of unpleasant experiences. Let us first consider the relationship between the two estimates of DRF and then evaluate the success of the correlational approach.

Operational Definition of Dream-Recall Frequency

In my own early work in this area, I made use of both the questionnaire and home dream-diary methods for assessing dream-recall frequency (DRF). The questionnaire included an eight-step item requesting an estimate of DRF during the prior 2 weeks from "not once" (scored 0) through "every morning" (scored 14). The three lowest steps on the scale, up to "about one morning each week" (scored 2) were usually used to define "infrequent DRF," and the three highest steps, from "most mornings of the week" (scored 10) to "every morning" usually defined "frequent DRF." A variety of "dream-diary" methods was used as well. For example, a subject might be asked to describe in as much detail as possible the content of each dream on a single diary sheet each night for any number of consecutive nights. A second method involved a diary checklist to allow the subject to indicate for each of 30 mornings the recall of details, recall of having dreamed but not details, or total failure to recall. The use of diary methods constituted a validational check on the questionnaire estimates.

Table 8.1 shows the intercorrelation matrix for three measures of DRF, male correlations above and female correlations below the diagonal. In addition, we obtained evidence of reasonable temporal consistency in the checklist diary when recall for the 2nd and 4th weeks of recording were correlated (.64 and .52 for 125 males and 203 females respectively).

Table 8.2 shows the subjects divided into frequent and infrequent recallers on the basis of the already described criteria applied to questionnaire estimates. On both kinds of diary measure, frequent recallers report from two to four times as much dream recall on diary measures as do infrequent recallers.

TABLE 8.1
Intercorrelations for Dream Recall Questionnaire
(Q-DRF), 25-Day Recall Checklist (25-Day),
and 3-Day Dream Diary (3-Day)

	Q-DRF[a]	25-Day[b]	3-Day[c]
Q-DRF	– –	.54	.56
25-Day	.69	– –	.54
3-Day	.37	.47	– –

Note. Data from males above the diagonal, data from females below. Based on a sample of 133 males and 205 females. All scores are based on the frequency of dreams recalled estimated from each measure. All correlations are significant ($p < .01$).

[a]Range of possible scores: 0–14.
[b]Range of possible scores: 0–25.
[c]Range of possible scores: 0–3.

TABLE 8.2
Mean 25-Day Recall Checklist and 3-Day Dream Diary Performance
of Highest and Lowest Self-Rated Dream Recallers (Q-DRF)

Criterion	High Recallers[a]	Low Recallers[b]	p <	r_{pb}
25-Day				
Males ($N = 65$)	13.9	6.1	.0001	.65
Females ($N = 118$)	16.4	5.8	.0001	.77
3-Day				
Males ($N = 59$)	2.1	0.5	.0001	.70
Females (N = 118)	1.8	0.9	.0001	.42

[a]Recall most mornings of the week or more.
[b]Recall less than once a week.

An additional test of the validity of the DRF estimate from questionnaires comes from comparisons of REM and NREM dream recall in the laboratory. Frequent recallers do in fact demonstrate more recall than do infrequent recallers, especially after NREM awakenings. These findings are elaborated later.

Individual Differences in DRF: Correlational Studies

An initial approach to the question of determinants of dream recall is to ask if individuals of similar dispositions and/or those who are subject to similar

socialization conditions are similar in DRF. Understanding how those dispositions and situations influence cognitive behavior would lead to testable predictions regarding the effect on dream recall of experimental manipulation of those
conditions. One example of this kind of approach to individual differences in
DRF is represented by a study that pitted a behavior-genetic against a social-
learning hypothesis (Cohen, 1973). Male and female identical twin (MZ) pairs
($N = 54$), same-sex dizygotic (DZ) twin pairs ($N = 34$), same-sex nontwin
sibling pairs ($N = 32$), and same-sex friend pairs ($N = 42$) were each divided into
subgroups depending on whether they were currently living together or apart.
Results shown in Table 8.3 indicated that there was significantly greater
similarity in questionnaire-estimated DRF for individuals living together compared to those living apart and significantly greater similarity in DRF for all
related vs. unrelated individuals. Although MZ were more similar than DZ twins,
the similarity between nontwin siblings, comparable to that of MZ twins, ruled
out the tempting conclusion that there might be a strong genetic factor in DRF.

Field Independence, Repression-Sensitization, and DRF

If there is a similarity in DRF among individuals sharing life experiences and
therefore presumably sharing similar dispositions, what are those dispositions,
and what are their implications for a theory of DRF? In fact, correlational work
reviewed in more detail elsewhere (Cohen, 1974c) suggests that there is a
relatively small association between personality dimensions and DRF and that
certain cognitive abilities are more strongly associated with DRF than are
estimates of emotionality or repression. For example, an early study (Schonbar,
1959) purporting to demonstrate a high correlation between emotionality (interpreted as the relative absence of repression) and DRF was not confirmed by later
studies (Domhoff & Gerson, 1967; Tart, 1962). Studies using field-dependence
estimates of the tendency to use repression, which suggested a psychodynamic
influence over DRF (Schonbar, 1965; Witkin, Dyk, Faterson, Goodenough, &
Karp, 1962), were subsequently challenged by other findings (Cohen & Wolfe,
1973). These low and somewhat unreliable correlations between estimates of the
disposition toward repression and DRF do not necessarily constitute evidence

TABLE 8.3
Similarity in Dream Recall Frequency: Family Study

	MZ Twin	DZ Twin	Sibling	Friend
Living together	2.37	3.18	2.00	4.33
Living apart	4.00	5.57	3.81	5.62

Note. Low scores index greater similarity in DRF. (Adapted from
Cohen, 1973, Table 1.)

against the validity of the repression scales (Byrne, 1964; Witkin et al., 1962.), but they do constitute evidence against the hypothesis that repression is an important determinant of DRF in the nonclinical population.

Let us consider a more sophisticated correlational approach to the relationship between repression and DRF. Antrobus, Antrobus, and Singer (1964) reported that requests for the suppression of ongoing fantasy elicited increased eye movement activity. This result suggested that hypothesis that infrequent recallers should demonstrate more eye movement activity during REM dreaming, i.e., a tendency to suppress (presumably ego-threatening) content "on line." In fact, Antrobus, Dement, and Fisher (1964) did find more eye movement activity during the REM sleep of infrequent compared to frequent recallers. However, there are at least three problems with the argument that REM eye movement density is an external indication of repression of imagery. First, the initial Antrobus et al. (1964) study did not employ a control condition to assess the effect of *effort* with respect to fantasy control on eye movement density during wakefulness. Would instructions to *increase* rather than inhibit intensity or activity or variability of fantasy also yield higher rates of eye movement? Second, imagery intensity is often *inversely* related to eye movement activity (Lavie & Kripke, 1975; Marks, 1972). Hiscock (1977) obtained some evidence of a sharp increase in eye movements when subjects shifted from imagining static images to thinking about verbal meanings.

These findings, which are apparently consistent with those reported by Antrobus, Antrobus, and Singer (1964), are readily interpretable within the context of hypotheses other than that of repression. For example, high eye movement activity may indicate that thoughtlike mentation, inherently difficult to recall, is operative. It is not necessary to conclude that the latter is being suppressed by the former in order to serve a "defensive" purpose. Were it established that infrequent recallers do have significantly more eye movement activity during REM, their poor recall could be explained as a function of the dominance of inherently less recallable thoughtlike mentation over visually salient dream imagery. On the other hand, if it could be demonstrated within subjects that ego threat is associated with within-subject decrease in dream recall, increase in eye movement, and increase in dream content that is more mundane or psychodynamically "safe," the repression argument would be strengthened. However, a subsequent study (Cohen, 1975; Cohen & Cox, 1975) found no relationship between habitual DRF and eye movement density, no relationship between DRF and repression-sensitization, and no relationship between REM dream recall and REM density. Although repressors in the ego-threatening situation did have relatively high eye movement density, this phenomenon was not associated with markedly low REM dream recall. Finally, it should be noted that two earlier studies obtained evidence of a positive relationship between eye movement density and dream recall (Baekeland, 1970; Goodenough et al., 1974), whereas another study (Molinari & Foulkes, 1969) found no relationship at all.

Other correlational findings cast doubt on the hypothesis that repression is more important than salience or interference as a determinant of dream recall. Goodenough et al. (1974) obtained somewhat more dream recall after awakenings from REM periods characterized by relatively high amounts of physiological turmoil. Like an earlier study (Shapiro, Goodenough, Biederman, & Sleser, 1964), this study found more dream recall to be associated with higher levels of respiratory irregularity. Similarly, Bell and Stroebel (1973) found no dearth of dream recall for REM awakenings characterized by the kind of scrotal muscle activity previously found during clinical interviews to be associated with anxiety content. Finally, four questionnaire studies (MacNeilage, Cohen, & MacNeilage, 1972) revealed higher DRF for frequent sleep talkers. Thus, evidence of high physiological activity indicating salience is associated with relatively high levels of dream recall. This is more consistent with a salience interpretation than with one based on repression.

These and other results do not challenge either the concept of repression and its importance in waking personality functioning or the hypothesis that under certain situations and for certain groups (e.g., clinic populations undergoing psychodynamic therapy) repression may indeed operate on dream recall. The results do seriously question the importance of repression in accounting for individual differences in dream recall for the population at large. Even if it were established that there is a strong relationship between certain measures of the disposition toward repression and DRF, it could not be concluded that repression determines DRF. It could be argued that such a tendency toward the use of repression during wakefulness correlates with poor imagery ability, certain physiological sources of interference with memory for imagery, or undeveloped skills in the retrieval of "inner life." For example, one psychoanalytic view is that repressiveness is an aspect of "character armor" and is expressed as muscular tension (Reich, 1949). Bugelski (1971) has suggested that motorically restless individuals are less likely to be able to sustain intense imagery.[4] Sleep laboratory research (Dement & Wolpert, 1958) suggests an inverse relationship between dream recall and movement during the REM period. In fact, one empirically unexploited possibility is that there is a correlation between dream recall and reduction in submental EMG recordings typical of the transition from stage 2-NREM to REM and dream recall. Such hypothetical correlations might reflect only the salience and interference factors that influence ability to recall, not active rejection (repression) of dream material.

---

[4]This suggestion is consistent with the popular notion that dream recall immediately upon awakening is facilitated by relaxation rather than effort (the latter possibly correlating with neuromuscular tension that interferes with imagery). It also fits with the concept of state-dependent learning. If dream imagery is associated with a unique neuromuscular relaxation, wakefulness associated with tension may correspond to a biological state whose qualitative difference from the sleep-dream state prevents good recall of material encoded in that state.

It is also possible that the dreams of some individuals might be less recallable because they are less "interesting" (Barber, 1969). Evidence of lower DRF and less situational recall for individuals with less ability to recall visual information, convergent rather than divergent cognitive styles, and with an interest in practical and scientific rather than intuitive and subjective information (what might be called left-, rather than right-, hemisphere-related activities) suggests a cognitive style rather than a repression hypothesis (Austin, 1971; Barber, 1969; Cohen, 1971; Cory, Ormiston, Simmel, & Dainoff, 1975; Orlinsky, 1966; Schechter, Schmeidler, & Staal, 1965; Singer & Schonbar, 1961).

Imagery Ability and DRF

The cognitive style factor is consistent with evidence that individual differences in DRF are associated with corresponding differences in imagery ability, i.e., vividness of, and ability to use, imagery. First, although some initial evidence (Cohen, 1971) suggested otherwise, it now seems clear that frequent recallers have better visual memory than infrequent recallers (Cory et al., 1975), although there is little difference between the groups in auditory memory (Hiscock & Cohen, 1973). Second, there are data suggesting that brain damage that interferes with waking imagery ability (i.e., the right occipital–parietal areas) is associated with diminished dream recall (Humphrey & Zangwill, 1951). Conversely, congenitally deaf individuals, who are especially tuned to and skilled at processing visual information, have good dream recall (Mendelson, Siger, & Solomon, 1960). In addition, frequent daydreamers tend to be frequent dream recallers (Singer & Schonbar, 1961). Evidence that good imagers are relatively insensitive to external sources of visual information concurrent with internally generated imagery (Singer, 1975) indirectly suggests that they would be less susceptible to interference from external events on the retrieval of dream imagery.

Hiscock and Cohen (1973) indirectly demonstrated an association between individual differences in DRF and imagery ability. From a group of 648 undergraduates who completed a DRF questionnaire, 268 indicated either especially frequent or infrequent DRF. Samples of these subgroups (15 male and 19 female frequent recallers and 26 male and 11 female infrequent recallers) were run in a verbal learning task. Each subject learned two matched lists of 10 concrete nouns, each paired with a number from 1 to 10. After learning the first list, each subject was tested for recall by random presentation of a number and a call for the appropriate noun. Prior to the trial with the second list, each subject was assigned to an "imagery" or an "association" condition. In the imagery condition, the subject learned a rhyme word for each number (1−*bun*, 2−*shoe*, etc.) and was instructed to form an image of the rhyme word and the List 2 word, which were each associated with a given number (e.g., for "1, *pencil*," visualizing a pencil in a bun). In the association condition, the subject learned the rhyme words but was asked merely to say that word associatively with the corresponding List 2 words elicited by the number (e.g., say "1−*bun−pencil*"). Both groups of subjects were told that their respective instructions were designed to facilitate recall of List 2 words.

Figure 8.1 reproduces the results produced by the four subgroups. No significant differences in recall were produced on Trial 1. On Trial 2, better recall was associated with high DRF and with imagery instructions. The expected interaction (favoring frequent recallers given imagery instructions) was not significant. However, it should be pointed out that this failure is in part the effect of an unanticipated poor performance on Trial 2 by the low-DRF subgroup receiving association instructions. This result artifactually increased the difference between the two low-DRF subgroups. In fact, although there was no difference between frequent and infrequent recallers on Trial 1, the former group

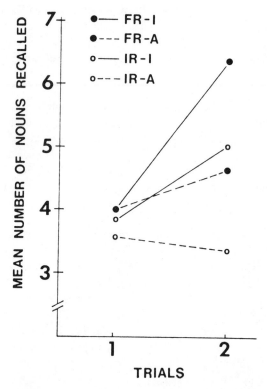

FIG. 8.1. Mean number of words recalled by frequent (FR) and infrequent (IR) dream recallers. Trial 1 is the baseline condition; on Trial 2, subjects received imagery (I) or association (A) instructions. (Reprinted from Hiscock & Cohen, 1973, Figure 1.)

TABLE 8.4
Dream Salience Indices of Content
Reported by Frequent and Infrequent Recallers

	Frequent	Infrequent	t	r_{pb}
Vividness	1.00	.67	1.86*	.44
Bizarreness	.36	.25	1.21	.31
Emotionality	.61	.25	2.34**	.53
Activity	.77	.79	1	— — —
Composite[a]	.69	.46	2.32**	.53

Note. N = 7 per group. (Adapted from Cohen & MacNeilage, 1974, Table 2.)
* $p < .10$.
**$p < .05$.
[a]Composite refers to the mean of the four ratings or [Viv + Diz + Emo + Activ]/4.

did perform significantly better under imagery instructions. In addition, frequent recallers obtained significantly higher scores than infrequent recallers on post-sleep questionnaires of visual, *but not auditory*, imagery during dreams. These differential questionnaire results provide a pattern that is commensurate with the differential results on Trial 1 vs. Trial 2 in the experimental situation. Thus, there is some support for the initial assumptions about the relationship between ability and utility of imagery and individual differences in DRF.

In a more direct test of the relationship between imagery ability and DRF (Cohen & MacNeilage, 1974), the REM dream recall of 16 male subjects across four laboratory nights was studied. Eight frequent and eight infrequent recallers were preselected by a combination of questionnaire and subsequent dream-diary methods prior to the laboratory condition. A total of 131 REM awakenings were made, 68 for frequent and 63 for infrequent recallers. Not unexpectedly, the percentage of REM awakenings yielding at least fragmentary recall was significantly greater for the frequent (96%) than for the infrequent (75%) recallers. These percentages are virtually identical to those reported by Lewis, Good-enough, Shapiro, and Sleser (1966). There was, however, no difference in the *amount* of scorable content yielded by the two groups. That is, when material was recalled, about the same amount was recalled by each type of individual. Table 8.4 shows that frequent recallers scored higher than the infrequent recallers on two of four content dimensions defined a priori- as salience characteristics. Some of these comparisons suggest that differences in habitual recall may be a function of the salience of the material.

An interesting difference between the two groups emerged on spontaneous dream-diary recall estimates obtained independent of experimenter control at the end of the night and written just after alarm clock awakenings. Of the 64 alarm clock awakenings (16 subjects, 4 nights each), 24 occurred from REM (12 for each group), and 26 occurred from NREM sleep (16 for frequent, 10 for infrequent recallers). REM diary recall was 95% for frequent and 75% for infrequent recallers; NREM recall was 75% for frequent but only 25% for infrequent recallers. Although these differential results are based on a relatively small sample, they are consistent with a pattern revealed in two other sets of data concerned with the association between recall for REM vs. NREM awakenings and variation in abruptness of the waking stimulus (Shapiro, Goodenough, Lewis, & Sleser, 1965; Zimmerman, 1970).

Individual Differences in DRF: Implications

This apparently consistent pattern of differential results suggests two potentially powerful explanations for DRF. One is that the difference between frequent and infrequent recallers in dream salience and interference during awakening is maximal during NREM sleep. Thus, if both groups tend to awaken with an equal probability from REM or NREM sleep, minimal salience differences during REM and maximal salience differences during NREM will, on the average, yield lower recall for infrequent recallers. A second possibility is that infrequent recallers tend more often than frequent recallers to awaken from NREM sleep. Although there is insufficient evidence for such a difference, the question should be of interest to investigators who are concerned about individual differences in the functional importance of REM sleep and its temporal integrity (Cohen, 1977b; Fiss, 1969).

For example, Webb and Kersey (1967) argued that if dream recall is largely a function of awakening from REM rather than from NREM sleep, then the percentage of subjects reporting dream recall on any particular day should be predictable on the basis of a multiplicative function of: (a) the probability of awakening from REM sleep, and (b) the probability of dream recall given a REM awakening. These investigators found that 37.5% of a group of 762 subjects reported having had a dream on a designated morning. The probability of awakening from REM (about .45) and the probability of REM recall (about .85) were derived from laboratory data. These combined probabilities yielded a figure of .37, remarkably close to the questionnaire findings.[5] The Webb and Kersey paper suggests that a difference in the tendency habitually to awaken at the end of the night from REM or NREM sleep would yield a most parsimonious explanation of differences in DRF, since it is well known that interruption of

---

[5]A recent study (Webb, 1977) showed that subjects in general did not necessarily awaken spontaneously from any specific stage of sleep; indeed the awakening stage reflected the distribution of sleep stages that would be expected after about 7 or 8 hours of sleep. This study confirms one of the assumptions that these estimates are based on, though they do not directly reflect on the dream-recall hypothesis. Unfortunately, a sleep laboratory study formally testing the proposed relationship has yet to be reported.

REM sleep yields far more dream recall than awakenings from NREM sleep. The intense physiological and cortical activation of the REM period provides a biological basis for empirically established differences in the salience and recallability of REM dreams compared to NREM mentation. Likewise, it may be tentatively asserted that to some extent, the low dream salience and "depth" characteristics of NREM sleep are two factors that contribute to an explanation of low DRF.

HYPOTHETICAL DETERMINANTS OF DREAM RECALL

The correlational data on individual differences in DRF have suggested that two factors, dream salience and interference with dream retrieval, provide a parsimonious and more reliable explanation for dream recall than does the repression hypothesis. In this section, experimental studies are described that include manipulations that are designed to affect these factors. Some of the studies represent an attempt to assess the operation of salience and interference factors by focusing on the interaction of presleep situation with individual differences. The review is selective and does not attempt to include all the literature.

Repression and Dream Recall

The repression hypothesis of dream recall has been proposed by investigators influenced by psychodynamic psychology. One variant that has prompted a great deal of research is that failure to recall dreams is an overt manifestation of a deliberate expulsion from consciousness of ego-threatening experience. A reaction by a more critical and defensive waking ego to the products of its more relaxed sleep counterpart eventuates in fragmentary recall, awareness of only having been dreaming (contentless reports), or complete recall failure (dreamless reports). Freud (1900/1953) describes this hypothetical process: "during the night the resistance loses some of its power . . . [and] . . . having gained its full strength at the moment of awakening, it at once proceeds to get rid of what it was obliged to permit while it was weak, [p. 526]." This "afterexpulsion" variant of the repression hypothesis suggests two kinds of predictions that have been subject to a great deal of empirical testing:

1. Repressor-type individuals (i.e., individuals who tend to forget unpleasant personal events) will tend to have less dream recall.
2. Conditions that increase the probability that dreaming will be unpleasant or disturbing will, especially in repressors, tend to reduce dream recall.

A few studies have been carried out specifically to test the idea that conditions presumed to be associated with more unpleasant or ego-threatening dream content would be, especially in repressor-type individuals, associated with the inhibition of dream recall (Cartwright, Bernick, Borowitz, & Kling, 1969; Goodenough, 1967; Witkin, 1969). A good example is that of Cartwright et al. (1969). Ten male volunteer subjects each spent five consecutive nights in the sleep laboratory, during which REM periods were interrupted to obtain dream content. Prior to the second sleep session (during the afternoon), the subject was shown an erotic movie involving explicit sexual acts. Differential dream recall yielded evidence interpreted as a repression effect. Specifically, following the viewing of the experimental film, on the second night, a lower percentage of REM content reports (68.5%) was obtained than on the first night (82.7%).

Before one could conclude that this cross-night difference in recall was an indication of repression, a number of questions would have to be answered. First, why should it be assumed that an erotic film shown in the afternoon increases the motive to repress dreams? No questionnaire or physiological evidence was reported that demonstrated that the film induced stress. In fact, it was reported that the sleep characteristics observed on the second night were normal. Also, no individual-difference measures relevant to repressiveness were reported though clinical and questionnaire data were obtained as part of the subject selection procedure. If repression were operating on Night 2, it would be expected that, say, repressors rather than sensitizers would show the greatest effect. If, for example, the small difference in content-report percentages were a function of a large difference for repressors but a small or negative difference for sensitizers, other things being equal (e.g., sleep quality), this would be strong evidence for the repression hypothesis. Finally, how do we explain the decrease in content reporting (72.7%) on Night 5? The difference between Night 2 and Night 5 does not appear to be significant. It is possible that a psychological factor or some quality of sleep not evident in the sleep data reported in the paper could account for the dream-recall fluctuations. Night 2 represents a kind of "rebound" from the anxiety of "first night effects" (Agnew, Webb, & Williams, 1966). Night 5 may involve relaxation at the end of a demanding study. It might have been that *positive* rather than negative presleep mood on those two nights accounted for the relatively low dream recall. (I discuss the relationship between presleep mood and dream recall later.) In short, there are too many factors other than repression that could account for these results.

A second, in some ways more powerful, test of the repression hypothesis was given preliminary discussion by Witkin (1969) and then reported in full by Goodenough et al. (1974). Preselected field-independents ($N = 16$) or field-dependent ($N = 12$) subjects were run for five nights in the sleep lab. During the last four, each subject saw either one of two "stress" films (either a subincision ritual or a birth) or either one of two control films (travelogues).

Although there appeared to be some evidence for the repression hypothesis in the increase in contentless reporting by field-dependent subjects on the stress nights, there are other possibilities. For example, there was no film condition to arouse *positive* effects. What if the level of contentless reporting under such high-positive arousal had been comparable to that induced by the high-stress condition? Second, if contentless recall is a sign of repression, why were the levels of contentless recall for field-independent subjects (supposed nonrepressors) in both stress and nonstress conditions comparable to those of the field-dependent subjects under the stress condition? True, the major comparison is the within-group one, and contentless recall in field-independent subjects may have been due to different factors (see discussion of contentless recall findings by Cohen and Wolfe, 1973). But such differences were not expected. Third, the investigators themselves point out that the psychophysiological correlate data do not fit a priori expectations generated by the repression hypothesis adopted in this experiment. That is, the REM periods associated with the highest degree of respiratory activity (a sign of distress observed in the presleep stress condition) were associated with *more*, rather than less, dream recall.

These investigators provide an important contribution to dream-recall theory in their post hoc analysis of the results; it represents an alternative to the repression hypothesis that initially guided the study. They suggest that anxiety regarding the stress condition may have distracted attention to the external aspects of the laboratory situation, especially in field-dependent subjects. Thus, an interference hypothesis is offered as a more parsimonious explanation. This revision is commensurate with the following evidence. First, both groups were apparently equally affected by the stress condition in terms of the questionnaire and physiological measures taken. Second, dream salience differences that might have accounted for obtained differences in recall were not obtained. Third, field-dependent subjects are more subject to interference from distracting information interpolated between initial learning (on which they do not differ from field-independent subjects) and later recall of that learning (for which they do show significant decrements relative to field-independent subjects; Goodenough et al., 1974). It is thus suggested that attention distracted to external information leads to more faulty recall when attention is later directed back to the task of retrieving dream information. This seems like a reasonable explanation, though it does not seem commensurate with the finding of only the slightest decrement of morning recall of previously reported content for field-dependent subjects in the stress, as compared to the control, condition.

Another study (Cohen, 1972) was modeled on Witkin's preliminary description (1969) of work reported in detail later by Goodenough et al. (1974). It represents a third example of an experimental approach guided by the repression hypothesis for dream recall. This study assessed the effect of a presleep stress manipulation on home dream reports written immediately upon awakening. The stress was the anticipation of participating the next morning in a difficult learning task including electroshock for error. In order to impress upon the subject the nature of the learning task he would be engaged in, he observed simulated learning by an accomplice the evening prior to dream recording. (Pilot subjects provided Rorschach data clearly indicating that the observation of the learning task, complete with "shocks," was indeed impressive. For example, whereas a control pilot subject described card III of the Rorschach immediately after the observation as "a couple of girls pulling on something," a stress pilot subject described "a frog stabbed with a knife. There is blood pouring over the sides.")

Frequent recallers tended to have more diary-dream recall (scored by reliable raters on a 5-step amount scale) than infrequent recallers, but this difference was significant only for the stress condition. Although my original interpretation was that the results lent support to a repression hypothesis, a more careful perusal of the results in the context of follow-up studies suggests alternative possibilities. For example, there was statistically nonsignificantly less dream recall for infrequent recallers in the stress, compared to the control, condition. That is, the major effect of the stress manipulation was to affect relatively more dream recall· in the frequent recallers rather than to depress recall in the infrequent recallers. In addition, I have subsequently come to believe that this kind of stress, namely external threat of a more or less physical nature, is less relevant to the hypothesis of repression than would be an internal (ego) threat (Cohen, 1976). These preliminary results may therefore be reinterpreted in terms of hypothetical influences on both individual differences in dream-recall ability and external sources that alter the probability that an individual will pay attention to dream material.

Dream Salience and Dream Recall

Salience refers to the quality of the experience, the nature of the encoding. The salience hypothesis suggests that more intense, emotionally exciting, consciously vivid dreams will tend to be more readily recalled, that individuals with good waking imagery will tend to be better dream recallers, and that conditions that increase dream intensity (e.g., presleep distress, REM as opposed to NREM physiology) will more likely be associated with dream recall.

Two studies on the relationship between home dream recall and presleep mood in female undergraduates can be interpreted within the framework of the salience hypothesis. In the first (Cohen, 1974b), a positive association was found between presleep dysphoric mood and morning dream recall, especially for habitual infrequent recallers. Within-subject comparisons of the amount of dream recall associated with days of highest and lowest self-confidence are shown in Table 8.5. Content, but not contentless, recall is associated with relatively low self-confidence ratings. On the basis of the proposal that the contentless report (recall of dreaming but no details) is an indication of repression (Goodenough, 1967; Witkin, 1969), one would have expected contentless recall to have been associated with low self-confidence. However, these results and those of a study described shortly (Cohen & Wolfe, 1973) suggest an alternative view, that contentless reports are merely indications of interference with recall, rather than

TABLE 8.5
Percentage of Type of Dream Report
Associated with Presleep Level of Self-Confidence

Type of Report	High Self-Confidence	Low Self-Confidence
Content	34**	63**
Contentless	36*	18*
Dreamless	29	19

Note. Test of difference between two proportions. (Adapted from Cohen, 1974b, Table 1.)

* $p < .06$.
**$p < .01$.

psychodynamically motivated rejection of dream material. The follow-up study (Cohen 1974a) again found a negative relation between presleep self-confidence ratings and dream recall for infrequent recallers, but not for frequent recallers.

These results were based on relatively uncontrolled conditions of home dream reporting. It is possible that presleep mood influences the quality of sleep and the stage of sleep from which an individual awakens. There is evidence that subjectively poor sleep in otherwise "normal" individuals is associated with more frequent awakenings from REM sleep and more frequent termination of sleep out of, or in close proximity to, a REM period (Baekeland, Koulack, & Lasky, 1968; Tanaka, 1975). If low self-confidence is associated with lighter sleep or a tendency to awaken more readily from REM than from NREM sleep, a ready explanation for the relationship to dream recall would be available. That is, REM dreams are naturally more salient and more readily recalled, and lighter sleep would reduce any state-dependent (interference) effects on recall. Of course, it is also true that such events would provide a more parsimonious explanation than "failure of repression."

A more direct and controlled test of salience and interference hypotheses for recall is provided by data from the Cohen and Cox (1975) experiment. Male undergraduates preselected on the basis of Maudsley Personality Inventory high (sensitizer) vs. low (repressor) neuroticism were randomly assigned to either an ego-threatening or control situation. The former included perfunctory treatment, social isolation, little information, and ostensible "failure on an IQ test." Postexperimental questionnaire data provided external validity for the manipulation. If repression were a significant factor in determining dream recall, repressors who are subjected to presleep stress should have had less recall. However, for neither REM nor NREM awakenings was there an interaction effect of personality and presleep conditions on dream recall. Rather, a pattern similar to that obtained in the two home dream-diary studies was obtained for diary dream recall in the laboratory in response to alarm clock awakenings in the morning (uncontrolled by the experimenter). The proportion of subjects with diary dream recall in the positive conditions was .38 (.50 for REM, and .27 for NREM, awakenings); in the negative condition the respective figure was .61 (.89 for REM and .43 for NREM). When preexperimental questionnaire data for only the least frequent recaller subjects were used,[6] the relationship was even stronger: .33 for the positive condition and .74 for the negative condition. That the facilitory effect of presleep stress on dream recall can be washed out under "ideal" conditions of dream retrieval suggests that attentional factors (interference) are important determinants of dream recall under typically informal conditions. That is, under conditions in which both internal (dispositional) and external sources of distraction are minimized, dream salience differences will have minimal impact on recall. However, under conditions in which potential sources of interference are maximized, differences in dream salience will produce noticeable differences in dream recall. It is interesting to note that presleep conditions in the Cohen and Cox experiment did have a differential impact on the dream salience of infrequent and frequent recallers that was commensurate with expectation.

Ten infrequent and 10 frequent recallers were selected, such that half of each group had been run in the positive and half in the negative condition. Under the positive condition, there was a marked and significant difference in mean sum salience scores, which largely replicated the Cohen and MacNeilage (1974) findings. However, under the negative condition, there was virtually no difference in salience between the two groups. The latter finding was due to higher dream salience for the infrequent recallers in the negative condition compared to the positive condition rather than any difference across conditions for the frequent recallers. These differential results support the contention derived from the earlier home dream study data that the effect of presleep stress on dream recall is mediated by a change in the salience of the dream material produced by subjects (infrequent recallers) who typically have low-salient dreams. Such mediation is moderated by the relative strength of interference factors, maximized at home and minimized in the laboratory where experimenters elicit and control the reporting process by encouraging attention to the dreaming experience.

These studies of the interaction of conditions designed to produce arousal and individual differences in dream recall are consistent with the hypothesis that there are individual differences in imagery ability or salience whose effects can be changed under certain conditions. The effects obtained in these studies are similar to those obtained in studies of individual differences in the responsiveness to hallucinatory drugs; individuals whose imagery is estimated to be relatively weak require higher doses of LSD to produce the psychedelic intensity comparable to that produced by lower doses given to individuals with good imagery (Barber, 1971).

---

[6]There was virtually no correlation between neuroticism scores and dream-recall scores.

Interference with Dream Recall

The interference hypothesis posits a variety of sources that interfere with encoding and with retrieval (decoding). An obvious example is distraction by external stimuli just after awakening. Dispositional factors include poor recall skills primarily with respect to visual material. A more speculative though potentially important source of interference is state dependency, the inability to retrieve in one physiological state (wakefulness) information that was acquired in a physiologically different state (REM or NREM). Operationally distinguishing between salience and interference is often difficult. For example, is better dream recall after awakening from REM than from NREM sleep evidence of the effect of intense and vivid dream consciousness (salience) or physiological state similarity between REM sleep and wakefulness (low interference), or both?

There is relatively little information on factors that might interfere with encoding (e.g., by reducing dream salience) and decoding (e.g., by distracting attention) dream experiences. Correlational data reviewed above suggest that to some extent, dream recall is a kind of skill that includes interest in, and practice at, paying attention to and communicating information about dream experiences. The phenomenon is, of course, more complicated than this, since it is clear that, under some conditions, trying very hard to recall a dream at the moment of awakening may be futile. I have suggested the possibility that neuromuscular arousal may account for such interference. Nevertheless, other things being equal in theory (they never are in fact), conditions that distract attention from the task of dream perception should be associated with diminished recall. (Conclusions about whether distracting attention reduces recall more than encouraging attention increases recall over neutral conditions will require more data than are available.)

Cohen and Wolfe (1973) studied a sample of 86 male and female undergraduates who were randomly assigned to an experimental (distraction) or control condition. Subjects filled out a dream-diary sheet the next morning. Experimental subjects were asked to call the weather bureau number immediately upon awakening the next morning and to write down the temperature for the day *prior to* writing a detailed description of any dream experiences they could recall. Control subjects were asked to lie in bed quietly for roughly 1.5 minutes (corresponding to the time required by the experimental subjects to carry out the telephone task) prior to describing their dream experiences. Of 40 control reports, 63% were content, 18% were contentless, and 20% were dreamless. Of 46 experimental reports, 33% were content, 43% were contentless, and 24% were dreamless. The difference in the pattern of the results for the two groups was significant. Note that the experimental manipulations had virtually no differential impact on the percentage of dreamless reports, a result commensurate with that obtained in the correlational study of presleep mood and home dream reporting previously described (Cohen, 1974b).

A follow-up study (Cohen & Wolfe, 1973) included a replication of the telephone distraction manipulation, which was combined with a manipulation designed to maximize or minimize fear of dream reporting. Roughly half of each distraction (telephone manipulation) or nondistraction (dream focus) group of subjects was assigned to a high, and half to a low, "dream salience" condition. In the high dream-salience condition, subjects were told that dreams provide information on latent or manifest psychopathology, that their dream reports (to be returned the next day) would be assessed in the light of personality data that were also to be obtained and discussed with them. The rest of the subjects (low-salience condition) were told that they were participating in a study of normative dream content of students of the University of Texas.

Results of this second study are shown in Table 8.6. Note that again, the distraction manipulation had the expected effect (diminution of recall of dream content). However, the effect of the high-salience manipulation was to *increase* rather than to decrease dream recall. The obvious conclusion is that either the threat manipulation increased dream salience or it produced a greater interest in and curiosity about dream content. There was no evidence of any attempt to suppress (if not to repress) dream reporting, even for the subgroup of habitual infrequent recallers, who, according to the repression hypothesis, ought to have suppressed dream reporting. Consider the following results from the dream-focus (nondistraction) condition. Subjects were divided into frequent and infrequent recaller subgroups on the basis of DRF questionnaire estimates obtained prior to their participation in the experiment. Whereas 67% of the frequent recallers reported dream content under the high-salience condition compared to 54% under the low-salience condition, 58% of the infrequent recallers reported dream content under high salience conditions vs. only 36% under low salience conditions. This differential result is similar to others found for comparable groups under conditions that differ with respect to "stress" or "threat" (Cohen, 1974b; Cohen & Cox, 1975; Cohen & MacNeilage, 1974) or with respect to other conditions (Shapiro et al., 1965). That is, rather than maintaining low levels or

TABLE 8.6
Percentage of Diaries Showing Dream Content
Under Various Conditions[a]

	Postsleep Condition		
Presleep Condition	Dream Focus	Distraction	Combined
High dream salience	63	26	43
Low dream salience	45	32	39
Combined	54	29	– –

[a]Adapted from Cohen & Wolfe, 1973, Table 1.

reducing levels of recall in individuals who supposedly repress dreaming (infrequent recallers), stress conditions tend to elicit more dream recall.

Of course, it could be argued that the increased recall in individuals prone to repression is the product of the failure of that repression. However, an increase in dream salience combined with more careful attention to the experience (lowered interference) seems like a more reasonable explanation. After all, if failure of repression were a factor in the increased recall of infrequent recallers, the recalled dreams should show some sign of threatening content. They don't. It might be argued that they don't because repression occurs ''on line'' to affect a censorship, a cleaning-up operation to make the dreams more acceptable to waking recall. Then it would have to be explained why recall is so poor under conditions that are not ego threatening and therefore not hypothesized to elicit a censorship of potentially threatening impulses. Aside from the alternative explanations of salience and interference that are clearly supported by data, the repression hypothesis can not account for much of the variance in dream recall, because more people in our culture do not accept responsibility for, nor typically pay much attention to or worry about, dreams. Why would they be motivated to repress them? If evidence of repression of dreams could be obtained from subjects who are deeply involved with their dreams (e.g., psychoanalytic patients), such evidence could not necessarily be generalized to explain individual differences in dream recall in the ''normal'' population.

It is relatively easy to demonstrate the effect of postsleep distraction on dream retrieval. There is virtually no direct evidence for the operation of factors that might interfere with dream retrieval by operating directly on the dream experience (e.g., preventing dream consciousness) or during the transition from the dreaming to the waking state. On a speculative level, it might be argued that interference with dream recall might be a partial function of the state dependency of dream-experience encoding. Investigators have noted electrophysiological similarities between REM sleep, for example, and wakefulness (Johnson, 1973). This similarity could account for high dream recall after awakening from REM sleep. Others have noted certain unique peculiarities of the REM period such as low muscular tonus and high electrocortical phasic activity (pontine-geniculate-occipital spiking). These peculiarities could account for difficulty in recalling experiences associated with such a state. From a psychobiological perspective, one could argue that the difficulty we have in recalling dreams is related to the psychological differences between the encoded experience and the retrieval mechanisms of wakefulness. In metaphorical terms, the key of waking memory does not fit the lock of dream experience.

For example, it could be argued that individuals with overdeveloped skills of a convergent, objective, analytical nature; skills developed at the expense of, or in the relative absence of, more intuitive, subjective skills, would be especially likely to have difficulty recalling dreams. Such an analysis is consistent with both correlational evidence of individual differences in DRF and evidence of the sharp decrease in dream recallability shortly after awakening. I have suggested elsewhere (Cohen, 1976) that the fading of the dream (more specifically, the fading of a REM dream and the possible substitution in consciousness of a "pseudo-dream" or hypnopompic experience) represents a biological transition from sleep to wakefulness; that in a very real sense, the dream does not slip away from the dreamer upon awakening but rather the dreamer slips away (into wakefulness) from the dream. Evidence from Zimmerman's (1970) study of differences in REM and NREM dream recall between light and deep sleepers, and the Shapiro et al. (1965) data on the effect of abrupt and gradual awakening on dream recall provide some indirect evidence for the kind of process that I am suggesting. However, there are really no good sources of direct evidence. Perhaps, following Bugelski (1971), a good place to start would be to evaluate the correlation between intensity of the preawakening EMG of REM sleep and the ability to recall the experience. If it could be shown that under highly directed conditions of dream retrieval, the correlations among EMG, dream salience, and recall are minimal, whereas under "looser" conditions, there is a highly negative relationship between EMG and recall, this would constitute relatively strong support for the kind of state-dependency interference hypothesis I am proposing.

A general assumption is that the encoding of the dream (determined by the physiological state with which the dream is associated) will affect its retrievability (decoding). In general terms, if the dream is the product largely of spatial encoding (due to the predominant influence of the right hemisphere) whereas postsleep recall is dominated largely by sequential encoding (due to the predominant influence of the left hemisphere), then decoding the dream experience will be particularly difficult. From the perspective of retrieval, good spatial ability would enhance the probability of dream recall. Presumably, there are individual differences in the ability to adopt a "spatial style" that are associated with the ability to recall dreams. From the perspective of encoding, any dream that is influenced by sequential coding without affecting its salience should more likely be recalled.

Therefore, we should expect that dreams that include substantial verbal activity (from which we infer sequential coding) should more likely be recalled. Whereas the right hemisphere may play a major role in determining the salience of the dream, the left hemisphere may play a relatively greater role in determining certain qualities (e.g., verbal) that favor retrieval and certainly *reporting*, which are usually dominated by the left hemisphere. There are two sets of data that directly support this speculation. First, we have published evidence that sleep talkers consistently report higher estimates of dream-recall frequency (MacNeilage et al., 1972). Sleep talking may provide a sign of an active role of the left hemisphere in the modification of the dream. Second, dream recall increases across REM periods during the night. I have obtained consistent evidence that, even controlling for the quality of dream reporting, categories of dream content that can be thought of as reflecting the predominant influence of the left hemisphere also increase across the REM periods of a night (Cohen, 1977a). The increase in significant verbal activity (e.g., conversation rather than isolated words) is the most consistent and statistically significant change. On the other hand, there is no evidence that categories of dream content presumed to reflect the influence of the right hemisphere change in any systematic fashion. Therefore, given the evidence of increasing autonomic activation during later REM dreams and the evidence of increasing left-hemisphere predominance, it is not surprising that there is an increase in dream recall. This increase would presumably be affected by an increase both in the salience and in the verbal encoding of the experience.

These distinctions among the various sources of influence over the encoding of the dream (left and right hemisphere plus subcortical activation) would explain why it is so difficult to obtain large correlations between dream recall and our rather crude measures of individual differences. The recallability of the dream, i.e., its state dependency, would be the joint function of spatial, sequential, and intensity factors during encoding and similar factors that affect decoding. These may be largely independent; they certainly defy operational definition, let alone experimental control, and are only crudely represented by the measures that we typically employ when we consider individual differences. Hypothetically, a good match between spatial/temporal encoding and decoding would—other things (e.g., intensity of the experience) being equal—favor dream recall. But how could we demonstrate such a relationship empirically?

Figure 8.2 summarizes the various factors that could have an effect on dream recall. These factors are organized from the perspective of a general interference hypothesis for two reasons. First, it is not always clear that we are capable of operationally distinguishing salience from interference. Second, although there are far more data apparently relevant to the salience than the interference hypothesis, many of the findings that I previously interpreted as evidence for the operation of salience may be interpreted as easily from the perspective of interference. Third, it is my suspicion that interference, despite its more scanty data base, is potentially a more powerful explanatory construct with respect to dream recall than is the construct of salience. The figure suggests, then, that the recall of dreams will be impeded by some combination of vague dream consciousness, too little verbal encoding, high awakening thresholds, high neuromuscular activation, and inattention to dream material. These in turn may be at least tentatively operationally defined both organismically (e.g., electrophysiologically) and psychologically and are assumed to operate at various "levels" from encoding during dreaming sleep through the awakening process to the decoding stage during immediate postsleep wakefulness. It is further presumed that such factors underlie both amount of dream recall in any particular situation and individual differences in amount and frequency of dream recall.

STAGE OF DREAM   TYPE OF INTERFERENCE   SOURCES OF INTERFERENCE

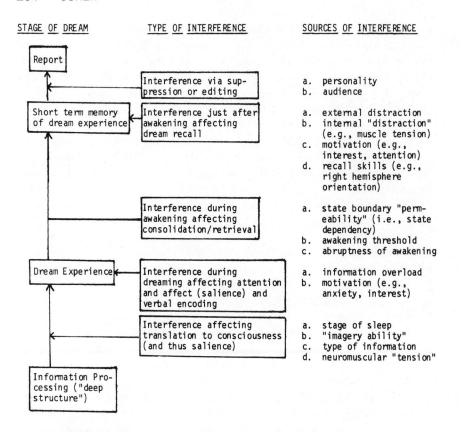

FIG. 8.2.   Hypothetical sources of interference at different stages of a dream report. (Reprinted from Cohen, in press, Figure 6-3.)

UTILITY OF DREAM RECALL DATA

I have reviewed some of the empirical bases of the hypothesis that memory for dream experiences is largely determined by the salience characteristic and by internal and external kinds of interference with the consolidation or retrieval of that information. I would like to suggest that within-subject changes in dream recall may be useful in research on the significance or importance of the dream experience. I use for an example some data obtained in a recent study of individual differences in the ''need'' for REM sleep. There now exists a body of research results strongly suggesting that individuals who score at the repression, low neuroticism, low anxiety end of various ''sensitization'' scales appear to react more stongly to conditions that interfere with or restrict REM sleep (Cohen, 1977b). For example, REM deprivation on one night is followed by a greater increase in REM sleep the following night (greater REM rebound) for low- than for high-neuroticism subjects (Nakazawa, Kotorii, Kotorii, Tachibana, & Nakano, 1975). On the basis of these kinds of findings, I ran a study that included the prediction that REM deprivation would have the following effects, especially for low-neuroticism subjects: (a) progressively shorter onset latency for REM periods during the deprivation night; (b) poorer postsleep performance on the Block Design subtest of the WAIS; and (c) relatively more dream recall (reflecting higher salience of the dreaming process). The latter prediction is particularly relevant, because it provides an example of the utility of the dream-recall datum in the study of the significance of the REM period.

The study included two conditions, a REM-deprivation condition, under which each REM period of a night was interrupted at its onset, and a REM non-deprivation condition, under which each REM period was interrupted at its estimated endpoint. After each awakening, the subject either described a recalled dream experience or, in the absence of recall, current fantasy. (The latter procedure was used to control the fantasy content of the interval.) Six subjects high in neuroticism were run in the deprivation, and six in the nondeprivation, condition; eight subjects low in neuroticism were run in the deprivation condition, and five were run in the nondeprivation condition.

Two of the three predictions were clearly supported by the data. Although there were no differences among the four subgroups on presleep Block Design items, there was a significant interaction for postsleep performance; whereas high-neuroticism subjects in the deprivation condition performed slightly (but nonsignificantly) better than in the nondeprivation condition, low-neuroticism subjects performed strikingly more poorly under the deprivation condition than under the nondeprivation condition.

There were virtually no differences in dream recall (7-step scale representing a combination of amount and clarity and scored from 0 to 6) for the four subgroups on the first REM period awakening. However, by the last REM period, there was a significant interaction. This interaction effect of condition and trait on late REM period dream recall is shown in Fig. 8.3. To what can be attribute this high level of REM dream recall for a group (low neuroticism, high "repressiveness") normally not expected to demonstrate such behavior? Perhaps in the early stages, REM deprivation interrupts a process that is particularly important for this group of individuals. As a consequence, there is a buildup of a kind of organismic pressure represented in part by an intensification of the salience characteristic of the dreaming aspect of the REM process. Although change in salience seems the best explanation, it is also possible that an alteration in the state-dependency characteristic of the dreaming process also occurs. That is, there may be a persistence into wakefulness of some of the qualities normally confined to REM sleep in these individuals. Such a persistence would reduce what might be called the organismic state boundaries between REM and wakefulness and therefore make it easier to recall material encoded at the onset of the interrupted REM period.

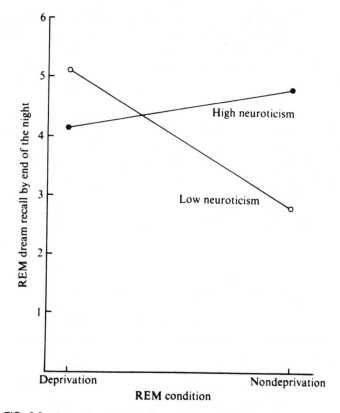

FIG. 8.3.   Interaction of level of neuroticism and REM-deprivation status on dream recall from the last REM period. (Reprinted from Cohen, 1977b, Figure 4.)

I have suggested how dream recall might be explained within the context of a state-dependency hypothesis that includes the constructs of dream salience and interference with recall (for an arousal-retrieval hypothesis including these same constructs, see Koulack & Goodenough, 1976). If this analysis is essentially correct, then differences in dream recall may, to some extent, be used to stand for the degree to which the sleeping and waking states are psychobiologically distant or distinct.

Consider the preliminary results shown in Fig. 8.4 which we obtained from a small group of habitual short (less than 7.0 hours per night) and long (more than 7.5 hours) sleepers. An interesting question is suggested by these differential dream-recall patterns. Is the major difference between these two kinds of individuals that short sleepers get "efficient sleep" (deep sleep, sleep that is psychobiologically most different from wakefulness)? Is it possible that the less efficient the sleep (i.e., the closer it is to wakefulness and therefore the less it carries out its special function), the longer one needs to sleep to maximize the function? (If such were the case, it would be true only for that subset of short and long sleepers whose sleep duration is more determined by differences in "neurotic" disturbances rather than differences in genetic programming.) Such hypothesis could be tested by assessing changes in dream recall concomitant with treatments that induce shorter sleep times in long sleepers, or longer sleep times in short sleepers.

One further potential use for dream-recall data might be mentioned. It is known that there is a decline with age in the amount of REM sleep (Williams, Karacan, & Hursch, 1974). Independent of age, the decline in REM sleep in the aged is associated with low-performance IQ scores (Feinberg, Koresko, Heller, & Steinberg, 1973). There are other observations with regard to aged populations that we need to consider. There is evidence that "fluid" rather than "crystallized" intelligence tends to decline in old age (Horn, 1970; Horn & Cattell, 1966). These data lend indirect support for the hypothesis that there tends to be a relatively greater decline in the sorts of intellective function mediated more by right- than by left-hemisphere processes. If the salience of waking imagery and dreaming is mediated to a large degree by the right hemisphere, then it would be predicted that capacity for imagery and dream recall should be noticeably diminished in aged populations. Kahn and Fisher (1968) have documented

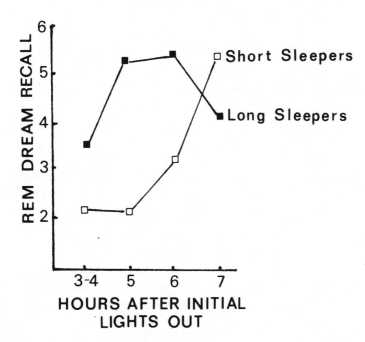

FIG. 8.4. Quality of REM dream report for short and long sleepers at various points in a night of laboratory sleep.

the latter. In a group of 19 male subjects aged 71 to 87, 108 REM awakenings (2 to 11 per subject) yielded 43% dream recall, a figure roughly half that observed for younger samples.

It should be noted that dream recall is also a short-term memory function for which the relationship between right- and left-hemisphere influence is unknown. Since there is reasonably good documentation of a short-term memory decline in the aged (Anders, Fozard, & Lillyquist, 1972; Inglis, Ankus, & Sykes, 1968), it is not surprising that dream recall should diminish as well. Thus, whether one views dream-recall data from the perspective of short-term memory or from the more speculative perspective of a presumed decline in right-hemisphere function, it may be possible to consider *changes* in dream recall as a potentially convenient diagnostic sign of aging. Incidentally, the observation of diminished REM dream recall in the aged is in marked contrast to the evidence that sleep per se is "lighter" (more fitful, less delta, less REM, more awakenings, etc.) (Williams et al., 1974). Normally, lighter sleep ought to be associated with *more* dream recall. That is, the evidence suggests that although there is a diminution of the state dependency of dreaming (which should increase dream recall), there may be a diminution of the salience of the dream (which should decrease dream recall). A combination of reduced salience and impaired short-term memory could go a long way in explaining poor dream recall in the aged.

RECALL OF, IN, AND THROUGH DREAMING

Having completed this review of research on determinants of dream recall, I should make clear that I have been discussing recall *of* dreaming. There are at least two other tangentially related questions. They are what might be called recall *in* dreaming and recall *through* dreaming.

By "recall in dreaming" I refer to the phenomenon of recall of information, apparently nonretrievable during wakefulness, within the context of the dream experience. Transformed by the "dreamwork" of sleep, this information might be described as "available" (in the altered state of consciousness of the dreaming sleep) but not "accessible" (during waking states) unless retrieved from the recalled dream. For examples of retrieval of typically inaccessible information under other kinds of altered states, we may refer to recall produced by hypnosis, psychedelic drugs, and brain stimulation. Of course, we may question the "accuracy" or validity of the products of recall (e.g., their correspondence to the original experience). And I should emphasize my view that the importance of the dreaming process in humans, to the degree that it is adaptive (and this is one of the most difficult of the intriguing problems for scientific dream research), is in the transformation and recombination of information rather than in merely the storage or retention of information.

The point is that the recall of information in dreaming may indeed be useful.

Let me give an anecdotal example: My wife, Leslie, was playing a game in which one tries to recall well-known individuals whose names are represented by quasi-random combinations of pairs of letters in a 26-pair list. It is a timed game that is particularly challenging when unusual initials appear in the list. The most difficult are the combinations of two vowels, e.g., *AA, EE, II, OO, UU*. Some, like *UU*, can be written off as virtually impossible. Others, like *EE*, are most interesting, since they are very difficult but not apparently impossible. For Leslie, the *EE* combination came up, and she was clearly obsessed by it. Prior to sleep she could think of no examples. About 6:00 A.M. the next morning she awakened me in order to recount a dream. Her former high school math teacher (whom she hadn't thought about for years) was in a seat at the end of a row of seats that she had been arranging. Upon awakening she realized that his last name was *E*wing, but it wasn't till over a month later (when we got around to checking the old year-book) that we discovered that his first name was *E*arl!

We have much anecdotal evidence in the dream literature of creativity in dreaming and its usefulness to highly creative individuals (Krippner & Hughes, 1970). How much useful information recalled *in* dreaming is lost to us because of the many factors that induce a failure of recall *of* dreaming? And to what extent has the much touted construct of "incubation" failed to achieve empirically acceptable status because we have paid too little attention to the relationship between specific problems confronted by motivated and gifted people and the content of their dreams? And finally, to what extent does recall in dreaming of typically nonretrievable information laid down early in development, now re-experienced in the dream and responded to *as if it were really happening*, continue to affect the development of waking personality?

By "recall through dreaming," I refer to the question of the extent to which the dreaming process contributes to consolidation and subsequent retrievability of new information (Cohen, in press). The question has been dealt with both theoretically and empirically in a number of forms. For example, it has been proposed that dreaming is a process by which new information is integrated with older information and that this process is particularly influenced by personal dynamisms (Breger, 1967). Others have discussed and designed studies to explore the contribution of REM (i.e., dreaming sleep rather than dreaming in the phenomenological sense) to learning and memory of certain kinds of information (e.g., Chernik, 1972; Dewan, 1969; Grieser, Greenberg, & Harrison, 1972). In other words, rather than thinking of sleep states as passive vehicles contributing to memory of information in the negative sense of providing minimal sources of interference, these investigators think of states of sleep as making an active contribution to the consolidation and retrievability of new information. Of course, another question related to the subject of recall in dreaming is to what extent does the dreaming process contribute to the kinds of transformations of original material that Bartlett (1932) insisted were so much a part of the memory process (Berger, 1963)? To what extent do such transformations differ through dreaming in comparison with transformations through wakefulness? And to what extent, under what conditions, and for which kinds of information are the transformations produced by dreaming (in comparison to wakefulness) better (e.g., more interesting, creative, useful) than the original information?

The implications of problems in the research on dream recall for understanding the dream process and related problems in the area of information processing are broad. They are yet to be sufficiently explored.

ACKNOWLEDGMENTS

Preparation of this paper was supported in part by Grant MH 26613 from the National Institute of Mental Health, United States Public Health Service.

REFERENCES

Agnew, H. W., Webb, W. B., & Williams, R. L. The first night effect: An EEG study of sleep. *Psychophysiology*, 1966, *2*, 263–266.

Anders, T. R., Fozard, J. L., & Lillyquist, T. D. Effects of age upon retrieval from short-term memory. *Developmental Psychology*, 1972, *6*, 214–217.

Antrobus, J. S., Antrobus, J. S., & Singer, J. L. Eye movements accompanying daydreaming, visual imagery, and thought suppression. *Journal of Abnormal and Social Psychology*, 1964, *69*, 244–252.

Antrobus, J., Dement, W., & Fisher, C. Patterns of dreaming and dream recall: An EEG study. *Journal of Abnormal and Social Psychology*, 1964, *69*, 341–344.

Arkin, A. M., Toth, M. F., Baker, J., & Hastey, J. M. The degree of concordance between the context of sleep talking and mentation recalled in wakefulness. *Journal of Nervous and Mental Disease*, 1970, *151*, 375–393.

Aserinsky, E., & Kleitman, N. Regularly occurring periods of eye motility, and concomitant phenomena during sleep. *Science*, 1953, *118*, 273–274.

Aserinsky, E., & Kleitman, N. Two types of ocular motility occurring during sleep. *Journal of Applied Physiology*, 1955, *8*, 1–10.

Austin, M. D. Dream recall and the bias of intellectual ability. *Nature*, 1971, *231*, 59–60.

Baekeland, F. Exercise deprivation: Sleep and psychological reactions. *Archives of General Psychiatry*, 1970, *22*, 365–369.

Baekeland, F., Koulack, D., & Lasky, R. Effects of a stressful presleep experience on electroencephalograph-recorded sleep. *Psychophysiology*, 1968, *4*, 436–443.

Barber, B. Factors underlying individual differences in rate of dream reporting (Doctoral dissertation, Yeshiva University, 1969). *Dissertation Abstracts International*, 1969, *30*, 1351. (University Microfilms No. 69-15, 215)

Barber, T. X. Imagery and "hallucinations": Effects of LSD contrasted with the effects of "hypnotic suggestions." In S. J. Segal (Ed.), *Imagery: Current cognitive approaches*. New York: Academic Press, 1971.

Bartlett, F. C. *Remembering*. Cambridge, England: Cambridge University Press, 1932.

Bell, A. I., & Stroebel, C. F. The scrotal sac and testes during sleep: Physiological correlates and mental content. In W. P. Koella & P. Levin (Eds.), *Sleep: Physiology, biochemistry, psychology, pharmacology, clinical implications*. Basel, Switzerland: S. Karger, 1973.

Berger, R. J. Experimental modification of dream content by meaningful verbal stimuli. *British Journal of Psychiatry*, 1963, *109*, 722–740.

Breger, L. Function of dreams. *Journal of Abnormal Psychology Monograph*, 1967, *72* (5, Whole No. 641), 1–28.

Bugelski, B. R. The definition of the image. In S. J. Segal (Ed.), *Imagery: Current cognitive approaches*. New York: Academic Press, 1971.

Byrne, D. Repression-sensitization as a dimension of personality. In B. A. Maher (Ed.), *Progress in experimental personality research* (Vol. 1). New York: Academic Press, 1964.

Cartwright, R. D., Bernick, N. Borowitz, G., & Kling, A. Effect of an erotic movie on sleep and dreams of young men. *Archives of General Psychiatry*, 1969, *20*, 262–271.

Chernik, D. A. Effect of REM sleep deprivation on learning and recall by humans. *Perceptual and Motor Skills*, 1972, *34*, 283–294.

Cohen, D. B. Dream recall and short-term memory. *Perceptual and Motor Skills*, 1971, *33*, 867–871.

Cohen, D. B. Presleep experience and home dream reporting: An exploratory study. *Journal of Consulting and Clinical Psychology*, 1972, *38*, 122–128.

Cohen, D. B. A comparison of genetic and social contributions to dream recall frequency. *Journal of Abnormal Psychology*, 1973, *82*, 368–371.

Cohen, D. B. Effect of personality and presleep mood on dream recall. *Journal of Abnormal Psychology*, 1974, *83*, 151–156. (a)

Cohen, D. B. Presleep mood and dream recall. *Journal of Abnormal Psychology*, 1974, *83*, 45–51. (b)

Cohen, D. B. Toward a theory of dream recall. *Psychological Bulletin*, 1974, *81*, 138–154. (c)

Cohen, D. B. Eye movements during REM sleep: The influence of personality and presleep conditions. *Journal of Personality and Social Psychology*, 1975, *32*, 1090–1093.

Cohen, D. B. Dreaming: Experimental investigation of representational and adaptive properties. In G. E. Schwartz & D. Shapiro (Eds.), *Consciousness and self-regulation: Advances in research* (Vol. 1). New York: Plenum. 1976.

Cohen, D. B. Changes in REM dream content during the night: Implications for a hypothesis about changes in cerebral dominance across REM periods. *Perceptual and Motor Skills*, 1977, *44*, 1267–1277. (a)

Cohen, D. B. Neuroticism and dreaming sleep: A case for interactionism in personality research. *British Journal of Social and Clinical Psychology*, 1977, *16*, 153–163. (b)

Cohen, D. B. Sources of bias in our characterization of dreams. *Perceptual and Motor Skills*, 1977, *45*, 98. (c)

Cohen, D. B. *Sleep and dreaming: Origin, nature, and functions*. Oxford, England: Pergamon, in press.

Cohen, D. B., & Cox, C. Neuroticism in the sleep laboratory: Implications for representational and adaptive properties of dreaming. *Journal of Abnormal Psychology*, 1975, *84*, 91–108.

Cohen, D. B., & MacNeilage, P. F. A test of the salience hypothesis of dream recall. *Journal of Consulting and Clinical Psychology*, 1974, *42*, 699–703.

Cohen, D. B., & Wolfe, G. Dream recall and repression: Evidence for an alternative hypothesis. *Journal of Consulting and Clinical Psychology*, 1973, *41*, 349–355.

Cory, T. L., Ormiston, D. W., Simmel, E., & Dainoff, M. Predicting the frequency of dream recall. *Journal of Abnormal Psychology*, 1975, *84*, 261–266.

Dement, W. Report IV(B): Comments to Report IV. In G. C. Lairy & P. Salzarulo (Eds.), *The experimental study of human sleep: Methodological problems*. Amsterdam, The Netherlands: Elsevier, 1975.

Dement, W., & Kleitman, N. The relation of eye movements during sleep to dream activity: An objective method for the study of dreaming. *Journal of Experimental Psychology*, 1957, *53*, 339–346.

Dement, W., & Wolpert, E. The relation of eye movements, body motility, and external stimuli to dream content. *Journal of Experimental Psychology*, 1958, *55*, 543–553.

Dewan, E. M. The programming (P) hypothesis for REMs. *Physical Science Research Papers*, No. 388. Cambridge, Mass.: Air Force Cambridge Research Laboratories, Project 5628, 1969.

Domhoff, B., & Gerson, A. Replication and critique of three studies on personality correlates of dream recall. *Journal of Consulting Psychology*, 1967, *31*, 431.

Evans, F. J. Personal communication, 1977.

Feinberg, I., Koresko, R. L., Heller, N., & Steinberg, H. R. Sleep EEG and eye-movement patterns in young and aged normals and in patients with chronic brain syndrome. In W. B. Webb (Ed.), *Sleep: An active process: Research and commentary*. Glenview, Ill.: Scott, Foresman, 1973.

Fiss, H. The need to complete one's dreams. In J. Fisher & L. Breger (Eds.), *The meaning of dreams: Recent insights from the laboratory*. Research Symposium No. 3, Sacramento, California: Bureau of Research, California Department of Mental Hygiene, 1969.

Foulkes, D. *The psychology of sleep*. New York: Scribner's, 1966.

Foulkes, D., & Pope, R. Primary visual experience and secondary cognitive elaboration in state REM: A modest confirmation and extension. *Perceptual and Motor Skills*, 1973, *37*, 107–118.

Freud, S. The interpretation of dreams. In J. Strachey (Ed.), *The standard edition of the complete psychological works of Sigmund Freud* (Vols. 4–5). London: Hogarth Press, 1953. (Originally published, 1900.)

Gardiner, R., Grossman, W. I., Roffwarg, H. P., & Weiner, H. The relationship of small limb movements during REM sleep to dreamed limb action. *Psychosomatic Medicine*, 1975, *37*, 147–159.

Goodenough, D. R. Some recent studies of dream recall. In H. A. Witkin & Helen B. Lewis (Eds.), *Experimental studies of dreaming*. New York: Random House, 1967.

Goodenough, D. R., Witkin, H. A., Lewis, H. B., Koulack, D., & Cohen, H. Repression, interference, and field dependence as factors in dream forgetting. *Journal of Abnormal Psychology*, 1974, *83*, 32–44.

Grieser, C., Greenberg, R., & Harrison, R. H. The adaptive function of sleep: The differential effects of sleep and dreaming on recall. *Journal of Abnormal Psychology*, 1972, *80*, 280–286.

Hartmann, E. *The functions of sleep*. New Haven, Conn.: Yale University Press, 1973.

Hiscock, M. Eye-movement asymmetry and hemispheric function: An examination of individual differences. *Journal of Psychology*, 1977, *97*, 49–52.

Hiscock, M., & Cohen, D. B. Visual imagery and dream recall. *Journal of Research in Personality*, 1973, *7*, 179–188.

Horn, J. L. Organization of data on life-span development of human abilities. In L. R. Goulet & P. B. Baltes (Eds.), *Life-span developmental psychology: Research and theory*. New York: Academic Press, 1970.

Horn, J. L., & Cattell, R. B. Age differences in primary mental ability factors. *Journal of Gerontology*, 1966, *21*, 210–220.

Humphrey, M. E., & Zangwill, O. L. Cessation of dreaming after brain injury. *Journal of Neurological and Neurosurgical Psychiatry*, 1951, *14*, 322–325.

Inglis, J., Ankus, M. N., & Sykes, D. H. Age-related differences in learning and short-term memory from childhood to the senium. *Human Development*, 1968, *11*, 42–52.

Johnson, L. C. Are stages of sleep related to waking behavior? *American Scientist*, 1973, *61*, 326–338.

Kahn, E., & Fisher, C. Dream recall and erections in the healthy aged. *Psychophysiology*, 1968, *4*, 393. (Abstract)

Karacan, I., Goodenough, D. R., Shapiro, A., & Starker, S. Erection cycle during sleep in relation to dream anxiety. *Archives of General Psychiatry*, 1966, *15*, 183–189.

Koulack, D., & Goodenough, D. R. Dream recall and dream-recall failure: An arousal-retrieval model. *Psychological Bulletin*, 1976, *83*, 975–984.

Krippner, S., & Hughes, W. Dreams and human potential. *Journal of Humanistic Psychology*, 1970, *10*, 1−20.

Lavie, P., & Kripke, D. F. Ultradian rhythms: The 90-minute clock inside us. *Psychology Today*, 1975, *8*, pp. 54−56; 65.

Lewis, H. B., Goodenough, D. R., Shapiro, A., & Sleser, I. Individual differences in dream recall. *Journal of Abnormal Psychology*, 1966, *71*, 52−59.

MacNeilage, P. F., Cohen, D. B., & MacNeilage, L. A. Subjects' estimations of sleeptalking propensity and dream recall frequency are positively related. *Journal of Consulting and Clinical Psychology*, 1972, *39*, 341.

Marks, D. F. Individual differences in the vividness of visual imagery and their effect on function. In P. W. Sheehan (Ed.), *The functon and nature of imagery*. New York: Academic Press, 1972.

Mendelson, J. H., Siger, L., & Solomon, P. Psychiatric observations on congenital and acquired deafness: Symbolic and perceptual processes in dreams. *American Journal of Psychiatry*, 1960, *116*, 883−888.

Molinari, S., & Foulkes, D. Tonic and phasic events during sleep: Psychological correlates and implications. *Perceptual and Motor Skills*, 1969, *29*, 343−368.

Murphy, G. *Personality: A biosocial approach to origins and structure*. New York: Harper & Brothers, 1947.

Nakazawa, Y., Kotorii, M., Kotorii, T., Tachibana, H., & Nakano, T. Individual differences in compensatory rebound of REM sleep, with particular reference to their relationship to personality and behavioral characteristics. *Journal of Nervous and Mental Disease*, 1975, *161*, 18−25.

Orlinsky, D. E. Rorschach test correlates of dreaming and dream recall. *Journal of Projective Techniques and Personality Assessment*, 1966, *30*, 250−253.

Rechtschaffen, A. Dream reports and dream experiences. *Experimental Neurology, Supplement 4*, 1967, 4−15.

Rechtschaffen, A. The psychophysiology of mental activity during sleep. In J. McGuigan & R. A. Schoonover (Eds.), *The psychophysiology of thinking*. New York: Academic Press, 1973.

Reich, W. *Character analysis*. New York: Noonday, 1949.

Schechter, N., Schmeidler, G. R., & Staal, M. Dream reports and creative tendencies in students of the arts, sciences, and engineering. *Journal of Consulting Psychology*, 1965, *29*, 415−421.

Schonbar, R. A. Some manifest characteristics of recallers and nonrecallers of dreams. *Journal of Consulting Psychology*, 1959, *23*, 414−418.

Schonbar, R. A. Differential dream recall frequency as a component of life style. *Journal of Consulting Psychology*, 1965, *29*, 468−474.

Shapiro, A. Dreaming and the physiology of sleep: A critical review of some empirical data and a proposal for a theoretical model of sleep and dreaming. *Experimental Neurology, Supplement 4*, 1967, 56−81.

Shapiro, A., Goodenough, D. R., Biederman, I., & Sleser, I. Dream recall and the physiology of sleep. *Journal of Applied Physiology*, 1964, *19*, 778−783.

Shapiro, A., Goodenough, D. R., Lewis, H. B., & Sleser, I. Gradual arousal from sleep: A determinant of thinking reports. *Psychosomatic Medicine*, 1965, *27*, 342−349.

Singer, J. L. *The inner world of daydreaming*. New York: Harper & Row, 1975.

Singer, J. L., & Schonbar, R. Correlates of daydreaming: A dimension of self-awareness. *Journal of Consulting Psychology*, 1961, *25*, 1−6.

Snyder, F. The phenomenology of dreaming. In L. Madow & L. H. Snow (Eds.), *The psychodynamic implications of the physiological studies on dreams*. Springfield, Ill.: Charles C Thomas, 1970.

Stoyva, J., & Kamiya, J. Electrophysiological studies of dreaming as the prototype of a new strategy in the study of consciousness. *Psychological Review*, 1968, *75*, 192−205.

Tanaka, M. Characteristics of poor sleep with the normal human being. *Folia Psychiatrica et Neurological Japonica*, 1975, *29*, 149−167.

Tart, C. T. Frequency of dream recall and some personality measures. *Journal of Consulting Psychology*, 1962, *26*, 467–470.

Tversky, A., & Kahneman, D. Judgment under uncertainty: Heuristics and biases. *Science*, 1974, *185*, 1124–1131.

Webb, W. B. The spontaneous termination of sleep. *Sleep Research*, 1977, *6*, 118.

Webb, W. B., & Kersey, J. Recall of dreams and the probability of stage 1—REM sleep. *Perceptual and Motor Skills*, 1967, *24*, 627–630.

Williams, R. L., Karacan, I., & Hursch, C. J. *EEG of human sleep: Clinical applications.* New York: Wiley, 1974.

Witkin, H. A. Presleep experience and dreams. In J. Fisher & L. Breger (Eds.), *The meaning of dreams: Recent insights from the laboratory* (California Mental Health Research Symposium No. 3) Sacramento, Calif.: Bureau of Research, California Department of Mental Hygiene, 1969.

Witkin, H. A., Dyk, R. B., Faterson, H. F., Goodenough, D. R., & Karp, S. A. *Psychological differentiation: Studies of development.* New York: Wiley, 1962.

Zimmerman, W. B. Sleep mentation and auditory awakening thresholds. *Psychophysiology*, 1970, *6*, 540–549.

9 State-Dependent Learning and Retrieval: Methodological Cautions and Theoretical Considerations

James M. Swanson
Marcel Kinsbourne
The Hospital for Sick Children, Toronto

In many experiments with drugs a subject learns new information in one of two "states": when the drug in question is given and is exerting its effect on the central nervous system, or when a placebo is given and the drug is not exerting its effect. In the same way, retention may be tested in either the drug or placebo state. In such a paradigm it is important to consider the possibility of state-dependent learning (SDL)—that is, whether retention is better when the subject is tested in the same state as that in which learning originally occurred. Table 9.1 shows the 2 × 2 factorial design that is standard in the SDL literature and describes the outcomes that may be observed. If SDL occurs, retention in the drug–drug (DD) combination should be superior to that in the placebo–drug (PD) combination, and retention in the placebo–placebo combination (PP) should be superior to that in the drug–placebo combination (DP). If only SDL occurs, the two control conditions (PP and DD) should be equivalent. However, invariably the drug treatment has some other effect as well, and it is important not to confuse these effects with SDL. A drug may either impair or facilitate initial learning or subsequent retention, which would be reflected in the analysis of variance as a significant main effect of either learning or retention state (separately or in combination); evidence for SDL emerges only when the learning and retention states interact.

State-dependent learning has received considerable attention in the recent literature (for extensive reviews, see Bliss, 1974; Eich, 1977; Keppel & Zubrzycki, 1977; Overton, 1968, 1971, 1973, 1977), and it is commonly associated with drug-induced changes in the behavior of animals and humans. That association is probably due to a convenient property of many drugs, whose rapid onset and end of effectiveness can be used by the experimenter to alter the

275

TABLE 9.1
The Standard 2 × 2 Design Used to Evaluate Hypothetical
Drug-Induced Effects on Acquisition and Retention

Acquisition State	Retention State	Combination	Interaction Effect	Main Effects of Drug	Combined Effects
Placebo (P)	Placebo (P)	PP (same states)	No effect (control)	No effect (control)	No effect (control)
Placebo (P)	Drug (D)	PD (different states)	Impairment due to SDL	Retention effect	Retention effect plus SDL effect
Drug (D)	Placebo (P)	DP (different states)	Impairment due to SDL	Acquisition effect	Acquisition effect plus SDL effect
Drug (D)	Drug (D)	DD (same states)	No effect (control)	Acquisition effect plus retention effect	Acquisition effect plus retention effect

organism's state in a clear and controlled manner. However, state-dependent learning is not restricted to drug-induced changes in state, and a variety of mechanisms can produce "dissociated" states: sleep (Evans, Gustafson, O'Connell, Orne, & Shor, 1966, 1970), time of day (Holloway, 1977; Jones, 1974), arousal level (Fischer & Landon, 1972), mental illness (Weingartner, 1977), simple context in experimental settings (Gooden & Baddeley, 1975; Pan, 1926), incentive motivation and electroconvulsive shock (Robbins & Meyer, 1970), and spreading cortical depression (Schneider, 1968). Appropriate acquisition-retention combinations of these states produce SDL-like effects that are as theoretically interesting and practically important as drug-produced SDL. In this paper we concentrate on those methodological and theoretical issues raised by drug related state-dependent learning that have important implications for a general theory of memory.

Before starting, a distinction must be made between learning through extended practice and the memory of a single experience. A traditional definition suggests that "learning is a relatively permanent change in a behavioral tendency that occurs as a result of reinforced practice" (Kimble & Garmezy, 1968, p. 262). All of the SDL research done with animals has been with tasks that are designed to investigate this type of learning, and some of the SDL research in humans has followed this format. Recently, some interesting research on humans has departed from this practice by employing a task that requires the recall of an event presented only *once*. This type of investigation is related to a construct called *episodic memory* (Tulving, 1972), and it may be qualitatively different from the research on associations acquired through repeated practice. Since state-dependent effects have been reported in both paradigms, both are discussed in this chapter.

The purpose of the present chapter, then, is to discuss drug-induced changes in "states" that may be responsible for dissociated learning or retrieval. This chapter is divided into four parts. First, the standard paradigms used to demonstrate drug-induced state-dependent learning are reviewed. This is necessary because the problems associated with measuring SDL are so great that the very existence of SDL is sometimes questioned on methodological grounds. The criticism of this paradigm is relevant to the research on non-drug-induced states, too. Second, the task specificity of SDL effects is covered, because not all measures of performance reflect state changes. Third, the relationship of SDL to theories of memory is discussed. Fourth, the adaptive significance of SDL-like effects is discussed.

DEMONSTRATIONS OF STATE-DEPENDENT LEARNING

Overton (1974), in one of the most important papers in this area, discussed in detail some of the methodological problems associated with measuring SDL. The problems he discussed there warrant additional coverage here. Part of Overton's (1974) discussion centers around the 2 × 2 design outlined in Table 9.1, which yields four combinations (DD, PD, PP, DP) of acquisition and retention states. This design was a major advance in the investigation of drug effects, because in most studies before 1960 (and many after then), only the PP and PD combinations were used to determine drug effects. Miller (1957) was one of the first to point out that impaired performance due to an interaction of acquisition and retention states could be mistaken for the main effect of the drug if only the PP and PD conditions were used. By adding the DD and DP conditions, he reasoned, performance effects (reflected by the main effects of the drug on retention) could be differentiated from a state-dependent effect (reflected by the interaction of the learning and retention states).

The 2 × 2 design suggested by Miller (1957) yields four distinct conditions, so only three independent questions may be asked of the data. Overton (1974) pointed out that more comparisons than three are often necessary to evaluate an SDL effect. According to his argument, drugs are expected to have a variety of effects on behavior, and in general, state-dependent effects occur *only* in conjunction with other drug effects. Thus, these "other" drug effects must be adjusted for before identifying a residual SDL effect.

Adjusting for One Main Effect

Concrete examples of this adjustment procedure are necessary to make Overton's (1974) approach clear. First, consider the expected main effect of alcohol on acquisition, which Overton (1974) labels a "memorization deficit." Such an effect appeared in one of the initial SDL studies on the effect of alcohol on learning (Storm & Caird, 1967). The performance scores (trials to criterion on a serial-learning task) for the four combinations of acquisition and retention states are provided in Table 9.2. Impairment of retention performance in the PD and DP conditions (relative to the DD and PP conditions) should be apparent if simple SDL occurred. But performance in the PD condition was better than

TABLE 9.2
Effects of Alcohol on Trials to Criterion in a Serial Learning Task
(from Storm and Caird, 1967)

Combination	Performance on Acquisition Task	Performance on Retention Task	Hypothetical Drug Effects (Overton, 1974)
PP	20.7	5.8	Control
PD	20.7	7.5	SDL
DP	24.8	11.2	SDL plus memorization deficit
DD	24.8	8.5	Memorization deficit

performance in the DD condition. Obviously, the simple outcome did not materialize, and more than an SDL effect is reflected in the retention data. What other effects did occur? The slight drug-induced impairment during acquisition, along with the overall poorer performance of retention in the two conditions associated with alcohol during acquisition (DP and DD), suggest that a main effect of the alcohol treatment is a "memorization decrement." What pattern of performance is expected if a main effect of acquisition state occurs in conjunction with an SDL effect? By summing the effects of a memorization deficit and SDL, Overton (1974) has presented a theoretical pattern of retention performance (p. 1802, Table 2, panel 8) showing *slightly* impaired performance in the PD condition (due to a SDL effect alone) and the DD condition (due to a memorization deficit alone), and *severely* impaired performance in the DP condition (due to both an SDL effect and a memorization deficit). The observed results of Storm and Caird (1967) fit this pattern.

This pattern is consistent across experiments in which alcohol has been investigated. Using a rote learning task, Goodwin and his colleagues obtained a similar pattern of performance presented in another experiment on alcohol and SDL (Goodwin, Powell, Bremer, Hoine, & Stern, 1969). The data (errors to criterion on a rote learning test) are presented in Table 9.3. The patterns of performance in acquisition and retention in this experiment are virtually the same as in the Storm and Caird (1967) experiment. An alcohol-induced memorization deficit impairs performance in the DP and DD conditions during the acquisition and retention phases of learning, and an SDL effect acts to impair performance in the PD condition and to compound the impairment in the DP condition.

In the two studies cited, the drug used was a depressant (alcohol) that impaired performance of the learning task. SDL has also been demonstrated in a situation in which a drug improved performance. We investigated the effect of stimulant drugs on the learning of hyperactive children (Swanson & Kinsbourne, 1976). A paired-associate learning task was administered in drug and placebo conditions, and retention was tested in the four combinations of acquisition and retention. The data (errors to criterion), are presented in Table 9.4. It was

TABLE 9.3
Effects of Alcohol on Errors to Criterion in Rote Learning Task
(from Goodwin, Powell, Bremer, Howie, and Stern, 1969)

Condition	Performance on Acquisition Task	Performance on Retention Task	Hypothetical Drug Effects (Overton, 1974)
PP	12.05	13.75	Control
PD	12.29	15.10	SDL
DP	20.56	24.55	SDL plus memorization deficit
DD	16.96	16.45	Memorization deficit

TABLE 9.4
Effects of a Stimulant Drug (Methylphenidate) on Errors to Criterion
in a Paired-Associate Learning Task (from Swanson and Kinsbourne, 1976)

Condition	Performance on Acquisition Task	Performance on Retention Task	Hypothetical Drug Effects (Overton, 1974)
PP	33.0	15.9	Control
PD	33.0	12.9	SDL plus performance facilitation
DP	24.4	20.3	SDL
DD	24.4	9.1	Performance facilitation

expected from previous work by Conners (Conners, Eisenberg, & Sharpe, 1964; Conners, Rothschild, Eisenberg, & Schwartz, 1969) that a drug-induced facilitation of performance would occur when hyperactive children were given stimulants, and the acquisition data confirmed that prediction. Apparently, as shown above in Table 9.4, an SDL effect also impaired performance in the PD and DP conditions, but the performance-facilitation effect compensated for that SDL effect in the PD condition. Thus, performance was not different in the PD condition than in the control (PP) condition, despite an SDL effect. This is in contrast to the effect of alcohol in the previous examples, in which the control (PP) condition produced the best performance.

What comparisons are most meaningful among the four acquisition–retention-state combinations? This question logically arises when main effects are considered as uninteresting in themselves. Should retention state be held constant to inspect the SDL effect, or should the acquisition state be held constant? If the retention state is held constant, then the proper SDL comparisons are (a) DD−PD and (b) PP−DP. If acquisition state is held constant, then the proper SDL comparisons are (a) DD−DP and (b) PP−PD. Which method is best?

If one main effect is significant in the retention data and the other is not, then the factor that is responsible for that effect should be held constant. This may differ for various drugs and for different populations. For example, with alcohol, the acquisition effect may be significant but not the retention effect; but for amphetamine, the retention effect may be significant but not the acquisition effect. Thus, the most meaningful set of comparisons among the four combinations of acquisition and retention states depends on the pattern of significant main effects.

In each example provided, only one main effect was considered. What happens if both main effects are considered at the same time, rather than adjusting for *only* the acquisition effect (e.g., the "memorization deficit" in the Storm and Caird [1967] and the Goodwin et al. [1969] studies) or for *only* the retention effect (e.g., the "performance facilitation" in the Swanson and Kinsbourne [1976] study)? The limitation of the 2×2 design becomes apparent when both adjustments are made.

Adjusting for Two Main Effects

In the three studies used in the foregoing examples, the SDL effect may appear to be greater when comparing the retention performance from the DP condition to retention performance from the PD condition. That pattern in the retention data is often attributed to *asymmetrical SDL*, a term used to characterize situations in which learning appears to transfer from the nondrug state to the drug state (PD) but not from the drug to the nondrug state (DP). The existence of asymmetrical SDL has been questioned, because a combination of drug effects could summate to produce an asymmetrical pattern in the retention data that may obscure the actual occurrence of *symmetrical* SDL or the absence of an SDL effect. (Deutsch & Roll, 1973; Overton, 1974). This possibility may be demonstrated concretely with reference to the studies cited in Tables 9.2, 9.3 and 9.4 by following Overton's suggested procedure for adjusting the means from the three cells in the 2×2 design that contain a drug treatment (PD, DP, DD) for comparison with the control condition (PP). First, the acquisition effect of the drug may be estimated by taking the difference between the average score associated with placebo during acquisition (PP + PD)/2 and the average score associated with drug during acquisition (DD + DP)/2. Next, the retention effect of the drug may be estimated by taking the difference between the average score associated with placebo during retention (PP + DP)/2 and the average score associated with drug during retention (DD + PD)/2. Those effects were estimated and added to the means for the four conditions to determine the adjustments and adjusted scores shown in Table 9.5.

TABLE 9.5
Examples of Adjusting for Main Effects of Acquisition and
Retention in the 2 X 2 Design

	Condition	Score	Adjustment for Acquisition Effect	Adjustment for Retention Effect	Adjusted Scores
Storm and	PP	5.8			5.8
Caird (1967)	PD	7.5		+0.5	8.0
	DP	11.2	−3.2		8.0
	DD	8.5	−3.2	+0.5	5.8
Goodwin et al.	PP	13.75			13.750
(1969)	PD	15.10		+3.375	18.475
	DP	24.55	−6.075		18.475
	DD	16.45	−6.075	+3.375	13.750
Swanson and	PP	15.9			15.9
Kinsbourne	PD	12.9		+7.1	20.0
(1976)	DP	20.3	−0.3		20.0
	DD	9.1	−0.3	+7.1	15.9

Inspection of the four conditions (PP, PD, DP, DD) in the examples given in Table 9.5 will show that in all cases, after adjusting for the two main effects, a *symmetrical* SDL effect emerges. Of course, this is no accident: For any set of scores assigned to the four combinations of the 2 × 2 design, a symmetrical SDL effect will *always* be reflected in the adjusted means. Consider the hypothetical scores presented in Table 9.6, representing number of words correctly recalled, which were chosen to reflect the extreme cases of asymmetrical SDL, in which no transfer occurs following a state change from drug to placebo and perfect transfer occurs following a state change in the opposite direction from placebo to drug. Even this extreme example, which we manufactured to represent an asymmetrical SDL, will show symmetrical SDL following adjustment for main effects.

The limitations of the 2 × 2 design become apparent when one realizes that the adjustment procedures suggested by Overton (1974) are no different in principle from the adjustment procedures applied automatically in the usual analysis of variance of the data from a 2 × 2 design. This issue is treated in more detail by Swanson and Kinsbourne (in press). Given this knowledge, consider the report of Deutsch and Roll (1973). They assert that "It is not permissible to conclude that there is asymmetrical dissociation of memory unless the existence of row and column effects has been adequately excluded" [p. 276]. But if a 2 × 2 design is used and adjustments are made for row (acquisition) and column (retention) effects, then it is *impossible* to conclude statistically that asymmetrical SDL occurs. Only the presence or absence of an SDL effect can be evaluated in the standard analysis of variance, since only one degree of freedom is available to test the interaction.

We have proposed a way to explicitly test for bidirectional SDL, which is the first step in demonstrating symmetrical SDL (Swanson & Kinsbourne, 1976). Instead of using the three degrees of freedom in the usual way specified by analysis of variance, we specified three orthogonal contrasts to test for: (a) performance facilitation, (b) transfer from the drug to the placebo state (DP versus PP), and (c) transfer from the placebo to the drug state (PD versus DD). In addition to this use of planned comparisons in our analysis, we altered the task procedures too.

TABLE 9.6
A Hypothetical Example of Adjusting for Main Effects When
Asymmetrical SDL Exists

Condition	Hypothetical Score	Acquisition Effect	Retention Effect	Adjusted Score
P	4 (perfect recall)			4
PD	4 (perfect recall)		−2	2
DP	0 (no recall)	+2		2
DD	4 (perfect recall)	+2	−2	4

Usually, in transfer paradigms in which the paired-associate learning procedure is used, several lists of items are learned in each of the acquisition states, and then the same lists are relearned in one of the possible retention states. Then the "savings" associated with relearning the initial lists are calculated. In our procedure, we did not require relearning of the initial lists in their original form. Instead, we combined several initial lists learned in different states into a single longer list for relearning. Then, instead of calculating the savings associated with relearning, we observed the difference in relearning items *within the same list* that were initially learned in different states. During acquisition, subjects learned four lists of six paired associates in each state. For retention, half the items from each list were combined to produce a 24-item list for testing in one retention state, and the remaining half of the items from each list were combined to produce a 24-item list for testing in the alternate retention state. Due to the short-acting characteristics of the drug being used (methylphenidate), drug and placebo conditions were established within a single day. Our arrangement allowed for a test of SDL within a single test session, and thus the main effect of the drug on retention was held constant. Across the two test sessions within a day, all four combinations of the acquisition and retention states were tested. This procedure, however, does not hold constant (within a given SDL comparison) differences in initial learning of the items across the two acquisition states.

Since only three degrees of freedom were available for statistical evaluation, an explicit test of the effect of the acquisition state *on retention* could not be made in the context of either SDL test. But in addition to the arrangement already described, we attempted to hold memorization factors constant by requiring subjects to learn, in both states, to the same criterion of two perfect recitations of each list. However, as Overton (1974) noted, this adjustment procedure is not without problems and may be inadequate. Thus, our explicit tests for bidirectional SDL were made at the expense of an explicit test of the main effect of the acquisition state.

This highlights the problems of the 2 × 2 design; as Overton (1974) noted, there is not enough information in the design to sufficiently test various models of SDL. For example, even in our tests for bidirectional SDL, we did not adequately address the question of symmetrical SDL. To do that in the context of planned comparisons, we would first have to demonstrate the existence of bidirectional SDL and then contrast the magnitude of the SDL effect across the two retention sessions in which an effect could occur. This test can be made orthogonal to the bidirectional tests, and the exact procedure is discussed in more detail by Swanson and Kinsbourne (in press), but its use precludes any test of a main effect.

It should be remembered that although the limitations of the 2 × 2 design are serious in discussions of characteristics (such as asymmetry) of the SDL effect, they are not necessarily damaging when merely the existence of an SDL effect is in question. For the purpose of this chapter, it is the existence of an overall SDL effect that is important to establish. The 2 × 2 design, despite its limitations, has been used successfully to provide statistical support for an over-all SDL effect, even though question of the symmetry of this effect remains unanswered.

The Drug Discrimination Paradigm

Despite the difficulties with the 2×2 design, it remains the usual one in human SDL research. That is not the case in animal SDL research. Most studies on animals now use another paradigm called the *drug discrimination* paradigm. The paradigm is derived from the basic procedures in instrumental learning. The usual task has two alternative responses (e.g., a T-maze). Animals are taught to make one response when in the drug state and the other response in the placebo state. Over repeated training sessions, the appropriate response comes to be made reliably in each state, and a drug discrimination is said to be learned. The drug is thought to act as a discriminative stimulus that has acquired response control. In other words, the drug appears to be a discriminative cue that sets the appropriate occasion for the behavior that leads to reinforcement.

The basic difference between the SDL paradigm and the drug discrimination paradigm is that the repeated training procedure is not necessary in the SDL paradigm. In the 2×2 design, after a single administration of drug in the PD and DP conditions, the response learned in one state fails to transfer to the alternate state or only does so partially. In the drug discrimination paradigm, evidence for dissociation is built up gradually by repeated training that occurs over several administrations of the drug.

Overton (1964) hypothesized that SDL effects and drug discrimination effects are manifestations of the same process; and over the years his hypothesis has become generally accepted. During this time, several desirable features of the drug discrimination paradigm were noted (e.g., the ability to use a lower dose of drug to demonstrate dissociation), and several weaknesses of the 2×2 design were delineated and acknowledged. The result is that today the drug discrimination paradigm has virtually replaced the 2×2 design in research on animals. Overton's (1968, 1974, 1977) detailed summaries of techniques and data derived from the drug discrimination paradigm make it clear that drugs that act on the central nervous system are potent discriminative cues; this is taken by some as strong evidence for the existence of SDL.

SPECIFICITY OF SDL EFFECTS

Even when all the known design problems are considered, the existence of overall SDL effects is well established (Eich, 1977; Overton, 1968, 1974, 1977; Weingartner, 1977). But SDL effects do not *always* occur. The magnitude of any effect in a drug study is dependent on the dose of drug used, and drug-induced SDL is no exception to this rule. In addition, task specificity of any drug response must be recognized (Weiss & Laties, 1962). For example, over the last 40 years, it has been repeatedly asserted that stimulant drugs improve learning of normal adults (see Grinspoon & Hedbloom, 1975 and Kolata, 1978). But it has been convincingly shown (Burns, House, Fensch, & Miller, 1967; Smith, 1967) that the same dose of amphetamine, for example, that *improves* performance on a "low-level" intellectual task (e.g., a reaction-time or a digit-letter-coding task) will *impair* performance on a "high-level" intellectual task (e.g., paired-associate learning). Thus, any drug-induced effect must be evaluated with careful consideration of both the task used and the dose of drug given. The relationships of dose and tasks to SDL effects are considered separately below. Logically, the task × dose analysis would be ideal to evaluate the SDL effect, but such a complicated analysis is not possible at the present time due to the limited amount of research that has been done.

Dose Effects

In research on human subjects, a variety of centrally acting drugs has been used to demonstrate SDL. In general, moderate doses of drugs such as alcohol (8 to 10 oz. of 80-proof vodka; Goodwin et al., 1969), marijuana (one cigarette containing 7.5 mg THC; Stillman, Weingartner, Wyatt, Gillin, & Eich, 1974) and amphetamine and amobarbital (20 mg d-amphetamine and 200 mg amobarbital; Bustamante, Rossello, Jordan, Pradera, & Insua, 1968; Bustamante, Jordan, Vila, Gonzales, & Insua, 1970) are sufficient to produce an SDL effect in subjects who have not developed tolerance to the drugs. Those who chronically abuse these drugs (e.g., alcoholics; Goodwin, 1974; Weingartner & Faillace, 1971) may require higher dosage to experience the same effects. Some clinical patients may require lower doses than normal subjects to show SDL effects (Swanson & Kinsbourne, 1976).

It is clear that not all drugs produce SDL; for example, Overton (1971) has shown that peripherally acting drugs do not, at least in the drug discrimination paradigm with rats as subjects. And not all doses of centrally acting drugs produce SDL; for example, Swanson and Kinsbourne (1976) have shown in children that the dose of methylphenidate administered must be sufficient to produce a significant main effect of the drug both in the acquisition and retention phases of the learning paradigm before an SDL effect emerges at retention. This held for both hyperactive and control children and may account for earlier failures to demonstrate SDL with amphetamine (Aman & Sprague, 1974; Hurst, Radlow, Chubb, & Bagley, 1969). A similar dose-related effect of alcohol was described by Goodwin (1974). When a dose of alcohol given to alcoholics was insufficient to produce overt intoxication, no evidence of SDL was observed using a word-association task. However, the same dose of alcohol in non-alcoholic subjects produces clear signs of intoxication, and an SDL effect was demonstrated with the same word-association task.

The common failure to show an SDL effect with a recognition task may be due to the doses of drug given. Adam, Castro, and Clark (1974) used the general anesthetic isoflurane and reported that SDL occurs in a recognition paradigm, but only for high doses of the drug. The demonstration of SDL was not with the usual 2 × 2 design because a "study−test−test" design was used. Subjects received word lists during the drug condition and were tested later after the drug effect dissipated (Test 1). When the dose was sufficient during the study session (as reflected by EEG changes), recognition performance on this test suffered. This represents the DP condition of the 2 × 2 SDL design. After demonstrating this impairment, the drug was given again to establish the DD condition. On a subsequent test, recognition performance improved, indicating that the material previously inaccessible in the different-state condition (DP) was now accessible in the same-state condition (DD). It should be emphasized that this pattern suggesting an SDL effect on a recognition task held for a high-dose condition and not a low-dose condition of the drug and then only for those subjects (7 out of 10) who showed a clear physiological response to the high dose.

Consideration of dose-related effects are certainly important, especially in evaluating failure to demonstrate SDL. But the drug conditions that produce SDL are not difficult to establish, so we do not dwell on those conditions that fail to produce SDL. Instead, we emphasize the tasks that reliably produce SDL when an appropriate drug and an adequate dose are used.

Recognition Tasks

In several studies, tests of recognition memory have failed to show state-dependent effects. For example, Goodwin et al. (1969) gave several learning and memory tasks to each subject who participated in their experiment on the effects of alcohol. All their tests *except* a picture-recognition test showed SDL effects. Wickelgren (1975), in another experiment on the effects of alcohol on memory, also failed to show a state-dependent effect using a recognition-memory paradigm in which a word list rather than pictures was the stimuli. Darley, Tinklenberg, Roth, and Atkinson (1974) also used a verbal recognition task in an investigation of the effects of marijuana on memory retrieval. Consistent with the alcohol studies, they reported an SDL effect for performance on a recall task, but not for the recognition task. In that study, the same initial acquisition phase served for both the recognition and recall tests, but only the recall test showed a state-dependent effect. However, as discussed before, it is not impossible to show SDL effects with a recognition task. As discussed earlier, Adam et al. (1974) showed that only by increasing dose could a significant SDL be elicited.

As Eich (1977) has pointed out, a recognition task seems to be the least likely task to show an SDL effect; but this may be due to the use of low doses of drugs. Only a dose-response investigation of multiple tasks could answer a question of this sort, and no such study has been done yet. Until it is, the question of task sensitivity to SDL effects must be qualified and restricted to low doses of drugs.

Paired-Associate and Serial Learning

In the original SDL experiments on animals, learning tasks were used that required repeated practice to master (Overton, 1964). The initial learning tasks used in the SDL research on human subjects followed the pattern set by the animal research (Storm & Caird, 1967; Goodwin et al. 1969). For example, when either serial or paired-associate learning tasks are used, *practice* during the acquisition phase is required until a criterion (usually perfect recitation of a list of items) is attained.

It is clear that SDL occurs in this paradigm in human subjects as well as in animal subjects. The examples already presented (Goodwin et al., 1969; Storm & Caird, 1967; Swanson & Kinsbourne, 1976) clearly demonstrate the effect with learning tasks that require repeated practice. Rickles, Cohen, Whitaker, and McIntyre (1973), in an investigation of marijuana, used a paired-associate learning task with a criterion of 100% overlearning. Even in the face of this extended practice, clear evidence for SDL was obtained.

Eich (1977) has pointed out that in some instances, paired-associate and serial learning tests fail to show SDL effects. He attributed this to the "cue-specific" nature of SDL, suggesting that SDL occurs when the utilization of stored information depends on subject-generated or "invisible" cues and not when retrieval is mediated by an overt cue. He considered the stimulus item of the S−R pair to be an overt cue for retrieval of the response item. Keppel and Zubrzycki (1977, note 5, p. 85) also suggested that SDL may be difficult to document on the paired-associate paradigm.

It is instructive to review the studies in which a paired-associate learning task was used and SDL was *not* observed. Hurst et al. (1969) used amphetamine to induce changes in state in normal adults and found no evidence for SDL on a paired-associate task or any of the other tests they used. Aman and Sprague (1974) reported a similar experience with hyperactive children as subjects. However, in these studies, no main effect of the drug during acquisition occurred either. As pointed out by Swanson and Kinsbourne (1976), this (instead of task insensitivity) could account for the lack of an SDL effect in this study. Lisman (1974) also reported a failure to demonstrate SDL effects for a paired-associate learning task and for a free-recall task, a hidden-picture task, and a recognition task as well. However, Lisman's (1974) failure to demonstrate SDL may have been due to design choices that resulted in masking SDL—a small sample size (four patients) and an easy task that produced a ceiling effect (mean recall = 5.8 out of 6 items). Osborn, Bunker, Cooper, Frank, and Hilgard (1967) required subjects to "learn" to associate 6 words (responses) with the first letters of the words (stimuli) (eg. C-Camel, W-Water, and F-Flower). They acknowledged that the task was too easy for adults, since perfect "learning" occurred on the first trial. This task is more like a cued recall task than a paired-associate learning task.

It is obvious, upon close inspection, that a variety of explanations come to mind to account for those failures to show SDL. However, the conclusion that paired-associate learning is an insensitive task for demonstrating SDL effects on the basis of the negative instances available in the literature does not seem warranted at this time. The lack of significant SDL effects cannot be attributed to deficiencies in the paired-associate procedure until the other obvious possibilities are discounted.

Cued and Uncued Free Recall

In the typical free-recall paradigm employed by Tulving (1974), a list of words is presented to the subject, blocked by categories to emphasize the organization of the list. Thus, the subject may have two things to remember the categories represented in this list and the individual words that fit into each category. Later, two attempts to recall the items are typically given: First, the subject is asked to remember the items from the list without any aids provided by the experimenter; then the subject is given the category names as aids to remember the items from the list. Cued recall is dramatically superior to uncued (free) recall (Tulving & Pearlstone, 1966).

As Roediger (1975) pointed out, the use of retrieval cues is one of the most potent experimental factors yet discovered to control memory performance. What component of memory is affected by this experimental operation? In free- and cued-recall conditions, the acquisition and storage components of memory are held constant. Only the retrieval component differs between the two conditions, so the dramatic differences in recall are attributed to this component of memory. During the past several years, considerable research has been conducted to investigate the effects of drugs on retrieval processes in memory.

In the free-recall paradigm, the acquisition phase is often a single presentation of a list of words. When this single trial free-recall paradigm is used, the term *learning* may be inappropriate. As mentioned earlier, the term learning is usually restricted to situations that involve repetition or practice. Recall, then, is a retrieval of a unique episode. To emphasize this, the term state-dependent learning (SDL) sometimes has been replaced by the term state-dependent retrieval (SDR) in the research using the free-recall paradigm.

Eich, Weingartner, Stillman, and Gillin (1975) showed that the single-trial free-recall task was very sensitive for demonstrating SDR. They also showed that by merely providing the appropriate retrieval cue (the category names) for the verbal items (words) in the free-recall list, the SDR effect could be overcome. Weingartner, Miller, and Murphy (1977) also showed that SDR could be obtained using the free-recall paradigm. In the same experiment, they showed that SDR could be modified by the nature of the stimuli presented: When high-imagery words were used, the SDR effects were small, but when low-imagery words were used, SDR effects were large.

These SDR effects have been described in detail by Eich (1977) and

Weingartner and Murphy (1977). Their studies are important demonstrations of a state-dependent effect, and they have considerable importance for theories of human memory. Eich (1977) even suggested an organization of the literature based on these results. He noted that: (a) most studies using the uncued free-recall task show SDR; (b) not all studies using the paired-associate or serial learning task show SDR; (c) very few studies using the recognition task show SDR; and (d) no studies using cued recall show SDR. Rather than implicating dose factors or design deficiencies (as suggested earlier) to account for some of those failures to show state dependency, he evaluated the characteristics of the tasks from the studies he reviewed and classified them into three types: (a) uncued recall tasks, (b) cued recall tasks, and (c) recognition tasks. On the basis of this post hoc organization, he concluded that human state dependency "clearly appears to be a cue-specific phenomenon: evidence of dissociative effects is far more likely to emerge in tasks where utilization of stored information critically depends on the operation of an invisible of subject-generated retrieval cues (i.e., tasks involving uncued recall) than in tasks where retrieval is mediated by either intralist or copy cues (i.e., tasks involving either cued recall or recognition) [p. 151]."

Recently Eich has tested his earlier proposal that human SDL is a "cue-specific phenomenon" and has found it lacking (personal communication, 1978). This later work supports the view that the manner in which order information is utilized in the free-recall task makes it sensitive to SDL effects. Apparently, cuing alters the order of recall and in that way negates the SDL effect, but certain ways of cuing actually potentiate the SDL effect.

THEORIES OF SDL

How do current theories of human memory and learning relate to theoretical accounts of state dependency? In the following section, we review two types of theories: First, we consider standard theories of memory developed primarily on the basis of nondrug research on normal human subjects (e.g., college sophomores); second, we relate those standard theories to specific theories of state-dependent learning developed primarily from research with drugs (and often with animals as subjects). Our intent is to use the constructs from standard theories to better describe the SDL effect.

Roediger (1975) emphasized consideration of the common three-stage model of learning in memory to aid in understanding state-dependent learning. The stages are: (1) initial encoding of material; (2) storage of the encoded material; and (3) retrieval of the stored material.

It is clear that some drugs, especially alcohol, affect the storage of new information. Ryback (1971), Wickelgren (1975), and Birnbaum and Parker (1977) have described how drugs affect the storage component of memory. SDL effects were not always apparent in their studies, but the issue is complicated by the design factors mentioned earlier. For that reason, the relationship between storage effects and SDL is not discussed here. Instead, both an encoding theory and a retrieval theory are discussed, and they are related to a widely accepted class of theories that Overton (1977) labeled the "stimulus theory" of SDL.

The stimulus theory of SDL suggests that the drug treatment in SDL experiments either produces internal stimuli (e.g., dry mouth, changes in heart rate, etc.) or alters perceptual processing of the to-be-remembered stimuli. Compared to the placebo state, these drug-produced stimuli alter the stimulus complex experienced by the subject. In the drug discrimination paradigm, the drug-produced stimuli are hypothesized to serve as mediators that allow the choice of the appropriate response. In the SDL paradigm, the drug-produced stimuli are present only once in the DP and PD conditions, so the to-be-remembered stimulus complex is different in the acquisition and retention phases of learning.

How does the stimulus theory of SDL relate to standard theories of human learning? Since its emphasis is on the stimulus properties of drugs, we consider theories from the human learning literature that are concerned with stimulus properties.

Encoding Variability

Not all information in a complex stimulus is used during acquisition (Underwood, 1963). The differential selection of or attention to certain components of the stimulus is called *stimulus encoding*. Martin (1972) has suggested that variables that affect stimuli in the paired-associate learning paradigm exert their effect on learning by changing the stability of the encoded version of the stimulus. It is possible that the stimulus effect of a drug is sufficient to alter encoding.

If a drug affects stimulus encoding, then the change can be conceptualized as a change in the functional stimulus. In the jargon of verbal learning, the same-state conditions (PP and DD) represent an A−B, A−B transfer paradigm (since the functional stimulus does *not* change between acquisition and retention), and the different-state conditions (DP, PD) represent an A−B, C−B transfer paradigm (since the functional stimulus *does* change in these conditions). Under these conditions (Kausler, 1974), maximum positive transfer is expected in the same-state conditions (DD and PP), and zero or slightly negative transfer is expected in the different-state conditions (DP and PD). Of course, this would be reflected as relative impairment in the DP and PD conditions, compared to the PP and DD conditions. This is the usual pattern of performance attributed to SDL, which is here attributed to a drug-induced variability in encoding.

This explanation of SDL in terms of encoding variability is a variant of stimulus generalization theory. Explanation of SDL effects on the basis of stimulus generalization decrements have been suggested often before. Miller (1957) and Hilgard and Bower (1975) have proposed explanation of this type, and Overton (1977) and Bliss (1974) have discussed stimulus generalization theories based on research on animals.

Keppel and Zubrzycki (1977) discuss a variant of the stimulus generalization theory with specific reference to state-dependent learning. Their suggestion, too, is that a drug-induced change in physiological state of subject results in a change in stimulus encoding. In the different-state combinations (DP and PD) of the 2 × 2 design, it is assumed that inappropriate encodings are elicited by the changed context, and this results in forgetting. Thus, the DP and the PD conditions suffer impairment (due to selective forgetting) relative to the DD and PP conditions (in which little forgetting occurs).

Keppel and Zubrzycki (1977) as well as Overton (1977) relate the stimulus generalization theory of SDL to the considerable literature on the effect of changes in the testing environment between acquisition and recall. As the similarity between test states is decreased, performance declines. Pan (1926) reported this phenomenon long ago, and Bilodeau and Schlosberg (1951), Greenspoon and Ranyard (1957), Rand and Wapner (1967), and Godden and Baddeley (1975) have contributed to the literature over the years. The Godden and Baddeley (1975) study shows this effect most clearly: Divers learned lists of words above or below the water and then recalled the words above or below water. This factorial arrangement of acquisition and retention states yielded a 2 × 2 design just as in the SDL 2 × 2 design. Consistent with the drug-induced SDL effects, they found poorer recall in the different-environment conditions (learn above water, recall below water; or learn below water, recall above water) than in the same-environment conditions.

Encoding Specificity and Retrieval

The principle of encoding specificity states that retrieval cues, given during the retention test, facilitate recall of material only if the retrieval cues were encoded and stored at the time of acquisition (Tulving & Pearlstone, 1966). Apparently, the context provided by the acquisition state (e.g., Bower, 1972) is used as a retrieval cue. If the drug state is the same at acquisition and retention (as it is in the PP and DD conditions in the SDL paradigm), then the drug-related retrieval cue is appropriate and should facilitate recall. However, when the drug state is different during acquisition and retention, then the drug-related retrieval cue is not appropriate, and no facilitation (or even impairment) of recall is expected.

Both Overton (1974) and Roediger (1975) view this retrieval theory of SDL as being a special case of stimulus generalization. Whether changes in the functional stimulus or in the functional retrieval cue are hypothesized, both theories predict that as the similarity of the acquisition and retention conditions increases, the performance on the recall test improves.

Eich et al. (1975) has extended the retrieval theory of SDL beyond the concept of stimulus generalization. In Overton's (1977) treatment of the retrieval theory, the drug-produced stimuli are considered to produce a context that serves as a retrieval cue. Eich et al. (1975) established an uncued-recall condition and in addition a recall condition in which category names were provided as retrieval cues. Clear evidence for SDR was found for uncued recall, but no evidence of SDR was found in the *cued*-recall condition.

Roediger (1975) could not fit this result into the framework of SDL. He correctly noted that the retrieval cue did not provide a reinstatement of the drug context and questioned how providing such a cue could overcome the SDL effect attributed to drug-produced stimuli. What "cues" are theoretically available for recall in the four conditions of the 2 × 2 design? Drug-produced stimuli provide context cues in the PD and DD conditions. Also, the nondrug state must provide alternate cues for the PP and DP condition. However, in the DD and PP condition, the context cues are appropriate (same-context stimuli), whereas in the PD and DP conditions, the context cues are not appropriate (different-context stimuli). This, then, may be the basis for the SDL effect in uncued recall.

What effects do the category names have? As Roediger (1975) pointed out, these cues presented at the retention test do not provide the missing drug-produced stimuli in the DP condition, nor do they remove the inappropriate drug-produced stimuli in the PD condition. Instead, they provide an additional cue that is much more effective than the drug-produced context stimuli. Why, then, is the benefit of the appropriate context cue not apparent still in the cued-recall test? There are several possibilities:

1. The category cues may evoke a memory of the acquisition state, which acts to provide the appropriate context in all the four conditions. This is unlikely, since the category cue results in much greater improvement in performance than the context cue based on the actual drug-produced stimuli themselves.

2. Only one of these two cues (either the context cue or the category cue) can be used at a time, and the category name takes priority due to its greater effectiveness. Thus the context cue may be available but not used in the PP and DD conditions when a category cue is provided.

3. The SDL effect is small, and any operation that increases retention will mask it. Thus, providing the category cue has the same effect as overtraining (Iwahara & Noguchi, 1972), which in animals improves retention in all four conditions but removes the SDL effect.

4. The category cues provide more of the same type of information than the context cues and render the small amount of information provided by the context cues redundant. The possibility has been suggested by Eich (personal communication, 1978), who found that the category cues provide lost "order" information that may be partially present in the PP and DD conditions.

5. SDL may occur only for recall of category names, not for items within a category. Thus giving the category names as cues may produce a ceiling effect, since all category names are made accessible and therefore recall of them cannot be state dependent.

The fact that category cues negate the SDL effect is important, but it does *not* mean that SDL occurs only when "invisible cues" direct recall. As discussed before, the evidence from the drug discrimination paradigm and from several studies with serial and paired-associate learning is sufficient to counter that argument.

Levels of Processing

The stimulus theory of SDL is easily related to encoding and retrieval theories of memory. Another theory, the brain function theory of SDL (Overton, 1977), is readily related to Craik and Lockhart's (1972) levels-of-processing theory of memory. Weingartner and Murphy (1977) discuss the role of state-specific strategies in producing SDL in humans. Overton (1973) had presented a similar idea based on animal SDL experiments.

Overton's (1973) idea seems to have derived from Sachs' (1967) work. He found that drugs impair cognitive functions, and as a result, the animal's approach to the task is less sophisticated in the drug state than in the placebo state. Apparently, Pusapulich (1974) documented this in rats, finding that they learn to escape a maze by learning specific response patterns in the drug state and by learning position habits in the placebo state. If the strategy used to learn a task in one state is not used to perform the task when the other state is established at recall, then performance should suffer. Thus, impairment should occur in the different-state conditions (DP and PD) and not in the same-state conditions (PP and DD). This model from the SDL literature is close to Craik's (1977) concept of memory. He suggests that an item is encoded in terms of the mental operations performed during acquisition. Retrieval is accomplished by performing the same operations to reconstruct a "percept uniquely similar to the encoded percept [p. 13]." If the type of operation performed changes between acquisition and retention, retrieval should fail or be impaired.

Craik's (1977) theory fits with the known effects of various drugs. For example, stimulant drugs act to make an individual less impulsive and more reflective in his approach to any task. If a reflective strategy is used during learning, the benefit of training may be lost if an impulsive strategy is used at the retention test. Kinsbourne (1977) has speculated that this is the basis for the state dependency associated with the drug treatment of hyperactive children. A recent study by Fischer (1978) has provided data to support this view.

Summary: The Generalization Gradient

At some level of analysis, all the theories we have discussed here rely on a generalization gradient to account for the SDL effect. In the encoding variability theory it is hypothesized that learning fails to generalize because a change in state alters the functional stimulus. In the encoding specificity theory, the drug is assumed to alter the context and thus the functional retrieval cue. In the levels-of-processing theory, the drug is assumed to alter the similarity of the reconstructive cognitive processes used to encode the presented stimulus. In each of the examples, if acquisition and retention states are held constant, then "similarity" is assumed to be high and recall is good. If the acquisition and retention states change, their "similarity" is assumed to be low and recall suffers.

Our reference to theories up to this point has been on a descriptive level. We have used the language of the various approaches merely to describe the SDL effect. The question of why the SDL effect exists was not addressed, but it will be considered in the next section.

ADAPTIVE CONSIDERATIONS

The state-dependence of learning, if viewed in isolation, seems like an arbitrary limitation on memory, the adaptive advantage of which is difficult to discern. But its biological origins become comprehensible if it is viewed within the broader context of human memory. Regardless of the details of the mechanisms and theories discussed above, we can regard state-dependence as one of the range of phenomena that reveal the effect of context on remembering.

Bower's (1972) idea of context is relevant to this discussion: he regarded context as the "background external and interoceptive stimulation prevailing during presentation of the phasic experimental stimuli" (p. 93). In a discussion of list differentiation, he suggested that context allowed subjects to relate items in a specific list to a designated cue by a paired-associate procedure. A list cue, then, served as a stimulus for recall of a particular set of items; in this way, the list cue provided the appropriate "response set". Even though Bower's (1972) work was based on "time tagging" of lists, he specifically included in his theory a notion of nontemporal list cues. In our present discussion, the drug state may be considered a nontemporal list cue of the sort suggested by Bower (1972).

Consider the implication of the effect of a list (or context) cue on two previously learned lists presented in different contexts (e.g., drug and placebo states). A particular list cue (e.g., the drug state) presented at the retention test would provide the appropriate response set for one list, and an inappropriate response set for the other. Thus, the drug-drug combination would provide the appropriate response set (and superior performance), while the placebo-drug combination would provide an inappropriate response set (and poorer performance). Essentially, this equates the mechanism responsible for state-dependent learning with the mechanism that established "response set," and it differs little from the usual discussion of similarity effects and the concepts of stimulus and response generalization (Hilgard & Bower, 1975).

What is the adaptive significance of "response set" and of stimulus and response generalization? Since the total capacity of any organism is limited, these processes are important for biasing the probabilities of particular responses at a particular point in time. Utilization of context is one way that the "appropriate" response may be chosen, and the "inappropriate" response may be suppressed. This effect of context may occur automatically, leaving the full processing capacity of the organism available for processing of more specific environmental stimuli. If this type of response selection is automatic it would have a profound biological significance. It would allow complete attention to the here-and-now, and thus minimize the chance of the organism falling prey due to its lack of vigilance, while at the same time providing use of prior experience.

What memory mechanisms are responsible for making responses readily available? Pribram (1969) has suggested a distinction between context free and context bound memories, which is related to Tulving's (1972) distinction between episodic (context bound) and semantic (context free) memory. One way that episodic memory and other memory systems differ is that the former represents unique personal experiences and the latter represents general rules. Precisely because general rules may be called upon to guide behavior at virtually any time and place, they have to be readily accessible by a mechanism that is automatic and context-free (Pribram, 1969). Therefore, information in semantic memory is rehearsed until it is highly overlearned. On the other hand, precisely because particular events (episodic memories) are characterized by their distinctiveness, their recovery has to be context-bound (Pribram, 1969). It is confined to settings which bear a sufficiently striking "family resemblance" to the original episode to provide the contextual cues that trigger recall of the event. The rarely experienced situation, by virtue of its uniqueness and non-recurrent nature, is not learned through repetition. Furthermore, it would be pointless to keep recollecting such an unique event which would not render the individual's general pattern of responding more adaptive. Episodic memories apparently are readily accessible only at times when they are likely to be utilized to direct response selection. In terms of infrequent events, this utilization is directed by the context which recurs and is shared with a previous event.

It is clear from the several theories of coding in memory (Martin, 1972; Tulving, 1972; Keppel & Zubrzycki, 1977; Craik, 1977) that remembering a prior event is not cost free. As Hilgard and Bower (1975, p. 547) point out, the reinstatement of the original context is important because it "isolates interpolated material and prevents interference at the time of recall of some originally learned material."

In the state-dependent learning paradigm, what is considered interpolated material? The SDL paradigm may result in material that is experienced in the different state conditions (DP and PD) being affected by the same underlying process that isolates interpolated material in the traditional verbal learning paradigms. This mechanism, which certainly exemplifies a phenomenon of profound biological significance, may be responsible for the observation of SDL in the laboratory.

We do not suggest that drug-induced state-dependent learning is adaptive. It is presumably a rare phenomenon in nature, and unlikely to have provided a basis for natural selection. But we do suggest that it is a subset of the range of episodic remembering, and that it reflects the economy of episodic forgetting. Episodic remembering is so broadly based that a unitary mechanism for state-dependent learning based on it may be credible.

REFERENCES

Adam, N., Castro, A., & Clark, D. State-dependent learning with a general anesthetic (isoflurane) in man. *Journal of Life Sciences*, 1974, *4*, 125–134.

Aman, M. B., & Sprague, R. L. The dissociative effects of methylphenidate and dextroamphetamine. *Journal of Nervous and Mental Disease*, 1974, *158*, 268–279.

Bilodeau, I. M., & Schlosberg, H. Similarity in stimulating conditions as a variable in retroactive inhibition. *Journal of Experimental Psychology*, 1951, *41*, 199–204.

Birnbaum, I. M., & Parker, E. S. Acute effects of alcohol on storage and retrieval. In I. M. Birnbaum & E. S. Parker (Eds.), *Alcohol and human memory*. Hillsdale, J. J.: Lawrence & Erlbaum Associates, 1977.

Bliss, D. K. Theoretical explanations of drug-dissociated behaviors. *Federation Proceedings*, 1974, *33*, 1787–1796.

Bower, G. H. Stimulus sampling theory of encoding variability. In A. W. Melton & E. Martin (Eds.), *Coding processes in human memory*. Washington D.C., Winston, 1972.

Burns, J. T., House, R. F., Fensch, F. C., & Miller, J. G. Effects of magnesium pemoline and dextroamphetamine on human learning. *Science*, 1967, *152*, 849–851.

Bustamante, J. A., Jordan, A., Vila, M., Gonzalez, A., & Insua, A. State-dependent learning in humans. *Physiology and Behavior*, 1970, *5*, 793–796.

Bustamante, J. A., Rossello, A., Jordan, A., Pradera, E., & Insua, A. Learning and drugs. *Physiology and Behavior*, 1968, *3*, 553–555.

Conners, C. K., Eisenberg, L., & Sharpe, L. Effects of methylphenidate (Ritalin) on paired-associate learning and Porteus Maze performance in emotionally disturbed children. *Journal of Consulting Psychology*, 1964, *28*, 14–22.

Conners, C. K., Rothschild, G., Eisenberg, L., & Schwartz, L. S. Dextroamphetamine sulphate in children with learning disorders: Effects on perception, learning, and achievement. *Archives of General Psychiatry*, 1969, *21*, 182–190.

Craik, F. I. M. Similarities between the effects of aging and alcoholic intoxication on memory performance, construed within a "levels of processing" framework. In I. M. Birnbaum & E. S. Parker (Eds.), *Alcohol and human memory*. Hillsdale, N.J.: Lawrence Erlbaum Associates, 1977.

Craik, F. I. M., & Lockhart, R. S. Levels of processing: A framework for memory research. *Journal of Verbal Learning and Verbal Behavior*, 1972, *11*, 671–684.

Darley, C. F., Tinklenberg, J. R., Roth. W. T., & Atkinson, R. C. The nature of storage deficits and state-dependent retrieval under marihuana. *Psychopharmacologia*, 1974, *37*, 139–149.

Deutsch, J. A., & Roll, S. K. Alcohol and asymmetrical state-dependency: A possible explanation. *Behavioral Biology*, 1973, *8*, 273–278.

Eich, J. E. State-dependent retrieval of information in human episodic memory. In J. M. Birnbaum & E. S. Parker (Eds.), *Alcohol and human memory*. Hillsdale, N.J.: Lawrence Erlbaum Associates, 1977.

Eich, J. E. Personal communication, 1978.

Eich, J. E., Weingartner, J., Stillman, R. C., & Gillin, J. C. State-dependent accessibility of retrieval cues in the retention of a categorized list. *Journal of Verbal Learning and Verbal Behavior*, 1975, *14*, 408−417.

Evans, F. J., Gustafson, L. A., O'Connell, D. N., Orne, M. T., & Shor, R. E. Response during sleep with intervening waking amnesia. *Science*, 1966, *152*, 666−667.

Evans, F. J., Gustafson, L. A., O'Connell, D. N., Orne, M. T., & Shor, R. E. Verbally induced behavioral responses during sleep. *Journal of Nervous and Mental Disease*, 1970, *150*, 171−187.

Fischer, M. A. Dextroamphetamine and placebo practice effects on selective attention in hyperactive children. *Journal of Abnormal Psychology*, 1978, *6*, 25−32.

Fischer, R., & Landon, G. M. On the arousal state-dependent recall of "subsconscious experience": Stateboundedness. *British Journal of Psychiatry*, 1972, *120*, 159−172.

Godden, D. R., & Baddeley, A. D. Context-dependent memory in two natural environments: On land and underwater. *British Journal of Psychology*, 1975, *66*, 325−331.

Goodwin, D. W. Alcoholic blackout and state-dependent learning. *Federation Proceedings*, 1974, *33*, 1833−1835.

Goodwin, D. W., Powell, B., Bremer, D., Hoine, H., & Stern, J. Alcohol and recall: State-dependent effects in man. *Science*, 1969, *163*, 1358−1360.

Greenspoon, J., & Ranyard, R. Stimulus conditions and retroactive inhibition. *Journal of Experimental Psychology*, 1957, *33*, 55−59.

Grinspoon, L., & Hedblom, P. *The speed culture*. Cambridge, Mass.: Harvard University Press, 1975.

Hilgard, E. R., & Bower, G. H. *Theories of learning* (4th ed.). Englewood Cliffs, N.J.: Prentice-Hall, 1975.

Hill, S. Y., Schwin, B., & Goodwin, D. W. State-dependent effects of marihuana on human memory. *Nature*, 1973, *243*, 242.

Holloway, F. A. State-dependent retrieval based on time of day. In B. Ho, D. Chute, & D. Richards (Eds.), *Drug discrimination and state-dependent learning*. New York: Academic Press, 1977.

Hurst, P. M., Radlow, R., Chubb, N. C., & Bagley, S. K. Effects of d-amphetamine on acquisition, persistence, and recall. *American Journal of Psychology*, 1969, *82*, 307−319.

Iwahara, S., & Noguchi, S. Drug-state dependency as a function of overtraining in rats. *Japanese Psychology Research*, 1972, *14*, 141−144.

Jones, B. M. Circadian variation in the effects of alcohol on cognitive performance. *Quarterly Journal of Studies on Alcohol*, 1974, *35*, 1212−1219.

Kausler, D. H. *Psychology of verbal learning and memory*. New York: Academic Press, 1974.

Keppel, G., & Zubrzycki, C. R. Selective learning and forgetting. In. I. M. Birnbaum & E. S. Parker (Eds.), *Alcohol and human memory*. Hillsdale, N.J.: Lawrence Erlbaum Associates, 1977.

Kimble, G. A., & Garmezy, M. P. *Principles of general psychology* (3rd ed.). New York: Ronald Press, 1968.

Kinsbourne, M. The mechanism of hyperactivity. In M. Blau, I. Rapin, & M. Kinsbourne (Eds.), *Topics in child neurology*. New York: Spectrum Press, 1977.

Kolata, G. E. Childhood hyperactivity; a new look at treatments and causes. *Science*, 1978, *199*, 515−517.

Lisman, S. A. Alcoholic "blackout": State dependent learning? *Archives of General Psychiatry*, 1974, *30*, 46−53.

Martin, E. Stimulus encoding in learning and transfer. In A. W. Melton & E. Martin (Eds.), *Coding processes in human memory*. Washington, D.C.: Winston, 1972.

Miller, N. E. Objective techniques for studying motivational effects of drugs on animals. In S. Garettine & V. Ghetti (Eds.), *Psychotropic drugs*. Amsterdam, The Netherlands: Elsevier, 1957.

Osborn, A. G., Bunker, J. P., Cooper, L. M., Frank, G. S., & Hilgard, E. R. Effects of Thiopental sedation on learning and memory. *Science*, 1967, *157*, 574−576.

Overton, D. A. State-dependent or "dissociated" learning produced with pentobarbital. *Journal of Comparative and Physiological Psychology*, 1964, *57*, 3–12.

Overton, D. A. Dissociated learning in drug states (state-dependent learning). In D. H. Efron, J. O. Cole, J. Levine, & R. Wittenborn (Eds.), *Psychopharmacology: A review of progress, 1957–1967*. Washington, D.C.: United States Government Printing Office, 1968.

Overton, D. A. Discriminative control of behavior by drug states. In T. Thompson & R. Pickens (Eds.), *Stimulus properties of drugs*. New York: Appleton-Century-Crofts, 1971.

Overton, D. A. State-dependent learning produced by addicting drugs. In S. Fisher & A. M. Freedman (Eds.), *Opiate addiction: Origin and treatment*. Washington, D.C.: Winston, 1973.

Overton, D. A. Experimental methods for the study of state-dependent learning. *Federation Proceedings*, 1974, *33*, 1800–1813.

Overton, D. A. Major theories of state-dependent learning. In B. Ho, D. Chute, & D. Richards (Eds.), *Drug discrimination and state dependent learning*. New York: Academic Press, 1977.

Pan, S. Context effects on memory. *Journal of Experimental Psychology*, 1926, *9*, 468–491.

Pribram, K. H. The ammestic syndromes: Disturbances in Coding? In G. A. Talland & N. C. Waugh (Eds.), *The pathology of memory*. New York: Academic Press, 1969.

Pusakulich. R. L. Analysis of cue use in state dependent learning. *Dissertation Abstracts International* (Part B), *34*, 4095, 1974 (abstract).

Rand, G., & Wapner, S. Postural states as a factor in memory. *Journal of Verbal Learning and Verbal Behavior*, 1967, *6*, 268–271.

Rickles, W. H., Cohen, M. J., Whitaker, C. W., & McIntyre, K. E. Marihuana-induced state-dependent verbal learning. *Psychopharmacologia*, 1973, *30*, 349–354.

Robbins, M., & Meyer, D. Motivational control of retrograde amnesia. *Journal of Experimental Psychology*, 1970, *84*, 220–225.

Roediger, H. L. Current status of research on retrieval processes in memory. *Polygraph*, 1975, *4*, 304–310.

Ryback, R. S. The continuum and specificity of the effects of alcohol on memory: A review. *Quarterly Journal of Studies on Alcohol*, 1971, *32*, 995–1026.

Sachs, E. Dissociation of learning in rats and its similarities to dissociative states in man. In J. Zubin & H. Hunt (Eds.), *Comparative psychopathology*. New York: Grune & Stratton, 1967.

Schneider, A. M. Stimulus control and spreading cortical depression: Some problems reconsidered. *Psychological Review*, 1968, *75*, 353–358.

Smith, R. G. Magnesium pemoline: Lack of facilitation in human learning, memory, and performance tests. *Science*, 1967, *152*, 603–605.

Stillman, R. C., Weingartner, H., Wyatt, R. J., Gillin, J. C., & Eich, J. E. State-dependent (dissociative) effects of marihuana on human memory. *Archives of General Psychiatry*, 1974, *31*, 81–85.

Storm, T., & Caird, W. K. The effects of alcohol on serial verbal learning in chronic alcoholics. *Psychonomic Science*, 1967, *9*, 43–44.

Swanson, J. M., & Kinsbourne, M. Stimulant-related state-dependent learning in hyperactive children. *Science*, 1976, *192*, 1354–1357.

Swanson, J. M., & Kinsbourne, M. The 2 × 2 design reconsidered: limitations imposed by the statistical model. In F. C. Colpaert and J. A. Rosecrans (Eds.), *Drugs as Discriminative Stimuli*, North Hollard Publishing Co., in press.

Tulving, E. Episodic and semantic memory. In E. Tulving & W. Donaldson (Eds.), *Organization of memory*. New York: Academic Press, 1972.

Tulving, E., & Pearlstone, Z. Availability versus accessibility of information for words. *Journal of Verbal Learning and Verbal Behavior*, 1966, *5*, 381–391.

Underwood, B. J. Stimulus selection in verbal learning. In C. N. Cofer & B. S. Musgrove (Eds.), *Verbal behavior and learning: Problems and processes*. New York: McGraw-Hill, 1963.

Weingartner, H. Human state-dependent learning. In B. T. Ho, D. Richards, & D. L. Chute (Eds.), *Drug discrimination and state-dependent learning*. New York: Academic Press, 1977.

Weingartner, H., & Faillace, L. A. Alcohol state-dependent learning in man. *Journal of Nervous and Mental Disease*, 1971, *153*, 395–406.

Weingartner, H., Miller, H., & Murphy, D. L. Mood-state-dependent retrieval of word associations. *Journal of Abnormal Psychology*, 1977, *86*, 276–284.

Weingartner, H., & Murphy, D. Brain states and memory: State-dependent storage and retrieval of information. *Psychopharmacology Bulletin*, 1977, *13*(1), 66–67.

Weiss, B., & Laties, V. G. Enhancement of human performance by caffeine and the amphetamines. *Pharmacological Reviews*, 1962, *14*, 1–36.

Wickelgren, W. A. Alcoholic intoxication and memory storage dynamics. *Memory & Cognition*, 1975, *3*, 385–389.

III PSYCHODYNAMIC FACTORS IN MEMORY

10 Dissociative Amnesia: A Clinical and Theoretical Reconsideration

John C. Nemiah
Beth Israel Hospital and Harvard Medical School

> To explore the most sacred depths of the unconscious, to labor
> in . . . the subsoil of consciousness, that will be the principal task
> of psychology in the century which is opening. I do not doubt that
> wonderful discoveries await it there, as important perhaps as
> have been in the preceding centuries the discoveries of the
> physical and natural sciences.
>
> Henri Bergson, *Dreams*

At the time that Bergson wrote, Freud had just published his *Interpretation of Dreams* (Freud, 1900/1953). Janet (1889, 1893, 1904) had already given to the scientific world several volumes based on his studies of dissociative phenomena, and Prince (1906) and others (Sidis & Goodhart, 1905) in America were beginning extensive investigations into the nature of unconscious mental processes. The promise of important discoveries was in the air, and one is not surprised either at Bergson's enthusiasm or at his failure to see that the promise was fated not to be immediately fulfilled. For reasons that we examine later, the direction of those pioneering investigations was diverted, and only now are we beginning to refocus our attention on the observations and concepts that animated clinical investigators nearly a hundred years ago.

CLINICAL OBSERVATIONS

Hysterical Amnesia

A central concern in these earlier studies of mental functioning was the fact of hysterical amnesia. Recognized by clinicians from the beginning of the 19th

303

century onward, it was most fully explored and described by Janet in the 1880s and 1890s. Typical of the patients he studied was Madame D. Janet (1904) tells us:

On the 28th of August, 1891, while in perfect health, she was the victim of a lamentable practical joke, which completely upset her mental equilibrium and produced a most remarkable psychological illness. While sitting alone in her house working at her sewing machine, she saw the door suddenly open. A stranger approached and said abruptly. "Get a bed ready, Madame D. They are carrying your husband home quite dead." When Madame D. failed to move but sat quietly sobbing, her head resting on her machine, he tapped her on the shoulder and added, "Stop crying so much and go upstairs to get a bed ready." Then he departed, leaving her to her despair.

Her neighbors came running in response to the poor woman's cries. They tried to calm her down, and in order to reassure her they sent off to fetch her husband. Shortly afterwards they returned with the latter (who was perfectly all right) and yelled out to Madame D., "Don't worry—here he is!" Misinterpreting their cries she thought they were really bringing back her dead husband's body and fell into a major [hysterical] convulsive crisis [pp. 116–117]. (Author's translation)

The hysterical attack lasted for two days, characterized by episodic convulsive movements, periods of lethargy, occasional attempts at suicide, and recurrent hallucinations reproducing the precipitating event and its sequelae. During the last, she would cry out, "Oh, my husband! He was such a good father—cry for him, my children! Poor Jean—she has no mourning clothes. Let me go back to him—let me watch over him." (Janet, 1904 [p. 117], author's translation)

On coming to herself at the end of the two-day period, the patient was completely composed, but it was then discovered that she had no memory of the emotional turmoil of the prior two days or the cruel prank that had caused it. What is more, she had lost her memory for all the events of the preceding six weeks as well. On careful examination during the weeks following the onset of her amnesia, it became apparent that the memories were not completely erased but could be recalled under special circumstances. Occasionally the patient would have brief hysterical alterations of consciousness (i.e., somnambulistic episodes) during which, with a show of terror, she would cry out about her "dead" husband. She also had repeated nightmares that, it was disclosed under hypnosis, reproduced the appearance of the anonymous practical joker and his commands to prepare a bed for her husband's corpse. Similarly, if she were left to her self when hypnotized, she would frequently reenact the same traumatic scene.

In this tragic vignette are to be found the salient characteristics of hysterical amnesia:

1. The patient manifests a complete oblivion for certain past events.
2. Though inaccessible to voluntary recall during normal consciousness, the memories are not obliterated from the totality of mental processes and can

be recovered in special states of consciousness (e.g., under hypnosis or in dreams) or by special techniques, such as automatic writing.

3. The unconscious memories may at times make themselves felt in such pathological states as somnambulism, nightmares, or hysterical hallucinations.

Hysterical amnesia may take several forms. In *localized* amnesia the period covered by the oblivion ranges from a few hours to a few weeks. In the *generalized* form the individual loses memory for the whole of his past life. *Systematized* amnesia affects the memories concerning specific and related past events only (such as those connected with a person with whom one has had an argument), the memory of other contemporaneous events remaining intact. Finally, in *continuous* (or *anterograde*) amnesia the patient forgets events as rapidly as they occur. This striking and unusual form of the disorder was well exemplified by Madame D., whose localized retrograde amnesia we examined earlier. After her recovery from the attack of somnambulism, she had not only forgotten the events of the prior six weeks, but in addition she appeared to fail to register events that ensued after the attack. She could not recognize people whom she had seen a few moments before, could not remember how to get from one part of the hospital to another, and she forgot even unusual and significant events such as having been severely bitten by a dog, or traveling to the Salpêtrière Hospital for a consultation with the famous Dr. Charcot. At the same time it was observed that memories of these happenings, however unavailable to voluntary recall, returned in her dreams. Like the memories of occurrences prior to her emotional trauma, they were preserved in a latent, unconscious state.

In the conditions we have been considering thus far, the amnesia is the primary feature of the clinical disorder. The individual comes or is brought to the doctor because of a loss of memory and has little else in the way of symptoms and signs. The history of Madame D., indeed, is a bit unusual in the fact that there was a well observed and documented attack of somnambulism preceding her memory disorder. The majority of patients when seen after the amnesia has appeared are aware merely of suddenly coming to themselves with a gap in memory that is not infrequently accompanied by a transient loss of personal identity (Abeles & Schilder, 1935; Gillespie, 1937). At most they can recollect only a brief period of confusion before realizing that they are amnesic. It should be remembered, however, that there may have been an unobserved alteration of consciousness as a prelude to the memory disturbance that, because of the amnesia itself, the patient is unable to recall. One cannot, therefore, speak with certainty about the prodromata of hysterical amnesia.

Fugue States

Less commonly, amnesia may be found in clinical syndromes that are more complex in form, and we must now turn our attention to *fugue states* and *multiple personalities*.

In a fugue state the individual not only develops a total amnesia for his past along with a complete loss of personal identity but, unconcerned by the internal revolution that has taken place, he complacently enters upon a new life and a new identity, often far removed from all that has gone before. Suddenly totally ignorant of his former life, occupation, family, and friends, he leaves home and, to the dismay of those left behind, seems to have disappeared from the face of the earth. In fact, he has merely wandered, often many miles, to a new location, sometimes with a vague sense of escaping from an intolerable situation, sometimes impelled by an inner fantasied goal. Then after weeks or months in his new life, he suddenly "comes to" as his former self with a complete amnesia for the events covered by the period of the fugue. The patient's dismay at finding himself in unfamiliar surroundings is equaled by the surprise of his new acquaintances at his sudden change of identity, for during the fugue his state of consciousness and behavior have in no way appeared unusual to observers.

The drama attending the fugue state can best be savored in the description of a famous victim of this singular phenomenon, Ansel Bourne, as reported by Hodgson (1892).

[He] was an itinerant preacher sixty-one years old, and residing in the small town of Greene, in the state of Rhode Island. One morning (January 17, 1887), whilst apparently in his usual state of health, he disappeared, and in spite of the publicity which the newspapers gave to the fact, and the efforts of the police to find him, he remained undiscovered for a period of two months, at the end of which time he turned up at Norristown, Pennsylvania, where for the previous six weeks he had been keeping a small variety store under the name of A. J. Brown, appearing to his neighbors and customers as a normal person. . . .

"On the morning of Monday, March 14th, about five o'clock" he awoke to find "a ridge in his bed not like the bed he had been accustomed to sleep on." On pulling back the curtains and looking out the window, he was alarmed to find his surroundings quite unfamiliar to him, and was immediately overcome with fear "knowing that he was in a place where he had no business to be."

The last thing he could remember before waking was seeing the Adams express waggons at the corner of Dorrance and Broad Streets, in Providence, on his way from the store of his nephew in Broad Street to his sister's residence in Westminster Street, on January 17th.

He waited to hear someone move, and for two hours he suffered great mental distress. Finally he tried the door, and finding it fastened on the inside, opened it. Hearing someone moving in another room, he rapped at the door. Mr. Earle opened it and said, "Good-morning, Mr. Brown." Mr. B: "Where am I?" Mr. E: "You're all right." Mr. B.: "I'm all wrong. My name isn't Brown. Where am I?" Mr. E.: "Norristown." Mr. B.: "Where is that?" Mr. E.: "In Pennsylvania." Mr. B.: "What part of the country?" Mr. E.: "About seventeen miles west of Philadelphia." Mr. B.: "What time of the month is it?" Mr. E.: "The 14th." Mr. B.: "Does time run backward here? When I left home is was the 17th." Mr. E.: "It's the 14th of March."

Mr. Earle thought that "Mr. Brown" was out of his mind, and said that he would send for a doctor. He summoned Dr. Louis H. Reade, to whom Mr. Bourne told the story of his doings in Rhode Island on the morning of January 17th. . . . "These persons," he said, "tell me I am in Norristown, Pennsylvania, and that I have been here for six weeks, and that I have lived with them all the time. I have no recollection of ever having seen one of them before this morning." He requested Dr. Reade to telegraph to his nephew, Andrew Harris. Dr. Reade telegraphed "Do you know Ansel Bourne? Please answer." The reply came, "He is my uncle. Wire me where he is, and if well. Write particulars" [pp. 221, 231– 232].

The "particulars" were ultimately pieced together, in part from the testimony given by those who had known Mr. Bourne during the period of his fugue and in part from a subsequent clinical examination by William James (1907), who through hypnosis was able to uncover in Mr. Bourne memories of his life as Mr. Brown that corresponded with the accounts supplied by others. It should be pointed out that though present in the hypnotic state, these memories never became available to Mr. Bourne while fully awake, and he remained amnesic for the events that had occurred during the six weeks of his fugue.

If we compare these two clinical disorders, hysterical amnesia and hysterical fugue, it is apparent that there are similarities and differences. Common to them both is a curious disturbance in memory, in which the normal voluntary recall of memories of past events is impossible, even though it can be shown (through hypnosis, for example) that the memories are preserved outside of ordinary conscious awareness. The memory disturbance in hysterical amnesia, however, is a relatively simple affair. It affects a set of associated events that are usually circumscribed and limited to a brief period of time. If there is a loss of personal identity, it is transitory in nature. Furthermore, except for a possible brief state of somnambulistic alteration of consciousness ushering in the amnesia, there has been no observable change in the patient's behavior, personality, or state of awareness during the period of events that is eventually lost to conscious recall.

In the fugue states, on the other hand, a change in the sense of identity is a central characteristic. As the fugue begins, the patient loses all memory whatsoever for the events of his entire past life. His origins, his family, his upbringing, wife, children, friends, occupation, all dissolve into the mists of forgetfulness, and the patient assumes a new name and life without any evident awareness or concern over the internal upheaval. Driven by often half-veiled inner urgings, he wanders far from his familiar surroundings to start a fresh existence, his conscious mind a virtual *tabula rasa*. It should be noted, however, that it is only the mental elements related to his personal identity that have disappeared. Basic functions such as language, general knowledge, and the skills of coping with the tasks of everyday living remain under his command, and there is no alteration in his state of consciousness of the new world of people and things around him. Only those who have known him in his previous existence would recognize the catastrophic changes in his being; to strangers, he appears in no way out of the ordinary. But ultimately and inevitably, a second revolution overtakes him. In the twinkling of an eye, he wakes to his old self, puzzled and dismayed to find himself in an alien world. His old identity is recaptured, but he is totally amnesic for all the events of the period of fugue and frighteningly ignorant of how he came to be where he is.

Multiple Personality

As we turn now to a consideration of the syndrome of *multiple personality*, we find some features reminiscent of those of the fugue, especially in the realm of changes in personal identity, which in the multiple personality form the hallmark of the disorder. This is strikingly exemplified by the Reverend Mr. Hanna, whose experiences were extensively investigated and presented by Sidis and Goodhart (1905) some 70 years ago.

On the evening of April 15, 1897, Mr. Hanna, aged 25, lost his footing while alighting from his carriage and fell, striking his head. Unconscious for nearly two hours, he awoke suddenly and began struggling with those in attendance upon him. It was soon discovered that he was totally amnesic for the entirety of his past life—for biographical events, family, and friends. What is more, he could no longer speak, read, write, and comprehend spoken language, and he had lost the motor skills and fund of knowledge of the average, normal adult. Indeed, both from direct observation as well as from his own later retrospective account, his state of being appeared to be that of a newborn infant.

Sidis and Goodhart (1905) wrote:

> Although the functions of the sense-organs remained intact, and the peripheral sensory processes remained normal, so that he experienced all the sensations awakened by external stimuli, yet there was a loss of all mental recognition and of interpretation of incoming sensations; all recognition of the external world was lost. Stimuli from without acted upon his sense-organs, gave rise to sensations, but perceptions and conceptions were entirely absent. The man was mentally blind. He could feel, but could not understand. He was as a newly-born infant opening his eyes for the first time upon the world.
>
> The world was to Mr. Hanna but a chaos of sensations not as yet elaborated and differentiated into a system of distinct percepts and concepts; neither objects, nor space, nor time, in the form as they are presented to the developed adult mind, existed for him. So totally obliterated from memory were the experiences of his past life that even the requirements of the simplest mental processes by which the appreciation of distance, form, size, magnitude is acquired, were effaced from his mind.
>
> Movement alone attracted his attention. He did not know the cause and meaning of movement, but a moving object fastened his involuntary attention and seemed to fascinate his gaze. He made as yet no discrimination between his own

movements and those of other objects, and was as much interested in the movement of his own limbs as in that of external things. He did not know how to control
his voluntary muscles, nor had he any idea of the possibility of such control.

From the more or less involuntary, chance movements made by his arms and
legs, he learned the possibility of controlling his limbs. The full voluntary power
over his muscles he only learned from instruction by others. He could not coordi-
nate the movements of his legs, hence he could not walk.

Unable to discriminate between his own activity and that of others, the world
was not as yet differentiated into the objective and subjective, and he had no idea
of ego activity. Movements had for him no differential coefficient—all were alike
to him. The three dimensions, length, width and depth, were as yet not appreciated; they really did not exist for him.

Although impressions were received by his sense-organs, still the only sensations prominent in his mind were darkness, light and color. Everything was close
to his eyes—objects near and far seemed equally distant.

He did not have the least conception of the flow of time—seconds, minutes,
hours were alike to him. His knowledge and adaptations to environment were so
completely obliterated that, like an infant, he most unceremoniously responded to
the calls of nature [pp. 92–93].

During the several weeks after his injury, Mr. Hanna rapidly regained his ego
functions, recovered his ability to use language, and "learned" a number of
special skills that had been his in his previous life. He developed a rapidly
growing store of conscious memories for the events and people associated with
the period following his accident and in addition was observed to have patterns of
behavior quite different from those of his former life. He now enjoyed, for
example, an occasional cigar or glass of beer—simple pleasures previously
forbidden to him as a clergyman. However, he remained totally without memory
of all that had occurred in the 25 years before the accident. Family, fiancée, and
friends were complete strangers to him; his lifelong surroundings were utterly
unfamiliar, and he had no recollection of having been a preacher. His life and
memories existed only for the time subsequent to his carriage mishap. It was as if
he were a totally new person inhabiting a body that had once belonged to
someone else.

Then, suddenly, in the small hours of the morning of June 9, nearly eight
weeks after the onset of his amnesia, Mr. Hanna woke his brother, who was
caring for him, and demanded to know where they were. It rapidly became
evident that he had recovered all the memories of his life prior to the accident but
that now he had an amnesia for the period between April 15 and June 9. From
that time on, the patient switched back and forth from State A (preaccident
personality) to State B (postaccident personality). The cluster of memories of
each of these alternating personalities remained isolated from one another, so
that in each state there was amnesia for the other. There were in effect two
separate persons living alternately in Mr. Hanna's body, at least as far as the

memory clusters and the sense of identity associated with each were concerned. Eventually, through the psychotherapeutic techniques of his doctors, both memory systems were reunited under the control of one ego, and Mr. Hanna was relieved of his distressing and disabling amnesia.

There was one significant exception to the isolation of the memory systems from one another. In his B State, Mr. Hanna would have vivid dreams of people and places that his family recognized as references to events that had occurred during his A State. For Mr. Hanna as B, however, the dream images were alien and meaningless. For example (Sidis & Goodhart, 1905), he described a dream picture in which he was with a

> . . . companion, whom he called, for no known reason, Ray W. Schuyler. In his dream he heard that the name of the place was "Morea." (We learned that Schuyler was the name of an old companion of Mr. Hanna's school-days; that they had been together in Morea, a town in Pennsylvania.) . . . The father, who was present when the dreams were related by the son, could identify the places spoken of as well as their names and also the persons mentioned. . . . When the father happened to mention the name of "Martinoe," Mr. Hanna at once said, "Oh, yes, that was the name of the place I passed through, but," exclaimed he, "how do you know of it?" When the father interposed and described more fully what Mr. Hanna saw, the latter with great wonder and amazement exclaimed, "How can you know all this, it was only a dream!" [p. 139].

In many patients manifesting multiple personalities, memory is not so tightly partitioned into separate cells. Most commonly, although the primary, or A, personality is unaware of the events that occur during the ascendancy in consciousness of the secondary, or B, personality, the limits of the memories of the latter encompass the events occurring when the primary personality holds sway. Simply put, B knows A, but A does not know B.

Such was the case with Mrs. Martha G., a 36-year-old woman admitted to the hospital with a hysterical inability to walk following a minor automobile accident some 6 months before her admission (Frankel, 1976). In addition to her motor disturbance, the patient complained of hearing a voice "that is not me, telling me to say things and do things," such as "to say mean things to my husband or to get mad at the doctors." If she tried to resist the commands of the voice, she would feel it "overcrowd me and overshadow me, as if it wanted to take over."

During an early diagnostic interview, when she spoke of pressure from the voice, she was told to "let it take over." She responded immediately with a clenching of her fists, a rolling of her head, and writhing of her body and appeared to be in an altered state of consciousness. After some 30 seconds of this behavior, she suddenly opened her eyes and began to speak to the interviewer. A marked change in her mien and behavior was immediately evident. Before the short lapse of consciousness, she had been listless, apathetic if not depressed, unable to walk, and complaining of headache, backache, and fatigue. Now she was bright, smiling, and cheerful. She had lost her aches and pains, was full of energy, and was able to rise off her chair and walk easily across the room and back.

The presence of a different person as judged by her appearance and behavior was confirmed by the patient herself. Her name, she said, was "Harriet." She expressed pleasure that "we have got rid of that other one who stays sick all the time," and then added in a confidential tone of voice, "They don't know I'm here." When asked to explain more fully who she was, she replied that she and Martha had been friends when they were little. "When we were six, I got sick and died. She didn't want me to die; she wanted to die, but I died, and she doesn't know I'm still alive inside of her." She had, Harriet continued, been quite content existing quietly inside of Martha until three years ago. At that time, Martha, along with her husband, was converted to a small, puritanical Christian sect, gave up smoking and drinking because "the Lord didn't like that," and spent the greater part of her waking hours in church activities until her inability to walk confined her to her home. Harriet expressed great resentment and scorn at Martha's behavior since her conversion. "She and that husband of hers, all they do is go to church and read the Bible and go to church. We like different things; I like to go drinking and dancing and night-clubbing, and she likes to go to church, and I don't. But I make her miserable!" When asked how it was that she could walk and Martha could not, though they shared the same body, Harriet replied, "I'm not sick. She's the one that stays sick, see, but I'm not sick. I'm an altogether different person."

At length it was suggested to Harriet that she let Martha return. After protesting briefly that "they should let her stay where she was," Harriet assented, clenched her fists, and with the same rolling and twisting of her head and body as before, accompanied by plaintive cries of "No! No!," she became momentarily out of contact with the interviewer, then suddenly relaxed, and with a big sigh opened her eyes and said, "Oh, I've been asleep on you." Asked how she felt, she replied, "Tired and cold and sleepy. And I've got a backache and my head's aching." It was evident that Martha had returned and that she had no memory for what had transpired in the preceding quarter of an hour. She showed no concern over the lapse in time and carried on with the interview as if nothing had happened.

Let us examine the salient characteristics in the relation between Martha and Harriet—characteristics that are similarly to be found in many of the multiple personalities who have been described over the past century. Although Martha was unaware of the existence of Harriet and was amnesic for the events that occurred while Harriet dominated consciousness, Harriet was aware of all that Martha knew, thought, and did. Each was a distinct personality, different from the other in terms of attitudes, likes, and dislikes, emotions and mood. The secondary personality (Harriet) experienced herself as an individual in her own right. Furthermore, she viewed the primary personality (Martha) with dislike and scorn and did what she could to annoy, disrupt, and dismay the other. Indeed, once Harriet came to light, the origin of Martha's hallucinatory symptoms could be seen in Harriet's teasing manipulations.

Co-Consciousness

In Mrs. G., only two personalities were to be observed. Not uncommonly, several such personalities may be found holding the stage of consciousness in turn and with varying degrees of awareness of one another (Prince, 1906, 1924; Schreiber, 1974; Thigpen & Cleckley, 1957). The nature of the secondary personalities when they are not dominating consciousness is not clearly understood. Presumably, in many cases, they are merely lying fallow and inactive in their unconscious state. There is evidence in some instances, however, that a well-developed secondary personality may continue to be active, to think, to experience, to feel, to grow in complexity—in short, to live a separate existence beneath the surface while the primary personality dominates ordinary consciousness and is in contact with the external world. This paradoxical state of *co-consciousness* can best be understood through an examination of the relevant clinical phenomena.

B. C. A., a patient described by Prince (1924), exhibited three separate personalities at the height of her illness. A and C had amnesia for each other, and both of them were amnesic in regard to B. On the other hand, B was fully aware of the memories and experiences of both A and C. Furthermore, B claimed to be an independent person in her own right and to retain a full co-consciousness of her own while either A or C was in conscious contact with the external world. At Prince's request, B wrote an autobiographical account based on her introspective observations of these co-conscious phenomena ("B," 1908–09):

> When I am not here as an alternating personality [i.e., dominating external consciousness], my thoughts still continue during the lives of A and C, although they are not aware of them. . . . That is to say, my mental life continues independently of theirs. . . . I think my own thoughts, which are different from theirs, and at the same time I know their thoughts and what they do. . . . [p. 322]
>
> Now nearly everything that happens is perceived by some part of C's mind— the rustle of a paper, the cracking of a stick in the fire, the sound of a bird chirping, the smile or frown on the face of a person whom we meet, the gleam of their teeth, etc., everything that can be seen or heard is recorded in her mind whether she is conscious of it or not. . . . Now into my stream of consciousness most of these perceptions are absorbed, but C is conscious of only the more important ones. For example: Dr. Prince comes into the room and C rises and greets him, shakes hands and says, "Good morning;" she is conscious of nothing but a sense of relief at seeing him, and is thinking only of the woes she has to tell him; but I perceive thinks like this: Dr. Prince's hand is cold; he looks tired or rested; he is nervous today; he has on such and such clothes or cravat, etc. These perceptions

become my thoughts. C does not take them into her consciousness at all. Later, if she were asked if she shook hands with Dr. Prince she might or might not remember it; as to his hand being cold and all the rest of it, she would not have noticed. . . . When C's mind is concentrated on any one thing, like reading or studying, it is closed to every other perception. She does not notice the sounds in the house or out of doors, but I, being co-conscious, do. I hear the blinds rattle, I hear the maid moving about the house, I hear the telephone ring, etc. She hears none of these things. She does not know that she is tired, and that she ought to stop reading, but all these things I know and think of. When she stops reading she becomes conscious that she is tired, but of the sounds in the house she knows nothing. I have read the book also, but these other things are added to my stream of conscious thought. So, you see, I know all C's thoughts, and think my own beside. When she is talking with any one, I often disagree with what she says. She does not think at all the same about many things. I think of replies I would make quite different from the ones she makes. Then sometimes I do not pay very much attention to her conversations, though I know all she says, but go on with my own thoughts. . . . (pp. 324−325) My train of thought may be, and usually is, quite different from C's. When C is ill, for instance, she is thinking about her headache, and how hard life seems and how glad she will be when it is over, and I am think-ing how tiresome it is to lie in bed when I am just aching to go for a long tramp or do something gay. We rarely have the same opinion about any book we are reading, though we may both like it. C, however, enjoys some writers whom I find very tiresome, Maeterlinck, for example. She considers him very inspiring and uplifting, and I think he writes a lot of nonsense and is extremely despressing . . . [p. 326].

Furthermore, as B informs us, she not only differed from A and from C in regard to perceptions, thoughts, interests, moods, and predilections, but at times she could influence their sensorimotor functions from her co-conscious position.

As an example of involuntary influence, I will take the following incident, as it is fresh in my memory. A few days ago Dr. Putnam kindly allowed C to see a patient of his who is suffering from a form of hysteria. She could not put her feet down flat on the floor, but turned her toes up and tried to walk on her heels and the sides of her feet, and as she walked she trembled all over and breathed irregularly. I was much interested in the matter, and after we got home kept wondering how the girl managed to walk that way—it seemed so difficult. There was in my mind a picture of the girl with her toes turned up, trembling and breathing hard; I was imagining how it would seem to walk that way and to tremble all over, etc. I was not paying any attention to C's train of thought, being absorbed in my own, and did not consider at all how my thoughts might affect her until I became aware that she was trembling from head to foot, that her toes were all curled up, and that she could hardly keep her feet flat on the floor. She was in great distress of mind, as she thought her condition was caused by her extreme suggestibility [pp. 331−332].

C's effect on A's motor function was matched by the influence she could occasionally exert on A's sensory apparatus, as evidenced by the following incident.

> I one day wrote something in the diary, which has been kept by all of us, which A did not understand, and she took the book to Dr. Prince. I did not care to have him read what I wrote in my diary, so that night I wrote a note to A, saying that I was going to put the diary where she could not find it and that she should never see it again. I did not, however, do so, but left it in the drawer where it was always kept. A found this note from me in the morning and went at once to see if the diary was gone. It was right there, but she could not see it; she took it in her hand several times in searching through the drawer but could not see it . . . [pp. 332–333].

The concept of co-consciousness perhaps raises more questions than it answers, and were B's autobiographical account the sole instance of the phenomenon, one might be tempted to dismiss it as the subjective and fanciful reverie of a suggestible mind. Credence in what she relates is strengthened, however, by other subjectively obtained evidence for what she describes (Prince & Peterson, 1908) and by the fact that similar phenomena are to be found in other patients with multiple personalities (Prince, 1906; Schreiber, 1974). Furthermore, her account is consonant with the observation (as we see shortly) that in certain unusual states of dissociation, highly complex logical and creative mental processes can operate independently, outside of normal conscious awareness. Before developing these trains of thought, let us turn our attention to the relation of the phenomena of hysterical amnesia to those of conversion hysteria, and to the relation of both to hypnosis and dissociation.

THEORETICAL CONSIDERATIONS

Hysteria, Hypnosis, and Dissociation

In the modern classification of the neuroses, hysteria is divided into two categories: *conversion hysteria* and *dissociative hysteria*. To the former are relegated those patients with sensorimotor phenomena such as paralyses and anesthesias; the latter includes individuals with amnesias, fugues, and multiple personalities. The boundaries of the two diagnostic categories do not, however, absolutely and sharply delimit separate clinical entities, for both forms of the disorder may be found in one and the same patients, as we have seen in Martha G., who manifested both a hysterical motor disorder and a hysterical splitting of her personality. Indeed, as was observed in Mrs. G., one may find that behind the patient who comes to the clinic with incapacitating hysterical conversion symptoms, there lies a secondary personality that is free of sensorimotor disturbances and is ostensibly a healthy, well-adapted, though entirely different person. The primary personality, in other words, may be truncated, diminished fragment of the secondary (Mitchell, 1912). Furthermore, one can often find that the sensorimotor symptoms exhibited by the primary personality are the direct result and representation of the mental activities of the secondary personality. Such was true of Mrs. G., whose auditory hallucinations as Martha stemmed from the underlying, unconscious influence of Harriet. Similarly, B. C. A.'s hysterical gait was immediately related to its being imagined by the secondary personality, B.

Further evidence for the intimate relation between the two forms of hysteria is to be found in the phenomena of hypnosis. The marked hypnotizability of hysterical patients has been repeatedly observed (Frankel, 1976; Janet, 1904), a fact that led many clinicians, particularly Janet and his associates, mistakenly to view the susceptibility to hypnosis itself as a hallmark of hysteria and, therefore, as pathological. This extreme position has been modified by the more extensive study of hypnotic phenomena in recent decades that has shown us that individuals are hypnotizable in varying degrees, ranging along a continuous scale from absent or low hypnotizability to those who are markedly susceptible to hypnotic trance induction. It is only at the upper end of the scale that one finds some individuals manifesting the clinical symptoms of hysteria.

What is of special interest is the fact that, particularly in susceptible subjects, hypnosis can produce all the phenomena that constitute hysteria when they occur spontaneously. Paralyses and automatic movements are the common coin of hypnotic states, as are anesthesia and analgesia—the insensitivity to pain, reaching a degree in some individuals that enables them to undergo major surgical procedures without awareness of discomfort. Total or selective blindness and deafness can likewise be induced. Furthermore, temporary alterations in personality and behavior can be elicited by the hypnotist's suggestion, and occasionally what appears to be an already-formed secondary personality emerges in the hypnotic state. Another important aspect of hypnosis in highly susceptible persons is the amnesia for the events of the trance that follows a return to normal consciousness, whether this occurs spontaneously or as the result of the hypnotist's suggestion. It should further be noted that just as the memory of events hidden by hysterical amnesia can be recovered under hypnosis, so too those concealed by posthypnotic amnesia may be recalled in subsequent hypnotically induced trances.

It must be emphasized that neither hysterical nor hypnotic amnesia is absolute. Modern investigation of hypnotic amnesia has shown experimentally that there may be partial recall by hypnotizable subjects of their experiences under hypnosis (Evans, Kihlstrom, & Orne, 1973). Of particular interest is what has been termed "source amnesia"; that is, a subject may remember a fact he has learned in a hypnotic state but have no memory whatsoever for where, when, and how he learned it (Evans & Thorn, 1966). Analogues of these hypnotic phenomena can be seen in the various forms of naturally occurring amnesia we have reviewed earlier. Mr. Hanna's recollection of the names of actual persons and places without recognition of their origin is strongly reminiscent of the experimentalist's "source amnesia"; and, along with other evidence of the intrusion of unconscious mental elements into conscious awareness, it indicates that the partitioning wall of dissociation is not impermeable.

It is not our purpose here to review the facts of hypnosis in detail but merely to indicate their striking similarity and close relation to hysterical phenomena. The connection between them was a major focus of attention of clinical investigators in the last decades of the 19th century and the early decades of this, and the diverse observations concerning them were united into an intelligible whole by the concept of dissociation.

Janet's Theoretical Model

Before it paled in the rising sun of psychoanalytic observation and theory, dissociation reached its apogee in the theoretical formulations of Pierre Janet (1904). For Janet, the process of dissociation, pathological in nature and ultimately genetic in origin, is the central mechanism in the production of neurotic symptoms. In the psychologically normal individual, he postulated, all of the mental functions, including memories of past events, are integrated in a unified personality dominated by the ego, whose central feature is the awareness of personal identity. In Janet's theoretical scheme, there are no unconscious (or subconscious, as he termed it) mental contents in the healthy psyche. It is only when a pathological state supervenes that ordinarily conscious mental events escape the control of the ego and are lost to conscious awareness—that is, they are dissociated. In this way the individual becomes amnesic for specific, often emotionally traumatic events in his life. The memory of these events, though now dissociated and unavailable to conscious recall, nonetheless retains the power to afflict the individual with pathological, ego-alien symptoms, such as somnambulistic states that recreate the traumatic event, hallucinations, sensory and motor disturbances, and alterations in personality. Dissociation and the concomitant unconscious mental events were for Janet and those who subscribed to his formulations evidence of a pathological diminution and fragmentation of the normal ego through the splitting off of portions that rightfully belonged to it.

According to Janet, the tendency to dissociation is basically genetic in origin. The normal individual, in his view, is born with a sufficient amount of nervous or mental energy to permit his ego to bind together all the psychic elements into a unified, functioning whole. In certain persons predisposed by heredity, however, the quantum of mental energy is lower than normal. Under the stress of an emotional trauma or a serious physical illness, the already inadequate store of energy will be further depleted to a level at which it is insufficient for the task of binding the psychic elements in a single stream of consciousness under the ego's domination. As a consequence, dissociation will result and symptoms will follow.

Freud's Theoretical Model

Janet's explanation of dissociation invoked a theoretical model that was mechanistic in nature and viewed the neurotic individual as the passive victim of an unfortunate heredity legacy and of the accidental buffets of stressful events. Freud, whose early theoretical formulations (Breuer & Freud, 1895/1955), like those of Janet, were aimed at accounting for the phenomena of dissociation, introduced an explanatory model that was revolutionary in character and that set the stage for the entire subsequent development of psychoanalysis. In *Studies on Hysteria* (Breuer & Freud, 1895/1955) as well as in the shorter clinical papers (Freud, 1894/1962, 1896/1962) that immediately followed, Freud proposed the term *defence hysteria* to designate a form of the disorder that comprised some if not most of the hysterical patients he studied. In defence hysteria, the patient is confronted with ideas that for a variety of reasons, moral and otherwise, are incompatible with and unacceptable to the rest of his ego. Motivated by the painful conflict aroused by this incompatibility, the individual *represses* the unacceptable ideas, a process that leads to their being split off from the ego and becoming unconscious. Dissociation occurs, in other words, not as the result of the passive falling away of an idea from a weakened ego, but through its active, forceful rejection from consciousness by an ego strong enough to banish it from sight.

The Unconscious in Psychoanalysis

In this explanation of dissociation, Freud made a radical departure from the contemporary theories of symptom formation, and the concept of psychological conflict became the foundation for the rapidly developing edifice of psycho-analysis. It should be noted, however, that Freud's discoveries, his clinical interests, and his evolving theoretical concepts led him along lines of investigation quite different from those of his contemporaries. As we know, he gave up hypnosis and developed the technique of free association as his basic tool of observation and investigation. He turned his attention away from memories of traumatic events as a major etiological factor in the production of neurotic symptoms, and he focused his sights on the instincts (mainly libidinal) and their derivative affects and fantasies as being the source of conflict and the basic motivation for defensive repression. At the same time he turned to a study of dreams as providing the "royal road to the unconscious."

Freud's investigations, in other words, shifted from a concern with the process of dissociation and its effect on the ego to the dark underworld of forbidden desire and primitive human strivings—a world in conflict with the reality-oriented ego of the civilized and socialized adult human being. There he discovered modes of thought and psychological functioning that led him to define the characteristics of the Unconscious that have been essential to our conception of it ever since. (Freud, 1900/1953, 1912/1958, 1915/1957, 1923/1961, 1940/1964) Let us review these briefly here:

1. Among the contents of the Unconscious are to be found not only what has been repressed from consciousness but many mental elements as well that have never been conscious at all.
2. The Unconscious is intimately related to human instinctual life and to the drives, affects, and fantasies that derive from instinctual energy.
3. The Unconscious is dominated by the pleasure principle—that is, it strives for the immediate expression and gratification of its instinctual needs and drives.
4. It manifests characteristics of thought that are in marked contrast to those of the ego. Under the dominance of the primary process (in which condensation and displacement are primary modes of thinking), it operates with a chaotic illogic, without regard for time, for contradictions, or for the orderly structure and dictates of the real, external world.

It is, in sum, a universe of wishes, fantasies, and desires that must be modified and controlled by other parts of the mind if the individual is to survive the demands of the social and physical environment in which he is forced to live.

The Unconscious of Dissociation

It would be hard to overstate or to overemphasize the impact of psychoanalytic concepts on 20th-century psychiatry or their importance for our understanding and treatment of emotional illness. The value of psychoanalytic thought as a general theory of human behavior, normal and abnormal, was recognized early in the century, and it soon attracted a growing band of clinical investigators who found that the breadth of its scope and explanatory power allowed them to apply psychoanalytic techniques and psychoanalytic concepts to a broad spectrum of clinical disorders.

At the same time, the rapid rise to predominance of the psychoanalytic approach diverted attention from the more restricted area of dissociation and the phenomena related to it and put a premature closure to the investigations and ideas of Janet and others who shared his views and interests. As Morton Prince rather petulantly complained in 1928, "Freudian psychology had flooded the field like a full rising tide, and the rest of us were left submerged like clams buried in the sands at low water" (Murray, 1956, p. 293). There was justification for Prince's grumblings, for in his descent into the unconscious disclosed by a study of psychological conflict, Freud plunged so quickly into the lower depths that he hardly got a glimpse of the regions of the unconscious revealed to us by a study of the nature of dissociative amnesia. As suggested by Prince (1921) himself, the unconscious produced by dissociation is quite different from that disclosed by psychoanalytic investigation. As we have seen in our earlier review of the clinical observations, it is an area of often extensive divisions and splitting of the ego itself—phenomena that, despite the earlier attention paid to them by Janet, Sidis, Prince, and others (Hart, 1929; McDougall, 1926), have not yet been adequately and fully explored. A brief survey of their general characteristics will indicate these differences.

First and foremost, dissociation leads to a splitting off of ego functions that may originally have been under voluntary control. The elements thus rendered unconscious range in organization from the simplest to the most complex. At one end of the spectrum, one sees separated from consciousness a limited series of related memories, a localized motor function, or a sensory modality or two, resulting clinically in a circumscribed amnesia, a hysterical paralysis, or a hysterical anesthesia. At the other, one may find a highly integrated and richly complicated set of mental elements constituting a complete person divorced from ordinary consciousness and existing side by side (as has been observed in the case of the dissociative multiple personality) with a primary personality of a totally different cast and hue. In each personality, there exists a full or nearly full range of ego functions enabling each to adapt and relate to its physical and human environment. To use a spatial metaphor, in dissociation the cleavage plane is along a vertical axis of the psyche; in psychoanalytic concepts, the division between conscious and unconscious lies in a horizontal direction.

Certain elements of ego functioning may be found in the unconscious that have never been in the purview of ordinary conscious awareness before being raised into consciousness by special measures such as hypnosis or automatic writing. We have seen in the autobiographical account given us by the secondary personality of B. C. A. how she was aware of sensory stimuli of which the primary personality had no knowledge or perception whatsoever. Similarly, using automatic writing in an experimental setting with the same patient, Prince was able to show that in the artificially altered state of consciousness, she could recall the minute details of objects she had recently seen of which neither she nor Prince had any knowledge when they tried voluntarily to remember what they had just perceived (Prince, 1924). Furthermore, an entire personality may exist, grow, and develop underground for years, undetected by the normal consciousness, and indeed may have no place in the normal and usual life of the person who harbors it. The famous multiple personality, Sally Beauchamp, for example, extensively studied and reported by Morton Prince during her long illness with dissociative hysteria, exhibited at the height of her disorder three separate and distinct personalities: BI, BII, and BIV. When, through Prince's psychotherapeutic skill, the elements of her psyche were reintegrated and she was restored to her normal premorbid state, this was found to consist of an amalgam of BI and BIV, the BIII personality, with its idiosyncratic characteristics having completely and permanently disappeared from view (Prince, 1906).

The dissociative unconscious is capable of orderly, rational, and logical mental operations that are totally unlike the chaotic, primary process thinking of the psychoanalytic unconscious. As a consequence of posthypnotic suggestion, complex mathematical calculations may be carried out without any conscious awareness of the steps taken to arrive at the answer. The correct solution appears suddenly in the individual's awareness, unbidden and out of the blue. Inductive logical processes are also found occurring unconsciously, providing an often surprised and delighted individual with a solution to a problem that has long eluded his conscious attempts to unravel it. The Assyriologist H. V. Hilprecht provides us with a striking example (Myers, 1954). Baffled by the nature and significance of two apparently unrelated fragments of Babylonian agate, he went to sleep exhausted by his fruitless conscious attempts to find a clue to the puzzle. In a long, richly textured, and dramatic dream, and ancient priest appeared before him and showed him how the two fragments fitted together into a single votive cylinder. Subsequent examination of the pieces themselves proved the truth of the vision and enabled the dreamer to read and translate the inscription on the cylinder that had been unintelligible in its fragmentary state.

The dissociative unconscious can be inventive and creative, casting up from the depths highly elaborate and fully fashioned artistic creations. Stevenson's well-known "Brownies," which often gave him long, complicated plots as he dreamed, are a case in point. This was, indeed, as he tells us in "A Chapter on Dreams," a source of *Dr. Jekyll and Mr. Hyde* (Stevenson, 1910). Even more remarkable are the productions of Mme. Hélène Smith as reported by Théodore Flournoy (1900). While in a dissociated trance state, she transmitted both orally and in writing an imaginative series of romantic tales concerning her previous incarnations. Perhaps unique are the literary creations of Mrs. Pearl Curran. As "Patience Worth," she emitted a spontaneous and automatic outpouring of words in the form of volumes of poetry and novels of striking literary merit that far transcended her education, apparent knowledge, and ordinary linguistic skills (Prince, 1927).

Although dissociation may often be the result of a defensive exclusion from consciousness of painful or unacceptable ideas, it need not stem from psychological conflict. The phenomena of hypnosis, whether self-induced or produced by a hypnotist, do not necessarily involve the dissociation of conflictual ideas, and the same may be said of the dissociative phenomena occurring during intense concentration in susceptible individuals.

Not only is the unconscious of dissociation different from that disclosed by psychoanalytic observations; but, as has been often suggested, the concepts of dissociation and repression are not entirely synonymous (Hart, 1926; McDougall, 1938; Mitchell, 1920; Rapaport, 1942; Sears, 1936). Repression is the preeminent defense mechanism of the psychodynamic structure that constitutes the psyche and is centrally involved in the control of instinctual processes and their derivatives. Dissociation, though it may often have a defensive function, can be set in motion by factors unrelated to psychological conflict, and its effects are felt more within the ego than in the psychic apparatus as a whole.

The differences in the two conceptions of the unconscious that have been highlighted here do not imply any basic or inherent conflict between them. On the contrary, each involves a study of separate areas of mental functioning, the results of which are complementary and help to complete our picture of the human mind. In the disorderly and often capricious progression of history, human thought advances along a meandering course, and the evolution of psychological ideas is no exception. It is not surprising, therefore, as we have already remarked, that with few exceptions, clinical investigators have paid little attention to the concept of dissociation during the past three-quarters of a century. Recently, however, it has been suggested that a renewed exploration of the facts and theories concerning it might prove rewarding, especially for a clarification of the functions of the ego (Hilgard, 1973; Nemiah, 1967, 1974). The nature of memory, the mechanisms of identification, the development of personal identity, the mystery of creativity, the process of dissociation itself, and its neurophysiological correlates—all and more stand to be elucidated by the further study of dissociative phenomena. By focusing attention on a realm of mental functioning different from, yet complementary to, the areas illuminated by the contributions of psychoanalytic investigations, a resurgence of interest in dissociation can bring us yet closer to a realization of Bergson's earlier hopes.

ACKNOWLEDGMENTS

I should like to thank my colleagues, Dr. Fred H. Frankel and Dr. Peter E. Sifneos, for their helpful suggestions.

The editors of this volume and myself also wish to express our appreciation and our thanks for permission to reproduce several passages in this chapter:

Extract from the case of Ansel Bourne from Hodgson, F. A case of double consciousness. *Proceedings of the Society for Psychical Research*, 1892, 7, 221–257.

Extract from the case of Madame D from Janet, P. *Nevroses et idees fixes*. 2nd Ed. Paris: Felix Alean, 1904.

Extract from the case of Mr. Ha-na from Sidis, B., & Goodhart, S.P. *Multiple personality: An investigation into the nature of human individuality*. New York: Appleton, 1905.

Extract from the case of B. C. A. from "B." An introspective analysis of co-conscious life, by a personality (B) claiming to be co-conscious. *Journal of Abnormal and Social Psychology*, 1908–1909, *3*, 311–334.

REFERENCES

Abeles, M., & Schilder, P. Psychogenic loss of personal identity Amnesia. *Archives of Neurology & Psychiatry*, 1935, *34*, 587–604.

"B" An introspective analysis of co-conscious life, by a personality (B) claiming to be co-conscious. *Journal of Abnormal Psychology*, 1908–1909, *3*, 311–334.

Bergson, H. *Dreams.* New York: B. W. Huebsch, 1914.

Breuer, J., & Freud, S. *Studies on hysteria.* In J. Strachey (Ed.), *The standard edition of the complete psychological works of Sigmund Freud* (Vol. 2). London: Hogarth Press, 1955. (Originally published, 1895.)

Evans, F. J., Kihlstrom, J. F., & Orne, E. C. Quantifying subjective reports during posthypnotic amnesia. *Proceedings of the 81st Annual Convention of the American Psychological Association*, 1973, *8*, 1077–1078.

Evans, F. J., & Thorn, W. A. F. Two types of posthypnotic amnesia: Recall amnesia and source amnesia. *International Journal of Clinical and Experimental Hypnosis*, 1966, *14*, 162–177.

Flournoy, T. *From india to the planet mars.* New York: Harper & Bros., 1900.

Frankel, F. *Hypnosis: Trance as a coping mechanism.* New York: Plenum Press, 1976.

Freud, S. The neuro-psychoses of defence. In J. Strachey (Ed.), *The standard edition of the complete psychological works of Sigmund Freud* (Vol. 3). London: Hogarth Press, 1962. (Originally published, 1894.)

Freud, S. Further remarks on the neuro-psychoses of defence. In J. Strachey (Ed.), *The standard edition of the complete psychological works of Sigmund Freud* (Vol. 3). London: Hogarth Press, 1962. (Originally published, 1896.)

Freud, S. The interpretation of dreams. In J. Strachey (Ed.), *The standard edition of the complete psychological works of Sigmund Freud* (Vols. 4–5). London: Hogarth Press, 1953. (Originally published, 1900.)

Freud, S. A note on the unconscious in psychoanalysis. In J. Strachey (Ed.), *The standard edition of the complete psychological works of Sigmund Freud* (Vol. 12). London: Hogarth Press, 1958. (Originally published, 1912.)

Freud, S. The unconscious. In J. Strachey (Ed.), *The standard edition of the complete psychological works of Sigmund Freud* (Vol. 14). London: Hogarth Press, 1957. (Originally published, 1915.)

Freud, S. *The ego and the id.* In J. Strachey (Ed.), *The standard edition of the complete psychological works of Sigmund Freud* (Vol. 19). London: Hogarth Press, 1961. (Originally published, 1923.)

Freud, S. *An outline of psychoanalysis.* In J. Strachey (Ed.), *The standard edition of the complete psychological works of Sigmund Freud* (Vol. 23). London: Hogarth Press, 1964. (Originally published, 1940.)

Gillespie, R. D. Amnesia. *Archives of Neurology and Psychiatry*, 1937, *37*, 748–764.

Hart, B. The conception of dissociation. *British Journal of Medical Psychology* 1926, *6*, 241–263.

Hart, B. *The psychology of insanity.* Cambridge: Cambridge University Press, 1929.

Hilgard, E. R. Dissociation revisited. In M. Henle, J. Jaynes, & J. J. Sullivan, (Eds.) *Historical conceptions of psychology.* New York: Springer, 1973.

Hodgson, F. A case of double consciousness. *Proceedings of the Society for Psychical Research*, 1892, *7*, 221–257.

James, W. *The principles of psychology* (2 vols.). New York: Henry Holt, 1907.

Janet, P. *L'Automatisme Psychologique.* Paris: Félix Alcan, 1889.

Janet, P. *État Mental des Hystériques* Paris: Rueff et cie, 1893.

Janet, P. *Névroses et idées fixes* (2nd ed.). Paris: Félix Alcan, 1904.

McDougall, W. *Outline of abnormal personality.* New York: Scribner's, 1926.

McDougall, W. The relations between dissociation and repression. *British Journal of Medical Psychology* 1938, *17*, 141–157.

Mitchell, T. W. Some types of multiple personality. *Proceedings of the Society for Psychical Research*, 1912, *26*, 257–285.

Mitchell, T. W. Psychology of the unconscious and psychoanalysis. *Proceedings of the Society for Psychical Research*, 1920, *30*, 134–173.

Murray, H. A. Morton Prince: Sketch of his life and work. *Journal of Abnormal and Social Psychology*, 1956, *52*, 291–295.

Myers, F. W. H. *Human personality and its survival of bodily death* (Vol. 1). New York: Longmans, Green, 1954.

Nemiah, J. C. Conversion reaction. In A. M. Freedman & H. I. Kaplan (Eds.), *Comprehensive textbook of psychiatry*. Baltimore, Md.: Williams & Wilkins, 1967.

Nemiah, J. C. Conversion: Fact or chimera. *International Journal of Psychiatry in Medicine*, 1974, *5*, 443–448.

Prince, M. *The dissociation of a personality*. New York: Longmans, Green, 1906.

Prince, M. A critique of psychoanalysis. *Archives of Neurology and Psychiatry*, 1921, *6*, 610–633.

Prince, M. *The unconscious*. New York: Macmillan, 1924.

Prince, M., & Peterson, F. Experiments in psycho-galvanic reactions from co-conscious (subconscious) ideas in a case of multiple personality. *Journal of Abnormal Psychology*, 1908, *3*, 114–131.

Prince, W. F. *The case of Patience Worth*. Boston: Boston Society for Psychical Research, 1927.

Rapaport, O. *Emotions and memory*, Baltimore, Md.: Williams & Wilkins, 1942.

Schreiber, F. R. *Sybil*. New York: Warner Books, 1974.

Sears, R. Functional abnormalities of memory with special reference to amnesia. *Psychological Bulletins*, 1936, *4*, 229–274.

Sidis, B., & Goodhart, S. P. *Multiple personality: An experimental investigation into the nature of human individuality*. New York: D. Appleton & Co., 1905.

Stevenson, R. L. *Across the plains*. London: Chatto & Windus, 1910.

Thigpen, C. H., & Cleckley, H. M. *The three faces of eve*. New York: McGraw-Hill, 1957.

11 The State Conducive to Momentary Forgetting

Lester Luborsky
University of Pennsylvania School of Medicine

Harold Sackeim
Columbia University

Paul Christoph
Yale University

As members of the post-Freudian generation, we have in common, at the least, the concept of motivated forgetting. At times we all stop to wonder about our state of mind and our motives when we experience disruptions in cognition. For slips and trips of the tongue and many memory dysfunctions, we might sometimes attribute the disruptions to factors such as inattention, distraction, or attentional overload, which do not necessarily imply motivational determinants. With one kind of forgetting, momentary forgetting, the thought that is forgotten was just in awareness before vanishing. After the disappearance it may obligingly reappear or it may resist recovery. The whole sequence of forgetting, followed by a remembering or a giving up of the effort to remember, may take just a few seconds, perhaps tempting us to dismiss our reflection about its motivation by attributing it to inattention, distraction, or attentional overload. However, this type of explanation may not quiet our doubts, since the momentary forgetting calls attention to itself by abruptly damming up our flow of speech in midstream, often without any external distraction to explain the blockage.

Our general aim has been to understand such fluctuations in memory functioning. Momentary forgetting, as compared with other memory dysfunctions, is an attractive choice for several reasons. Its form is stereotyped—the thought that was just in awareness is forgotten and then recalled again, or not recalled. It occurs while speaking, so that the context of spoken words can be examined. Finally, the symptom-context method, a procedure that seems exquisitely suited to the examination of clinically derived concepts, can be applied to the investigation of the conditions associated with momentary forgetting. The milieu of psychotherapy provided the context in which the clinical concepts explaining memory dysfunction were originally generated. The symptom-context method is a type of controlled clinical observation applicable to the study of any recurrent event appearing in a recordable verbal and/or physiological context, in which behavior before and after critical events—as well as before and after other comparison events—can be examined. We review the main areas in which observations have previously been made about momentary forgetting, as well as adding new analyses of old data. Patients' instances of momentary forgetting during the course of psychotherapy comprise our data base. From the findings on these data we abstract the main factors involved in the state conducive to momentary forgetting.

THE DATA AND ITS PREPARATION

Samples

The preliminary work on momentary forgetting involved a pilot study based on one therapist's process notes (Luborsky, 1964, 1967). This study examined a near-verbatim record of 67 instances of momentary forgetting together with their contexts—that is, the patient's words before and after each instance. The collection was derived from 2,085 psychotherapy sessions with 19 patients.

The better controlled work on momentary forgetting that followed the initial pilot studies was based on transcripts of tape recordings of psychotherapy sessions and drew from the work of several therapists. Two of these better controlled studies were a report of a "new sample" of a few instances of momentary forgetting for each of 10 patients (Luborsky, 1973) and a report of 13 instances of momentary forgetting in a single patient (Luborsky & Mintz, 1974).

The present report includes findings from an extension of the data analysis for the "new sample" of 10 patients plus 5 additional patients. In this "enlarged new sample" of 15 patients, one to four instances of momentary forgetting were obtained in each case, making a total of 31 instances (see Table 11.1).[1] Of the 15 patients, 8 were treated by one of the authors (L.L.) and 7 by other therapists who volunteered tape recordings of their psychotherapy. The patients were mainly young adults (age range $20-39$, $M = 27$). Almost all were in the neurotic

---

[1] The analyses in the 1973 report were computed in terms of mean patient scores on dependent measures. However, in this paper we are interested in the phenomenon itself, and therefore the results have been analyzed so that each instance of momentary forgetting is an independent data point.

TABLE 11.1
An Enlarged New Sample of Momentary Forgettings

Subject	Age	Sessions Observed	Instances Observed	Recovered	Nonrecovered	HSRS[a]	Rate (Instances/ Session)
1	20	15	2	1	1	60	0.13
2	29	193	4	0	4	55	0.02
3	23	230	2	2	0	70	0.01
4	39	176	3	3	0	60	0.02
5	27	146	2	0	2	65	0.01
6	26	117	2	2	0	65	0.02
7	23	205	2	1	1	68	0.01
8	26	194	2	2	0	50	0.01
9	19	68	2	1	1	55	0.03
10	29	66	2	1	1	75	0.03
11	26	179	2	1	1	64	0.01
12	30	61	1	1	0	70	0.02
13	24	225	1	1	0	65	0.00
14	35	31	1	1	0	75	0.03
15	28	259	3	3	0	70	0.01

[a]HSRS = scores on Health–Sickness Rating Scale.

range, and they were almost all in intensive, long-term psychotherapy or psycho-analysis in private practice settings. Consistent with the patients' being mainly in the neurotic range, their health–sickness global ratings (Luborsky, 1962, 1975) ranged from 50 to 75 (M = 64).

Method

The first step in preparing the data was to match each forgetting point with a comparable point in another session of the same patient that did not contain momentary forgetting (a "control session"). For each of the control sessions, a "control point" was marked off that was as far along in time on the control tape as the matched instance of momentary forgetting was situated. The contexts for the momentary forgetting, as well as for the control point, were marked off into 50-word units. The onset of the momentary forgetting is taken as the beginning of the pause before the patient says, "I forgot what I was going to say." Eleven hundred words of the patient were counted—550 before and 550 after the momentary forgetting point—and similar units were selected before and after the control point. There are then eleven 50-word units before and after the real (momentary forgetting) and control (nonforgetting) points. The time interval for 550 words is approximately 6 minutes. The basis for choosing approximately 12 minutes of time to investigate the factors associated with momentary forgetting was arbitrary. Since we could not be sure where "the action" was, we felt it necessary to sample a rather large section of the immediate context of instances of momentary forgettings.

The transcriptions of the tape recordings of therapy sessions were done with great care. Two people independently listened to the 1,100-word segment. The final transcripts were accurate records of what the patients had said, exactly as they said it, with all the slips, pauses, mispronunciations, etc., included. Our procedures and results are clearer when verbatim examples are examined. We have, therefore, included as specimens three extensive examples from Mr. D (Sessions 12, 68, and 137) in the Appendix.

FINDINGS: OLD AND NEW

In this section we present empirical results for each of the 15 aspects of momentary forgetting that have been examined over the course of the study (pilot sample, new sample, and enlarged new sample).

Frequency of Occurrence

The majority of the patients in the pilot sample (Luborsky, 1964, 1967) experienced momentary forgetting during the course of psychotherapy. Of 19 patients studied, 15 produced one or more instances of momentary forgetting during the total of 2,085 sessions. The rate of momentary forgetting in the enlarged new sample was somewhat less than in the pilot work. In 2,165 sessions there were 31 instances of momentary forgetting.

Momentary forgetting happens to the majority of people during therapy, although it is an infrequent phenomenon even for those who do show it. We have no clues to help account for the differences in the two samples in the incidence of momentary forgetting; they may be due to differences in therapist and/or patient variables. Likewise, we do not know what factors distinguish the minority who do not produce momentary forgetting from the majority who do provide instances. Within our sample. rate of forgetting was not related to health-sickness (Table 11.1). However, since momentary forgetting is an infrequent behavior even for those patients who do produce it, it may be the case that if a longer observation period were taken, those patients who do not seem to show momentary forgetting would be found to produce instances of it.

"Goodness of Fit" of Forgetting Instances to an Ideal Form

The price of using a naturalistic or observational method to sample behavior is that of having to cull through possible instances of the behavior to select those that fit the definition of the phenomenon to be studied. Even after the instances are selected, there may be some variation in the quality of each of the instances— that is, in the "goodness of fit" between the instances and the criteria for selection. Fortunately, momentary forgetting tends to occur in stereotypic form: The patient typically pauses at the moment of forgetting and explains, "I just had a thought which I was about to tell." For such an instance to be included in the sample, two criteria had to be met. First, there must have been evidence that the thought was in awareness before it was forgotten. The more fully the thought was in awareness before the forgetting, the better the judged fit between the instance and our working conceptualization of momentary forgetting. The second criterion concerns the suddenness of the loss of the thought. The more sudden the loss, the more likely the patient had been fully and faithfully speaking his thoughts before the forgetting and the better the fit between the instance and the conceptualization.

For the new sample, instances of momentary forgetting were selected by one of the authors (L.L.) and three other judges. Each judge independently rated how well the proposed instances met each of the two criteria and how well each instance overall fit the working conceptualization of momentary forgetting, on 5-point scales. Similarly, the judges rated other variables that might be related to the "goodness of fit": the degree to which the forgotten thoughts were subsequently recovered, the amount of cognitive disruption associated with the forgetting, the amount of external distraction present during the forgetting episode, and the degree to which the therapist promoted recall. For "goodness of fit," the judges showed high levels of agreement; the range of correlations among the judges for ratings of overall goodness of fit, for example, was .63 to .87. As expected, ratings of the two components of the definition of goodness of fit (clarity of thought prior to its forgetting and suddenness of the forgetting) correlated highly with ratings of overall goodness of fit (.59 and .78, respectively, $p < .001$). Recovery of the thought was not included as a criterion in the definition of goodness of fit; nevertheless, the ratings of degree of recovery turned out to be substantially correlated with goodness of fit (.64, $p < .001$).

Location of Momentary Forgetting Episodes

For the enlarged new sample, the distribution of momentary forgetting episodes was calculated for 10 units of 5 minutes each (during the 50-minute therapy sessions). Forgettings were found to be most likely to occur in the first and last 15 minutes of the therapeutic hour.

Because the patients varied in the length of their treatment, the number of sessions they attended was divided into units of 10%. The greatest number of momentary forgetting episodes occurred at the beginning of treatment, with a decrease in frequency as treatment proceeded. There was also a tendency for momentary forgetting to increase again in the latter part of treatment.

The distributions of instances of momentary forgetting within sessions and across treatments appear to be parallel. Momentary forgetting was especially likely at the beginning of sessions and at the beginning of treatment. The increase in forgettings toward the end of sessions resembles the increase toward the end of treatments. These distributions of momentary forgettings suggest that the occurrence of the memory dysfunction is intimately related to the patient's sense of security about the relationship with the therapist. It is natural that when the patient is beginning and ending contact with the therapist, there are higher levels of insecurity about the relationship. We might put this in the form of a proposition: Whatever interferes with the patient's sense of security about the relationship with the therapist increases the frequency of momentary forgetting. We have not yet examined the relationship between the temporal distribution of momentary forgetting and interruptions in treatment due to vacations, illness, etc. If the hypothesis is correct that the frequency of occurrence of momentary forgetting is associated with heightened insecurity about the relationship with the therapist, then it would be expected that rates of momentary forgetting increase before and after interruptions in treatment.

It is of considerable interest that other types of recurrent symptoms expressed during psychotherapy have been found to have similar temporal distributions. For example, reports of stomach pain by a patient with a stomach ulcer followed a similar frequency distribution across treatment (Luborsky, 1953; Luborsky & Auerbach, 1969). The same type of across-treatment distribution was found with a patient who presented a rapid buildup of cluster headaches (Luborsky & Auerbach, 1969), and a similar within-session distribution was found for frequency of petit mal epilepsy attacks in a psychotherapy patient (Luborsky, Docherty, Todd, Knapp, Mirsky, & Gottschalk, 1975). Indeed, this type of patterning may characterize a variety of individual patients' behaviors that may not be clearly symptom related, such as Blacker's (1975) report of one patient's recurrent memory for a crucial game of Chinese checkers. In a study of the dream reports of three patients, Zabarenko (1972) found that after an initial peak, such reports decreased during the first one-third to one-half of treatment and then increased again toward the end.

Frequency of Recovery of the Forgotten Thought

Two judges rated the degree to which patients recovered forgotten thoughts after instances of momentary forgetting. Typically, their judgments were directly based on what the patients said about their thoughts. For example, patients usually remarked when there were recoveries and made comments about the extent to which the recoveries were complete and exact. The reliability of the pooled ratings was .94. The forgotten thoughts were observed to be recovered in 68% of the cases (21 out of 31) in the enlarged new sample; this figure compares favorably with the 74% frequency of recovery obtained in the pilot sample.

Elapsed Time Until Recovery of the Forgotten Thought

In the pilot sample, the therapist routinely made an estimate of the elapsed time between the onset of momentary forgetting and the recovery of forgotten thoughts. The range of recovery intervals was estimated to vary from 5 to 70 seconds, with a mean estimated interval of about 20 seconds. For the enlarged new sample, the intervals between the onset of the forgetting and the recovery of the forgotten thoughts were timed from the tape recordings of the therapy sessions. The range of recovery intervals varied from 7 to 210 seconds, with a mean of 57 seconds and a median of 26.5 seconds. Thus, the vast majority of recoveries of momentarily forgotten thoughts occurred within 1 or 2 minutes after the forgetting. After this short period, recovery of forgotten thoughts was very unlikely.

Levels of Certainty and Abstraction of the Recovered Thought

Inspection of patients' transcripts in the pilot sample had revealed that there was a considerable range of certainty that the recovered thoughts matched the momentarily forgotten thoughts. Sometimes the identity between lost and recovered thoughts seemed vague and uncertain, and sometimes the patient claimed with absolute certainty that the exact forgotten thought had been re-covered. At times, the uncertainty about the recovered thought was so great that neither the patient nor the therapist could discern whether, in fact, a particular thought was actually the forgotten one. These uncertainties very much resemble the uncertainties expressed in recalling dreams.

Many of the recovered thoughts appeared to be high-level abstractions from the presumably more specific thoughts that had been forgotten. This abstract quality of some recovered thoughts suggested that they were often not exactly the thoughts that had been forgotten but were derivatives of them. The variations in certainty about the exactness of the recovery and in levels of abstraction of recovered thoughts might reflect the operation of a defensive process and/or the fact that the thoughts were difficult to apprehend due to attentional overload or similar reasons.

Cognitive Disturbance and Momentary Forgetting

Since momentary forgetting is one of many types of cognitive disturbance, we decided to examine whether the onset of momentary forgetting was associated with other types of disturbance. An a priori scale was constructed that measured the frequency of occurrence of three main types of dysfunctions: disturbances in the recall of memories, disturbances in the certainty of thoughts, and disturbances in the ability to express thoughts clearly. Since difficulties in recall are far less common than the other two types of disturbance, the scores on the scale are primarily composed of the second and third types of cognitive disturbance (Luborsky, 1966). The scoring manual lists 25 subtypes of such disturbances with examples of each. Each 50-word unit of the real and control segments was scored for degree of cognitive disturbance by two judges. The reliability of these judgments was high, ranging from 71% to 84% agreement, with an overall figure of 78%. (Almost all the disagreement occurred when one judge noted an item and the other judge missed it.)

Cognitive disturbance scores for real and control instances, taken from the eleven 50-word units before and eleven 50-word units after the momentary forgetting points, were compared in a repeated-measures analysis of variance. The main effect of groups (real vs. control) was not significant ($F < 1$), and no relevant interactions were significant.

Since the effects on levels of cognitive disturbance might be more proximal to the forgetting, the three units before and after real and control instances of forgetting were explored more intensively (Fig. 11.1). An analysis of variance, real vs. control $\times$ before vs. after $\times$ units with repeated measures on the last factor, revealed no significant main effects. Importantly, however, the interaction between groups and before vs. after forgetting approached significance ($F(1,60) = 3.14, p < .08$); and the interaction between groups and units was clearly significant ($F(2,120) = 3.88, p < .025$).

Our main expectation, however, based on our previous work, was that the immediate onset conditions were crucial and that cognitive disturbance would increase just before forgetting. Inspection of Fig. 11.1 suggests that the interaction between groups and the factor of before vs. after forgetting were primarily due to differences between the groups *before* instances of momentary

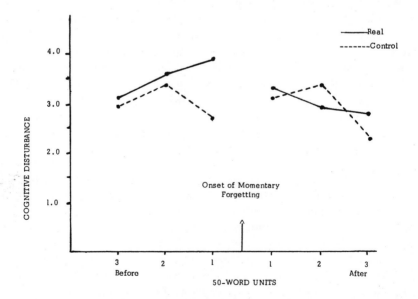

FIG. 11.1   Interactions between levels of cognitive disturbance before and after real and control instances of momentary forgetting.

forgetting. This impression was supported by the results of a repeated-measures analysis of variance for the scores of real and control groups for the three units before forgetting. The effects of groups approached significance ($F(1,60) = 3.80$, $p < .06$); and the interaction between groups and units was clearly significant ($F(2,120) = 3.38$, $p < .05$).

The cognitive disturbance scale is composed of three main types of disturbance: in the recall of memories, in the certainty of thoughts, and in the clear expression of thoughts. Only scores for certainty and clarity were examined in these analyses, and the two subscales of cognitive disturbance were found to be uncorrelated. Comparisons of real and control instances of momentary forgetting for scores on the two subscales indicated that both types of disturbance tended to increase before real instances of forgetting.

Thus, momentary forgetting is temporally associated with other cognitive disturbances, particularly in the 150-word unit prior to the forgetting (about 1 or 2 minutes) and especially in the 50 words before momentary forgetting. Prior to forgetting, patients demonstrated greater uncertainty about their thoughts and greater disturbance in clearly expressing their thoughts. This indicates, of course, that the designation *momentary* for this type of forgetting is not entirely apt, since the process clearly begins more than momentarily before the forgetting.

It might be expected that those instances that were judged to best fit the concept of momentary forgetting should most clearly show the relationship between momentary forgetting and other types of cognitive disturbance. However, our working definition of "ideal" instances of momentary forgetting, necessarily arbitrary, posits that the clearer the person has the to-be-forgotten thought in mind, the better the instance is as an example of the phenomenon. Thus there is some tension between our definition and the empirical findings; we found that momentary forgetting is associated in general with a greater unclarity of *expression* of the thoughts prior to the forgetting as measured by the Cognitive Disturbance Scale (Luborsky, Sackeim, & Christoph, in preparation).

Real instances of momentary forgetting were divided into two groups—those above ($N = 15$) and those below ($N = 15$) the median of mean ratings of overall goodness of fit. A repeated-measures analysis of variance on cognitive disturbance scores for the three 50-word units before and after forgetting (good vs. poor fit × before vs. after forgetting × units) revealed that instances judged to have poor fit with the concept of momentary forgetting showed increased cognitive disturbance scores as forgetting approached, whereas instances judged to have good fit did not change in cognitive disturbance scores (Fig. 11.2).

Thus, differences in the rated quality (goodness of fit) of each instance of momentary forgetting among those accepted into the sample had a negative predictive power in relation to levels of cognitive disturbance prior to forgetting: The poorer-quality instances showed greater levels of cognitive disturbance before forgetting. Two points should be made in reference to this result. First,

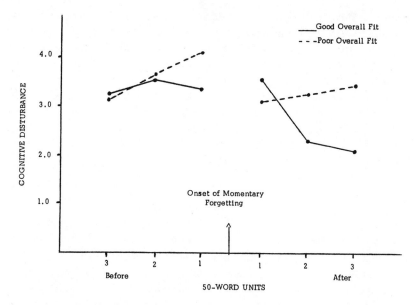

FIG. 11.2.   Interactions between good vs. poor fit and before vs. after momentary forgetting, on cognitive disturbance.

the ratings of goodness of fit were only distinctions among instances of the phenomenon, all of which were considered to be acceptable examples. Second, our working definition of an ideal instance of momentary forgetting was arbitrary. In fact, from these findings we might think of the lack of clarity of the thought as another impact of the high cognitive disturbance that our previous findings indicated was associated with the forgetting. In essence, the assumption that the clarity of the thought that is to be forgotten would be or should be a criterion of an ideal instance of momentary forgetting may be inappropriate.

Recovery of the Momentarily Forgotten Thought and Cognitive Disturbance

Ratings of the degree to which momentarily forgotten thoughts were recovered were bimodally distributed in the enlarged new sample, permitting instances of momentary forgetting to be divided into recovered and nonrecovered groups. The nonrecovery group ($N = 10$) was comprised of instances of forgetting that received mean ratings of 2 or below on a 5-point scale, and the recovery group ($N = 21$) was comprised of instances of forgetting that received mean ratings of 4 or above.

A repeated-measures analysis of variance (recovered vs. nonrecovered groups × before vs. after forgetting × units) on cognitive disturbance scores for the three units before and after forgetting showed a significant main effect for recovery groups (F (1,29) = 4.51, p < .05). As is seen in Fig. 11.3, the cognitive disturbance scores for the group that was judged not to have recovered momentarily forgotten thoughts were higher before and after forgetting. This suggests that greater cognitive disturbance is associated with the nonrecovery of momentarily forgotten thoughts.

This finding indicates that levels of cognitive disturbance are associated not only with the occurrence of momentary forgetting but also with the recovery or nonrecovery of momentarily forgotten thoughts. The implication is that where there is a high level of cognitive disturbance, there will be interference in the underlying process involved in retaining thoughts.

Momentary Forgetting and Speech Disturbance

Mahl (1956) presented as a measure of anxiety a scale that measures the frequency of disruptions in speech. The scale is composed of seven types of speech disruptions: sentence correction, incomplete sentences, word repetition, stuttering, intruding incoherent sounds, slips of the tongue, and omission of words or parts of words. Each 50-word unit of real and control segments was scored for the amount of speech disturbance by one judge (in view of the high reliability of the scale reported by Mahl).

Although none of the seven categories of the speech disturbance scale overlaps in content with the categories of the cognitive disturbance scale,

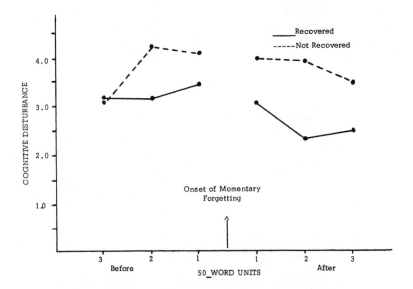

FIG. 11.3. Interactions between recovered vs. nonrecovered momentary forgetting and before vs. after forgetting, on cognitive disturbance.

moderate correlations were expected between the two scales because of similarities in concept. The correlation of mean scores on the speech disturbance and cognitive scales for the eleven 50-word units prior to forgetting for the total sample of real and control instances was $r = .17$ ($p > .05$, n.s.) in the enlarged new sample. The correlation for scores after forgetting was $r = .40$, $p < .01$.

In order to examine the relationships among cognitive disturbance, anxiety, and momentary forgetting, the analyses already reported on cognitive disturbance scores were repeated for speech disturbance scores. Repeated-measures analyses of variance showed no significant main effects or interactions for real vs. control instances of forgetting on speech disturbance scores (either 11 or 3 units before and after forgetting). When real instances of forgetting were grouped by ratings of goodness of fit or by ratings of recovery of forgotten thoughts, no significant main effects of group and no significant interactions with the factor of group were found. It appeared that momentary forgetting and speech disturbance scores were not related.

Thus, a speech disturbance scale that was reported to measure anxiety did not show any significant relation to momentary forgetting. If the scale actually measures anxiety, we could conclude that variations in levels of anxiety are not related to the occurrence of momentary forgetting.

External Distraction and Momentary Forgetting

Two judges read the transcripts and rated on a 5-point scale the extent to which any external distraction occurred during the real and control segments. The reliability of their pooled ratings was .77. External distraction was correlated with neither the overall "goodness of fit" rating of the forgetting (.25) nor with the degree of recovery of the forgotten thoughts (.17). The average rating of external distraction for all instances was quite low ($M = 1.8$). In only 7 of the 31 instances was there any evidence for the presence of external distraction, and these 7 instances received only moderate ratings.

There is little support, then, for the explanation of momentary forgetting as due to the disruptive effects of external distraction. Very few of the instances have evident external distraction before the momentary forgetting. The paucity of evidence for the role of external distraction in producing momentary forgetting reinforces our view that the determining processes are largely internal to the patient.

Relationship with the Therapist and Other Important Relationships

In our earlier pilot work, the number of references to important relationships was rated for the recovered thoughts in forgetting sessions and for comparison sentences in control sessions. It was found that references to important relationships were more prevalent in the recovered thoughts than in comparison sentences. The important relationships generally included father, mother, spouse, and boy or girl friend.

It was not until the data for the enlarged new sample was examined, however, that the significance of the relationship with the therapist became apparent. Since forgetting occurs in the presence of the therapist, the forgetting *may* indicate compunction about saying or thinking something in his or her presence. As the involvement in the relationship with the therapist changes, so also may the frequency of forgetting change. Therefore, we had two judges rate the variable "involvement with the therapist" for six 50-word units before momentary forgetting. The reliability of these ratings had been shown to be high in the Luborsky and Mintz (1974) study. In addition, a more objective measure of involvement with the therapist was examined: the number of explicit references to the therapist by the patients in real and control instances.

As is seen in Fig. 11.4, there is a steep increase in ratings of involvement around 150 words before real instances of forgetting. It was also found that it was unnecessary to have judges rate the degree of involvement with the therapist, as similar results were obtained when the number of explicit references to the therapist was counted. As is seen in Fig. 11.5, patients made more references to the therapist as forgetting approached.

In an intensive single-case analysis (Luborsky & Mintz, 1974) of Ms. RM, we showed this effect in a striking way. For example, the patient revealed in Session 36 that her forgotten thought was, "It struck me that you weren't really listening." This thought reflects a high degree of involvement in the relationship with the therapist around the idea that the therapist would reject her by inattention.

Momentary forgetting is temporally associated with increased involvement with the therapist (as measured by judges' ratings) and with increased explicit references to the therapist (as measured by counting references) before the forgetting occurs. These findings support the explanation offered earlier for the distribution of momentary forgettings within sessions and across treatments. Furthermore, they imply that it is not just the content of what is being talked about but also the heightened involvement in the relationship at the moment that may be instrumental in momentary forgetting. What has been noted, therefore, for some psychophysiological functions may also be true for this memory phenomenon. It is not only the psychological content per se that is an important determinant of a psychophysiological change (such as diastolic blood pressure; see Williams, Kimball, & Williard, 1972) but also the direction of attention and the amount of interpersonal interaction during an interview (Hardyck, Singer, & Harris, 1962; Singer, 1967, 1974).

Other Content Variables Distinguishing Real vs. Control Contexts

Judges rated real and control instances for the degree of presence of several content variables. The variables that were most discriminating in the pilot sample

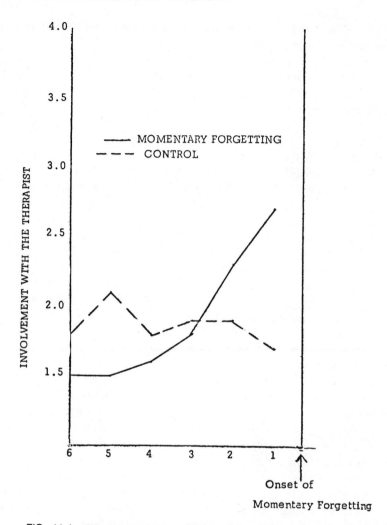

FIG. 11.4. Fifty-word units of patients' speech: involvement with therapist scores before momentary forgetting (means for 10 patients; 26 momentary forgetting instances and 26 controls, scored by an independent judge).

were, in decreasing order of importance (as indicated by the size of the associated *t* value): (a) new attitude or behavior, (b) difficulty with attention, (c) guilt, (d) lack of control and competence, and (e) Oedipal conflict. These findings were based on the two- or three-sentence contexts immediately adjacent to the momentary forgetting or matched control contexts. A similar analysis was performed for recovered thoughts vs. control thoughts. The discriminating variables were approximately the same with the addition of high level of abstraction, observation about oneself, references to an important relationship, and elated mood.

The discriminating variables in the new sample (Luborsky, 1973) were cognitive disturbance, involvement with the therapist, and explicit reference to the therapist. For the case of Ms. RM (Luborsky & Mintz, 1974), the differentiating variables for the unit preceding the forgetting were rejection, high involvement with the therapist, helplessness, explicit reference to the therapist, and inferred hostility toward the therapist.

Time Intervals of Related Qualities Before and After Onset

For those qualities that build up before momentary forgetting, the increase tended to be greater, the nearer it was to the onset. The interval for most related

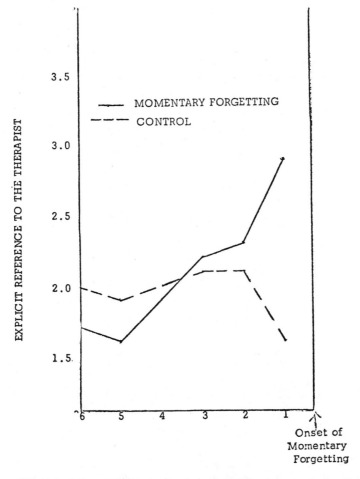

FIG. 11.5. Fifty-word units of patients' speech: explicit reference to the therapist before momentary forgetting (means for 10 patients; 26 momentary forgetting instances and 26 controls, scored by an independent judge).

variables (e.g., cognitive disturbance, involvement with the therapist, reference to the therapist) was 1 to 2 minutes before the momentary forgetting. Those qualities that build up before the momentary forgetting tend to decline within 1 to 2 minutes after the episode (Luborsky, 1973; Luborsky & Mintz, 1974). As mentioned earlier, the process underlying momentary forgetting is not really "momentary"—it requires a minute or two to build up and a comparable time to decline.

Consistency and Type of Recurrent Core Relationship Theme

In our earlier work (Luborsky, 1964, 1967), we attempted to identify the consistency and the type of the most frequent recurrent themes, both in the immediate context and in the forgotten thought for each of the patients. The most general formulation of the content emerging from the pilot sample was that it dealt with a potential anxiety about letting oneself and/or the therapist become aware of a thought. Each patient had a specific recurrent theme. The most frequent of these recurrent themes were: (a) showing lack of control, loss of self-mastery, weakness, and dependence; (b) showing control, mastery, strength, and independence; (c) showing one's anger to (and receiving anger from) a parent, parental figure, or other significant person; and (d) anxiety about showing sexual, affectionate, or loving inclinations.

The enlarged new sample also gave evidence of a special recurrent core relationship for each patient. (For those 3 patients among the 15 who had only one instance of momentary forgetting each, it is impossible, of course, to try to show consistency. It can be done with most confidence for those with three or more instances of forgetting.) The repeated theme was determined clinically by a single judge. It is important to emphasize that the theme is usually transparent in the sense that no high-level abstraction is necessary to discern it, and the theme formulation sticks very close to the manifest material. This can be confirmed by the reader by reviewing the examples from Mr. D given in the Appendix. For Mr. D, the most redundant theme was anger at the therapist and the expectation of anger in return from the therapist. For Mr. PB, it was the imminence of anger toward the therapist (usually based on anger about not getting attention, or concern, or affection from the therapist). For Ms. MF, another patient in our sample, the theme was anxiety and potential fright and guilt about revealing forbidden sexual and oral thoughts. For Ms. RM (Luborsky & Mintz, 1974), the theme was experiencing and expressing a thought concerning expectation of rejection. The themes for these patients were of a similar type to those found in the pilot sample.

Both in the pilot and new samples a consistent recurrent theme is prominent in the context of each series of instances for each patient. Each patient has a special theme, and these special themes are not the same from patient to patient. This conclusion is based on the clinical examination of one judge, except for the report by Luborsky and Mintz (1974) on Ms. RM's main theme, which was based on independent assessments of two judges.

Why should there be a patient-specific special supertheme? One way to get a perspective on this theme is to examine its function. An examination of the relationship repertoire of each patient reveals that the theme is part of the core conflict in relationships. This can be verified by applying the core conflictual relationship theme method, a new method for abstracting the main themes in relationships (Luborsky, 1977). This type of analysis has been done on a few patients by following the steps outlined for the core theme method: abstracting the relationship episodes in four sessions for each patient and then getting clinical judgments about the common denominator in these relationship episodes. That common denominator is the same as the core theme, which is the same as the core theme in the momentary forgettings. In conclusion, the supertheme found in the momentary forgetting instances is not just one among many important themes but is the quintessence of the conflictual relationship themes.

Qualities of Whole Sessions in which Momentary Forgetting Occurs

Some of the factors conducive to momentary forgetting may also be evident in the large context of the complete therapy session rather than just in the context immediate to the momentary forgetting that we have taken to be, in most of the studies, 6 minutes before and 6 minutes after the forgetting. The entire session context was first studied systematically in the Luborsky and Mintz (1974) study of a single patient by means of Dahl's factor scores of word categories (1972). These did not discriminate between symptom vs. control sessions. However, in studies of other symptoms, the entire session usually contained content similar to that of the immediate context (Luborsky & Auerbach, 1969).

For the nine patients of one therapist (L.L.), at the end of every session the therapist completed a form containing forty-five-point scales describing aspects of the whole session. The variables included those from the pilot study as well as from the study of ratings of tape-recorded sessions (Auerbach & Luborsky, 1968). The principal limit of this method is that of estimating the single judge's reliability. However, on many of these same variables, this judge has shown high reliability with other judges (e.g., Auerbach & Luborsky, 1968, etc.).[2] Since all the sessions were tape-recorded, our hope is that the results will yield leads to be

---

[2]In a study of the reliability of the session variable ratings (Freedman, Luborsky & Harvey, 1970), three raters judged a set of 38 sessions of one patient on most of the same variables. Some of these could be judged with considerable agreement: for example, the reliability of pooled ratings for a mean of three raters for depression−elation was .91. However, a few were poor; for example, separation concern was only .51, and receptiveness was only .23.

tested further by independent judges who will use the same tapes and transcripts on which to base their judgments. One other limit may influence the results: All the momentary forgetting sessions were included on the basis of a notation by the therapist of the presence of momentary forgetting. The quality of each instance of momentary forgetting was not rechecked by relistening to the tape recording.

Each "real" momentary forgetting was paired with two to four "control" nonmomentary forgetting sessions. For each variable, the significance of differences between mean ratings for the "real" vs. the "control" sessions was tested. This was done both for the group of nine patients as a whole as well as for each individual patient. The across-patient analyses yielded findings similar to those of the pilot study (Luborsky, 1964, 1967). Those variables that significantly discriminated the "real" from the "control" sessions were: attention difficulties (p < .001), elation (p < .005), and new attitude or behavior (p < .05).

The analyses were also repeated for each patient separately. New attitude was significantly discriminating for three patients. Several other variables discriminated for no more than two patients each: elation, separation anxiety, receptiveness, shame (less shame with the reals for two patients), helplessness, therapist's warmth, and therapist responds effectively. Several other variables were discriminating for only one patient. The variables that discriminated within each patient usually make instant clinical sense for that patient. As reported before (Luborsky, 1967, 1970; Luborsky & Auerbach, 1969), the main themes of the momentary forgetting are recurrent for a particular patient and coincide with an important repressed memory system for that patient. For one patient, the discriminating variables were guilt and shame. The points in the treatment at which he had been most upset were those in which he experienced guilt and shame, directly or indirectly, in relation to his father. Recurrently from the beginning to the end of the treatment, this was the theme that had to be worked out. It was both the most difficult for him to accomplish and the most necessary to change. For another patient, separation anxiety and helplessness were tremendously prominent. Separation anxiety, which precipitated her into feelings of helplessness, might be thought of as her presenting problem and as part of her core conflict. For still another patient, fears about homosexuality were part of the presenting problem and remained central throughout the treatment. Similar statements can be made about some of the other patients.

The whole-sessions analyses turned up two main leads to understanding the larger context in which momentary forgetting occurs. It was found that greater feelings of elation and the expression of new attitudes or behavior characterized sessions in which momentary forgetting occurred. The presence of elation further supports the concept that a changed state of consciousness is associated with the occurrence of momentary forgetting. (The presence of increased cognitive disturbance also provides evidence for a changed state of consciousness.) Possibly the emission of new attitudes or behavior are increased by the elated state; that is, the elated state may make it more possible for the patient to venture new attitudes or behavior. In any case, the concept "new attitude or behavior" suggests that the person is able to express a content that has been previously withheld. Furthermore, one might expect compensatory defensive processes, including momentary forgetting, to occur in sessions showing greater elation and new attitude or behavior because of the greater venturing of new thoughts and a consequent concern about going too far. The concept of the emergence of previously withheld contents is central to the thinking of the psychoanalytic research group of the Mount Zion Hospital, San Francisco (Sampson, Weiss, Mlodnosky, & Hause, 1972; Horowitz, Sampson, Siegelman, Wolfson, & Weiss, 1975, as reviewed by Luborsky & Spence, 1978).

Further work must be done using these two concepts in the studies of the immediate context of momentary forgetting. They were found to be present in the pilot sample but not studied thereafter. The concept of new attitude or behavior is a difficult one to apply, since it requires a judge who is familiar with the entire treatment so that he or she can decide whether a particular attitude or behavior is new or not.

WHAT EXPLAINS MOMENTARY FORGETTING?

After all of this naturalistic observation based on old and new research, how near have we come to discerning the significant factors related to the momentary forgetting of thoughts? The varied observations we have made can be interpreted as revealing three main classes of factors.

Three Factors in Momentary Forgetting

Factor 1. A cognitively disturbed state: Just before the momentary forgetting, there is an increase in cognitive disturbance. The types of cognitive disturbance that increase before forgetting refer to uncertainty in ideation and unclarity of expression. Individuals become more unclear in communicating their thoughts and make more qualifications on the content of their thinking before instances of momentary forgetting. Importantly, greater disturbances of this type are associated with reduced recovery of forgotten thoughts. It appears that the type of disturbance that occurs before momentary forgetting is somewhat specific; the level of anxiety, as measured by speech disturbance scores (Mahl, 1956), does not predict either forgetting or recovery of forgotten thoughts.

Factor 2. A heightened insecure involvement with the therapist: Just before momentary forgetting, patients show *a heightened insecure involvement with the therapist* as evidenced by ratings and by the fact that they make more explicit references to the therapist before instances of forgetting. The heightened involvement with the therapist generally reflects feelings of insecurity about the relationship and possibly feelings of helplessness. For example, for the momentary forgetting in Session 36, Ms. RM explains that she had had the thought, "It struck me you weren't really listening."

Some data related to the temporal patterning of instances of momentary forgetting both within sessions and over the treatment provide further evidence for the significance of this factor. One might expect greater intensity of feelings of insecurity about the relationship with the therapist when the relationship is reinitiated and temporarily broken off, that is, at the beginnings and ends of sessions. It is at these points that the incidence of momentary forgetting is greatest. Over the course of the treatment, one might expect greater intensity of feelings of insecurity in the beginning phase. In fact, it is in the earlier stages of treatment that frequency of momentary forgetting is highest.

Factor 3. An activated, individually specific core relationship theme: Around the moment of the forgetting, *a specific core relationship theme or conflict is activated* in the context of the relationship with the therapist. This theme differs among patients. For example, for Ms. RM, the expectation of rejection was associated with instances of momentary forgetting (Luborsky & Mintz, 1974); for Mr. D, the theme was anger at the therapist or expectation of anger in return from the therapist. Content analysis indicates that although the themes differ among patients, they are relatively consistent within patients.

In presenting these three factors, we are not claiming that they provide an exhaustive list of the conditions necessary and sufficient for the onset of momentary forgetting. It is quite conceivable, for instance, that all three factors may be present at a point in therapy, after which a symptom other than momentary forgetting may occur or even no symptom at all. Examination of the conditions preceding other symptoms as well suggest that this is the case (Luborsky & Auerbach, 1969; Luborsky et al., 1975; Luborsky, Sackeim, & Christoph, in preparation). The list of factors explaining the occurrence of momentary forgetting was essentially derived from the sets of measures that discriminated between instances of momentary forgetting and control periods. The decisions to examine particular variables were determined by previous findings concerning onset of symptoms and clinical intuitions about the nature of momentary forgetting. It is quite possible that examining other variables that have not yet been tested would reveal additional factors. Furthermore, our method of investigation precludes any claims about the independence of the factors that have been established. The factors may operate together; e.g., a cognitively disturbed state (Factor 1) may result from a patient's heightened insecure involvement with a therapist (Factor 2), and may not independently contribute to momentary forgetting. In order to discern the independence of the factors as well as the question of whether momentary forgetting is motivated, the use of alternative methodologies may be valuable. We discuss some of these issues now.

Why Is the Particular Thought Selected to Be Forgotten?

The particular thought that is forgotten is a derivative of a specific core relationship theme, as Factor 3 indicates. The themes or conflicts that patients present during episodes of momentary forgetting differ among patients but are consistent within patients. Luborsky (1977) has shown that over the course of treatment, patients show remarkable consistency in the themes or conflicts that emerge when they discuss interactions with other people. Comparisons for a few patients of the themes related to instances of momentary forgetting with this core conflictual relationship theme for interactions with people yield striking congruence. Further research should be directed toward examining this issue. For the moment, it appears that patients generally demonstrate momentary forgetting of thoughts that are central to the core conflicts they have in their interpersonal relationships.

A related issue concerns whether the forgotten thought is a deviant version of the core theme or whether there is continuity in thought before and during the forgetting. Inspection of the contexts of forgetting suggests that there is continuity in the stream of associations between what is said before the forgetting and what is recovered. There is no marked break or shift in topic. The lost thought appears to be a specification of the immediately prior-to-forgetting thought. It may be selected for forgetting because it is experienced as a little more dangerous to think or express in the relationship than the prior thought.

Selection of the Symptom: Why Momentary Forgetting?

The conditions that precede the onset of momentary forgetting and other symptoms appear to be similar. Evidence for this view is derived from applying the symptom context method in case studies of single patients: momentary forgetting (Luborsky & Mintz, 1974), petit mal attacks (Luborsky et al., 1975), stomach pains (Luborsky & Auerbach, 1969), headaches (Luborsky & Auerbach, 1969), and depressive mood shifts (Luborsky, Singer, & Hartke, in preparation). For these five patients, the three factors appear to predict the onset of symptoms. In addition, unlike the across-group results of the enlarged new sample of instances of momentary forgetting, the variable that most uniformly predicted symptom onset for the five intraindividual case studies was the intensity of the patients' feelings of helplessness. Helplessness is the central factor in Freud's theory of symptom formation (Freud, 1926/1959). In sum, although not supported by the new sample findings, previous case study research suggests that helplessness is predictive of the appearance of both psychological and somatic symptoms during the course of psychotherapy.

Given the premise that there is some uniformity in the factors that relate to the onset of diverse symptoms, what additional factors might determine the selection of symptoms? We can only share speculations about this issue. Individuals differ in their "preferred" symptoms. With somatic symptoms such as petit mal attacks, genetic and constitutional factors may underlie the individual differences. Situational variables may also play a role in symptom choice. Moreover, it is doubtful that patients frequently forget their own names or even the names of their therapists; thoughts or concepts that are well rehearsed or overlearned are naturally more difficult to forget (Neisser, 1967). On the other hand, the thoughts that are momentarily forgotten during the course of therapy appear to be derivatives or examples of the patient's core interpersonal conflicts that are being reenacted at the moment with the therapist. The forgotten thoughts are, therefore, not only threatening but also more "flimsy" or fresher than thoughts that are well rehearsed or overlearned. This may contribute to the susceptibility of these thoughts to momentary forgetting.

Why Is the Lost Thought Recovered?

Another issue that remains unresolved concerns the recovery of momentarily forgotten thoughts. Since one of our assumptions is that the forgotten thoughts are potentially threatening, one may wonder why these thoughts do not stay lost.

In addressing this issue, it should be kept in mind that not all lost thoughts are recovered. Nonrecovery is especially likely, the higher the preforgetting level of cognitive disturbance. It may be possible that the interval between forgetting and recovery is a "cooling-off" period and that the conditions that generate the forgetting subside in intensity, thereby promoting recovery. Indeed, following the forgetting, patients may become less involved with the therapist. Furthermore, there appears to be no objective way to examine the degree of similarity between the forgotten thought and the recovered thought. Not only may the conditions that contribute to forgetting change, but the recovered thought may be more uncertain or less concrete than the original and, therefore, perhaps less threatening.

Alternative Methodologies: What Are the Roles of Laboratory vs. Naturalistic Studies of Momentary Forgetting?

The findings reported here are of value in coming to a better understanding of the factors that produce momentary forgetting. However, although our results are supportive, they do not demonstrate the claim that momentary forgetting is motivated. For instance, it could be that the activation in the relationship with the therapist (Factor 2) of a patient's specific "hot theme" (Factor 3), rather than motivating forgetting directly, instead establishes a distracted state or introduces attentional overload (Factor 1) and that this results in momentary forgetting. By this alternative view, the conditions prior to the forgetting increase the likelihood of forgetting but not with the purpose of avoiding the "hot theme."

In order to demonstrate that momentary forgetting is motivated, it is necessary to show that under the same conditions, individuals prefer the consequences of forgetting to those that would occur if forgetting did not take place and, furthermore, that the forgetting ensues in order to achieve those consequences (Irwin, 1971). Indeed, in order to firmly establish a motivational basis for momentary forgetting, it must be shown that when the contingencies between the gains, (positive consequences of forgetting) and forgetting behavior, and the contingencies between the negative consequences and nonforgetting behavior are reversed, the frequencies of both behaviors alter appropriately. The method of controlled naturalistic observation that we have employed has not settled some questions concerning the purposeful nature of forgetting. Possibly, an experimental investigation of momentary forgetting might have added further knowledge.

The huge literature on experimental studies on motivated forgetting has been reviewed elsewhere (Holmes, 1974; Kline, 1972; Madison, 1961; Sears, 1943a, 1943b). The general conclusion appears to be that the evidence in favor of the existence of motivated forgetting as derived from laboratory studies is equivocal at best, and that "there is no consistent research evidence to support the hypothesis derived from the theory of repression" (Holmes, 1974, p. 649). However, it can be argued that laboratory investigators who have attempted to demonstrate the existence of motivated forgetting have used methodologies that were inherently inadequate for that purpose. For example, Freud (1915/1957) claimed that contents of consciousness that are repressed are highly individual and that repression itself is mobile, varying with the motivational concerns of the individual. Indeed, the findings presented here indicate that thoughts that are forgotten during the course of therapy refer to the individual patient's specific core relationship theme. With a few exceptions (e.g., Sackeim & Gur, 1978), experimental studies of defensive phenomena have not attempted to relate manipulations of motivational circumstances to individual dynamics. The failure to establish suitable experimental analogues of clinical phenomena may have contributed to the failure to confirm predictions derived from theories based on such phenomena. Another difficulty that besets the experimental investigation of motivated forgetting was alluded to above. Typically, studies concerned with motivational control of behavior attempt to demonstrate behavior and outcome independence. In order to show that behavior is emitted in order to achieve a goal, the contingencies between behaviors and outcomes must be manipulated (cf. Irwin, 1971). The consequences of forgetting are presumably intra-psychic and may pertain to the warding off of threatening thoughts, the avoidance of anxiety, etc. It is difficult to see how the contingencies between forgetting, not forgetting, and this type of outcome might be manipulated experimentally.

In sum, although it requires a conceptual leap to use extant research findings to claim that momentary forgetting is motivated, our results certainly do not contradict, and seem to support, such a view. Failure to find differences in the conditions that precede instances of forgetting and control points might have suggested that momentary forgetting was epiphenomenal or random in nature. The finding that the contents of forgotten thoughts are related to individual specific conflicts, although subject to several interpretations, is supportive of motivational accounts of momentary forgetting. *These observations should be useful in constructing experimental designs that will bear more decisively on this issue.*

Disruptions in the flow of cognition, such as the "tip of the tongue phenomenon," have proven to be valuable preparations in coming to understand normal cognitive functioning (e.g., Brown & McNeill, 1966). Similarly, a greater understanding of the state conducive to momentary forgetting can also aid us in elucidating these processes. Based on clinical observation and theory, Freud claimed that the investigation of the psychopathology of everyday life provides a road into the "psychic apparatus." We have shown that one way to travel this road is to return to the clinical setting and everyday life recurrent behaviors, from which Freud generated such concepts as motivated forgetting, but be guided in testing them by controlled observational methods.

APPENDIX: THREE INSTANCES OF MOMENTARY FORGETTING FOR MR. D

The text that follows contains three excerpts from the momentary forgetting protocols of Mr. D, a patient in this study. Because of space limitations, only 200 patient words before and after the forgetting are included here.

Session 12

P: . . . boy in high school—was brighter than I and it always used to bother me that my mother compared us—and now when I actually feel in this group of students that I am—the brightest (hesitates) that I am number one, it bothers me (hesitates). Maude (?) is the name of a homosexual magazine (p. 7.5 sec). Just had a thought (wheezes) you know, I've got to preface things by "I've just had the thought"—I'm picking it up myself—that this is a way of leading into—something which is embarrassing for me. (hesitates) I don't know why it sort of displaces the thought but it does, or lessens its impact. But I wanted to be in bed with you. Crikes. (p. 4 sec).

T: That little remark has another meaning, too, and it means that rather than saying things as you think them, you're thinking about them first and then saying them.

P: Yes, that's what I was trying to say (p. 8.5 sec). I'm still not free associating well. (p. 3 sec). That gives me some element of control. (p. 3 sec). I was thinking—the other day that (hesitates) when I—the day that I—I walked out of here I felt so shitty that I hadn't performed or that—nothing had come out (hesitates) (slight wheeze?) God I—everything's coming out in anal terms: shitty, hadn't performed, nothing had come out. (p. 2.5 sec). And I felt (p. 2 sec) that you just—eh—just—hated me (p. 4 sec) (wheeze?) (bangs table)

I forgot what I was gonna to say. I just forgot what I was gonna say again (p. 4.5 sec). Oh (p. 2 sec) um (p. 2 sec) I began having—resentment towards you (p. 2 sec) (wheezes) having resentment feeling resentment (p. 3 sec) and I had the feeling although there a—I didn't have (p. 2 sec) I was very much aware at the time that there were—there was nothing you had done (p. 2.5 sec). But I had the feeling (p. 3 sec) again that if I let loose (p. 4 sec) whatever there is inside me here we go again (p. 2 sec) I could almost kill you with my words (p. 2 sec) that you couldn't stand the onslaught. (p. 6 sec) (wheeze). And I don't want to do that to you. (p. 2.5 sec). I'm not talking about anything in specific that I'm hiding, I'm not (p. 3 sec) but particularly this I—I'm in a way I think I'm afraid of the time that I know is going to come when I am gonna resent you. (p. 4 sec) It's much harder for me to dislike you (hesitates) than anybody—much harder (p. 2 sec) 'Cause you're such a darn decent guy. (p. 7 sec) In a way, that's gonna make the analysis more difficult because I know about you from the County. And I know that you're a decent guy; this isn't just fantasy (hesitates). And also in this situation already. You haven't kicked me out yet. (p. 6 sec) You know I. . . .

Session 68

P: . . . wish for immediate gratification I want that other car. I don't want to have to worry about starting this car in the winter-time again (hesitates). I have too many—other things—to be concerned about—which is a rationalization. I just want the other car (p. 3 sec). Like a child. (p. 2 sec) I actually can't afford it I suppose but (p. 27 sec). It has been bucking an awful lot though (p. 22.5 sec). I'm gonna be honest with you. I'm getting off solf—all these subjects that

T: Why?

P: Why?

T: Yeah. (hesitates) What are your thoughts about that? (p. 11 sec).

P: I'm through with it that's all. Well probably (slight laugh) it bothers me too much to talk about it or I just sorta feel—wrung—dry on the subject (p. 3 sec) as if I've been dried (p. 9 sec). You know, I must think of you—in some way in these terms too, what you're going to do to me (p. 8 sec). You know, are you gonna rape my mind (p. 14.5 sec). Maybe that's one of the reasons why I have trouble l-letting go completely on the couch. "Letting go" sounds to me just like crapping—I mean, like becoming incontinent—. And I think that's perhaps the way I conceive of it, that if I let go I'll shit all over this place (p. 5 sec). *I've just (snaps fingers) lost a thought.* (p. 4.5 sec) I just lost that thought (p. 14.5 sec). It had something to do with letting go, that if I lower my guard (p. 4 sec), you will penetrate me (p. 2 sec), rip me to pieces, tear me apart. (p. 13 sec). You're a nice guy, you wouldn't do that (p. 10 sec). Again I have a thought of—biting your genitals off—. It's a terrible thought.

T: Was that the thought you'd lost? No.

P: No (hesitates). The thought I'd lost (p. 4 sec) it had to do with with uh being on guard here (p. 4.5 sec). It's almost as if my mind becomes a sphincter and I've got to—tightly control that (hesitates) so that—you can't get in and all this shit can't come out. (p. 2 sec) It was that thought (p. 7.5 sec). You know, I just have the—the image of—letting myself go, and this whole room literally being—filled to the ceiling—and it's a big room—with with all kinds of horrible internal products, vomit and shit and piss. (p. 6.5 sec) That whatever's inside is filthy. (p. 16 sec) You know, I'm in a period now where I'm not resisting the analysis so much, just in the last two days, and I don't understand why but it's been different the last two days than it has been (hesitates) in the last couple of. . . .

Session 137

P: . . . around and Sue—was riding by on a bicycle (hesitates). And she stopped and ish she was so tense she was ready to hit the ceiling (hesitates). And she—I—and she sort of—took me aside and asked me whether this was serious with Nancy et cetera (p. 6.5 sec). If Nancy is a castrater the way most of the women whom I've taken out have turned out to be she's a hell of a lot more subtle about it (p. 5 sec).

T: Doesn't seem to me that you're responding to her being a castrater. You're responding to her being a manipulator (hesitates) and, and, uh, now wanting things from you and placing demands upon you and pretending she's not (p. 3 sec).

P: And this Friday we meet her father and stepmother. (p. 6.5 sec) (sighs) (p. 7 sec) It's like sleep over if you want to sleep over, I'm not placing any demands on you and that's a lot of crap. She wants to sleep with me.

T: (overlapping with above) Of course it's crap. (p. 4 sec) I'm struggling to put into words—my sense that some of that same interaction goes on between you and me. (p. 3 sec) And that I think—I th—I really think that some of the time maybe a lot of the time maybe a little perhaps none—but that some of the time—

P: (laughing) Boy, you've got yourself covered there.

T: Yeah. Well (P still laughing) I'll st— (T laughs) I'll crawl out on a limb. I think that some of the time—you have to be deliberately—naughty in here (p. 2.5 sec), uncooperative, silent, not free associating, abusive (p. 3.5 sec) i-i-i-in order to assure yourself that I don't need anything from you. (p. 2.5 sec) Tha− that thing that Dr. S. said to you last week uh that you couldn't make any sense of. I think—rang bells on other levels about—the therapist needing nothing from the patient and, uh, taking no pleasure other than (hesitates) whatever pleasure she said was, was kosher to take.

P: She said no pleasure was kosher.

T: No pleasure. Pleasure of seeing him get well? (hesitates) Not even that.

P: Just the money.

T: Just, oh that's right, just the money. The pleasure of taking the money.

P: Getting well was the last that she said you should look for.

T: (sniffs) Yea. (p. 2 sec) I—I do think she's speaking to you as a patient (p. 2 sec) that you are terrifically concerned—unconsciously—with what I get out of this. With the question of you being used. (hesitates) And it's so terribly hard for you not to feel used. (p. 4 sec) And that sometimes, well, d—I just now going back to home base—that sometimes you have to be deliberately a crummy patient (hesitates) in order to see what it is I need from you (p. 10.5 sec). But of course you can feel—then manipulated if I don't respond to that (p. 2 sec) can feel I'm just then treating you like a little boy and humoring you along. I—it's it's a vicious cycle—in which the essential reassurance is awfully hard to get (sniffs). (p. 5 sec)

P: It's such a paradox. I—I mean (hesitates) you're—if you do want me to get better (p. 3 sec) it's for me but I can only conceive of it in terms of for you.

T: That's right. (p. 6 sec)

P: And you're right. I'm just sort of rephrasing this to understand it myself— the other side of that is (hesitates). *Oh, shit, now I lost that thought.* (p. 6 sec) Oh (p. 2 sec) n− and, and what investment can you possibly have in my getting better. No, that isn't what I was g− (p. 7.5 sec). If you don't want me to get better I'm pissed off and if you do I'm pissed off. (p. 2 sec) If you don't you don't care and if you do you want something from me. (p. 15 sec) I just had a thought I'm gonna get sick this weekend—. Not really—I'm just not gonna take her out. (p. 9 sec) She sure spends my money easily. (p. 3 sec) It's funny 'cause I just had a thought as I came up here this morning (p. 4.5 sec). As I looked at your house, I kinda walked away from it (hesitates) and (p. 2.5 sec.) I was thinking to myself either, you know, I'm sure you don't the way I would do in my obsessive way well this patient's money is for this, this is for that and this is for that—what do you do with the money I give you? (p. 4.5 sec) What's it for? (p. 20.5 sec.) She does use me. That bitch. (p. 14.5 sec) And I'm damn good to her and it bothers me. I'm always a very solicitous date. (p. 2 sec) Are you too hot? Are. . . .

The Recurrent Theme

In Session 12 the patient had just said, "And I felt that you just, uh, just hated me." At that point, he forgot what he was going to say. What he was going to say was, "I began having resentment toward you." In Session 68 he had just said, "I'll shit all over this place" when he lost his thought. He did not recover it precisely but said, "It had something to do with letting go, that if I lower my guard you will penetrate me, rip me to pieces." The next instance occurs in Session 137. The patient is obsessing about getting better for himself or for the therapist when he forgets the thought, and what he recovers is, "If you don't want me to get better I'm pissed off, and if you do I'm pissed off." In all three instances, therefore, the content clearly deals with anger. The anger is either directed at the therapist or is an expectation of receiving anger from the therapist.

The theme for this patient is, therefore, very much like that found for Mr. PB. The fear of rejection could be seen as a related content; even for Ms. MF, the danger in revealing sexual or oral thoughts was that the therapist would hurt the patient when this was revealed.

ACKNOWLEDGMENTS

This study was supported in part by Grant MH 15442 and Research Scientist Award MH40710 from the United States Public Health Service.

The authors wish to thank Justin Simon and Philip G. Mechanick for supplying some of the data; Roberta Harvey, who did many of the original analyses; and Marjorie Cohen for help with sorting out the data and preparation of the manuscript.

REFERENCES

Auerbach, A. H., & Luborsky, L. Accuracy of judgments of psychotherapy and the nature of the "good hour." In J. Shlien, H. F. Hunt, J. P. Matarazzo, & C. Savage (Eds.), *Research in psychotherapy* (Vol. 3). Washington, D.C.: American Psychological Association, 1968.

Blacker, K. H. Tracing a memory. *Journal of the American Psychoanalytic Association*, 1975, *23*, 51−68.

Brown, R., & McNeill, D. The "tip of the tongue" phenomenon. *Journal of Verbal Learning and Verbal Behavior*, 1966, *5*, 325−337.

Dahl, H. A quantitative study of a psychoanalysis. In R. Holt & E. Peterfreund (Eds.), *Psychoanalysis and contemporary science* (Vol. 1). New York: Macmillan, 1972.

Freedman, A., Luborsky, L., & Harvey, R. B. Dream time (REM) and psychotherapy. *Archives of General, Psychiatry*, 1970, *22*, 33−39.

Freud, S. Repression. In J. Strachey (Ed.), *The standard edition of the complete psychological works of Sigmund Freud* (Vol. 14). London: Hogarth Press, 1957. (Originally published, 1915.)

Freud, S. *Inhibitions, symptoms, and anxiety.* In J. Strachey (Ed.) *The standard edition of the complete psychological works of Sigmund Freud* (Vol. 20). London: Hogarth Press, 1959.

Hardyck, G., Singer, M. T., & Harris, R. E. Transient changes in affect and blood pressure. *Archives of General Psychiatry*, 1962, *7*, 15−20.

Holmes, D. S. Investigations of repression: Differential recall of material experimentally or naturally associated with ego threat. *Psychological Bulletin*, 1974, *81*, 632−653.

Horowitz, L. M., Sampson, H., Siegelman, E. Y., Wolfson, A. W., & Weiss, J. On the identification of warded-off mental contents. *Journal of Abnormal Psychology*, 1975, *84*, 545−558.

Irwin, F. W. *Intentional behavior and motivation: A cognitive theory.* Philadelphia: Lippincott, 1971.

Kline, P. *Fact and fantasy in Freudian theory.* London: Methuen, 1972.

Luborsky, L. Repeated intra-individual measurements (P-Technique) in understanding symptom structure and psychotherapeutic change. In O. H. Mowrer (Ed.), *Psychotherapy: Theory and research.* New York: Ronald Press, 1953.

Luborsky, L. (with Benjamin Rubinstein, Gerald Aronson, Paul Bergman, Michalina Fabian, Robert Holt, Helmuth Kaiser, Gardner Murphy, and Donald Watterson). *The Health−Sickness Rating Scale and sample cases.* Topeka, Kansas: The Menninger Foundation, 1962. (a)

Luborsky, L. A psychoanalytic research on momentary forgetting during free association. *Bulletin of the Philadelphia Association for Psychoanalysis*, 1964, *14*, 119−137.

Luborsky, L. *A cognitive disturbance scale.* Unpublished manuscript, 1966.

Luborsky, L. Momentary forgetting during psychotherapy and psychoanalysis: A theory and research method. In R. R. Holt (Ed.), *Motives and thought: Psychoanalytic essays in honor of David Rapaport. Psychological Issues*, 1967, *5* (2−3), Monograph 18/19.

Luborsky, L. New directions in research on neurotic and psychosomatic symptoms. *American Scientist*, 1970, *58*, 661−668.

Luborsky, L. Forgetting and remembering (momentary forgetting) during psychotherapy: A new sample. In M. Mayman (Ed.), Psychoanalytic research: Three approaches to the experimental study of subliminal processes. *Psychological Issues, Monograph 30*, 1973, *8*(1).

Luborsky, L. Clinicians' judgments of mental health: Specimen case descriptions and forms for the Health-Sickness Rating Scale. *Bulletin of the Menninger Clinic*, 1975, *35*, 448−480.

Luborsky, L. Measuring a pervasive psychic structure in psychotherapy: The core conflictual relationship theme. In N. Freedman & S. Grand (Eds.), *Communicative structures and psychic structures*. New York: Plenum Press, 1977.

Luborsky, L., & Auerbach, A. H. The symptom-context method: Quantitative studies of symptom formation in psychotherapy. *Journal of the American Psychoanalytic Association*, 1969, *17*, 68−99.

Luborsky, L., Docherty, J., Todd, T., Knapp, P., Mirsky, A., & Gottschalk, L. A context analysis of psychological states prior to petit-mal seizures. *Journal of Nervous and Mental Disease*, 1975, *160*, 282−298.

Luborsky, L., & Mintz, J. What sets off momentary forgetting during a psychoanalysis? Methods of investigating symptom-onset conditions. In L. Goldberger & V. Rosen (Eds.), *Psychoanalysis and contemporary science* (Vol. 3). International Universities Press, 1974.

Luborsky, L., Sackeim, H., & Christoph, P. *A cognitive disturbance scale: Reliability and validity.* Manuscript in preparation, 1978.

Luborsky, L., Singer, B., & Hartke, J. Testing theories of depression: The symptom-context method applied to patients with precipitous shifts in depressive mood. Manuscript in preparation, 1978.

Luborsky, L., & Spence, D. Quantitative research on psychoanalytic therapy. In S. L. Garfield & A. E. Bergin (Eds.), *Handbook of psychotherapy and behavior change*. New York: Wiley, in press.

Madison, P. *Freud's concept of repression and defense*. Minneapolis: University of Minnesota Press, 1961.

Mahl, G. F. Disturbances and silences in patient's speech in psychotherapy. *Journal of Abnormal and Social Psychology*, 1956, *53*, 1−15.

Neisser, U. *Cognitive psychology*. Englewood Cliffs, N.J.: Prentice-Hall, 1967.

Sackeim, H., & Gur, R. Self-deception, self-confrontation and consciousness. In G. E. Schwartz & D. Shapiro (Eds.), *Consciousness and self-regulation: Advances in research*. (Vol. 2). New York: Plenum Press, 1978.

Sampson, H., Weiss, J., Mlodnosky, L., & Hause, E. Defense analysis and the emergence of warded-off mental contents: An empirical study. *Archives of General Psychiatry*, 1972, *26*, 524−532.

Sears, R. R. Experimental analyses of psychoanalytic phenomena. In J. McV. Hunt (Ed.), *Personality and behavior disorders*. New York: Ronald Press, 1943. (a)

Sears, R. R. *Survey of objective studies of psychoanalytic concepts*. New York: Social Science Research Council, 1943. (b)

Singer, M. T. Enduring personality styles and responses to stress. *Transactions of the Association of Life Insurance Medical Directors of America*, 1967, *51*, 150−166.

Singer, M. T. Engagement-involvement: A central phenomenon in psychophysiological research. *Psychosomatic Medicine*, 1974, *36*, 1−17.

Williams, R. B., Jr., Kimball, C. P., & Williard, H. N. The influence of interpersonal interaction on diastolic blood pressure. *Psychosomatic Medicine*, 1972, *34*, 194−198.

Zabarenko, L. *The context of reported dreams during psychoanalysis*. Paper presented at Psychoanalytic Institute, Pittsburgh, Pa., 1972.

12

Let's Not Sweep Repression Under the Rug: Toward a Cognitive Psychology of Repression

Matthew Hugh Erdelyi
Benjamin Goldberg
Brooklyn College of the City University of New York

> *Every man has reminiscences which he would not tell to everyone but only to his friends. He has other matters in his mind which he would not reveal even to his friends, but only to himself, and that in secret. But there are other things which a man is afraid to tell even to himself, and every decent man has a number of such things stored away in his mind.*

Fyodor Dostoyevsky, Notes from Underground

The problem of repression—and we introduce it gingerly as "the problem," since no consensus has yet emerged about whether we are dealing with an everyday "fact," a "theory," or a discredited "hypothesis"—poses some unique difficulties. These difficulties are profound as well as far-ranging, involving intractable issues of methodology, theory, and even semantics. Beyond these types of problems, which perhaps are really not that unusual but simply the burden of any truly seminal concept in psychology, there exists an additional difficulty that probably is unique to repression among major psychological constructs.

DEFINING THE PROBLEM

Affect and Bias Toward Psychodynamic Formulations

We might as well confront the fact at the outset: Repression is an emotionally loaded term. As the "foundation-stone on which the whole structure of psychoanalysis rests" (Freud, 1914/1957, p. 16), repression is willy-nilly caught

355

up in psychology's problematical attitude toward psychoanalysis in general, which of late (particularly among contemporary personality and clinical psychologists) has once more entered a negative phase inclined toward indiscriminate and often vitriolic rejection.

The emotional stakes are high. For the committed, whether pro or con, the fate of the repression concept may represent nothing less than a lifetime's investment in a particular psychological Weltanschauung. It may not come altogether as a surprise, therefore, given such highly charged emotional considerations, to discover certain peculiar aberrations in the conceptual treatment of repression. These are hardly novel manifestations to psychodynamicists, for they include such cognitive "vicissitudes" as regressive logic, displacement of accent, concretism, euphemistic symbolic representation, syncretism (condensation), and especially, censorship by omission (cf. Freud, 1900/1953; 1915–16/1961).

Consider, for example, the fate of the repression concept in mainstream cognitive psychology. For a specialty that takes thought as its subject matter and information processing as its principal metaphor, one might suppose that the topic of tendentious *mis*thinking—or motivated information *mis*processing—would be of central concern. Nothing could be further from the facts. Despite a remarkably far-flung range of concerns, often on topics of a decidedly exotic nature, not a single article on repression has appeared in this decade in any of the major speciality journals of cognition and memory. The broader topic of defense mechanisms and indeed the whole field of psychodynamics (concerned with the interaction of motives and cognition) have similarly been relegated to silence. (An exception, a computer simulation of paranoid thinking by Faught, Colby, and Parkinson [1977], has appeared at this writing and is discussed later.) Recent textbooks on memory and cognition, many of them encyclopedic efforts spanning the whole history of psychology, as a rule fail even to index the term.

What is to be made of this blanket silence? It would certainly be a mistake to suppose that the problem of motivation itself was of no current interest. On the contrary, one of the most influential developments in modern psychology has been the mathematical elaboration, as in signal detection theory, of motivated decision processes in psychophysical tasks (Green & Swets, 1966; Swets, 1964; Swets, Tanner, & Birdsall, 1961). This application of mathematical decision theory has given rise to a full-fledged psychodynamic psychophysics concerned focally with the effects of motives ("costs" and "payoffs") upon response production and inhibition. From the methodological standpoint at least, decision theory techniques have become a virtual sine qua non in the analysis of performance in perceptual, learning, and memory experiments. Yet despite the much vaunted "cognitive revolution," this psychodynamic approach to response processes has not been extended into the domain of thought itself. Although the "availability–accessibility" distinction (Tulving & Pearlstone, 1966)—originally proposed by Freud (1912/1958; 1915b/1957) as the "unconscious–

preconscious'' distinction—has become a virtual truism in modern cognitive psychology, no attention has been directed at the motivated decision processes that might determine the accessing or nonaccessing of unconscious (but available) ideas into conscious thought.

How is this neglect to be explained? Is it really a reflection of bias against psychoanalytic notions in general and, through guilt by association, against psychodynamics in particular? Or is there perhaps some other simpler or more reasonable explanation? In the face of cognitive psychology's pervasive silence on the matter, we cannot know for sure; we would need more data to draw a defensible conclusion. At this point we have only the fact: The concept of repression in cognitive psychology is—to use the expression Freud so often borrowed from Charcot—treated as *non-arrivée*.

More palpable evidence of biased thinking on repression is to be found in the contemporary personality and clinical literatures that, if nothing else, have at least broached the repression issue overtly.

Bandura's position over the last decade is instructive (e.g., Bandura, 1969, 1971, 1977). In his influential book on behavior modification (Bandura, 1969), he devotes several pages (pp. 587–594) to the intertwined problems of unconscious processes and repression. There can be no doubt that Bandura thinks poorly of psychoanalytic constructs. Yet there is a paradox here. A careful reading of his explicit stance suggests that at bottom, he might well be espousing the very concepts he seems to be rejecting and that the disagreements are really more terminological than conceptual. Thus, for example, although the notion of unconscious contents is dismissed as "psychotherapists' speculations" of "questionable validity," he nevertheless embraces the unconscious concept under alternate labels such as "implicit," "inhibited," "automatic," or "covert." Elsewhere, he excoriates "traditional explanations [which] invoke a potent psychic entity in the form of an 'unconscious mind' which supposedly possesses sensitive discriminating capacities [p. 588]." Yet a major emphasis of his own work (Bandura, 1971, 1977) is the existence and operation of "cognitive controls" that modulate thought processes and ultimately behavior. In this emphasis on cognitive controls, it turns out, Bandura is actually subscribing to a well-established "ego-psychology" tradition within psychoanalysis, which has already elaborated—and coined—the "cognitive control" concept (e.g., Holzman & Klein, 1954; Klein, 1958; 1970; Klein & Schlesinger, 1949). Cognitive psychology itself has recently rediscovered such executive control processes (e.g., Atkinson & Shiffrin, 1968; Kahneman, 1973). Interestingly, both the contemporary cognitive tradition and the psychoanalytic one assumes that such cognitive control processes typically operate outside of awareness (cf. Erdelyi, 1974; Posner & Warren, 1972). As to the existence of unconscious "sensitive discrimination capacities," it must be emphasized that despite experimental psychology's failure to demonstrate such effects in the laboratory (e.g., Eriksen, 1962), the notion in modern cognitive psychology is taken not only to be true but truistic. As linguists easily demonstrate without the paraphernalia of the laboratory, we can make exceedingly complex syntactic discriminations without being able to articulate consciously the rules by which we make them (e.g., Slobin, 1971). The very same point was made by Helmholtz (1850/1925), a major influence on Freud, with respect to distance perception and constancy scaling; since the perceiver is not aware of the complex inference rules he uses, which he nevertheless uses exceedingly well, the process must necessarily be one of "unconscious inference."

Bandura's actual position on repression is similarly perplexing. He states (1969): "there is no doubt that thoughts and other implicit activities can be effectively inhibited. Thought inhibition is traditionally attributed to the mechanism of repression, which is believed to operate largely outside of conscious levels [p. 591]." He goes on to suggest that "In behavior theory the phenomenon ascribed to repression is conceptualized in terms of the process of avoidance conditioning. . . . Once certain thoughts come to function as conditioned aversive stimuli, their occurrence generates anxiety and their elimination allays it [p. 591]." Is Bandura rejecting or paraphrasing the repression concept here? Is "thought inhibition" meant to be synonymous with "repression," or is another meaning intended? Is "traditionally" used in the sense of "classic" or "outmoded"? Are *terms* or *concepts* at issue? Or is there perhaps a theoretical divergence? For example: "In social learning interpretations of repression incompatible responses rather than psychic agents are considered to be the inhibitory forces. . . . Social learning theory . . . makes no appeal to prohibitive psychic agents in accounting for inhibitory processes [p. 592]." But what is a "cognitive control" if not a psychic agent? What are "incompatible responses"? Are they any different from "antithetical ideas" (Freud, 1892–1893/1966)?

In the end we seem to have a position involving the "coexistence of opposites," a kind of "white black dog" phenomenon: behavioristic dogma against mentalistic notions in psychoanalysis coexisting with the mentalisms of the currently fashionable cognitive orientation. Logic would seem to require a consistent stance; one either accepts mentalisms (images, models, thought, consciousness, etc.), or one rejects them.

Bandura's position is at least in one respect unequivocally like Freud's. By whatever label it is to be designated, whether "repression" or "thought inhibition," it is asserted that "there is no doubt" about the existence of the phenomenon itself. A radically different point of view, perhaps best exemplified by the recent work of Holmes (1972, 1974), holds to the contrary, that "there is no evidence that repression does exist" (Holmes, 1974, p. 650). The conclusion follows from methodological flaws uncovered in laboratory attempts to demonstrate repression. Since, it is averred, no unassailable evidence exists for the repression phenomenon, it is only reasonable to espouse the null hypothesis, i.e., there is no repression. Such a position is straightforward and powerful. If true, it immediately explains, and in logical rather than psychological terms, the silence surrounding repression in the modern literature; after all, why should researchers invest their energies in a nonexistent phenomenon? There are, however, a variety of problems in experimental critiques of repression such as Holmes'. Let us briefly examine three of these.

First, there exists a sampling problem: Holmes' analysis is based on a biased sample of the evidence undergirding the repression concept. His review focuses on the laboratory tradition involving recall inhibition as a function of presumed "ego-threat" (cf. Rosenzweig, 1933, 1943, 1952; Zeigarnik, 1927; Zeller, 1950a, 1950b, 1951) about which there have been perennial doubts from the very beginning (see, for example, Freud's own critical note of 1934 to Rosensweig [in MacKinnon & Dukes, 1964]). Holmes quite thoroughly ignores a variety of other evidence that might bear negatively on the null hypothesis. For example, he bypasses the perceptual defense literature by suggesting that others, specifically Eriksen and Pierce (1968), have already exposed its methodological shortcomings. This, however, is a misleading construction of Eriksen's position (Eriksen, 1958, Eriksen & Pierce, 1968). Although Eriksen has argued against the *perceptual* nature of perceptual defense (Erdelyi, 1974), he has specifically assumed the existence of nonperceptual defensive cognitive processes—e.g., "cognitive avoidance," his synonym for repression (Eriksen & Pierce, 1968). More serious, however, is Holmes' complete neglect of the wealth of clinical evidence for repression, which is the empirical foundation of the repression concept to begin with (Breuer & Freud, 1895/1955). It is not impossible, of course, that the clinical evidence itself might be flawed, but such shortcomings must be demonstrated, not assumed. It certainly would be misleading to imply that repression was a piece of philosophic or artistic speculation; Freud was quite adamant on this score (e.g., Freud, 1914/1957), emphasizing that repression was not an assumption but a "theoretical inference legitimately drawn from innumerable observations [p. 17]."

Another flaw in Holmes' analysis arises from a logical misconception, the faulty notion that the existence of repression must be judged by the success of experimental psychologists in producing the phenomenon in the laboratory. But since when, and by what philosophy of science, is a phenomenon's existence predicated on the laboratory scientist's ability to create it? Astronomy has been, at least until very recently, a nonlaboratory science for millennia; the reality of its subject matter has not been denied as a result. If a misguided "experimental" astronomer had attempted to measure the gravitational pull between two golf balls in the laboratory, it would have been his method, not the phenomenon, that would have been rejected. It is, of course, convenient to be able to produce and study effects in the laboratory, and this is sometimes possible, but existence arguments can hardly be settled on the basis of laboratory failures in creating the phenomenon—whether we are concerned with the existence of Mt. Everest, the rings of Saturn, or, for that matter, the white rat. This is a logical point. We presently take up the more practical question of laboratory experimental psychology's actual contribution to the problem of repression.

A third and final point should be made about Holmes' analysis of repression. The methodological critique comprising the bulk of his paper turns out to be quite irrelevant. This is so, because none of the experiments surveyed by Holmes satisfies his own initial definition of repression—e.g., that the mechanism itself be unconscious. Consequently, the methodological exercise is superfluous; the analysis was predetermined, by definition, to yield a negative conclusion. It would have sufficed to spell out his four minimal criteria (pp. 632–633) and to point out—quite correctly—that no experiments exist (and we would add, *could* exist) that simultaneously satisfied his fourfold conceptualization.

Now this is an intriguing problem, immediately bringing two questions to the fore: the intrinsic limits of laboratory experimental psychology as we know it today (a topic only beginning to be confronted by experimental psychology— e.g., Bregman, 1977; Deese, 1972; Neisser, 1976; Norman, 1973) and the problem of correctly defining repression. We take up the definitional problem first.

Definition and Development of the Repression Concept

The meaning of repression has been a subject of great and continuing confusion, both within as well as outside of psychoanalysis (Brenner, 1957b; Eriksen & Pierce, 1968; Holmes, 1974; MacKinnon & Dukes, 1964; Madison, 1956, 1961; Wolitzky, Klein, & Dworkin, 1976). Indeed, it may turn out eventually that most controversies about the existence of repression constituted not controversies in the true sense of the word, i.e., *differences in opinion*, but rather *different opinions about different things*. Although Freud, who developed the concept of repression, has deservedly gained a reputation for impressionistic, even loose, articulation of technical terms, we believe that in the case of repression he was unusually clear, certainly so by the standards of clarity associated with any fundamental psychological construct such as attention, aggression, behavior modification, intelligence, and consciousness. The key to the confusion lies in a general failure to distinguish between the phenomenon itself and theories of the phenomenon, about which it is only natural to find differences.

What, then, constitutes the phenomenon of repression? It would be difficult to put the matter any more clearly than Freud (1915a/1957) himself did: "*the essence of repression lies simply in the function of rejecting and keeping something out of consciousness* [p. 105]." Note that this basic definition does not stipulate the method or methods of rejection from consciousness—whether by inhibition (e.g., "counter-cathexes"), attention withdrawal, or some other single or combined set of techniques; nor does the definition stipulate that the process must be conscious or unconscious. The definition does not even commit itself to the nature of the "something" that is rejected nor to the reason or purpose behind the rejection, though in virtually all of his writings, including the article in which this quote occurs, it is made clear that repression *as a defense* seeks to eliminate or prevent some form of psychological "pain [p. 105]," variously conceptualized as "trauma," "intolerable ideas," "unbearable affect," "anxiety," "guilt," or "shame" ("moral anxiety"), etc. However, the irreducible essence of the phenomenon is nothing more than what Freud has stated. Extensions of the concept—e.g., that it must be unconscious, that it applies only to sexual or aggressive impulses, that it must concern infantile traumas, that it requires constant expenditures of psychic energy, that it results in symptoms, that it constitutes an ego or superego mechanism—all these, and many other notions, are theoretical elaborations, not the "essence" of the phenomenon itself.

To place too much reliance on any single quote of Freud's may not be an altogether satisfactory way of proceeding, however; Freud's proclivity toward self-contradiction is only too well known. Ultimately the best way to gain a clear conception of the meaning of repression is through an examination of the origin and development of the concept. This "genetic" (i.e., historical or developmental) approach, after all, is precisely the psychoanalytic strategy for penetrating problematical meanings.

It is generally believed, probably because Freud himself suggested it, that repression was a fortuitous discovery resulting from the abandonment of hypnosis in favor of the free-association technique. This is not really so, however, for the repression concept was clearly central to Freud's earliest psychological writings, preceding both the free-association technique and the development of psychoanalysis. In his 1892–1893 report of "A Case of Successful Treatment by Hypnotism" (a technique that antedates not only psychoanalytic therapy but also the earlier cathartic method of Breuer), Freud sets forth a conflict theory of hysteria in which one element of the conflict is intentionally barred—"suppressed," "excluded," "dissociated"—from consciousness: "the distressing antithetic idea, which has the appearance of being inhibited, is removed from association with the intention and continues to exist as a disconnected idea, often unconsciously to the patient himself" (Freud, 1892–1893/1966, p. 122). In a posthumously published letter to Breuer, written in 1892, Freud states: "an hysterical patient intentionally seeks to forget an experience, or forcibly repudiates, inhibits, and suppresses an intention or idea" (Freud, 1940b/1966, p. 153). In his joint "Preliminary Communication" with Breuer (Breuer & Freud, 1893/1955) the term *repression—verdrängt* (repressed)—appears for the first time, casually intermixed with a number of synonyms: "it is a question which the patient wished to forget, and therefore intentionally repressed from his conscious thought and inhibited and suppressed [p. 10]."

In the *Studies on Hysteria* (Breuer & Freud, 1895/1955), repression comes to play a central theoretical role. It constitutes, as it did before under different labels, Freud's explanation of the psychogenesis of hysteria—"an idea must be *intentionally repressed from consciousness* [p. 116]." Also, repression serves to explain the ubiquitously found "resistance" encountered in "talking cures," seen with special clarity in "free associations," against openly and freely broaching painful memories. The "free" associations of the patient are thus never really free; they reflect not only a form of "outward dishonesty" in which he self-censors painful *responses* but also a form of "inward dishonesty," involving ultimately the *cognitive* counterpart of the response censorship, repression. Freud's work with free associations led him to emphasize that memory is organized not only *thematically* but *psychodynamically* as well (Breuer & Freud, 1895/1955):

> I have described such groupings of similar memories into collections arranged in linear sequences (like a file of documents, a packet, etc.) as constituting "themes." These themes exhibit a second kind of arrangement. Each of them is— I cannot express it in any other way—stratified concentrically round the pathogenic [traumatic] nucleus. . . . The contents of each particular stratum are characterized by an equal degree of resistance, and the degree of resistance increases in proportion as the strata are nearer to the nucleus. . . . The most peripheral strata contain the memories (or files) which, belonging to different themes, are easily remembered and have always been clearly conscious. The deeper we go the more difficult it becomes for the emerging memories to be recognized, till near the nucleus we come upon memories which the patient disavows even in reproducing them [pp. 288–289].

Freud seems to be outlining here a notion of gradients of inhibition or avoidance, to be elaborated more formally some half a century later (see succeeding) by Dollard and Miller (1950). The critical point, however, is that inhibition of response and inhibition of thought are manifestations of the same process. There is no discontinuity between response processes and cognitive processes. Free associations—freely thinking aloud—constitute therefore a "microscope" for cognition in that what they reveal about overt responses presumably reflects also the covert process of thought.

It should be quite clear, then, that Freud's earliest conception of the phenomenon of repression, initially formulated under a remarkable profusion of interchangeable rubrics—"repression," "inhibition," "exclusion," "dissociation," "removal," "censorship," "defense," "resistance," "forcible repudiation," "intentional forgetting"—unmistakably corresponds to his conception of two decades later. The intervening developments in psychotherapeutic technique and the accumulation of clinical data thus served merely to corroborate the original observation. The only real change was a finer-grained articulation of the manifold ways in which it was possible to achieve the "function of rejecting and keeping something out of consciousness." As early as 1894, for example, Freud observed that a painful ideational complex might be dealt with, not through a blanket, indiscriminate inhibition of the whole complex, but through the inhibition or repression of only its *emotional* component: "[the] defense against the incompatible idea was effected by separating it from its affect; the idea itself remained in consciousness" (Freud, 1894/1962, p. 58). This affective form of repression came later to be known in psychoanalysis as the defense mechanism of "isolation." With the accumulation of clinical experience, an increasing spectrum of special cognitive techniques for distorting consciousness of reality (and therefore in some sense "rejecting and keeping something out of consciousness") was delineated by Freud, sometimes formally and sometimes in passing. In just two published case histories, the "Rat Man" (1909/1955) and the Psychotic "Dr. Schreber" (1911/1958), Freud delves into more than a dozen such devices (though not always by actual name), including omissions and ellipses, symbolization, isolation, displacement, doubt, regression, reaction formation, undoing, rationalization, denial, and projection.

As the specific techniques or combination of techniques proliferated, Freud began to revert to the construct of "defense" (*Abwehr*) (Freud, 1894/1962; 1896/1962) as the generic rubric for all the diverse mechanisms for rejecting painful aspects of reality from consciousness (e.g., Freud, 1926/1959). Freud was never too consistent in this regard, however, and frequently continued using "repression," especially "repression in the broadest sense," as a synonym. This inconsistency may best be understood, perhaps, by appreciating the fact that all specific "defense" techniques involve "repression" (rejection from consciousness) in some sense, even though they may be discriminable from one another. Thus, for example, the mechanism of "projection" (Freud, 1909/1955) excludes some piece of psychological reality from consciousness by the transposition of 'subject and object of a proposition (e.g., "I love you" → "you love me"), whereas "reaction formation" transposes the predicate of the proposition into its opposite (e.g., "I love you → "I hate you"). Since both transformations, though different, exclude the original reality from consciousness (i.e., "I love you), they may be properly conceived of as "repression"—in the broadest sense. These specific mechanisms, however, are clearly distinct from one another and may also be distinguished from a narrower conception of "repression" as the direct inhibition of an idea's access to consciousness. It has become customary within psychoanalysis (e.g., Fenichel, 1945; A. Freud, 1936/1946) to adopt this narrower view of repression—the direct inhibition of a thought, impulse, memory, etc.—and to treat it as only one of a myriad of cognitive devices for tampering with reality for the purpose of avoiding pain.

Whether this latter, "narrow" sense of repression ultimately conveys a distinct meaning is problematical, however, despite its superficial plausibility and widespread adoption (Madison, 1961). What, after all, could we mean when we say "direct" or "inhibit" or, indeed, "thought" or "memory"? What would be the effect on the notion of "direct memory inhibition" if we adopted Tulving's (1972) distinction between episodic vs. semantic memory (see, for example, Wolitzky, Klein, & Dworkin's [1976] conceptualization of repression as "failure of comprehension" rather than merely "memory failure"). What would "thought or memory inhibition" constitute if we emphasized the constructive, generative nature of all cognitive processes? Would not most or all specific defense mechanisms revert to being variants of this now peculiarly broad "narrow" conception of repression (based on a "broad" construction of thought or memory)?

Consider, for example, the fate of the superficially straightforward notion of "intentional forgetting" in the recent experimental literature (discussed later) that in less than a decade has spawned such varied conceptualizations as "selective rehearsal," "differential grouping," "selective search," "dumping," "erasure," "differential encoding," "differential depth of search," "blocking," "report withholding," "active inhibition," "output interference" (cf. Bjork, 1972; Epstein, 1972; Rakover, 1975; Roediger & Crowder, 1972; Weiner, 1968). Even at this point—and we shall no doubt witness further conceptual proliferation, perhaps even the rediscovery of some Freudian mechanisms—it would be perplexing in the extreme to propound a notion of intentional forgetting in the "narrow sense." It is no different, we believe, with "repression." The only clear meaning of repression is the general one—i.e., "the function of rejecting and keeping something out of consciousness"—with narrower formulations representing hypothesized variants, of the overall phenomenon. In our view, therefore, the expression "processes of defense" (Freud, 1926/1959) (usually known as the "mechanisms of defense," after Anna Freud [1936/1946]) is synonymous with repression, having perhaps the nomenclatural advantage of emphasizing the multifaceted nature of the overall phenomenon and also the distinction, remarkably unappreciated in the literature, between the *mechanisms* involved and the *purpose* that they serve, i.e., defense. This latter distinction, of little immediate relevance in clinical contexts, assumes a major significance for laboratory approaches, for, as we shall see, it is much easier to prove by standard experimental paradigms the existence of mechanisms than the existence of purposes.

A last issue remains to be broached before concluding this examination of the meaning of repression. We have seen that the clearest definition of repression is the general one, namely, the overall function of rejecting something from consciousness. We now raise the question of whether the function *itself* is something that is excluded from consciousness; i.e., is repression—are the defense mechanisms—unconscious? An almost universal consensus has emerged on this issue. Probably as a result of *Anna* Freud's (1936/1946) exceptionally influential monograph on the topic, it is believed that the mechanisms of defense, without exception, operate unconsciously. So widespread is this belief, that by now most theorists treat the notion not as a hypothesis but as an integral component of the definition of the phenomenon. The most significant exception to this rule, curiously, is *Sigmund* Freud.

The unconscious nature of repression was simply not a critical theme in Freud's treatment of the topic, certainly not before his relatively late "structural" theorizing (Freud, 1923/1961; 1933/1964). Although defenses were often treated as unconscious processes (as early as Freud, 1896/1962), there was no consistent suggestion that they had to be unconscious; indeed, repression was often portrayed as a conscious or sometimes conscious process (Breuer & Freud, 1895/1955; Freud, 1894/1962; 1915a/1957; 1915b/1957). In "Repression" Freud (1915a/1957) specifically speaks of the "censorship of consciousness [pp. 149–150]" and, in fact, feels obliged to warn the reader not to assume that repression is always a conscious undertaking ("it is a mistake to emphasize only the repulsion which operates from the direction of the conscious upon what is to be repressed [p. 148]"). Although it is appreciated by psychoanalytic scholars that in his very earliest writings (e.g., Freud 1894/1962) repression was treated as a potentially conscious mechanism, it is mistakenly assumed that by 1895 (Breuer & Freud, 1895/1955) Freud had shifted to the now orthodox view of repression as unconscious. There is even a regrettable tendency toward retrospective reinterpretations—secondary elaborations—of Freud's original intended meanings (the laws of psychodynamics are not suspended for psychodynamicists). Thus, for example, a lengthy editorial footnote appears (p. 10) in the English translation of Breuer and Freud's (1895/1955) *Studies on Hysteria* in which the reader is warned against falsely construing terms such as *deliberate* or *intentional* as implying *conscious*. Although the logic of the point is unassailable, it nevertheless remains the case that the contexts in which the terms occur make it very clear that at least at times, repression is a conscious, deliberate act. Thus, in the case of Miss Lucy R., where Freud states that for a hysterical symptom to develop, "an idea must be *intentionally repressed from consciousness* [p. 116]," he goes on to quote the following exchange: " 'But if you knew you loved your employer why didn't you tell me'?—'I didn't know—or rather I didn't want to know. I wanted to drive it out of my head and not think of it again; and I believe latterly I have succeeded' [p. 117]." In the case of Katherina, Freud speaks directly of "conscious rejection [p. 134]." Nor do we need to restrict ourselves to the *Studies on Hysteria* for such examples, for in numerous subsequent articles, including "Repression" (1915a/1957), Freud implies or directly indicates that repression may be conscious. In his discussion of Schreber (Freud, 1911/1958), for example, Freud states that repression "emanates from the highly developed systems of the ego—systems which are capable of being conscious [p. 67]." In a footnote added to *The Interpretation of Dreams* (1900/1953) in 1914 Freud remarks: "In any account of the theory of repression it would have to be laid down that a thought becomes repressed as a result of the continued influence upon it of two factors: It is pushed from the one side (by the censorship of *Cs.*) and from the other (by the *Ucs.*) [p. 547]."

But did not Freud specifically distinguish between unconscious and conscious forms of consciousness rejection by using "repression" for the former and "suppression" for the latter? The answer is no. Although many psychoanalytic and nonpsychoanalytic scholars have advanced such a distinction (though careful scrutiny reveals that "suppression" is by no means used uniformly—compare, for example, Brenner [1975], Dollard & Miller [1950], Holmes [1974]), the distinction is simply not one that Freud himself made. The closest he comes to so doing is in an isolated footnote in *The Interpretation of Dreams* (1900/1953) where he suggests that repression "lays more stress" than suppression "upon the fact of attachment to the unconscious [p. 606]." Such an amorphous passing hint is not a particularly serviceable foundation on which to build a formal distinction, particularly since elsewhere, from his earliest psychological writings (e.g., Breuer & Freud, 1893/1955) to his last (Freud, 1940a/1964), Freud uses "suppression" and "repression" interchangeably.

Nor is there any conspicuous theoretical need to make the distinction. Let, for example, R refer to the conscious operation of repressing something—i. Let us further consider the possibility that consciousness of the operation of repressing i, that is, R(i), is itself aversive; by again using the same operation R the subject need only repress R(i), that is, R(R(i)), to escape residual pain. This constitutes nothing other than an intrapsychic version of the "cover-up of the cover-up," hardly a novel notion in this post-Watergate era.

We have laid such emphasis on the issue of whether repression is, or need be unconscious for two reasons. First, from the historical standpoint, we have here an almost universally accepted notion—a truism—that is not clearly true. Although a particular repression may indeed be unconscious, our point is that not every repression need be unconscious; moreover, a particular repression that is unconscious may have originally started out as a conscious process (Eriksen & Pierce, 1968). For the clinician, such concerns can hardly be of major import. For the laboratory scientist, however, it may well be one of the most critical, for we believe that contemporary laboratory experimental psychology can, despite its many limitations, easily demonstrate the phenomenon of motivated forgetting; it may even be in a position to demonstrate, though this becomes immeasurably more difficult, that such motivated forgetting is used instrumentally to avoid pain, i.e., for defense. But to prove simultaneously all this and, in addition, that such a process operates unconsciously is simply beyond the scope of experimental psychology's current methodological perimeters. A laboratory attempt to demonstrate unconscious defensive processes with current techniques is foredoomed to failure. Such a failure, however (and here we radically part with Holmes and other experimentalists), may be more of a reflection on today's experimental psychology than on unconscious defensive processes.

THE EVIDENCE FOR REPRESSION:
CLINICAL AND EXPERIMENTAL[1]

Clinical Evidence

Excepting a transitory fascination with Jung's reaction-time studies of word associations, Freud saw little need or value in laboratory demonstrations of repression. (Jung himself was later to turn against the experimental approach to complex mental processes [1928/1953]: "whosoever wishes to know about the human mind will learn nothing, or almost nothing, from experimental psychology [p. 246].") The basic phenomenon (if not its varied manifestations and consequences) was too obvious, ubiquitously observed in the clinic and outside it, partaken by all human beings (even psychologists). For this reason, Freud did not feel obliged to elaborate in any great detail the evidentiary basis of repression, viewing with alternate bemusement and incredulity the insistence of experimental psychologists to foist the ceremonial rigors of the laboratory upon the obvious. For example, responding in 1934 to reprints sent to him by Rosenzweig on attempts to demonstrate repression experimentally, Freud stated bluntly that he could not "put much value" on such confirmations because repression was based on a "wealth of reliable observations" that made it "independent of experimental verification," adding, with little apparent confidence, that the exercise could at least "do no harm" (cf. MacKinnon & Dukes, 1964).

Hypermnesia

The clinical observations supporting the notion of repression are basically of two kinds, direct and indirect. The former, the direct data, involve those not infrequent situations where the subject (in therapy, hypnosis, or with just the passage of time) manages finally to remember some heretofore inaccessible painful idea, including in many instances the original resolve to reject the material from consciousness (see, for example, the foregoing quote from the case of Miss Lucy R. [Breuer & Freud, 1895/1955]). This is a direct form of what Freud sometimes referred to as "the return of the repressed" and as such, constitutes the most straightforward proof of the existence of repression. There are numerous instances of such hypermnesias (i.e., the lifting of amnesias) scattered across Freud's clinical reports (e.g., Breuer & Freud, 1895/1955; Freud 1918/1955). In Freud's famous case, "The Wolfman" (Freud, 1918/1955), the patient, after some premonitory dreams, suddenly recalled his sister's

---

[1]Space limitations require us to be highly schematic and selective in this section. Our major purpose is not in any sense to detail the clinical and laboratory data relating to repression but rather to provide a summary overview of the major types of empirical evidence available and the kinds of problems and limitations to which these are subject.

seduction of him ("Let's show one another our bottoms," etc.). In the case of Elizabeth von R. (Breuer & Freud, 1895/1955), the patient experienced excruciating physical pain whenever she began to broach the idea that she was eventually to retrieve into consciousness, the wish that her beloved sister should die so she might marry her brother-in-law. Even before the climactic hypermnesia, Elizabeth was aware that she had "carefully avoided" certain thoughts (e.g., the possibility that her sister might die of her illness); after the hypermnesia, she was overwhelmed by excruciating guilt (psychic pain), the motive for "fending off" the idea. Getting at the painful psychological material was a "layer by layer" process, akin to "excavating a buried city [p. 139]," except that the patient fought the "work of recollection" at every step. We have already had occasion to cite Freud's summary of his observations of the retrieval process involving painful mentation: Memories are "stratified concentrically" about a traumatic "nucleus," the material becoming progressively more inaccessible as the subject gets closer to the traumatic nucleus.

Such hypermnesia-based evidence for repression is not, of course, limited to Freud's observations. It is a virtually standard feature of any long-term clinical interaction, whether the therapist is psychoanalytically oriented (e.g., Deutsch, 1965; A. Freud, 1936/1946; Lindner, 1955) or otherwise (e.g., Thigpen & Cleckley, 1957). In Thigpen and Cleckley's famous case, *The Three Faces of Eve*, for example, the patient, with the initial help of hypnosis, achieved a remarkable array of hypermnesias of aversive memories (e.g., the terrifying experience of being forced by her mother to touch the face of her dead grandmother). Moreover, the patient was able to recall in some instances the hitherto unconscious undertaking of the repression itself, an effort experienced consciously as headaches (e.g., p. 29). Similarly, there is an abundance of reports in the literature on traumatic neurosis of recoveries from amnesias of unbearable memories through hypnosis, drugs, or dynamic therapies (e.g., Gillespie, 1942; Grinker & Spiegel, 1945a, 1945b; Janis, 1969; Kardiner & Spiegel, 1947). Gillespie (1942), for example, reports the case of a man buried alive by an explosion. After his rescue, the man developed symptoms of cramps and bed wetting that could be neither cured nor explained until the patient recalled, under Evipan narcosis, the terrible leg cramps from which he had suffered while trapped in the debris and his desperate effort to avoid the shame of wetting his pants while thus trapped. Grinker and Speigel (1945a) report the permanent cure of a patient's vomiting symptom after the patient was able to gain consciousness (under the influence of sodium pentathol) of hitherto unconscious resentment toward his superior officers (case 30). Another patient (case 43) was cured of his symptoms of depression, moodiness, and insomnia after gaining consciousness (again under sodium pentathol) of his unconscious resentments against his family, particularly his younger brother. Without hypnosis or drugs, another patient (Kardiner & Spiegel, 1947) was eventually able to recall, after several years of intermittent dynamic therapy, the actual details of the airplane crash he survived, for which he had been hitherto amnesic. Typically, patients experience great anxiety in achieving hypermnesias of traumatic materials and struggle against the work of recollection.

Hypermnesias of traumatic materials in combat neurotics have been construed by some experimentalists as constituting unambiguous corroboration of "the reality of repression" (Dollard & Miller, 1950, p. 201). Actually, experiences of this nature are by no means restricted to such recondite settings or, for that matter, to the special conditions of the clinic. It appears that the vast majority of ordinary people can recollect the past use of one form of defense or another for the purpose of avoiding "psychic pain" (anxiety, guilt, shame, etc.). In a recent informal survey of undergraduates by the senior author, virtually every subject (85 of 86) reported having used "conscious repression" ("excluding painful memories or thoughts from consciousness for the purpose of avoiding psychological discomfort"). Moreover, a remarkably high percentage of subjects were able to recall past use of unconscious defenses; that is, they were now conscious of previous unconscious use of defense techniques such as unconscious projection (72%), unconscious reaction formation (46%), unconscious displacement (86%), and unconscious rationalization (93%). Clearly, then, the direct hypermnesia paradigm of repression yields not only abundant but almost universal support for repression: Most people, inside or outside clinical settings, can recall materials they had previously excluded from consciousness in order to avoid psychic pain and can, moreover, recall the specific techniques of defense by which the rejection from consciousness was achieved.

It remains only to ask whether such broad-based evidence allows any continuing doubt about the reality of repression. There are, actually, two methodological issues that must be confronted, both related to the problem of shifting *report criteria* with pressures (demand characteristics, etc.) to retrieve initially inaccessible materials (Egan, 1958; Erdelyi, 1970, 1972; Green & Swets, 1966). The first of these is, in the terminology of signal detection theory, the problem of "false alarms," or in Freud's system the problem of "paramnesias" or "false recollections." It is possible that subjects purportedly recovering lost memories are in fact generating not memories of true events but fanciful guesses, fantasies, or plain confabulations. Such data would then constitute evidence not of repression but imagination.

There can be little question that clinicians have seriously underestimated this problem, no doubt because subjects will frequently generate false recollections with every sign of believing in them themselves (cf. Erdelyi, 1970). Freud himself felt prey to this methodological trap when, being too credulous of his early patients' apparent hypermnesias of childhood seductions, he rushed into his "infantile seduction theory" of hysteria only to be obliged to recant it in short order (Freud, 1906/1953). Hypnotic hypermnesias are similarly suspect. Thus, Bernstein (1956) has reported success in retrieving inaccessible memories not only from childhood but from previous reincarnations! Those not inclined to dismiss reincarnation out of hand may well have to contend with time travel or clairvoyance as well, for experiments have shown (Kline, 1958; Rubenstein & Newman, 1954) that subjects imaginatively responding to hypnotic suggestions will confidently recall events not only from the past but from the future as well. As Bernheim used to warn his students, "when a physician employs hypnosis with a patient it is wise always to be aware who may be hypnotizing whom" (cited in Thigpen & Cleckley, 1957, pp. 136–137). Even Penfield's dramatic hypermnesias brought on by temporal lobe stimulation may turn out, at least in some cases, to have been highly elaborate concrete fantasies (Neisser, 1967).

The methodological solution to this problem is to obtain some independent verification of the accuracy of the hypermnesias produced by the subject. Unfortunately, this is not always possible; moreover, even when feasible, clinicians have not as a rule made efforts to verify their patients' hypermnesias, partly because it is difficult, partly because clinicians are not sensitized to the methodological issue, but mainly because it is of little clinical import. If the patient is cured, it matters little whether he has "worked through" traumatic memories or traumatic fantasies. Nevertheless the problem is not insurmountable. Careful search will turn up specific hypermnesias of painful materials that are consistent with already-known facts (as in the details of the air crash for which Kardiner and Spiegel's patient was amnesic) or which are independently confirmed by relatives and acquaintances (e.g., Schreiber, 1973; Thigpen & Cleckley, 1957).

Even if the recovered memories can be shown to be veridical (i.e., to constitute "hits" rather than "false alarms"), there remains the residual methodological issue of whether the subject is actually recalling (i.e., remembering) more or merely reporting more (Erdelyi, 1970; Erdelyi & Becker, 1974; Erdelyi & Kleinbard, 1978). For example, it is possible that Elizabeth von R. was from the beginning aware of her shameful wishes concerning her sister and brother-in-law but could not initially bring herself to acknowledge them to her therapist. This brings us to the murky frontier between deception and self-deception (Sackeim & Gur, 1977): report bias vs. memory bias. Despite the impressive contribution of signal detection theory, which might yet find profitable application in the clinic, the fact remains that no absolutely foolproof technique exists for resolving the problem. This is tantamount to saying that psychology—clinical or experimental—has not yet devised a fully reliable technique for reading minds. In the interim we must remain content with a Bayesian approach, involving probabilities rather than certainties. Fortunately, there are myriad clinical situations in which we are able, by virtue of our combined knowledge of the subject, the context of events, and the types of events involved, to dismiss with (virtual) certainty the possibility of gross initial withholding of eventually recovered materials. Laboratory data, moreover, with maximal controls over shifting report criteria—and total control over false-alarm effects—have confirmed the feasibility of achieving extensive hypermnesias of hitherto inaccessible materials through multitrial recall techniques (Erdelyi & Becker, 1974; Erdelyi, Finkelstein, Herrell, Miller, & Thomas, 1976; Erdelyi & Kleinbard, 1978; Erdelyi & Stein, in preparation). Erdelyi and Kleinbard (1978) for example, repeatedly testing subjects' recall over periods of days, were able to obtain memory functions resembling upside-down versions of the classic Ebbinghaus (1885/1964) curve of forgetting (see Fig. 12.1). (Curiously, for reasons not yet understood, the hypermnesias seem to be largely restricted to pictorial or imagistic materials.)

Manifest and Latent Contents

If the *direct* (hypermnesia) evidence for repression is common, the indirect type of evidence is downright commonplace. It is as routinely observed in the clinic as in everyday life and is as much a source of fascination to psychologists as to the artist, whether he be Dostoyevsky or the creator of *True Romance* comic books. The evidence in question involves a form of psychological dissociation: The subject is aware of one set of ideas (wishes, attitudes, etc.) yet, unbeknownst to himself, betrays by a multitude of minor but converging signs a quite different point of view that is antithetical and repugnant to the conscious position. The subject then is emitting double messages while being aware of only one. Thus, a conscious belief p (e.g., "I hate him") is, or gives the appearance of being, dissociated from an unconscious belief $\bar{p}$ ("I love him"). This kind of

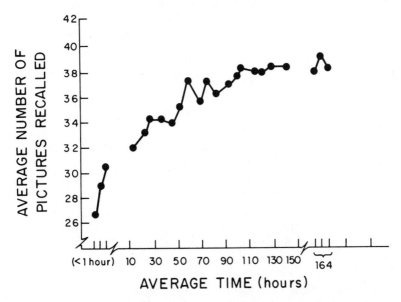

FIG. 12.1.   Long-term hypermnesia: "Unforgetting" over time with repeated recall efforts. (Adapted from Erdelyi & Kleinbard, 1978.)

phenomenon has been explored in some detail by Bateson (1972), though it comes down in the last analysis to Freud's "depth psychology" distinction between *latent contents* and *manifest contents* (e.g., Freud, 1900/1953).

The psychotic Dr. Schreber (Freud, 1911/1958), for example, initially claimed to be grateful to his physician (p), but both the manner in which he stated his gratitude and the wider context of his case suggested the contrary disposition ($\bar{p}$). He did not want to be homosexually assaulted by his physician or God (father?)—p—but gave every sign of desiring precisely that—$\bar{p}$.

The senior author knows at first hand a patient in many ways similar to Schreber but in whom the dissociation between conscious and unconscious belief is even more clear-cut. This patient continually rails against homosexuals, whom he detests with a violent passion. After a brief, unsuccessful marriage, followed by impotence, he began to experience delusions of persecution, according to which the CIA and the FBI were continually observing him with the ultimate purpose of getting him to submit to the sexual advances of Richard Nixon. He gave up all attempts at heterosexual sex, because he "would not make love in public," i.e., in front of the lurking agents. He soon came to understand also that his impotence had been imposed on him, via laser rays, by Nixon's agents. Satellites specifically sent up for this purpose began to bombard him with homosexual messages. Finally he constructed a special protective hat fitted with a highly complex electrical jamming device. He wore this hat continually, at home and in public places, including restaurants and work (he was soon dismissed). Even so, the messages that he should submit to Nixon increased in intensity and began to "penetrate" at times. Around this period he took all his jackets to a tailor and had the tailor sew up the slits (or flaps) in the back of the jackets. He implored his male acquaintances to do likewise, lest they be taken for "slot-jacket ass panderers" (note: "slot," not "slit"). He deplored tight dungarees because they revealed buttocks too openly and therefore constituted a disgraceful invitation to sodomy. He complained that the CIA was spreading rumors that he was a homosexual; indeed they had contrived to find a "double" for himself and a friend and photographed them—the doubles—in "disgusting" homosexual acts, all for the purpose of blackmail, so that he might submit to the homosexual importunings of the "anarcho-communist sodomite" Gerald Ford, who, as he now came to realize, was really "behind" the conspiracy (Nixon, it now turned out, was just a "front"). Ford, he believed, succeeded in having his landlord evict him from his apartment, so that he would be forced to live in the local YMCA among "faggots." This was meant to be a "softening-up" tactic. Without any possible doubt, he consciously hated homosexuals; indeed the extent of his hatred was worrisome, particularly since he began to speak of destroying them, seeing himself an innocent heterosexual victim of homosexual persecution (p). Yet all the contextual signs suggested that he in fact was homosexually inclined ($\bar{p}$)—though he would have met such a suggestion not only with vehemence but probably violence.

Though not everyone is likely to have had firsthand experience with such dramatic delusional systems, probably most readers can recall instances in their own lives or that of their acquaintances in which a conscious disposition, p, was contradicted by a confluence of concurrent behaviors implying the contrary, but not necessarily conscious, disposition, $\bar{p}$. (We have found that in normal people, troubled romantic relations are a particularly fecund source for the observation—or remembrance—of such motivated psychological dissociations, i.e., repressions.) Despite the ubiquity of this type of occurrence in everyday life, experimental psychology has thoroughly ignored it in its approach to the problem of repression. Perhaps the reason is that this type of evidence is indirect and, more serious, based on *interpretation*. It could be argued that there exists no formal method by which the existence of latent dispositions can be logically proven. Thus, the attribution of unconscious homosexual desires to the paranoid patient just discussed is really a matter of mere inference or interpretation but not logical demonstration, the stuff of which science is made. Moreover, outlandish interpretations carelessly bandied about by psychoanalysts from Freud on have deservedly rendered the interpretative process a suspect art, to say nothing of science.

Although criticisms of interpretation, by which psychoanalysts appear to be able to prove anything and everything is thoroughly merited, there nevertheless is something profoundly wrong about going to the other extreme and excluding interpretation as a semantic instrument in experimental psychology. The reason is really quite obvious: All of us, regardless of theoretical predisposition, engage in psychological interpretation for *normal* communication; indeed, the overliteral communicator is aberrant. Thus, though there is no logical technique for proving that a sarcastic remark, p (e.g., "Brutus is an honorable man"), actually means $\bar{p}$ ("Brutus is *not* an honorable man"), the real but latent meaning is obvious to psychoanalyst, behaviorist, and social-learning theorist. Indeed, the understanding of a whole family of communication modalities such as nuance, irony, sarcasm, innuendo, and humor is predicated on the ability to interpret latent meanings; not "getting a joke," for example, constitutes a failure of interpretation. To prove the existence of such latent meanings to a person who has a sense of humor is superfluous; it is obvious without laboratory demonstrations. But to prove such latent meanings to a person who operates at a purely literal level—an insight-blind person—is beyond the pale of any logic or methodology, as would be the proof of the existence of green grass to a sightless person. The same is the problem of attempting to prove logically that a person who consciously detests homosexuality (p) latently is attracted toward homosexuality ($\bar{p}$) while avoiding awareness of the latent fact $\bar{p}$.

The ultimate solution to bringing interpretation into the corpus of scientific psychology is to discover the grammar of interpretation. Just as there are formal grammars (rules) for perceiving depth, there must also be formal rules for perceiving depth of *meaning*; it is simply a question of moving from mere *sight* to *insight*. There is no logic to perceiving 3-D from a 2-D retinal image, only psychological rules. Similarly, there is no logic to perceiving deep (latent) meanings from surface (manifest) presentations; only *psychological* rules—as yet undiscovered and hence only intuitively or artistically applied by a process, in Helmholtz's analogous formulation for sight, of "unconscious inference." We attempt in our theoretical section to suggest some preliminary steps toward a science of interpretation. It suffices to say at this point that experimental cognitive psychology has begun to rediscover at least the *existence* of latent meanings, though typically under alternate labels such as "deep semantic structures," "abstracted meanings," "tacit knowledge," "tacit meanings," "pragmatic implications," "polysemy," "meaningful entities versus brute things" (Bransford & Franks, 1971; Bransford & McCarrell, 1974; Dooling & Lachman, 1971; Franks, 1974; Harris & Monaco, 1978; Loftus & Zanni, 1975; Martin, 1975; Monaco & Harris, 1978; Polanyi, 1966).

Laboratory Evidence

The Jung–Riklin Word-Association Studies

The earliest laboratory studies applied to the repression problem were those of Jung and Riklin (1904–1905; Jung, 1906/1908) both then at the famed Burghölzli Clinic of Eugen Bleuler. Perhaps the best way to grasp the rationale of these studies is first to consider some of Jung's related work on lie detection (Jung 1935/1968), from which all modern lie-detection systems are derived.

Jung and his colleagues found that a dissimulating criminal—or patient— could unwittingly give himself away through certain anomalous responses, such as changed pulse rates, depth of breathing, elevated galvanic skin responses, or a variety of abnormalities in word associations (unusually long reaction times to critical stimuli; superficial, repetitive, or clang associations, etc.). The emotionally toned topics about which the subject was deliberately (and consciously) trying to lie nevertheless produced emotional reactions that these more subtle "indicators" gave away. For example: Three nurses suspected of stealing some money from their hospital were individually administered word-association tests by Jung. One of the nurses gave unusually slow reactions to stimulus words related to the crime (e.g., *money*), on which basis Jung accused her of the theft. Thereupon she broke down and confessed. The emotional ideation, despite the subject's attempt at dissimulation, had leaked through into the more sensitive indicator system.

The question now arises: What if a subject gives the appearance through these indicators of emotionality of lying, but is not conscious of any attempt of lying or even of what it is about which he is presumably lying? One may infer, as Jung did, that the subject is engaged in a private lie, that he is lying to himself. In this view, then, the patient is treating his own consciousness as an outside agent from which some emotional facts are being hidden but that, as in the case of the public lie, more sensitive indicators register and reveal. It was such evidence of emotional reactivity in the absence of awareness for the ideas behind it (and, often, unawareness for the emotional reaction itself) that led Jung to construe his experiments as demonstrating the existence of "emotionally-toned ideational complexes" existing in dissociation from consciousness.

Though interesting, and certainly heuristic for the field of lie detection, the research program cannot be said to shed much light on the problem of repression. A careful reading of this work reveals a plethora of methodological as well as conceptual flaws that are too numerous to attempt detailing here. We may cite a few of the more major issues. First, anomalous reactions such as delayed reaction times need not indicate emotionality; other factors, such as familiarity or complexity, might yield similar effects, a possibility for which Jung was criticized and for which he had no answer (Jung, 1935/1968, p. 65). Then, even if the indicator correctly reveals emotionality as opposed to some other factor (i.e., an emotional hit vs. a false alarm), it still does not follow that the subject is unconscious of the ideation that triggers the emotion. Indeed, a careful reading of Jung's writings on the topic typically shows Jung unveiling a conscious rather than an unconscious secret (i.e., a secret withheld from others rather than from the self). Moreover, in those cases where the subject reports no awareness for the ideation producing emotional reactions, it is never clear what it is he is repressing, if anything. Jung often supplies some inferred complex, but one can never be certain whether the subject's unawareness of it reflects repression or faulty interpretation on the part of the therapist. Thus, it is by no means clear how—if at all—these experimental data extend the insights obtainable in straightforward clinical settings, especially if the demonstration must also hinge eventually on interpretation.

Disturbed Memory for Unpleasant or Anxiety-Provoking Events

Another early experimental approach to repression was the attempt to demonstrate that memory for unpleasant events is poorer than for pleasant events (e.g., Koch, 1930; Meltzer, 1930; Moore, 1935). Perhaps no other research effort in the area has been as universally criticized by opponents as well as proponents of psychoanalysis. Again, the problems are conceptual as well as methodological (for an in-depth review, see Rapaport, 1942/1971). Perhaps the most obvious experimental issue is whether in fact it is true that memory for the unpleasant is inferior to that for the pleasant. Thus, Cason (1932) demonstrated that extremely pleasant and unpleasant experiences tend to be remembered equally but in both cases better than mildly pleasant or unpleasant experiences.

At the theoretical level, it has been claimed that such laboratory work rests on a basic misunderstanding of Freud's concepts in that not all unpleasant, but only anxiety-provoking, materials tend to activate repression (Eriksen & Pierce, 1968;

MacKinnon & Dukes, 1964; Sears, 1936, 1942). Wolitzky, Klein, and Dworkin (1976) have extended the point by insisting that conflict must also be present. This line of criticism, we feel, is probably unjustified. It could be said that in this regard Freud himself had basic misunderstandings about Freud. Certainly not until 1926 (in *Inhibition, Symptoms, and Anxiety*, 1926/1959), near the end of his career, did Freud specifically formulate his notion that anxiety instigates repression. Moreover, a broad conception of "anxiety" (including guilt, shame, worry, etc.) is hard to disentangle from the unpleasant, especially in the light of Freud's "Pleasure−Unpleasure Principle," in which unpleasure is defined generally as tension (and pleasure as the reduction of tension). We believe that the more serious theoretical problem with this research approach is the erroneous assumption that unpleasant things in general are repressed. This certainly was never Freud's position. It does not follow that because things that *are* repressed are unpleasant (or lead to unpleasure)—a position that Freud did hold— unpleasant things therefore are necessarily repressed. Such a conclusion is based on a faulty syllogism of the form:

> All philosophers are men (or women)
> Therefore, all men (or women) are philosophers.

Freud (1915−1916/1961) actually addressed this problem directly: "Aren't unhappy memories the hardest to forget, as for example the recollection of grievances or humiliations? This fact is quite correct, but the objection [with respect to the repression notion] is not sound. It is important to begin early to reckon with the fact that the mind is an arena, a sort of tumbling ground, for the struggles of antagonistic impulses [pp. 76−77]." Here Freud is emphasizing that the psychological system is not unitary, based solely on the "Pleasure-Unpleasure Principle." The "Reality Principle" opposes the developmentally primitive "Pleasure−Unpleasure Principle," and it is precisely with respect to the relatively innocuous events experienced or reported in the laboratory that contact with reality is likely to prevail, and perhaps be even amplified. Thus, the innocuous stimuli of the laboratory are precisely the least likely to activate defenses. (Moreover, even if activated, a variety of defensive devices, such as intellectualization, would not necessarily yield a diminution of episodic memory.)

In an effort to come to grips with the problem of ineffective laboratory stimuli, researchers cast about for some experimental manipulation that would be disturbing enough psychologically to activate defensive reactions. A major breakthrough (or so it was thought) was provided by what MacKinnon and Dukes (1964) have aptly termed "Zeigarnik's unintentional study of repression, [p. 675]." Zeigarnik is best known, of course, for her famous, if often disputed, Zeigarnik Effect, the discovery that uncompleted tasks tend to be better remembered than completed tasks. The relevance of this work for repression is Zeigarnik's (1927) discovery of a systematic exception to the Zeigarnik Effect:

When the noncompletion of a task was construed by the subject as a personal failure rather than just merely a consequence of insufficient time, that is, when the subject felt stupid, awkward, or inferior because of the failed task, then it was the uncompleted rather than the completed task that tended to be "extremely often forgotten." These tasks—Zeigarnik called them "repressed tasks"—were thought to produce an "ego-threat" of sufficient seriousness as to mobilize repression, accounting for the forgetting of failed tasks.

This approach was systematically explored and extended by subsequent researchers (e.g., Buss & Brock, 1963; Eriksen, 1952; Flavell, 1955; Glixman, 1949; Gould, 1942; Holmes, 1972; Holmes & Schallow, 1969; Lazarus & Longo, 1953; Rosenzweig, 1933, 1943, 1952; Rosenzweig & Mason, 1934; Zeller, 1950a, 1950b, 1951), though the emphasis soon shifted away from the interruption of tasks per se to direct manipulation of anxiety through laboratory induction of feelings of failure or success, guilt, psychopathology, etc. (for recent reviews, see Eriksen & Pierce, 1968; Holmes, 1974; MacKinnon & Dukes, 1964).

The performance decrement effects for anxiety-related materials are reasonably robust, particularly if individual differences in defense strategies are taken into account (cf. Eriksen, 1952; Lazarus & Longo, 1953). Nevertheless, the findings—or the conclusions derived from the findings—have been subjected to a variety of criticisms: that diminution in memory is in itself an insufficient demonstration of repression unless the return of the repressed, i.e., hypermnesia for the forgotten, can be effected by the removal of the associated anxiety (Zeller, 1950a, 1950b, 1951); that performance decrements in themselves need not arise from repression but might result instead from other mechanisms, such as disturbed attention (Aborn, 1953), response "interference" or "competition" (Holmes, 1972; Holmes & Schallow,1969; Russell, 1952), or the general effect of anxiety upon the performance of complex tasks (Truax, 1957); that since subjects have been found to ruminate about their anxiety-provoking experience before recall trials, that the subsequent memory decrements cannot be a consequence of repression (D'Zurilla, 1965); that the memory decrement effect cannot involve repression, since it appears to be subject to conscious control (Aborn, 1953); that the studies in question do not tap repression, since the ego- or superego-threat manipulations produced in the laboratory are simply not powerful enough to mobilize repression (Kris, 1947/1951) or at least not such gross defensive reactions as outright amnesias (Wolitzky, Klein, & Dworkin, 1976); and that—and here we add our own criticism—it has not been demonstrated that the obtained performance decrements reflect true memory rather than merely report bias processes (cf. Erdelyi, 1970, 1974; Erdelyi & Becker, 1974).

Although there is merit in some of these criticisms, many of them may also be shown to be flawed or downright misguided. Aborn's (1953) objection, for example, that repression must be a process beyond conscious control is simply wrong. Freud's earliest nonhypnotic technique for recovering repressed materials was nothing other than conscious effort (Breuer & Freud, 1895/1955). D'Zurilla's (1965) observation that subjects ruminate about their failures is most interesting and certainly in accord with clinical experience, as with the "repetition-compulsion" nightmares of war neurotics, but it simply does not follow logically that the resultant memory failures for parts of the experience are therefore not a result of repression. Zeller's (1950a) critique has been exceptionally influential but is probably off the point, having more to do with the demonstration of the existence of *the repressed* than the existence of *repression*. At a rote level it is true, of course, that at least some repressed materials should be subject to recovery. This, after all, is the goal of psychoanalytic psychotherapy. However, the return of the repressed is not a necessary condition for the assumption of repression; psychoanalysis in fact maintains that most repressed materials are never recovered. A modern conception of memory, moreover, would specifically suggest that, contrary to Freud, some repressed materials will in fact be lost irretrievably. Thus, although materials rejected from long-term memory are likely to remain available for subsequent retrieval, rejection from other memory buffers, as, for example, iconic memory stores (Neisser, 1967), would result in permanent loss of the material—not because repression erases the memory trace, but because the memory trace in buffers other than long-term memory tend to decay precipitously if not subjected to conscious processing (Erdelyi, 1974).

The "response interference" or "disturbed attention" arguments per se cannot be viewed as criticisms of repression but only—at best—as theoretical conceptualizations of repression (or at worst, terminological wrangles). Without any doubt, Freud's own concept of repression is an interference one (though he did not, of course, use behavioristic terminology); moreover, Freud specifically viewed the withdrawal of attention ("attention cathexis") as one means by which repression is effected (Freud, 1915b/1957). The really important criticism behind Holmes' response interference position, however, is the question of whether the interference is tendentious, i.e., purposeful, as opposed to being merely a "non-defensive attentional process." This, Holmes is right to assert, has not been proven. His own research has shown, for example, that performance decrements can be obtained not only with ego-threat but with ego-boosting manipulations as well. Unfortunately, it is not obvious how the experimental paradigm under discussion could be adapted to yield the requisite proof of intent. Thus, the fact that the paradigm does not yield such a proof may, as we have already intimated, reflect on the experimental paradigm, not necessarily on repression.

Perceptual Defense: Is it Repression?

Probably no topic in the recent history of experimental psychology has led to as bitter and sustained a controversy as the issue of perceptual defense (Dixon, 1971; Erdelyi, 1974), the purported tendency of subjects to resist perceiving anxiety-provoking stimuli. (With certain identifiable subjects, at certain levels of stimulus emotionality, an opposite, sensitization phenomenon may be observed, termed *perceptual vigilance*.) The exceptional attention lavished on the topic by a generation of psychologists has produced what is perhaps the most profound and wide-ranging analysis of the issues confronting the study of repressionlike phenomena in the laboratory. Probably every question to have arisen in other laboratory literatures on repression has cropped up in the perceptual defense area, where it is likely to have been subjected to deeper and more articulated analysis than elsewhere. The contested issues have ranged from the most technical methodological matters to questions of logic and philosophy.

For example, it was thought initially by some critics that the very notion of perceptual defense rested on a logical absurdity, for it seemed altogether paradoxical to conceive of a subject defensively *not perceiving* a stimulus without first *perceiving* the stimulus to be defended against. This issue, as Sackeim and Gur (1977) have pointed out, is analogous to certain philosophic objections (e.g., Sartre, 1958) to the general notion of repression and the unconscious. Even a psychological version of Zeno's paradox arose, wherein it was argued that perceptual defense implied a censoring homunculus, which in turn had to imply a homunculus within the homunculus, and thus an infinite (and therefore impossible) regress of homunculi. Such arguments were a natural consequence of the now-abandoned behavioristic Weltanschauung of experimental psychology of those days (which now dominates personality and clinical psychology a generation later).

It is worth noting that these philosophic difficulties of perceptual defense were resolved neither by experimental psychology (i.e., laboratory research) nor by philosophy but, instead, by an analogy. As soon as the rat gave way to the computer as cognitive psychology's central metaphor, the problems dissolved of their own weight, since it now became clear, indeed trivially obvious, that computers could selectively regulate their own input (and thus perceive at one level without perceiving at another level) through the operation of "control processes" that were neither mystical nor eternally regressive.

On the methodological side, there was a wide assortment of issues. The most fundamental of these was the question of whether the phenomenon was in fact "perceptual" in nature, a problem of little consequence for the issue of repression, particularly in those cases where critics maintained that the effect was not a *perceptual* but a *memory* or *cognitive* phenomenon, which is tantamount to saying that it is not *perceptual* defense but rather *memory* or *cognitive* defense— i.e., standard repression. The trivializing criticism in this family of criticisms was that the phenomenon constituted not a *perceptual* bias, but a *report* bias, resulting from the subject's embarrassment at having to report taboo items. The application of signal detection techniques to this area, together with its theoretical reconceptualization in terms of modern *non*tachistoscopic work on selective attention (Erdelyi, 1974), have cast doubt on the latter criticism, so that after almost a decade of general disrepute, perceptual defense is regaining wide credibility (Nisbett & Wilson, 1977).

Has the laboratory literature on perceptual defense, then, finally accomplished the task of proving the existence of repression in the laboratory? Some issues remain to be answered. First, is it proper to view perceptual defense as a form of repression? Note, for example, that it does not pass Zeller's (1950a) criterion, since there is no evidence that the defended-against input can be recovered. We feel, as we have already indicated, that Zeller's notion is not well taken. Though the "return of the repressed" might be a reasonable goal for clinicians, accustomed as they are to exploring long-term memory, an effect based on the "function of rejecting and keeping something out of consciousness" from a fleeting memory buffer will result in the permanent loss of that "something." We feel, then, that perceptual defense conforms to Freud's fundamental definition of repression and may be properly regarded as a form of repression.

Another issue, however, is more problematical. It is essentially the same as that applied by Holmes to the memory studies of the previous section. Granted that perception and cognition may be disrupted in the processing of emotional stimuli, does it necessarily follow that the disruption is tendentious; i.e., does lowered sensitivity necessarily imply a defensive intention not to see, as opposed to a general disruption of processing by emotionality? Thus, for example, in a perceptual experiment reminiscent of some of Holmes' own work, Erdelyi and Appelbaum (1973) demonstrated that the perception, by religious Jews, of a neutral tachistoscopic display was as much disrupted by a contiguous swastika as by a contiguous Star of David. The subjects presumably were not "defending" against the stimulus items associated with the Star of David.

In the case of tachistoscopic stimuli, on which the vast bulk of the perceptual defense literature rests, the methodological problem of proving intention is even more intractable than before; the disruption processes occur so rapidly that the perceiver would not even be in a position to give subjective reports of their cognitive activities or intentions during the disruption. Thus though it is probably safe to conclude, despite the weight of past controversies, that brief emotional stimuli may yield disrupted perception, it does not necessarily follow that the disruption occurs because of a deliberate rejection of the emotional material.

Much more helpful in this regard is the vast modern literature on selective attention (e.g., Broadbent, 1958, 1971; Moray, 1970; Norman, 1976), which, though never pursued with repression in view, has nevertheless demonstrated beyond any lingering doubt that the perceiver can intentionally reject selected perceptual inputs. Neisser and Becklen (1975), for example, have recently extended the auditory shadowing paradigm to the visual modality, demonstrating a similarly remarkable selectivity in visual processing. Thus, subjects were shown capable of massively blanking out an unfolding visual scene at which they were actually staring, in order to attend to another overlapping scene that had been superimposed on the same visual field.

Two separate facts, then, have been demonstrated in the laboratory, both critical to the repression concept. It has been experimentally shown that (a) emotional stimuli may yield impaired perception and (b) that the perceiver can intentionally and selectively reject perceptual inputs. What has *not* been demonstrated in the laboratory, however, is the conjoint fact that the perception of emotional stimuli is disrupted *because* of intentional rejection by the perceiver. It is highly plausible of course, that such may be the case. It would be unthinkable that such remarkable cognitive capabilities would not be put to instrumental use.

At least it may be said for once that a demonstration of the conjoint fact is not beyond the reach of the experimental paradigm in question, for it may probably be shown without much difficulty (especially if individual differences are taken into account at the outset) that a traumatic visual sequence (e.g., a lung cancer operation) superimposed over a neutral sequence will result, without any prompting from the experimenter, in an intentional rejection of the aversive material. This would be the cognitive counterpart of closing or averting one's eye in order not to see some unbearable scene.

We might conclude this section on a small sophistry (one man's sophistry being another's sophistication). Supposing the foregoing experiment were successfully executed, demonstrating the compound fact that subjects will on their own volition reject perceiving aversive visual inputs. Would it necessarily follow that the rejection of emotional input was undertaken for the purpose of defense, i.e., to escape psychic pain? The inference seems overwhelmingly plausible, almost mandatory, but how could we prove it? Pressed on this point, one could think only of asking the perceiver for a subjective report about why he rejected the emotional material, a type of data that Nisbett and Wilson (1977) have quite properly warned us is fraught with peril.

Hypnotic and Non-hypnotic Studies of Intentional Forgetting

If the frequency with which Freud refers to Bernheim's work on hypnotically directed forgetting (which Freud personally witnessed during a brief visit to Bernheim's clinic in 1889) is any indication, research on intentional forgetting played a significant role in the development of the repression concept. In "astonishing experiments upon his hospital patients" (Freud, 1925a/1959, p. 17), Bernheim would hypnotize a patient, subject him to a variety of experiences and posthypnotic suggestions, direct the patient *not* to recall the hypnotic experiences (but nevertheless to carry out the indicated posthypnotic behaviors), awaken him from the trance, and then question him about the to-be-forgotten, though just experienced, hypnotic events (cf. Freud, 1916–1917/1963, p. 277). The patient typically would recall little or nothing (posthypnotic amnesia), though Bernheim also showed that with unrelenting pressure the subject could be made gradually to recover the lost material (hypermnesia), a fact that Freud was later to turn to clinical account (Breuer & Freud, 1895/1955) and Zeller (1950a), as we have seen, into a criterion of repression.

Bernheim's loose hypnotic demonstrations have since been extensively replicated in the laboratory (for two recent studies, see Kihlstrom & Evans, 1976; Spanos & Ham, 1973). Further, as we have already indicated, a major experimental program on *non*hypnotic "directed forgetting" ("intentional forgetting," "voluntary forgetting," "selective amnesia," etc.) has arisen in the modern cognitive literature, though with few exceptions (Roediger & Crowder, 1972; Weiner, 1968), the relationship of this work to either Bernheim's research or to the issue of repression has been ignored or brushed aside (Bjork, 1972; Bjork, LaBerge, & Legrand, 1968; Davis & Okada, 1971; Epstein, 1972; MacLeod, 1975; Rakover, 1975; Shebliske & Epstein, 1973). Nevertheless, this contemporary work on selective amnesia, like the modern research on selective attention and inattention, tends to confirm the basic repression mechanism—if not the defense—posited by Freud, i.e., "the function of rejecting and keeping something out of consciousness." Both literatures, however, have heretofore focused on the rejection of information from unstable memory buffers, iconic stores in the case of selective attention—inattention and short-term stores in the bulk of selective amnesia studies. Only recently (e.g., MacLeod, 1975; Rakover, 1975) have researchers begun to extend the selective amnesia paradigm to long-term memory; it is this latter direction, we predict, that will yield hypermnesia, i.e., "return-of-the-repressed" effects.

Space does not permit a detailed discussion of the methodological or theoretical issues impinging on the selective amnesia literature. In many respects (and for no good apparent reason) the field appears to be recapitulating some of the unfortunate either—or proclivities of perceptual defense theorizing. Thus, a great deal of experimental effort is being invested in attempts to show that a particular locus or a pet mechanism is the critical (or interesting) underpinning of the phenomenon. There is little doubt, however, that the selective amnesia phenomenon, like all complex cognitive phenomena, is multiprocess in nature and that a series of overlapping and sometimes redundant mechanisms operate sometimes singly, other times in unison, in producing the amnesia effects. It is only reasonable that complex phenomena should have complex determinants (Erdelyi, 1974).

There are, of course, a variety of methodological problems, the major one, once again, being the question of whether the effect is a report bias ("response withholding") or memory bias phenomenon. Especially in early efforts (Weiner, 1968), as in Bernheim's work, where subjects are first instructed to forget, then to remember, one is led to wonder about the crosscurrent of demand characteristics impinging on the subject and the problematical consequence of these conflictual demands upon what the subject is willing to say he does and does not remember.

In order to bypass these obvious problems, many of the recent studies have used indirect measures, e.g., the reduction of interference by (presumably) forgotten items or the memory enhancement of the to-be-remembered items as a function of to-forget instructions for other list items. The disadvantage of these more indirect approaches is that the conclusions that can be drawn are necessarily more indirect as well.

Fortunately, however, despite many unresolved problems, there can be no doubt of the existence of intentional forgetting in at least short-term memory tasks. The very nature of the demonstration of short-term memory (Brown, 1958; Peterson & Peterson, 1959)—namely that nonrehearsal of new inputs inevitably results in rapid memory loss—necessarily means that the subject can voluntarily effect selective forgetting through selective nonrehearsal. Archer & Margolin (1970) have experimentally confirmed this expectation.

Granted, then, that certain types of memories can be intentionally rejected and kept from consciousness, may these experimental demonstrations be construed as proofs of repression? Scholars in the field, to the extent that they have allowed themselves to broach the matter, have tended to dismiss the bearing of selective amnesia on repression (or vice versa) while simultaneously offering up notions that, to us at least, bear remarkable similarities in conception, if not wording, to Freud's own ideas. Thus, Epstein's (1972) "selective search" or selective "depth of search" hypothesis may be thought of as recapitulating Freud's (1915b/1957) attention cathexis notion; similarly, Bjork's "differential grouping" hypothesis appears to be a variant of Freud's early (e.g., 1892–1893/1966) "dissociation" theory; Rakover's "blocking" notion sounds like Freud's (1900/1953) "censorship."

Leaving terminological issues behind, the answer to the question ultimately rests on the same considerations that confronted us in the case of selective inattention. The mechanisms clearly exist for the undertaking of the defense; also, aversive stimuli may be shown to disrupt memory (Erdelyi & Blumenthal, 1973; Suedfeld, Erdelyi, & Corcoran, 1975); yet, as before, the compound fact, as plausible as it might appear, has not been experimentally demonstrated, i.e., that the available mechanism is in fact deployed for defense against aversive stimuli. It is, moreover, less likely that such a laboratory demonstration will be achieved in the memory realm, since, on account of the immediacy and consequent impact of perception, it is easier to introduce an unbearable visual stimulus than an unbearable memory in the laboratory.

Conclusion on the Evidence for Repression with Some Observations on Methodology

What has been shown? The answer would seem to depend on whether one looks at the clinical or laboratory data, for the two approaches have had palpably different yields. Such differences, we believe, reflect inherent differences in the two approaches, not some peculiar inconstancy of the phenomenon itself.

The genius of the clinical approach is its ability to reveal truly complex cognitive processes. It can uncover compound facts such as the conjoint occurrence of (a) tendentious rejection from awareness of (b) aversive materials (c) for the purpose of avoiding pain (d) often by unconscious means (though the latter fact is not essential for the proof of repression). From the clinical standpoint, the evidence for repression is overwhelming and obvious.

The weakness of the clinical approach, on the other hand, is its looseness of method. The most ubiquitous evidence is the indirect one, based on unregimented interpretation, which up to now has been more of an art form than a scientific instrument—though we should not forget that we use that "art," like syntax, for daily communication. The more direct evidence, namely hypermnesia effects, is methodologically more solid. Quite clearly, people at times forget traumatic events and then subsequently remember both the forgotten material and the defensive intent to forget. Even so, some features of these data cannot be fully verified. Report bias effects have not been formally controlled. Moreover, as far as the paramnesia problem is concerned, one may verify the objective truth of an objective event (e.g., "my mother died") but not the objective truth of a subjective intent (e.g., "I wished not to face the fact that my mother died"). Scientific psychology has yet to develop a methodology of purpose.

The strength of the laboratory-experimental approach, unlike the clinical, is its methodological rigor; its overriding weakness is its inability to deal with truly complex processes. Thus, none of the four critical facts in themselves are in any doubt within experimental psychology: (a) that there can be selective information rejection from awareness; (b) that aversive stimuli tend to be avoided; (c) that organisms strive to defend themselves against pain; and (d) that many psychological processes occur outside of awareness. All these facts, independently, are not in dispute; what is in dispute, and what has not been demonstrated experimentally, is the conjoint fact, i.e., all the component facts integrated into a higher-order fact. In the absence of a clear-cut demonstration of the compound phenomenon, experimental psychologists have reflexively held the phenomenon accountable. How curious that they should never question the method instead.

Methodology, after all, is only an applied epistemology; as such it is a band of philosophy and, therefore, theory; as such it is subject to verification—and, hopefully, to falsification. If an applied epistemological theory fails, it should be discarded or modified, like any theory. There is nothing sacrosanct or final about theories, whether about the mind (psychological theory) or about how the mind should pursue truth (methodological theories). Like any theory (Kelly, 1955) a particular methodology has its "focus of convenience." Rats, pigeons, nonsense syllables, sensory processes, and the like are the focus of convenience of current experimental methodologies. If it now should blur suddenly when applied to new domains—complex cognitive processes like poetry, intention, love, repression— we should hardly be surprised. Nor should we helplessly cling to the hapless methodology, shaping reality to fit the method. Better to search for something in the darkness than to search for nothing in the light (J. B. Watson notwithstanding).

A methodological crisis is upon modern cognitive psychology. The crisis was inevitable once the field broke away from the safe moorings of nonsense syllables and other such ecological irrelevancies and moved toward the study of complex events (first words, then sentences, and now extended prose). The crisis has been apprehended up to now by only a few (e.g., Bregman, 1977; Deese, 1972; Neisser, 1976; Norman, 1973). Ponderous experiments, bristling with technical competence, continue to be churned out at an ever greater pace, fostering the illusion of a scientific enterprise. What has been overlooked over the last few years, however, is that the experiments have less and less to do with proofs of theory. The experiments might confirm a minuscule feature of this or that theoretic system, but modern theories about the higher mental processes are, in truth, non sequiturs. The laboratory data tend to prove nothing anymore; they are mere anecdotes foraged from the laboratory, much like Freud would pluck supporting anecdotes from Shakespeare or some telling case. The pathetic faddishness of contemporary cognitive psychology, remarkably unremarked, is the clearest proof of the breakdown of its methodological underpinnings. Roughly every five years (the approximate life span of the average graduate student), the "facts" of the field change. Short-term memory is in, short-term memory is out; imagery is a true phenomenon, no it's an epiphenomenon; psycholinguistics is in, psycholinguistics is out; depth of processing is the new metaphor of information processing, but by the time this chapter appears in print, it will already ring with time.

We should not be misunderstood. We do not turn against the methodology of conventional experimental psychology because of its failure to confirm repression. We turn against that methodology as an arbiter of the phenomenon because it is inherently incapable of addressing the problem of repression—or any other truly complex mental process.

We cannot here speculate on the likely shape of future methodologies for cognitive psychology—and we expect it will be a psychodynamic cognitive psychology—but we have a strong hunch that a hybrid epistemological system, combining the vigor of the clinic and the rigor of the laboratory, will emerge.

THE COGNITIVE PSYCHOLOGY OF REPRESSION

Freud's Cognitive Approach

Freud's approach to repression, like so much of psychoanalysis, is quintessentially cognitive, though this fact has been remarkably unappreciated (Erdelyi, in preparation). The theory is a theory of thought, or rather tendentious thought, in which reality is regularly misperceived, misremembered, or misconstrued for the purpose of defense. Its cognitive foundations were laid down in the famous Chapter 7 of *The Interpretation of Dreams* (Freud, 1900/1953). Figure 12.2, an

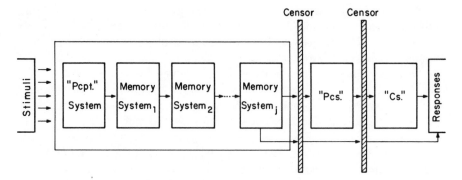

FIG. 12.2. Adaptation of Freud's (1900/1953, Chapter 7) "compound instrument" model of the "psychical apparatus."

adapted version of Freud's own flow diagram (p. 541), serves to encapsulate the essential features of the approach. The scheme is remarkably prescient, resembling in its basic features the types of information-processing diagrams that were to become the hallmark of the cognitive revolution more than half a century later (Broadbent, 1958, 1971; Erdelyi, 1974; Haber, 1968, 1969; Moray, 1970; Neisser, 1967, 1976; Norman, 1976; Shiffrin & Atkinson, 1969; Sperling, 1960, 1967).

The "Pcpt." system is essentially the homologue of what is known today as "iconic" memory (Neisser, 1967), an extremely fleeting but high-capacity buffer. It is a tribute to Freud's brilliance that, on purely theoretical grounds, he should have posited such a system before its experimental discovery (actually rediscovery, in view of Baxt's work of 1871) by Sperling (1960) and Averbach and Coriell (1961). The basic theoretical consideration giving rise to the system "Pcpt." was that a mechanism had to be postulated for receiving perceptual stimuli that nevertheless "retained no trace of them and thus had no memory [p. 538]"—Freud should have said no *lingering* memory—so that past traces should not interfere with the extraction of new inputs. For the details of this line of reasoning, see Freud (1900/1953; 1925b/1961).

Like all contemporary information-processing models, Freud's posits a multiplicity of memory buffers, though these do not correspond to the typical short—intermediate—long-term variety. Freud's conception is probably closer in spirit to the depth-of-processing approach (Craik & Lockhart, 1972), emphasizing the element of "psychical topography" or "dimension of depth" (Freud, 1915b/1957, pp. 174—175) and underemphasizing the specific identity or number of stages except for the suggestion that there are many. The memory systems represent microdevelopmental memory stages through which information is not only transmitted but also transformed. Information may be stored at different levels (topographies); also, different memory systems may hold different types of information in different representational formats (e.g., imaginal vs. verbal). Information in these memory systems is unconscious and must traverse at least a pair of "censors" ("critical agencies," "screens," etc.) in order to reach consciousness. Herein lies the psychodynamic feature of the model. Materials that would produce unbearable anxiety are not allowed through the censors ("filters" would be the name given them today). Interestingly, the two types of "censors" operate according to different principles. The first edits out unwanted "communications" from the preceding memory system. The second "censor," however, the one between Pcs. (accessible memory) and Cs. (accessed memory, i.e., conscious memory), operates by a principle of selective "attention" deployment (cf. Freud, 1900/1953, Chap. 7; Freud, 1915b/1957). Thus, aversive materials that might get through the editing censor may still be expunged from consciousness by a second line of defense, namely, selective inattention.

Censorship is not an all-or-none affair. Unacceptable information may not be altogether blocked from consciousness but, more typically, subjected to editing processes (i.e., defense mechanisms) that render the original meaning unrecognizable to Cs., and therefore innocuous. Physical symptoms, such as paralyses, tics, anesthesias, etc., are a subclass of these indirectly expressed and sanitized materials (which continue to exist in their original forms in long-term memory systems, inaccessible to consciousness). Physical symptoms, then, are *alternate forms of remembering*, a type of nonconscious recall (see Fig. 12.2) expressed in the recondite dialect of body language, which the subject himself fails to comprehend. Hence Breuer and Freud's (1895/1955) formula: "Hysterics suffer mainly from reminiscences "[p. 7]."

Freud's general model, then, is remarkably modern in conception, obviously reflecting his neurological training, to which information-processing notions such as temporal microdevelopment, multiple stages and stores, control processes, inhibition–facilitation processes, capacity limits, selectivity, and so forth were hardly foreign (Freud, 1895/1966; Pribram & Gill, 1976). Perhaps the greatest limitation to Freud's approach, for which he can hardly be faulted, was the unavailability at the time of the computer analogy. The primitive information-processing systems to which he could resort for analogies—e.g., photography and photo-processing, optical systems like the microscope or telescope, a nascent neuron theory—were inevitably limiting and at times misleading. The medium was not up to the message. In order to articulate a highly complex theory, Freud was obliged to fracture his mode of expression, utilizing different metaphors for different conceptual features, resulting in a veritable Babel of mixed and mutually foreign metaphors—and inevitable confusion. If the computer analogy were not a daily feature of our thinking, Freud's "compound instrument" model would necessarily strike us as bizarre (as it did the preceding generation of behaviorists)—a microscope or telescope with intervening memory systems and censors! Freud desperately groped for a unifying analogic scheme such as the computer (see his fascinating conception of a "truly magical magic pad'' [Freud, 1925b/1961]) but was not to have it. Consequently, the finer-grained articulations of this theory were scattered across different works and different analogic systems, relatively independent of his potentially unifying scheme of Fig. 12.2, which—if it had been based on a truly compound instrument, the computer—would easily have encompassed most of the disparate components (e.g., Erdelyi, 1974; Faught, Colby & Parkinson, 1977).

Thus, the "censors" in the model necessarily imply a complex semantically tuned control mechanism, capable of making decisions based on expected consequences. This mechanism formally emerged as the "Ego" in Freud's late writings (Freud, 1923/1961; 1933/1964) and was specifically assigned the control of defensive processes. The actual processes themselves were again formulated through a multiplicity of analogic devices. Direct inhibition, i.e., blocking of information—what many would conceive of as repression in the narrow sense—and displacement, were typically formulated in terms of vector dynamics involving "forces" or neurological "excitations" ("cathexes" and "countercathexes"). In other cases, as we have seen, "attentional" mechanisms were imported. In still other cases, as in projection and reversal (Freud, 1911/1958), transformational notions were introduced (for a mathematical articulation of this approach, see Suppes, & Warren, 1975). Political concepts such as "compromise," "censorship," "suppression−repression" were also frequently invoked, as were analogies from the arts ("symbolism," "deep meanings," "interpretation," "displacement of accent," "condensations," "plastic word representation," etc.). This wild sprawl of incompatible metaphor sketches indicates to us that Freud had pushed too far ahead of his time and had outrun—and run out of—sensible linguistic vehicles through which to give coherent expression to his theory. In support of this contention, we offer the fact that so many of the apparently intractable problems and contradictions besetting Freud's patchwork system dissolve, with not the slightest effort, with the application of the computer analogy.

Neobehavioristic Cognitive Formulations

The neobehavioristic approach to repression—indeed to all cognitive processes—may be conceived of as a new analogic departure; it takes the extensively investigated behavior of laboratory animals, such as rats, dogs, cats, and pigeons, as a model of human thought processes. Perhaps the most brilliant, certainly the most influential, version of this perspective is that of Dollard and Miller (1950). Consciousness (associated with covert verbal labels) is treated as behaving much like a rat in the Miller box: It can learn (through classical conditioning) to fear hitherto innocuous materials, like the white electrified compartment of the box; and moreover, it can learn (through instrumental conditioning) to escape and avoid the anxiety-provoking area. Extrapolated to the cognitive realm, we have, then, a simple formulation of repression: It is basically a form of avoiding certain painful thoughts (Dollard & Miller, 1950, pp. 200−201), i.e., "cognitive avoidance" (Eriksen & Pierce, 1968; Mischel, 1976). The subject, moreover, may remain unconscious of the thoughts he is avoiding because (Dollard & Miller, 1950):

> the response of stopping thinking [tends] to become anticipatory like any other strongly reinforced response. Therefore the patient should tend to stop thinking, or veer off onto a different line of thought, before he reaches the memory of the traumatic incident. He should learn to avoid not only thoughts about the fear-provoking incident but also the associations leading to those thoughts [p. 202].

The formulation appears quite close to Freud's earlier quoted notion of "concentric stratification" of traumatic materials (Breuer & Freud, 1895/1955, p. 289), particularly when we take into account the avoidance gradients demonstrated experimentally with laboratory animals (the closer a harnessed rat gets to an aversive region, the more force he exerts to get away).

More subtle versions of defense may also be generated from this mode of analysis. Thus, *regression* may be thought of as the dropping-out of recent dominant responses (because of nonreinforcement, frustration, punishment) in favor of older response patterns, hitherto submerged in the subject's response hierarchy. *Displacement* may be viewed as a special form of generalization, arising from bivalent goal situations (approach−avoidance conflicts), where the actual response is a compromise (equilibrium point) between avoidance and approach tendencies. This mode of analysis, however, becomes increasingly strained, cumbersome, and post hoc as it attempts to deal with more sophisticated, semantic types of defenses (projection, reversal, rationalization). Analogic systems, like theories, also have their focus of convenience, beyond which they obscure rather than illuminate the ideas they are meant to convey.

In retrospect, it is difficult to discover any conceptual breakthroughs in the neobehavioristic approach to defense mechanisms, as clever as some of the formulations may be ("miraculous" might be the apter description, for it seems to us that theorists like Dollard and Miller succeed often in squeezing theoretic juice out of behavioristic rock). Psychologically, i.e., rhetorically, the approach did have a major impact. Since the theoretical principles were extrapolated from a highly experimental laboratory base, the altogether illusory impression was gained that the extrapolated principles themselves were somehow experimentally valid through a kind of "rigor by association." Although it could often be shown that humans behaved like laboratory animals behaved, only in the rarest instance was there experimental confirmation that cognitive processes recapitulated behavioral processes (e.g., Miller, 1950). Thus, the experimental rigor of animal research has little to do with the rigor or even the truth value of the analogic extrapolations to which they give rise.

The senior author, as a graduate student, once broached the issue with Neal

Miller: On what basis could one justify the extrapolation of animal behavior to human thought? Miller's reply, coming with no apparent hesitation, was a simple word: "Faith."

Biased Information-Processing Conceptualization

The approach under consideration was first set forth by Erdelyi (1974). Although the manifest purpose of this effort was to reevaluate the issue of perceptual defense, its deeper intent was to lay the conceptual foundation for a modern, psychodynamic cognitive psychology. This undertaking may be correctly viewed as yet another analogic departure, involving the application of the computer metaphor to Freud's scattered psychodynamic principles.

Although it would be ingenuous to suppose that the computer analogy provides a conceptual panacea for the theoretical problems in the field, it nevertheless yields a momentous breakthrough. First, as we have already indicated, it makes possible a grand unification, into a single coherent scheme, of the hitherto unwieldy patchwork of component theories, which are often redundant, sometimes contradictory, and invariably expressed in incompatible metaphor languages. The computer, then, provides a theoretical *lingua franca*. There is probably no defense process discussed by Freud that does not naturally lend itself to a computer articulation. Moreover. the postulated mechanisms supporting defense processes (see Fig. 12.2), such as control processes, perceptual systems, memory buffers, censors (filters, decision nodes), and so forth, are not only not bizarre; they are obvious and essential features of any of today's "compound instruments."

The other fundamental advantage conferred by the computer analogy is the possibility of simulation of any feature of the theory. Though such simulations would not provide proof that the mind works in the same manner as the simulation (we extrapolate no less than Neal Miller by a leap of faith), nevertheless the simulation provides a hitherto unavailable methodology for testing the internal logic of the posited processes. We have already seen that certain logical and philosophic objections to defense processes collapsed with the advent of the computer analogy. If the computer could be programmed to simulate perceptual defense effects, than all the paradoxes that supposedly rendered the process impossible must be in error. Or if a persuasive philosopher such as Sartre proves that a system cannot lie to itself (and that, therefore, there cannot be self-deception and, therefore, no repression), the *idiot savant* computer can set matters straight immediately by showing that it can deceive itself and thereby undeceive us brighter human savants.

But can a computer actually simulate self-deception, i.e., the defense processes? Faught, Colby, and Parkinson (1977) have recently reported on a sophisticated self-deceiver, the paranoid PARRY 2 (a program), which manages to pass Turing-like tests of indistinguishability from human paranoids (Colby,

Hilf, Weber, & Kraemer, 1972). When PARRY is sufficiently threatened, its reality-testing routine (the "INFERENCE"process) is overridden by the reality-distorting "PARANOID MODE," which defends it against unbearable mental distress, "shame." Thus: "If shame crosses a threshold for paranoia (SHAME equal to 10), the paranoid mode is activated. The first consequence of the paranoid mode is the rejection of the belief that led to the increase in shame by resetting the truth value of the belief. . . . Instead an alternate belief is inferred" (Faught, Colby, & Parkinson, 1977, pp. 175–176). It should be noted, moreover, that in the simulation, the paranoid intention is "activated outside the normal intention process on condition of extreme shame affect. Such a process is a clear example of unconscious processing, an intentional process that is not available to conscious inspection either during or after its performance [p. 179]."

Using similar programming techniques, it would be a relatively straight-forward matter to simulate the whole gamut of well-known defenses, including dynamic amnesia, displacement (actually, PARRY engages in that already), reaction formation, regression, and physical symptoms (stuttering, tics, apha-sias, etc.). Indeed, it would be possible to construct an all-purpose psycho-dynamic entity (PSYCHO ?) that could selectively use any one or a combination of defense techniques, depending on the "psychodynamic cognitive style" programmed into it.

Erdelyi's (1974) processing-bias model is an attempt to articulate the fundamental theme upon which such a complex, all-purpose, psychodynamic entity—the human mind—is actually based. The effort is made to bring some psychological facts to bear on the model, so that, unlike mere simulations, the resultant model should be not only logically possible but psychologically plausible.

The fundamental principle underlying the approach is that biased (selective, tendentious) processing is a ubiquitous characteristic of the psychological system, observable in input regions of processing (e.g., biased eye-fixation strategies, closing of one's eyes, biased encoding from iconic memory into short-term memory, biased rehearsal and consolidation processes for storage in long-term memory) as well as in "output space" (e.g., biased retrieval, biased reporting strategies). Although the actual mechanisms through which biased processing is effected vary widely (as should be obvious from the foregoing examples), the underlying principle—the strategy if not the tactics—is constant and pervasive. Thus, there is no single locus or set of loci at which tendentious processing (censoring, filtering, etc.) occurs; rather, *bias begins at the beginning and ends only at the very end of information processing* (Erdelyi, 1974). This position is not really different from Freud's. Although Freud's formal model (Fig. 12.2) is based on merely two sites of bias (censorship), his real intent was probably not to suggest that there were merely two, but rather that there were more than one: "We shall do well . . . to assume that to every transition from one system to that immediately above it (that is, every advance to a higher stage of psychical organization) there corresponds a new censorship'' (Freud, 1915b/ 1957, p. 192).

Such an approach does not make for a neat, compact theoretical accounting (or even counting) of specific defense processes. Indeed, it calls for a potentially endless assortment of specific biasing tactics, some of which may or may not be interesting in specific contexts. This corresponds pretty much to the treatment of ''defense mechanisms'' in the clinical literature. There is no set number of them; reality may be distorted (i.e., processed tendentiously) in countless ways for the purpose of defense. It is for this reason that we emphasize the basic theme or strategy (bias) rather than any specific tactic (a particular mechanism). The processing-bias point of view, then, holds that tendentious processing may occur across the entire cognitive continuum and be effected by a plethora of mechanisms active throughout processing space. Like corruption in government, corruption of thought is ubiquitous and multifaceted.

In regard to retrieval from long-term memory, for example, we would posit that any mechanism capable of affecting retrieval could be biased in the service of defense. Thus, we would expect for there to be tendentious depth (and breadth) of processing for different memory items. The subject could engage in biased search-termination strategies, searching extensively for some classes of items and not for others. Since recall can be shown to grow substantially for periods of days with protracted effort (Erdelyi & Kleinbard, 1978), it is likely (and we are now pursuing the issue experimentally) that the subject may effect selective (biased) hypermnesias as well as selective amnesias for different classes of materials as a function of differential search effort. The effect of retrieval cues of various kinds, including abstract organizational schemes, has been recently emphasized. The subject need not be passive in this regard; he can free associate to himself, self-administer category lists, try to recreate the original scene, etc., in a biased way, i.e., more for some recall efforts than others (Erdelyi & Kleinbard, 1978). Emphasis on the constructive or reconstructive nature of memory (Bartlett, 1932) suggests a wide variety of additional biasing mechanisms. E. Loftus and Zanni (1975), for example, have demonstrated dramatic effects of the mode of questioning upon recall of information (e.g., ''How fast was the car going when it smashed/bumped against the other car?''). Such leading questions need not, however, come from an external agent such as a psychologist or lawyer. After all, most of our retrieval queries are self-initiated and framed by our own selves according to our fears, needs, and prejudices. Our recollections would be predictably biased by the mode in which we framed our retrieval queries to ourselves (e.g., ''What was it that the faggot/gentleman whispered to me yesterday?'').

Up to now, we have focused upon episodic rather than semantic events (Tulving, 1972). Once, however, we move beyond mere ''brute facts'' into the realm of meaning, the possibilities for biased cognition become virtually limitless, for meanings are not objective events but subjective interpretations ("constructions," "abstractions," "information processing between the lines," "listening with the third ear," etc.) extracted from typically ambiguous information (cf. Bransford & Franks, 1971; Bransford & McCarrell, 1974; Dooling & Lachman, 1971; Franks, 1974; Harris & Monaco, 1978; Monaco & Harris, 1978). It is in this implicational realm that most tendentious thinking occurs, for it takes a more drastic bias to misprocess a clear episodic event (e.g., "my wife came home late yesterday") than an interpretation of that event ("she was visiting her mother/lover").

The interpretation of an event, x, depends on the contextual ecology in which x transpires, which includes not only other events but psychological intentions as well. It is contextual background, like depth cues in the extraction of 3-D from 2-D images, that gives rise to depth of meaning. However, the contextual surround of any semantic event is limitless, and the processor therefore can only sample the population of potential contextual cues. The processor, then, is forced to be selective not only with respect to the input but also with respect to the context he brings to bear on the input. It is here that interpretation can become altogether tendentious, for like two opposing lawyers (or two disagreeing scientists), biased samples of the contextual ecology may be applied to the ambiguous event, x, imparting quite different meanings to it. Moreover, certain contextual elements, like components of a picture, convey different amounts of implication (information?); some contextual elements considerably reduce uncertainty, others little or not at all, and others, still, increase it. By tendentiously focusing on different contextual cues, the processor can extract different meanings as well as different amounts of meaning.

Consider the following "semantic algebra" task. Its object is to find the one and only correct meaning of the semantic unknown, x. After each best "estimate" of x (guessing if necessary), the reader might assign a subjective confidence value $(0-100\%)$ to his or her response:

1. I broke my x.
2. I detest $x$ball.
3. He put his x in his mouth.
4. He really put his x in his mouth!
5. Gogol may have written a story about a nose, but he certainly never wrote anything about a x.
6. The Indian Chief's name was Little X.

Pilot studies with this material reveal what the reader has probably found already. By Item 3, x will have been interpreted as probably (but not certainly) constituting "foot." Item 4 further enhances the interpretation in favor of "foot" because of its emphasis of the idiomaticness of the expression. Note that there is no mandatory logic or certainty in interpretation; x could be foot, hand, basket, base, or pin, though pilot subjects are remarkably consistent in opting for foot. There must then be some consistently used interpretation rules, as hard as they are to articulate formally.

No single contextual item is decisive; a network of implications progressively excludes competing possibilities. However, not all contextual cues are clues; some of them carry little meaning. Item 5, for example, adds little new implicational information, nor does Item 6. Other contextual cues, however, seem to put an end to further doubt:

7. Is your x mending?
8. Try Bloomingdale's $x$wear department.
9. What's ax?
10. The movie director needs more $x$age of that scene.

This exercise demonstrates that a totally invisible meaning may be extracted—by some interpretative process, whatever it might be—from a sufficiently developed network of contextual clues. Context, then, is the key to interpretation. So powerful can context be, that it may turn an objective event into its semantic opposite—as in "Brutus is an honorable man." The psychoanalyst, through extensive personal knowledge of the patient and through the latter's free association (a form of context generation), is then often in the position of uncovering meanings that to the outsider, excluded from the vast network of contextual information, appear bizarre and unbelievable. The patient himself, though he has knowledge of his contextual universe, might be no less unconscious of the uncovered latent meanings, since the meanings of which he *is* aware are the consequence of tendentious sampling of an infinite contextual domain.

Interpretation, whether by the therapist or patient, cannot ever be a sure thing. Not only is bias a fundamental factor, but the contextual information itself is a more-or-less rather than an all-or-none affair—as is the processor's inherent "sensitivity," apart from bias, for contextual "signals." (Applications of signal detection theory to the problem of insight, currently in progress in our laboratory, reveal the expected individual differences in the ability to "see" invisible stimuli—i.e., to gain insight for latent contents. Some people are obviously more "sensitive" than others.)

Most contextual universes are not as convergent as the artificial constellation just devised. Indeed, it would not be difficult to undermine the reader's confidence in the semantic solution (x = foot) by appending some additional context:

11. The person who devised this exercise is a pathological liar; if he says "x" he means "y."
12. Actually, the "x" of Items 1−3 is different from the "x" of Items 4−6.

The real contextual world is typically fuzzy. Implications tend often to work at cross-purposes, and our inferences, bias apart, are only best approximations arrived at in a "field" of noisy implications. Since there is no absolute logic to interpretation or even a cognitive methodology for bias-free contextual sampling, it is quite possible to interpret the world tendentiously without giving up one's claim to reason—or memory, or perception. Here then is one of the most subtle but pervasive mechanisms of self-deception. Through biased sampling of our contextual ecology, we can escape intolerable meanings (insights) in favor of more acceptable ones.

All this is a far cry from rats and nonsense syllables. We are now confronting a realm of indefinite subjective processes—interpretations—for extracting physically nonexistent entities—meanings. As chancy and vague as it may seem, the progression from behavioristic concretism to cognitive abstraction is but a natural developmental progression (e.g., Werner, 1948). Complex cognitive systems—whether societies, human beings, or scientific theories—inevitably struggle from a concretistic "golden-cow" phase that is sure (because its materials can be seen, smelled, and touched—and measured) to a hard-to-grasp but infinitely more powerful stage of abstraction.

ACKNOWLEDGMENT

This work was supported by Faculty Research Award Program grants number 11189 and 11800 of the City University of New York.

REFERENCES

Aborn, M. The influence of experimentally induced failure on the retention of material acquired through set and incidental learning. *Journal of Experimental Psychology*, 1953, *45*, 225–231.

Archer, B. U., & Margolin R. R. Arousal effects in intentional recall and forgetting. *Journal of Experimental Psychology*, 1970, *86*, 8–12.

Atkinson, R. C., & Shiffrin, R. M. Human memory: A proposed system and its control processes. In K. W. Spence & J. T. Spence (Eds.), *The psychology of learning and motivation* (Vol. 2). New York: Academic Press, 1968.

Averbach, E., & Coriell, A. S. Short-term memory in vision. *Bell Systems Technical Journal*, 1961, *40*, 309–328.

Bandura, A. *Principles of behavior modification.* New York: Holt, Rinehart & Winston, 1969.

Bandura, A. *Social learning theory.* Morristown, N.J.: General Learning Press, 1971.

Bandura, A. *Social learning theory.* Englewood Cliffs, N.J.: Prentice-Hall, 1977.

Bartlett, F. C. *Remembering.* Cambridge: Cambridge University Press, 1932.

Bateson, C. *Steps to an ecology of mind.* New York: Ballantine, 1972.

Bernstein, M. *The search for Bridey Murphy.* New York: Lancer, 1956.

Bjork, R. A. Theoretical implications of directed forgetting. In A. W. Melton & E. Martin (Eds.), *Coding processes in human memory.* Washington, D.C.: Winston, 1972.

Bjork, R. A., LaBerge, D., & Legrand, R. The modification of short-term memory through instructions to forget. *Psychonomic Science*, 1968, *10*, 55–56.

Bransford, J. D., & Franks, J. J. The abstraction of linguistic ideas. *Cognitive Psychology*, 1971, *2*, 331–350.

Bransford, J. D., & McCarrell, N. S. A sketch of a cognitive approach to comprehension: Some thoughts about understanding what it means to comprehend. In W. B. Weimer & D. S. Palermo (Eds.), *Cognition and the symbolic processes*. Hillsdale, N.J.: Lawrence Erlbaum Associates, 1974.

Bregman, A. S. Perception and behavior as compositions of ideals. *Cognitive Psychology*, 1977, *9*, 250–292.

Brenner, C. *An elementary textbook of psychoanalysis*. Garden City, N.J.: Doubleday, 1957. (a)

Brenner, C. The nature and development of the concept of repression in Freud's writings. *Psychoanalytic Study of the Child*, 1957, *12*, 19–46. (b)

Breuer, J., & Freud, S. The psychical mechanism of hysterical phenomena: Preliminary communication. In J. Strachey (Ed.), *The standard edition of the complete psychological works of Sigmund Freud*. (Vol. 11). London: Hogarth Press, 1955. (Originally published, 1893.)

Breuer, J., & Freud, S. *Studies on hysteria* In J. Strachey (Ed.), *The standard edition of the complete psychological works of Sigmund Freud* (Vol. 2). London: Hogarth Press, 1955. (Originally published, 1895.)

Broadbent, D. E. *Perception and communication*. London: Pergamon Press, 1958.

Broadbent, D. E. *Decision and stress*. New York: Academic Press, 1971.

Brown, J. Some tests of the decay theory of immediate memory. *Quarterly Journal of Experimental Psychology*, 1958, *10*, 12–21.

Buss, A. H., & Brock, T. C. Repression and guilt in relation to aggression. *Journal of Abnormal and Social Psychology*, 1963, *66*, 345–350.

Cason, H. The pleasure–pain theory of learning. *Psychological Review*, 1932, *39*, 440–466.

Colby, K. M., Hilf, F. D., Weber, S., & Kraemer, H. C. Turing-like indistinguishability tests for the validation of a computer simulation of paranoid processes. *Artificial Intelligence*, 1972, *3*, 199–221.

Craik, F. I. M., & Lockhart, R. S. Levels of processing: A framework for memory research. *Journal of Verbal Learning and Verbal Behavior*, 1972, *11*, 671–684.

Davis, J. C., & Okada, R. Recognition and recall of positively forgotten items. *Journal of Experimental Psychology*, 1971, *89*, 181–186.

Deese, J. *Psychology as science and art*. New York: Harcourt Brace Jovanovich, 1972.

Deutsch, H. *Neuroses and character types*. New York: International Universities Press, 1965.

Dixon, N. F. *Subliminal perception: The nature of a controversy*. London: McGraw-Hill, 1971.

Dollard, J., & Miller, N. *Personality and psychotherapy*. New York: McGraw-Hill, 1950.

Dooling, D. J., & Lachman, R. Effects of comprehension on retention of prose. *Journal of Experimental Psychology*, 1971, *88*, 216–222.

D'Zurilla, T. Recall efficiency and mediating cognitive events in "experimental repression." *Journal of Personality and Social Psychology*, 1965, *3*, 253–256.

Ebbinghaus, H. *Memory*. New York: Dover, 1964. (Originally published, 1885.)

Egan, J. P. *Recognition memory and the operating characteristic*. Bloomington, Ind. Indiana University Hearing and Communication Laboratory Technical Note (Contract No. AF19(604)-1962, AFCRC-TN-58-51), 1958.

Epstein, W. Mechanisms of directed forgetting. In G. Bower (Ed.), *The psychology of learning and motivation* (Vol. 6). New York: Academic Press, 1972.

Erdelyi, M. H. Recovery of unavailable perceptual input. *Cognitive Psychology*, 1970, *1*, 99–113.

Erdelyi, M. H. The role of fantasy in the Pötzl (Emergence) phenomenon. *Journal of Personality and Social Psychology*, 1972, *24*, 186–190.

Erdelyi, M. H. A new look at the New Look: Perceptual defense and vigilance. *Psychological Review*, 1974, *81*, 1−25.

Erdelyi, M. H. *The cognitive psychology of Sigmund Freud*. Manuscript in preparation, 1979.

Erdelyi, M. H., & Appelbaum, G. A. Cognitive masking: The disruptive effect of an emotional stimulus upon the perception of contiguous neutral items. *Bulletin of the Psychonomic Society*, 1973, *1*, 59−61.

Erdelyi, M. H., & Becker, J. Hypermnesia for pictures: Incremental memory for pictures but not words in multiple recall trials. *Cognitive Psychology*, 1974, *6*, 159−171.

Erdelyi, M. H., & Blumenthal, D. Cognitive masking in rapid sequential processing: The effect of an emotional picture on preceding and succeeding pictures. *Memory & Cognition*, 1973, *1*, 201−204.

Erdelyi, M. H., Finkelstein, S., Herrell, N., Miller, B., & Thomas, J. Coding modality vs. input modality in hypermnesia: Is a rose, a rose, a rose? *Cognition*, 1976, *4*, 311−319.

Erdelyi, M. H., & Kleinbard, J. Has Ebbinghaus decayed with time?: The growth of recall (hypermnesia) over days. *Journal of Experimental Psychology: Human Learning and Memory*, 1978, *4*, 275−289.

Erdelyi, M. H., & Stein, J. Recognition hypermnesia: Growth of recognition memory with time and effort. Manuscript in preparation, 1979.

Eriksen, C. W. Individual differences in defensive forgetting. *Journal of Experimental Psychology*, 1952, *44*, 442−447.

Eriksen, C. W. Unconscious processes. In M. R. Jones (Ed.), *Nebraska Symposium on Motivation* (Vol. 6). Lincoln: University of Nebraska Press, 1958.

Eriksen, C. W. (Ed.). *Behavior and awareness*. Durham, N.C.: Duke University Press, 1962.

Eriksen, C., & Pierce, J. Defense mechanisms. In E. Borgatta & W. Lambert (Eds.), *Handbook of personality theory and research*. Chicago: Rand McNally, 1968.

Faught, W. S., Colby, K. M., & Parkinson, R. C. Inferences, affects, and intentions in a model of paranoia. *Cognitive Psychology*, 1977, *9*, 153−187.

Fenichel, O. *The psychoanalytic theory of neurosis*. New York: Norton, 1945.

Flavell, J. H. Repression and the "return of the repressed." *Journal of Consulting Psychology*, 1955, *19*, 441−443.

Franks, J. J. Toward understanding understanding. In W. B. Weimer & D. S. Palermo (Eds.), *Cognition and the symbolic processes*. Hillsdale, N.J.: Lawrence Erlbaum Associates, 1974.

Freud, A. *The ego and the mechanism of defense*. New York: International Universities Press, 1946. (Originally published, 1936.)

Freud, S. A case of successful treatment by hypnotism: With some remarks on the origin of hysterical symptoms through "counter will." In J. Strachey (Ed.), *The standard edition of the complete psychological works of Sigmund Freud* (Vol. 1). London: Hogarth Press, 1966. (Originally published, 1892−1893.)

Freud, S. The neuropsychoses of defence. In J. Strachey (Ed.), *The standard edition of the complete psychological works of Sigmund Freud* (Vol. 3). London: Hogarth Press, 1962. (Originally published, 1894.)

Freud, S. Project for a scientific psychology. In J. Strachey (Ed.), *The standard edition of the complete psychological works of Sigmund Freud* (Vol. 1). London: Hogarth Press, 1966. (Originally published, 1895.)

Freud, S. Further remarks on the neuro-psychoses of defence. In J. Strachey (Ed.), *The standard edition of the complete psychological works of Sigmund Freud* (Vol. 3). London: Hogarth Press, 1962. (Originally published, 1896.)

Freud, S. *The interpretation of dreams*. In J. Strachey (Ed.), *The standard edition of the complete psychological works of Sigmund Freud* (Vols. 4−5). London: Hogarth Press, 1953. (Originally published, 1900.)

Freud, S. My views on the part played by sexuality in the aetiology of the neuroses. In J. Strachey (Ed.), *The standard edition of the complete psychological works of Sigmund Freud* (Vol. 7). London: Hogarth Press, 1953. (Originally published, 1906.)

Freud, S. Notes upon a case of obsessional neurosis. In J. Strachey (Ed.), *The standard edition of the complete psychological works of Sigmund Freud* (Vol. 10). London: Hogarth Press, 1955. (Originally published, 1909.)

Freud, S. Psychoanalytic notes upon an autobiographical account of a case of paranoia (*dementia paranoides*). In J. Strachey (Ed.), *The standard edition of the complete psychological works of Sigmund Freud* (Vol. 12). London: Hogarth Press, 1958. (Originally published, 1911.)

Freud, S. A note on the unconscious in psychoanalysis. In J. Strachey (Ed.), *The standard edition of the complete psychological works of Sigmund Freud* (Vol. 12). London: Hogarth Press, 1958. (Originally published, 1912.)

Freud, S. The history of the psychoanalytic movement. In J. Strachey (Ed.), *The standard edition of the complete psychological works of Sigmund Freud* (Vol. 14). London: Hogarth Press, 1957. (Originally published, 1914.)

Freud, S. Repression. In J. Strachey (Ed.), *The standard edition of the complete psychological works of Sigmund Freud* (Vol. 14). London: Hogarth Press, 1957. (Originally published, 1915.) (a)

Freud, S. The unconscious. In J. Strachey (Ed.), *The standard edition of the complete psychological works of Sigmund Freud* (Vol. 14). London: Hogarth Press, 1957. (Originally published, 1915.) (b)

Freud, S. *Introductory lectures on psychoanalysis.* In J. Strachey (Ed.), *The standard edition of the complete psychological works of Sigmund Freud* (Vol. 15). London: Hogarth Press, 1961. (Originally published, 1915–1916.)

Freud, S. *Introductory lectures on psychoanalysis.* In J. Strachey (Ed.), *The standard edition of the complete psychological works of Sigmund Freud* (Vol. 16). London: Hogarth Press, 1963. (Originally published, 1916–1917.)

Freud, S. From the history of an infantile neurosis. In J. Strachey (Ed.), *The standard edition of the complete psychological works of Sigmund Freud* (Vol. 17). London: Hogarth Press, 1955. (Originally published, 1918.)

Freud, S. *The ego and the id.* In J. Strachey (Ed.), *The standard edition of the complete psychological works of Sigmund Freud* (Vol. 19). London: Hogarth Press, 1961. (Originally published, 1923.)

Freud, S. *An autobiographical study.* In J. Strachey (Ed.), *The standard edition of the complete psychological works of Sigmund Freud* (Vol. 20). London: Hogarth Press, 1959. (Originally published, 1925.) (a)

Freud, S. A note on the mystic writing pad. In J. Strachey (Ed.), *The standard edition of the complete psychological works of Sigmund Freud* (Vol. 19). London: Hogarth Press, 1961. (Originally published, 1925.) (b)

Freud, S. *Inhibitions, symptoms, and anxiety.* In J. Strachey (Ed.), *The standard edition of the complete psychological works of Sigmund Freud* (Vol. 20). London: Hogarth Press, 1959. (Originally published, 1926.)

Freud, S. *New introductory lectures on psychoanalysis.* In J. Strachey (Ed.), *The standard edition of the complete psychological works of Sigmund Freud* (Vol. 22). London: Hogarth Press, 1964. (Originally published, 1933.)

Freud, S. *An outline of psychoanalysis.* In J. Strachey (Ed.), *The standard edition of the complete psychological works of Sigmund Freud* (Vol. 23). London: Hogarth Press, 1964. (Originally published, 1940.) (a)

Freud, S. Sketches for the 'preliminary communication' of 1893: On the theory of hysterical attacks. In J. Strachey (Ed.), *The standard edition of the complete psychological works of Sigmund Freud* (Vol. 1). London: Hogarth Press, 1966. (Originally published, 1940.) (b)

Gillespie, R. D. *Psychological effects of war on citizen and soldier*. New York: Norton, 1942.

Glixman, A. F. Recall of completed and incompleted activities under varying degrees of stress. *Journal of Experimental Psychology*, 1949, *39*, 281–295.

Gould, R. Repression experimentally analyzed. *Character and Personality*, 1942, *10*, 259–288.

Green, D. M., & Swets, J. A. *Signal detection theory and psychophysics*. New York: Wiley, 1966.

Grinker, R. R., & Spiegel, J. P. *Man under stress*. New York: Blakiston, 1945. (a)

Grinker, R. R., & Spiegel, J. P. *War neurosis*. New York: Blakiston, 1945. (b)

Haber, R. N. (Ed.). *Contemporary theory and research in visual perception*. New York: Holt, Rinehart & Winston, 1968.

Haber, R. N. (Ed.). *Information-processing approaches to visual perception*. New York: Holt, Rinehart & Winston, 1969.

Harris, R. J., & Monaco, G. E. The psychology of pragmatic implication: Information processing between the lines. *Journal of Experimental Psychology: General*, 1978, *107*, 1–22.

Helmholtz, H. von. [*Physiological optics*] (J. P. C. Southall, Ed.). Rochester, N.Y.: Optical Society of America, 1925. (Originally published, 1850.)

Holmes, D. S. Repression or interference? A further investigation. *Journal of Personality and Social Psychology*, 1972, *22*, 163–170.

Holmes, D. S. Investigations of repression: Differential recall of material experimentally or naturally associated with ego threat. *Psychological Bulletin*, 1974, *81*, 632–653.

Holmes, D. S., & Schallow, J. R. Reduced recall after ego threat: Repression or response competition? *Journal of Personality and Social Psychology*, 1969, *13*, 145–152.

Holzman, P. S., & Klein, G. S. Cognitive system-principles of leveling and sharpening: Individual differences in assimilation effects in visual time-errors. *Journal of Psychology*, 1954, *37*, 105–122.

Janis, I. *Stress and frustration*. New York: Harcourt Brace Jovanovich, 1969.

Jung, C. G. *Studies in word-association*. London: Heinemann, 1918. (Originally published, 1906.)

Jung, C. G. Two essays on analytical psychology. In H. Read, M. Fordham, & G. Adler (Eds.), *The collected works of C. G. Jung*. Princeton, N.J.: Princeton University Press, 1953. (Originally published, 1928.)

Jung, C. G. *Analytical psychology: Its theory and practice*. New York: Pantheon, 1968. (Originally published, 1935.)

Jung, C. G., & Riklin, F. Experimentelle Untersuchung uber Associationen Gesunder. *Journal für Psychologie und Neurologie*, 1904–1905, *3–4*, pp. 24–67; 55–83; 109–123; 145–164; 193–214; 238–308.

Kahneman, D. *Attention and effort*. Englewood Cliffs, N.J.: Prentice-Hall, 1973.

Kardiner, A., & Spiegel, H. *War stress and neurotic illness*. New York: Hoeber, 1947.

Kelly, G. A. *A theory of personality*. New York: Norton, 1955.

Kihlstrom, J., & Evans, F. Recovery of memory after posthypnotic amnesia. *Journal of Abnormal Psychology*, 1976, *85*, 564–569.

Klein, G. S. Cognitive control and motivation. In G. Lindzey (Ed.), *Assessment of human motives*. New York: Holt, Rinehart & Winston, 1958.

Klein, G. S. *Perception, motives, and personality*. New York: Knopf, 1970.

Klein, G. S., & Schlesinger, H. J. Where is the perceiver in perceptual theory? *Journal of Personality*, 1949, *18*, 32–47.

Kline, M. V. The dynamics of hypnotically induced anti-social behavior. *Journal of Psychology*, 1958, *45*, 239–245.

Koch, H. I. The influence of some affective factors upon recall. *Journal of Genetic Psychology*, 1930, *4*, 171–190.

Kris, E. The nature of psychoanalytic propositions and their validation. In M. H. Marx (Ed.), *Psychological theory: Contemporary readings*. New York: Macmillan, 1951. (Originally published, 1947.)

Lazarus, R. S., & Longo, N. The consistency of psychological defense against threat. *Journal of Abnormal and Social Psychology*, 1953, *48*, 495–499.

Lindner, R. *The fifty-minute hour*. New York: Holt, Rinehart & Winston, 1955.

Loftus, E. F., & Zanni, G. Eyewitness testimony: The influence of the wording of a question. *Bulletin of the Psychonomic Society*, 1975, *5*, 86–88.

MacKinnon, D., & Dukes, W. Repression. In L. Postman (Ed.), *Psychology in the making*. New York: Knopf, 1964.

MacLeod, C. M. Long-term recognition and recall following directed forgetting. *Journal of Experimental Psychology: Human Learning and Memory*, 1975, *104*, 271–279.

Madison, P. Freud's repression concept. *International Journal of Psychoanalysis*, 1956, *37*, 75–81.

Madison, P. *Freud's concept of repression and defense, its theoretical and observational language*. Minneapolis: University of Minnesota Press, 1961.

Martin, E. Generation-recognition theory and the encoding specificity principle. *Psychological Review*, 1975, *82*, 150–153.

Meltzer, H. Individual differences in forgetting pleasant and unpleasant experiences. *Journal of Educational Psychology*, 1930, *21*, 399–409.

Miller, N. E. Learnable drives and rewards. In S. Stevens (Ed.), *Handbook of experimental psychology*. New York: Wiley, 1950.

Mischel, W. *Introduction to personality* (2nd ed.). New York: Holt, Rinehart & Winston, 1976.

Monaco, G. E., & Harris, R. J. Theoretical issues in the psychology of implication. A reply to Keenan. *Journal of Experimental Psychology: General*, 1978, *107*, 28–31.

Moore, E. H. A note on the recall of the pleasant vs. the unpleasant. *Psychological Review*, 1935, *42*, 214–215.

Moray, N. *Attention: Selective processes in vision and hearing*. New York: Academic Press, 1970.

Neisser, U. *Cognitive psychology*. Englewood Cliffs, N.J.: Prentice-Hall, 1967.

Neisser, U. *Cognition and reality*. San Francisco: Freeman, 1976.

Neisser, U., & Becklen, R. Selective looking: Attending to visually specified events. *Cognitive Psychology*, 1975, *7*, 480–494.

Nisbett, R. E., & Wilson, T. D. Telling more than we can know: Verbal reports on mental processes. *Psychological Review*, 1977, *84*, 231–259.

Norman, D. Discussion: Section 1. In R. L. Solso (Ed.), *Contemporary issues in cognitive psychology: The Loyola Symposium*. Washington, D.C.: Winston, 1973.

Norman, D. A. *Memory and attention* (2nd ed.). New York: Wiley, 1976.

Peterson, L. R., & Peterson, M. J. Short-term retention of individual verbal items. *Journal of Experimental Psychology*, 1959, *58*, 193–198.

Polanyi, M. *The tacit dimension*. Garden City, N.Y.: Doubleday, 1966.

Posner, M. I., & Warren, R. E. Traces, concepts, and conscious constructions. In A. W. Melton & E. Martin (Eds.), *Coding processes in human memory*. Washington, D.C.: Winston, 1972.

Pribram, K. H., & Gill, M. *Freud's 'project' reassessed*. New York: Basic Books, 1976.

Rakover, S. S. Voluntary forgetting before and after learning has been accomplished. *Memory & Cognition*, 1975, *3*, 24–28.

Rapaport, D. *Emotions and memory*. New York: International Universities Press, 1942. (Republished, 1971.)

Roediger, H. L., & Crowder, R. G. Instructed forgetting: Rehearsal control or retrieval inhibition (repression)? *Cognitive Psychology*, 1972, *3*, 255–267.

Rosenzweig, S. The recall of finished and unfinished tasks as affected by the purpose with which they were performed. *Psychological Bulletin*, 1933, *30*, 698.

Rosenzweig, S. An experimental study of "repression" with special reference to need-persistive and ego-defensive reactions to frustrations. *Journal of Experimental Psychology*, 1943, *32*, 64–74.

Rosenzweig, S. The investigation of repression as an instance of experimental idio-dynamics. *Psychological Review*, 1952, *59*, 339–345.

Rosenzweig, S., & Mason, G. An experimental study of memory in relation to the theory of repression. *British Journal of Psychology*, 1934, *24*, 247–265.

Rubenstein, R., & Newman, R. The living out of "future" experiences under hypnosis. *Science*, 1954, *119*, 472–473.

Russell, W. Retention of verbal material as a function of motivating instructions and experimentally induced failure. *Journal of Experimental Psychology*, 1952, *43*, 207–216.

Sackeim, H. A., & Gur, R. C. Self-deception, self-confrontation and consciousness. In G. E. Schwartz and D. Shapiro (Eds.), *Consciousness and self-regulation: Advances in research*. New York: Plenum, 1977.

Sartre, J. P. [*Being and nothingness: An essay on phenomenological ontology*] (H. Barnes, trans.). London: Methuen, 1958.

Schreiber, F. R. *Sybil*. New York: Warner Books, 1973.

Sears, R. R. Functional abnormalities of memory with special reference to amnesia. *Psychological Bulletin*, 1963, *33*, 229–274.

Sears, R. R. *Survey of objective studies of psychoanalytic concepts*. New York: Social Research Council, 1942.

Shebliske, W., & Epstein, W. Effects of forget instructions with and without the conditions of selective search. *Memory & Cognition*, 1973, *1*, 261–267.

Shiffrin, R. M., & Atkinson, R. C. Storage and retrieval processes in long-term memory. *Psychological Review*, 1969, *76*, 179–193.

Slobin, D. I. *Psycholinguistics*. Glenville, Ill. Scott, Foresman, 1971.

Spanos, N. P., & Ham, M. L. Cognitive activity in response to hypnotic suggestion: Goal-directed fantasy and selective amnesia. *The American Journal of Clinical Hypnosis*, 1973, *15*, 191–198.

Sperling, G. The information available in brief visual presentations. *Psychological Monographs*, 1960, *74*, (11, Whole No. 498).

Sperling, G. Successive approximations to a model of short-term memory. *Acta Psychologica*, 1967, *27*, 285–292.

Suedfeld, P., Erdelyi, M. H., & Corcoran, C. R. Rejection of input in the processing of an emotional film. *Bulletin of the Psychonomic Society*, 1975, *5* (1), 30–32.

Suppes, P., & Warren, H. On the generation and classification of defence mechanisms. *International Journal of Psycho-Analysis*, 1975, *56*, 405–414.

Swets, J. A. (Ed.). *Signal detection and recognition by human observers*. New York: Wiley, 1964.

Swets, J. A., Tanner, W. P., & Birdsall, T. G. Decision processes in perception. *Psychological Review*, 1961, *68*, 301–340.

Thigpen, C. H., & Cleckley, H. M. *The three faces of Eve*. McGraw-Hill, 1957.

Truax, C. B. The repression response to implied failure as a function of the hysteria-psychasthenia index. *Journal of Abnormal and Social Psychology*, 1957, *55*, 188–193.

Tulving, E. Episodic and semantic memory. In E. Tulving & W. Donaldson (Eds.), *Organization and memory*. New York: Academic Press, 1972.

Tulving, E., & Pearlstone, Z. Availability versus accessibility of information in memory for words. *Journal of Verbal Learning and Verbal Behavior*, 1966, *5*, 381–391.

Weiner, B. Motivated forgetting and the study of repression. *Journal of Personality*, 1968, *36*, 213–234.

Werner, H. *Comparative psychology of mental development*. New York: International Universities Press, 1948.

Wolitzky, D. L., Klein, G. S., & Dworkin, S. F. An experimental approach to the study of repression: Effects of a hypnotically induced fantasy. In D. P. Spence (Ed.), *Psychoanalysis and contemporary science* (Vol. 4). New York: International Universities Press, 1976.

Zeigarnik, B. Über das Behalten von erledigten und underledigten Handlungen. *Psychologische Forschungen*, 1927, *9*, 1–85.

Zeller, A. An experimental analogue of repression: I. Historical summary. *Psychological Bulletin*, 1950, *47*, 39–51. (a)

Zeller, A. An experimental analogue of repression: II. The effect of individual failure and success on memory measured by relearning. *Journal of Experimental Psychology*, 1950, *40*, 411–422. (b)

Zeller, A. An experimental analogue of repression: III. The effect of induced failure and success on memory measured by recall. *Journal of Experimental Psychology*, 1951, *42*, 32–38.

Author Index

Subject Index